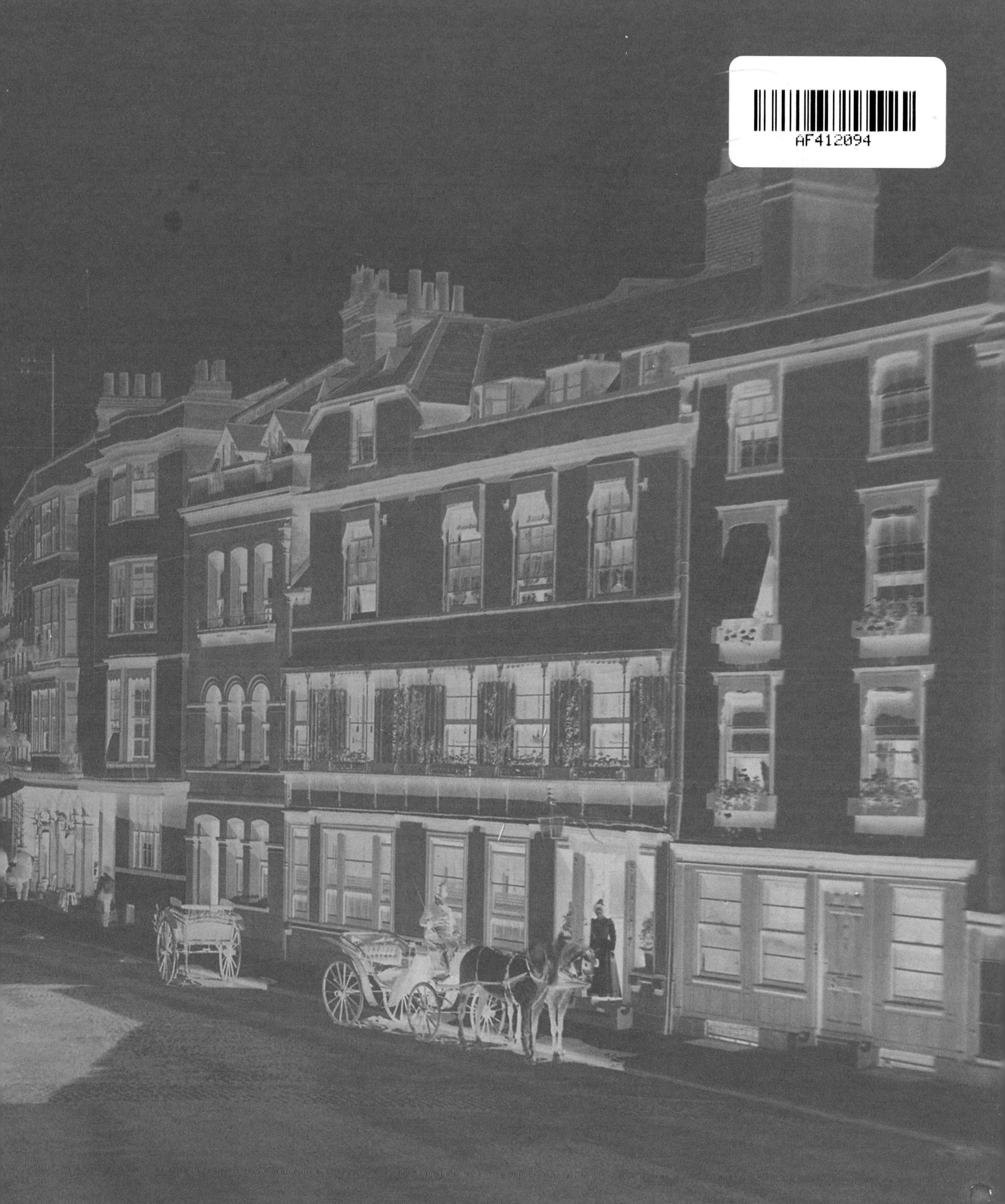
AF412094

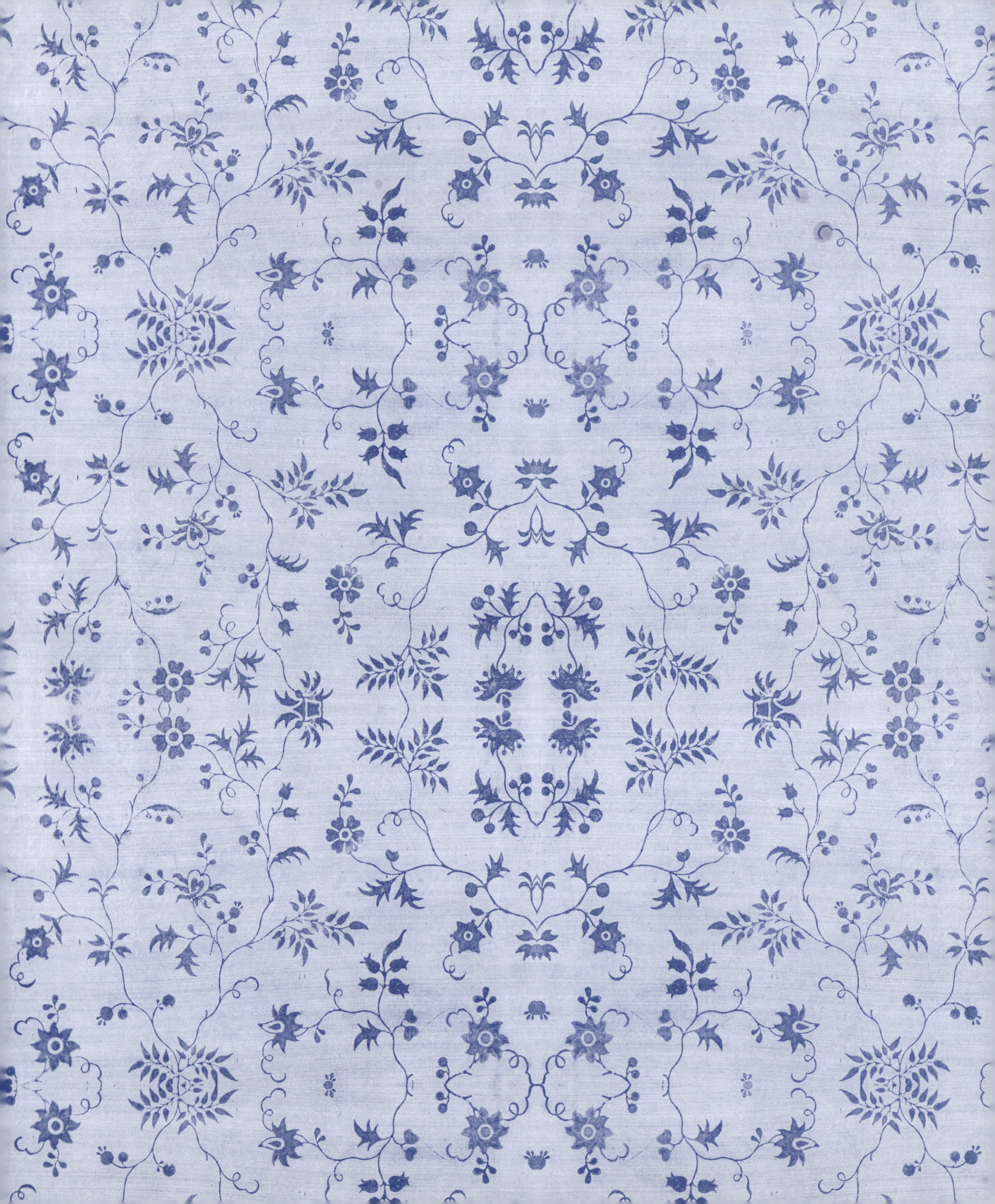

SARAH ANGELINA ACLAND

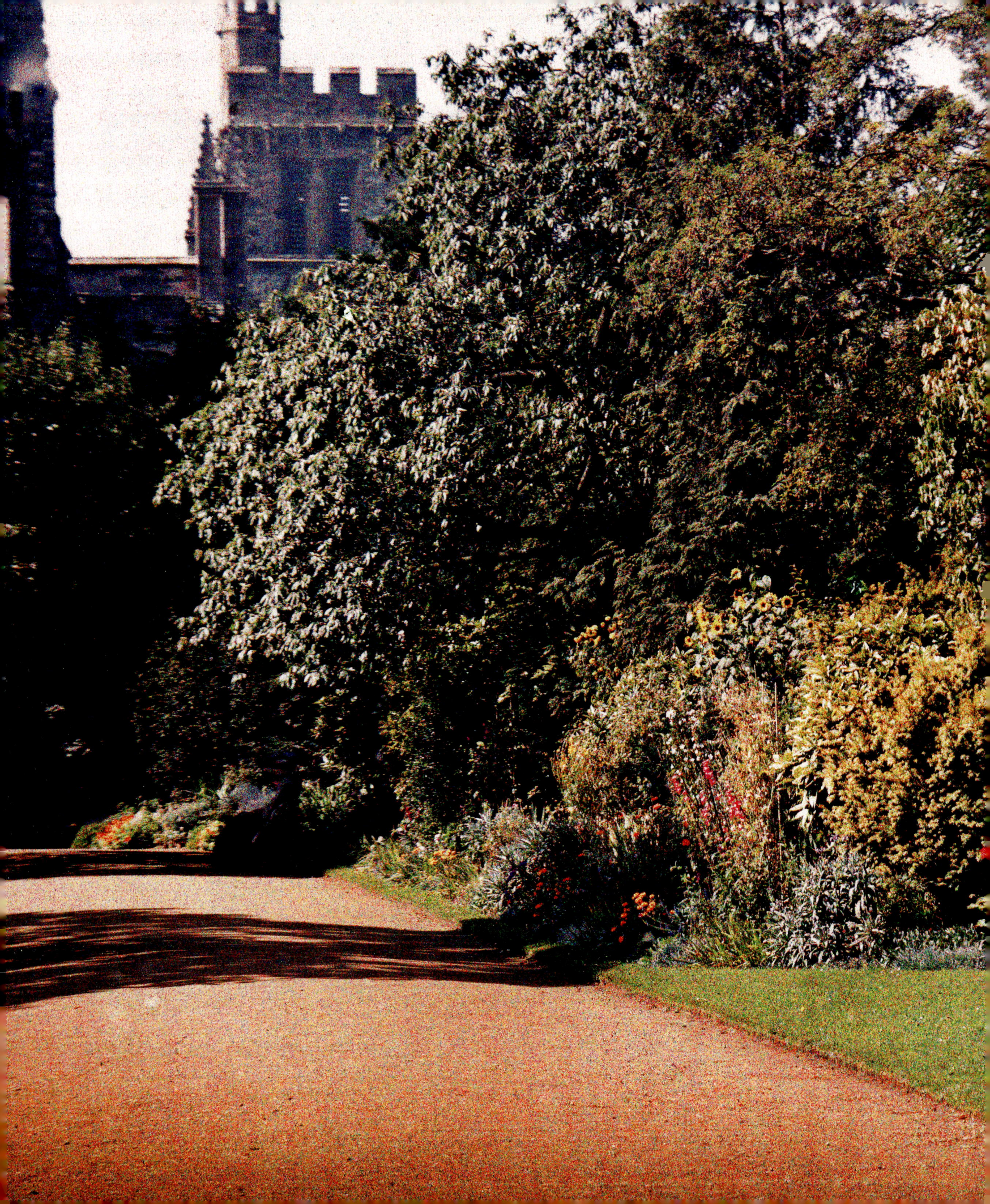

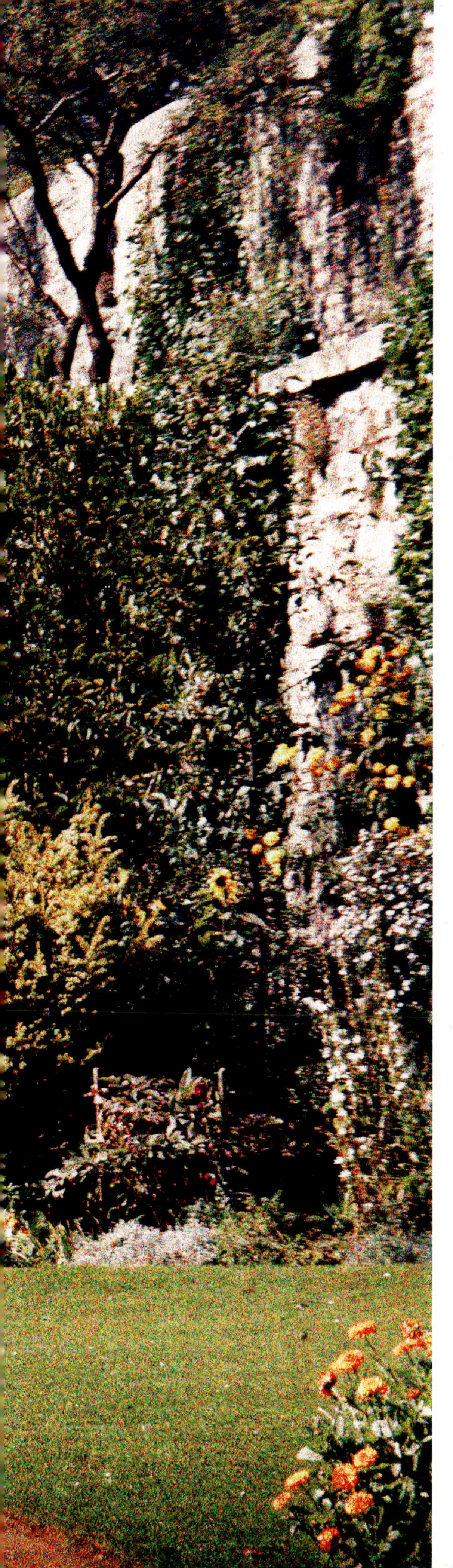

SARAH ANGELINA ACLAND

First Lady of Colour Photography, 1849–1930

Giles Hudson

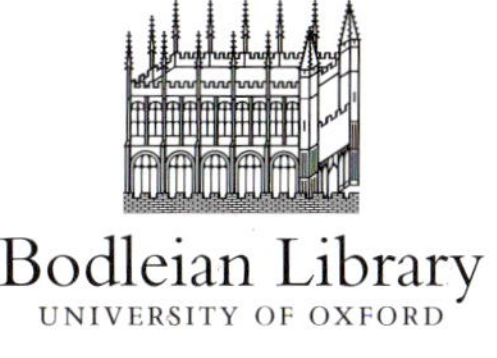

Bodleian Library
UNIVERSITY OF OXFORD

Atque hoc principio paucis, adverte, docebo,
Quod cupio posthac claris exponere verbis:
Sol tibi picturas reddet simulacraque certa.
Quod fieri tibi si potero pervincere, dictis
Dede manus, et pictorem solem venerare.

But listen now: here at the start I will tell you briefly
What I wish to explain in more detail later on:
the sun offers you pictures and unmistakable images.
If I can convince you that this is true, you must concede
the truth of what I say and venerate the sun as a painter.

Francisco Paget, *Sol Pictor* (Oxonii, T. Shrimpton et Filius, 1871), ll. 18–22, trans. C. White

The winning entry in the Chancellor's Prize for Latin Verse in 1871, a 210-line poem on the theory and practice of photography in the style of Lucretius, marked a rite of passage for photography in Oxford when it was delivered in the Sheldonian Theatre on 14 June by its author, Francis Paget (1851–1911). Francis was the son of Miss Acland's beloved physician, James Paget (1814–1899), and brother of her "greatest friend in this world", Catharine ('Katie') Paget (1846–1937). He went on to become Bishop of Oxford and Dean of Christ Church.

First published in 2012 by the Bodleian Library
Broad Street
Oxford OX1 3BG
www.bodleianbookshop.co.uk

ISBN: 978 1 85124 372 3

Photography, composites and reproductions by Giles Hudson, except fig. 7 Museum of the History of Science, fig. 30 National Media Museum, and figs. 51 & 93 Bodleian Library

British Library Catalogue in Publishing Data
A catalogue record for this publication is available from the British Library

Jacket design by the Bodleian Library, © University of Oxford, 2012
Designed and typeset by Giles Hudson in Garamond Premier Pro 10·5 on 14·5 pt
Printed and bound by Great Wall Printing Co. Ltd., Hong Kong, on 157gsm Gold East matt art paper

CONTENTS

Published by George Allen, 156, Charing Cross Road, London.

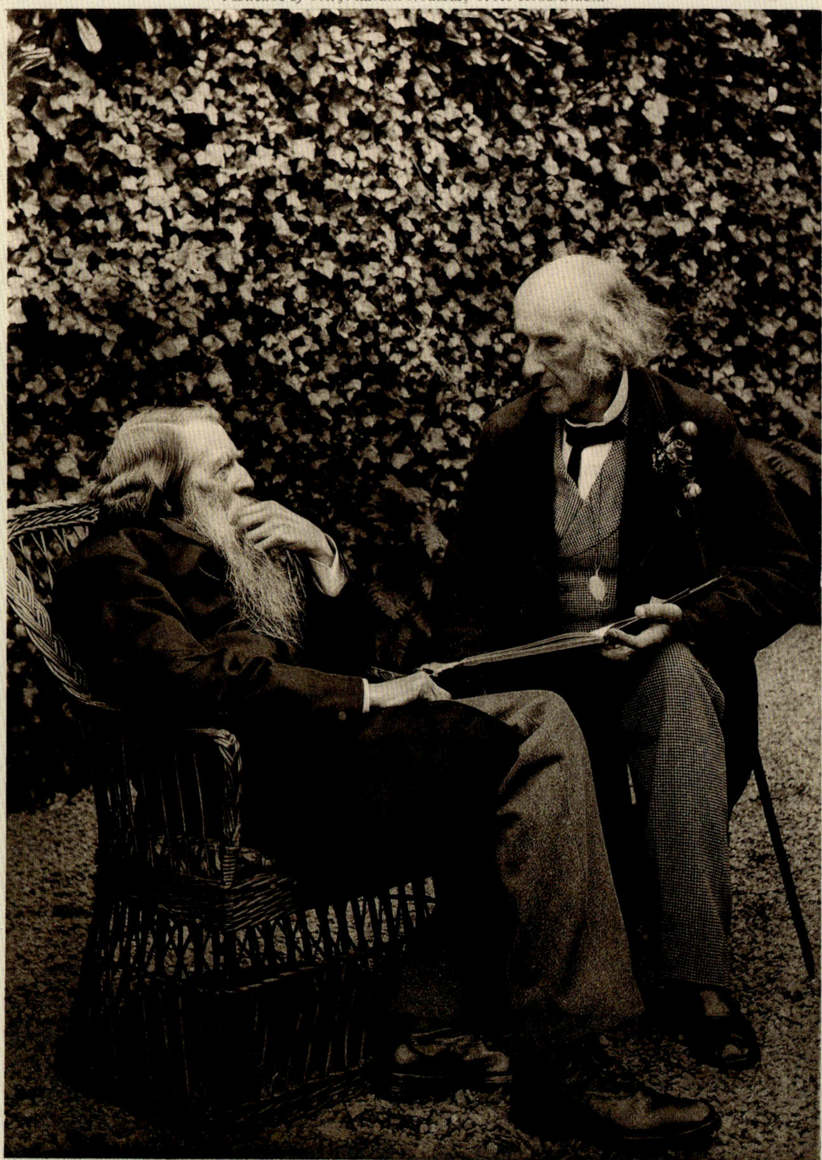

Professor Ruskin and Sir Henry Acland Bart.
From a Photograph taken by Miss Acland,
at Brantwood, August 1st 1893.

 Swan Electric Engraving Co.

CHRONOLOGY

26 June 1849	Sarah Angelina Acland born, Broad Street, Oxford
November 1856	Photographed by Lewis Carroll
June 1868	Suffers relapse of a childhood illness
24 November 1870	Begins lessons in art with John Ruskin
c. December 1870	Meets Julia Margaret Cameron
25 October 1878	Mother dies
26 June 1891	Receives Kodak No. 3 camera for her 42nd birthday
May or June 1892	Acquires Watson 'Acme' half-plate camera
25 October 1892	Photographs the Prime Minister, W. E. Gladstone
14 February 1893	Wins medal at the Torquay photographic exhibition
1 August 1893	Photographs Ruskin at Brantwood
11 June 1894	Elected the first woman member of the Oxford Camera Club
27 February 1899	Lectures on "Home Portraiture" at the Camera Club
25 September to 11 November 1899	Shows lantern slides at the Royal Photographic Society (R.P.S.) exhibition
12 December 1899	Elected a member of the R.P.S.
23 April 1900	Lectures on "Spectrum Plates" at the Camera Club
16 October 1900	Father dies
25 March 1901	Shows colour lantern slides at the Camera Club
23 May 1901	Moves to Clevedon House, Park Town, Oxford
30 September to 2 November 1901	Exhibits colour lantern slides at the R.P.S. annual exhibition
7 April 1902	Lectures on the Sanger Shepherd process at the Camera Club
29 September to 4 November 1902	Exhibits colour prints at the R.P.S. exhibition
May 1903 & May 1904	Photographs Gibraltar in colour
19 December 1904	Lectures on "A Visit to Gibraltar" at the Camera Club
1 February 1905	Elected a fellow of the R.P.S.
16 June 1905	Gives a 'demonstration' of colour photography at the R.P.S.
5 & 31 October 1905	Lectures on "A Visit to Gibraltar" during the R.P.S. exhibition
19 January to 17 March 1906	Exhibits at the *British Journal of Photography* colour photography exhibition
20 December 1906	Lectures on "A Visit to Gibraltar" during the R.P.S. exhibition
30 September to 26 October 1907	Exhibits an Autochrome at the Society of Colour Photographers exhibition
6 March 1908	Leaves for Madeira for the first time
2 June 1915	Arrives back from Madeira for the last time
January 1919	Begins disposing of her photographic equipment
11 February 1930	Completes her presentation albums of portraits and memoirs
2 December 1930	Sarah Angelina Acland dies, Park Town, Oxford, aged 81

OPPOSITE

"Old College Friends"

Miss Acland's most famous portrait was published in photogravure in 1894. It depicts the two most influential men in her life: her father and John Ruskin.

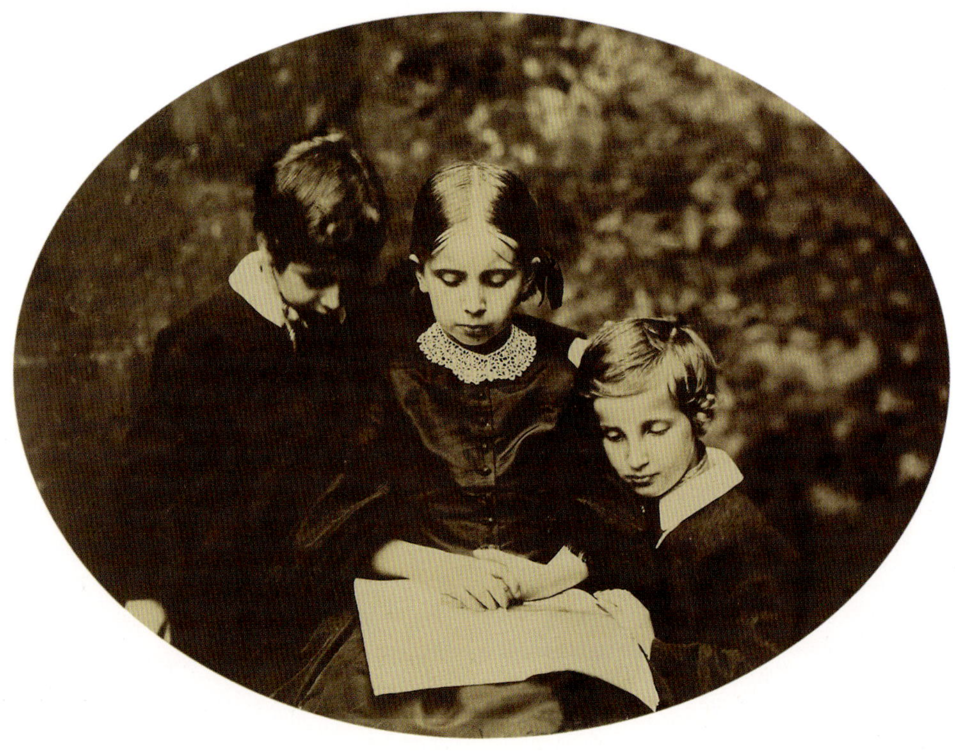

Fig. 1. *Theodore, Sarah Angelina and Henry Acland*
Charles Lutwidge Dodgson (1832–1898), albumen print, November 1856

Sarah Angelina Acland (1849–1930) was one of Lewis Carroll's earliest child sitters and appeared for him at least six times. After taking up photography in 1891 she too would become fond of photographing children.

During their childhood Angie, as she was known, and her brothers Harry and Theo were often to be found in the company of Dodgson's favourite child sitters, their great friends Ina, Alice and Edith Liddell. On Theo's birthday in 1858, for example, the Liddells were invited to a magic lantern show at the Acland house in Broad Street (Mrs Acland having failed to secure "Mr. Elmer the Conjuror"). In 1869 the Aclands visited the Christ Church Deanery for *tableaux vivants* acted by the sisters, Harry and his father having rowed Alice and Edith down the Thames to Sandford on the first summer evening earlier in the year.

INTRODUCTION

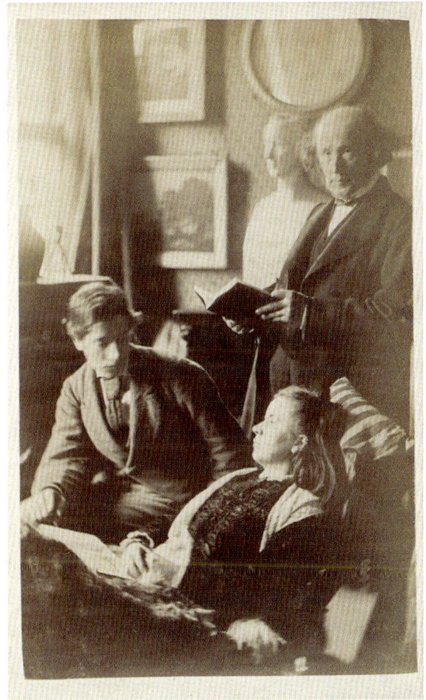

Fig. 2. *The Invalid*
Hills & Saunders, albumen print, *c.* 1868
In the week of her nineteenth birthday Miss Acland fell ill. A couch was arranged for her in the drawing room of her Oxford home, from where she could observe the ebb and flow of eminent visitors, many of whom she would later photograph. She is pictured here with Theodore and her father, whose bust, by the Pre-Raphaelite sculptor Alexander Munro, is in the background. The photograph records the scene much as Julia Margaret Cameron would have found it when she visited the Aclands.

In November 1856 Sarah Angelina Acland and her brothers Harry and Theodore sat for their photograph before an obscure Christ Church mathematician.[1] Aged seven, six and five, they were the second group of children to pose for the novice photographer in Oxford, missing out on first place to their close friends Ina, Alice and Edith Liddell. Later they would all partake of a different activity together: "going down the river with the Liddells taken by Mr. Dodgson (Lewis Carroll) who used to tell us stories bits of which became Alice in Wonderland".[1]

In the last year of her life, when Miss Acland came to compose her memoirs, she still had the "very quaint photographs Mr. Dodgson took of us when children", even though "he never kept up with us after we left childhood".[3] Dodgson, however, was not the only celebrated photographer she would meet as a girl, as she also recalled in an oft-quoted passage from her autobiography:

> During the time that Mr. Ruskin was with us Mrs. Cameron a well known artistic portrait photographer came to us on a visit and she and Mr. Ruskin had frequent skirmishes about photography. I was one day lying on my couch in the drawing room when Mrs. Cameron insisted on showing Mr. Ruskin some of the wonderful heads of well known people which she had taken. He got more and more impatient until they came to one of Sir John Herschel in which his hair all stood up like a halo of fireworks. Mr. Ruskin banged to the portfolio upon which Mrs. Cameron thumped his poor frail back exclaiming "John Ruskin you are not worthy of photographs". They then left the room.[4]

After witnessing such memorable photographic encounters as a child, it was perhaps inevitable that as an adult Miss Acland would be inspired to take up photography herself. Rather more remarkably, she too would rise to fame within her chosen art, becoming better known as a photographer in her own lifetime than Dodgson in his. Her celebrity rested on achievements in two very different genres. From 1891 to 1899 she followed in the footsteps of both Cameron and Carroll, specializing in portraiture and photographing (in monochrome) the eminent visitors to her Oxford home, including Ruskin, whose portrait she published to great acclaim in 1894. In 1899 she then turned to the problem of photography in colour, becoming the leading practitioner of the ground-breaking, but now largely forgotten, 'Sanger Shepherd process of natural colour photography'. Her magnificent results with the Sanger Shepherd process were achieved in the seven years before 1907 (the date conventionally ascribed to the 'birth of colour photography' by historians), her greatest triumph coming with a lecture on Gibraltar illustrated with colour slides, which she gave to overflowing audiences at the Royal Photographic Society an unprecedented four times in 1905 and 1906. Her reputation as a colour photographer was unrivalled: writing in the *Photogram* in 1905 the photographic journalist Catherine Weed Ward (1851–1913) described her work as "quite the best I have ever seen", while the *British Journal of Photography* judged it "the finest which has ever been publicly shown".[5] Two years later she became the first woman to exhibit a photograph by the revolutionary 'Autochrome' process of Auguste and Louis Lumière. In 1936, six years after her death, her work was still regarded as without match, the authority in the field Henry Oscar Klein declaring that "the colour transparencies of Miss Acland, done with the Sanger-Shepherd process, have never been surpassed in brilliancy and truthfulness of colour, and only Technicolor of to-day can approach them."[6]

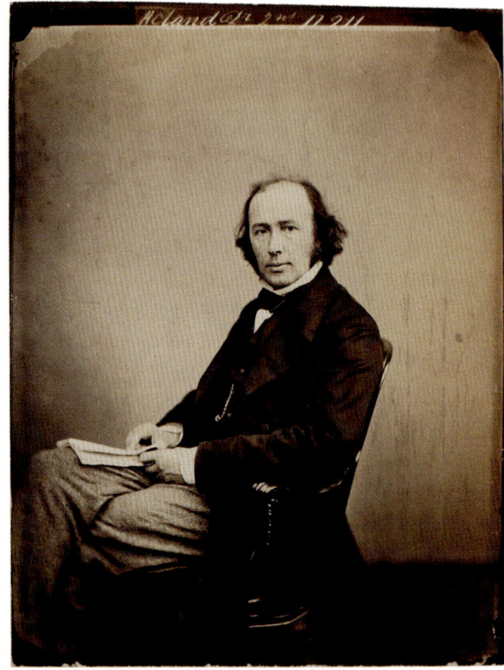

Fig. 3. *Henry Wentworth Acland*
Maull & Polyblank, albumen print, 1860

Art, Science and the Acland Family of Oxford

Sarah Angelina Acland — 'Angie' as she was known to family (never Sarah), or 'Miss Acland' as she was invariably addressed by contemporaries — was born on 26 June 1849 in Oxford, where she would live until her death on 2 December 1930. Her father, Henry Wentworth Acland (1815–1900), was the son of Thomas Dyke Acland, 10th baronet (1787–1871), a wealthy landowner with a seat at Killerton House in Devon (now a National Trust property). Her mother Sarah, née Cotton (1815–1878), was the daughter of William Cotton (1786–1866), a rich city merchant who served three times as Governor of the Bank of England. She therefore lived a life of relative comfort, security and privilege, on the fringes of the upper middle class and aristocracy, spared the need, or indeed the opportunity, to earn a living.

Miss Acland's parents were highly respected figures in Oxford. At the time of her birth Acland held the position of Lee's Reader in Anatomy at Christ Church and practised as a physician out of Broad Street. During his daughter's childhood he would be appointed to a string of influential University posts, including Regius Professor of Medicine, Radcliffe Librarian and Curator of the University Galleries (now the Ashmolean Museum). His two great passions, instilled in his daughter by example, were art and science, which he invariably pursued in close conjunction. At a time when neither had a formal place within the curriculum he fought for them both, and was responsible more than any other person for their advancement in the City and University, supported in his mission by his former tutor, Henry George Liddell (1811–1898), Dean of Christ Church and father of the famous sisters. Acland's lasting legacy was the creation of a new museum for Oxford, opened in 1860: a masterpiece of art and science in itself, now the University Museum of Natural History. The

Fig. 4. *"A Garden in Broad St."*
Photographer unknown, albumen print, 22 June 1865
Miss Acland is seen far right, wearing her riding habit. In the background is the revolving roof of her father's observatory.

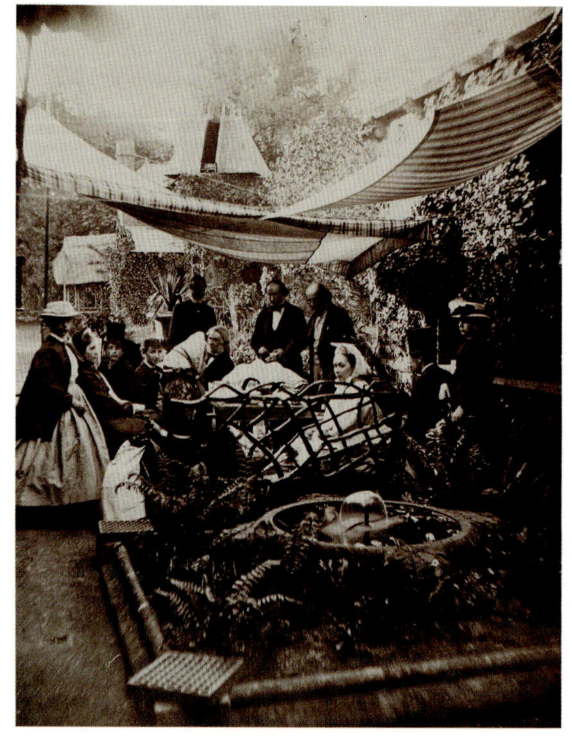

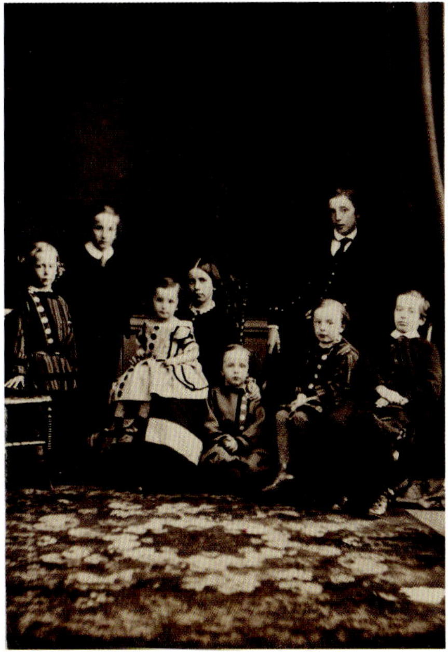

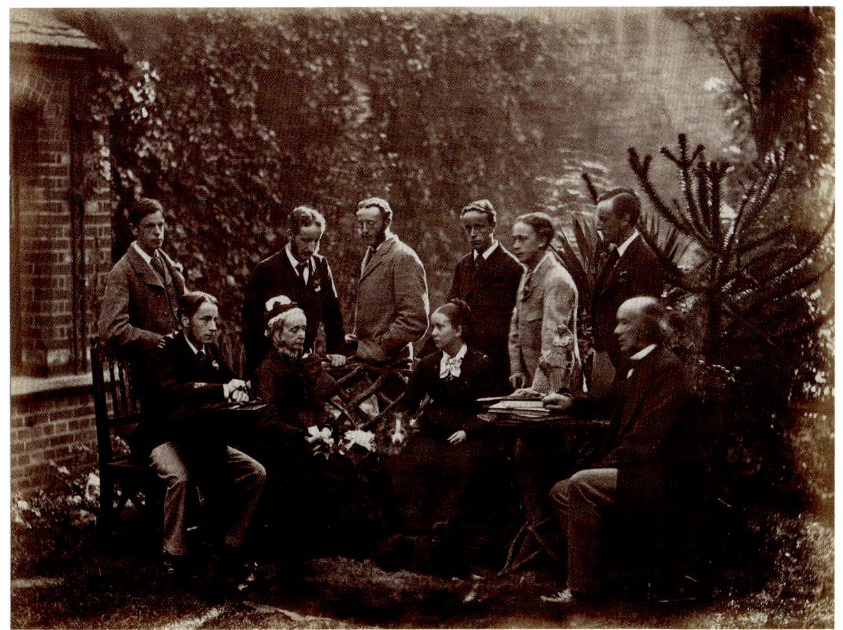

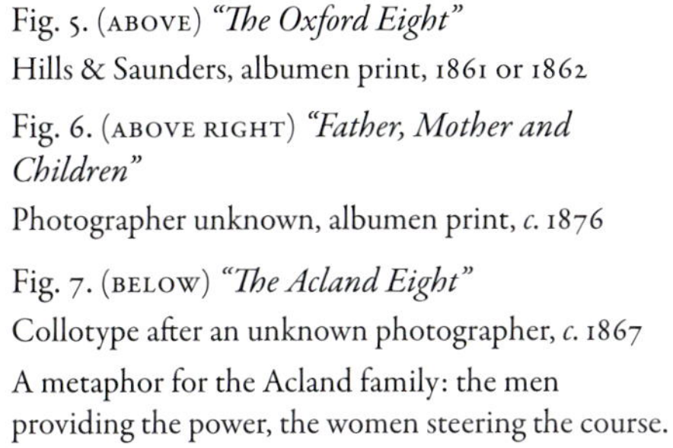

Fig. 5. (ABOVE) *"The Oxford Eight"*
Hills & Saunders, albumen print, 1861 or 1862

Fig. 6. (ABOVE RIGHT) *"Father, Mother and Children"*
Photographer unknown, albumen print, *c.* 1876

Fig. 7. (BELOW) *"The Acland Eight"*
Collotype after an unknown photographer, *c.* 1867
A metaphor for the Acland family: the men providing the power, the women steering the course.

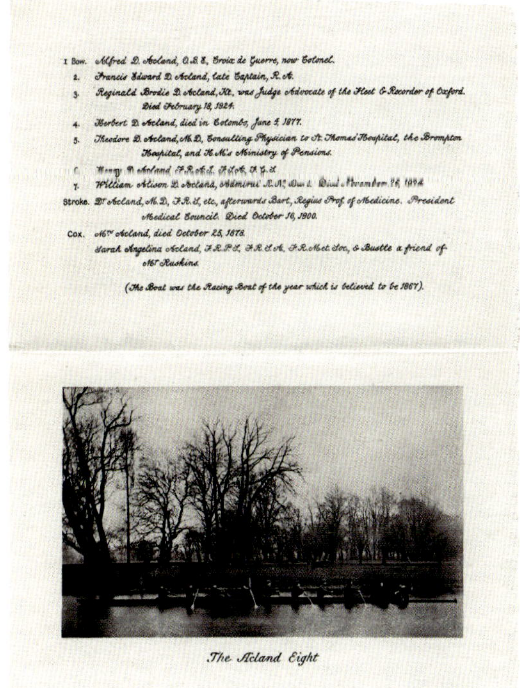

1 Bow. Alfred D. Acland, O.B.E., Croix de Guerre, now Colonel.
2. Francis Edward D. Acland, late Captain, R.A.
3. Reginald Brodie D. Acland, Kt., was Judge Advocate of the Fleet & Recorder of Oxford. Died February 18, 1924.
4. Herbert D. Acland, died in Colombo, June 5, 1877.
5. Theodore D. Acland, M.D., Consulting Physician to St. Thomas' Hospital, the Brompton Hospital, and H.M.'s Ministry of Pensions.
6. Henry D. Acland [illegible]
7. William Alison D. Acland, Admiral R.N., [illegible] Died November 18, 1924
Stroke. Dr Acland, M.D., F.R.S., etc., afterwards Bart., Regius Prof. of Medicine. President Medical Council. Died October 16, 1900.
Cox. Mrs Acland, died October 25, 1878.
Sarah Angelina Acland, F.R.P.S., F.R.S.A., F.R.Met.Soc., & Bustle a friend of Mr Ruskins.

(The Boat was the Racing Boat of the year which is believed to be 1867).

Museum was designed by his "charming and beloved" friend, the architect Benjamin Woodward (1816–1861), in consultation with Ruskin, the most revered critic of the century and Acland's mentor on matters artistic.[7]

Miss Acland's home for the first fifty-two years of her life was a large house on Broad Street, directly overlooking the Sheldonian Theatre (cat. no. 4). The house occupied a central position in Oxford, socially as well as geographically, playing host to a constant stream of visitors from near and far, many of unequalled repute, princes and prime ministers among them. The appeal of the Aclands' drawing room owed much to Mrs Acland, who was admired for her grace, culture and learning. The Aclands were credited with creating a new kind of society in Oxford, in which traditional divides between town and gown, dons and undergraduates, and men and women were broken down, all meeting in their home "on easier terms than they would have otherwise done".[8] Their hospitality extended to individuals of modest birth, in fulfilment of the family's deeply held social, moral and religious beliefs, which also found expression in their many charitable and philanthropic undertakings.

For Miss Acland the 'Old Home' embodied the ideals of her parents, which she took as her own, and which represented much of what she valued in life. When she was forced to leave after her father died in 1900, having devoted herself to his service for twenty-two years since her mother passed away in 1878, the wrench was traumatic. As well as sharing Broad Street with a staff of a dozen servants (cat. no. 54), she had seven brothers for company: William Alison Dyke ('Willie') Acland (1847–1924), Henry Dyke ('Harry') Acland (1850–1936), Theodore Dyke ('Theo') Acland (1851–1931), Herbert Dyke ('Herbie') Acland (1855–1877), Reginald Brodie Dyke ('Reggie') Acland (1856–1924), Francis Edward Dyke ('Frank') Acland (1857–1943), and Alfred Dyke Acland (1858–1937). Herbert died at the age of 22 in Ceylon, having emigrated as a coffee planter, but his brothers had long and successful careers, all but Harry making it into *Who's Who* with their father. Willie joined the Royal Navy at 14, retiring with the rank of Admiral after serving as Naval A.D.C. to Queen Victoria. Harry followed the profession of his great grandfather, the banker Henry Hoare (1750–1828), becoming manager of the Old Bank in Malvern. Theodore chose medicine, his career culminating as Governor of St Thomas's Hospital; Reggie was called to the bar and knighted in 1914; Frank served in the Royal Artillery and as director of the Maxim-Nordenfelt Gun Company; and Alfred trained as a civil engineer before joining the business of his father-in-law, the newsagent W. H. Smith.

As a Victorian woman, Miss Acland led a more circumscribed life than her brothers. Her opportunities for marriage were limited by poor health — a childhood illness left her lame and requiring the use of a wheelchair for lengthy periods — and by service to her father: she died a spinster. Her education took place at home under a succession of governesses, in the schoolroom of her uncle near Killerton, and from the age of 16 to 18 at a girls' boarding school, Mayfield, in Southgate, North London. Typically for a woman of her class, her lessons revolved around languages, literature, music and religious instruction. However, in Oxford she was also exposed to the wonders of science, whether observing the planets through a telescope in the observatory in the back garden or witnessing electrical experiments performed by George Griffith (1833–1902), deputy to the Professor of Experimental Philosophy, who married her cousin Harriet Dyke ('Ettie') Troyte, née Acland (1838–1921). Her mother was as keen as her father to encourage her scientific curiosity, in 1869 corresponding with her on Helmholtz's *Popular Lectures on Scientific Subjects*, and taking her to lectures on microscopy in the Museum. Although of academic bent, Miss Acland belonged to a generation of women denied access to higher education. Her ambitions therefore had to be satisfied by other means, art and photography offering such possibilities.

Art was an important part of Miss Acland's life from an early age. In 1930 she could still remember the 'Pre-Raffaelite days' in Oxford and the painting of the Union murals by Dante Gabriel Rossetti (1828–1882), Edward Burne-Jones (1833–1898) and William Morris (1834–1896). "Rossetti would occasionally let me have his palette", she wrote.[9] Other artists she knew through her father included Holman Hunt (1827–1910) (see cat. no. 45), William Edwards Miller (1851–1940) (from whom Acland commissioned an *Oxford Gallery of Portraits* in 1876), and William Blake Richmond (1842–1921) (cat. no. 60). Her artistic training began under her father, who was an avid painter in watercolours, before being placed on a formal footing in 1864 (aged 15) when she started lessons with the Oxford art master William Riviere (1806–1876). At Mayfield her instruction continued under the watercolourist David Hall McKewan (1816–1873); after leaving she enrolled in the Oxford School of Art, where Alexander Macdonald (1839–1921), who became a lifelong friend, was drawing master. Her father had been one of the leading lights in the foundation of the School (now Oxford Brookes University), which had 360 pupils by 1868, including the Liddell sisters and another of their close friends, Alice Emily Donkin (1849–1940), daughter of the Professor of Astronomy, William Fishburn Donkin (1814–1869). In March Miss Acland passed the second grade government art examinations. At the prize-giving in the Town Hall in October seven of her watercolours were exhibited: two landscapes, *Ptarmigan*, *Pigeon*, *Herring*, *Basket of Fruit*, and *Florence Flask*.

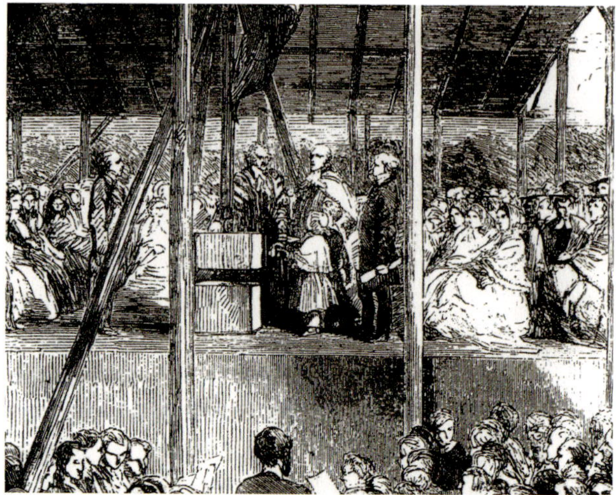

Fig. 8. *Laying the 'Chief Stone' of the Oxford University Museum*
The building of the new Oxford University Museum loomed large over Miss Acland's early childhood. At the laying of the foundation stone on 20 June 1855 she was given responsibility for presenting the ceremonial trowel to the Earl of Derby, former Prime Minister and Chancellor of the University. Ten days later an engraving of the ceremony appeared in the *Illustrated London News*, but failed to win her approval. "I was deeply offended because I was represented wearing a bonnet whereas I was wearing a hat!", she wrote in her memoirs. Her position in the scene is indicative of the place she would occupy in Oxford over the next half century: at the centre of University life but never a formal member of the institution.

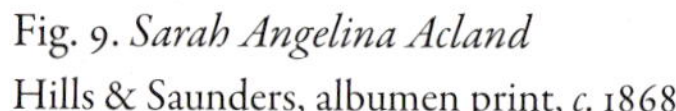

Fig. 9. *Sarah Angelina Acland*
Hills & Saunders, albumen print, *c.* 1868

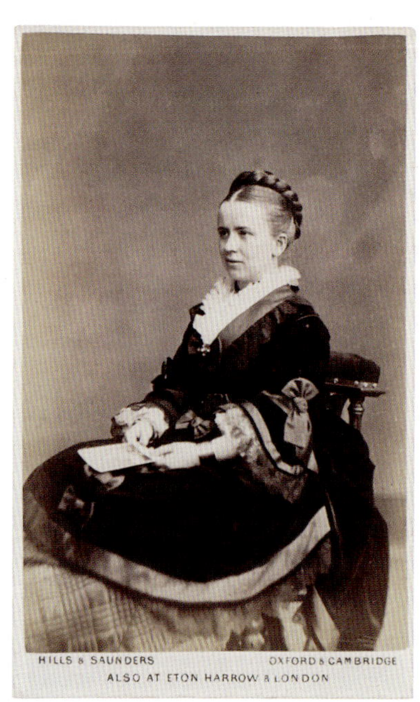

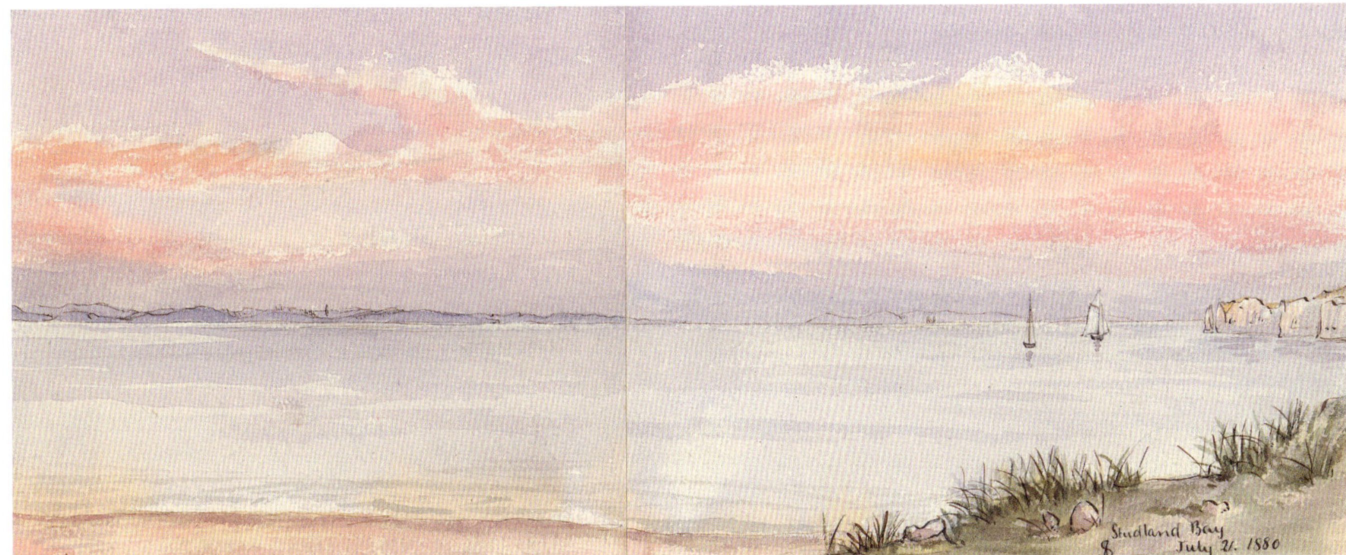

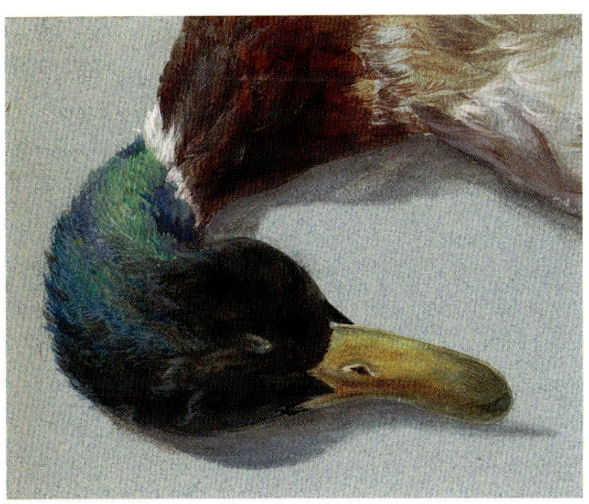

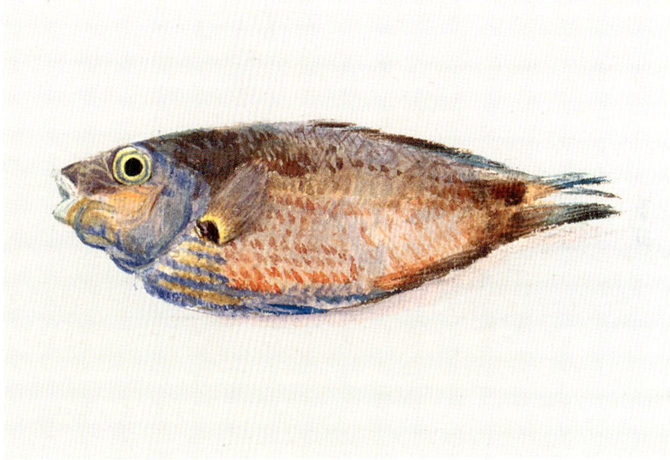

Figs. 10–12. *Watercolours by Sarah Angelina Acland* "Bournemouth & Isle of Wight from Studland Bay, July 21, 1880"; "Wild duck, Dec. 1878, Oxford"; Study of a Fish, "Mentone, April 24 [1877]"

Miss Acland was a capable watercolourist. Her photography would later be preoccupied with the Pre-Raphaelite doctrine of "truth to nature", just as under Ruskin her drawing and painting had been.

According to Miss Acland's obituary in *The Times*, Ruskin, who was Harry's godfather, "exercised great influence on her artistic powers, which were considerable".[10] Her education under the critic, both practical and moral, began after her father engineered his appointment to the chair of Slade Professor of Art in 1869. Ruskin lodged in the Acland house whilst giving his first professorial lectures, providing the opportunity for Miss Acland, aged 21, to take lessons from him. Inevitably perhaps, she soon became emotionally attached to her "Cricket", as she called him, Ruskin doing little to discourage her by addressing her as "my darling Teaze" and similarly affectionate terms.[11] Worries about the relationship soon led Mrs Acland to eject Ruskin to college rooms, but from 1872 Angie continued her lessons at his Drawing School in the University Galleries, where he had taken over the upper and middle class pupils of the School of Art. She also continued to serve as his 'secretary' of sorts, undertaking (paid) commissions at his request, such as colouring plates for his published works and making enlarged drawings for his lectures. Examples of her work that survive reveal the strength of his influence by their similarity of style and subject matter. Her abilities can also be judged from her success in getting *The Intruder*, a portrait of her dog Fez, accepted for the Royal Academy exhibition in 1875.

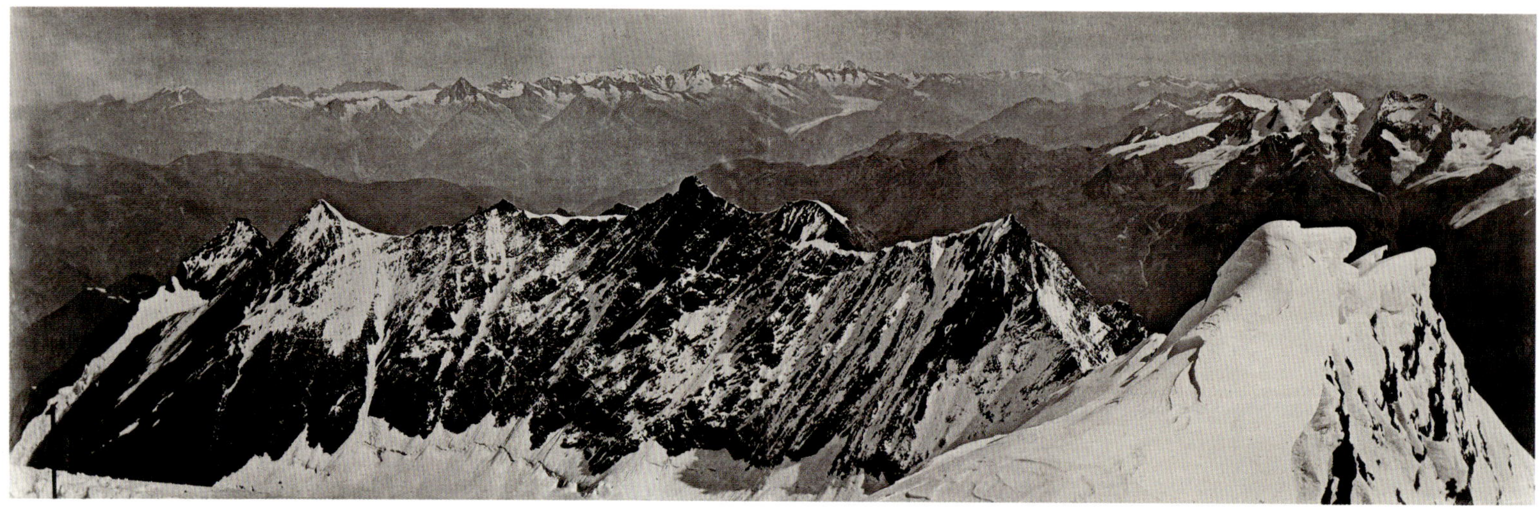

An Oxford Education in Photography, 1849 to 1891

During Miss Acland's upbringing in Oxford a greater variety and concentration of photographic activity could be found within a mile of her home than almost anywhere else in the world. Without leaving the street on which she was born she could witness the full range of photography's manifestations, commercial, scientific, scholarly and recreational. Directly opposite her house, for example, in what was then the Ashmolean Museum (now the Museum of the History of Science), Nevil Story Maskelyne (1823–1911), Reader in Mineralogy, used photography to investigate irradiation and other phenomena during the 1850s. In his shop two doors down John Henry Parker (1806–1884) compiled a catalogue of 3,391 photographs of the antiquities of Rome between 1864 and 1877, exhibiting them to the public in the Ashmolean after he became Keeper. At the west end of Broad Street Henry Taunt (1842–1922) ran his photographic business from 1874 to 1895, while at the east end, in a house on the site of the future Indian Institute, William Frederick ('Willie') Donkin (1845–1888), brother of Alice Donkin, honed the skills that would see him become the foremost alpine photographer of the day — "the Millais of the Matterhorn" — and with it secretary of both the Alpine Club and the (Royal) Photographic Society.[12]

Oxford's introduction to photography had taken place on 6 April 1839, two months after its announcement by Fox Talbot and Daguerre, when Joseph Plowman (1811–1867), an influential local tradesman, advertised "photogenic or sun drawing paper" for sale at his shop on the Corn Market.[13] By this date Talbot's 'photogenic experiments' were already familiar to Oxford's men of science, Baden Powell (1796–1860), Savilian Professor of Geometry, having corresponded with him in February about their relevance to the wave theory of light. Talbot would become a familiar figure on the streets of Oxford in the ensuing years, visiting to photograph her picturesque buildings. In 1844 he chose Queen's College for the first plate of *The Pencil of Nature* — a scene Miss Acland returned to half a century later (cat. no. 104).

The most conspicuous manifestation of photography in Oxford was undoubtedly commercial portraiture. Oxford's first studio, the "Photographic &

Fig. 13. *"The Nadelgrat from the Summit of the Dom"*
William Frederick Donkin, 'Autotype print', between 1879 and 1881
Donkin died tragically during a photographic expedition to the Caucasus in 1888. His plates were posthumously exhibited at the Gainsborough Gallery.

Fig. 14. *"Colossal Head of Domitian, now in the Courtyard of the Palazzo de' Conservatori on the Capitol"*
Albumen print, by or for John Henry Parker, *c.* 1863

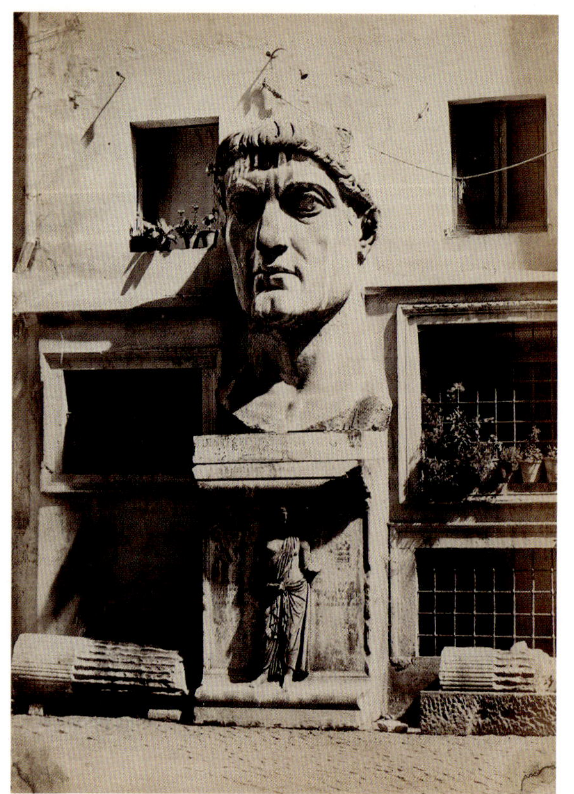

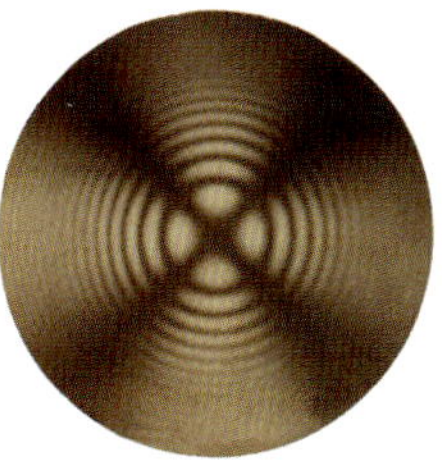

Fig. 15. *Interference Pattern of Polarized Light through Calcite*
William Crookes, albumen print (in Acland's album), *c.* 1853

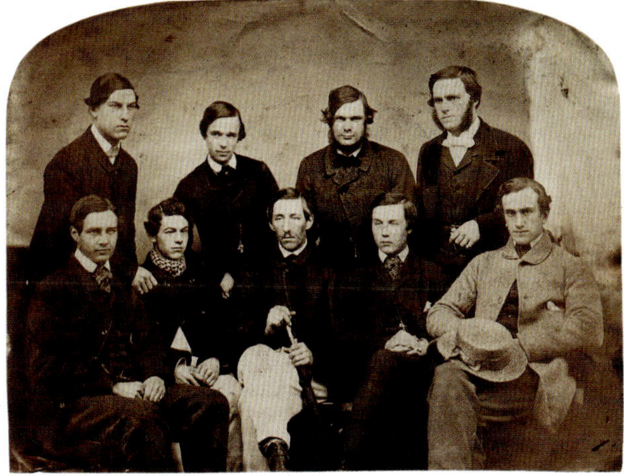

Fig. 16. *"The Magdalen College Eight Oar, 1859"*
Albumen print, probably by Robert Hills

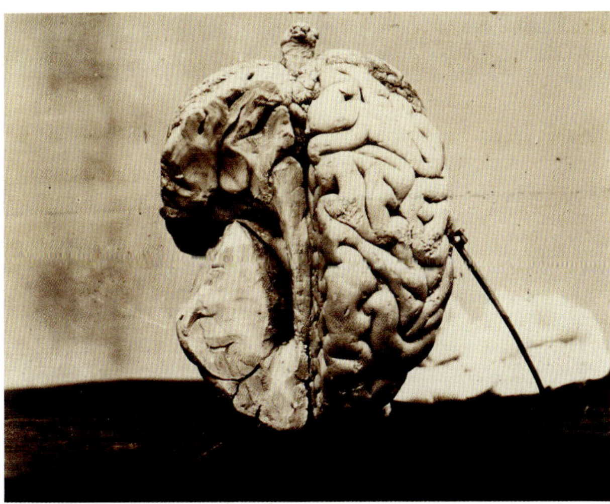

Fig. 17. *"Brain of Orang dissected so as to show the lateral ventricle of the right side, its three cornua and the hippocamus minor"*
Hills & Saunders for George Rolleston, albumen print, 1860 or 1861

Whether the brain of man and monkey differed anatomically was at the heart of the Darwinian debate, over which Samuel Wilberforce and Thomas Henry Huxley argued in Acland's new museum in 1860. This print is evidence of the similarity. Its place in Acland's album betrays his opposition to the stance of his friend the Bishop of Oxford and his belief in the power of photography as witness to 'anatomical matters of fact'.

Daguerreotype Portrait Institution", opened on the High Street on 17 October 1842, under the proprietorship of the landscape painter John Akers (1802/3–1879) (not, as often stated, William Tuckwell). Akers retired from photography in 1846, but his successor, Edward Bracher (1823–1887), would remain in business for almost two decades, trading first in daguerreotype and calotype portraits, adding collodion and 'enamelled' photographs from 1854, and exploiting the craze for the carte de visite when it reached Oxford in 1861. Bracher's first permanent rival set up in 1856: Robert Hills (1821–1882), a former "artist in hair", who with John Henry Saunders (1836–1890) founded one of the longest-lived studios in all England. During the 1860s Bracher and Hills were joined by a host of competitors, their profits buoyed by undergraduates eager to be portrayed with their fellow oarsmen and other college friends. A consequence of the growth in studios was the employment of significant numbers of women in photography, the census recording seventeen in Oxford by 1891. Most were engaged in subordinate roles, such as retouching prints; it was not until 1895 that the trade directories list a woman with her own studio: Alice Emma Buttrum (b. 1865), who was briefly in business at 18 Market Street.

The scientific basis and applications of photography were recognized as a fertile field for exploration in Oxford not only by Baden Powell but by the Professor of Chemistry and Botany, Charles Giles Bridle Daubeny (1795–1867). On 7 May 1839 Daubeny exhibited photogenic drawings at the Ashmolean Society, the University's principal scientific forum. Photography would feature regularly at the Society in subsequent decades. In May 1847, for example, Maskelyne discoursed on its bearings on chemical philosophy, while in June 1848 the influential amateur William Thomson (1819–1890), Archbishop of York, presented the results of his investigations with the collodion process.[14] Photography proved of particular value in Oxford's observatories. At the Radcliffe Observatory William Crookes (1832–1919), discoverer of thallium and founder of the *Photographic News*, invented a waxed paper process to facilitate the 'self registration' of meteorological instruments; at the University Observatory Charles Pritchard (1808–1893), Savilian Professor of Astronomy, and his assistants used gelatine plates to capture images from a 13-inch telescope donated by the pioneer celestial photographer Warren De La Rue (1815–1889). Miss Acland later developed interests in both fields, photographing eclipses (cat. no. 119) and making records of the weather, which earned her a fellowship at the Royal Meteorological Society in 1916.

In the arts in Oxford photography was slower to gain a footing. The first reference to a print being shown at the Architectural and Historical Society — the counterpart of the Ashmolean Society — dates from 1846, when William Basil Jones (1822–1897), future Bishop of St David's, exhibited a Talbotype of Oriel College. However, another decade would pass before photographs secured a regular place in the Society's proceedings, when they eventually ousted plaster casts for illustrating architecture. One member of the Society who did recognize their value earlier was Ruskin. Ruskin's use of daguerreotypes in art historical research is well known, his use of calotypes and albumen prints as teaching aids less so. At the Drawing School he assembled a large collection of prints, the majority intended for consultation by pupils (Miss Acland included) as part of their instruction in the elements of drawing. For his wider public he arranged for photographic copies of the artworks discussed

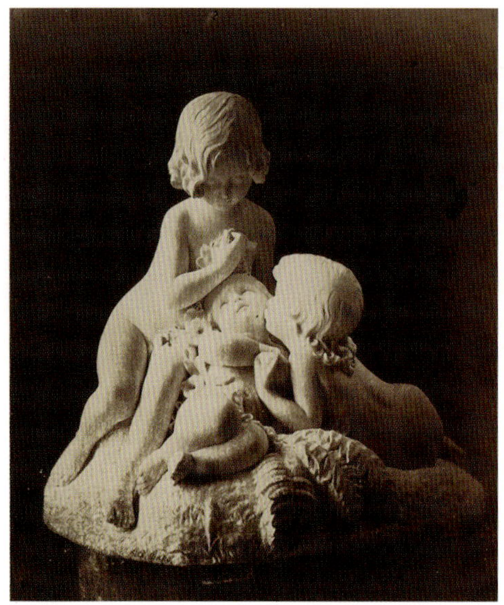

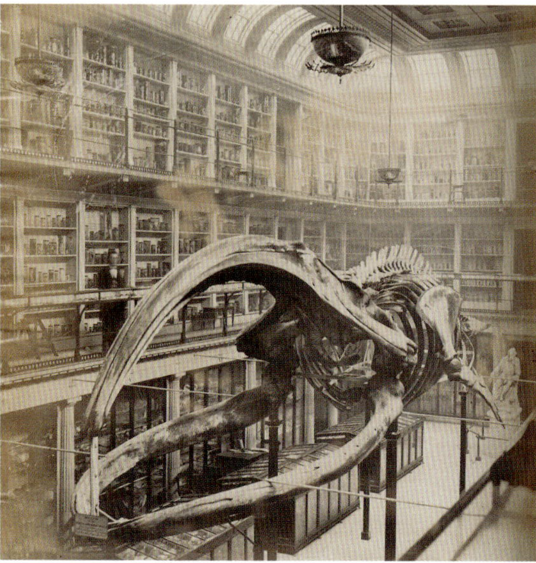

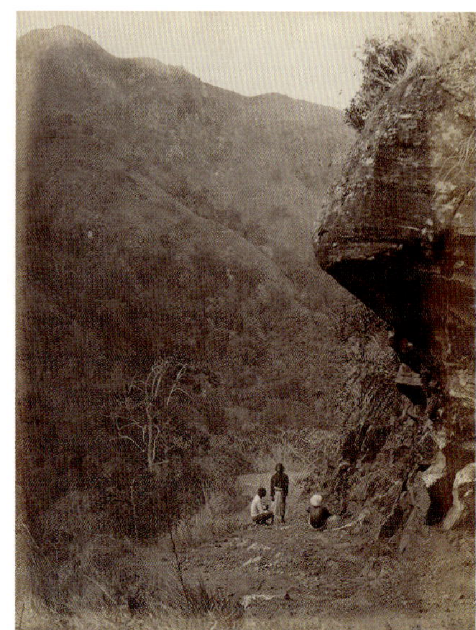

in his lectures to be made available through his agent William Ward (1829–1908) and at the shop of the printseller Albert Davis (1840–1884) in Turl Street.

As well as in shop windows and at the Drawing School, Miss Acland could see photographs in the comfort of her own home. Soon after her birth her father assembled an exceptional collection of prints in an album Ruskin had given him. The prints span the spectrum of photographic genres, from portraiture by Maull & Polyblank to views of a dissected orang-utan brain by Hills & Saunders, landscapes acquired in 1860 whilst accompanying the Prince of Wales to Canada, and architectural studies of prototypes for the University Museum. Among the most notable are a variant of *Waves Breaking* by John Dillwyn Llewelyn (1810–1882) and a salt print (now faded almost into oblivion) of sheep following the shepherd, the gift of Elizabeth Siddal (1829–1862) (see cat. no. 95). The value of photography for copying artworks particularly engaged Acland's attention, as it later would his daughter (cat. nos. 95–99). The largest group of prints in his album, thirty-six in total, depicts works by his close friend the sculptor Alexander Munro (1825–1871). A print of Munro's *Child Play* has a special place in the history of photography, since it was seen by Dodgson at a party at the Aclands in November 1857, prompting him to embark on a fruitful collaboration of his own with the sculptor (see cat. no. 81).

Acland had been keen to encourage Dodgson in photography even before showing him *Child Play*. Aside from allowing him to take portraits of the children, in May 1857 he asked Dodgson to photograph a tuna skeleton he had recently acquired in Madeira. The commission led Dodgson to make several more anatomical photographs, including a famous portrait of Reginald Southey (1835–1899), Acland's student, posed with human and ape skeletons. Southey, like Dodgson, was both a Christ Church man and a photographer. Salt prints from his hand can also be seen in Acland's album but were not, surprisingly, the first by a member of the college to find their way there. This honour went instead to work by Acland's brother-in-law, Arthur Benjamin Cotton (1832–1918). 'Uncle ABC', as he was known to the children, matriculated at Christ Church in 1850 and received a first in Mathematics and Physics in 1854,

Fig. 18. (ABOVE LEFT) *Child Play*
William Jeffrey (1826–1877)?, albumen print, *c.* 1853

Prints from Mrs Acland's Album
Fig. 19. (ABOVE MIDDLE) *"Museum at the College of Surgeons"*
Photographer unknown, albumen print, *c.* 1870
Fig. 20. (ABOVE RIGHT) *"A 'bit' on the Ella Pass Road, Ceylon"*
Bourne & Shepherd?, albumen print, *c.* 1877 or 1878
Fig. 21. (BELOW) *"Mr. Combe and Cyril Hunt"*
Charles Lutwidge Dodgson, albumen print, 24 or 25 July 1872
An unrecorded portrait by Dodgson of Holman Hunt's son, Cyril Benoni Holman Hunt, with Thomas Combe.

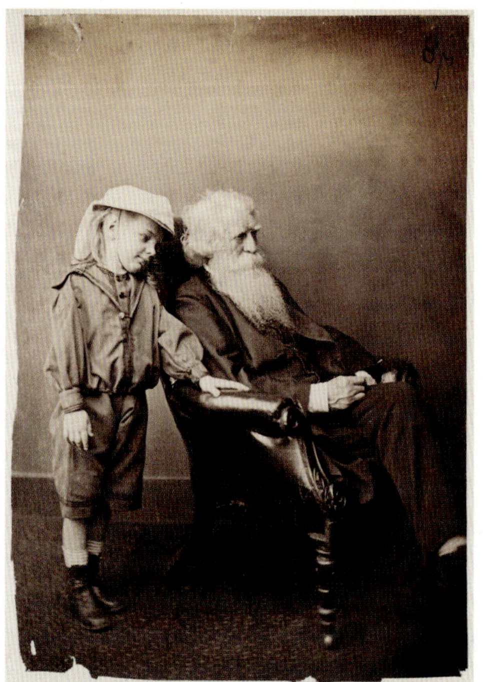

Fig. 22. *"Walwood, N.E."*
Arthur Benjamin Cotton, albumen print, April 1863
Walwood House, Leytonstone, was the home of the Cotton family. In this photograph Mrs Acland is sitting under a lime tree in the grounds, listening to her husband read a poem to her wheelchair-bound mother Sarah Cotton, née Lane (1790–1872). Miss Acland's 'Uncle ABC' took up photography earlier and was arguably more capable than either of his Christ Church contemporaries, Dodgson and Southey.

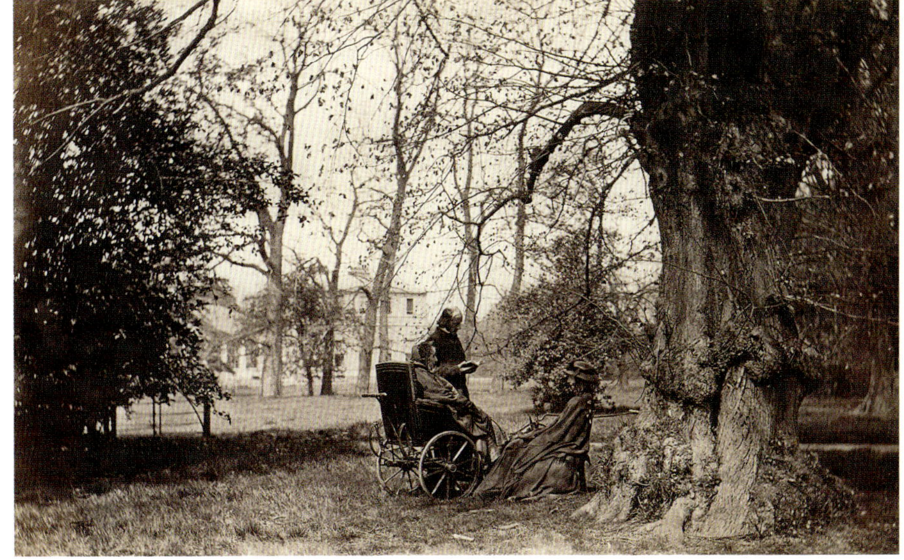

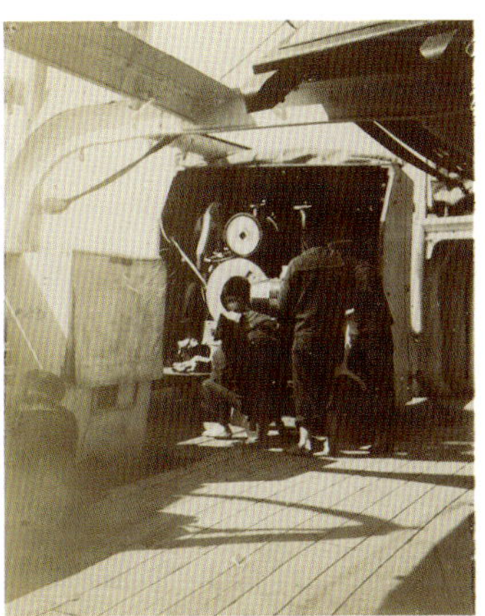

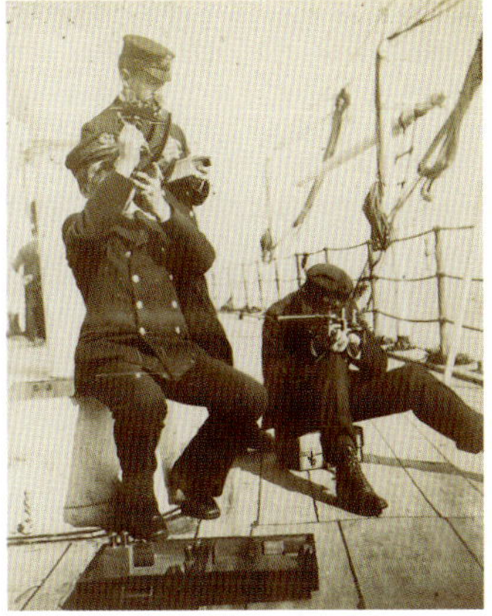

Figs. 23 & 24. *On H.M.S. Edgar*
Francis Edward Dyke Acland, albumen prints, April 1893

Fig. 25. *"Natives & Idols, Mallicollo"*
William Alison Dyke Acland, albumen print, Vanuatu, 1884

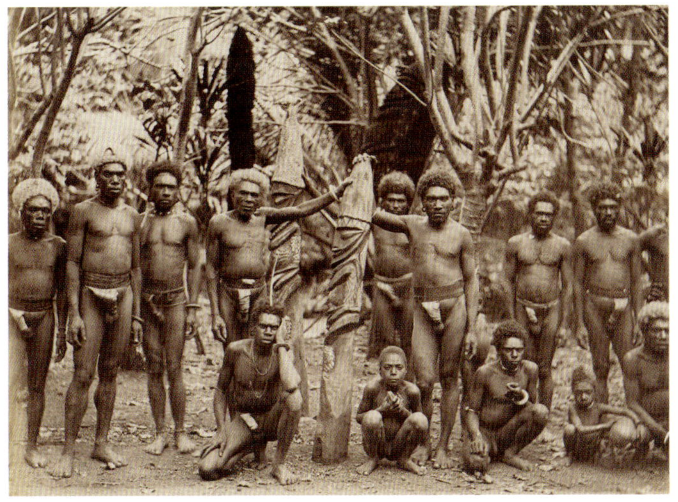

by which time he was already an accomplished photographer, more than a year before Dodgson. Three years later he invited his friend on a photographic tour of France. Dodgson did "not much fancy the plan", but Cotton went regardless, one product of the trip, a salt print of *L'Eglise de St Pierre à Caen*, finding its way into the Photographic Exchange Club album for 1858.[15] Cotton's photographs also feature in a volume compiled between 1860 and 1878 by his sister. Mrs Acland's album is different in character from her husband's, but no less remarkable, containing over 500 prints, by Cameron, Dodgson and others. The album was a fixture of the drawing room at Broad Street, where Mrs Ackland used it to entertain guests, young and old: "Violet Liddell is sitting by my side making a drawing of Mr. Conybeare from the Photograph in my Book!", she told Angie in 1878.[16]

Encouraged by her mother and father, Miss Acland had already developed a taste for photography by 1857, when she can be found asking for a portrait of her late aunt Phoebe Cotton (1817–1857). In the early days of her collecting she kept her prints in "pretty little portfolios" she bound herself.[17] On starting school at Mayfield a more respectable album became a necessity and was duly provided on her sixteenth birthday. This she filled with photographs of "people and places" begged from friends. While staying in the spa town of Wildbad in the Black Forest in 1869, for example, she was given two signed cartes de visite. However, these she preferred to have mounted in a bespoke, velvet-lined case, complete with the envelope in which they came, which bore the treasured inscription "For Miss Acland from the Prince & Princess of Wales with their best wishes for her recovery".[18] Later she used photographs to illustrate her travel journals, also sending home images of treasures seen in Italy and elsewhere, prints of which her father specifically asked her to obtain.

By the time Miss Acland came to entertain thoughts of taking up photography herself, there were several capable photographers in her close family from whom she could seek inspiration and advice. Continuing the family photographic dynasty at Christ Church inaugurated by her uncle were three cousins: Arthur Herbert Dyke Acland (1847–1926), John Dyke Acland (1863–1944) and Henry Dyke Acland

(1867–1942). Arthur showed seventeen prints at the Photographic Society in 1883 and 1884, including the intriguingly titled *A Vivâ-voce Examination in the University of the Future*. John, who exhibited at the Society in 1886, and Henry were both leading lights of the University Photographic Club (their sisters contributed to the family photographic enterprise at home back in New Zealand).[19] Miss Acland could also learn from her brothers, at least four of whom took up photography before her. Herbert, who matriculated at Christ Church in 1874, had been the first to do so, asking his Uncle ABC for "a photographic apparatus to amuse himself with" in 1870, whilst at school at Charterhouse with one of Cameron's sons (see cat. no. 1).[20] Frank and Harry followed later and would eventually give lectures at the Oxford Camera Club: Frank on the 'Transvaal War', Harry on a visit to Africa with the B.A.A.S. Although not the first, undoubtedly the most celebrated of Miss Acland's brothers as a photographer was Willie, who learnt to use a camera on his appointment to H.M.S. *Miranda* in 1883. Over the next two years he exposed numerous plates whilst sailing the remote islands of Melanesia and Polynesia, photographing the indigenous peoples, their material culture and encounters with Europeans.[21] Miss Acland was captivated by the images he sent back to Oxford, commissioning Hills & Saunders to mount them in albums so she could show them to friends.

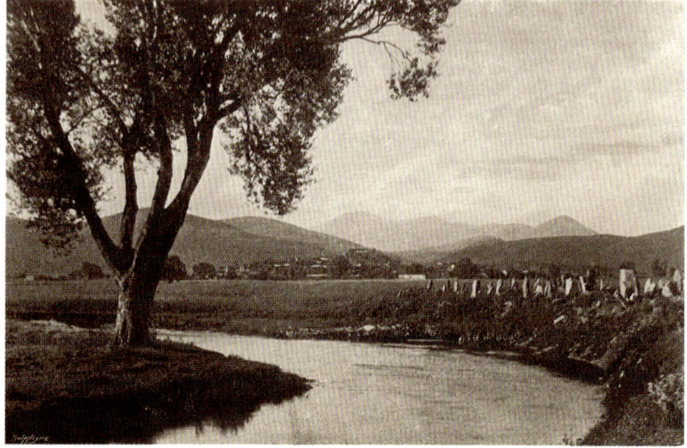

Fig. 26. *"View of Gyuksun (Cocusus) in the Anti-Taurus"*
John Arthur Ruskin Munro (1864–1944), 'Swantype', 1891

J. A. R. Munro was the son of Alexander (sculptor), the ward of Acland, and Rector of Lincoln College. In 1891 he travelled to Asia Minor with the archaeologist David George Hogarth (1862–1927), mentor of T. E. Lawrence (1888–1935). He belongs to a long line of Oxford archaeological photographers, in which Lawrence also stands, and was one of several friends to whom Miss Acland could turn for advice when starting out in photography.

First Photographs

Miss Acland began her career as an amateur photographer on 26 June 1891, when her father gave her a camera for her birthday. The timing of her turn to photography was not untypical of a woman of her class. At 42 she was still six years younger than Cameron had been in 1863 when her daughter gave her a similar present. However, like Cameron, she benefitted from the fact that, as the *Queen* explained, the gift of a camera was "equally acceptable to the older and wiser amongst us as to the more juvenile of our acquaintances".[22] Despite its long-standing status as the "scientific amusement of the higher classes", photography had become fashionable as a pastime for middle-class women only in the late 1880s: amateur photography *per se* had seen huge growth after the release of dry plates in 1878, but women lagged behind men in embracing the hobby.[23] In October 1884, for example, in the first issue of *Amateur Photographer*, the editor concluded that women photographers were still an unknown quantity: "like the guests at a well-arranged dinner party, numbering more than the Graces and less than the Muses".[24] Nevertheless, by 1889 their numbers had increased significantly, the tally exhibiting at the Photographic Society jumping from three to twelve, among them Ellen Anne Boyer Brown (1848–1927), the headmistress of Miss Acland's old school, Mayfield.

The camera Miss Acland received for her birthday was a Kodak No. 3. The original Kodak, later called the No. 1, had been launched by George Eastman in 1888 and sold in unprecedented numbers with the help of the famous advertising slogan "You press the button, we do the rest" (albeit with the now forgotten caveat, "or you can do it yourself"). The No. 3 was similar, but took rectangular rather than round photographs, 3¼ × 4¼ inches in size, on celluloid roll film. At £8 14*s* 6*d* (about £706 at 2012 values) it was a luxury item. Miss Acland put hers to use for the first

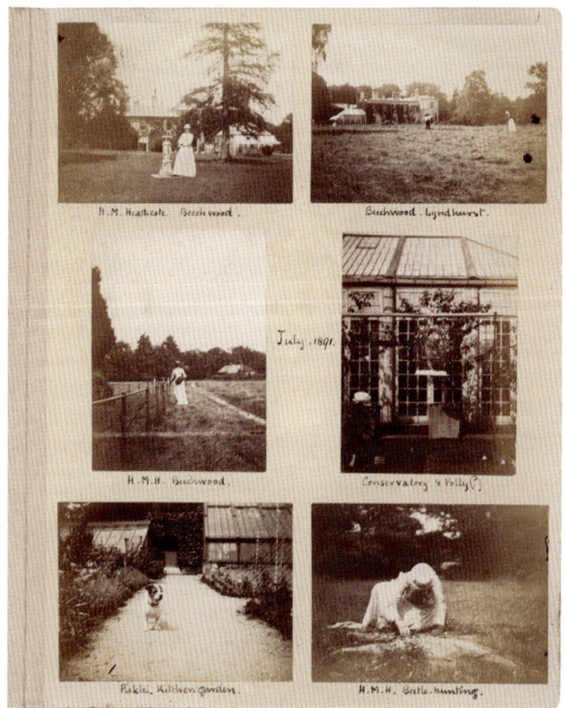

Fig. 27. *"July 1891"*
The first page of Miss Acland's first album

Miss Acland's first photographs were taken at the home of her friends Ellie and Be Heathcote, daughters of William Heathcote, M.P. for the University. The two at the bottom of the page make good use of the low viewpoint possible with a 'hand camera'.

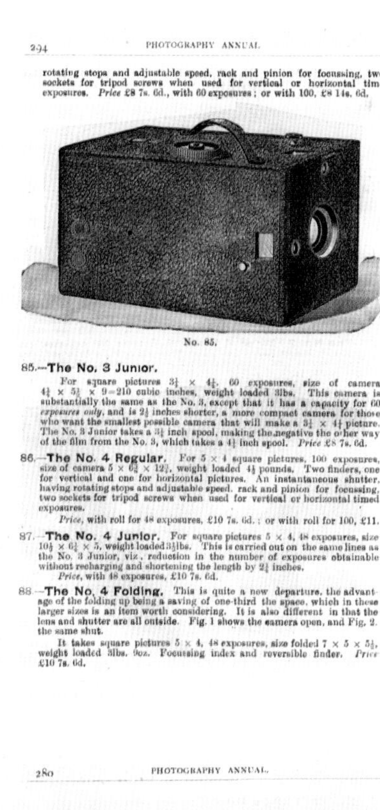

294 PHOTOGRAPHY ANNUAL.

rotating stops and adjustable speed, rack and pinion for focussing, two sockets for tripod screws when used for vertical or horizontal time exposures. *Price* £8 7s. 6d., with 60 exposures; or with 100, £8 14s. 6d.

No. 85.

85.—**The No. 3 Junior.**

For square pictures $3\frac{1}{4} \times 4\frac{1}{4}$, 60 exposures, size of camera $4\frac{1}{4} \times 5\frac{1}{2} \times 9 = 210$ cubic inches, weight loaded 3lbs. This camera is substantially the same as the No. 3, except that it has a capacity for 60 *exposures only*, and is $2\frac{1}{2}$ inches shorter, a more compact camera for those who want the smallest possible camera that will make a $3\frac{1}{4} \times 4\frac{1}{4}$ picture. The No. 3 Junior takes a $3\frac{1}{4}$ inch spool, making the negative the other way of the film from the No. 3, which takes a $4\frac{1}{4}$ inch spool. *Price* £8 7s. 6d.

86.—**The No. 4 Regular.** For 5×4 square pictures, 100 exposures, size of camera $5 \times 6\frac{3}{4} \times 12\frac{3}{4}$, weight loaded $4\frac{1}{2}$ pounds. Two finders, one for vertical and one for horizontal pictures. An instantaneous shutter, having rotating stops and adjustable speed, rack and pinion for focussing, two sockets for tripod screws when used for vertical or horizontal timed exposures.

Price, with roll for 48 exposures, £10 7s. 6d.; or with roll for 100, £11.

87.—**The No. 4 Junior.** For square pictures 5×4, 48 exposures, size $10\frac{1}{2} \times 6\frac{3}{4} \times 5$, weight loaded $3\frac{1}{2}$lbs. This is carried out on the same lines as the No. 3 Junior, viz., reduction in the number of exposures obtainable without recharging and shortening the length by $2\frac{1}{4}$ inches.

Price, with 48 exposures, £10 7s. 6d.

88.—**The No. 4 Folding.** This is quite a new departure, the advantage of the folding up being a saving of one-third the space, which in these larger sizes is an item worth considering. It is also different in that the lens and shutter are all outside. Fig. 1 shows the camera open, and Fig. 2 the same shut.

It takes square pictures 5×4, 48 exposures, size folded $7 \times 5 \times 5\frac{1}{2}$, weight loaded 3lbs. 9oz. Focussing index and reversible finder. *Price* £10 7s. 6d.

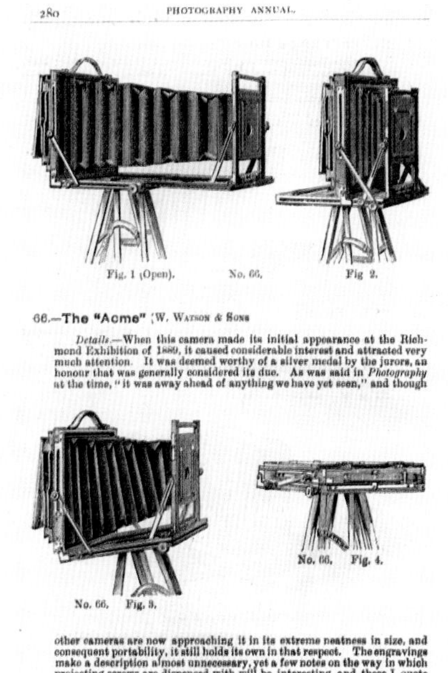

280 PHOTOGRAPHY ANNUAL.

Fig. 1 (Open). No. 66. Fig 2.

66.—**The "Acme"** (W. Watson & Sons

Details.—When this camera made its initial appearance at the Richmond Exhibition of 1889, it caused considerable interest and attracted very much attention. It was deemed worthy of a silver medal by the jurors, an honour that was generally considered its due. As was said in *Photography* at the time, "it was away ahead of anything we have yet seen," and though

No. 66. Fig. 4.

No. 66. Fig. 3.

other cameras are now approaching it in its extreme neatness in size, and consequent portability, it still holds its own in that respect. The engravings make a description almost unnecessary, yet a few notes on the way in which projecting screws are dispensed with will be interesting, and these I quote from the makers' list.

Figs. 28 & 29. *Hand and Stand Cameras*

Reviews from the *Photography Annual*, 1892 and 1891

The Kodak No. 3 was one of a number of new models marketed by Eastman in early 1890 in Britain. Miss Acland probably owned the 'Junior' version, which had a detachable back capable of taking glass plates in addition to roll film. The 'Acme', which she used for her formal portraiture, had been released by Watson & Sons in 1889. Most commentators regarded it as fully worthy of its name.

time during a summer vacation in the south of England, her father writing to her on 12 July 1891 to convey his love to friends and family "who are I suppose already Kodaked".[25] Fifty-six prints from this first period of her photography survive, the Kodak No. 3 being supplied pre-loaded with film for sixty exposures, although it was capable of taking up to a hundred in the 'Junior' model.

Miss Acland's earliest photographs reveal her to have been a competent photographer from the outset, with a good eye for composition. She continued to use her Kodak for several years, including during a visit to Brantwood to photograph Ruskin in 1893 (cat. nos. 18 & 19). However, having rapidly acquired a taste for her new hobby and developed ambitions to do more than was possible with a 'hand-camera', in early summer 1892 she purchased a more serious instrument: a Watson half-plate 'Acme' camera. The Acme combined the best of a 'field' and 'studio' camera, taking 6½ × 4¾ inch film and glass plates. Complete with Rapid Rectilinear lens and iris diaphragm, three double dark slides, tripod stand and 'solid leather travelling case' (all of which Miss Acland owned) it sold for £17 9*s* (approximately £1,410 at 2012 values). The earliest dated photograph Miss Acland made with the camera was taken on 6 June 1892 and depicts a cast of the Kaufmann head of the Aphrodite of Knidos by Praxiteles of Athens: a suitable test subject with which to begin. The photograph she later claimed to be "the first portrait she ever took" (an assertion that ignored her earlier Kodak portraits) dates from soon afterwards and depicts her father, posed in the garden, in front of a fabric background (cat. no. 1).[26] Around the same date he also sat for her indoors (cat. no. 2), as did Dean Liddell (cat. no. 3).

Portraiture would dominate Miss Acland's monochrome photography in the years to come but was far from the only genre in which she excelled, architecture, genre studies, seascapes, animals and 'instantaneous work' also bringing her success. In the 1908 Camera Club exhibition, for example, one of her landscapes impressed judge John Furley Lewis (1867–1939), a leading pictorial photographer, who wrote that "one seldom finds a composition framed by an archway so satisfactory".[27] In 1905, using Willie's whole-plate camera, first loaned to her in 1897, she ventured into the realm of advanced pictorial photography with *Sunset in the Bay*, over-painting the negative in ink on translucent paper. After portraiture the most frequent subject in her early work was the domestic interior (cat. nos. 5–10). Interiors were characteristic of women's photography during the late nineteenth century. As Catherine Weed Ward argued in 1889, they made "peculiarly suitable work for ladies who possess the requisite taste and patience" and were "exceedingly satisfactory when well done".[28] Their popularity was partly due to convenience and partly the influence of two pervasive Victorian cultural phenomena: the domestic ideal, which privileged the home above all other social structures, especially in the lives of women; and its artistic offshoot, the 'renaissance of art in the home', which was part of the Aesthetic Movement more widely. In Miss Acland's home both influences were everywhere to be felt, the message of the value of domesticity inscribed in the very fabric of the building (cat. nos. 10 & 50). Photographing her 'house beautiful' not only allowed Miss Acland to record its artistic qualities for posterity, but also to demonstrate her belief in everything the domestic ideal entailed, and to prove that her new pastime could be undertaken in a manner compatible with her traditional role as a woman.

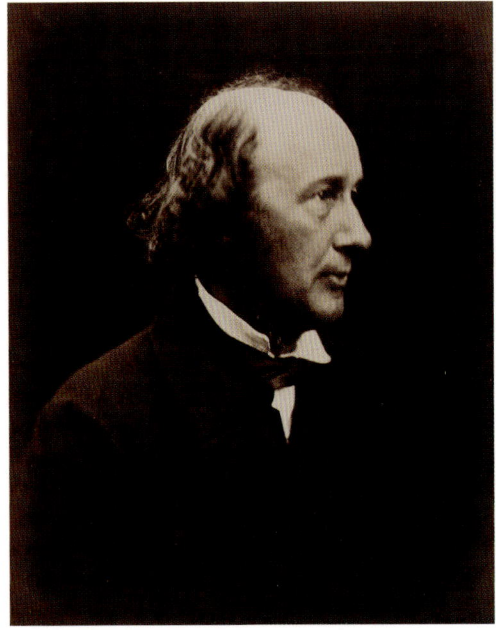

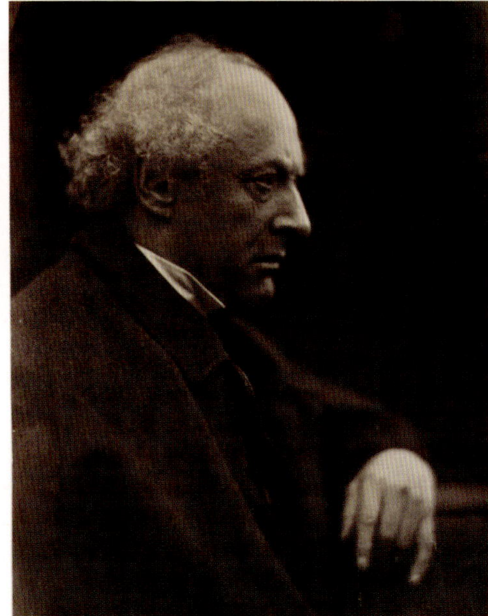

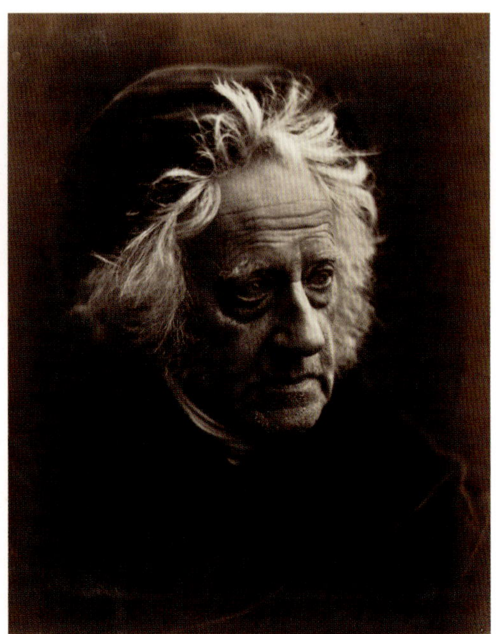

Figs. 30–32. *Portraits by Julia Margaret Cameron*

"Dr Acland of Oxford", albumen print, 1867; "The Dean of Christ Church", albumen print, 1865; "J. F. W. Herschel", albumen print, 1867

Cameron's portrait of Liddell is present in Mrs Acland's album; her study of Herschel hung in the drawing room at Broad Street.

Portraiture after Cameron and Carroll

Writing in *Amateur Photographer* in March 1899, 'Lux' described Miss Acland as "a lady amateur photographer who has applied herself chiefly to portraiture with quite extraordinary success".[29] Her reputation as a portraitist had been established soon after she acquired her half-plate camera, as a result of an opportunity that arose in October 1892 to photograph the most influential man in the land: the Prime Minister, William Ewart Gladstone (1809–1898). Gladstone was in Oxford to give the first Romanes Lecture. As old friends of the Aclands, he and his wife visited Broad Street for luncheon, when Miss Acland made six portraits: two of the Premier alone, two of Mrs Gladstone, and two of the couple together (cat. nos. 11 & 12). The sitting was a great success, her preferred portrait of Gladstone receiving the approval of his family, his niece Constance Gladstone (1850–1928) writing that she was "immensely struck with it".[30] Wider public recognition followed after the portrait was entered in the first Torquay Photographic Association exhibition in February 1893, where it won a bronze medal and held its own against the work of many of the acknowledged masters of the day.

With their strong contrasts of lighting, uniform diffusion of focus and dark backgrounds, Miss Acland's studies of Gladstone and his wife are stylistically similar to her earliest portraits of her father and Dean Liddell. They also have much in common with the work of Julia Margaret Cameron. The similarity is far from accidental: thirteen years after her death, Cameron still exercised a dominant influence over women photographers, Miss Acland in particular. The tendency of women to imitate their illustrious predecessor, whose achievements remained the gold standard of artistic portraiture, was widely recognized. In 1889, for example, when Eveleen Myers, née Tennant (1856–1937), published a selection of portraits of celebrities, *The Times* described them as "reminding us of the work which used to be done 20 years ago by

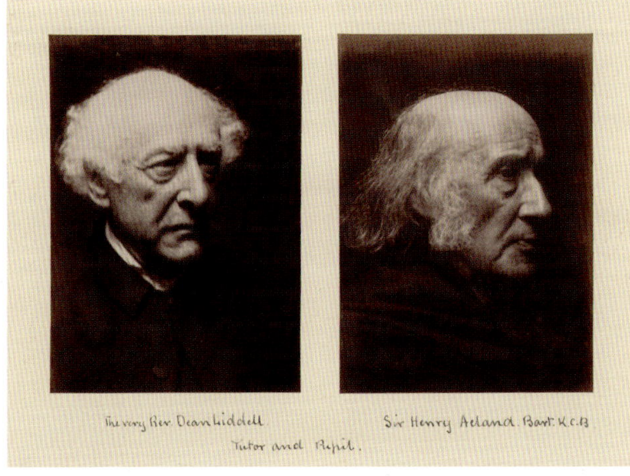

Fig. 33. *"Tutor and Pupil"*

Henry George Liddell and Henry Wentworth Acland, 1892

Miss Acland's early portraiture takes its inspiration from Julia Margaret Cameron.

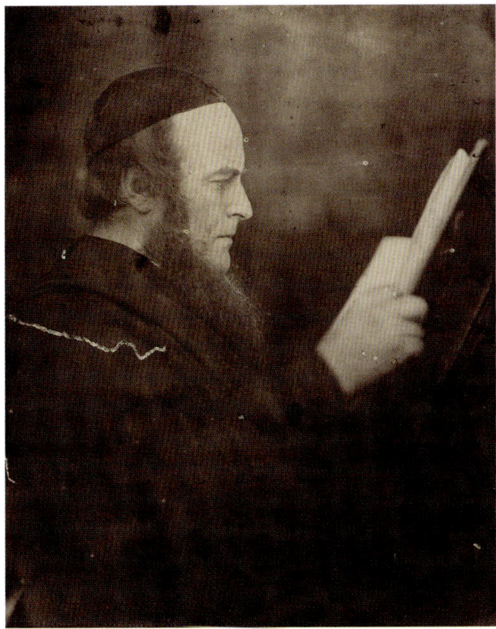
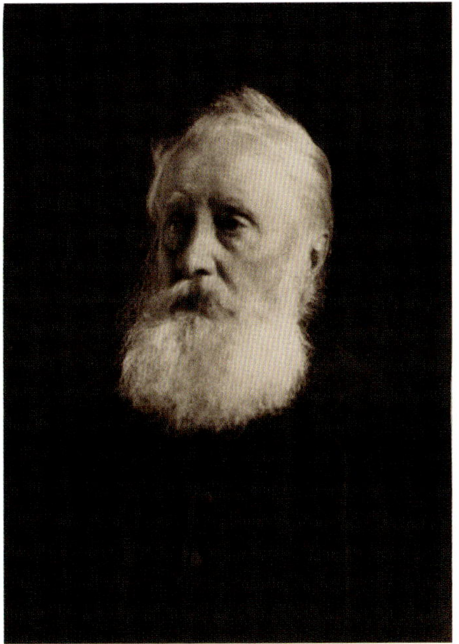
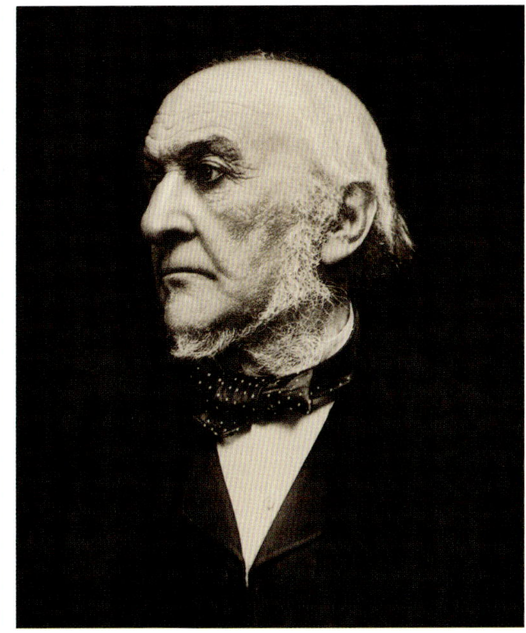

Figs. 34–36. *Portraits after Julia Margaret Cameron*

"Rev Charles Conybeare", photographer unknown, albumen print, before 2 January 1878; "B.H. Hodgson", by Susan Hodgson, photogravure engraved by W. J. Colls, published in 1888; "Mr. W. E. Gladstone", by Eveleen Myers, photogravure, published in 1890
Cameron exercised a powerful influence on portraitists in the two decades after her death, especially women. The pencil scar on Conybeare's shoulder was inflicted by Violet Liddell when she copied the print in Mrs Acland's album.

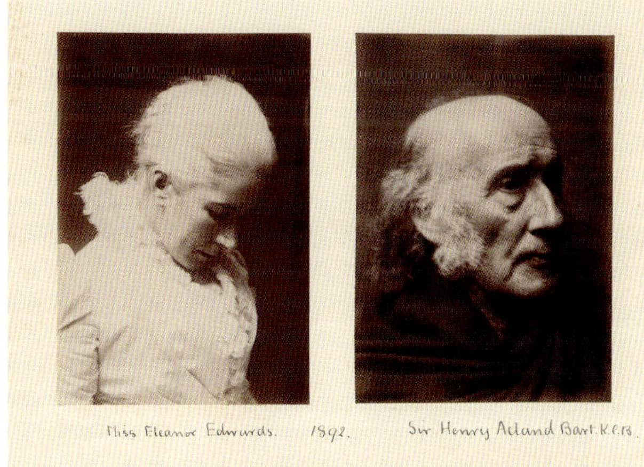

Fig. 37. *Early Formal Portraits*
Eleanor Dorothea Edwards and Henry Wentworth Acland

the late Mrs. Cameron".[31] For Andrew Pringle (1850–1929), writing in his seminal article "The Naissance of Art in Photography" in the *Studio* in 1893, Myers had "evidently and happily followed in the steps of Mrs. Cameron".[32] Another woman whose work was destined to be viewed in the same light was Susan Hodgson, née Townsend (1844–1912). Hodgson rose to attention in 1889 by winning third prize in the *Amateur Photographer* 'Home Portraiture' competition, a success that prompted the journal to hold its first 'Ladies' Photographic Competition' the following year. Her portraits bore "a strong resemblance to the late Mrs. Cameron's work", the judges concluded, even going as far as to describe them as "after Mrs. Cameron".[33]

Aside from having met Cameron in person, Miss Acland had numerous opportunities to see her work both before and after taking up photography. In 1868 Liddell lent a *Madonna and Child* to the School of Art exhibition in the Town Hall, where it hung on the same walls as her watercolours. Cameron's portrait of the Dean himself appears in Mrs Acland's album, as do studies of Henry Taylor (1800–1886) and Miss Acland's second cousin by marriage, Cameron's maid Mary Ryan (1848–1914). Her father sat for Cameron in 1867, as did Ina, Alice and Edith Liddell in 1872 (Mrs Liddell gave "most amusing accounts of the photographing" on their return from Freshwater).[34] Although not over-enamoured with his own likeness, Acland admired Cameron's portraits generally, personally securing at least three for the University Galleries and hanging her iconic study of John Frederick William Herschel (1792–1871), over which Ruskin quarrelled, in a prominent position in the drawing room at Broad Street (cat. no. 5). Miss Acland is known to have held the Herschel portrait in high regard, as it was one of the few photographs not from her own hand she chose to exhibit when lecturing on portraiture at the Oxford Camera Club in 1899. Herschel is clearly the model for her head studies of her father (in which he too is portrayed as sage, cloak wrapped around his shoulders), just as Cameron's work provides the inspiration for her early portraiture as a whole.

Encouraged by her success with Gladstone, between 1892 and 1900 Miss Acland went on to take more than 250 formal portraits in monochrome. The majority were accomplished in the 'Mess room' at home — an old tool shed at the back of the house that had been converted to her drawing studio in 1877. Her sitters were drawn from the distinguished acquaintances of her father who visited Broad Street, from near and far, as well as from her own friends, many of whom were of more humble birth. At one end of the scale, for example, belonged Mary Barney (1825/6–1903), the widow of an Oxford chimney sweep (cat. no. 72); at the other John Shaw Billings (1838–1913), first Director of the New York Public Libraries (cat. no. 61). Family also sat — her father more than any other person — as did the servants (cat. nos. 54 & 55).

Among Miss Acland's many notable portraits two groups stand out. The first is the photographs she took at Brantwood, Ruskin's home on Coniston Water, during a month-long vacation in the Lake District in August 1893. The holiday was arranged for the purpose of meeting Ruskin again, eight years after his ignominious departure from Oxford, and for what all concerned must have known would be the last time. On the afternoon of 1 August Miss Acland made four portraits of her Cricket: two of Ruskin alone, one with her father, and one with the two men and Joan Severn, née Agnew (1846–1924), Ruskin's cousin and housekeeper. One of the studies of Ruskin alone and the portrait with her father would become her most famous photographs. At the suggestion of George Allen (1832–1907), Ruskin's publisher, the double portrait was engraved in photogravure for inclusion in a new edition of Acland and Ruskin's jointly authored work, *The Oxford Museum* (London, 1893). The plate was well received, Miss Acland boasting to Willie that a good review had appeared in the *Westminster Gazette*, "with a special mention of my photography", and that the notice in *The Times* also contained "a special mention too of my photograph, so I feel very proud".[35] Her portrait of Ruskin alone came to attention in February 1895, when it was reproduced in a new periodical, the *Windsor Magazine*. Touted as the "biggest and best sixpenny magazine published", the *Windsor Magazine* had a circulation of 100,000 and was heavily advertised, with Miss Acland's portrait mentioned as one of its most attractive features.[36] Other requests for the plate soon followed, the portrait appearing on the cover of *The Young Man* in July (as the 'Latest Portrait of Mr. Ruskin'), in Herbert Maxwell's *Sixty Years a Queen* in 1897, and in the *Review of Reviews* and other publications on Ruskin's death in 1900.

In her memoirs Miss Acland identified her "most interesting portraits" as a group taken a year after her visit to Coniston, during the 1894 meeting of the British Association for the Advancement of Science.[37] The Association met from 8 to 15 August, visiting Oxford for the fourth time in its history. Miss Acland photographed the more senior members in attendance, beginning well in advance of the opening session with the incumbent President, John Scott Burdon Sanderson (1828–1905). Sanderson, Waynflete Professor of Physiology at Oxford, is depicted as the epitome of the Victorian scientific type, in wing-collar, bow tie and gold-rimmed spectacles, posed either reading, or with hand to head, as if in contemplation of some obscure point of electrophysiology (cat. nos. 23–25). The first sitter Miss Acland obtained during the meeting proper was the incoming President and second Prime Minister to appear before her lens: Robert Gascoyne-Cecil, 3rd Marquess of Salisbury (1830–1903)

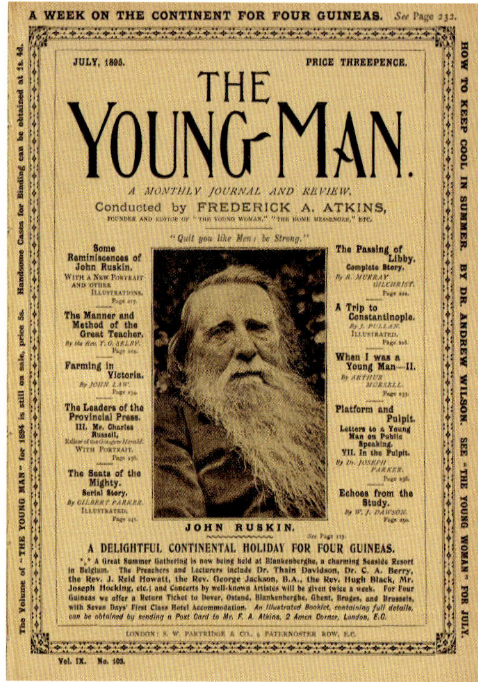

A WEEK ON THE CONTINENT FOR FOUR GUINEAS. *See Page 232.*

JULY, 1895. PRICE THREEPENCE.

THE YOUNG MAN.

A MONTHLY JOURNAL AND REVIEW.

Conducted by FREDERICK A. ATKINS,

FOUNDER AND EDITOR OF "THE YOUNG WOMAN," "THE HOME MESSENGER," ETC.

"Quit you like Men: be Strong."

Some Reminiscences of John Ruskin. WITH A NEW PORTRAIT AND OTHER ILLUSTRATIONS.

The Manner and Method of the Great Teacher. *By the Rev. T. G. SELBY.*

Farming in Victoria. *By JOHN LAW.*

The Leaders of the Provincial Press. III. Mr. Charles Russell, Editor of the *Glasgow Herald*. WITH PORTRAIT.

The Seats of the Mighty. Serial Story. *By GILBERT PARKER.* ILLUSTRATED.

The Passing of Libby. Complete Story. *By R. MURRAY GILCHRIST.*

A Trip to Constantinople. *By J. PULLAN.* ILLUSTRATED.

When I was a Young Man—II. *By ARTHUR MURSELL.*

Platform and Pulpit. Letters to a Young Man on Public Speaking. VII. In the Pulpit. *By Dr. JOSEPH PARKER.*

Echoes from the Study. *By W. J. DAWSON.*

JOHN RUSKIN.

A DELIGHTFUL CONTINENTAL HOLIDAY FOR FOUR GUINEAS.

*** A Great Summer Gathering is now being held at Blankenberghe, a charming Seaside Resort in Belgium. The Preachers and Lecturers include Dr. Thain Davidson, Dr. C. A. Berry, the Rev. J. Reid Howatt, the Rev. George Jackson, B.A., the Rev. Hugh Black, Mr. Joseph Hocking, etc.; and Concerts by well-known Artistes will be given twice a week. For Four Guineas we offer a Return Ticket to Dover, Ostend, Blankenberghe, Ghent, Bruges, and Brussels, with Seven Days' First Class Hotel Accommodation. *An Illustrated Booklet, containing full details, can be obtained by sending a Post Card to Mr. F. A. Atkins, 2 Amen Corner, London, E.C.*

LONDON: S. W. PARTRIDGE & CO., 9 PATERNOSTER ROW, E.C.

Vol. IX. No. 103.

The Volume of "THE YOUNG MAN" for 1894 is still on sale, price 5s. Handsome Cases for Binding can be obtained at 1s. 4d.

HOW TO KEEP COOL IN SUMMER. BY DR. ANDREW WILSON. SEE "THE YOUNG WOMAN" FOR JULY.

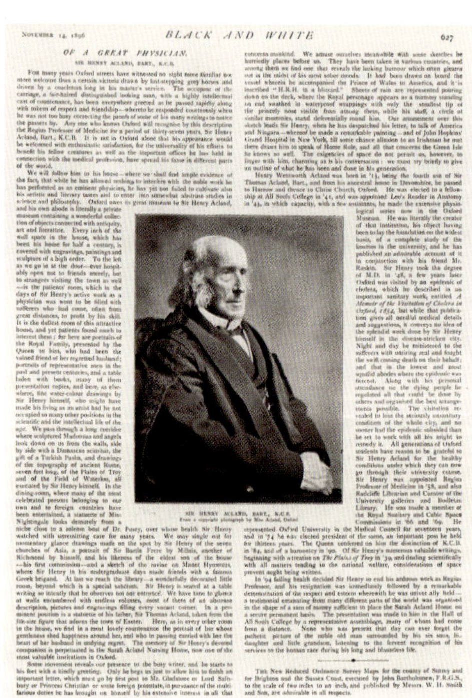

NOVEMBER 14, 1896 *BLACK AND WHITE* 627

OF A GREAT PHYSICIAN.

SIR HENRY ACLAND, BART., K.C.B.

Figs. 38 & 39. *Portraits in Print*

Miss Acland was no stranger to seeing her work published in print. Her portraits of Ruskin, her father, W.J. Herschel, Eleanor Smith, Gladstone, Salisbury and Burdon Sanderson were all reproduced in the press. Unfortunately, no negative survives of the magnificent study of Acland from *Black & White*.

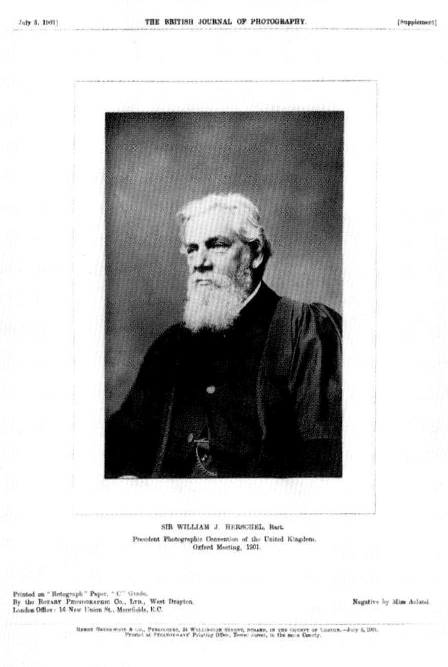

July 5, 1901] THE BRITISH JOURNAL OF PHOTOGRAPHY. [Supplement]

SIR WILLIAM J. HERSCHEL, Bart.

President Photographic Convention of the United Kingdom.
Oxford Meeting, 1901.

Printed on "Rotograph" Paper, "C" Grade,
By the ROTARY PHOTOGRAPHIC Co., LTD., West Drayton.
London Office: 14 New Union St., Moorfields, E.C.

Negative by Miss Acland

HENRY GREENWOOD & Co., PUBLISHERS, 24 WELLINGTON STREET, STRAND, IN THE COUNTY OF LONDON.—July 5, 1901.
Printed at STRANGEWAYS' Printing Office, Tower Street, in the same County.

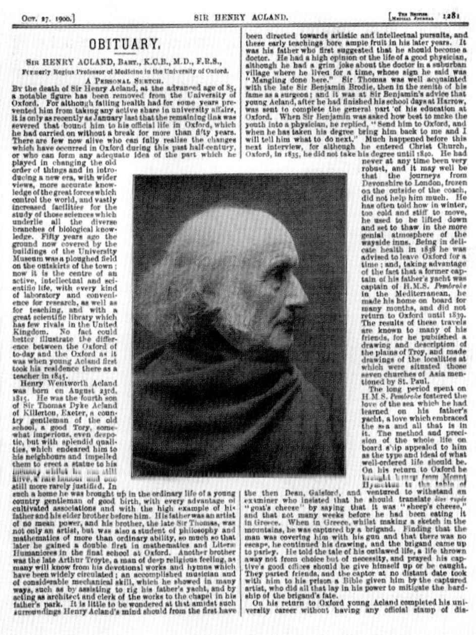

OCT. 27. 1900.] SIR HENRY ACLAND. [THE BRITISH MEDICAL JOURNAL 1281

OBITUARY.

SIR HENRY ACLAND, BART., K.C.B., M.D., F.R.S.,
Formerly Regius Professor of Medicine in the University of Oxford.

A PERSONAL SKETCH.

BY the death of Sir Henry Acland, at the advanced age of 85, a notable figure has been removed from the University of Oxford. For although failing health had for some years prevented him from taking any active share in university affairs, it is only as recently as January last that the remaining link was severed that bound him to his official life in Oxford, which he had carried on without a break for more than fifty years. There are few now alive who can fully realise the changes which have occurred in Oxford during this past half-century, or who can form any adequate idea of the part which he played in changing the old order of things and in introducing a new era, with wider views, more accurate knowledge of the great forces which control the world, and vastly increased facilities for the study of those sciences which underlie all the diverse branches of biological knowledge. Fifty years ago the ground now covered by the buildings of the University Museum was a ploughed field on the outskirts of the town; now it is the centre of an active, intellectual and scientific life, with every kind of laboratory and convenience for research, as well as for teaching, and with a great scientific library which has few rivals in the United Kingdom. No fact could better illustrate the difference between the Oxford of to-day and the Oxford as it was when young Acland first took his residence there as a teacher in 1845.

Henry Wentworth Acland was born on August 23rd, 1815. He was the fourth son of Sir Thomas Dyke Acland of Killerton, Exeter, a country gentleman of the old school, a good Tory, somewhat imperious, even despotic, but with splendid qualities, which endeared him to his neighbours and impelled them to erect a statue to his memory whilst he was still alive, a rare honour and one still more rarely justified. In such a home he was brought up in the ordinary life of a young country gentleman of good birth, with every advantage of cultivated associations and with the high example of his father and his elder brother before him. His father was an artist of no mean power, and his brother, the late Sir Thomas, was not only an artist, but was also a student of philosophy and mathematics of more than ordinary ability, so much so that later he gained a double first in mathematics and Literæ Humaniores in the final school at Oxford. Another brother was the late Arthur Troyte, a man of deep religious feeling, as many will know from his devotional works and hymns which have been widely circulated; an accomplished musician and of considerable mechanical skill, which he showed in many ways, such as by assisting to rig his father's yacht, and by acting as architect and clerk of the works to the chapel in his father's park. It is little to be wondered at that amidst such surroundings Henry Acland's mind should from the first have been directed towards artistic and intellectual pursuits, and these early teachings bore ample fruit in his later years. It was his father who first suggested that he should become a doctor. He had a high opinion of the life of a good physician, although he had a grim joke about the doctor in a suburban village where he lived for a time, whose sign he said was "Mangling done here." Sir Thomas was well acquainted with the late Sir Benjamin Brodie, then in the zenith of his fame as a surgeon; and it was at Sir Benjamin's advice that young Acland, after he had finished his school days at Harrow, was sent to complete the general part of his education at Oxford. When Sir Benjamin was asked how best to make the youth into a physician, he replied, "Send him to Oxford, and when he has taken his degree bring him back to me and I will tell him what to do next." Much happened before this next interview, for although he entered Christ Church, Oxford, in 1835, he did not take his degree until 1840. He had never at any time been very robust, and it may well be that the journeys from Devonshire to London, frozen on the outside of the coach, did not help him much. He has often told how in winter, too cold and stiff to move, he used to be lifted down and set to thaw in the more genial atmosphere of the wayside inns. Being in delicate health in 1838 he was advised to leave Oxford for a time; and, taking advantage of the fact that a former captain of his father's yacht was captain of H.M.S. *Pembroke* in the Mediterranean, he made his home on board for many months, and did not return to Oxford until 1839. The results of these travels are known to many of his friends, for he published a drawing and description of the plains of Troy, and made drawings of the localities at which were situated those seven churches of Asia mentioned by St. Paul.

The long period spent on H.M.S. *Pembroke* fostered the love of the sea which he had learned on his father's yacht, a love which embraced the sea and all that is in it. The method and precision of the whole life on board ship appealed to him as the type and ideal of what well-ordered life should be. On his return to Oxford he brought honey from Mount Hymettus to the table of the then Dean, Gaisford, and ventured to withstand an examiner who insisted that he should translate [illegible] "goat's cheese" by saying that it was "sheep's cheese," and that not many weeks before he had been eating it in Greece. When in Greece, whilst making a sketch in the mountains, he was captured by a brigand. Finding that the man was covering him with his gun and that there was no escape, he continued his drawing, and the brigand came up to parley. He told the tale of his outlawed life, a life thrown away not from choice but of necessity, and prayed his captive's good offices should he give himself up or be caught. They parted friends, and the captor at no distant date took with him to his prison a Bible given him by the captured artist, who did all that lay in his power to mitigate the hardship of the brigand's fate.

On his return to Oxford young Acland completed his university career without having any official stamp of dis-

Figs. 40 & 41. *Published Portraits*

Miss Acland's portrait of W. J. Herschel was published as a special supplement to the *British Journal of Photography* to coincide with the visit to Oxford, in July 1901, of the Photographic Convention of the United Kingdom. In an unusual move for the *Journal* it was reproduced as a true photograph rather than a half-tone, on 'Rotograph' bromide paper. The same portrait was used for the frontispiece of the Official Guide to the Convention.

(cat. no. 35). In the days that followed there was no let-up in the stream of eminent visitors to her studio. A third President, this time of the Royal Society, sat on 10 August: William Thomson, Baron Kelvin (1824–1907) (cat. no. 38).

Like her studies of Ruskin, Miss Acland's portraits of Sanderson and Lord Salisbury would eventually be seen by a large public. Sanderson's accompanied his obituary notice in the *Proceedings of the Royal Society* in 1907. Salisbury's was first published in 1899, during his lifetime, in *Photography*, after it won a certificate in the journal's 'Portraiture and Figure Subjects' competition. In 1903, the year of his death, Miss Acland exhibited the portrait again, as a bromide enlargement, at the Royal Photographic Society exhibition, prompting its appearance as the first plate in the catalogue. Her studies of Sanderson and Salisbury had both been seen at the R.P.S. before: in 1899, when they were two of the four lantern slides, along with her portraits of Gladstone and Ruskin, that marked Miss Acland's debut in the exhibition. She would show a total of thirty-seven photographs at the R.P.S. in the following years, making her the fourth most prolific woman amateur to exhibit there before 1915, after Cameron (with fifty-six photographs), the "pioneer of women bird photographers" Emma Louisa Turner (1867–1940) (with fifty-one), and the Birmingham amateur Emma Boaz Barton, née Rayson (1872–1938) (with forty-eight).[38] On 14 November 1899 Miss Acland was nominated for membership of the Society on the strength of her portraiture. Six years later, on 1 February 1905, she became a fellow, largely due to her achievements in colour photography, which also saw her elected to the Society of Arts in January 1903.

Miss Acland was by no means the first photographer to take advantage of the British Association to obtain sittings from the famous men and women who graced its meetings. In York in 1844 Hill and Adamson made calotype portraits of the delegates, while at Dundee in 1867 James Valentine (1815–1879) photographed them at the rate of forty per day. When the Association met in Oxford in 1860, in Acland's half-completed museum, members had a choice of two photographers to attend: Dodgson or Hills & Saunders. After the meeting both sought to profit from their endeavours, Dodgson adding his sitters' names to a printed list of his photographs available for purchase, Hills & Saunders circulating a flier announcing that their portraits could be "safely transmitted by Post to any Address" (in what must be an early example of photographic distance selling).[39]

In place of Miss Acland's Kelvin, Dodgson had secured Faraday at the B.A.A.S. Lord Salisbury would also sit for him, but not until June 1870, on his investiture as Chancellor of the University. When Miss Acland photographed Salisbury twenty-four years later he reminded her of the earlier sitting:

> Lord Salisbury was wearing his robes as Chancellor of the University of Oxford and told me that he had only been photographed in them once before, and that was by Mr. Dodgson (Lewis Carroll) author of Alice in Wonderland.[40]

That Miss Acland included this anecdote in the notes accompanying Salisbury's portrait in her presentation albums is testimony to her awareness that she was following in Dodgson's footsteps in Oxford. Other sitters she shared with Dodgson included Ruskin, Goldwin Smith (1823–1910) (cat. no. 22) and Friedrich Max Müller

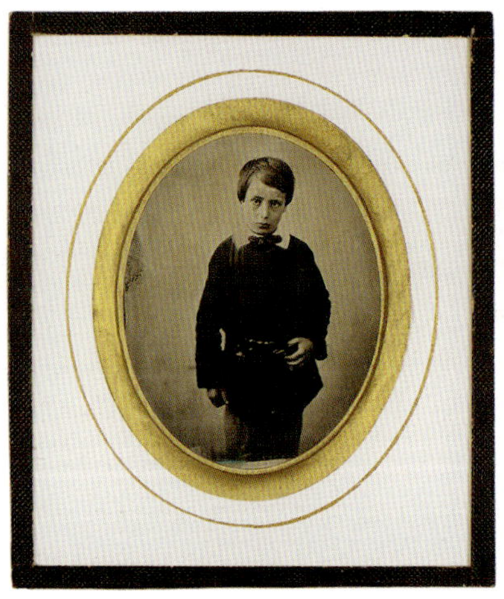
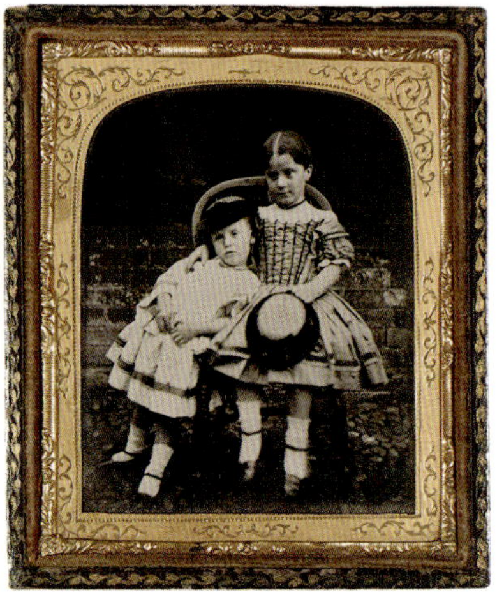
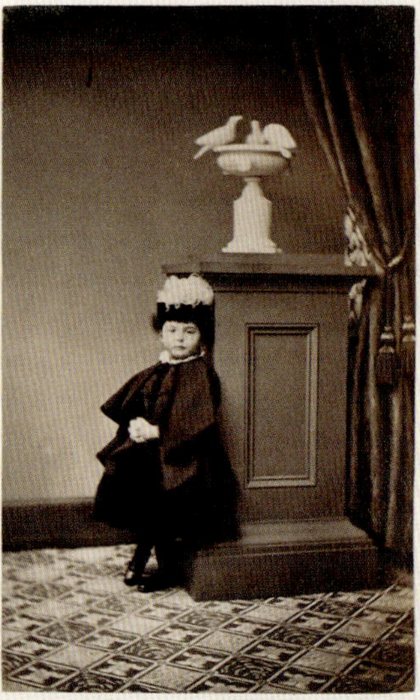
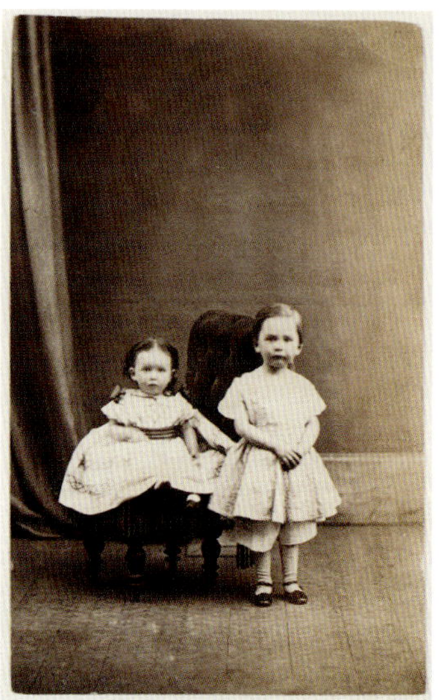

(1823–1900), as well as members of her family and her childhood friend Margaret Ann Huxley, née Brodie (1850–1944). This is perhaps fewer than expected, many of the Aclands' closest friends who sat for Dodgson being absent from Miss Acland's œuvre: Woodward, Munro and Professor Donkin, for example, as well as Charles Ranken Conybeare (1821–1885), William Jacobson (1803–1884) and Samuel Wilberforce (1805–1873). The reason for the omissions is simple and inescapable: these men were already dead by the time Miss Acland took up photography. Of friends still alive, several had long since left Oxford, often on their marriage, notably Ina and Alice (Edith had also died). Miss Acland did manage to secure two Liddells who escaped Dodgson: the Dean and his fifth daughter, Violet Constance Liddell (1864–1927). Mrs Liddell eluded them both.

Dodgson and Miss Acland lived in different photographic eras — the age of wet collodion versus the gelatine dry plate — and their portraits are visually quite different as a result (Dodgson's reflecting his need for the bright, uniform illumination of the Deanery garden or his rooftop studio). Something both photographers did have in common was a love of child photography. "Photographing children was fascinating," Miss Acland told the Camera Club in 1899, "but required an infinity of patience."[41] As a woman she was supposed to be at an advantage in such work: "Women are peculiarly successful as photographers of children, being rich in that love for and knowledge of childhood which lead direct to the hearts of children", the *Photo-Miniature* claimed in 1900.[42] As a spinster, she depended largely on access to her nephews and nieces (she had fifteen by 1902), as well as the sons and daughters of the servants, to obtain young sitters; Dodgson, as a bachelor, was aided by his reputation as a children's author. The fondness both of them displayed for the field was far from unusual, even if children are conspicuous in the extent to which they dominate Dodgson's output. Child portraiture was a popular branch of photography, especially in Oxford. Bracher and Hills & Saunders excelled in the genre and their commercial work has more in common with Dodgson and his fellow amateurs than is generally recognized. In Miss Acland's day the most successful

Figs. 42–45. *Portraits of Oxford Children*
LEFT TO RIGHT, ABOVE
George James Dew (1846–1928), by Edward Bracher, collodion positive, *c.* 1855; Henry Reynolds Knatchbull Rogers (1858–1876) and Annie Mary Anne Henley Rogers (1856–1937), photographer unknown, collodion positive, taken at Marcham church, June 1861; Rhoda Liddell, by James Saunders, albumen print, *c.* 1863; Frances Harriet Griffith (1866–1938) and Arthur Troyte Griffith (1864–1942), photographer unknown, albumen print, *c.* 1868

Henry and Annie Rogers were also photographed by Dodgson in June 1861; Annie was the first woman to sit Oxford examinations. Artie Griffith, Miss Acland's cousin, is the subject of the 7th of Elgar's *Enigma Variations* (see cat. no. 130).

Fig. 46. *A Son of Rokuichiro Masujima*
Rokuichiro Masujima (1857–1948), gelatine print, Tokyo, 1923
Rokuichiro Masujima, founder of the English Law School in Tokyo, now Chuo University, was one of Miss Acland's several Japanese friends. Another, Keimin, Viscount Matsudaira (b. 1883), whom she proposed for the Camera Club in 1905, eventually became Grand Chamberlain of the Japanese Imperial Household.

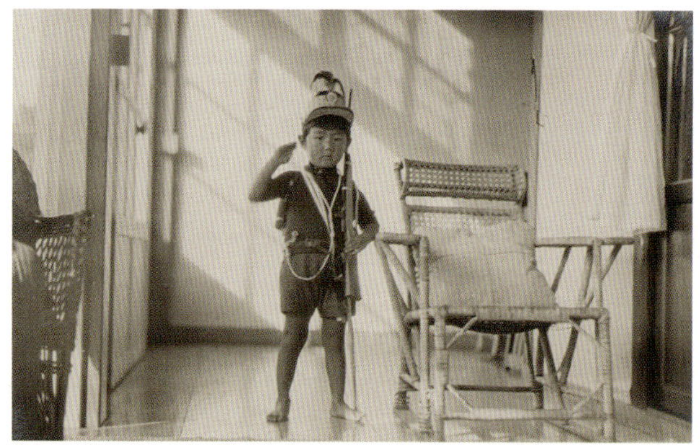

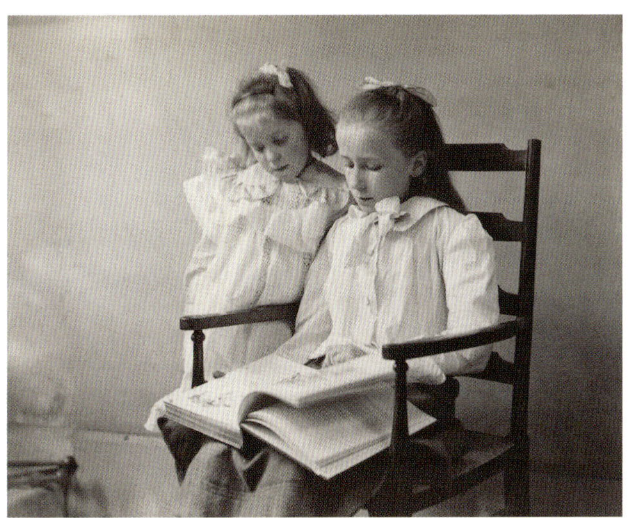

Fig. 47. *"Eva & Elsie Hewitt"*
Henry Michael John Underhill, platinum print, 1902
Underhill was the heir to Dodgson's mantle as a photographer of children in Oxford, as this beautiful portrait of Eva Beatrice (b. 1894) and Elsie Eugenie Hewitt (1890–1973) demonstrates.

Fig. 48. *"First Baron Kelvin"*
Frederick Hollyer, platinum print, exhibited in 1908
Miss Acland was guided in her mature portraiture by the same artistic principles as Hollyer and other leading professional artist-photographers of the 1890s.

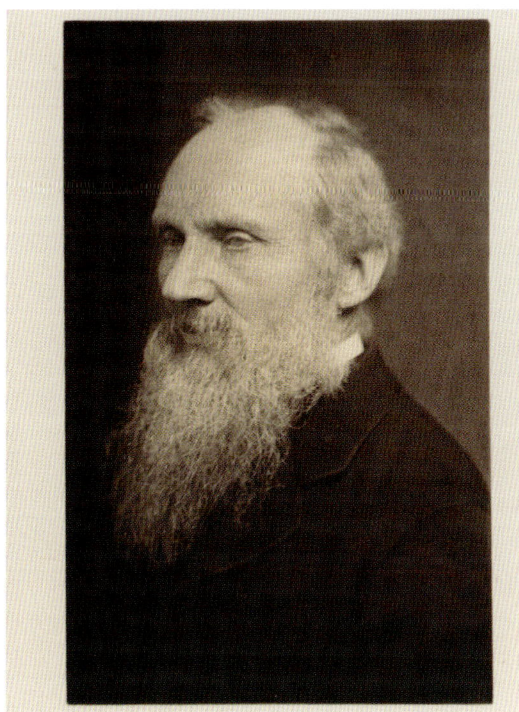

child photographer in the City was the amateur Henry Michael John Underhill (1855–1920). Underhill lectured on "The Artistic Possibilities in the Photography of Children" at the Oxford Camera Club in March 1902 and won several prizes in national competitions.

Miss Acland made her own debut as a public speaker, in any capacity, at the Camera Club on 27 February 1899, lecturing on the subject of "Home Portraiture". The lecture took place in the University Museum before a large audience "anxious to learn her methods".[43] She used the occasion to discourse on the principles and practice of amateur portraiture, as illustrated by sixty-one lantern slides from her finest portraits. The title she chose was highly significant. Although largely passed over by the canonical histories of photography, during the 1880s and 1890s 'home portraiture' became a distinct, widely recognized, and influential photographic genre. The term signified a technical and ideological approach that privileged the home as the location of the creation of artistic portraits and amateur photographers as their creators. Home portraiture would play a vital role in the advance of the 'Pictorial Movement' in photography in the late nineteenth century, 'at home portraits', 'home studies' and other synonymous types being exhibited by many champions of photography's claim to the status of a fine art, including Peter Henry Emerson (1856–1936), Frederick Evans (1853–1943), and Alfred Stieglitz (1864–1946). The private space of the home was viewed by these men as the antidote to the industrialized commercial studio: a place where sitters were more likely to reveal, and portraitists better able to capture, the individuality of character and expression sought in artistic portraiture.

The photographs Miss Acland exhibited during her lecture were described as "beautiful examples of portraiture" by the *British Journal of Photography*, which along with *Amateur Photographer* contained a detailed account of her remarks.[44] In addition to her early Cameronesque studies, the lecture included numerous examples of her mature work. Departing from the slavish imitation of Cameron, Miss Acland's mature portraiture dispensed with extremes of contrast and uniformly diffuse focus in favour of a broad range of mid-tones, retention of detail in the highlights and shadows, finely rendered chiaroscuro, and the careful use of selective focus, albeit with a very narrow depth of field (see, for example, cat. nos. 61 & 71). The style was one she shared with advocates of advanced "pictorial portrait photography", or the "new school of portraiture", as it was sometimes labelled.[45] In addition to Emerson, Evans and other amateurs, practitioners of this approach included the leading professional artist-photographers of the 1890s, namely Frederick Hollyer (1838–1933), William Crooke (1849–1928), Henry Walter Barnett (1863–1934) and Julia Margaret Cameron's son (Herbert Acland's schoolmate) Henry Herschel Hay Cameron (1852–1911). Attempting "to become, in the best sense of the term, amateurs", these men eschewed the trappings of commercial photography, fitting up their studios instead as home-like spaces.[46] Literally a 'domestication' of the portrait profession, and in so far as the domestic space was the sphere of women a 'feminizing' of photography, this transformation opened up commercial portraiture to a new class of 'lady photographers', such as Alice Mary Hughes (1857–1939) and Mary Olive Edis (1876–1955), who built on the success of earlier women amateurs to forge independent careers as professional portraitists in the 1890s and 1900s.

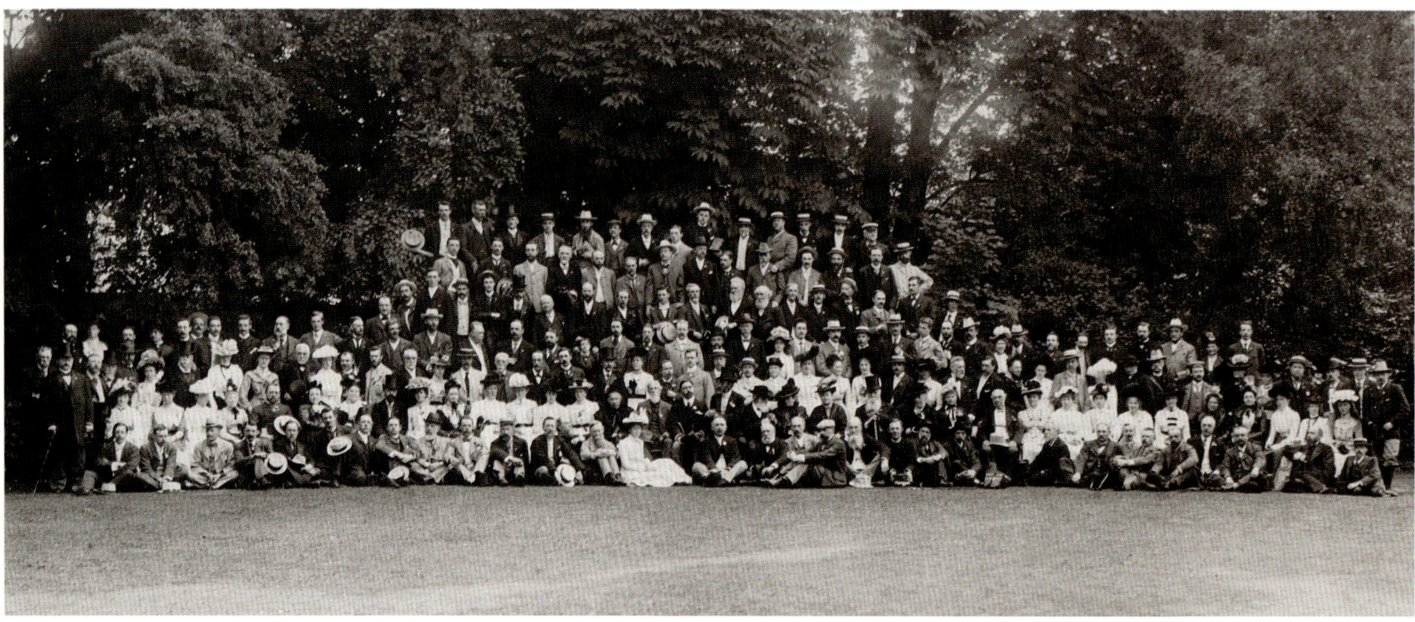

The Oxford Camera Club

The Oxford Camera Club had been an important part of Miss Acland's photographic life for several years before she delivered her Home Portraiture lecture, providing a place in which she could exhibit her work, compete and collaborate, learn from her peers, and, importantly, exercise powers of patronage. On 11 June 1894 she became the Club's first woman member; a year later she was the first to be elected to the committee, and for twenty-six years from 1896 she served as one of the Vice-Presidents, before being nominated for life. The Club had been founded in April 1894 but was only Oxford's third: in 1884 Charles William Dyson Perrins (1864–1958), heir to the Worcestershire sauce fortune, inaugurated the Oxford University Photographic Club, while in 1889 the first club open to non-University members, the Oxford Photographic Society, had been formed. The Photographic Society was relatively short-lived, folding in 1893 having "overrated its powers of endurance in that tender matter of £ s. d.", but was the direct precursor of the Camera Club.[47]

As the foundation of three clubs in Oxford suggests, the years 1884 to 1898 were the golden age of photographic societies in Britain, over 200 coming into existence. The Oxford Camera Club was similar to those elsewhere, its object, as defined in Rule 1, "the advancement of Photography in all its branches". This was achieved principally through fortnightly meetings, at which lectures and demonstrations were given, members' slides exhibited, and circulating portfolios from other societies examined. Lectures ranged from "A Tour through Oxfordshire" to the "Electrical Transmission of Portraits"; demonstrations from "Sepia-toning of Platinotypes" to "Photography by Röntgen's X Rays". Many were no more than thinly disguised marketing pitches by representatives of the trade, but all were highly valued even so. Predictably perhaps, the most popular meeting ever held, which attracted an audience of 250, was a promotion by the Eastman Company: a lecture by Henry Charles Shelley (1862–1936), correspondent of the *Westminster Gazette*, on "The

Fig. 49. *Photographic Community*
Hills & Saunders, platinum print, 10 July 1901
In July 1901 the Oxford Camera Club joined delegates of the Photographic Convention of the United Kingdom for a group photograph in Worcester College gardens. Miss Acland is the first woman right of centre in the second row, sitting next but one to the top-hat-clad portraitist William Crooke.

Fig. 50. *"A Young Princess"*
Eugene Clutterbuck Impey, collodion negative, *c.* 1862

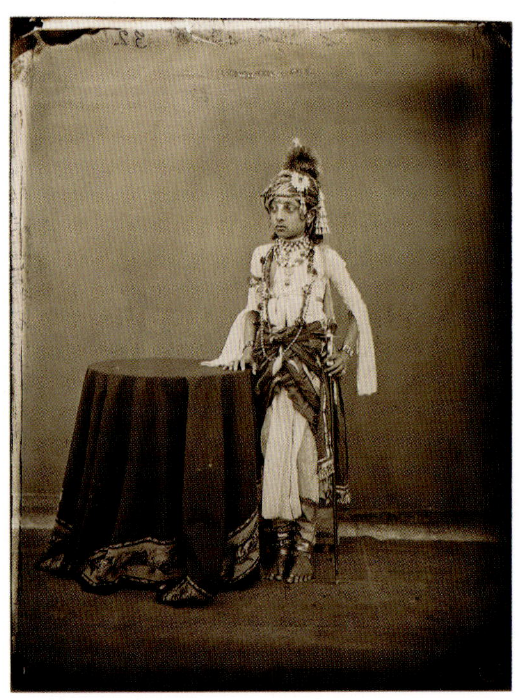

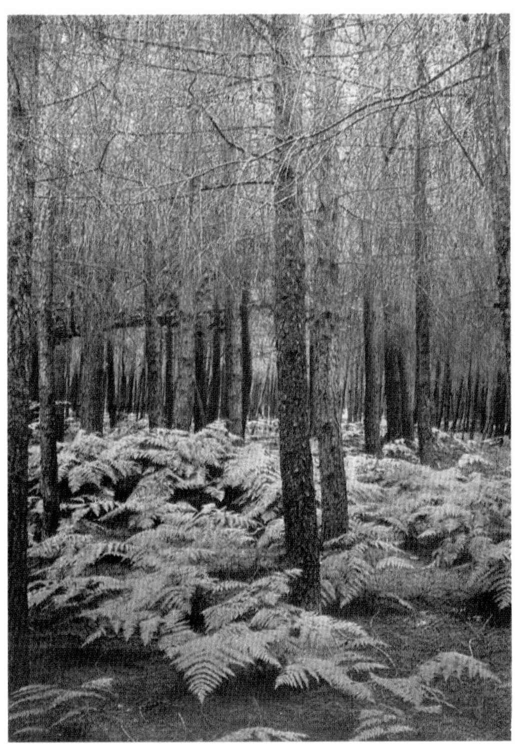

Fig. 51. *"Bagley Wood"*
Arthur Harry Church, half-tone, published in 1922

Fig. 52. *"Avila"*
John Reginald Homer Weaver, half-tone, published in 1943
In 1943 the R.P.S. honoured Weaver with a one-man show.

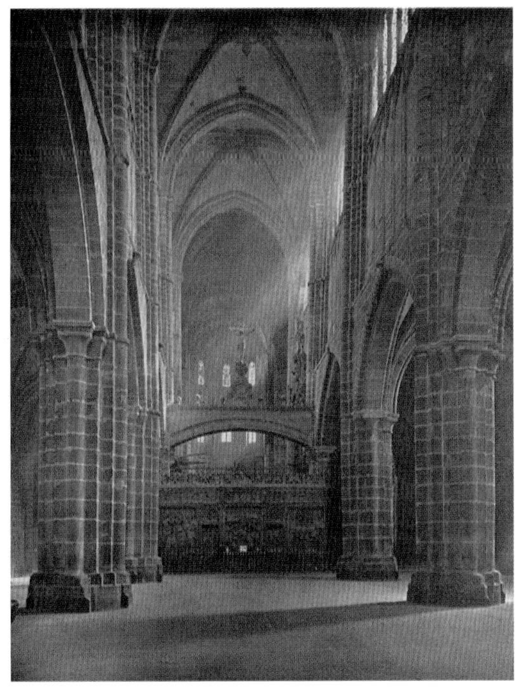

Kodak in Peace and War". As well as ordinary meetings, the Club organized more exceptional events, the most important of which was a biennial public exhibition, held in the Holywell Music Room or a gallery in the Clarendon Hotel. Miss Acland was a leading exhibitor, usually sweeping the board in the portraits class. The strong collaborative ethos of the Club also saw it embark on two unusual collective projects in which Miss Acland was closely involved: supplying the illustrations for a series of histories of the Oxford colleges for the London publisher Francis Edward Robinson (1865–1936) (see cat. no. 100 ff.) and an ambitious scheme for a 'Photographic Survey of Oxfordshire' (cat. no. 114). The most memorable (and financially lucrative) event in the Club's history took place from 8 to 12 July 1901, when it hosted 200 delegates of the Photographic Convention of the United Kingdom.

By its first 'annual meeting' in February 1895 the Camera Club boasted sixty-one members. President of the Club was William James Herschel (1833–1917) (cat. no. 86) (Dodgson had been first on the list to be asked if Herschel declined the nomination).[48] The most senior member of the Club in age was Julia Margaret Cameron's cousin, Eugene Clutterbuck Impey (1830–1904) (cat. nos. 70 & 71). Like Herschel, Impey had cut his teeth in photography in India during the early years of the British Raj. The ordinary members of the Club came from a wider range of social backgrounds, from dairymen to merchant bankers. Between these extremes were pharmacists, teachers, architects, lawyers, clerics and professional photographers. Artists and scientists were represented in approximately equal numbers. In the former category belonged Christopher Wyndham Hughes (1881–1962), who became Art Master at Marlborough College (where Anthony Blunt was his pupil), and Thomas Frederick Mason Sheard (1866–1921), future Professor of Art at Queen's College, London. Among the scientists were Arthur Harry Church (1865–1937), Demonstrator of Botany in the University; Gustav Mann (1864–1921), afterwards Professor of Physiology at Tulane University, New Orleans; and Albert Harry Hamm, né Ham (1862–1951), Assistant at the University Museum, whom *Nature* described as an "inseparable part of Oxford entomology".[49] Academics from other fields included David Samuel Margoliouth (1858–1940), Laudian Professor of Arabic; John Frederick Stenning (1868–1959), Reader in Aramaic and Warden of Wadham College; and John Reginald Homer Weaver (1882–1965), President of Trinity College and Editor of the *Dictionary of National Biography*. Notable for other reasons were Joseph Augustus Cooper (b. 1878), first business partner of William Morris (1877–1963), motor manufacturer, and Arthur Richard Burrows (1882–1947), 'Uncle Arthur', the first BBC presenter. The list could go on: of the 333 members elected before March 1909 no fewer than forty are mentioned in *Who's Who* or the *DNB*.

Unlike either of its predecessors, the Camera Club went out of its way to create an atmosphere attractive to women. Ladies' membership of learned societies (in which the Club classed itself) was the "burning question of the hour" in the 1890s, the women-haters apparently being well-organized and fighting with "the tenacity of despair".[50] Oxford prided itself in having the greatest proportion of women of any mixed photographic society in Britain. Miss Acland was joined by seven in the first year of the Club's existence; by 1906 sixty-four had been elected, making up 43 per cent of the active membership. The women tended to represent a narrower section of society than the men, the majority being gentlewomen 'living on own means'. However, their exact degree of means varied considerably. At the top of the scale were Mabel Pickersgill Cunliffe (1866–1932), daughter of a wealthy city banker, and Edith Forlonge (1851/2–1921), whose father owned vast tracts of land in Australia. Lower down was a large group of clergymen's daughters, of whom Evelyn Hamilton Gifford (1876–1920), daughter of the Archdeacon of London, was typical (Thomas Hardy was her cousin and wrote *Evelyn G. of Christminster* in her memory). Whether by choice or necessity a small minority of the middle-class women of the Club earned their own living: Jane Malvina Williamza Grimston (1869–1958), whose lawyer father had died when she was 17, as Miss Acland's lady's companion; Edith Margaret Argles (1853–1935), daughter of a canon of Peterborough, as the Vice Principal and Bursar of Lady Margaret Hall.

Argles, like Miss Acland, was one of several women in the Club photographed by Dodgson as children. Another, Agnes Grace Weld (1849–1915) (immortalized by Dodgson as *Little Red Riding Hood*) also sat for Cameron, who was a friend of her uncle, Alfred, Lord Tennyson. Frederica Harriette Morrell (1869–1908) appeared for Dodgson and for her sister-in-law, society hostess and photographer Ottoline Morrell (1873–1938). In 1879 Leila Campbell Taylor (1867–1960), daughter of James Taylor (1833–1900), organist of New College, became one of Dodgson's last sitters, twenty years before being proposed for membership of the Camera Club by Miss Acland, who also photographed her father, her piano teacher.

Like Miss Acland, many of the most influential women in the Club were the wives or daughters of academics. Several belonged to scientific households. Emily Poulton, née Palmer (1856–1939), for example, was the wife of Edward Bagnall Poulton (1856–1943), Hope Professor of Zoology. Gaining distinction in science on their own merit were Mabel Purefoy FitzGerald (1872–1973), who collaborated with John Scott Haldane (1860–1936) in physiological research, and Lilian Jane Veley, née Nutcombe Gould (1861–1936), assistant librarian at the Royal Society and one

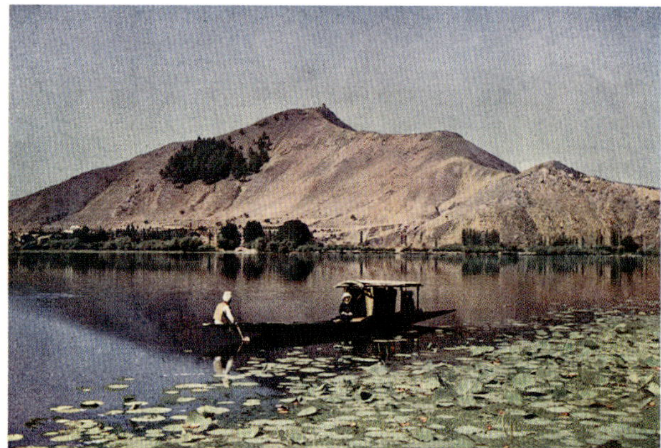

Fig. 53. *"The Dal Lake where the Lotus Lilies Grow"*
Bernard Okes Coventry (1873–1960), half-tone from an Autochrome, published in 1923

Coventry exhibited Autochromes with Miss Acland in the Camera Club exhibition in March 1908, having been proposed by her for membership five months earlier. A mature student at Balliol College, studying chemistry prior to taking up the appointment of Imperial Forest Chemist in Dehradun, India, he went on to use the Autochrome process to great effect in illustration of his *Wild Flowers of Kashmir* (3 series, London, 1923–30).

Figs. 54–56. *Women's Work*
Marjory Theodora Hardcastle (1876–1959) was closely associated with the Camera Club through her uncle, the President, but never a formal member. Her Autochrome portrait of Herschel (left) was taken in 1912. Other women in the Club had a taste for more avant-garde pictorial work. Magdalen Katharine Commeline, née Hopkins (1859–1934), the cousin of Gerard Manley Hopkins, exhibited *The Camp Fire* (middle), a gum print, at the R.P.S. in 1902, having shown at the Photographic Salon in 1900 and 1901. *Houses of Parliament* (right) by Gertrude Aitchison (1866/7–1961) was reproduced in *Photograms of the Year* in 1908.

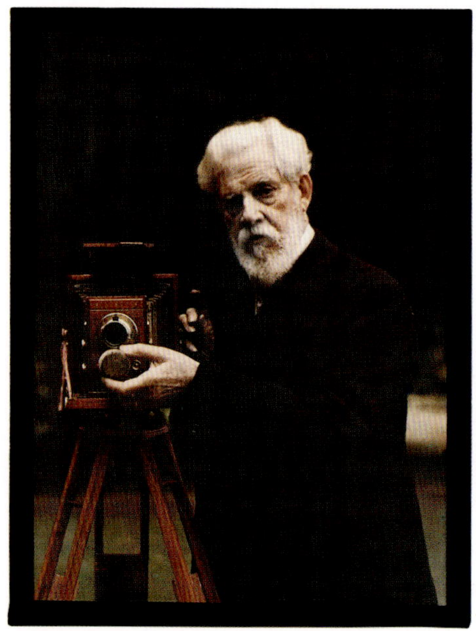

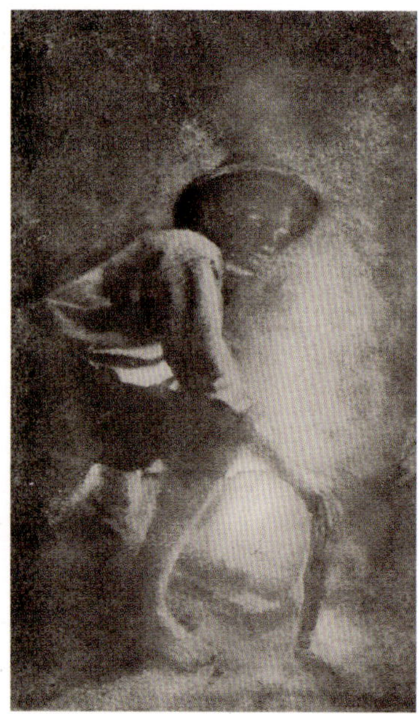

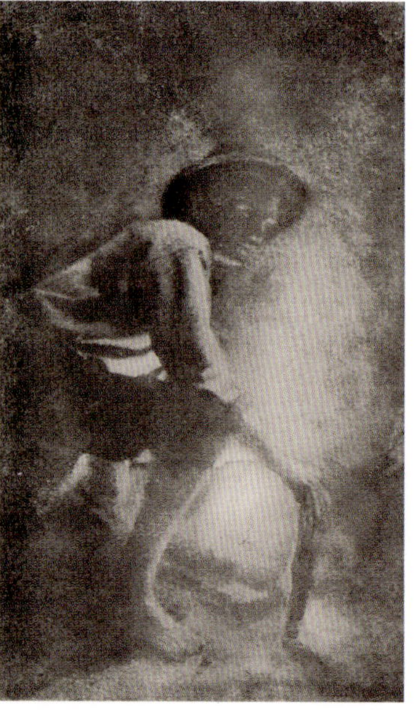

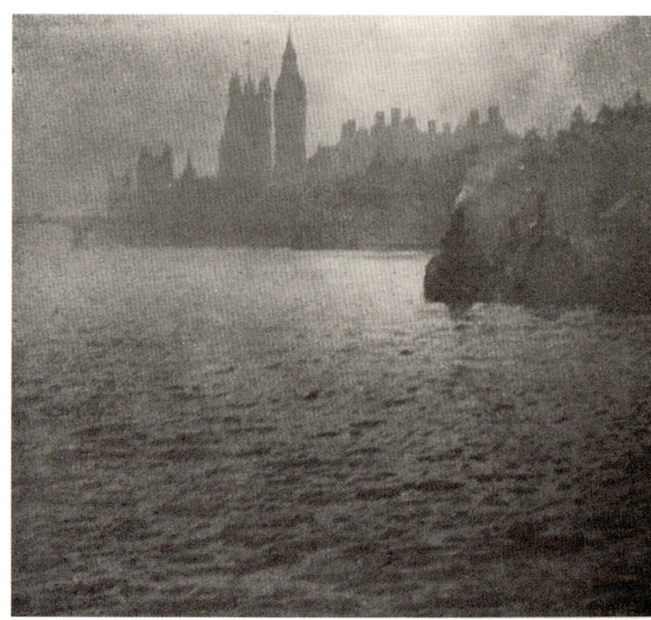

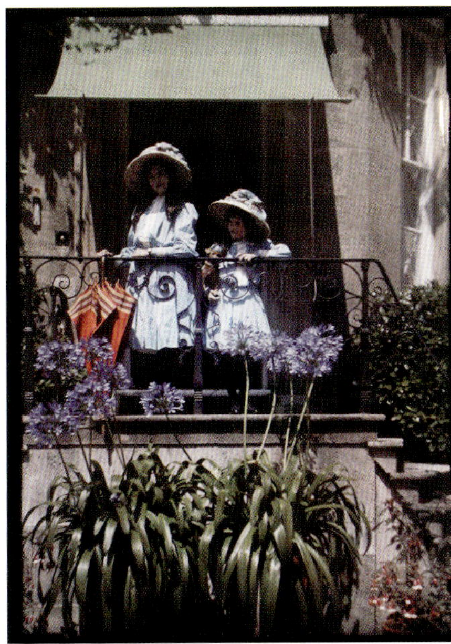

Fig. 57. *Blue Dresses and Agapanthus*
Etheldreda Janet Laing, Autochrome, *c.* 1909
That Laing is now better known as a colour photographer than Miss Acland would have shocked both women. She photographed her daughters Janet Marian (1898–1985) and Iris Carola (1903–1994) on the steps of Bury Knowle House, Headington.

of the first women to be elected to the Linnean Society. The most senior woman in the Club after Miss Acland was another clergyman's daughter: Edith Venables (1861–1938), whose father was a canon of Chester. Elected to the Club in September 1894, aged 32, Edith also served as one of the Vice-Presidents for twenty-one years. Her upbringing and education (at a school in Holland Park) were conventional enough, but otherwise she could hardly have been more unlike Miss Acland, her great passions being mountaineering and alpine photography.

Ironically, given her prominence in her own day, Miss Acland has been overshadowed in recent years by another of her Camera Club contemporaries: Etheldreda Janet ('Audrie') Laing, née Winkfield (1872–1960). Laing owes her celebrity to thirty-one Autochromes in the National Media Museum. By the time she was elected to the Club on 16 December 1901, aged 29, she was known to many of its members, her husband Charles Miskin Laing (1863–1939) having served on the City Council with Impey since 1889. Brought up in the Cathedral Close in Ely, where she had been the neighbour of another of the Club's members-to-be, Sophia Merivale (1853–1928) (cat. no. 176), Laing moved to Oxford on her marriage in 1895, already sharing links to the city through her uncle, Alfred Winkfield (1838–1917), House Surgeon to the Radcliffe Infirmary. She took a low-key role after joining the Club, but even before turning to the Autochrome her work had been admired. In the 1904 exhibition, for example, her "landscape, river and lake scenery, seascape and cloud studies" were deemed worthy of note, as was a "delightful study of a little girl", presumably one of her daughters, soon to be immortalized in colour.[51]

Orthochromatic Photography and the Cadett Spectrum Plate

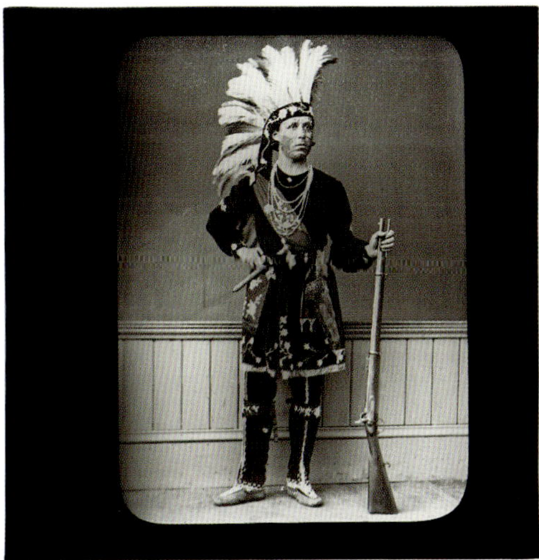

Fig. 58. *"Dr. Oronhyatekha"*
Lantern slide from a negative by Hills & Saunders of 1862
Miss Acland would later photograph Peter Martin, 'Burning Cloud', Chief of the Mohawks, in her garden, in traditional Oxford tribal dress: subfusc.

As well as exhibiting Cameron's study of J. F. W. Herschel after her Home Portraiture lecture, Miss Acland showed a daguerreotype and two ambrotypes of Ojibwe people, and an enlargement from a famous portrait by Hills & Saunders of her friend Oronhyatekha, 'Burning Cloud', Chief of the Mohawks (1841–1907). Also on display, in a special viewing device called a 'Krōmskōp' or 'Photochromoscope' that the Club had just purchased, was a 'Kromogram' (see p. 194) of what W. J. Herschel claimed was the first ever portrait to be taken in colour, made at his special request by the Anglophile American inventor Frederic Eugene Ives (1856–1937).

Miss Acland's decision to include a colour photograph in her lecture was a signal that she intended to turn away from portraiture and embark on a new direction in her photographic work. Over the next two decades she would dedicate herself with increasing devotion to the scientific side of photography and the challenge of colour in particular. Her first step along this path was an investigation not of photography *in* colour, but *of* colour: orthochromatic photography. The problem of orthochromatic photography was an old one, long known to photographers. As Elizabeth Eastlake (1809–1893) explained in a celebrated article in the *London Quarterly Review* in 1857, it stemmed from the insensitivity of silver salts to the red end of the spectrum:

> So impatient have been the blues and violets to perform their task upon the recipient plate, that the very substance of the colour has been lost and dissolved in the solar presence; while so laggard have been the reds and yellows and all tints partaking

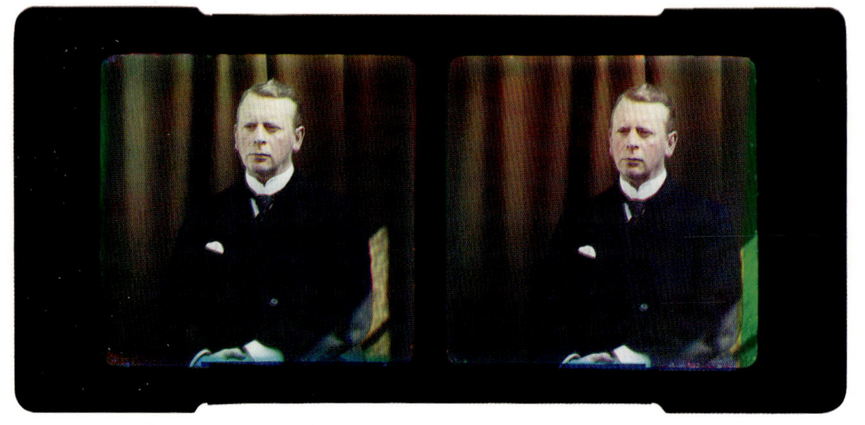

Fig. 59. *"Mr Robinson (Assistant to Mr Ives)"*
Digital composite from Kromogram positives, the originals made for William James Herschel by Frederic Ives, *c.* 1898
According to Herschel this was the first portrait ever taken with the three-colour process, but as he wrote on the label "Mr Ives deprecated exhibition of it".

> of them, that they have hardly kindled into activity before the light has been withdrawn. Thus it is that the relation of one colour to another is found changed and often reversed, the deepest blue being altered from a dark mass into a light one, and the most golden-yellow from a light body into a dark.[52]

The first commercial 'orthochromatic' or 'isochromatic' plates (the terms were used synonymously in the 1890s), in which colour sensitizers were added to the emulsion in an attempt to make them responsive to the entire spectrum, were released in Britain in 1883. However, they failed to gain much of a following, the tonal characteristics of 'ordinary' plates being so deeply imprinted in the eyes and minds of photographers that most were sceptical of the need for anything different, some even going as far as to ridicule orthochromatic photography as "the 'true translation of colour' twaddle".[53] In the late 1890s this attitude would begin to change. That it did so owed much to the efforts of the British plate manufacturer James William Thomas Cadett (1852–1949). In 1895 Cadett released the first in a series of 'Cadett Spectrum plates', which he claimed were capable of producing "absolutely correct representation of colour luminosities".[54] The Spectrum plate was a significant advance on anything that had gone before. Cadett advertised it heavily (for both scientific and artistic uses), promoting the cause of orthochromatic photography in the process.

Somewhat surprisingly, given his overtly commercial motives, in his campaign to promote the Spectrum plate Cadett was assisted materially by Miss Acland, who treated orthochromatic photography as synonymous with the use of his products. Miss Acland had been introduced to Cadett at the Camera Club in December 1897, where he spoke on "The Photographic Plate its present & future capabilities". When he returned in October 1898, to discuss "Latest views on Development", she lodged him in Broad Street. With her portraiture lecture out of the way, in spring 1899 she commenced a series of systematic trials of the Spectrum plate's pictorial capabilities (cat. nos. 87–92). Her experiments began with daffodils, which were peculiarly revealing of the need for a colour-correct emulsion, their yellow petals and orange trumpets appearing absurdly dark when rendered by ordinary plates. During a summer vacation in Boars Hill, a hamlet just outside Oxford, she then tested the Spectrum plate for landscape work, discovering its advantages in depicting the golden yellows of cornfields — an issue that also preoccupied George Bernard

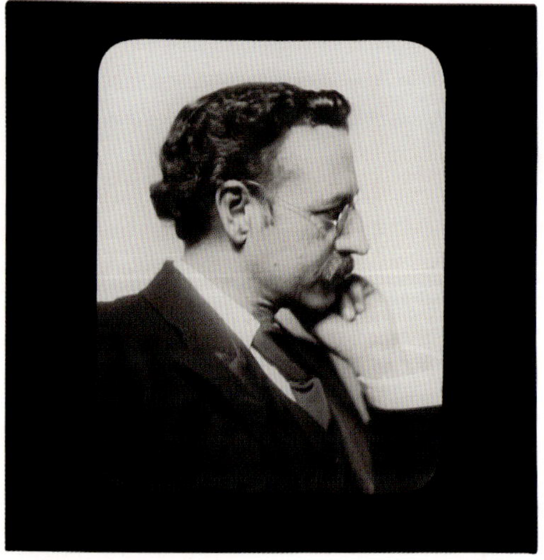

Fig. 60. *"James Cadett Esqr."*
Oxford, 9 or 10 October 1898
Miss Acland took Cadett's portrait on one of his own plates when he stayed with her in Broad Street prior to lecturing at the Camera Club in October 1898. Her relationship with the evangelistic manufacturer of the Spectrum plate is surprising given his overtly commercial interests, which might have been expected to threaten her amateur credentials and the genteel mores of her class.

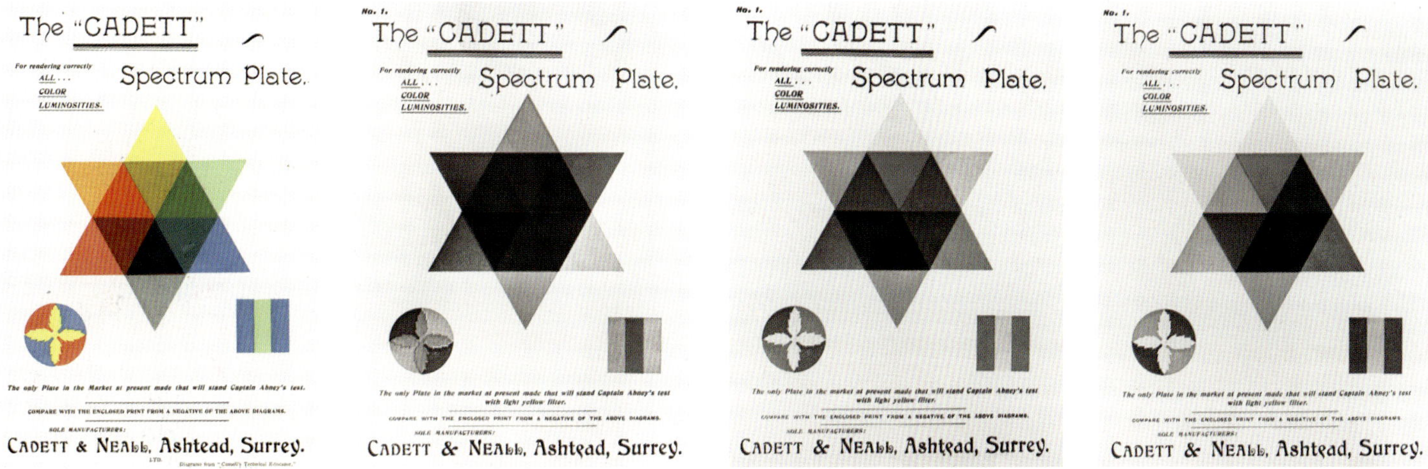

Figs. 61–64. *Ordinary Plate and Spectrum Plate Compared*
Before 23 August 1900
Cadett's printed test sheet exposed (from left to right) on an ordinary plate, a Spectrum plate with 'Gilvus' filter, and a Spectrum plate with 'Absolutus' filter. The reds are too dark on the ordinary plate, the blues too light. With the Spectrum plate and Gilvus filter an improvement is seen; with the Absolutus the change is dramatic. The Gilvus filter was yellow, the Absolutus deep orange and required ×5 the exposure.

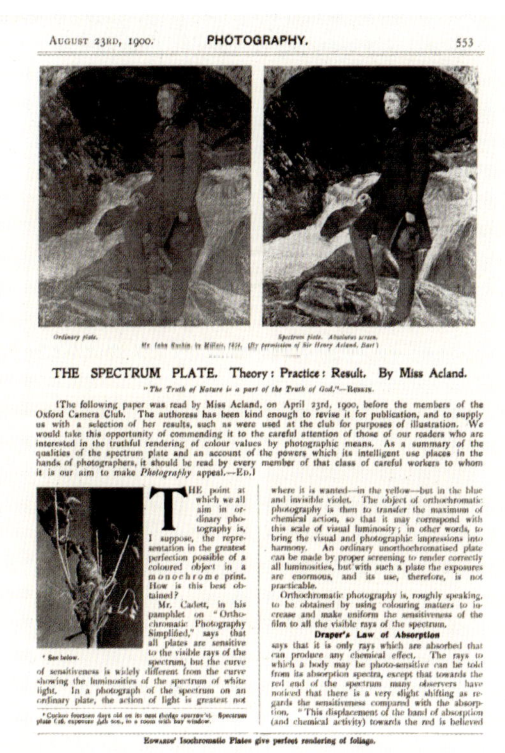

AUGUST 23RD, 1900. PHOTOGRAPHY. 553

Ordinary plate. Spectrum plate. Absolutus screen.
Mr John Ruskin, by Millais, 1854. (By permission of Sir Henry Acland, Bart.)

THE SPECTRUM PLATE. Theory: Practice: Result. By Miss Acland.

"The Truth of Nature is a part of the Truth of God."—RUSKIN.

[The following paper was read by Miss Acland, on April 23rd, 1900, before the members of the Oxford Camera Club. The authoress has been kind enough to revise it for publication, and to supply us with a selection of her results, such as were used at the club for purposes of illustration. We would take this opportunity of commending it to the careful attention of those of our readers who are interested in the truthful rendering of colour values by photographic means. As a summary of the qualities of the spectrum plate and an account of the powers which its intelligent use places in the hands of photographers, it should be read by every member of that class of careful workers to whom it is our aim to make *Photography* appeal.—ED.]

* See below.

THE point at which we all aim in ordinary photography is, I suppose, the representation in the greatest perfection possible of a coloured object in a monochrome print. How is this best obtained?

Mr. Cadett, in his pamphlet on "Orthochromatic Photography Simplified," says that all plates are sensitive to the visible rays of the spectrum, but the curve of sensitiveness is widely different from the curve showing the luminosities of the spectrum of white light. In a photograph of the spectrum on an ordinary plate, the action of light is greatest not where it is wanted—in the yellow—but in the blue and invisible violet. The object of orthochromatic photography is then to transfer the maximum of chemical action, so that it may correspond with this scale of visual luminosity; in other words, to bring the visual and photographic impressions into harmony. An ordinary unorthochromatised plate can be made by proper screening to render correctly all luminosities, but with such a plate the exposures are enormous, and its use, therefore, is not practicable.

Orthochromatic photography is, roughly speaking, to be obtained by using colouring matters to increase and make uniform the sensitiveness of the film to all the visible rays of the spectrum.

Draper's Law of Absorption

says that it is only rays which are absorbed that can produce any chemical effect. The rays to which a body may be photo-sensitive can be told from its absorption spectra, except that towards the red end of the spectrum many observers have noticed that there is a very slight shifting as regards the sensitiveness compared with the absorption. "This displacement of the band of absorption (and chemical activity) towards the red is believed

* Cuckoo fourteen days old on its nest (hedge sparrow's). Spectrum plate C16, exposure 1/25th sec., in a room with bay window.

EDWARDS' Isochromatic Plates give perfect rendering of foliage.

Fig. 65. *Truth to Nature*
The opening of Miss Acland's eight-page paper on the Spectrum plate in the journal *Photography*, 23 August 1900

Shaw (1856–1950), a keen photographer and advocate of orthochromatic film.[55] As an objective test of the Spectrum plate and the two different types of 'measured' light filters supplied with it — the 'Gilvus' and 'Absolutus' filters — she photographed Cadett's 'coloured star': a set of colour patches adapted from a diagram in *Cassell's Technical Educator* (2 vols., London, 1871–72), where it accompanied "Six Lessons on the Theory of Colour" by Arthur Herbert Church (1834–1915), graduate of Lincoln College, former student of Crookes, and the authority on the science of art.

Miss Acland's experiments in orthochromatic photography culminated in a second lecture to the Camera Club, on "Spectrum Plates", delivered in the Museum on 23 April 1900 and illustrated with forty-two lantern slides. In August 1900 this was published in extended form in *Photography* under the title "The Spectrum Plate. Theory: Practice: Result", accompanied by the unusual extravagance of nineteen half-tone plates. Also released as an offprint, the paper was widely praised, *American Amateur Photographer* judging it "a convincingly beautiful illustrated article".[56]

One of the most important real-world applications of the Spectrum plate Miss Acland addressed was the copying of artworks (cat. nos. 95–99). At the top of her published paper she included two reproductions of a painting her father owned, one on an ordinary plate, the other a Spectrum plate. The painting is one of the most celebrated of the nineteenth century: John Everett Millais's portrait of Ruskin at Glenfinlas (see cat. no. 111). The motto Miss Acland chose for the paper was taken from Ruskin's *Modern Painters*, "The Truth of Nature is a part of the Truth of God".[57] On one level her inclusion of portrait and motto functioned to cast orthochromatic photography as a Pre-Raphaelite undertaking: a quest for greater truthfulness of representation, but of colour rather than form. On another it enabled her to communicate her belief in the mutual interdependence of art and science, and her conviction that both ultimately served a higher moral purpose. Although artistic and scientific photography are conventionally portrayed as adversaries during the 1890s, no conflict existed between the two in Miss Acland's mind. Scientific photography was not to be depreciated, nor did it undermine the pursuit of artistic ideals. Technical advances such as orthochromatic plates could only advance pictorial ends, she believed, and with it photography's standing in the hierarchy of the arts.

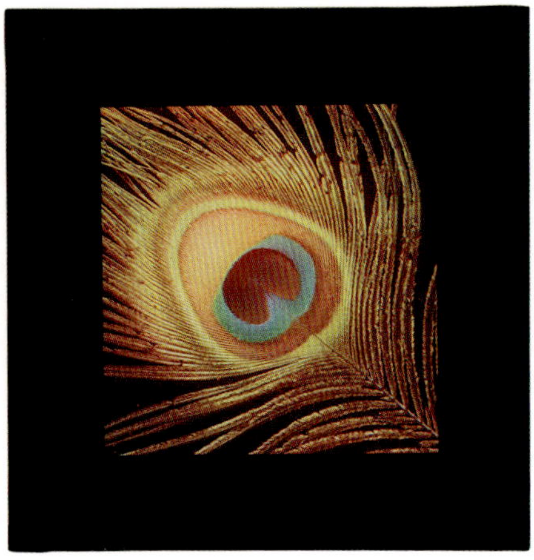

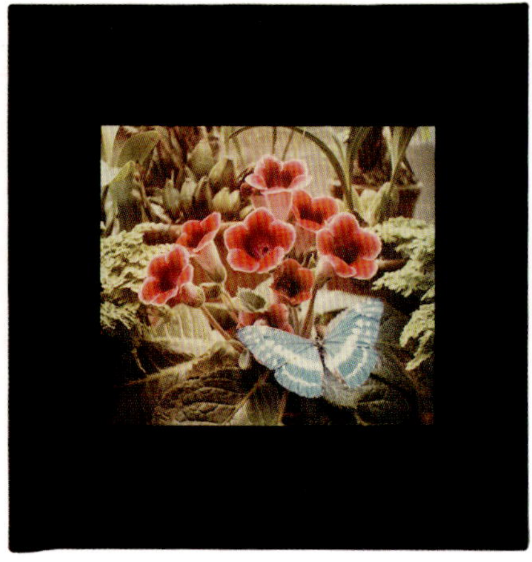

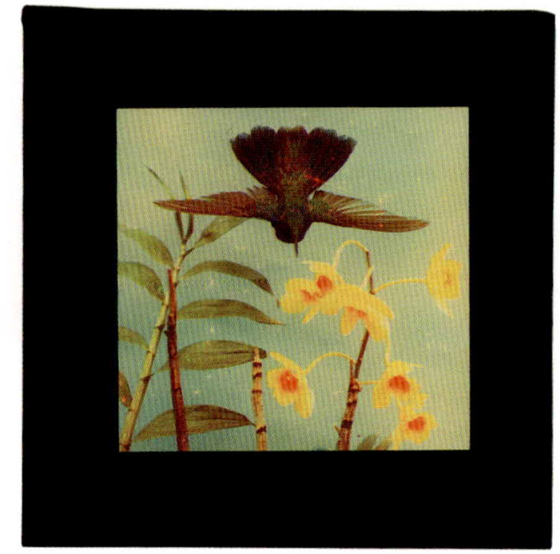

The Sanger Shepherd Process of Natural Colour Photography

For the last ten slides in her 1900 lecture Miss Acland exhibited examples of the Spectrum plate's most important application: colour photography. The appearance of colour slides at the Camera Club caused considerable excitement, Herschel speaking of their "wonderful beauty" and enthusing that the audience had been given "a pleasure that evening that they could hardly have expected in their lives".[58] Colour had long been the Holy Grail of photography. Potential solutions had been advanced for decades, Louis Ducos du Hauron (1837–1920) and Charles Cros (1842–1888) both publishing methods based on James Clerk Maxwell's trichromatic theory of vision as early as 1869. The 1890s saw work reach frenetic levels, claims to have solved the problem being put forward not only by Ives, but by Gabriel Lippmann (1845–1921) and John Joly (1857–1933), amongst others. Nevertheless, a truly practicable method remained elusive, leading many to doubt whether photography in 'natural colours' would ever be achieved. In an article on "Colour Au Naturel" in the *British Journal of Photography*, for example, the editor Thomas Bedding (1861–1936) equated the problem with the "Elixir Vitæ, the conversion of ferric oxide into gold, practical aerial navigation, the occurrence of two Sundays in one week" — it would be "a long time coming".[59] This was no bad thing, he argued: "that animals cannot tell us what they think of us, that a man is limited to one mother-in-law at a time, that Christmas falls but once per annum, let us be truly thankful, and not less truly, in sooth, than we are for the remoteness of the 'naturally' coloured photograph."

That Bedding would soon be forced to eat his words was due largely to one man and the process that bore his name: Edward Sanger Shepherd (1868–1927). A former assistant of Ives, Sanger Shepherd set up in business on his own in 1899 in order to promote his 'Sanger Shepherd Process of Natural Colour Photography'. The process was a method of producing colour lantern slides, viewable in the hand or using a normal lantern projector, and therefore differed from the 'Ives colour system', as seen after Miss Acland's Home Portraiture lecture, in dispensing with the need for a special viewing instrument. Simple in principle, the system was difficult in practice. The first step involved taking three separate photographs of the subject

Figs. 66–68. (ABOVE) *Sanger Shepherd Specimen Slides*
Sanger Shepherd & Co., 1899
Specimen slides were available from Sanger Shepherd for 10/6. Most were taken by his partners William Saville Kent (1845–1908), an established nature photographer, and Robert Lincoln Cocks (1876–1937), who became a respected worker in bromoil. The peacock feather and butterfly were shown by Miss Acland during her Spectrum Plates lecture.

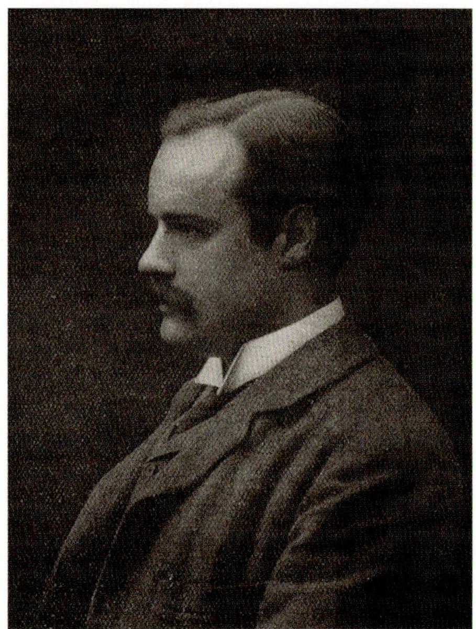

Fig. 69. *Edward Sanger Shepherd*
Edward Le Jeune, half-tone, published in 1907
When the *British Journal of Photography* began a 'Monthly Colour Supplement' in January 1907 the editor chose a biography of Ducos du Hauron for the first page. Sanger Shepherd's portrait appeared in the February issue, reflecting contemporary opinion that until his efforts "colour-photography as a craft cannot be said to have come into existence".

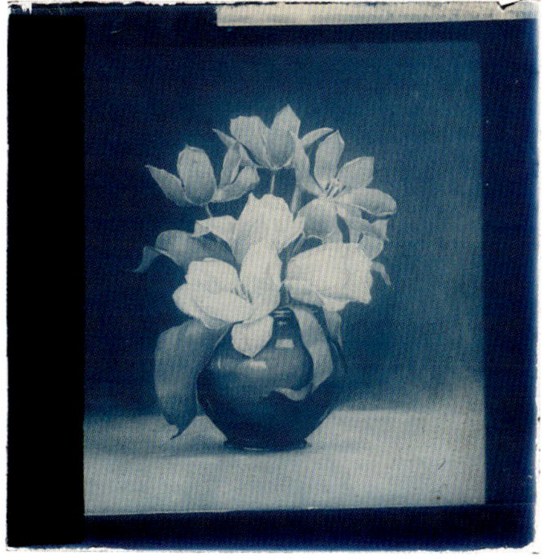

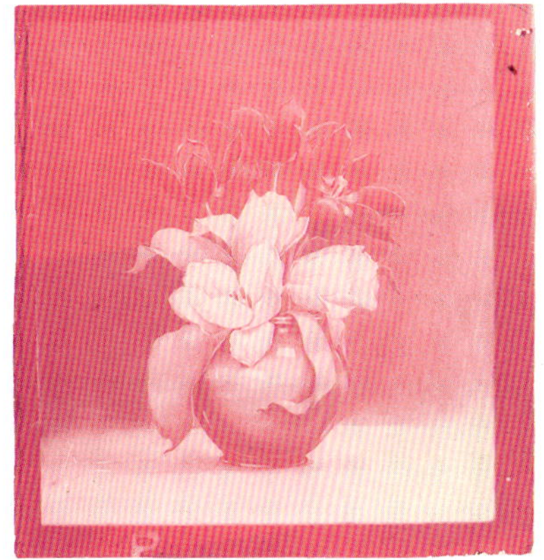

Figs. 70–72. *Components of a Sanger Shepherd Lantern Slide*

Sanger Shepherd & Co., *c.* 1899

Sanger Shepherd colour slides consist of a cyanotype on glass and two celluloid-mounted carbon prints dyed 'pink' and yellow after exposure and development. Contrary to their name, carbon prints are formed by the action of light in hardening a thin tissue of gelatine that has been sensitized in a bichromate solution.

A BRIEF EXPLANATORY NOTE.

We are often asked to state in the briefest manner how our method differs from that for Monochromatic Photography.

In reply it may be stated, that whereas in the latter the **whole of the white light** from the subject impresses itself on the sensitive plate in the camera **at one operation**; in the Sanger-Shepherd process **one third only of the spectrum** of white light **is allowed to reach the plate at a time**, the other two-thirds being excluded by accurately measured colour filters placed between lens and plate.

These three screens pass to the plate respectively the Red, Green and Violet thirds of the Spectrum. They are clipped in a frame to the front of the long-shaped dark slide, and after insertion in the Repeating-Back case on the camera are moved one after another, with the plate, past the single opening (*see fig.*) Development then gives three neutral grey negative images on the single plate, **differing however in densities according to the colours passed by the light filters** (*see fig.*)

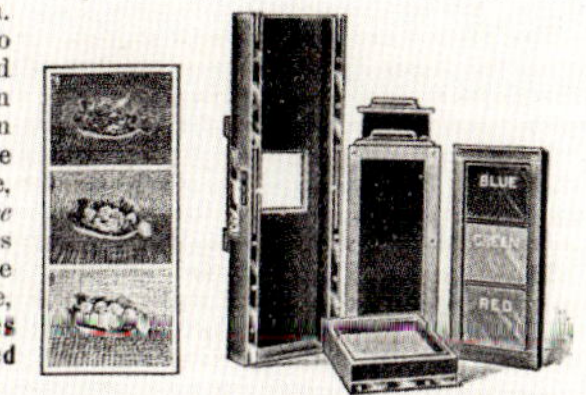

Sanger-Shepherd Repeating Back and One-Plate Triple Negative

COMPOSITION OF THE COLOUR PRINT.—A black and white photograph is a print opposite and complementary in its densities to those of its single negative, so also the colour photograph, though apparently a single positive, is really three superimposed thirds, **each third complementary in densities to its negative** and nearly **complementary in colour to its taking screen.** In other words we superimpose for our finished print, greenish-blue, pink and yellow thirds obtained respectively from the red, green and violet sensation negatives. As the whole of the Spectrum with every colour reaches the sensitive plate it will be seen that there is no loss whatever, and provided accurately measured screens are used, the system becomes one of the highest efficiency. *For method of making the prints, see previous page.*

Fig. 73. *Sanger Shepherd Repeating Back*

Sanger Shepherd separation negatives were exposed in a normal bellows camera, on a single narrow plate, using a 'repeating back' in which the dark-slide and colour filter assembly moved the width of the image between each exposure.

through red, green and blue filters. From the resulting negatives three positives were then printed: one as a cyanotype on glass, the others on celluloid as magenta and yellow carbon prints (prints in which the image is formed in hardened gelatine). These were then cemented together in 'optical contact' to create a full-colour image. Unlike other colour pioneers, Sanger Shepherd made no claim to any new scientific discovery. Instead, his goal had been to convert existing ideas into a reliable system of colour photography, capable of being worked by amateurs. To this end, in July 1900 he released complete sets of apparatus and materials for the process. Ready-made specimen slides could also be purchased from his company; when seen on his stall at the Royal Photographic Society in September 1900 they were described in the *Photographic Journal* by Henry Snowden Ward (1865–1911) as "very magnificent transparencies", the correspondent of the *Photographic Times* judging them "far superior to anything I have ever seen".[60]

The colour slides Miss Acland exhibited during her Spectrum Plates lecture were samples lent to her by Sanger Shepherd, to whom she had been introduced through Cadett. Ten weeks after the lecture, in a letter to Willie of 8 July 1900, she hinted at her intention to master the process herself: "I am very busy clearing off all my arrears so as to devote myself to 3 colour photography. I want to do it stereoscopically in time."[61] In the event, her first colour photograps would not be shown in public until 25 March 1901, when she sent six Sanger Shepherd slides to a members' lantern slide evening at the Camera Club. However, at least one of these — *Crimson Rambler in New College Gardens* (cat. no. 125) — must have been assembled from negatives taken the previous June or July, just as Sanger Shepherd's materials became available, because it depicts summer-flowering roses.

The delay in Miss Acland showing her colour slides was due to the death of her father on 16 October 1900, shortly after the Camera Club had reconvened for its autumn session. The trauma of Acland's passing, which necessitated her move of home in May 1901 to Clevedon House in Park Town, North Oxford, no doubt hampered Miss Acland's ability to progress in colour photography. However, it was not long before she began to display her work in public regularly. In July 1901, for example, several of her colour slides were exhibited at the Town Hall during a lecture on colour photography by Herschel before the 'large and brilliant assemblage' of delegates to the Photographic Convention.[62] These included a view from the Malvern hills (cat. no. 130) and "the first portrait of a lady by this process", which depicted a woman seated in a flower garden (untraced).[63] Later in the summer, during a visit to Willie's flagship H.M.S. *Magnificent* in Torbay, she took a photograph of the whole fleet (untraced), showing it at the Camera Club in November. In September she had made her debut as a colour photographer at the Royal Photographic Society exhibition, sending six slides: *Crimson Rambler in New College Gardens, Portrait of a Lady, View from Great Malvern, Queen's Chocolate Box* (untraced), *Strelitzia Regina — South African Plant* (cat. no. 128) and *Frogbowl, Ribbon and Fruit* (cat. no. 121).

The time and skill involved in making Sanger Shepherd slides was considerable. In early 1902 Miss Acland reported that on no occasion had she been able to complete one in less than a fortnight, "although two or three might be in preparation at one time".[64] By the end of the year her rate had risen slightly. "I have been working very hard at making up colour slides", she wrote to Willie in December, "and have made up 26 new ones since October which is very good for one pair of hands."[65] Some of these slides, only a small fraction of which survive, are mentioned elsewhere in the historical record. In January, for example, Henry Trueman Wood (1845–1929) borrowed examples to exhibit at his Christmas Juvenile Lectures on "Photography and its Applications" at the Society of Arts (where he was Secretary). In March 1903 Miss Acland entered *Foreshore, Southampton Water* (cat. no. 134) in the Royal Photographic Society "Affiliation Societies' lantern slides competition", where it won a certificate and was included in a set of photographs circulated around clubs and societies all over Britain and Ireland. The following year she submitted *Perseverance* (untraced) in the first competition ever held for colour photographs, which was organized by the journal *Photography*, coming first and winning a silver medal. This also travelled the country, as one of the 'Photography prize slides'.

Miss Acland's first opportunity to speak on the subject of colour photography arose in April 1902 when she was invited to give her third lecture to the Oxford Camera Club: a "Demonstration of the Sanger-Shepherd Method of Indirect Colour Photography". The lecture differed from her previous performances in being presented jointly with her fellow Camera Club member James Henry Hall ('Harry') Minn (1870–1961). Minn was also a keen colour photographer and collaborated closely with Miss Acland in her early experiments, having previously acted as a photographic factotum in regard to her monochrome photography. During the lecture Miss Acland and Minn discoursed on the theory and practice of colour photography by the Sanger Shepherd process, assembling a slide on the spot. In concluding their remarks they revealed that they had also been exploring a more innovative branch of colour photography still: the creation of colour prints on paper. The revelation attracted widespread notice. "That indefatigable lady amateur Miss Acland, of Oxford, England, has been experimenting in tri-color printing on paper", *Wilson's Photographic Magazine*, based in New York, reported in May.[66] In September 1902 Miss Acland became the first woman to exhibit colour prints at the R.P.S. exhibition, beaten to outright first place only by Walter Edwin Brewerton (1870–1947), son of the business partner of tea baron Frederick John Horniman. One of the five prints she submitted, *The X Fleet in Torbay* (untraced), had the unique distinction of being

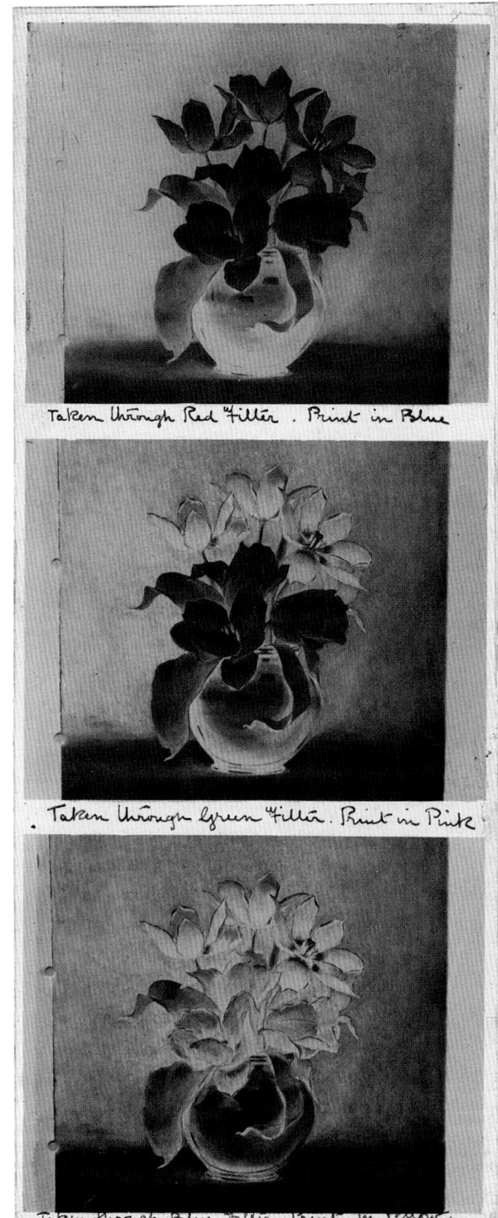

Fig. 74. *Sanger Shepherd Three-colour Negative*
Sanger Shepherd & Co., *c.* 1899
Sanger Shepherd separation negatives were created by making three exposures side by side on the same rectangular Spectrum plate, through (from top to bottom) red, green and blue filters. These were then printed in their complementary colours — cyan, magenta and yellow — either on glass and celluloid in the case of lantern slides (see figs. 70–72) or on paper when making prints.

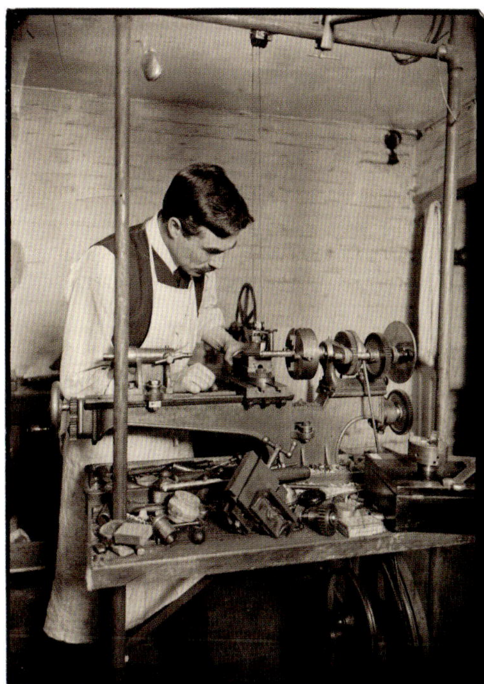

Fig. 75. *Harry Minn at his Lathe*
James Henry Hall Minn, half-plate negative, *c.* 1900
This study is sometimes attributed to Miss Acland but is probably a self-portrait by her friend and collaborator.

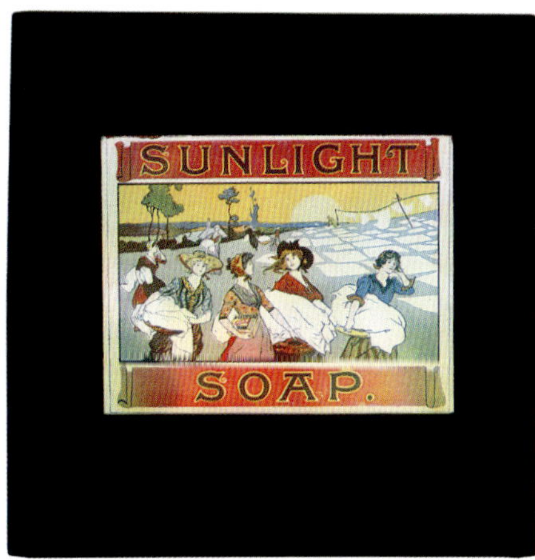

Fig. 76. *"Coloured Advertisement"*
James Henry Hall Minn, Sanger Shepherd lantern slide, 1901
Minn showed colour lantern slides at the Oxford Camera Club on two occasions while Miss Acland was absent in mourning for her father. This slide was exhibited after her return, in December 1901, when it was described as "remarkably accurate in tint".

hung in the 'Pictorial' rather than the 'Scientific' section of the exhibition. In its review of the show the *British Journal of Photography* gave details of her (elaborate) method of working, revealing that the prints were based on carbon printing in pink and yellow over a blue-toned bromide print, the superimposition achieved using collodion-coated rubber-edged glass transfer plates (see cat. no. 141).

Miss Acland's experiments on paper were highly original and put her at the vanguard of progress in colour photography. In subsequent years she would continue to refine her techniques, also experimenting with 'imbibition printing' — a process patented by Sanger Shepherd in 1902 (see cat. no. 156). However, it was not her paper prints that brought her to fame as a colour photographer. This she owed instead to the collection of colour slides she assembled from negatives taken during two visits to Gibraltar in May 1903 and 1904. Forty-two Sanger Shepherd slides formed the basis of her celebrated lectures on Gibraltar, the first of which was delivered at the Oxford Camera Club on 19 December 1904 under the title "A Visit to Gibraltar".[67] On 6 June 1905 they were seen again when she made her debut as a lecturer in the metropolis, in a crowded room of the R.P.S. in Bloomsbury. The slides were described in "eulogist terms" by the press after the London lecture, the success of the event earning her an invitation to show them again, to the general public, during the Society's exhibition in October.[68] Her exhibition lecture, given before overflowing audiences at the New Gallery in Regent Street, caused a sensation and was the most popular feature of the season. Its enthusiastic reception obliged her to give two repeat performances: as an unscheduled event on the closing night of the exhibition and "By special request" as the opening feature of the 1906 programme.[69] The photographs that proved so popular were a mixture of portraits (cat. nos. 140–145), views of Gibraltar (cat. nos. 135 & 136) and scenes in the beautiful gardens of 'The Mount', Willie's official residence as Admiral Superintendent of the Dockyard (cat. nos. 146–154). They were the "finest collection of slides in colour photography yet produced on one subject", according to one critic, the *Oxford Times* reporting that audiences went away "filled not only with wonderment at the possibilities of this new branch of photographic art, but with delight at having had the beauties of one of Britain's smallest but most jealously guarded possessions exhibited in the natural colours".[70] Miss Acland was "*facile princeps* amongst three-colour workers" the editor of *Photography* observed, her work leaving "nothing to be desired in the direction of perfect colour rendering".[71]

Despite these accolades Miss Acland's colour photography has largely been ignored by historians, the Sanger Shepherd process faring little better. In the orthodox account of the history of photography the birth of colour is said to have taken place at the Photo-Club de Paris on 10 June 1907, credit for the first commercially successful colour process going not to Sanger Shepherd but to Auguste and Louis Lumière, for their Autochrome process. This is clearly incorrect. The first practicable system of colour photography was an English rather than a French achievement, vested in a tradition of precision scientific-instrument making and its application in the arts. The Sanger Shepherd process was widely practised in the seven years before the Autochrome saw the light of day. Over 300 Sanger Shepherd colour photographs were shown at the R.P.S. annual exhibition alone between 1900 and 1906, by eighteen

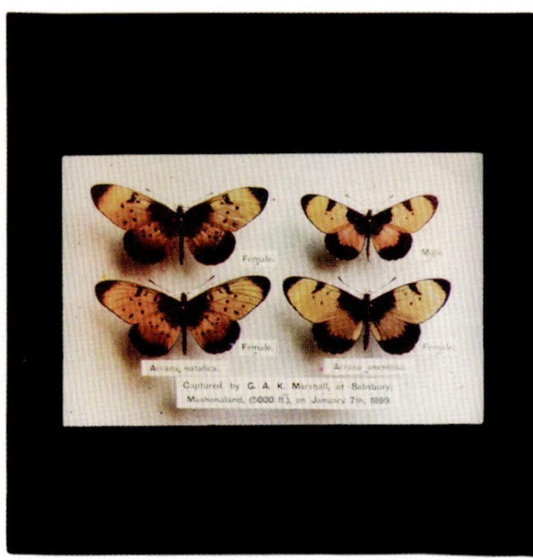

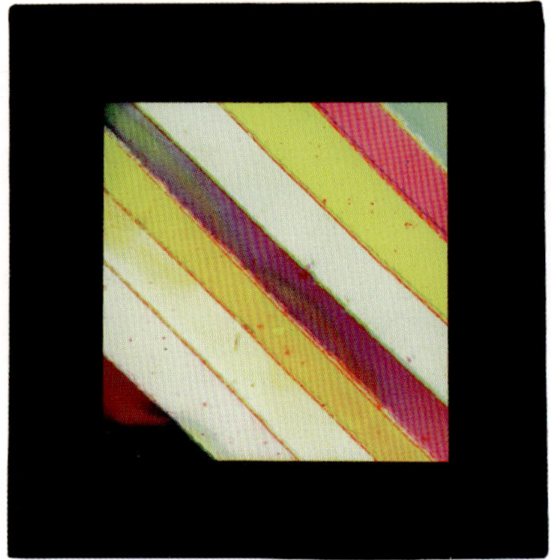

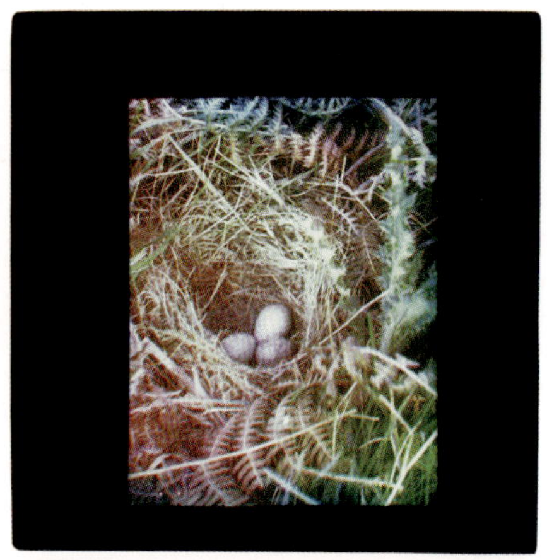

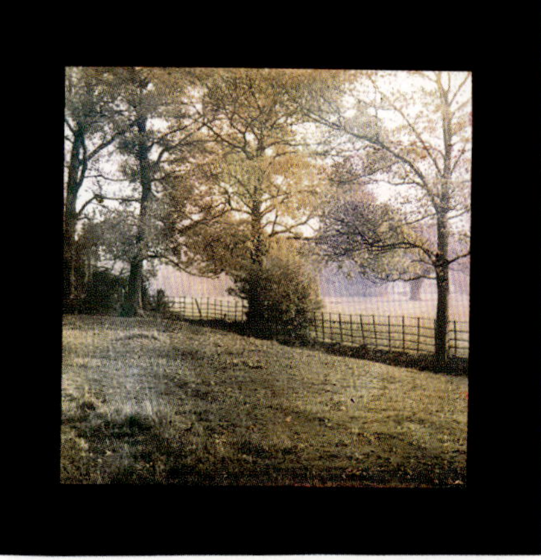

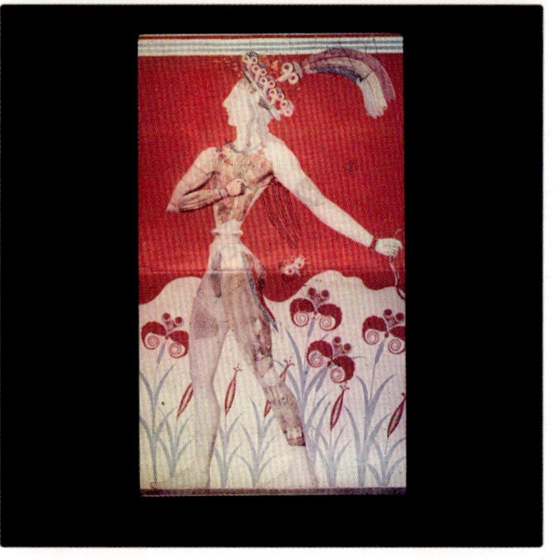

Sanger Shepherd Slides by Other Workers

Fig. 77. *Acraea natalica* and *Acraea anemosa*
Sanger Shepherd for Edward Bagnall Poulton, *c.* 1902

Fig. 78. *"¼-wave length Mica wedge"*
Edmund Johnston Garwood (1864–1949), *c.* 1903

Fig. 79. *"Nest of Wood Lark"*
Oliver Gregory Pike (1877–1963), 1904

Fig. 80. *Autumn Landscape*
William de Wiveleslie Abney (1843–1920), *c.* 1905

Fig. 81. *The Prince of the Lilies*
Sanger Shepherd for Arthur Evans, after Piet de Jong, 1923

different photographers. In the 1901 exhibition, for example, Miss Acland was joined by John Allen (1871–1944), William Edward Bond (1852–1938), Charles Barker Howdill (1863–1941), and Andrew Pringle. Allen, who was the son of Ruskin's publisher, no less, showed colour slides of Swiss scenes, including such favourites with Ruskin as the *Jungfrau* and *Mont Blanc, from the Mer de Glace*. Howdill, an architect by profession, exhibited slides of stained glass windows taken in Oxford. Bond, a fellow of the Society, contributed still lifes, Pringle slides of crystals. Sanger Shepherd slides could also be seen outside the exhibition context entirely: in 1901 Edward Bagnall Poulton included them in his lectures on protective colouration of insects at the Entomological Society; in 1906 Fred Enock (1845–1916) showed slides of plants at the Royal Horticultural Society. Some lecturers preferred Sanger Shepherd's system over the Autochrome for years to come, the archaeologist Arthur Evans (1851–1941) using it as late as 1923 to copy Piet de Jong's watercolours of his "spoils from Crete" (as they were described to Miss Acland).

Historians' blindness to the existence of practicable colour photography before the Autochrome extends to a number of important institutional initiatives that took place prior to the arrival of the process in England. The first exhibition devoted exclusively to colour photography opened at the offices of the *British Journal of Photography* in London on 16 January 1906, seventeen months before the Autochrome's release. Thirty-two exhibitors, including Miss Acland, showed 150 colour photographs between them, which were seen by Eveleen Myers, George Bernard Shaw and Alvin Langdon Coburn (1882–1966), among 200 other visitors in the first four days of the two-month opening. The exhibition attracted coverage in the general press, reviews appearing in such unlikely places as the *Daily Express*, *Westminster Gazette* and *Morning Advertiser*, the latter singling out Miss Acland's slides for praise. Following on the heels of the exhibition, in October 1906 a 'Society of Colour Photographers' was founded. A year later, by which time seventy-three members had joined, the Society held its own exhibition, attracting 1,000 visitors in the first week, who saw seventeen photographs by Miss Acland. Prompted by the burgeoning enthusiasm for colour, in January 1907 the *British Journal of Photography* inaugurated a "Monthly Supplement on Colour Photography". Miss Acland, as the undisputed leader of the field, was expected to bestow her blessing on the project: "I wish the Supplement every success", she wrote in a letter in the first issue.[72]

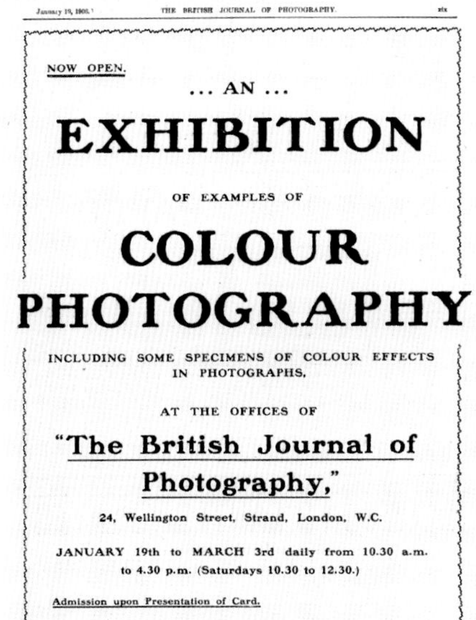

Fig. 82. *Colour Comes of Age*

The first exhibition of colour photography in Britain opened in January 1906, seventeen months before the Autochrome's release: a fact that exposes the error of the idea that the Lumières' process constitutes the 'birth of colour photography'.

Sept. 6, 1907.] THE BRITISH JOURNAL OF PHOTOGRAPHY. [Supplement.] 67

The Chemical Processes.

The operations which follow the first development of the plate in the special pyro-ammonia developer for 2½ minutes do not call for any remark other than those in the printed instruction for the process. As soon as the developer has been applied for the stated time, and a brief wash has been given to the plate, the acid permanganate solution (Solution C) is poured on, and the plate removed in it into daylight, or the lights in the dark-room turned up. Thenceforward the whole of the operation may be done in daylight; in fact, the re-development (of the positive image) must be done in a strong light, otherwise the silver may not be completely reduced, and will therefore become dissolved in the fixing bath, with consequent reduction of the image. The glass dish in which the succeeding operations are done is best rinsed when commencing work with a little fairly strong nitric acid to make it perfectly clean, being then well flushed with water. This, in conjunction with the several permanganate solutions which are used in it, keeps it free from organic dirt, and the intensifying bath of acid silver, which usually is a dirty mixture in use, works, in our experience, very

THE LUMIÈRE PROCESS AT A GLANCE.

The beginner in the use of Lumière "Autochrome" plates will appreciate the following condensed and tabulated instructions for their manipulation, which we have adapted for English workers from the latest French instructions, and have found very useful ourselves as a ready reference in carrying out the fourteen operations which are necessary from first to last:—

Operations.	Solutions used. Quantity about sufficient for a half-plate.	Time of Action.	Notes.
In the Dark-room.			
1. First development	A, 2 drams; B, 2 drams, water to 3 oz.	2½ mins. exact	Mix at last moment and use once only. If developer too warm, will eat away half-tones and destroy detail.
2. Washing		15 to 20 secs.	
3. Reversing the image: Dissolving the developed image	C (as made up), 3 oz.	3 to 4 mins.	Solution may be used several times. If the solution does not act fully, stains or dark patches are produced.
In Daylight.			
4. Reversing the image: Washing		30 to 40 secs.	
5. Reversing the image: Developing positive image	D (as made up), 3 oz.	3 to 4 mins.	Must be used in daylight. Solution can be employed once or twice.
6. Reversing the image: Washing		30 to 40 secs.	
7. Destroying developer	E (as made up), 3 oz., or D, ½ dram, water to 3 oz.	10 secs.	Use once only. If allowed to act too long, or if used too long, the detail in the high-lights suffers.
8. Washing		15 to 20 secs.	
9. Intensification	F, [illegible]; G, 100 minims	[illegible] mins., as necessary	Intensifier should not be used a second time
10. Washing		20 to 30 secs.	
11. Clearing	H (as made up), 3 oz.	30 to 60 secs.	Use once only. If solution H does not act fully, dichroic fog is produced, but is removed by applying H again.
12. Washing		20 to 30 secs.	
13. Fixing	I (as made up), 3 oz.	2 mins.	May be used repeatedly.
14. Final washing		5 mins.	

Note.—All solutions should be used at 60 to 65 deg. Fahrenheit.

First Developer (Negative).

A.	Pyro	3 gms.	260 grs.
	Pure alcohol	100 ccs.	20 oz.
B.	Potass bromide	3 gms.	310 grs.
	Ammonia (·880)	9 ccs.	17 drms.
	Water to	85 ccs.	20 oz.

The ammonia directed by MM. Lumière in solution B is that of specific gravity ·92, a weaker variety (20-21% of real ammonia) than strong liquor ammonia ·880. The lesser quantities, therefore, given in the formula suffice.

Reversing Solution.

C.	Potass permanganate	2 gms.	70 grs.
	Sulphuric acid	10 ccs.	6½ drams.
	Water	1,000 ccs.	80 oz.

The sulphuric acid in C is the strong acid of 1·98 specific gravity. It should be added to the water, not *vice versa*.

Second Developer (Positive).

D.	Soda sulphite (anhydrous)	15 gms.	130 grs.
	Diamidophenol*	5 gms.	45 grs.
	Distilled water	1,000 ccs.	20 oz.

In place of anhydrous sulphite of soda in solution D, double the weight of crystallised sulphite may be taken.

Destroying Second Developer.

E.	Solution C	20 ccs.	1 oz.
	Water	1,000 ccs.	50 oz.

Intensifier.

F.	Pyro	3 gms.	26 grs.
	Citric acid	3 gms.	26 grs.
	Water	1,000 ccs.	20 oz.
G.	Silver nitrate	5 gms.	90 grs.
	Distilled water	100 ccs.	4 oz.

Clearer.

H.	Water	1,000 ccs.	20 oz.
	Potass permanganate	1 gm.	9 grs.

Fixing Solution.

I.	Hypo	150 gms.	3 oz.
	Soda bisulphite (solution)	50 ccs.	1 oz.
	Water	1,000 ccs.	20 oz.

Potass metabisulphite (7 gms. or 60 grs.) may be used in place of the soda bisulphite solution in making the fixing bath.

Varnish.

J.	Gum dammar	20 gms.	1 oz.
	Benzole (crystallisable)	100 gms.	5 oz.

* Amidol, or Dianol.

Fig. 83. *"The Lumière Process at a Glance"*

The Autochrome process is often portrayed by historians, quick to adopt the Lumières' own rhetoric, as no more difficult than developing a black and white negative. In reality, in its first form, it was far more complex and notoriously unreliable.

One of Miss Acland's contributions to the Society of Colour Photographers' first exhibition is especially significant: a portrait of her god-daughter Mary Agnes Hope (b. *c.* 1872, d. after 1923) (cat. no. 169). As far as is known, the portrait was the first Autochrome by a woman ever shown in a public exhibition. Although not the earliest workable colour process, the Autochrome would have a huge impact on colour photography, opening the field to many more amateurs than before. Autochromes had several advantages over the Sanger Shepherd process, the most important of which was the fact that the final colour image was created in a single exposure on the same plate as exposed in the camera, thereby avoiding the need for the development and registration of three separate prints, with all the associated difficulties. This was possible because the required red, green and blue filters were incorporated within the plate itself, as (somewhat extraordinarily) a microscopic layer of coloured potato starch grains. The intense beauty of the Lumières' process — Autochromes are miniature jewels of photographs — and its relative simplicity also contributed to its popularity, photographers' enthusiasm tempered only by its high cost, the difficulty of making prints and duplicates, and the density of the plates, which meant they were unsuitable for showing in an ordinary lantern projector.

Miss Acland was quick to try the Autochrome when it became available in England in the first week of September 1907. Her early results were encouraging, despite several complete failures during development (see cat. no. 172). She exhibited at least five plates at the Camera Club in 1907, including beautiful views of Oxford gardens in the glory of their late summer and early autumn colours (cat. nos. 167–174). Before long she would come to prefer the Autochrome for most purposes. Although her earliest trials were made in England, over the next eight years the majority of her plates would be exposed 1,500 miles away, on the island of Madeira, which she visited for the first time in March 1908 for a three-month holiday, returning again in November and for five months every winter thereafter until 1915.

Miss Acland's sojourns in Madeira, where she lived in rooms in Reid's Palace Hotel in Funchal, were ostensibly for the benefit of her health. The lameness she suffered throughout her life reared its head when she was only eight, requiring a consultation with Charles West (1816–1898), physician to the Hospital for Sick Children in Great Ormond Street. The cause of the malady would never be clearly diagnosed, but its symptoms included periods of weakness, paralysis and 'nervous contractions' in her left leg and foot. Her condition deteriorated during her late teens and early twenties, necessitating intensive treatment under a string of eminent doctors, including William Withey Gull (1816–1890) and James Paget (1814–1899) in London (who both became close friends), Karl (von) Burckhardt (1818–1888) in Wildbad in the Black Forest, and the French surgeon Auguste Nélaton (1807–1873) in Paris. Nélaton advocated amputation, but this, thankfully, was rejected by her English doctors in favour of leg irons, manipulation, 'galvanism', and other novel therapies. Her health improved after her mother's death, but by then she was consigned to the status of an invalid. Her condition was well known, Catherine Weed Ward even mentioning it in the *Photogram*.

Madeira had long been frequented by invalids as an overwintering ground. In 1857 Acland accompanied Liddell to its warm climes, returning with the 'tunny fish' Dodgson photographed. The island was ideal for Miss Acland both as patient and as photographer. The bright light and warmth aside, its greatest advantage was the hammocks that were used for transport around the steep streets (see cat. no. 193). These enabled her to enjoy a mobility never experienced before. For photography Madeira offered splendid views and a paradise of exotic plants, many with startling masses of brightly coloured flowers, making ideal subjects for colour work. Much of Miss Acland's time was therefore spent being carried by her 'hammock men' from the beautiful gardens of one *quinta* to another, photographing as she went. Her social circle in Funchal rivalled that in England, her friends including the pillars of Madeira society, permanent and temporary, from the English physician Michael Comport Grabham (1840–1935) and his wife Mary, née Blandy (1843–1914) (sister-in-law of Lord Kelvin), to the Viscountess Torre Bella (1839–1925), widow of Russel Manners Gordon (1829–1906), of Cossart Gordon wine merchants.

Once she became established, other visitors to Madeira would seek out Miss Acland as an authority on the island and its gossip. In 1912, for example, she received a visit from the Archbishop of Cape Town, William Marlborough Carter (1850–1941); in 1913 from Clements Robert Markham (1830–1916), President of the Royal Geographical Society. From time to time she bemoaned the lack of 'real gentlefolks' in the hotel and the mass invasions of passengers from passing liners. Of the regular guests of whom she did approve among the most notable are the American family of Frederic Oakley Spedden (1867–1947). The Speddens' young son, Robert Douglas Spedden (1905–1915), was her "special friend", a "dear little boy".[73] Douglas stayed at Reid's in 1909 and 1910, and landed especially to see Miss Acland whilst in transit to Algiers on the *Caronia* in January 1912. Retuning to America exactly three months later, on 14 April 1912, he found himself in the unenviable position of being a passenger on another White Star liner. Miss Acland was greatly upset on learning of the sinking of the *Titanic*, but soon had cause to be thankful when a telegram was received announcing "Spedden family saved", the *Carpathia* having picked them up with the thirty-nine other occupants of Lifeboat No. 3 (capacity sixty-five).[74]

For the first few years Miss Acland's photography in Madeira was largely carried out on Autochrome plates, although she also took her Sanger Shepherd equipment with her on at least the first visit. Later she would experiment with a number of new 'screen-plate' processes as they were released onto the market. The principle of screen-plate processes, the Autochrome included, was the same as the digital camera and computer monitor of today. During exposure light from the subject was passed through a microscopic mosaic of red, green and blue filter elements, and the intensity of the colour at each point recorded (in the case of the photographic processes simply by means of a black-and-white negative). To display the image thus captured light was passed back through a positive from the negative and the same or a similar filter screen, creating the illusion, at a distance, of a full-colour image, due to the mixing of the primary colours. The processes, as such, were 'additive' systems of colour photography, as opposed to the 'subtractive' scheme of Sanger Shepherd lantern slides, in which colours were absorbed as white light passed through successive cyan, magenta and

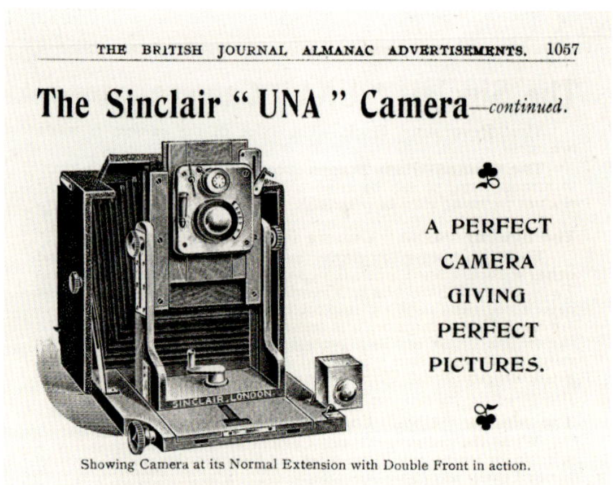

THE BRITISH JOURNAL ALMANAC ADVERTISEMENTS. 1057

The Sinclair "UNA" Camera—*continued.*

A PERFECT CAMERA GIVING PERFECT PICTURES.

Showing Camera at its Normal Extension with Double Front in action.

Fig. 84. *The Sinclair 'Una' Camera*
For her Autochrome work Miss Acland invested in a new camera, a Sinclair Una, which used metric plates, 12 × 9 cm.

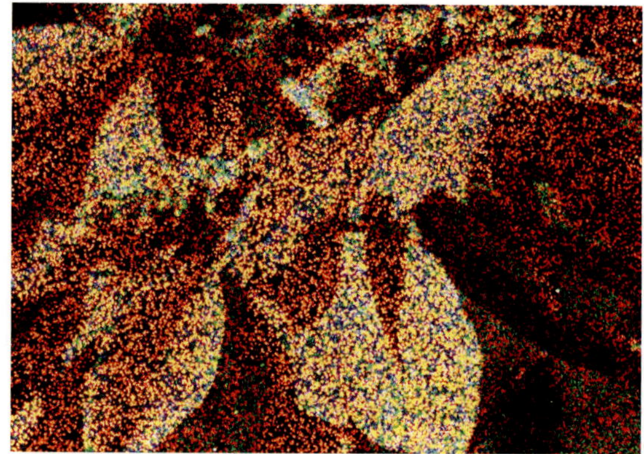

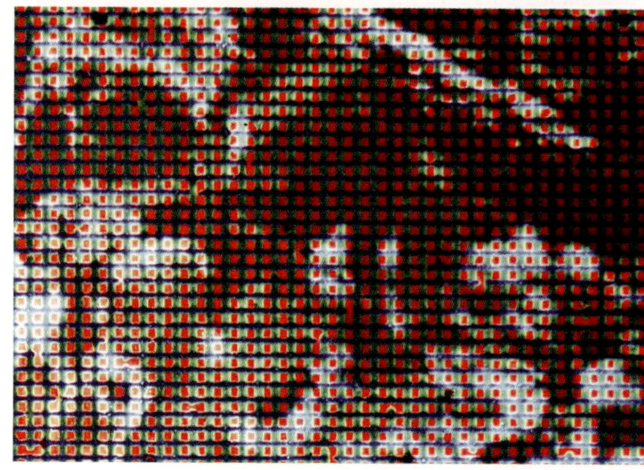

Figs. 85 & 86. *Autochrome and Omnicolore Screens Compared*
Details from cat. nos. 185 and 202, ×15
Autochrome images are formed from randomly distributed grains of potato starch stained orange, green and blue-violet. Omnicolore plates have a regular screen of filter elements, created by a grid of coloured lines. Both are additive systems, the colour elements positioned adjacent to one another, in contrast to the layered structure of Sanger Shepherd slides.

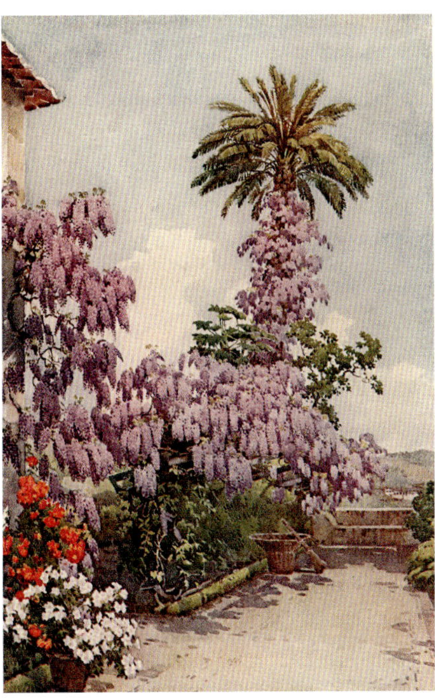

Figs. 87 *&* 88. *Wisteria in the Quinta da Levada*

Mildred Cossart, "Palm tree and Wistaria, Quinta Levada", half-tone, published in 1909; Ella Du Cane (1874–1943), "Wistaria, Quinta da Levada", half-tone from a watercolour, published in 1909

Several of the scenes Miss Acland photographed in Madeira were popular with other artists and photographers, such as this view of the Quinta da Levada, with its glorious wisteria (cf. cat. no. 180).

Fig. 89. *"Winter Sunshine at Funchal, Madeira"*

When not photographing in Madeira, Miss Acland made meteorological recordings. Twenty-five years earlier another woman with photographic interests, Jessie Piazzi Smyth, née Duncan (1815–1896), had done the same, her husband, the noted early photographer Charles Piazzi Smyth (1819–1900), publishing them in *Maderia Meteorologic* in 1882. Piazzi Smyth's sister, Henrietta Grace Smyth (1824–1914), married Baden Powell, Savilian Professor of Geometry at Oxford, and nursed Miss Acland when she was dangerously ill as a child.

Winter Sunshine at Funchal, Madeira.

The average daily sunshine recorded in the British Islands during the winter months, even in the most favoured parts, is comparatively so small that it is not surprising that a number of people find it necessary to leave these shores and seek brighter skies in more southern latitudes. The following sunshine figures for Funchal are taken from a MS. record kept by Miss Acland, F.R.Met.Soc., whose custom it has been for many years to winter in Madeira, and while there to make a number of meteorological observations. They illustrate the sunny conditions which prevail there.

MEAN DAILY SUNSHINE IN HOURS, FUNCHAL, MADEIRA.

Years.	December.	January.	February.	March.	April.	May.	Sunless Days whole Period.
1908–09	5·7	5·4	5·9	6·4	7·8	8·4	5
1909–10	...	6·4	6·7	5·4	8·4	...	1
1910–11	...	5·5	6·3	7·4	7·3	...	7
1911–12	4·9	5·2	5·6	6·0	6·8	...	6
1912–13	...	5·0	6·0	6·5	4·9	...	1
1913–14	5·3	4·2	6·6	7·2	7·1	...	3
1914–15	...	...	...	5·0	...	...	...
Mean .	5·3	5·3	6·2	6·3	7·1	...	4

yellow image layers. Just as with today's technologies, the rival manufacturers of the historic processes favoured slightly different shapes, sizes and arrangements of filter elements, and developed their own patent manufacturing techniques. In contrast to the Autochrome's randomly distributed starch grains, the newer processes were based on regular screens, arranged in geometric patterns, the filter elements printed or stained on the plate. The first alternative to the Autochrome Miss Acland tried was the Omnicolore process, released in spring 1909 (see p. 272). The second she experimented with, the Dufay Dioptichrome process (see p. 278), became available between May and July 1910. Both had highly transparent filter screens, and were therefore faster than the Autochrome, but they were also beset by other problems, such as strong colour casts and shrinkage of the screen after development (cat. no. 208). The fourth screen-plate Miss Acland used, which she would come to prefer over the Autochrome, was the Paget Colour process (see p. 280). Paget plates have a distinctive green bias to the modern eye, but Miss Acland found them eminently suited to her needs, as proven by the fifty-six examples from her hand that survive.

Miss Acland's unrivalled experience of colour photography made her a valuable source of information for photographers in Madeira, who would descend on Reid's to take her advice. In March 1912, for example, she could be found at "photographic play" with a Russian prince, Paul Arsenievitch Pontiatine. "He has never done any colour work so I have been helping him & it has been quite an amusement", she wrote.[75] The prince had been sent to her by Madeira's leading professional photographer, Manuel Olim Perestrello (1854–1929), whom she counted as a friend. In January 1914 another well-connected photographer visited to seek her advice on the Paget process: the Italian Consul, Ferdinando Maximiliano de Bianchi (1859–1920), godson of Maximilian, Emperor of Mexico.

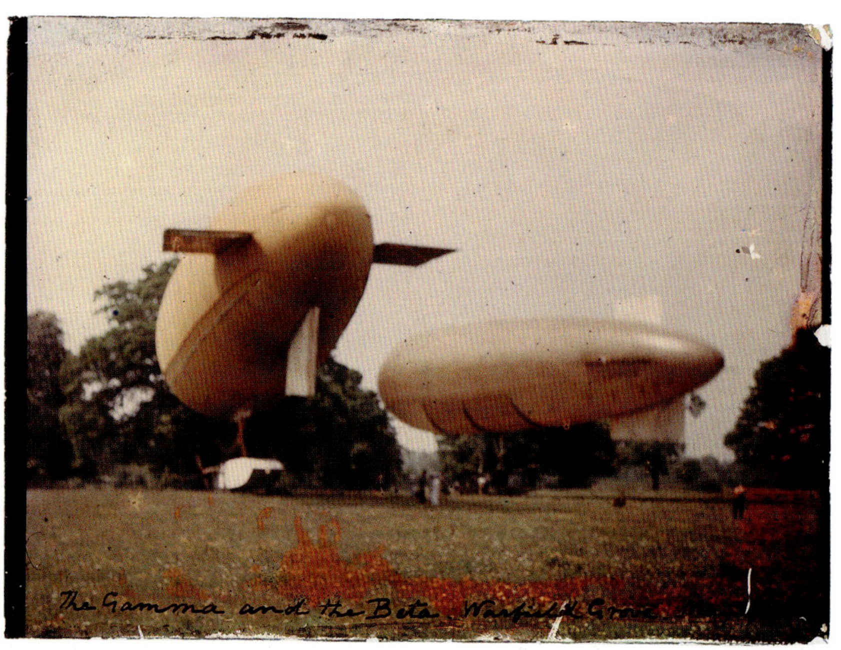

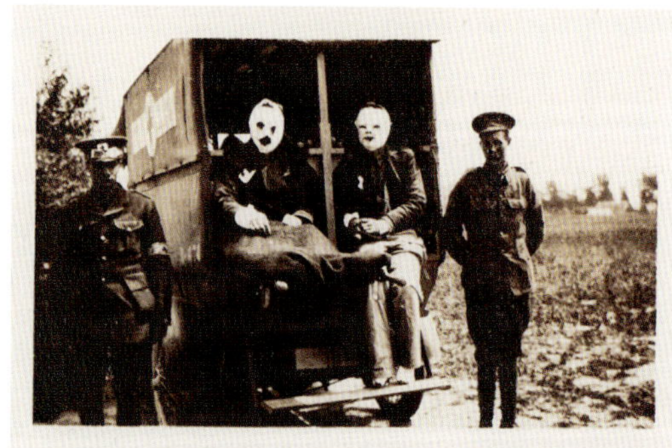

Last Years and Legacy

Miss Acland's winters in Madeira were brought to an end by the First World War. She visited for the last time in January 1915, the sinking of the *Lusitania*, while she was still on the island, making the decision not to return straightforward. The War was also the beginning of the end for her photography. Colour was an early casualty of the conflict, not only due to problems with the supply of materials, but also because photographers were put under moral pressure to restrict their spending to necessities, "among which assuredly colour photography, for example, does not come".[76] As hostilities dragged on Miss Acland was also faced with what seemed like insurmountable domestic difficulties: "I fear to run this house with less than three maids", she complained in May 1918.[77] With the prospect of photography becoming increasingly daunting as she approached the age of 70, in January 1919 she resolved to dispose of her equipment, "as it were preparing for my last journey".[78] The preparations were premature, as she saw out another dozen years of life, occasionally taking new photographs (cat. no. 119). She also devoted considerable time to consolidating her previous work, from 1923 to 1928 producing a series of photographic Christmas cards, in 1929 compiling two presentation albums of her finest portraits, and in 1930 completing a photographically illustrated volume of "Memories". The portrait albums contain 112 sepia carbon prints between them, each accompanied by handwritten reminiscences of the sitter; the memoirs thirteen platino-matt bromide prints. All are beautifully bound and presented, and works of art in their own right.

"Here end the day dreams of my beloved home & some of its visitors", Miss Acland wrote in the codicil to the portrait album she presented to the Bodleian Library, adding in a letter that "mine was a wonderful home & from force of circumstances there never could be another like it."[79] The words reflect portraiture's principal function for her: the commemoration of her home and the society that

Fig. 90. (ABOVE LEFT) *Army Airships Gamma and Beta*
William James Herschel, Autochrome, May 1913

Fig. 91. (ABOVE) *Roger de Halpert and Robin Acland, Invalided*
Photographer unknown, gelatine print, nr. Ypres, June 1915
Miss Acland's nephew William Henry Dyke ('Robin') Acland (1888–1970) matriculated at Christ Church in 1907, joining the Camera Club in the same year. In WWI he flew air reconnaissance missions in the Royal Flying Corps, until being shot down in flames with his 'photo man' Roger de Halpert (1885–1969).

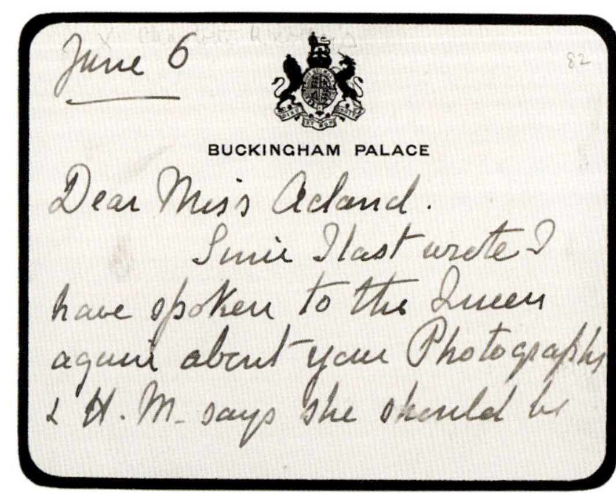
June 6

BUCKINGHAM PALACE

Dear Miss Acland.
Since I last wrote I have spoken to the Queen again about your Photographs & H. M. says she should be

Fig. 92. *Royal Command*
Miss Acland sent her photographs to friends in the highest places. This card from Charlotte Knollys (1844–1930), lady-in-waiting to Queen Alexandra, continued "very happy to see them if you could, at any time, send a small collection of them here". Miss Acland had known the Queen, who was also a photographer, from when they were both in Wildbad in 1869.

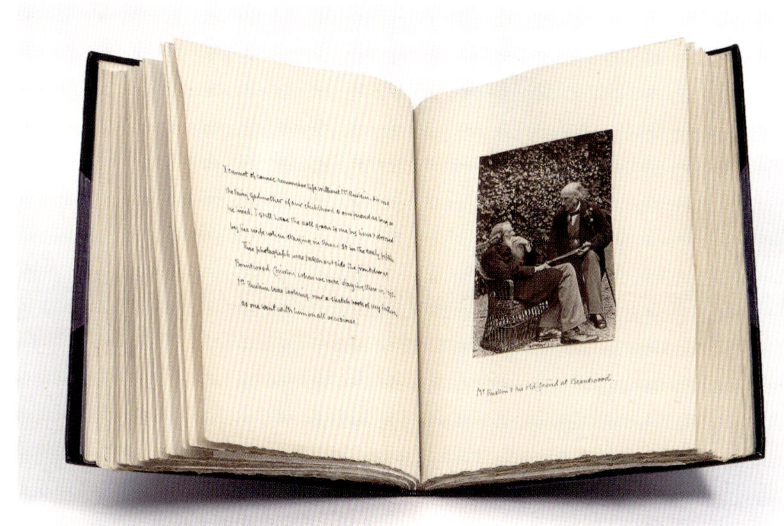

Fig. 93. *"Portraits by S.A. Acland"*
Miss Acland's beautiful presentation album of portraits, given to the Bodleian Library in 1930, is half-bound in gilt-lined morocco leather and fine blue fabric. A matching volume of her memoirs, illustrated with 'platino-matt' bromide prints, is now in the Devon Records Office.

congregated around it, by means of a personal, localized form of the 'hero worship' that defined the Victorian age. Her photography as a whole provided a form of creative expression compatible with her health, wealth and domestic circumstances; it allowed her to exercise skills of hand, eye and mind, and to obtain a wider degree of public recognition than possible as a woman in other spheres of life. Through the artistic aspects of her work she was able to honour one side of her father's legacy, with her contribution to its scientific advance another.

Miss Acland suffers the fate of other nineteenth-century women photographers in living in the shadow of Julia Margaret Cameron. However, her mature portraiture was guided by different aims and must be judged by different criteria. Her portraits occupy a transitional space between the extremes of Cameron and Victorian commercial portraiture on the one hand, and the new vision of Edwardian portraitists such as Lena Connell (1875–1949) and Clara Cooper (1877–1927) on the other. Her 750 monochrome photographs, 120 of which are reproduced in the catalogue that follows, provide an illuminating window on late-nineteenth-century photography, including the nature of its social organizations, the influence of the domestic ideal, and the role of women in shaping pictorial ideas. Her colour photographs, of which 100 examples from 350 surviving plates are included in the following pages, are one of the most important collections in the early history of the field. The significance of Miss Acland's colour photography with the Sanger Shepherd process is difficult to overstate. Her slides made her a household name among photographers, created an appetite for colour in the lecture-going public, and remained a point of reference for years to come. In the opinion of Roger Child Bayley (1869–1935), future champion of the Autochrome, her Gibraltar lecture was epoch-making, "marking as it did the definite assumption of three-colour work as a process for the travelling amateur".[80] Miss Acland's Sanger Shepherd slides are nothing less than the prototype of all subsequent attempts to photograph the world in colour, whether by her immediate successors, such as Sergei Mihailovich Prokudin-Gorskii (1863–1944) and the professionals employed by Albert Kahn (1860–1940) on his *Archives de la Planète*, or the myriad colour photographers who contribute to the global digital projects of today.

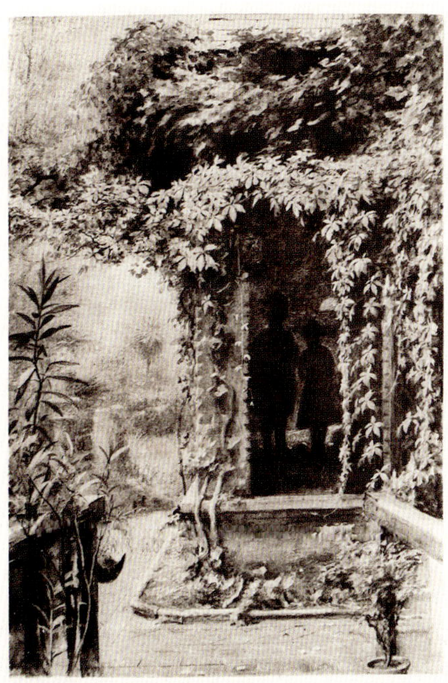

Fig. 94. *"It will rise again!"*
Collotype, after Alexander Macdonald, 1923
The fresco on the south wall of the library at Broad Street was painted by Acland and depicted Angie and Willie watching the sun set. In 1856, in one of the earliest references in his correspondence to photography, Acland had instructed his wife to get "E.C." to take them to be photographed in the same pose so he could paint them in oils. The collotype above, from a photograph of a watercolour of the fresco by Alexander Macdonald, was reproduced by Miss Acland as her 1923 Christmas card.

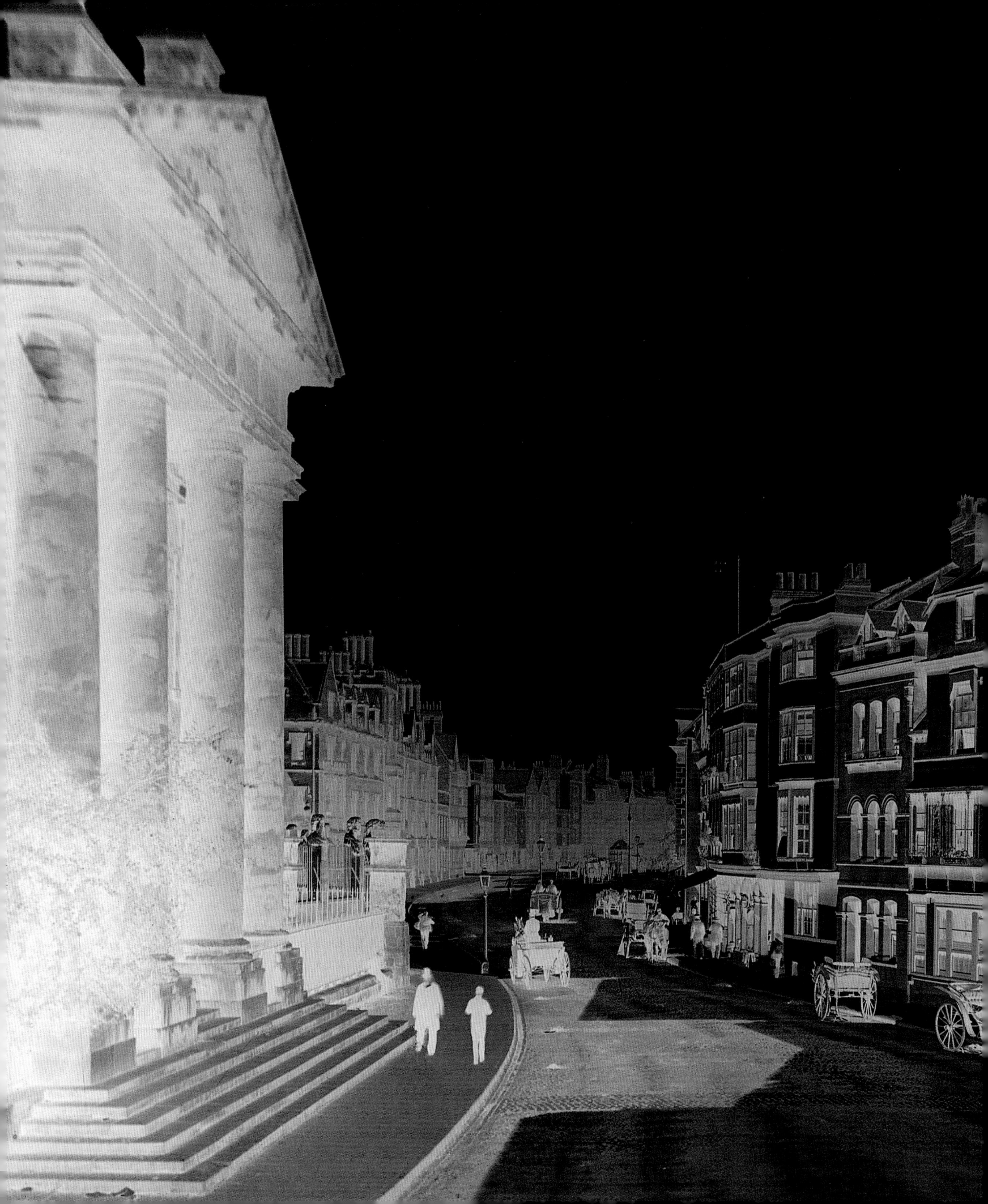

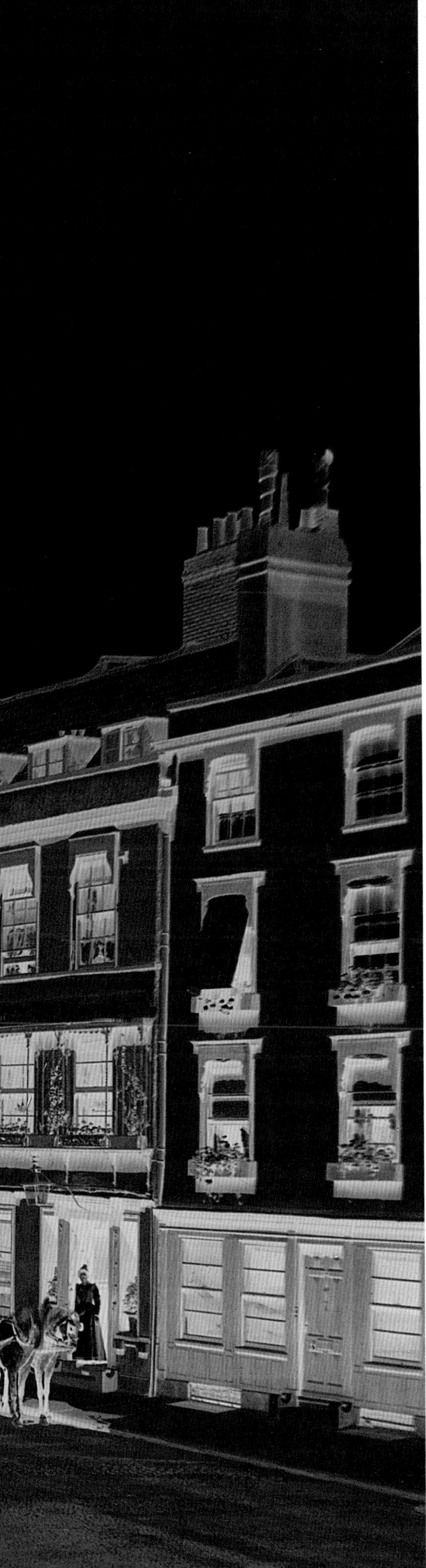

CATALOGUE NOS. 1–120

MONOCHROME PHOTOGRAPHS

In the catalogue that follows, titles of entries when enclosed within quotation marks are Miss Acland's own, as found in her albums or as exhibited; otherwise they are merely descriptive. References at the end of entries are to the passages in block quotes and double quotation marks in the text, and are listed strictly in order.

Miss Acland's photographs are reproduced as negatives, prints and lantern slides, and as digital positives created from her negatives. The negatives, prints and lantern slides are shown in their actual colours. When digital positives are used an appropriate contrast curve has been applied and a sepia tone added consistent with her surviving prints. Most of the illustrations have been sharpened, as necessary with half-tone reproductions. As this exaggerates dust, pinholes and scratches in the emulsion, they have also been 'spotted' to remove minor defects (as Miss Acland would have done), while ensuring that significant flaws, integral to the historic character of the plates, are retained.

Plate sizes and their metric equivalents are as follows: Lantern plate (3¼ × 3¼ inches; 83 × 83mm), Quarter-plate (4¼ × 3¼; 108 × 83), Half-plate (6½ × 4¾; 165 × 120), Whole-plate (8½ × 6½; 216 × 165). All are reproduced actual size unless a magnification factor is given in brackets.

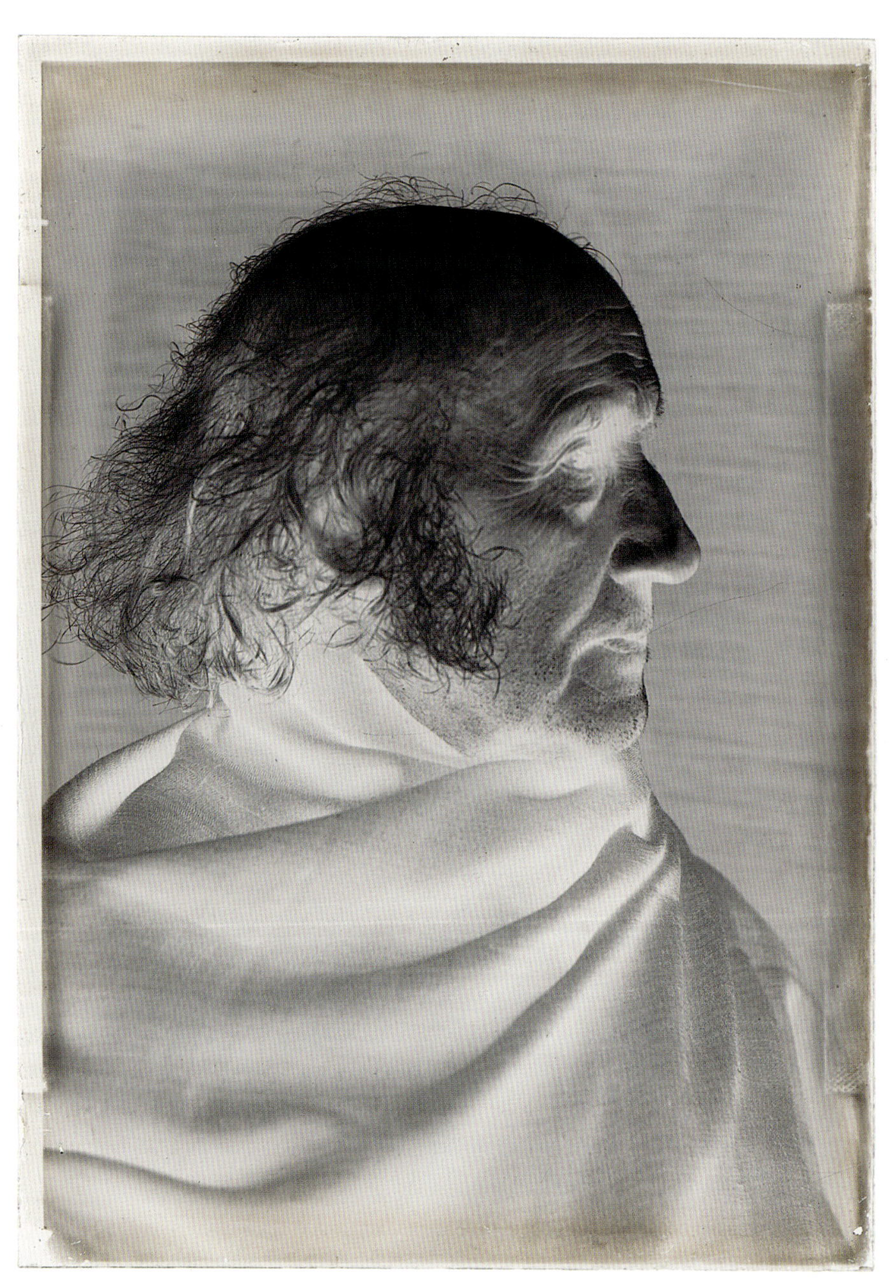

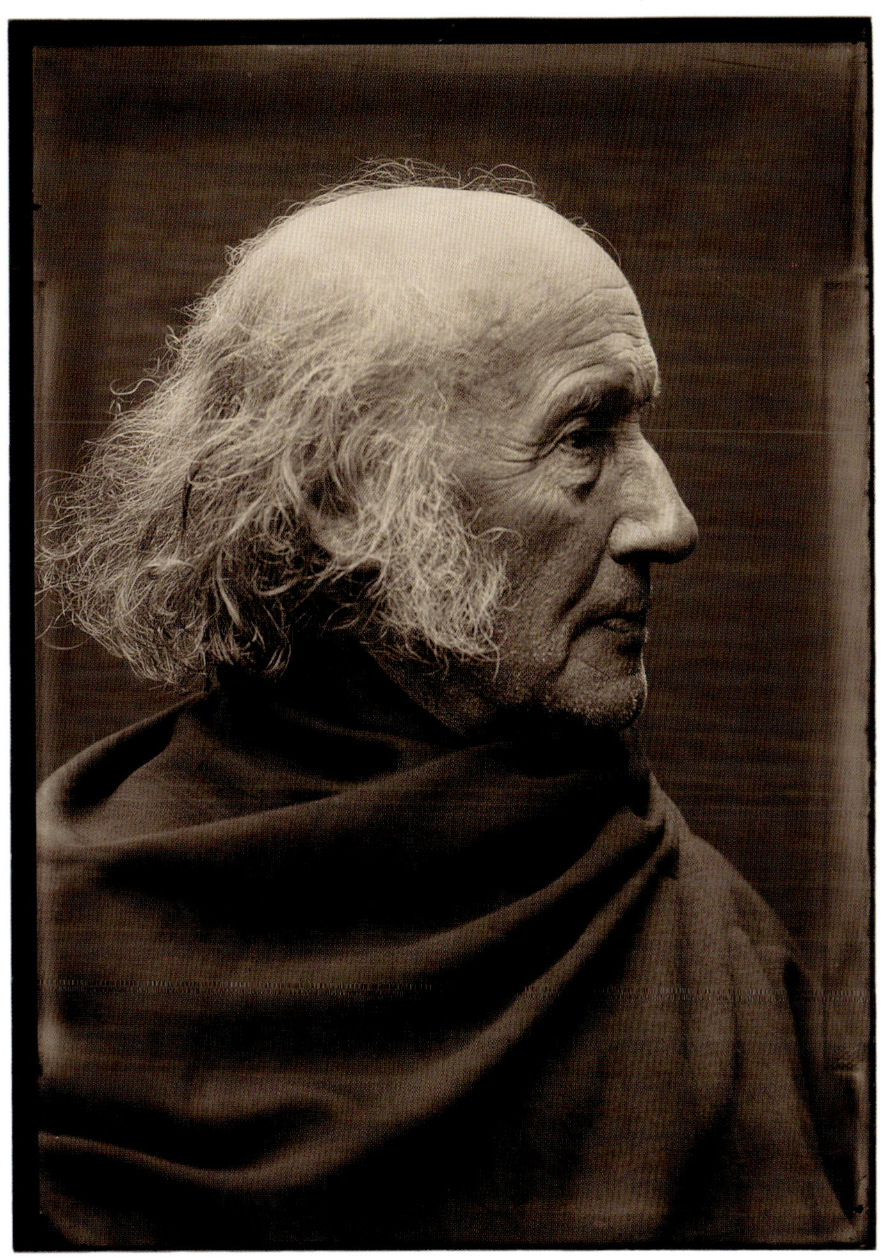

PREVIOUS OPENING & OPPOSITE

1 & 2. *"Sir Henry Acland, Bart., K.C.B."*

Henry Wentworth Acland (1815–1900)
Oxford, *circa* 6 June 1892

Half-plate negative
Bodleian Library, Minn negative 176/7

Albumen print from half-plate negative
Bodleian Library, MS. Photogr. c. 176, fol. 161

When Miss Acland exhibited the first of these portraits of her father (reproduced on the previous page with its negative) during her "Home Portraiture" lecture at the Oxford Camera Club in 1899, she described it as the "first portrait she ever took". This was not altogether true, as she had already taken a number of informal studies with her first camera, a Kodak No. 3. However, she appears to have regarded these small-format photographs as unworthy of ranking as portraits in the higher sense of the term.

Miss Acland's earliest formal portraits owe an obvious stylistic debt to Julia Margaret Cameron (1815–1879). Cameron exercised a dominant influence on nineteenth-century women photographers. Miss Acland felt the weight of her legacy more than most, having met the great woman at the age of 19. During her upbringing she was surrounded by Cameron's work, which could be found in abundance in Oxford. A copy of Cameron's iconic portrait of John Frederick William Herschel (1792–1871) hung in the drawing room of her Broad Street home (cat. no. 5), for example, and was clearly the model for these studies of her father. Both men are depicted in the guise of sage, enveloped in cloaks, their wild white air standing out against the dark background.

The lives of the Acland and Cameron families intersected on several occasions. Miss Acland's brother Herbert was at school at Charterhouse with one of Cameron's sons, Henry Herschel Hay Cameron (1852–1911), whom Mrs Acland admired in Tom Taylor's *Helping Hands* in the school theatricals in December 1869. After Charterhouse Henry Herschel went up to University College, Oxford, following in the footsteps of his brother Hardinge Hay Cameron (1846–1911) and Oxford's alpine photographer Willie Donkin. After going down (without a degree) he emigrated with his family to Ceylon to become a coffee planter. Herbert Acland followed a year later for the same purpose, moved in similar circles in Nuwara Eliya, and died on the island in 1877, two years before Mrs Cameron.

It was while visiting Oxford that Cameron spotted the Donkins' cook and invited her home to Dimbola Lodge on the Isle of Wight to be immortalized as Oenone and other women from mythology. Miss Acland's father had been photographed by Cameron in Freshwater in 1867, shortly before his wife's second cousin, Henry John Stedman ('Harry') Cotton (1845–1915), married Mary Ryan (1848–1914), her maid and favourite sitter. Miss Acland also had links to another of Cameron's favourite sitters, Elizabeth Louisa ('Topsy') Douglas, née Keown (1858–1951), employing her daughter Grace Helen Douglas (1885–1984) as a paid companion in 1911.

In his *Indian and Home Memories* Harry Cotton wrote that Acland and his wife were "both of them very kind to me, and their house in Broad Street was a home where I passed many pleasant hours with their children". His description of Acland mirrors the image Miss Acland attempted to present of her father: "Among all the Oxford dons of that day — and I do not forget Dean Liddell of Christ Church — Dr. Acland was, I think, the most striking and intellectual-looking."

"Miss Acland on Home Portraiture", *Proceedings of the Oxford Camera Club*, no. 1 (April 1899), pp. 3–5, p. 4; Henry Cotton, *Indian and Home Memories* (London & Leipzig, 1911), p. 21; Ibid.

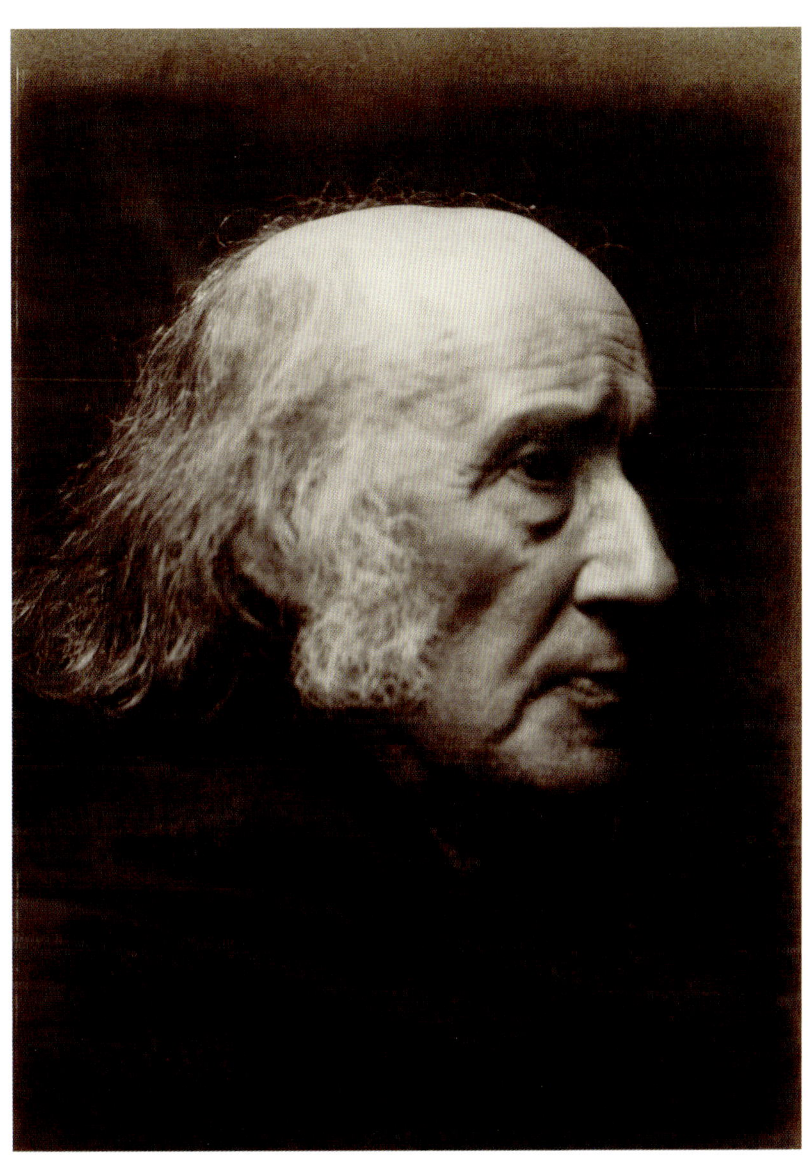

3. *"The Very Rev. Dean Liddell"*

Henry George Liddell (1811–1898)
Oxford, between 6 June and 30 July 1892
Albumen print from half-plate negative
Bodleian Library, MS. Photogr. c. 176, fol. 160

In her first album Miss Acland placed this study of Dean Liddell opposite the portrait of her father, catalogue no. 2, labelling the opening "Tutor and Pupil". In one of the presentation albums she compiled later in life she explained the allusion: "When Mr. Liddell, afterwards the Dean of Christ Church was made Tutor of his College, his first three pupils were John Ruskin, Charles Newton and Henry Acland." By the time she took this portrait Liddell had retired from the Christ Church Deanery, after thirty-six years as incumbent, and was living at Ascot Wood House, near Windsor.

On 30 July 1892, Liddell wrote to Miss Acland with his verdict on her efforts:

> My dear Angie
>
> Many thanks for the Photographs. They are very good as merciless representations of old people. I say this, without remorse, because I think your Father's is the most merciless. I have no doubt they portray us as we are. But I must confess I think we should be thankful for a little softening of the negatives. The same delineates all the lines & hollows in a somewhat exaggerated form, — at least I am inclined to think so.
>
> But all the same, it is well to see ourselves with all our defects, & I thank you. ...
>
> Ever yours most truly
>
> HG Liddell

By 1892 Liddell was already experienced in sitting for merciless women portraitists, Julia Margaret Cameron having taken his likeness in April 1865, in a portrait Miss Acland knew from her mother's photograph album. Miss Acland's portrait of Liddell is arguably more Cameronesque than Cameron's own, Liddell's brooding face emerging from the indistinctness of the dark background characteristic of her early studies.

"Mrs Cameron used to place her sitters inside a barn with large open doors", Miss Acland pointed out in her Home Portraiture lecture when discussing approaches to lighting. This portrait was also taken indoors, her strategy being to light Liddell's face strongly from one side only. Her mature portraiture has less extreme contrast, the depth of shadow moderated by a reflector, for which she favoured an ordinary white sheet or tablecloth. For outdoor work she recommended other household items. A piece of blue tarletan (muslin), for example, stretched over a hoop and suspended by a bamboo fishing rod, might serve as a good diffuser. The setting and the apparatus she chose for her portraiture underline the domestic nature of the undertaking.

Miss Acland described Liddell as "a very striking figure in Oxford in his day, rather feared, as his very reserved manner, due to shyness, made people think him to be haughty but he had the very kindest of hearts". When, on retiring, he visited to say goodbye, she asked him "what shall I do Mr. Dean when you have gone. I shall have no one left to scold Father"; to which he replied, "He is sure to give me plenty of opportunity by letter."

Although Liddell is now remembered principally as the father of the eponymous *Alice in Wonderland*, in his own day his name was synonymous with the *Greek–English Lexicon*, compiled in collaboration with Robert Scott (1811–1887). 'Liddell & Scott' was also the name of a tailors' shop in Newcastle, a salt print of which can be found in Acland's photograph album, where it was seen by Dodgson at a party at the Aclands in November 1857.

MS. Photogr. c. 176, fol. 159; MS. Don. d. 14, fol. 16v; MS. Acland d. 159, fols. 37–8; *British Journal of Photography*, vol. 46, no. 2027 (10 March 1899), p. 151; MS. Don. d. 14, fol. 17v; Ibid., fol. 16v.

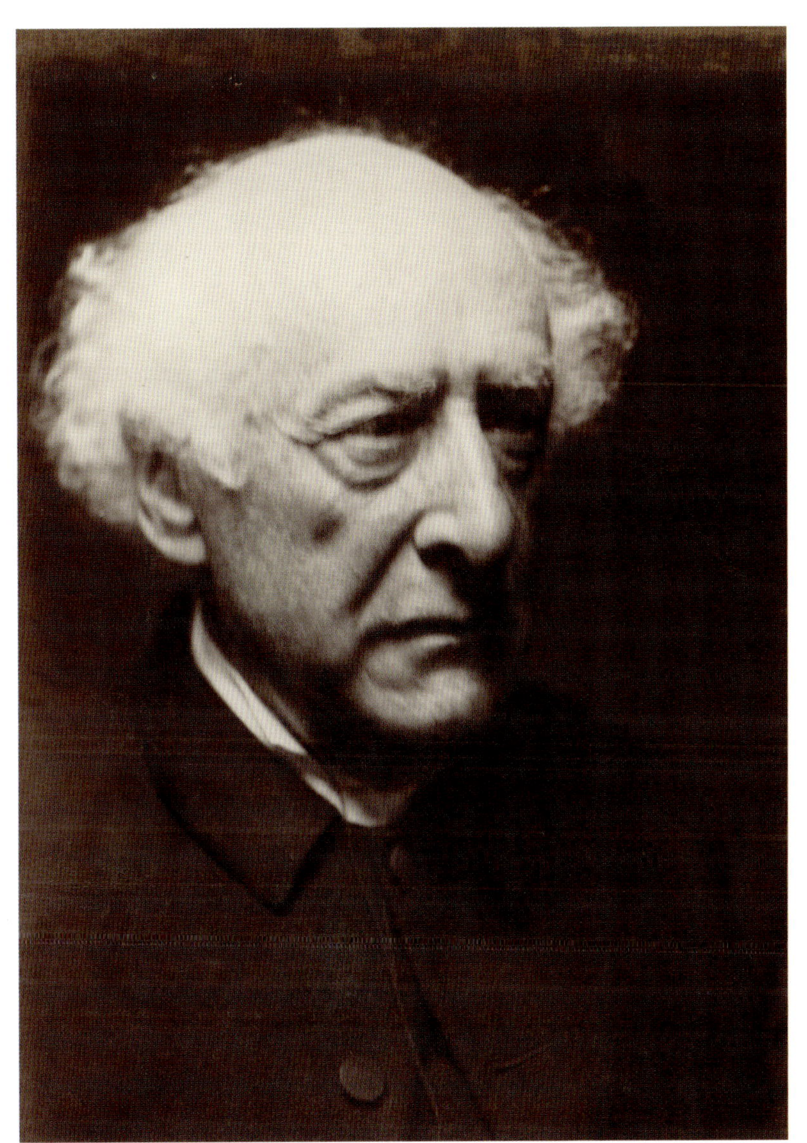

4. *"Broad St. from Prior's Windows"*

Broad Street from No. 32, looking due west
Oxford, 27 June 1892

Half-plate negative
Bodleian Library, Minn negative 184/1

Miss Acland was born and lived for the first fifty-two years of her life in her parental home on Broad Street, Oxford. The Acland house, No. 39–41, is the large building second from the right in this photograph. Standing in the doorway is a maid and in the street waits the Aclands' coachman, George Greening (1839–1927), with their Victoria carriage and two greys. The photograph gives a good indication of how centrally the house was located with regard to the principal institutions of the University: the Clarendon Building (the imposing portico on the left), former home of the University Press; the Sheldonian Theatre and original Ashmolean Museum (obscured behind the Clarendon's giant order); and the Bodleian Library, just out of sight to the south.

Acland and his new wife moved into Broad Street in autumn 1847, after he took over the medical practice of the previous occupant, John Wootten (1799–1847), physician to Tractarian Oxford. The frontage of the house was a composite of two timber frame properties dating from the early seventeenth century, the ground floor taken up by consulting and waiting rooms. The drawing room, from where Miss Acland took several notable photographs, was on the first floor, with the 'little drawing room' (cat. no. 111) at the west end. The top two storeys were sitting rooms and bedrooms, although Wootten previously had a laboratory in the attic. Acland made numerous alterations to the building after taking over the lease. According to William Tuckwell (1829–1919), "the graceful sunshade work outside Dr. Acland's windows found imitation in many another street" and was one of the key indicators "that Art was in the air" in Oxford in the 1850s.

Immediately to the west of the Acland house is No. 42, which Acland also owned. In 1867 this was rebuilt to a design by William Charles Clifford Bramwell (1817–1876), superintendent of works on the University Museum. Bramwell lived next door, at No. 43, the bay-fronted building, another of Acland's properties. Further down the street, in the distance, is the cabmen's shelter, with its pointed roof, that was erected with money raised by Miss Acland and opened by her in July 1885.

Miss Acland's Watson 'Acme' camera, with which she took this photograph, would usually have been used on a tripod. Focussing was carried out at full aperture on the ground glass screen at the back of the bellows by moving the lens board at the front with a rack and pinion (most of her lenses were fixed focus). In bright ambient light this was done under a black focussing cloth, which made for hot work in warm weather. After focussing the cap was replaced on the lens, the aperture stopped down (to f/22 for this scene), a dark slide inserted, the blind removed, and the negative exposed. She recorded the exposure for this plate as "Cap on & off", which highlights the fact that most of her photographs were taken without a shutter, even on bright, sunny days in the middle of summer. However, for exposure times of less than a second she had a Thornton-Pickard roller blind shutter, which fitted to the front of the lens and was released with a pneumatic ball.

Miss Acland availed herself of the opportunity to photograph Broad Street from this vantage point — the shop of the pharmaceutical chemist George Thomas Prior (1826/7–1904) — shortly before the building was knocked down to make way for an extension to the Indian Institute (later the Faculty of Modern History). She left Broad Street herself in May 1901 after the death of her father, moving to Park Town in north Oxford. As if to underline the intertwined nature of their lives, Ina Liddell then took over the house as Willie Acland's tenant, having married his rival in love William Baillie Skene (1838–1911) (see p. 122). Both women were spared the distress of seeing their old home demolished in 1937, along with the rest of the houses in the foreground of the photograph, to make way for Giles Gilbert Scott's new Bodleian building, now the Weston Library.

W. Tuckwell, *Reminiscences of Oxford* (London, 1900), p. 52; MS. Photogr. c. 176, fol. 152.

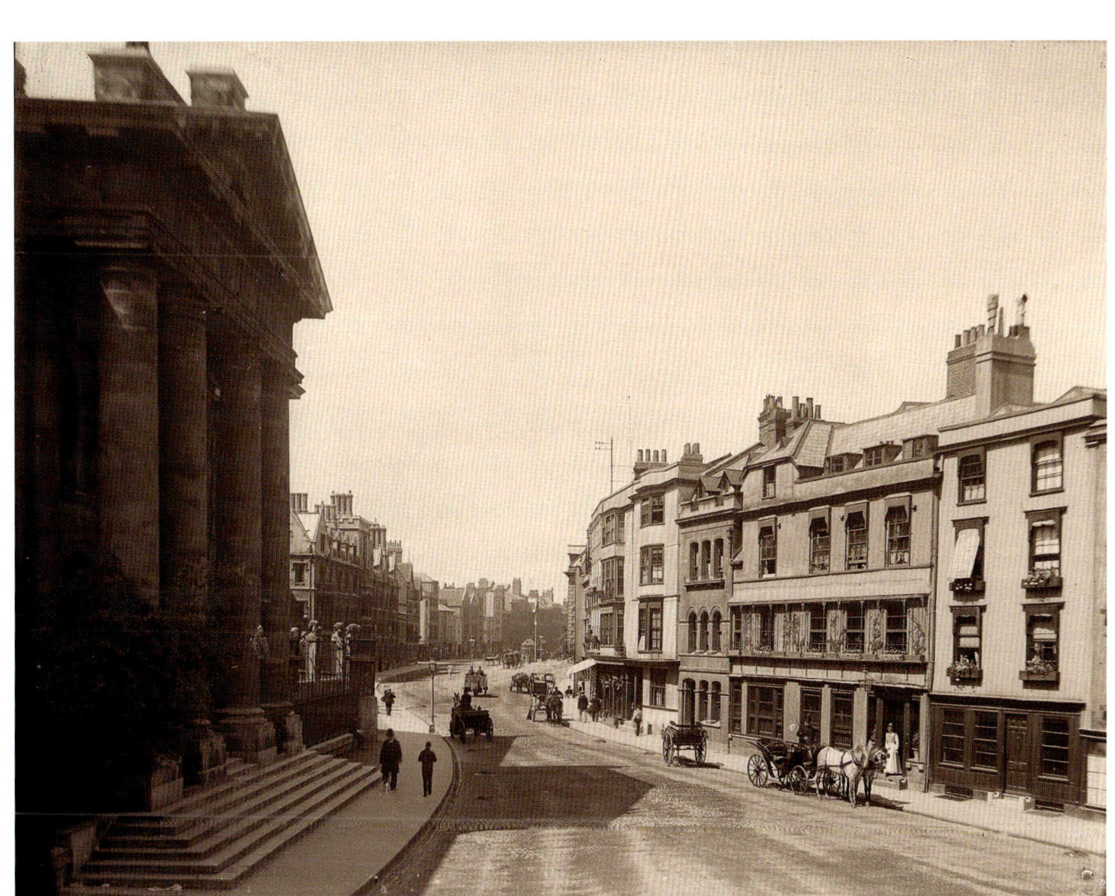

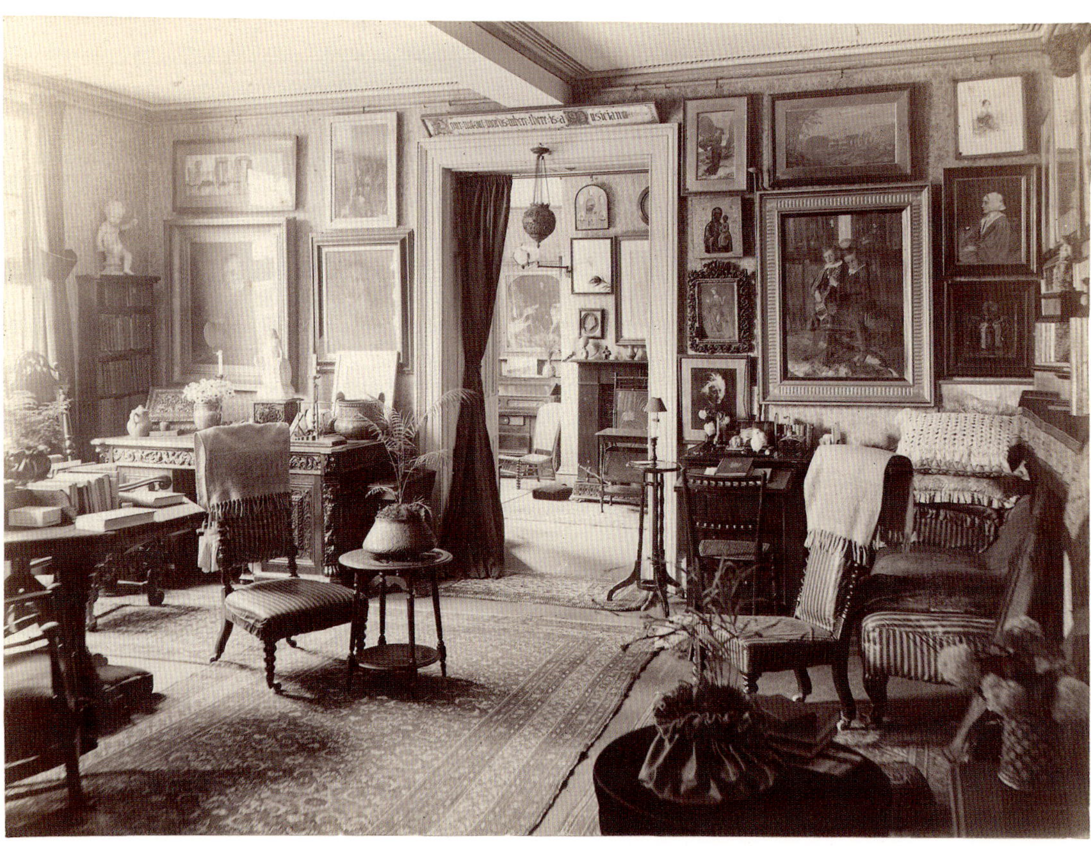

5 & 6. *"Drawing Room, Broad Street, Oxford"*

The drawing room, 39–41 Broad Street
Oxford, July 1892

Albumen prints from half-plate negatives
Bodleian Library, MS. Photogr. c. 176, fols. 135 & 132

The Acland drawing room was a *locus mirabilis* of Victorian Oxford: a place where men and women of different social rank and political persuasion from both sides of the divide between the University and the City could meet on easier terms than elsewhere or in an earlier age. The room was conceived by Acland, in advance of the Aesthetic Movement proper, as an artistic space, both in its furnishings and the (modern) artworks that hung on the walls. "Oxford owes its great museum to Sir Henry Acland," the author of an article in the magazine *Black & White* wrote in November 1896, "and his own abode is literally a private museum containing a wonderful collection of objects connected with antiquity, art and literature. Every inch of the wall space in the house, which has been his home for half a century, is covered with engravings, paintings and sculpture of the highest order."

Works of art visible in the west view of the room (above) include a self-portrait by George Richmond (under a drawing of Stonehenge by Acland); portraits by William Blake Richmond of Professor Donkin and of Frank and Alfred Acland (cat. nos. 98 & 99); J. F. W. Herschel by Julia Margaret Cameron; and, partly obscured by the crochet-covered cushion on the far right, a watercolour by Ruskin referred to by Acland as "Coast of Dorset (Geological)", but now in the Yale Centre for British Art as "Rocky Bank of a River". In the distance, in the little drawing room, is John Everett Millais's celebrated portrait of Ruskin at Glenfinlas (see cat. no. 111).

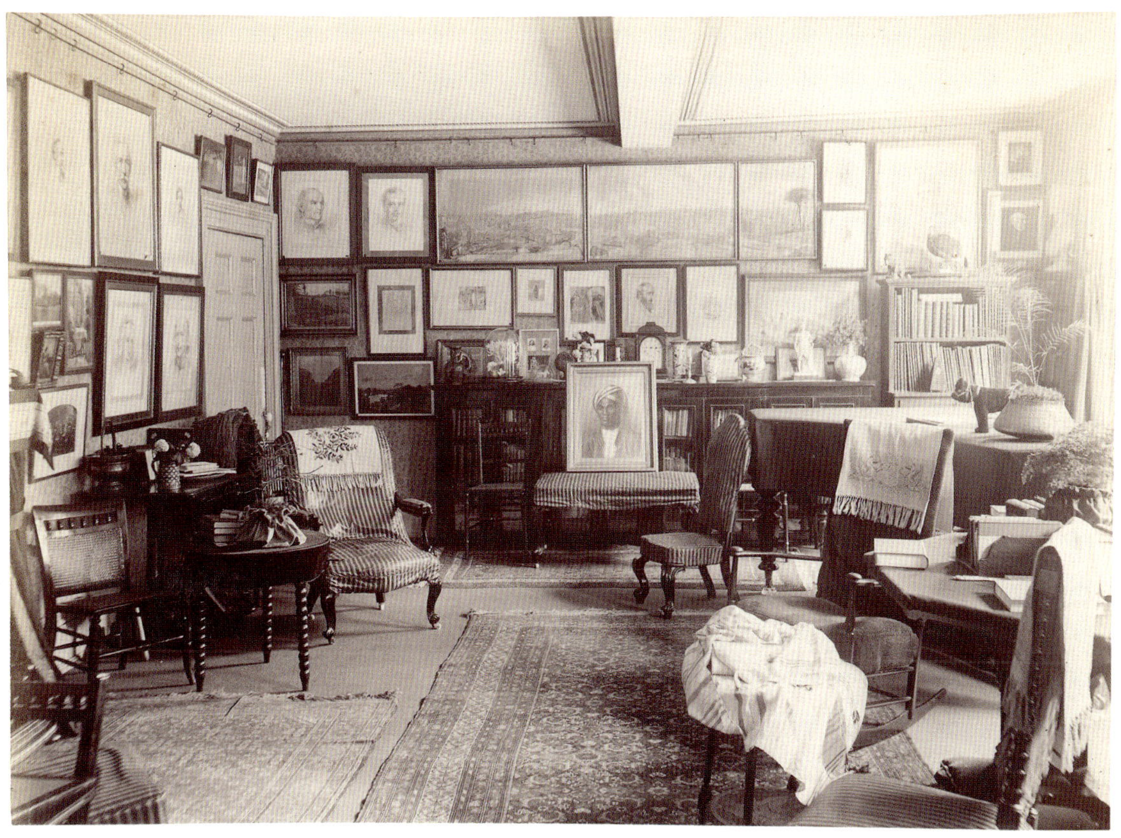

The east end of the Acland drawing room (above) was dominated by a 10-foot panorama of Rome, drawn by Acland in 1838. In the row of pictures below, from left to right, are works by the giants of nineteenth-century British art: a portrait of Mary Gladstone (1847–1927) by Burne-Jones; a drawing by Rossetti, *Gathering the Bitter Herbs* (cat. no. 95); a watercolour by Ruskin of one of the towers at Lucerne; Rossetti's *Eating the Passover*; a crayon drawing by George Richmond of Lord Salisbury; and *The Gate of Theseus, Athens*, a watercolour by J. M. W. Turner. Elsewhere are portraits of family and friends (including Gladstone and Prince Leopold) commissioned by Acland from William Edwards Miller. Framed on the chair is Miss Acland's portrait of 'Acland Sahera of Zanzibar' (see cat. no. 111). One of the photographs above the door, not easily made out, is a portrait of Benjamin Woodward by Dodgson.

Prior to taking these photographs Miss Acland painted an almost identical view of the west end of the room in watercolour. In 1887 she considered sending this to the Royal Academy, but after taking Richmond's advice decided to wait until 1892 before exhibiting it at the Oxford Art Society. Thirty-two years later, in 1924, she reproduced the painting in collotype for her Christmas card, as *A Room in the Old Home*.

Black & White, vol. 12, no. 302 (14 November 1896), p. 627; MS. Acland d. 100, fols. 199–200 ([H. W. Acland], "Among wayside gleanings for a quiet home" (Oxford, 1886?)).

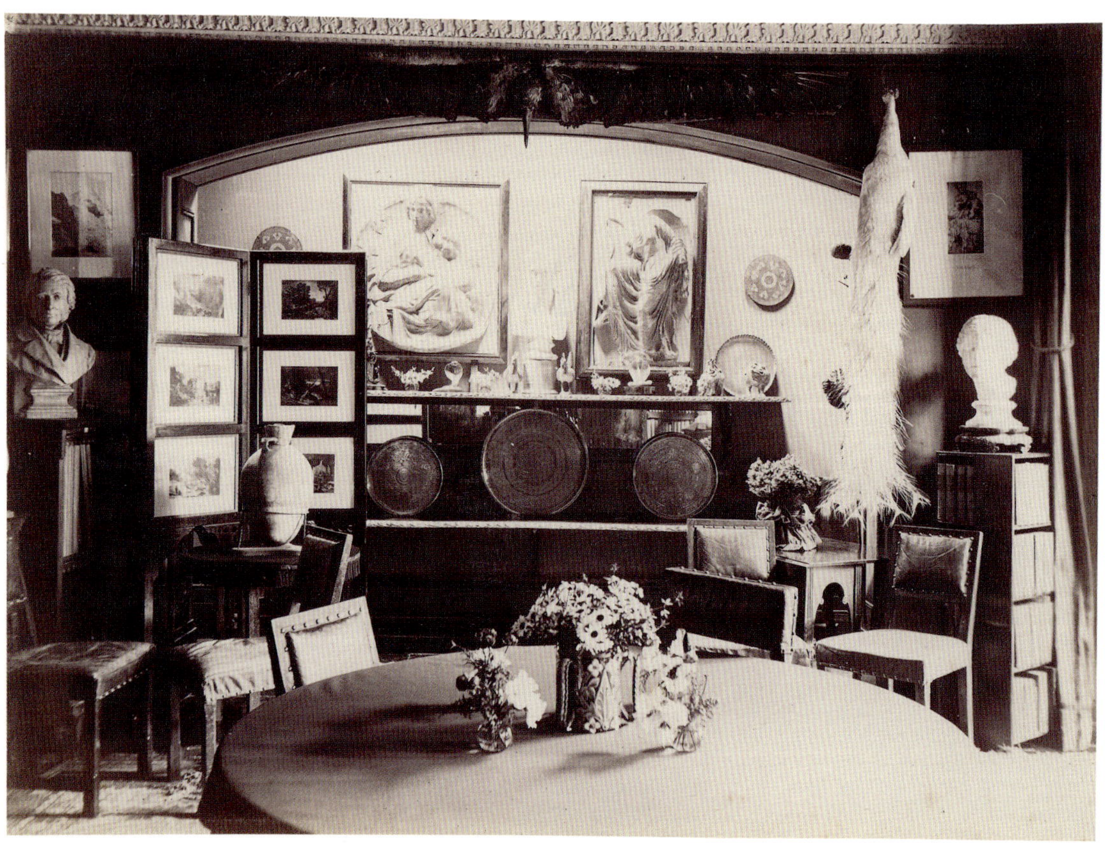

7 & 8. *"Dining Room, Broad Street, Oxford"*

The dining room, 39–41 Broad Street
Oxford, July 1892

Albumen prints from half-plate negatives
Bodleian Library, MS. Photogr. c. 176, fols. 136 & 133

Like the drawing room, the Aclands' dining room was a treasure trove of art and artefacts, placed on display for their many breakfast, luncheon and dinner guests. Visible in the west end of the room (above) are prints from Turner's *Liber Studiorum* and several casts: the Kaufmann head of the Aphrodite of Knidos; a terracotta bust of Ruskin by Joseph Edgar Boehm (1834–1890); the Nike Apteros ('Wingless Victory') from the Acropolis; and Michelangelo's Pitti Tondo (the last two given to Acland by Charles Newton when Keeper of Greek and Roman Antiquities at the British Museum). Hanging from the picture rail above the arch, which hid a skylight, are an albino peacock and ibis. These probably owed their place in the room to their anthropological significance, rather than as objects of natural history, and joined numerous other ethnological artefacts in the house collected by Acland and his sons. Among similar items presented by the family to the Pitt Rivers Museum are mummies from Peru and canoes from the South Sea Islands, sent home by Willie during his voyages around the world in the service of the Royal Navy.

On the east wall of the room (opposite) are four casts of sculpture by the Pre-Raphaelite sculptor Alexander Munro: alto-relievos of the *Four Seasons* (above the door); a high relief medallion of Agnes Gladstone (1842–1931); the only cast of a high relief of Agnes and her brother Herbert John Gladstone (1854–1930); and a high relief of Pauline Geneviève de Perusse des Cars, Duchess of Vallombrosa (1836–1886). On the

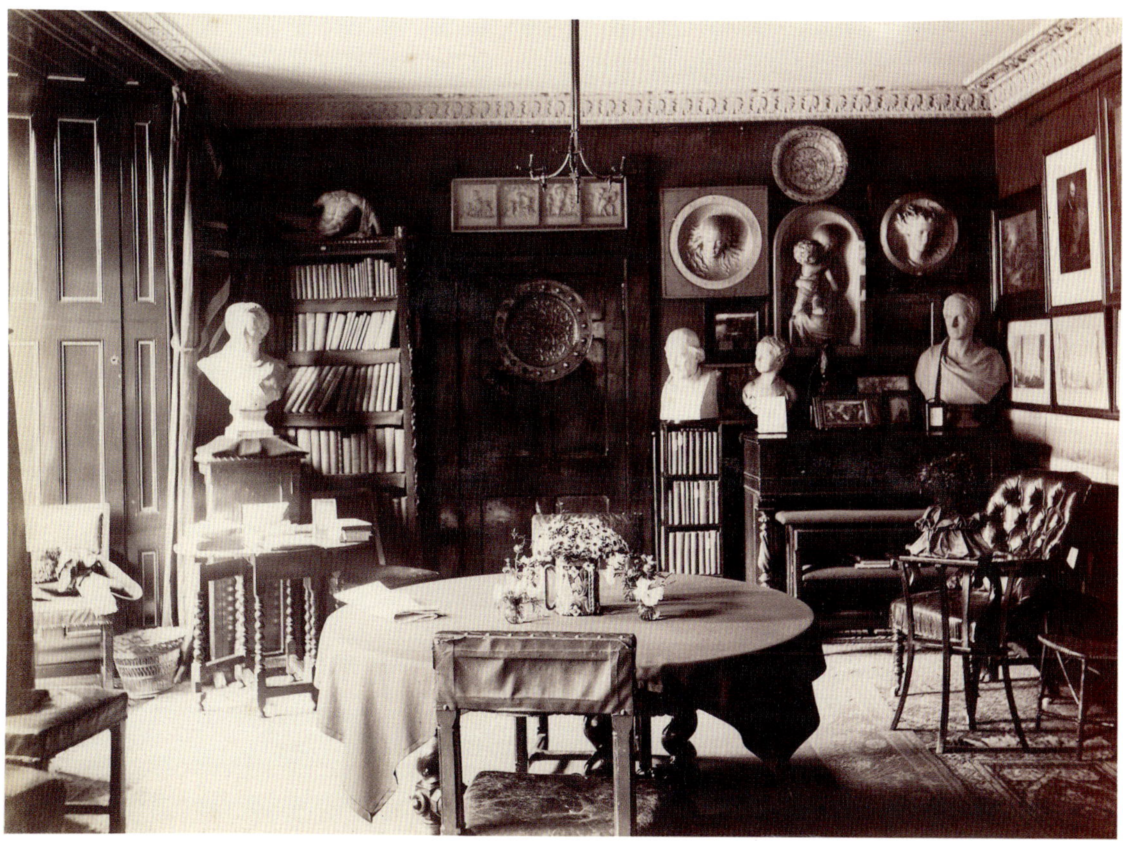

small revolving bookcase is a terracotta from George Richmond's posthumous bust of Edward Bouverie Pusey (1800–1882). Next to Pusey, on a harmonium given to Acland by Otto Goldschmidt (1829–1907), husband of the 'Swedish Nightingale' Jenny Lind (1820–1887), who sometimes stayed in Broad Street, stands a bust of Prince Leopold, and behind it a watercolour sketch, *We Are Seven*, the gift of Elizabeth Siddal in 1855 (see cat. no. 198). Also on the harmonium is a copy of a photograph of Benjamin Woodward sometimes attributed to Dodgson, but actually taken by Hills & Saunders (on the same occasion as a portrait of Acland now in his photograph album). Slightly above and to the right of the large bust (sitter unknown) is a pen and wash drawing of a woodland landscape by Thomas Gainsborough (1727–1788) given to Acland by a patient in lieu of payment. In the middle of the same wall are watercolours by Acland of the *Seven Churches of the Book of Revelation*, made in 1838, and under them a 7-foot engraving from his drawing *The Plains of Troy*. Also said to be in the room, but not easily identifiable, was an 'oil sketch' of Alice Liddell, artist unknown. The brass plate hanging on the door was bought in Italy by another of Acland's patients, Edward, Prince of Wales.

In the original negative a reflection of Miss Acland can be seen in the mirror under the shelf in the west end of the room, as can the tripod of the camera with which she was taking the photograph, in what was approximately a 15-minute exposure.

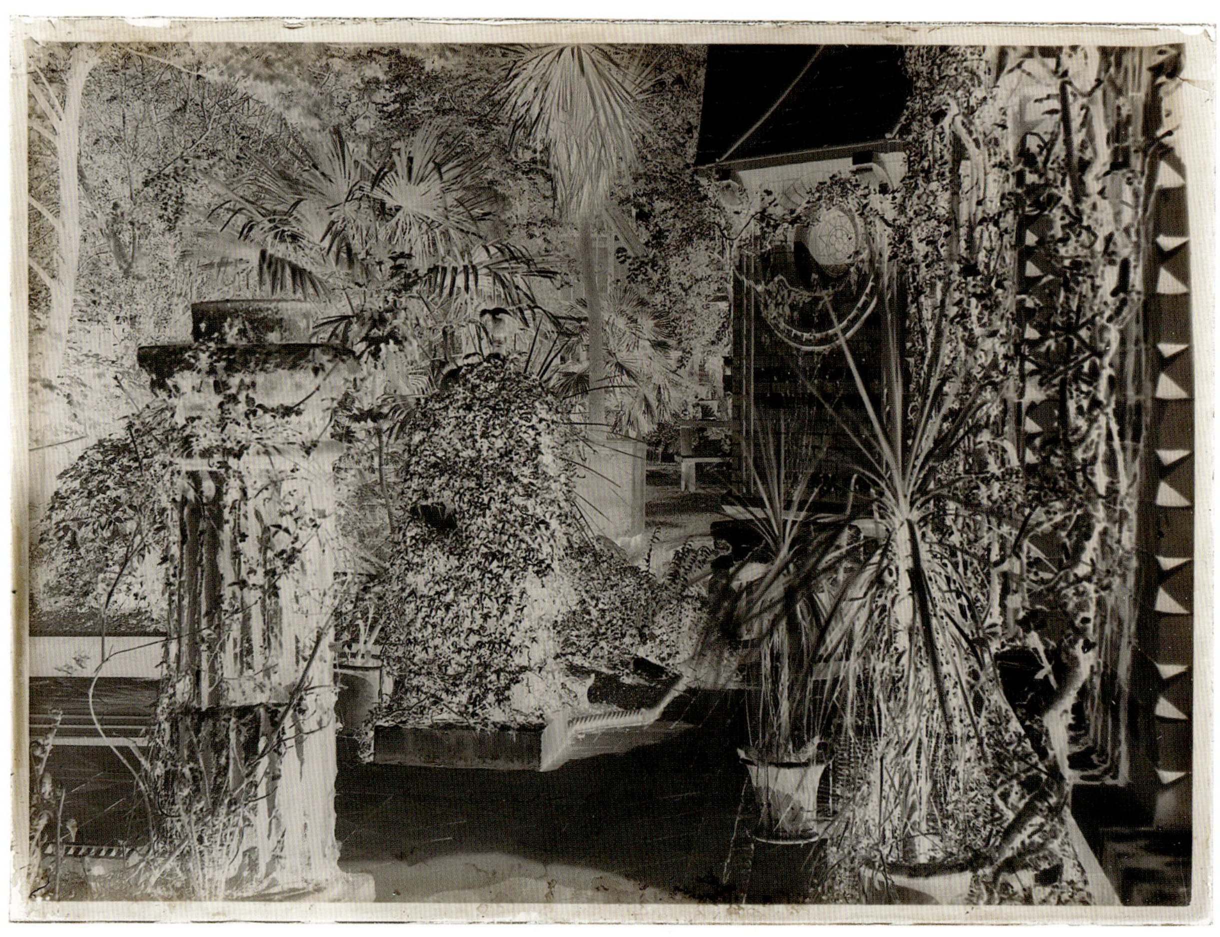

9. *"Our Garden"*

The garden, 39–41 Broad Street, looking north
Oxford, June or July ?, 1892

Half-plate negative
Bodleian Library, Minn negative 177/5

The garden of the Acland house, in which Miss Acland took several of her early portraits, was an oasis in the middle of Oxford, extending 150 feet to the wall of Trinity College. Halfway down on the left was a greenhouse, the eaves of which can just be seen in the centre of the frame. On the right-hand side a passage led past the Aclands' stables and coach house to Park Street (Parks Road), opposite Wadham College. On the corner of the passage Acland had an observatory, complete with 6-inch Dollond refractor and revolving roof, built on to the side of the cottage where Frances Wootten (1809–1876), John's widow, lived before moving to Birmingham to take up the post of matron in Newman's Oratory Schools.

During the summer the Aclands' garden functioned as an extension of the drawing room. A large tarpaulin was suspended over the courtyard between the east and west wings of the house, under which coffee, claret-cup and 'lemon aid' was served to guests at afternoon teas and garden parties. In May 1865 one of the guests was "Dr. Livingstone the African traveller", who sat under the awning for an hour in the afternoon in conversation with Acland. "He looks such a strong man, and as if

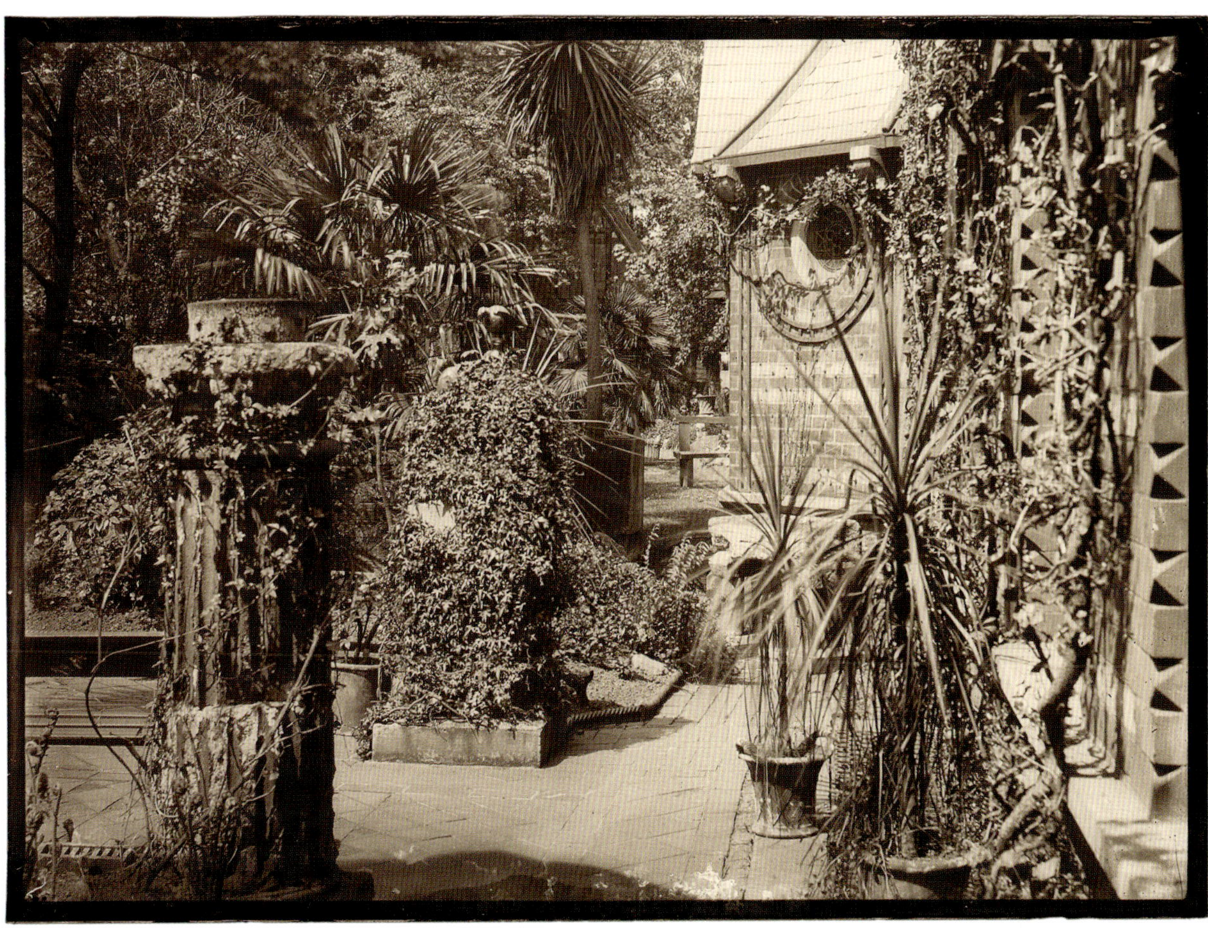

all his travels and labours had done him no harm", Mrs Acland told Willie. In 1869 Longfellow and his entourage visited, Mrs Acland writing that he was "a very pleasant unassuming, un-lion-like man & Papa & he enjoyed each other immensely".

Visible on the right-hand side of the photograph are the dog-tooth mouldings of the windows of Acland's library. The octagonal room with the circular window was a later addition, built between 1867 and 1873 by Bramwell and referred to as the North Library or 'Maalstofa' (after the Icelandic for 'meeting hall'). The eroded column is from the Tower of the Five Orders in the Old Schools Quadrangle, now the Bodleian Library, removed during the restoration of 1881–82. Further down the garden, visible in the distance through the back of a bench, is one of the old emperors' heads from outside the Sheldonian Theatre or Ashmolean on Broad Street, which were replaced in 1868 and 1875 respectively. This went with Miss Acland to Park Town, as did the columns and a pinnacle from the Bodleian seen in one of her colour photographs (cat. no. 161).

MS. Acland d. 42, fols. 156–64; Ibid.; Ibid., fols. 227–30.

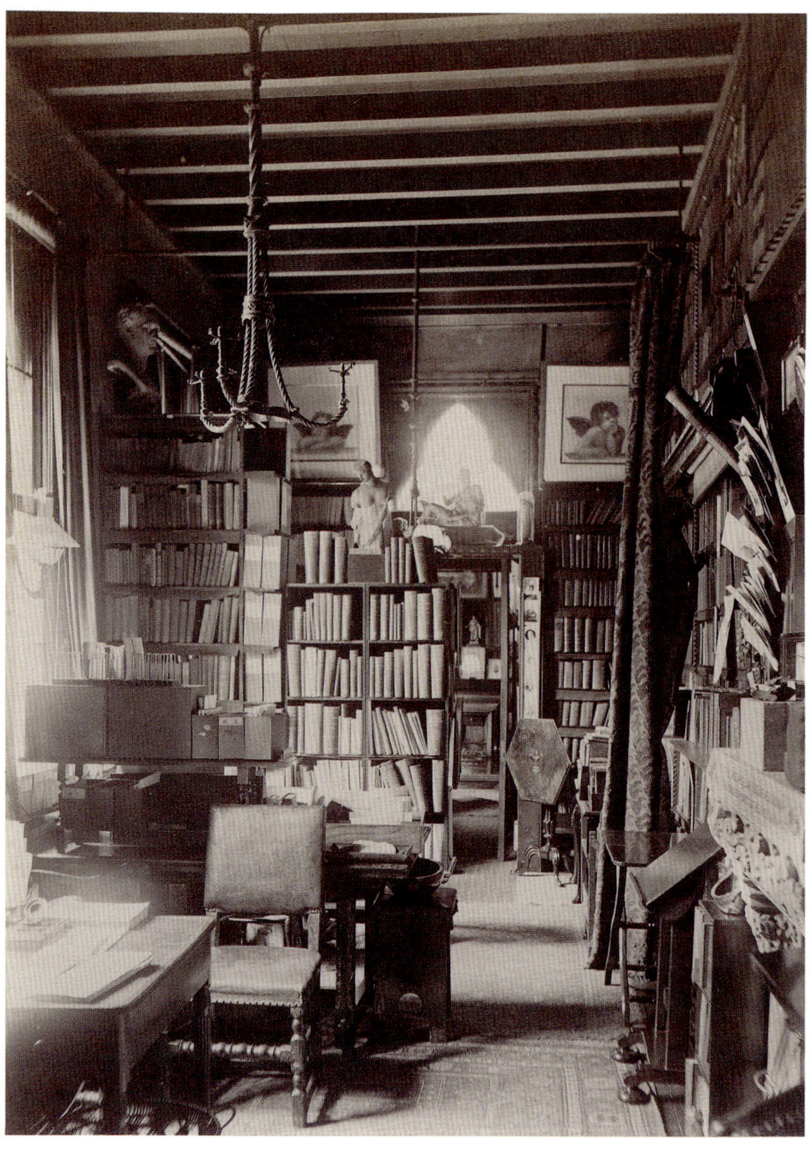

10. *Acland's Library*

The library, 39–41 Broad Street, looking north
Oxford, July 1892

Albumen print from half-plate negative
Bodleian Library, MS. Photogr. c. 176, fol. 137

In December 1857 the library at Broad Street was cited in the *Saturday Review* by the poet and critic Coventry Patmore (1823–1896):

> Mr. Woodward and his pre-Raphaelite friends are clearly of opinion that the use of colour in architecture may and ought to be revived to an extent at present almost undreamt of by most persons; and certainly, in the beautiful and original Gothic room which Mr. Woodward has just completed in the house of Dr. Acland at Oxford, the extremely bold chromatic decoration is entirely successful.

Patmore would also have approved of the inscription over the fireplace: 'Type of the wise, who soar, but never roam, True to the kindred points of Heaven and Home.'

Saturday Review, vol. 4, no. 113 (26 December 1857), pp. 583–4.

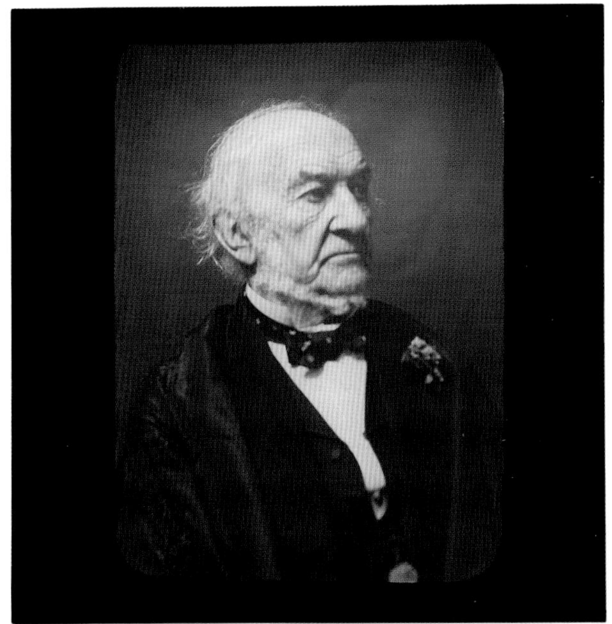

ABOVE RIGHT & OVERLEAF LEFT

11. *"The Right Honble. W. E. Gladstone"*

William Ewart Gladstone (1809–1898)
Oxford, 25 October 1892

Lantern slide
Museum of the History of Science, Inventory no. 26541

Half-plate negative
Bodleian Library, Minn negative 200/1

Gladstone's portrait was Miss Acland's first success as a photographer. James Paget, her physician, wrote that it was "certainly the best likeness of him that I have ever seen", while Liddell called it "very striking — very". The Prime Minister, who was no stranger to being photographed, sat a few months after she acquired a half-plate camera. "Had I at the time photographed for three years, I should have been afraid to attempt it", she remarked. Luckily, Gladstone was an "absolutely perfect and obedient sitter, saying, 'It is yours to command, I will obey.'"

Uniform softness of focus, which Gladstone's portrait displays in abundance, became fashionable with photographers (and notorious in wider circles) through Julia Margaret Cameron. As with Cameron, whether Miss Acland's use of the technique was entirely by choice may be questioned. In the slide she has corrected another fault of the plate, moving Gladstone towards the centre.

MS. Acland d. 162, fols. 41–2; MS. Acland d. 159, fols. 39–40; MS. Don. d. 14, fol. 4v; *Proceedings of the Oxford Camera Club*, no. 1 (April 1899), p. 5.

OVERLEAF RIGHT

12. *"Mrs W. E. Gladstone"*

Catherine Gladstone, née Glynne (1812–1900)
Oxford, 25 October 1892

Half-plate negative
Bodleian Library, Minn negative 200/11

Miss Acland's portraits of the Gladstones were made over a 40-minute period, from 12.20 to 1 p.m. She took six, limited by the number of dark slides she owned. Mrs Gladstone sat first, her head study taking 11 seconds at f/11 with a Rapid Rectilinear lens, on a 'Paget 5×' plate.

The Gladstones were often in Broad Street as the Grand Old Man was a political and religious confrère of Miss Acland's uncle, Thomas Dyke Acland (1809–1898). In 1890 Mrs Gladstone stayed to keep tabs on her husband, who, as Miss Acland explained,

> caused quite a flutter in Oxford by going into residence at All Souls. Mrs. Gladstone telegraphed to me to say that she was coming to stay with us. Happily we were able to take her & her maid in. Mr. Gladstone was constantly in & out in Broad St. though I cannot help feeling that he would have preferred to have made his visit to All Souls unaccompanied.

These portraits were reproduced in an account of the visit, C. R. L. Fletcher's *Mr. Gladstone at Oxford, 1890* (London, 1908), although they date from two years later.

Devon Records Office, 1148M/7/1, p. 111.

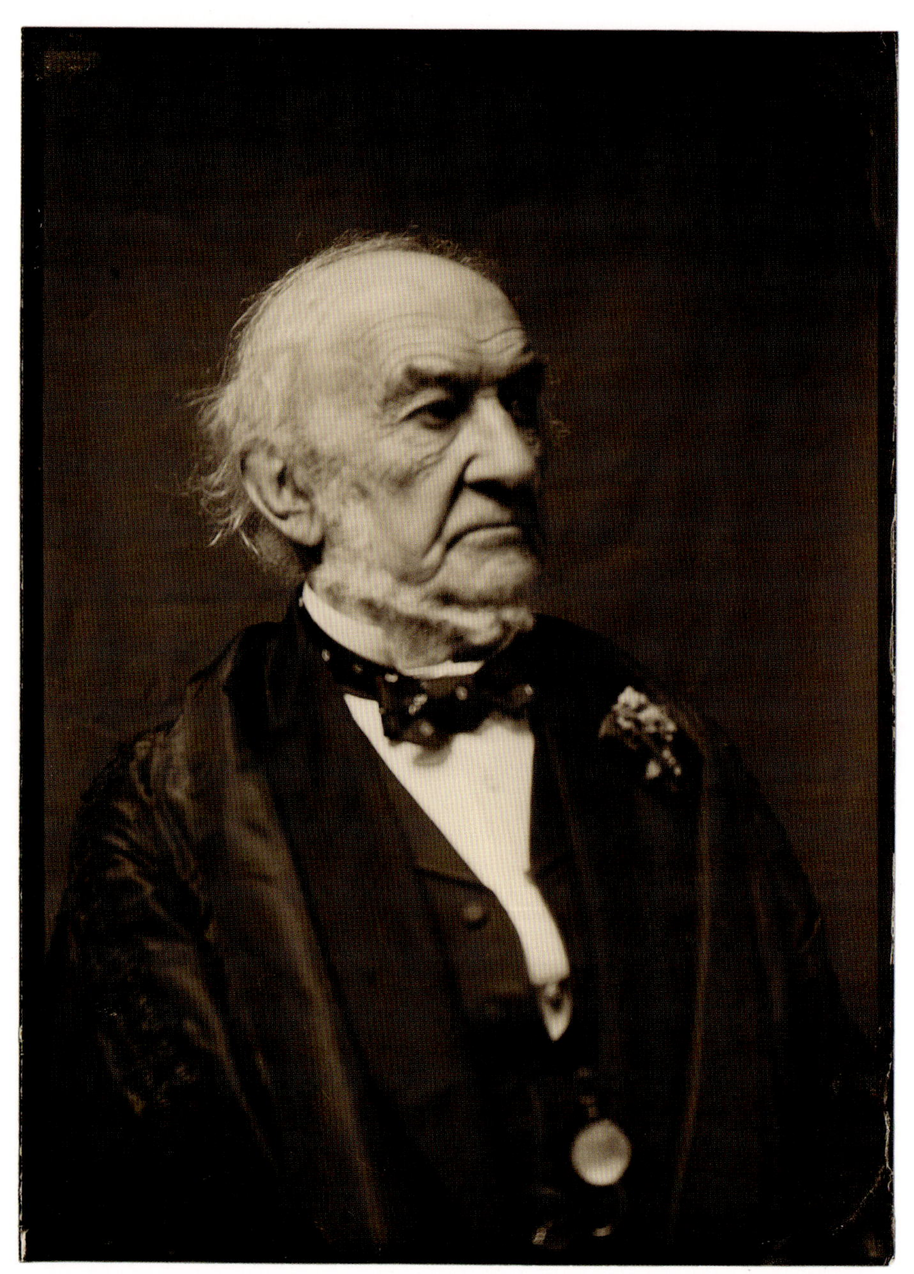

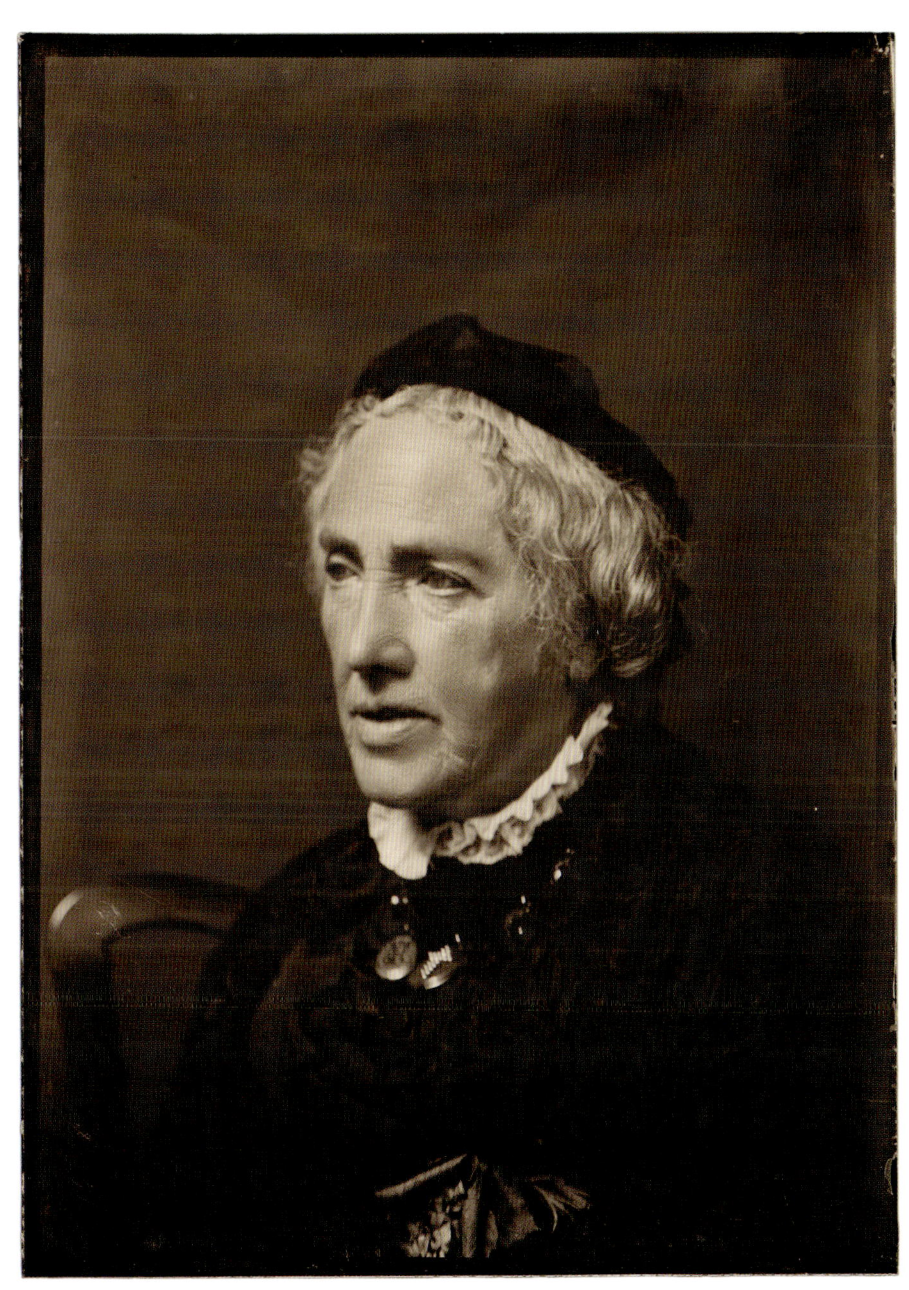

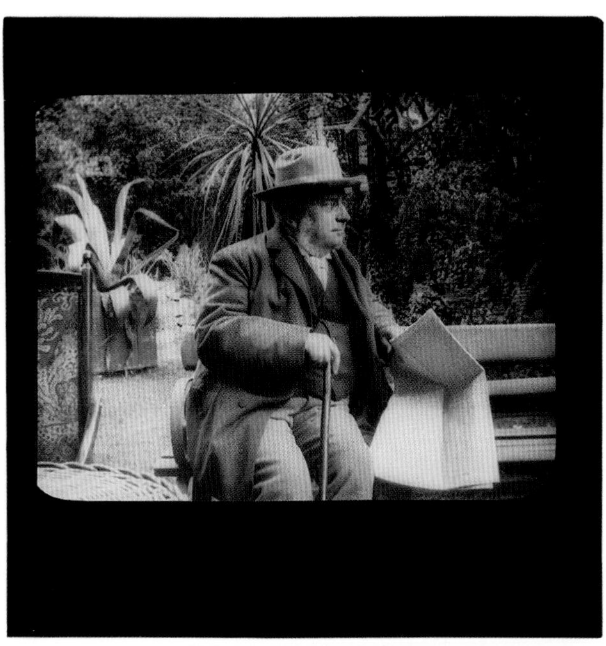

13. *"Isambard Brunel, Esq."*

Isambard Brunel (1837–1902), with a copy of *The Times*
Oxford, 1892 ?
Lantern slide
Museum of the History of Science, Inventory no. 20319

Miss Acland's portrait of Isambard Brunel, showing him as a kindly and unassuming man, a little portly perhaps, makes a stark and fascinating contrast with one of the most iconic photographs of the nineteenth century: the study by Robert Howlett (1831–1858) of his father, engineer Isambard Kingdom Brunel (1806–1859), standing in front of the launching chains of the *Great Eastern*.

Brunel *fils* trained as a barrister before becoming Chancellor of the Diocese of Ely. An "excellent man of business", he was relied upon by Miss Acland and her father for financial and legal advice. Like Miss Acland he was "somewhat crippled", apparently due to "congenital trouble in his knees", and could therefore empathize with her suffering.

When she later came to give her Home Portraiture lecture, Miss Acland was keen to stress that, the benefits of a large-format camera aside, good work could be done "even with the cheap — might she call them — toys". She exhibited this portrait of Brunel as proof, explaining that it was taken with "a pocket Kodak". Although she already owned a Kodak No. 3, in 1896 Miss Acland seems to have splashed out on a newer model: on 15 April her father wrote to her about a Russian whom he wanted to invite to a garden party, commenting that he had inspired her "to an Easter Kodak". Nahum Ellan Luboshey (1869–1925) was Eastman's representative and had spoken at the Oxford Camera Club two days earlier on "Platino-Bromide papers & Portraiture", showing fine examples of his own work.

One of the points Miss Acland stressed in her lecture was the need to adapt lighting to sitter, "in order to minimise defects that were hardly noticeable in life, with its varied expression". In the case of Brunel attention needed to be drawn away from his double chin "which in life in the interest and charm of the man and his character was rarely noticed".

MS. Eng. misc. d. 214, fols. 84–5; Ibid.; *Proceedings of the Oxford Camera Club*, no. 1 (October 1899), p. 4; Ibid.; MS. Acland d. 134, fols. 92–3; MS. Top. Oxon. e. 624, fol. 59r; *Proceedings of the Oxford Camera Club*, no. 1 (October 1899), p. 4; Ibid.

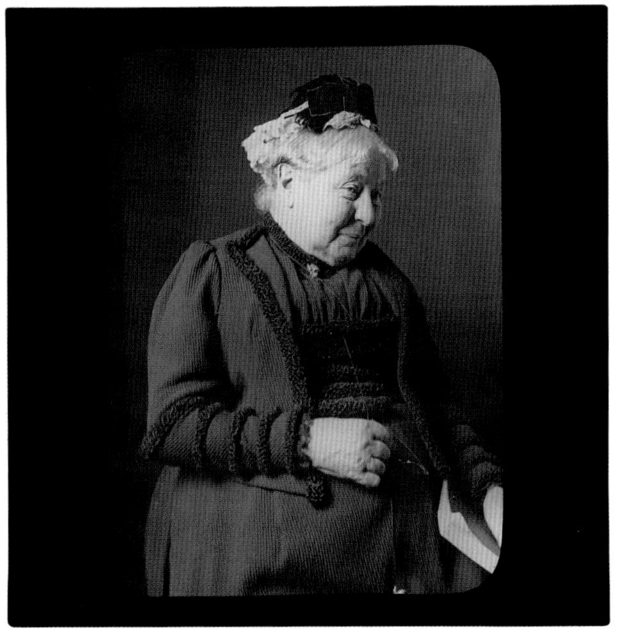

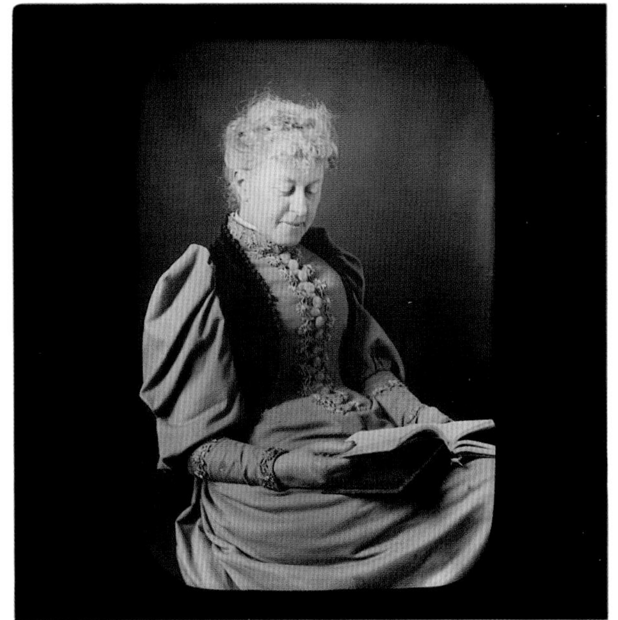

14. *"Mrs Peard"*

Frances Cooke Peard, née Ellicombe (1805–1895)
Torquay, 16 March 1893

Lantern slide
Museum of the History of Science, Inventory no. 69045

Miss Acland took this portrait of Mrs Peard relatively early in her photographic career, whilst overwintering in Torquay with her companion Eleanor Dorothea Edwards (1848–1903). "I have done three or four rather good portraits whilst she [Miss Edwards] has been here. A most successful one of Mrs Peard aged 88. Miss Peard is quite delighted with it", she wrote on 17 March.

Mrs Peard was the widow (of thirty-six years) of George Peard (1793–1857), Royal Navy commander and elder son of Shuldham Peard (1761–1832), Rear Admiral of the White. Her father, Hugh Myddleton Ellicombe (1777–1857), had been a respected solicitor in Exeter. Hawthornden, the house where the sitting took place, belonged to George Marsden Waterhouse (1824–1906), Premier of South Australia and of New Zealand.

This lantern slide is a duplicate of the one Miss Acland used in her Home Portraiture lecture and finds her experimenting with a warmer tone than she eventually settled upon, as seen by comparison with the following.

MS. Acland d. 107, fols. 201–2.

15. *"Miss F. M. Peard"*

Frances Mary Peard (1835–1923)
Torquay, 20 March 1893

Lantern slide
Museum of the History of Science, Inventory no. 29922

Frances Mary Peard was photographed by Miss Acland four days after her mother. The sitting took place in an "upstairs bedroom" and was accomplished with the aid of "brown paper to stop out the light from the lower panes, and a white blanket as a reflector".

Miss Peard was a novelist and is presumably seen reading one of her own works. As a young woman she had been a member of Charlotte Yonge's Gosling Society, which aimed to promote essay writing among girls educated at home. Her thirty-one works in the British Library catalogue include *The Rose Garden* (London, 1872), *The Secret of the Organ Loft* (n.p., [1891]) and particularly relevant to Miss Acland, *One Year; or, A Story of Three Homes* (London, 1869). Despite having fifteen novels published in the Tauchnitz edition, her biographer still had cause to complain that "had her lot been cast in a larger sphere no doubt her talents and personality would have made her name better known, and she would have had greater opportunities of developing them."

Proceedings of the Oxford Camera Club, no. 1 (October 1899), p. 4; Mary J. Y. Harris, *Memoirs of Frances Mary Peard* (Torquay, 1930), p. 73.

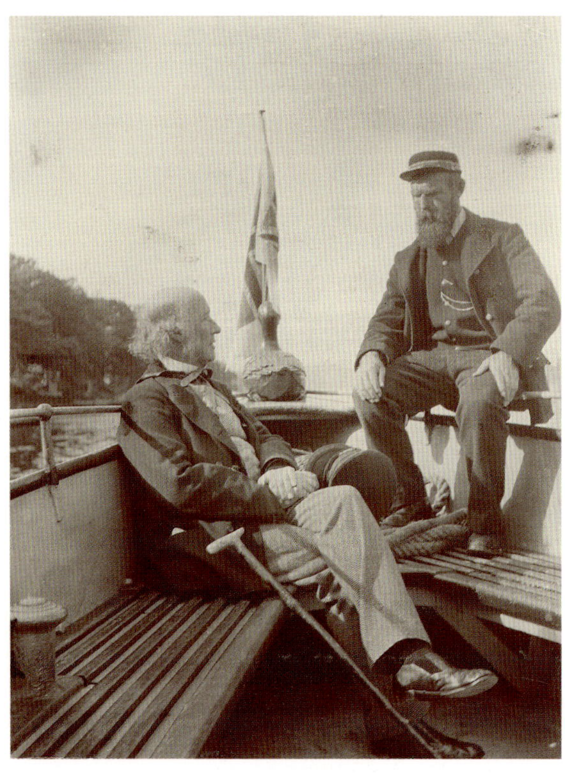

16. *"Father & the Captain of the Teale, Windermere"*

Henry Wentworth Acland (1815–1900) and an unidentified man, sitting in the bow of the *Teal*
Windermere, Cumbria, August 1893

Albumen print from quarter-plate negative
Bodleian Library, MS. Photogr. c. 177, fol. 60

In August 1893 Miss Acland and her father travelled to the Lake District in order to see their old friend John Ruskin. Setting out for Cumbria on Friday 29 July 1893, they stayed at the Low Wood Hotel on Windermere after the 9½ hour journey from Oxford before going over to Brantwood, Ruskin's home since 1871. The visit followed an invitation from Ruskin's cousin Joan Severn. Joan was the wife of Arthur Severn (1842–1931), whose father, Joseph Severn (1793–1879), artist and friend of Keats, Acland had known in Rome in the 1830s.

Miss Acland took both her Watson half-plate camera and Kodak No. 3 to the Lakes. With their small size and tendency to fade, the albumen prints from the Kodak are easily overlooked. This portrait, however, like many of her small-format photographs, is a fine piece of work, its charm heightened by the informality of the sitters. It was taken on the steam yacht *Teal*, which was built in 1879 to provide services on Windermere connecting with the Furness Railway. The *Teal* was scrapped in 1929, but a namesake, launched in 1936, still sails today.

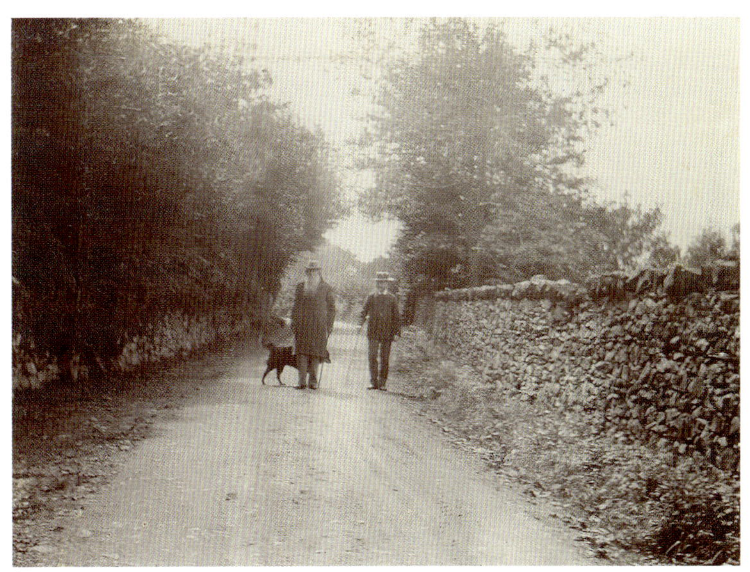

17. *"Mr. Ruskin, Bramble & Baxter"*

John Ruskin (1819–1900), Peter Baxter (1846/7–1918) and Ruskin's dog Bramble
Brantwood, Coniston, 1 August 1893

Albumen print from quarter-plate negative
Bodleian Library, MS. Photogr. c. 177, fol. 57

Taken on the third day of her holiday in the Lake District, this photograph records Miss Acland's first glimpse of Ruskin since he left Oxford in the midst of controversy nine years earlier. She also recorded the moment in words:

> Mr Ruskin was out when we arrived walking with his man Baxter & with an old Collie dog Bramble. So we went to meet him & as soon as he saw us he stretched out both hands & hastened his very slow step to welcome us. He is altered & has a very long & beautiful flowing beard — is very quiet & unemotional — speaks only in a whisper & does not often originate subjects but he seems & looks very well & is very happy. He was delighted to see us.

Ruskin grew his beard in 1881 during his second bout of "brain fever", as Mrs Acland described his illness to Angie; he previously sported impressive side whiskers.

MS. Acland d. 107, fols. 253–7; MS. Acland d. 142, fol. 141.

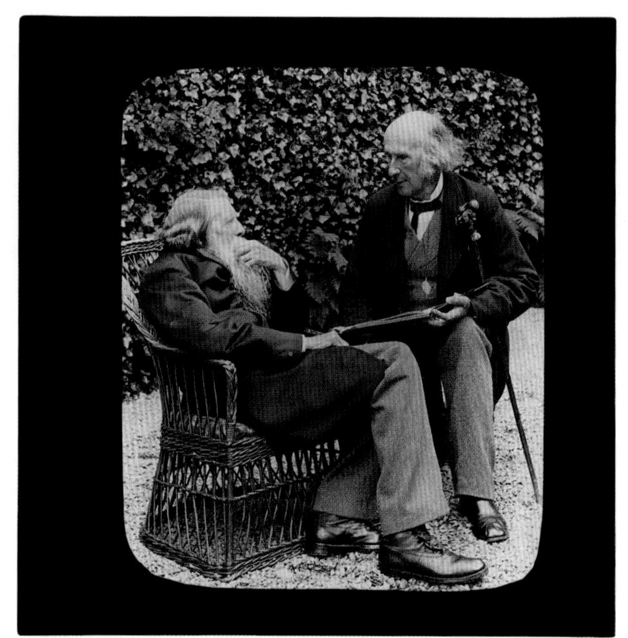

18. *"Mr. Ruskin & his Old Friend at Brantwood"*

John Ruskin (1819–1900) and Henry Wentworth Acland
Brantwood, Coniston, 1 August 1893

Lantern slide
Museum of the History of Science, Inventory no. 17293

Half-plate negative
Bodleian Library, Minn negative 169/11

Miss Acland's study of her father and his 'Old Friend' is her best-known photograph. The portrait was taken in the courtyard outside Ruskin's front door at Brantwood, where "the lighting was good, but ivy made nearly as bad a back-ground as could be".

"I cannot of course remember life without Mr. Ruskin", Miss Acland wrote when describing the portrait in her presentation albums. She had known the great man since childhood through his friendship with her father, who had taken him under his wing when they were both undergraduates at Christ Church. Ruskin, soon to become the most celebrated critic of the age, subsequently acted as Acland's guide in artistic matters, Acland exercising his powers of patronage to secure Ruskin's appointment as the first Slade Professor of Fine Arts at Oxford in 1869. During the period of fifteen years over which Ruskin occupied the chair he encouraged and instructed Miss Acland in art.

At the suggestion of George Allen, Ruskin's publisher, this portrait was included in photogravure in the 1893 edition of Acland and Ruskin's jointly authored work, *The Oxford Museum* (actually published on 17 January 1894, in two sizes, crown octavo and crown quarto). The plate was prepared by the Swan Electric Engraving Company, who did an excellent job, the *Studio* describing it as "exquisitely reproduced". According to *Amateur Photographer* the portrait became a familiar sight in London shop windows. Acland is showing Ruskin his sketch book, which accompanied him everywhere he went, according to his master's teachings.

Miss Acland took the portrait on a celluloid negative, preferring to carry film rather than plates whilst touring. The negative has since been destroyed, but not before two copies were made on glass. Miss Acland printed the lantern slide in 1898 in advance of her Home Portraiture lecture. In 1900 she sent a bromide enlargement to the Royal Photographic Society exhibition to mark Ruskin's death earlier in the year. During the exhibition her father also passed away.

Proceedings of the Oxford Camera Club, no. 1 (October 1899), p. 4; Presentation album, private collection, n.p.; "New Publications", *Studio*, vol. 2, no. 12 (15 March 1894), p. 222.

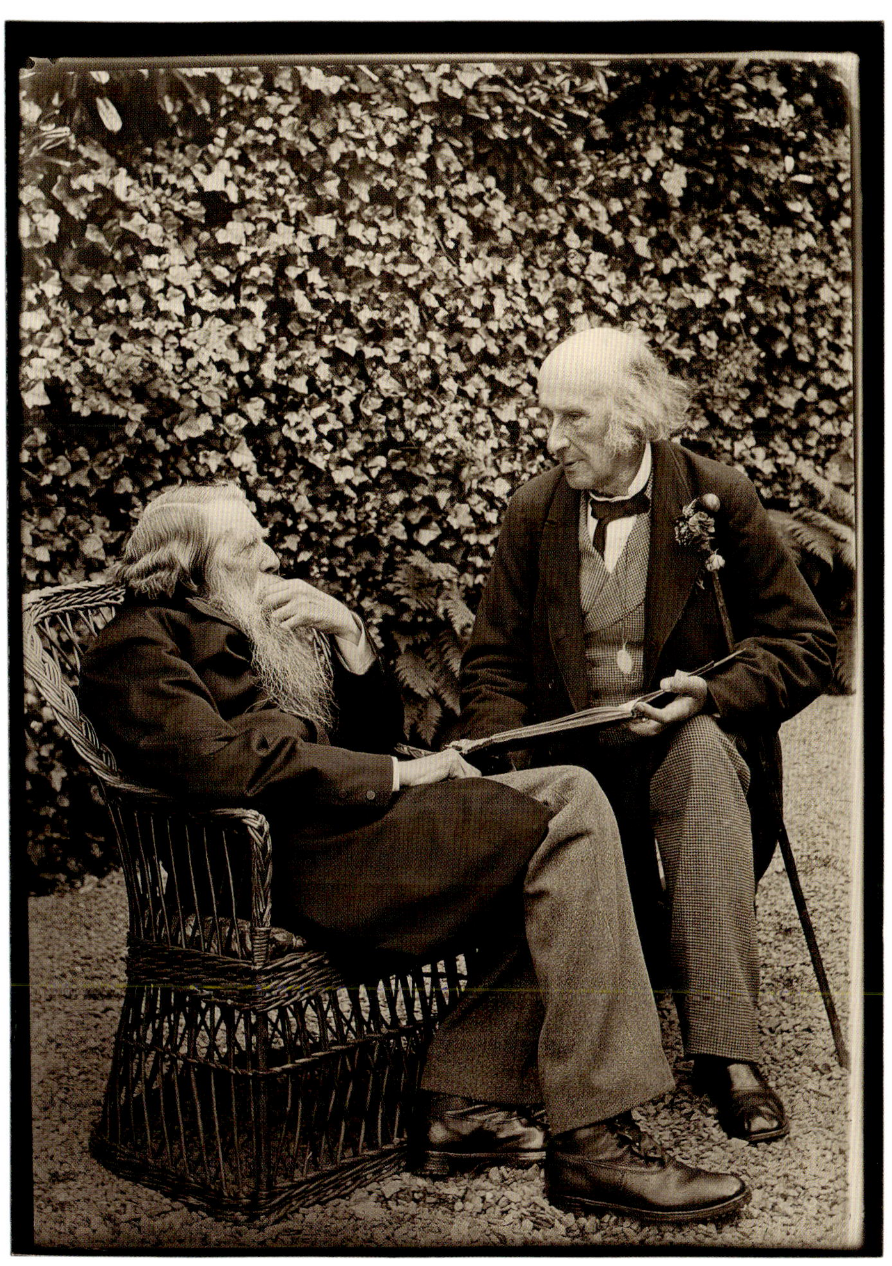

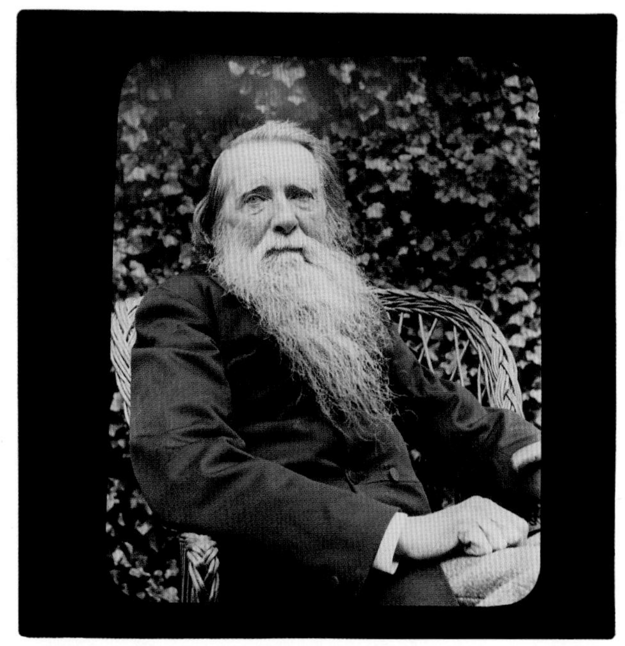

19. "*John Ruskin Esq.*"

John Ruskin (1819–1900), seated in a wicker chair
Brantwood, Coniston, 1 August 1893

Lantern slide
Museum of the History of Science, Inventory no. 17603

Half-plate negative
Bodleian Library, Minn negative 169/15

Miss Acland took Ruskin's portrait at 3 p.m., half an hour after she photographed him with her father. She used Carbutt 'Eclipse' film and a 3-second exposure at U.S. 64 (the 'Uniform System' of aperture measurement favoured by the Royal Photographic Society, equivalent to f/32). A slight fault can be seen in the negative: the fogging above Ruskin's head, which was probably caused by light entering the dark slide when she changed the film on her travels.

Like her double portrait, this study was originally intended by Miss Acland for release in photogravure. However, when the Swan Company eventually produced a proof it was found wanting. Responding to her concerns, William H. Ward (b. 1842), the manager, offered what appear to be ironic suggestions for its improvement:

> We might lower the shoulder a little, and alter the shadows in the coat, to bring the body into better proportion. I would advise the sleeve being lengthened and the cuff extended beyond it; and the forefinger might be reduced to a mere line, almost, the fingers being reduced carefully to a scale nearer to what they ought to represent. Such liberties would not quite be 'liberties', for the Camera has committed the faults, and if successfully corrected, the result would be much truer. Then we would try to bring out the eyes better, and soften the shadows.

To add to the difficulties Allen had begun to doubt whether the plate would sell. Exasperated, Miss Acland resolved to abandon the project, proposing instead "to get some forum to publish it as a photograph".

More by accident than design, the portrait eventually became the most widely circulated of Miss Acland's photographs (see p. 22). Unfortunately, it was not always reproduced with her approval. In October 1895 the *London Home* magazine used the plate without permission, prompting her to threaten legal action for copyright infringement. One of the last times it was seen during her lifetime was in 1923, in the unlikely context of an advertisement for the photographic dealer Robbins Manistre in the *British Journal Photographic Almanac.*

Miss Acland's portrait is undoubtedly an honest portrayal of Ruskin, if arguably too truthful, revealing him, in his declining years, to be a shadow of his former self.

MS. Acland d. 97, fols. 15–16; Ibid., fols. 18–19; Ibid.

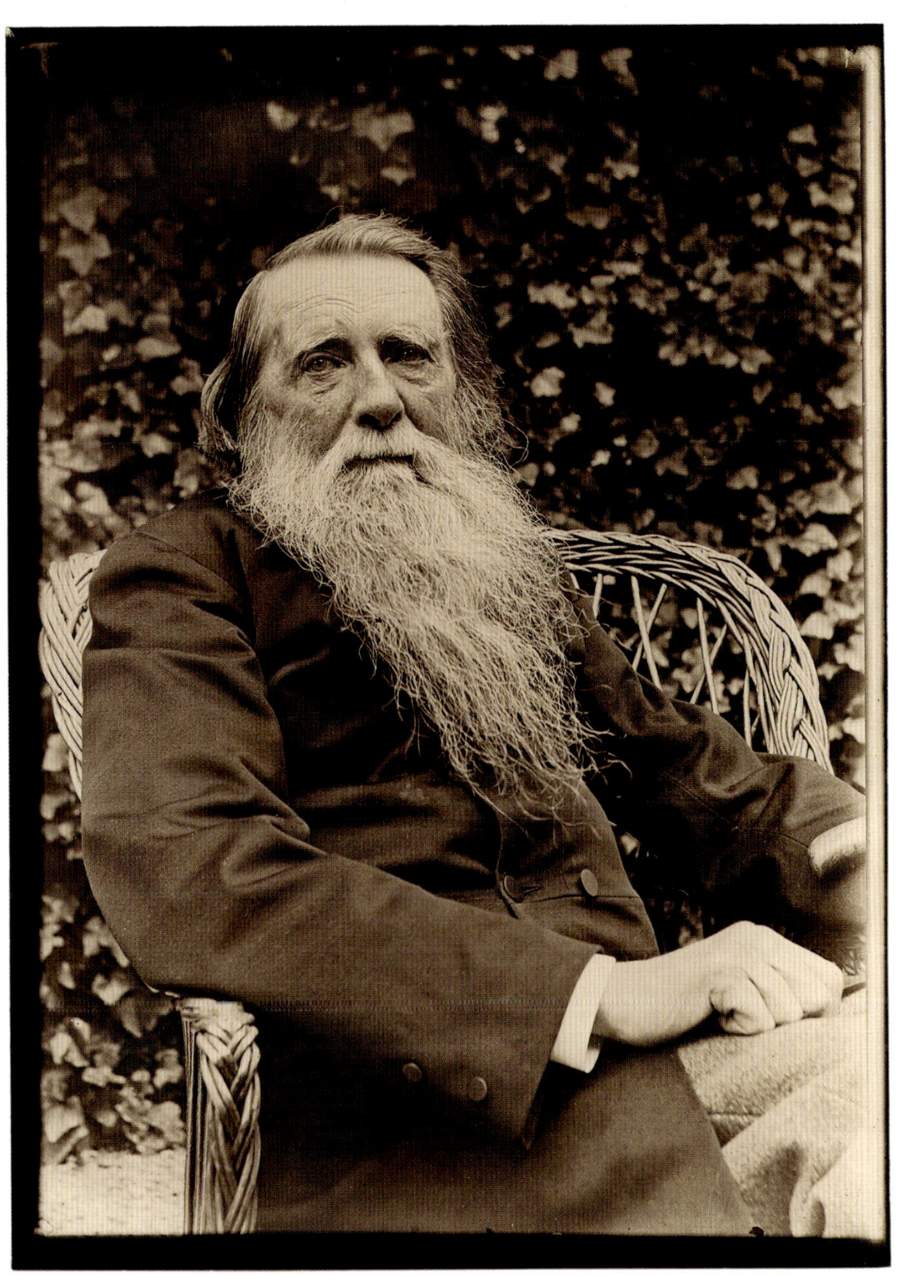

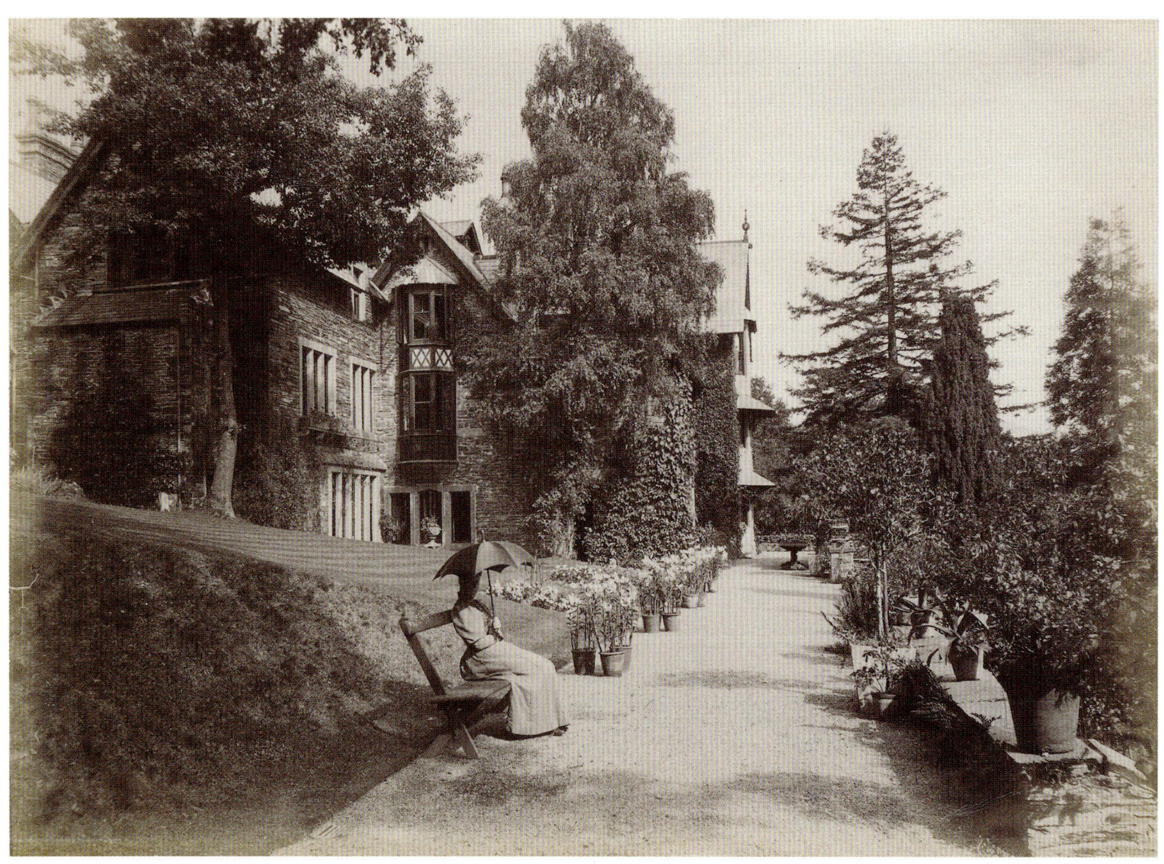

20. *"Fawe Park, Derwentwater"*

Fawe Park, with an unidentified woman holding a parasol
Keswick, Cumbria, 4 September 1893

Albumen print from half-plate negative
Bodleian Library, MS. Photogr. c. 177, fol. 68

Miss Acland spent several weeks at Fawe Park after visiting Ruskin, ostensibly to recover from a "slight poisoning" or "relaxation" of the stomach picked up at Brantwood, where there had been a "dreadful smell" emanating from the foul cellar. The house, on the shore of Derwentwater, had been rented for the summer by her doctor at the time, Richard Douglas Powell (1842–1925), Physician in Ordinary to Queen Victoria.

Another holiday visitor to Fawe Park during the 1890s was Beatrix Potter (1866–1943), who set *The Tale of Benjamin Bunny* in the kitchen garden. Beatrix's father, Rupert William Potter (1832–1914), was also an amateur photographer. Like Miss Acland he photographed Gladstone and exhibited at the Photographic Society.

MS. Acland d. 107, fols. 258–9.

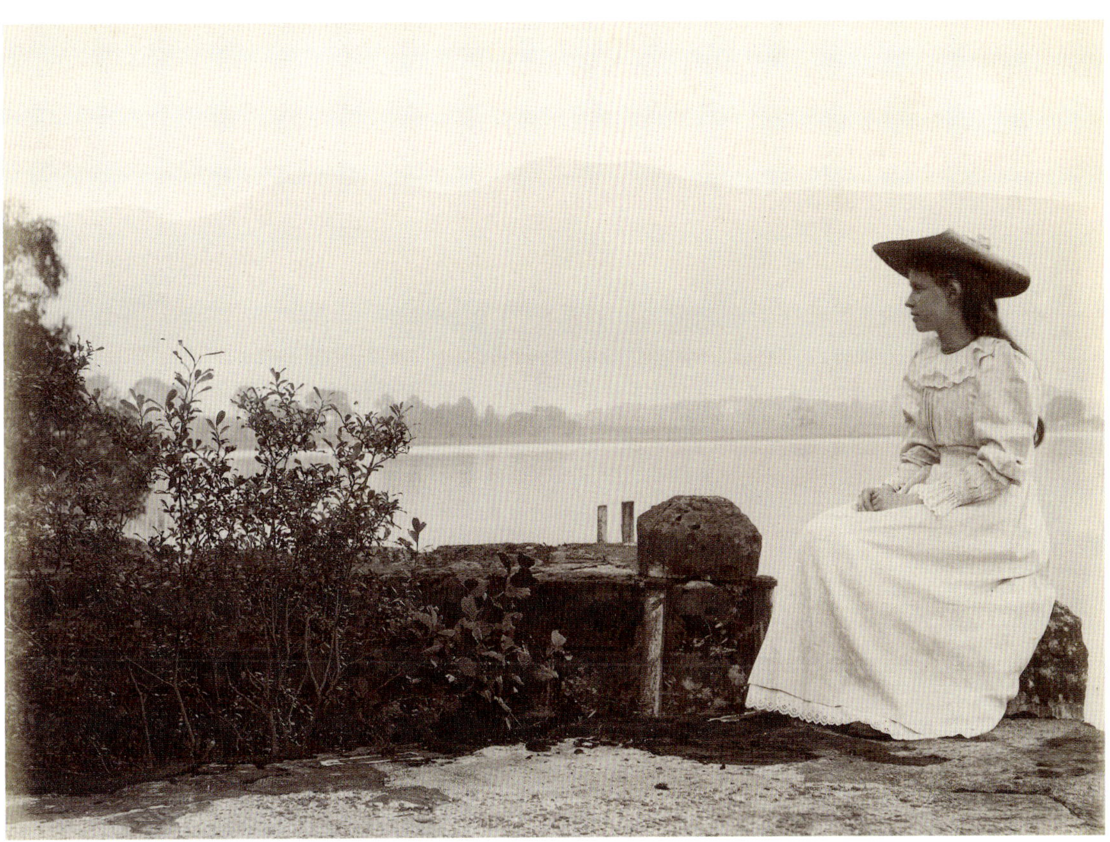

21. *"From the Boathouse, Fawe Park, with Skiddaw and Evelyn Powell"*

Evelyn Sydney Powell (1878–1921) at Fawe Park boathouse
Keswick, Cumbria, 4 September 1893

Albumen print from half-plate negative
Bodleian Library, MS. Photogr. c. 177, fol. 74

Only a small number of Miss Acland's portraits are taken against the backdrop of the natural landscape, but those that are prove highly effective. This pleasing composition was one of the earliest photographs for which she used orthochromatic plates, in this instance choosing not Cadett's, but those of B. J. Edwards. Orthochromatic plates were alleged by some, including Willie Donkin, to reduce the desirable effect of 'atmospheric perspective': the illusion of distance due to haze. Here, however, Skiddaw, the third highest mountain in England, is but a dim shadow in the background.

The boathouse at Fawe Park contained an unusual vessel: a Venetian gondola, in which Miss Acland and her camera were ferried around Derwentwater by two of her doctor's sons, Douglas Powell (1874–1932) and Scott Powell (1885–1916). "I am glad you are a Gondolier", her father wrote from Ireland on 4 September.

The Powell children were "bright and pleasant" and "well brought up", according to Miss Acland. In 1900, at the age of 22, Evelyn, pictured here, married Robert Malcolm McIlwraith (1865–1941), judicial adviser to the Egyptian Government. Douglas went up to Magdalen in 1893. Scott, an officer in the Royal Welsh Fusiliers, was killed in 1916 sitting on a Turkish trench signalling to the British guns to stop firing until the soldiers who had gone too far could get back. His death was all the more tragic because his brother Charles Folliott Borradaile Powell (1879–1901) had died in the Boer War.

MS. Acland d. 131, fols. 64–5; MS. Acland d. 107, fols. 258–9.

22. *"Mr. Goldwin Smith"*

Goldwin Smith (1823–1910)
Oxford, 13 December 1893
Half-plate negative
Bodleian Library, Minn negative 169/16

Goldwin Smith held the post of Regius Professor of Modern History at Oxford from 1858 to 1866. In 1868 he moved to the United States, having become well known as a liberal intellectual, a supporter of the northern states, and an advocate of the abolition of slavery. Three years later he settled in Toronto, where he married a rich widow, living the rest of his life in The Grange, a large Georgian house left by his wife to the municipality and now the Art Gallery of Ontario. Smith bequeathed his own fortune to Cornell University.

Miss Acland remembered Goldwin Smith from her childhood with great affection because of his enthusiasm for organizing children's parties at his house, the first to be built in Norham Gardens in north Oxford. When she grew older he gave her history lessons in the Christ Church Deanery in the company of her brothers Harry and Theodore and the three Liddell sisters. "The effect of the History classes was not altogether a success", she wrote, "as when he told us that Walter Tyrell did not kill William Rufus and the little princes were not murdered in the Tower, I gave up history, it seemed to me useless to learn and then unlearn." In later years Goldwin Smith never failed to visit Broad Street when in Oxford, although he disagreed with Acland on many subjects. This portrait was taken a few days after a dinner arranged in his honour, attended by the Vice Chancellor, the President of Magdalen, and other dignitaries.

The length of exposure required for Miss Acland's earliest portraits, according to the report of her Home Portraiture lecture, was as much as 66 seconds. By the time she came to record exposure details in her albums, presumably after acquiring a better lens, this value had dropped to around 3 seconds at f/22 outdoors, or 9 seconds at f/11 indoors, using the new brands of 'extra rapid' gelatine plates (the fastest plate Cadett had succeeded in manufacturing by 1896 had a speed of 244 on the Hurter and Driffield scale, equivalent to about ASA 10). This negative is particularly thin and underexposed, no doubt due to the weakness of the light available in Miss Acland's Mess-room studio in December, but Smith's commanding countenance is still very apparent. The flaw by his right breast was present when Miss Acland printed the negative for her first display album of portraits in about 1895.

MS. Don. d. 14, fol. 30v.

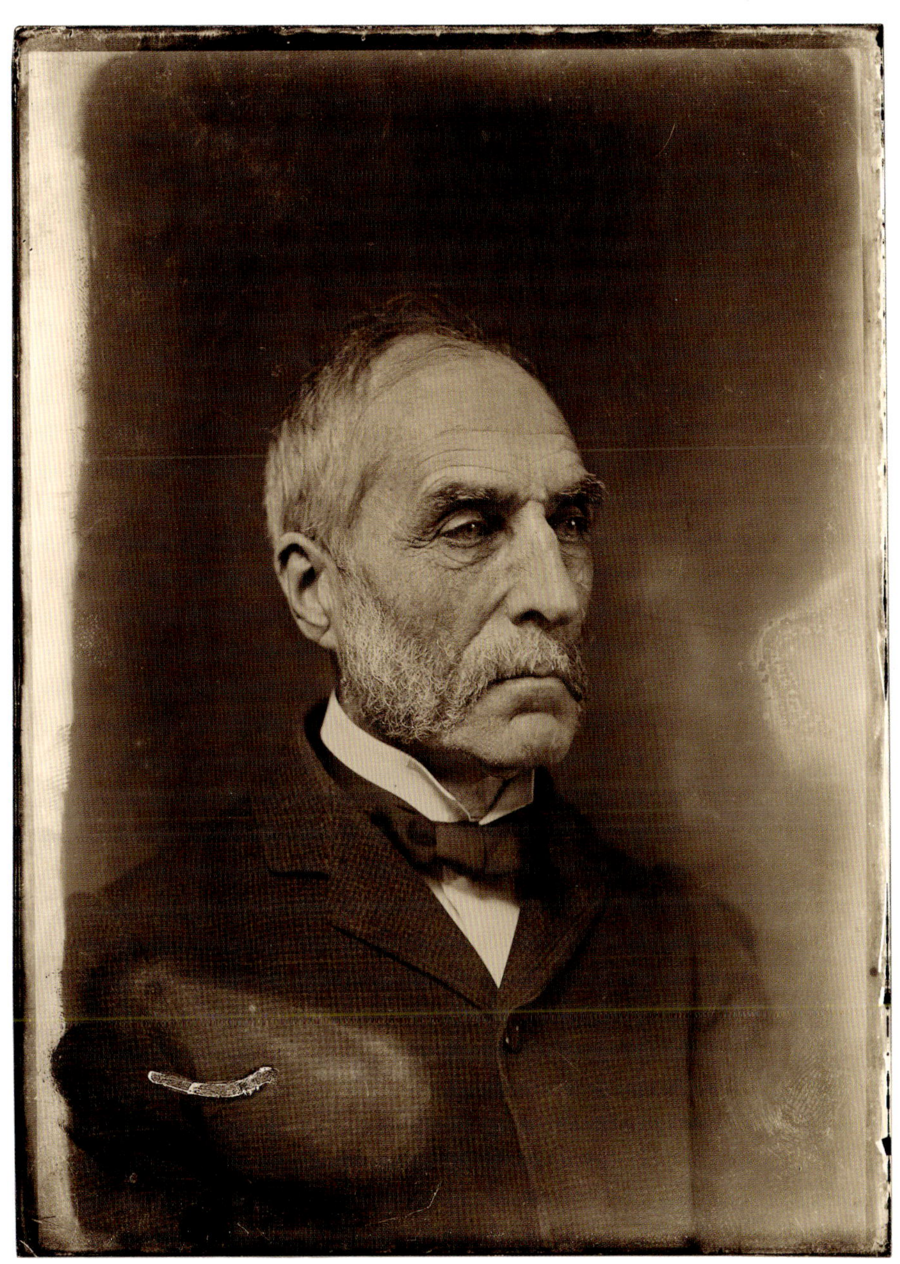

OPPOSITE & OVERLEAF

23–25. *"Professor Burdon Sanderson"*

John Scott Burdon Sanderson (1828–1905)
Oxford, 20 June 1894

Half-plate negatives
Bodleian Library, Minn negatives 144/2, 144/10 & 169/6

Burdon Sanderson became the first Waynflete Professor of Physiology in 1882. His appointment was largely in Acland's gift as Regius Professor of Medicine, to which chair Sanderson succeeded him in 1895.

The image of the preoccupied professor Miss Acland conveys with her camera is also the picture she painted of Sanderson in her memoirs:

> Always very absent minded one day having had his luncheon & gone out, the butler came running up to me soon after saying that Dr. Sanderson had come in again & had rung the dining room bell & asked for his luncheon but he had eaten it! What was he to do? I supposed he had not had enough & as the servants were having their dinner it was easy to provide him with some more. This was done & I went down & sat with him a second time. In those days not knowing him well & being rather alarmed at him I was afraid to tell him.

Sanderson was a controversial figure in Oxford on account of holding a Home Office licence to practise vivisection. A long campaign was waged against him, supported by Ruskin and Dodgson, amongst others, with frequent attempts made to block the allocation of monies to his department. In June 1883 a vote over funding for his laboratory was carried by a majority of three, Acland having telegraphed for Theodore to come up from London, who also persuaded the Dean of Westminster to vote. "Poor Dr. Sanderson was very much upset about it", Miss Acland told her brother Willie. The campaign reached its climax at a vote in the Sheldonian three years later, which she remembered as "the most stirring dramatic & exciting scene at which I was ever present".

Devon Records Office, 1148M/7/1, p. 88; MS. Acland d. 107, fols. 50–3; Devon Records Office, 1148M/7/1, p. 96.

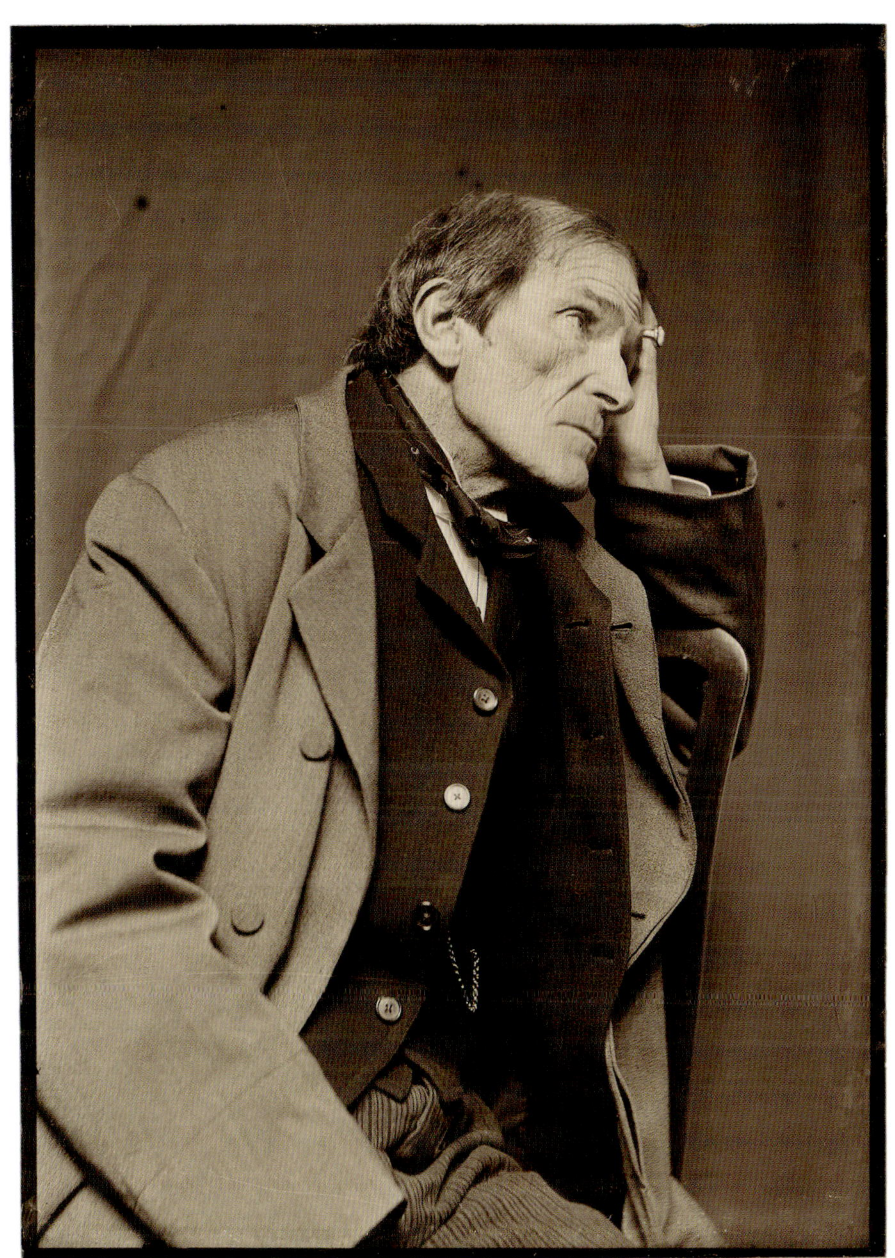

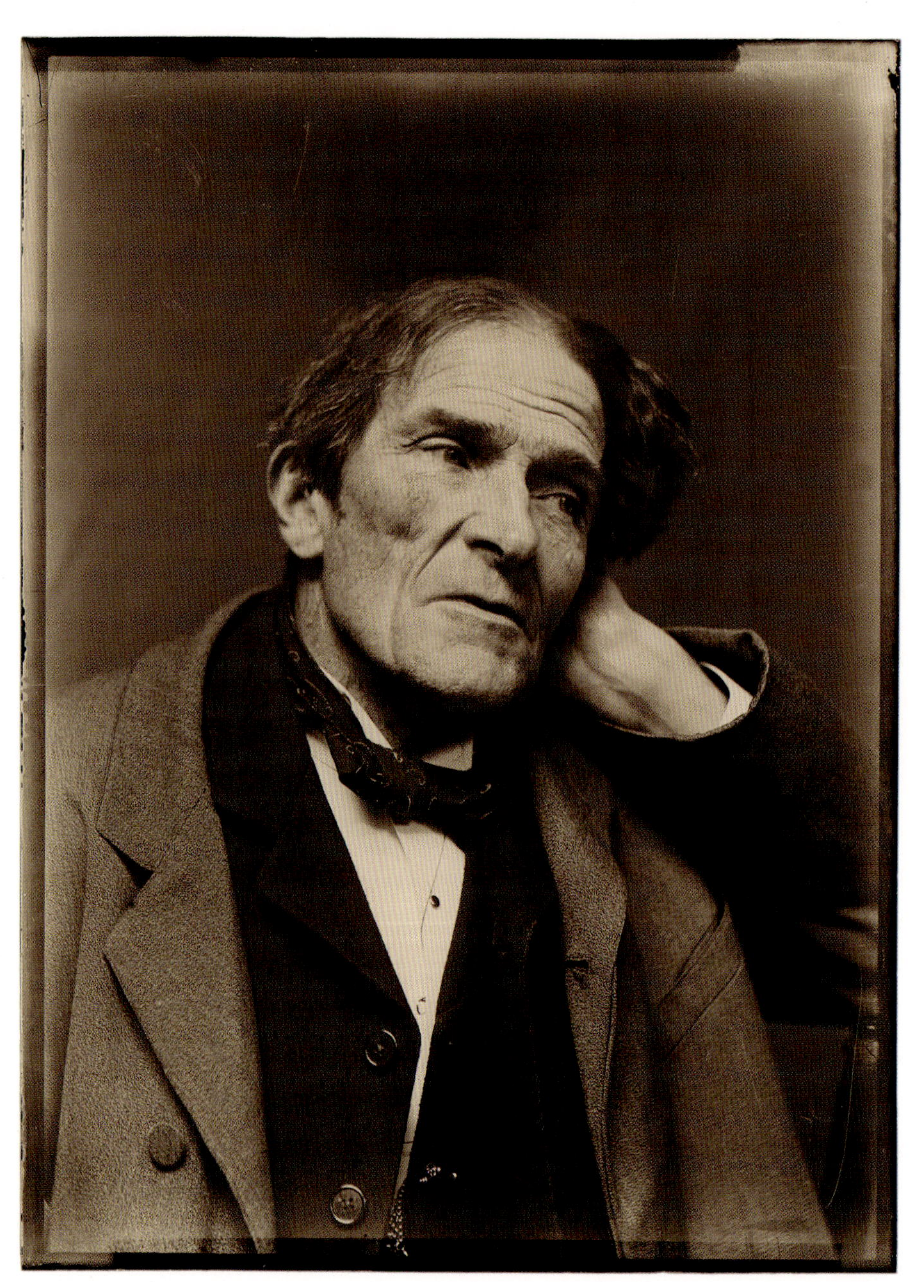

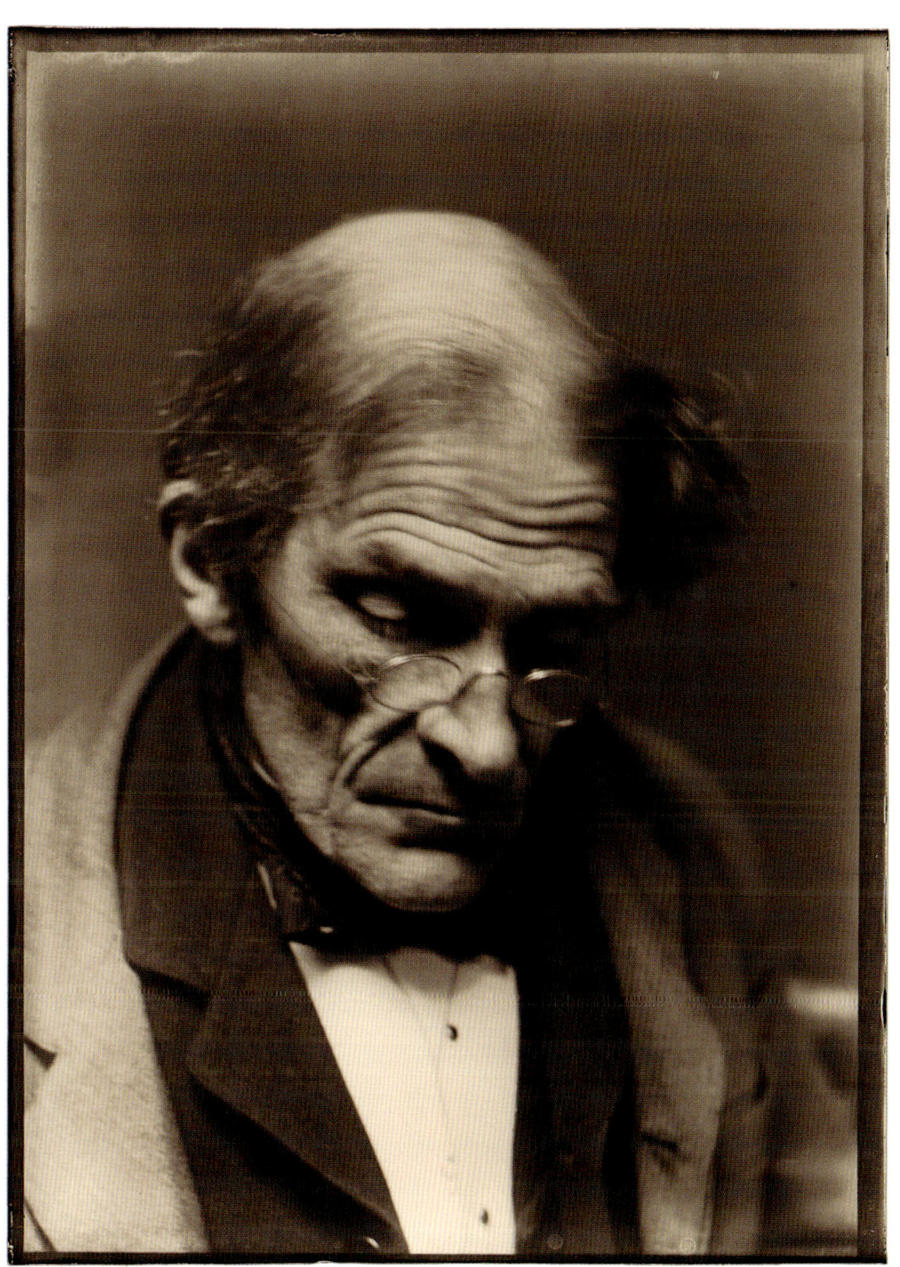

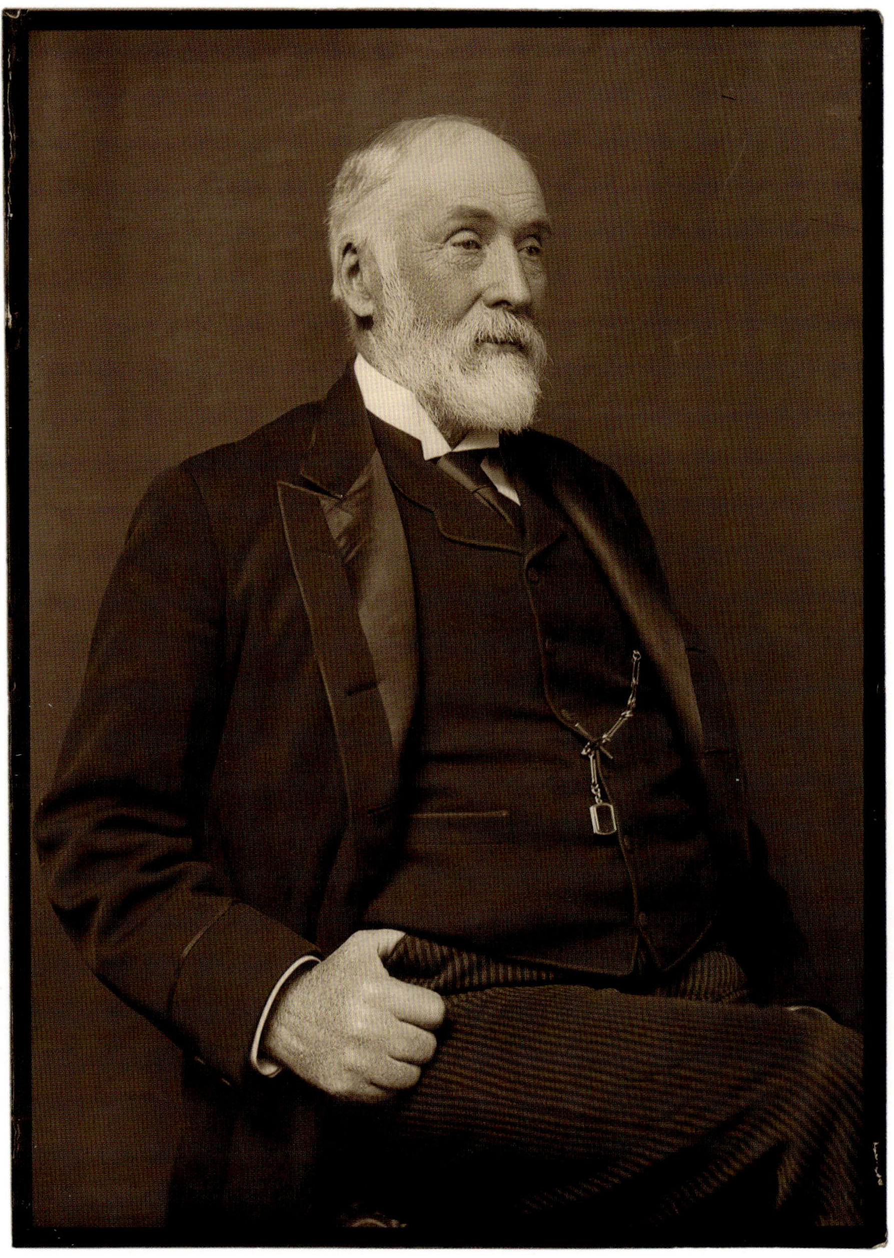

26. *"Edward L. Pierce, Milton, Massachusetts"*

Edward Lillie Pierce (1829–1897)
Oxford, 21 June 1894

Half-plate negative
Bodleian Library, Minn negative 203/12

Edward Pierce was a prominent Boston lawyer, Republican and philanthropist, the author of the standard text on railroad law and a biography of the anti-slavery campaigner Charles Sumner (1811–1874). By the time she compiled her presentation albums, Miss Acland could no longer remember how her father had made his acquaintance, but Pierce's interest in asylums provides a possible reason. She did, however, recall the more memorable fact that he was a director of the Walter Baker Chocolate Co. (the oldest in the United States), which was owned by his brother Henry Lillie Pierce (1825–1896), Mayor of Boston and U. S. Representative.

OVERLEAF LEFT

27. *"W. D. Walker, Bishop of North Dakota, U.S.A."*

William David Walker (1839–1917)
Oxford, 21 June 1894

Half-plate negative
Bodleian Library, Minn negative 203/9

Miss Acland took this portrait of Bishop Walker on the day the degree of Doctor of Divinity, *honoris causa*, was conferred on him in the Sheldonian Theatre. Walker was born in New York City and graduated from Columbia College. He was the first bishop of the Episcopal diocese of North Dakota, which was established in 1883, six years before the civil state of the same name was admitted into the Union. He served in the post until 1896. North Dakota was a frontier district, covering 70,000 square miles, and his ministry was therefore largely missionary in character. By 1891 the diocese had eighteen churches and twenty-five missions. Walker's cathedral was a Pullman railway carriage, complete with organ, in which he travelled from town to town — an idea borrowed from the Russian Orthodox travelling chapels on the Siberian railway.

Walker had a reputation as a "friend of the Indians". In 1887 he was appointed to the Board of Indian Commissioners, which was charged, under an evangelizing agenda, with providing better conditions for the indigenous peoples.

The 'reticulated' texture visible in Walker's face in the photograph is the result of extensive retouching to the negative in lead pencil. The same effect can be seen in the previous portrait of Edward Pierce. In Miss Acland's own print, made in 1895 or 1896, the retouching is absent, suggesting it was added by Harry Minn when, many years later, he made prints from the negative for her presentation albums, attempting to compensate for the lack of detail in his method of working the carbon process by adding his own.

"A Cathedral on Wheels", *Illustrated American*, vol. 6, no. 57 (21 March 1891), pp. 222–4, p. 224.

OVERLEAF RIGHT

28. *"W. S. Perry, Bishop of Iowa, U.S.A."*

William Stevens Perry (1832–1898)
Oxford, 21 June 1894

Albumen print from half-plate negative
Bodleian Library, MS. Minn 226, fol. 10r

Bishop Perry travelled with Bishop Walker during a six-month visit to Europe in 1894 to represent the American church at the Anglican Missionary Conference in London. A graduate of Harvard, he was the second Bishop of Iowa, serving from 1876 to 1898. His ministry centred on the foundation of schools, hospitals and other charitable institutions. By the time of this portrait he already held the degree of Doctor of Divinity, *honoris causa*, from Oxford.

Bishops Perry and Walker were two of numerous American and Canadian visitors to Broad Street, many of whom Acland had met whilst travelling in North America in 1860 as Honorary Physician to the Prince of Wales. Other friends of the Aclands from across the Atlantic included Justin Winsor (1831–1897), Librarian at Harvard, and his granddaughter Penelope Barker Noyes (1891–1977) (whom Miss Acland particularly liked); the botanist Asa Gray (1810–1888) and his wife (whom she described as a "charming couple"); Charles William Eliot (1834–1926), President of Harvard ("a very pleasant and intelligent person", according to Mrs Acland); Caroline Mastin Pope, née O'Fallon (1828–1917), whose father "practically owned the town of St. Louis it being built on his land"; and countless medical men, including Samuel David Gross (1805–1884), who wrote of Acland that there was "hardly an American of note who visits Oxford that is not entertained at his table".

No negative is known of this portrait. The reproduction overleaf is from an albumen print in Miss Acland's earliest volume of portraits and displays the fading and loss of detail in the highlights typical of the medium.

Presentation album, private collection, n.p.; MS. Acland d. 42, fols. 434–40; Devon Records Office, 1148M/7/1, p. 57; Samuel W. Gross and A. Haller Gross (eds), *Autobiography of Samuel D. Gross, M.D.* (2 vols., Philadelphia, 1887), vol. 2, p. 79.

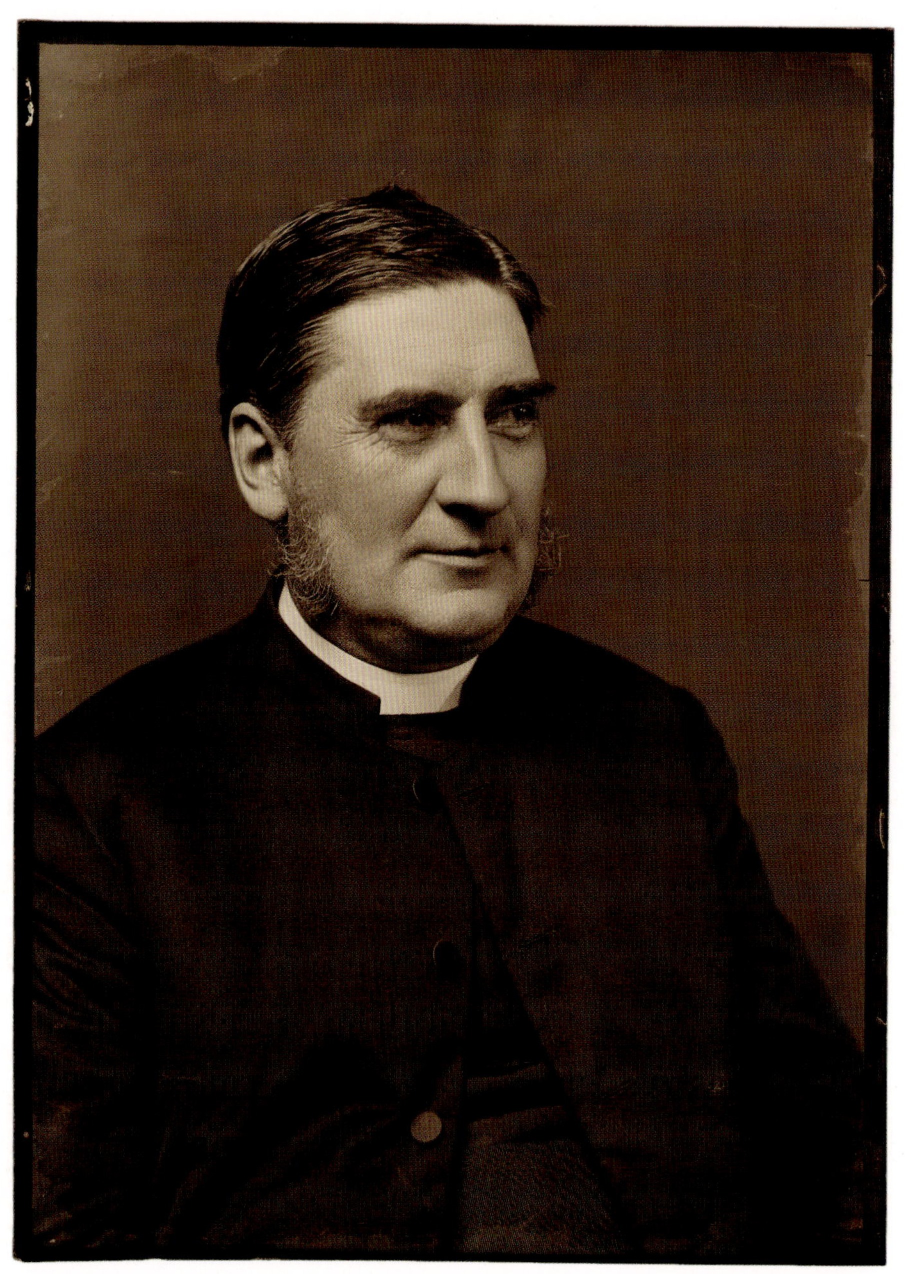

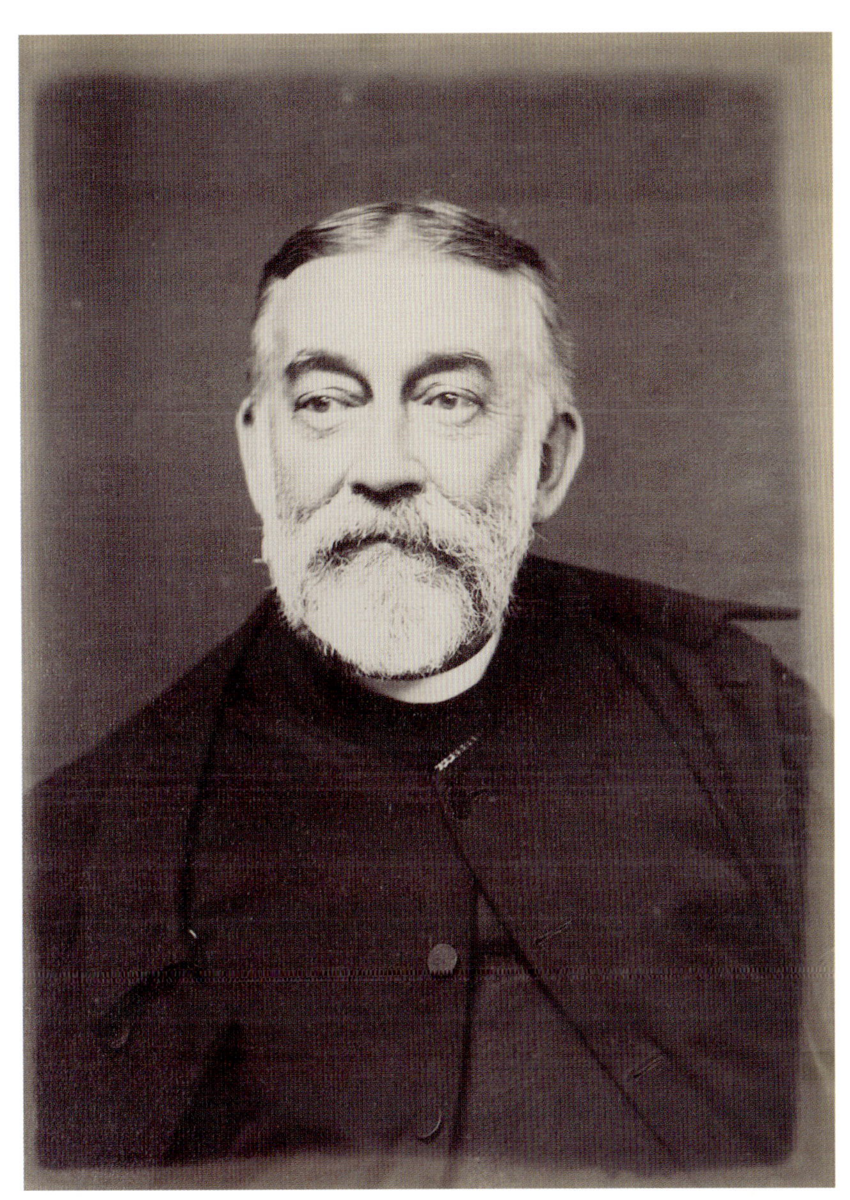

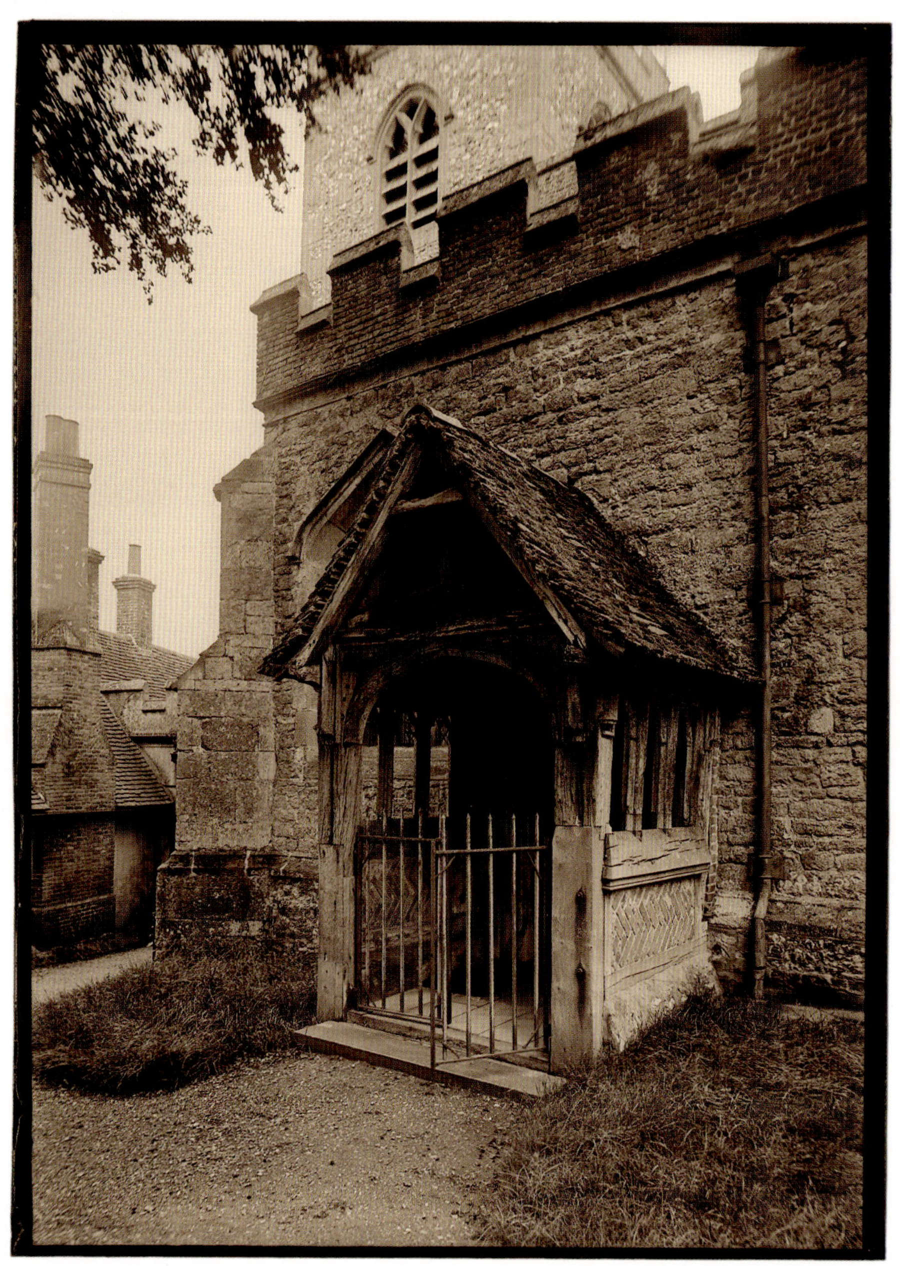

OPPOSITE

29. *Ancient Oak*

The south porch, St Mary the Virgin, and the almshouses
Ewelme, probably 7 July 1894

Half-plate negative
Bodleian Library, Minn negative 175/5

Although Miss Acland's photography before 1900 is dominated by portraiture, she was also an enthusiastic photographer in other genres. In the 1896 Oxford Camera Club exhibition, for example, she came first in the landscape class with *Summer Evening in Suffolk*, second in the 'Instantaneous' class with *Two Cyclists* (even though "under exposure was very apparent" in the print), and second in the 'Hand Camera' class with *A Day on H.M.S. Australia*. In the 1900 exhibition her "wonderfully clever and admirably printed" studies of a cuckoo secured her second prize in the animals class.

As Regius Professor of Medicine Acland was also Master of the Hospital of St John the Baptist in Ewelme, South Oxfordshire. The Hospital is an almshouse, established in 1442 for two priests and thirteen poor men, arranged around a cloister attached to St Mary the Virgin. The south porch of the church is tucked around the back of the building, but with its ancient timbers, perpendicular window openings, and herringbone brickwork it offers interesting pictorial possibilities.

St Mary's contains the tomb of Thomas Chaucer, son of the poet, which Miss Acland also photographed.

Oxford Times, no. 1786 (21 November 1896), p. 7c ; *Oxford Times*, no. 2044 (10 March 1900), p. 11f.

OVERLEAF

30. *Waifs and Strays*

Castle Mills and St George's Tower, from Paradise Street
Oxford, July 1894 ?

Half-plate negative
Bodleian Library, Minn negative 17/3

Miss Acland often attracted spectators when she ventured out with her half-plate camera, some of whom can be spotted in her photographs on close inspection. Rarely, however, did the onlookers add so much to the composition as the two young girls in this view of St George's Tower and the Castle Flour Mills. As well as the girls, in the distance in a doorway on the first floor of the Mill, two men can be seen looking at the camera, and below them a third, resting from loading his wagon, while his horse waits patiently by.

Castle Flour Mills was demolished in 1930. By the time Miss Acland took this photograph the Saxon St George's Tower, formerly part of Oxford Castle, had been incorporated into the County Gaol. It remained part of Oxford Prison until 1996.

This is a wonderful photograph: a fascinating and beautiful subject, perfectly lit, with human interest, the composition a subtle balance of lines and masses that lead the eye from the foreground to the background. It may have been intended by Miss Acland as a genre study or allegory, the more dishevelled girl on the right providing a contrast with her tidy friend on the left. The writing on the piece of paper propped up on the kerb is too small, even in the original negative, to be legible.

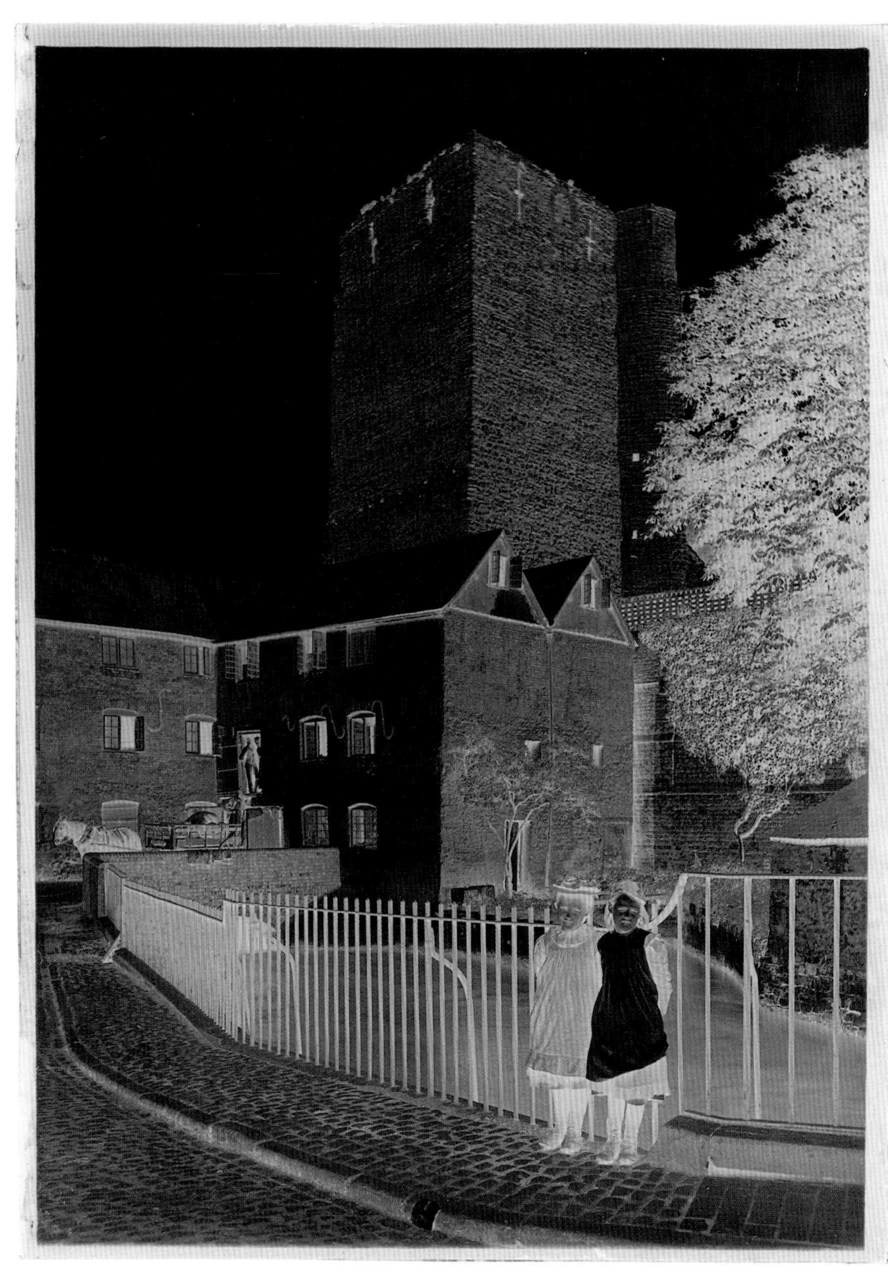

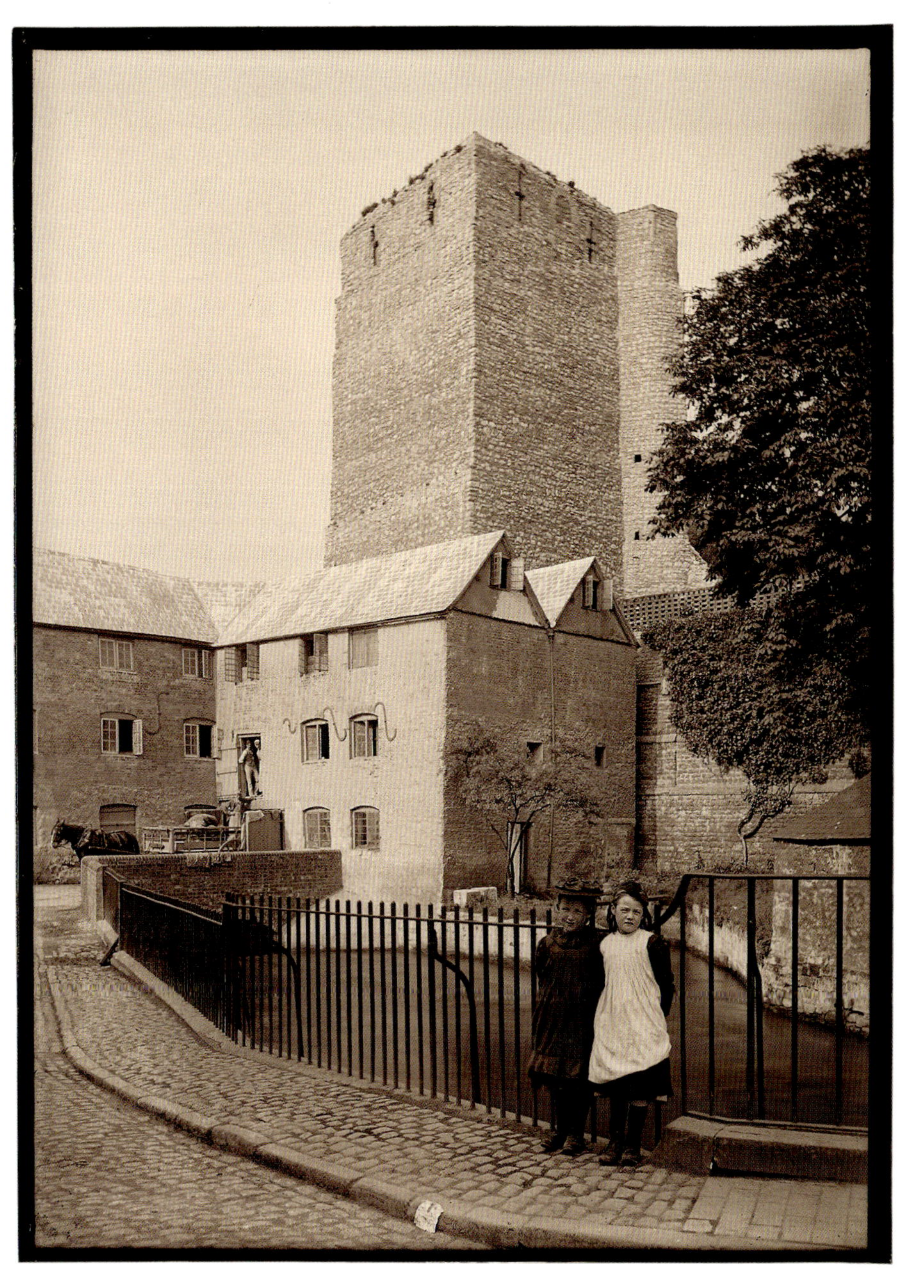

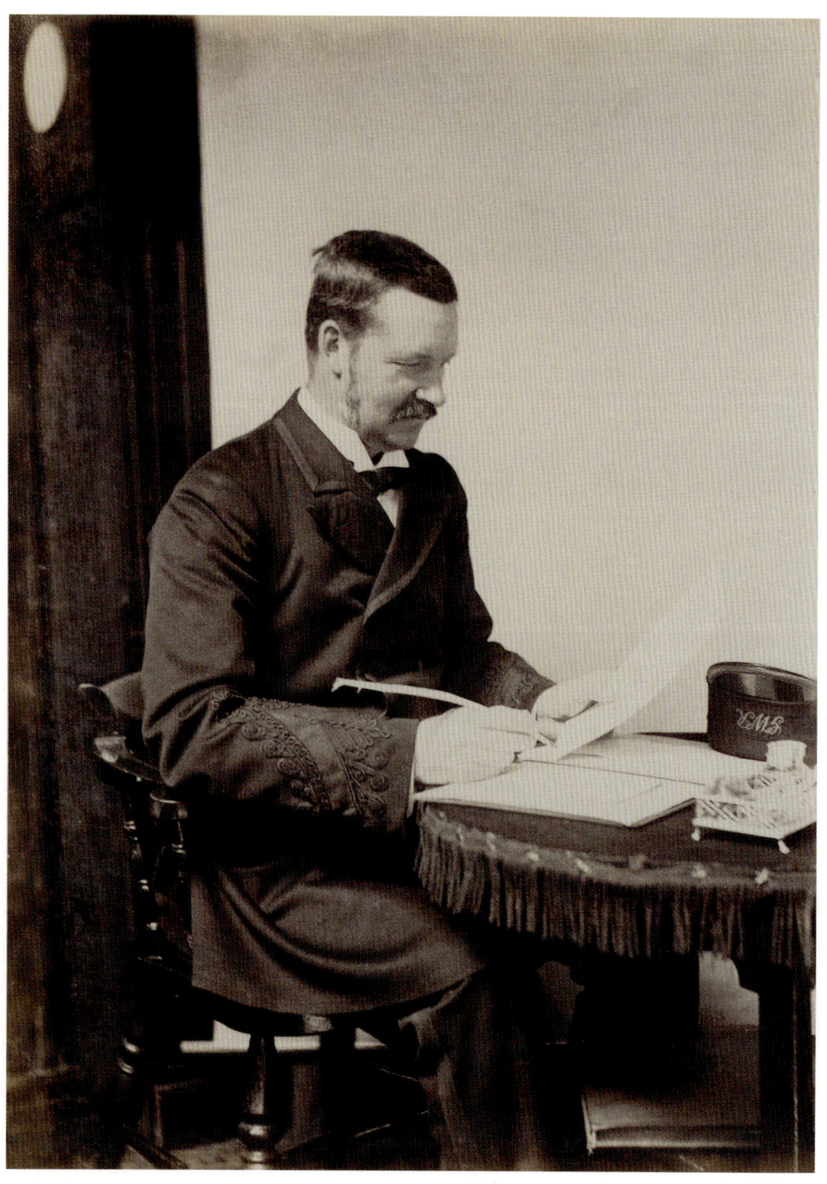

31. *"Mr. R. Davis, Station Master, G.W.R."*

Robert Davis (b. 1849, d. after 1911)
Oxford, 3 July 1894

Albumen print from half-plate negative
Bodleian Library, MS. Minn 226, fol. 6v

Robert Davis was born in Salisbury, but by the 1881 census is listed as a railway clerk living in Paddington. His appointment as Station Master at the Great Western in Oxford took place in 1883, when he was 34. Little else is known about him, but from occasional reports in which he is mentioned in *Jackson's Oxford Journal* he seems to have spent much of his time observing criminals' movements on the station and dealing with the aftermath of gruesome accidents on the line. Miss Acland's portrait gives the illusion that he is busy at work in his office, but the roller background behind suggests she may have photographed him closer to home.

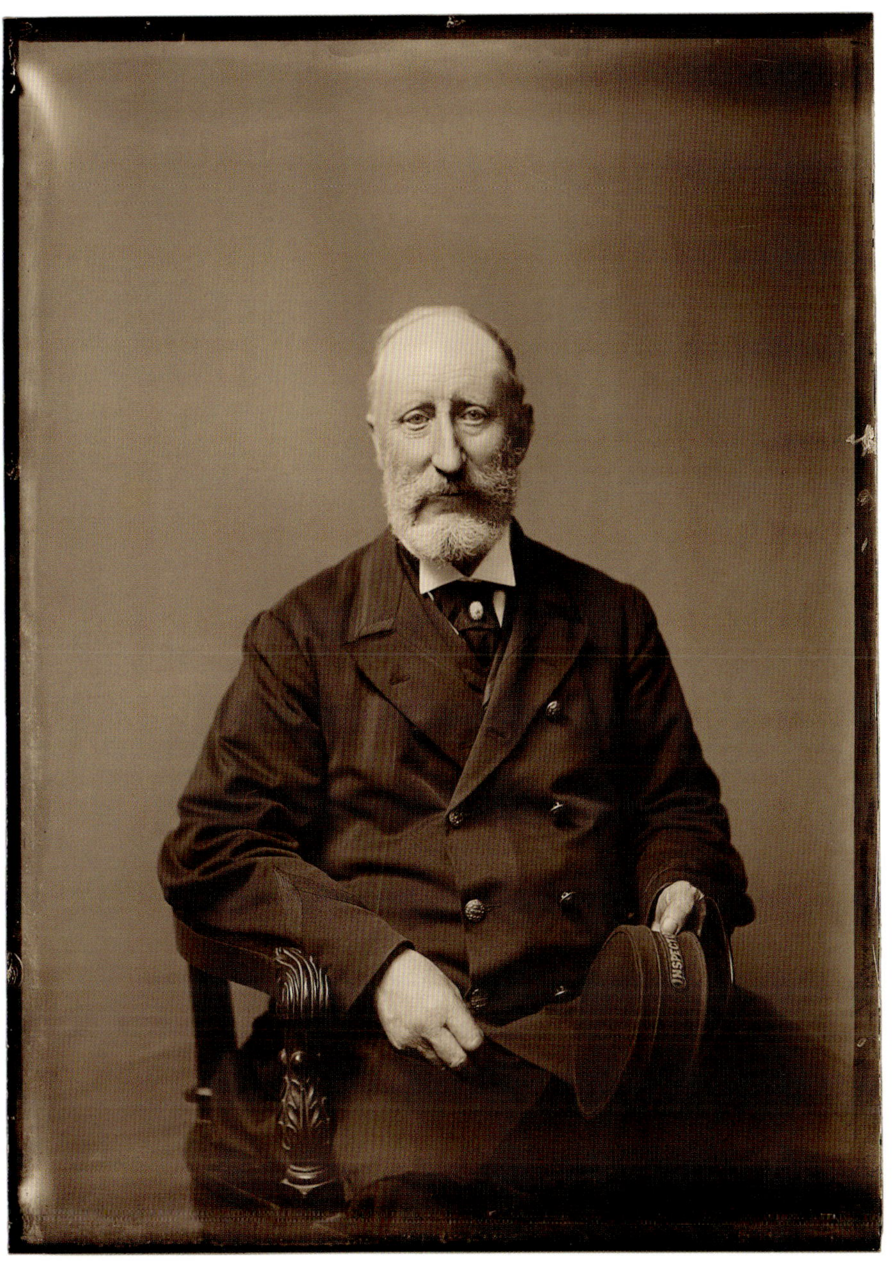

32. *Inspector Cooper, G.W.R.*

John Cooper (1830–1903), holding his Inspector's cap
Oxford, *circa* 3 July 1894 ? or perhaps 1898
Half-plate negative
Bodleian Library, Minn negative 183/7

Miss Acland photographed men and women of all classes, good character being the only qualification for a sitting. After Cooper retired from the G. W. R. in 1898 his moral well-being became a concern for her, since in order to provide a home for his daughters, Mary (1858–1902) and Alice (b. 1862), he took a public house. Both soon turned to drink, Mary dying from her alcoholism. Later Miss Acland delivered a letter from Cooper to the brewery surrendering the lease. "I have done a great many things but I never gave up a Public before!", she quipped.

MS. Acland d. 108, fols. 111–14.

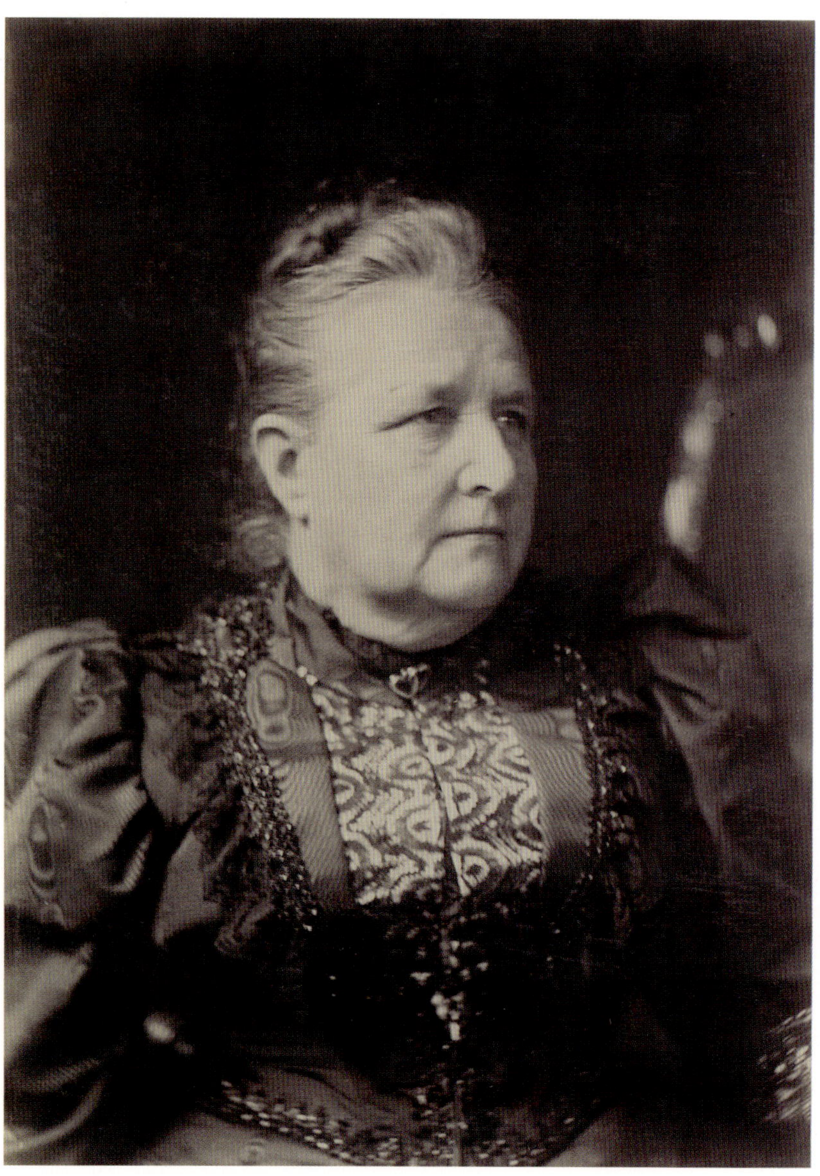

33. *"Mrs Billings, Georgetown, D.C., U.S.A."*
Katharine Mary Billings, née Stevens (1836–1912)
Oxford, 8 August 1894
Albumen print from half-plate negative
Bodleian Library, MS. Minn 226, fol. 18v

In 1894 Mrs Billings travelled to Oxford to be with her husband at the meeting of the British Association for the Advancement of Science, where ladies were welcome. She visited again in 1903, after Acland's death, staying with Miss Acland in Park Town. The daughter of Hestor Lockhart Stevens (1803–1864), a lawyer who served as a Democratic Congressmen for Michigan from 1853 to 1855, she married her husband on 3 September 1862 and bore him two sons and three daughters. Despite her formidable appearance she was described as an "ideal home maker", her "tactful sympathy" a foil to her husband's "imperious temper". Her sentimental side is seen in the interlocking hearts she has chosen to wear on her collar.

Fielding H. Garrison, *John Shaw Billings: A Memoir* (New York & London, 1915), p. 327.

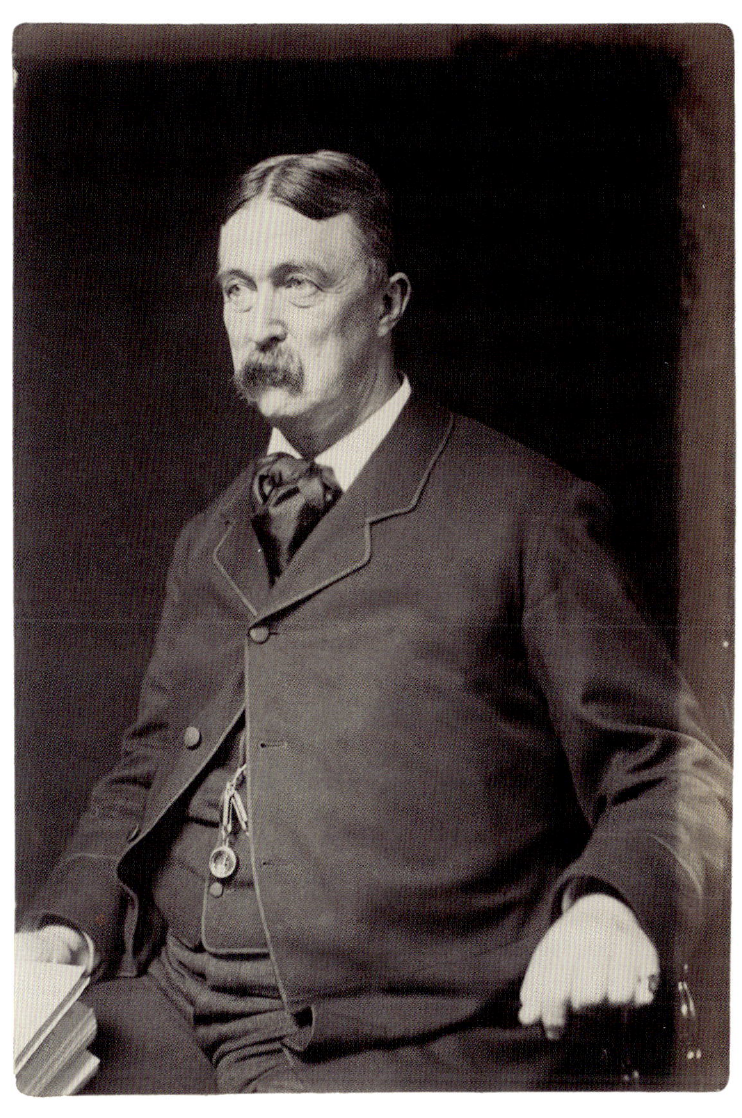

34. *"Dr. Billings, Deputy Surgeon General, U. S. Army"*

John Shaw Billings (1838–1913)
Oxford, 8 August 1894
Albumen print from half-plate negative
Bodleian Library, MS. Minn 226, fol. 27r

Billings, who served for nearly thirty years as Director of the Surgeon General's Library, was a treasured friend of the Aclands. Miss Acland remembered him coming to England in 1876 with Ezra Mundy Hunt (1830–1894) to discuss plans for the Johns Hopkins Hospital, which he designed. During his visits to Broad Street he "lived and fitted in like a member of the family", his "quiet and dignified manner, his unfailing sense of humour, combined with his clear and powerful intellect and great common sense" making him an ideal companion for the aged Acland.

Miss Acland quoted in Fielding H. Garrison, *John Shaw Billings: A Memoir* (New York & London, 1915), p. 388.

OPPOSITE

35. *"The Marchioness of Salisbury"*

Georgina Charlotte Gascoyne-Cecil, née Alderson, Marchioness of Salisbury (1827–1899)
Oxford, 9 August 1894

Half-plate negative
Bodleian Library, Minn negative 200/9

Lord Salisbury's marriage to Georgina Alderson in 1857 created a "double friendship" with the Aclands. Georgie had been an acquaintance of Mrs Acland from before her marriage, her father Edward Hall Alderson (1787–1857), Baron of the Exchequer, moving in the same circles as Miss Acland's grandfather, William Cotton.

When her husband was installed as Chancellor of the University in 1870 Lady Salisbury lodged her daughters Lady Gwendolen Cecil (1860–1945) and Lady Beatrix Maud Cecil (1858–1950) with the Aclands. Her sons were also in and out of the house, as Mrs Acland explained to Willie in a letter of 23 June:

> I have enjoyed having the two Salisbury little girls here, very much: And the little boys have been here also occasionally for their meals. Dear little boys in black velvet knickerbockers, who act as Pages to their Father holding up the main of his Gown on all State occasions.

Dodgson photographed the boys with their father on the same day, exactly as Mrs Acland described them.

Miss Acland had her own opportunity to spend time with the Salisburys in February 1877 whilst over-wintering in Mentone, on the French Riviera, where they stopped off on the way back from the Conference of Constantinople.

Lady Salisbury is holding a copy of James Moore's *Historical Handbook and Guide to Oxford* (Oxford, 1878), which is illustrated on the cover with an engraving of the baroque porch of the University Church.

MS. Eng. misc. d. 214, fol. 38; MS. Acland d. 42, fols. 196–7.

OVERLEAF

36. *The Marquess of Salisbury, K.G."*

Robert Arthur Talbot Gascoyne-Cecil, 3rd Marquess of Salisbury (1830–1903)
Oxford, 9 August 1894

Half-plate negatives
Bodleian Library, Minn negatives 200/10 & 200/6

Miss Acland secured Lord Salisbury — her second Prime Minister — during the meeting of the British Association for the Advancement of Science in Oxford. Salisbury wore his robes as Chancellor of the University especially for the occasion, the sitting taking place the day after his opening address in the Sheldonian, which was lighted by electricity for the first time, in his honour.

Like Gladstone, Salisbury was an old friend of the Aclands. After falling ill as an undergraduate at Christ Church he consulted Acland who, "much in advance of his day", advised him to go to Australia for a year to "live an outdoor life". The advice was taken, against the wishes of his father, and his health saved. Salisbury therefore felt he owed Acland "the whole of his career".

Salisbury's portrait won a certificate in the "Portraiture and Figure Studies" competition of the journal *Photography* in May 1899, the judges commenting that

> the technique of this photograph is excellent. The pose of the statesman, the bowed shoulders and slightly bended head, suggest an Atlas bearing a world of care. Miss Acland's rendering of her subject challenges comparison with many of the published portraits, and does not suffer in doing so.

When it was exhibited at the Royal Photographic Society in 1903, Albert Charles Robinson Carter (1864–1957), in his review for *Photograms of the Year*, wrote that "a few more portraits of this class, and fewer damp woods, would have been preferable".

From the row of books poking out above her fabric background it seems Miss Acland photographed Salisbury in the library, rather than her usual Mess-room studio. In 1911 the portrait appeared as part of the Oxford Camera Club's contribution to the Imperial Exhibition at Crystal Palace.

MS. Don. d. 14, fol. 3v; Ibid.; *Photography*, vol. 11, no. 549 (18 May 1899), p. 332; *Photograms of the Year*, 1903, p. 156.

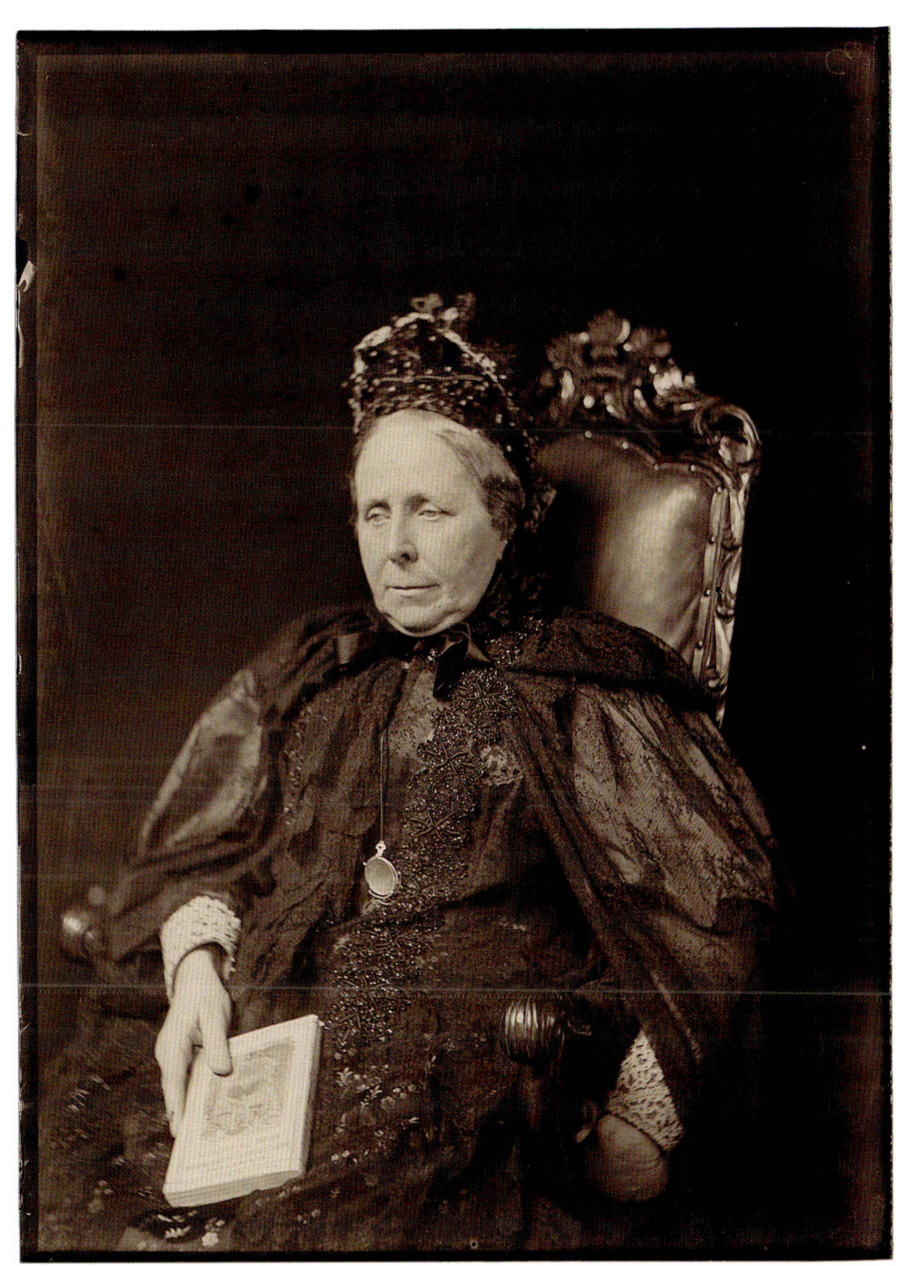

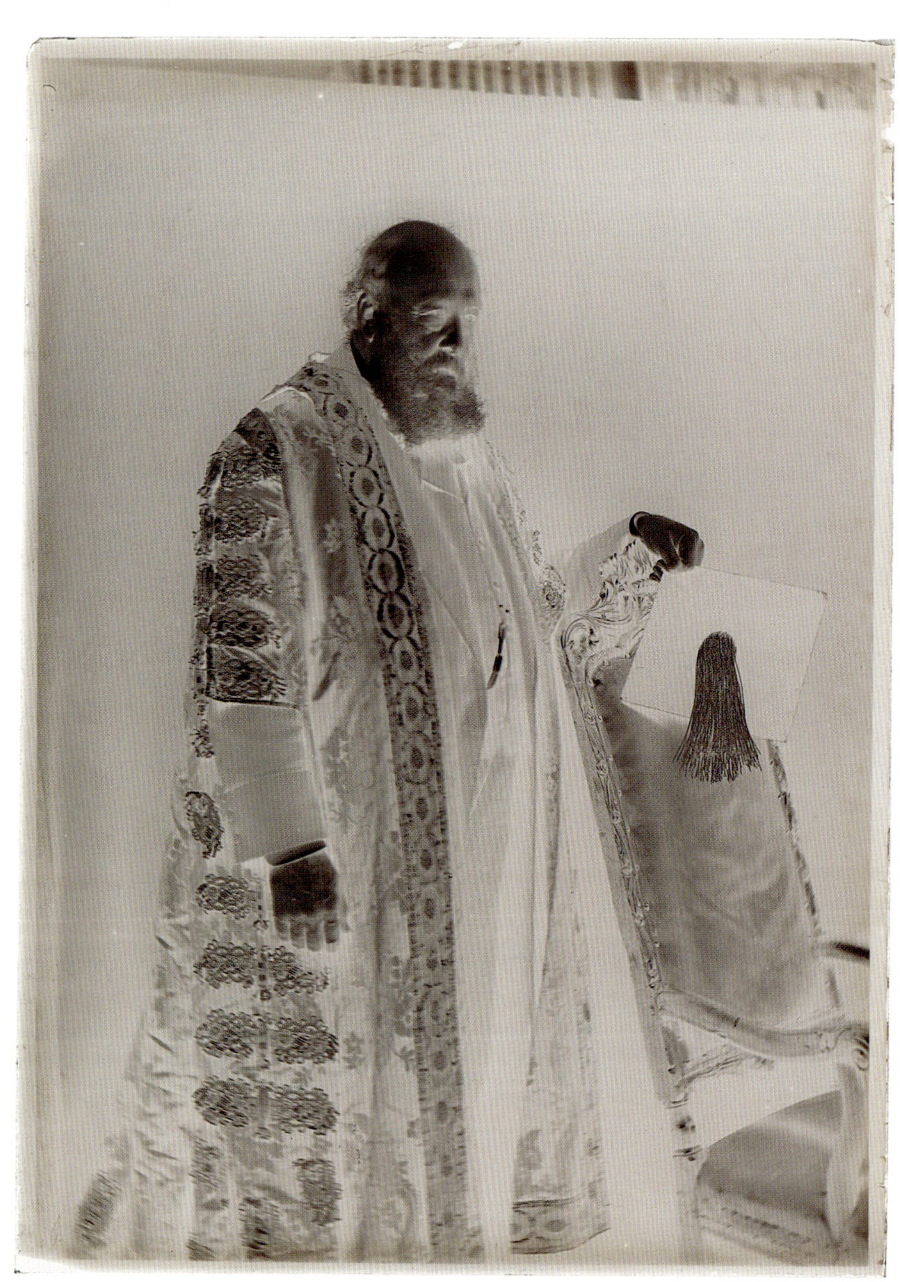

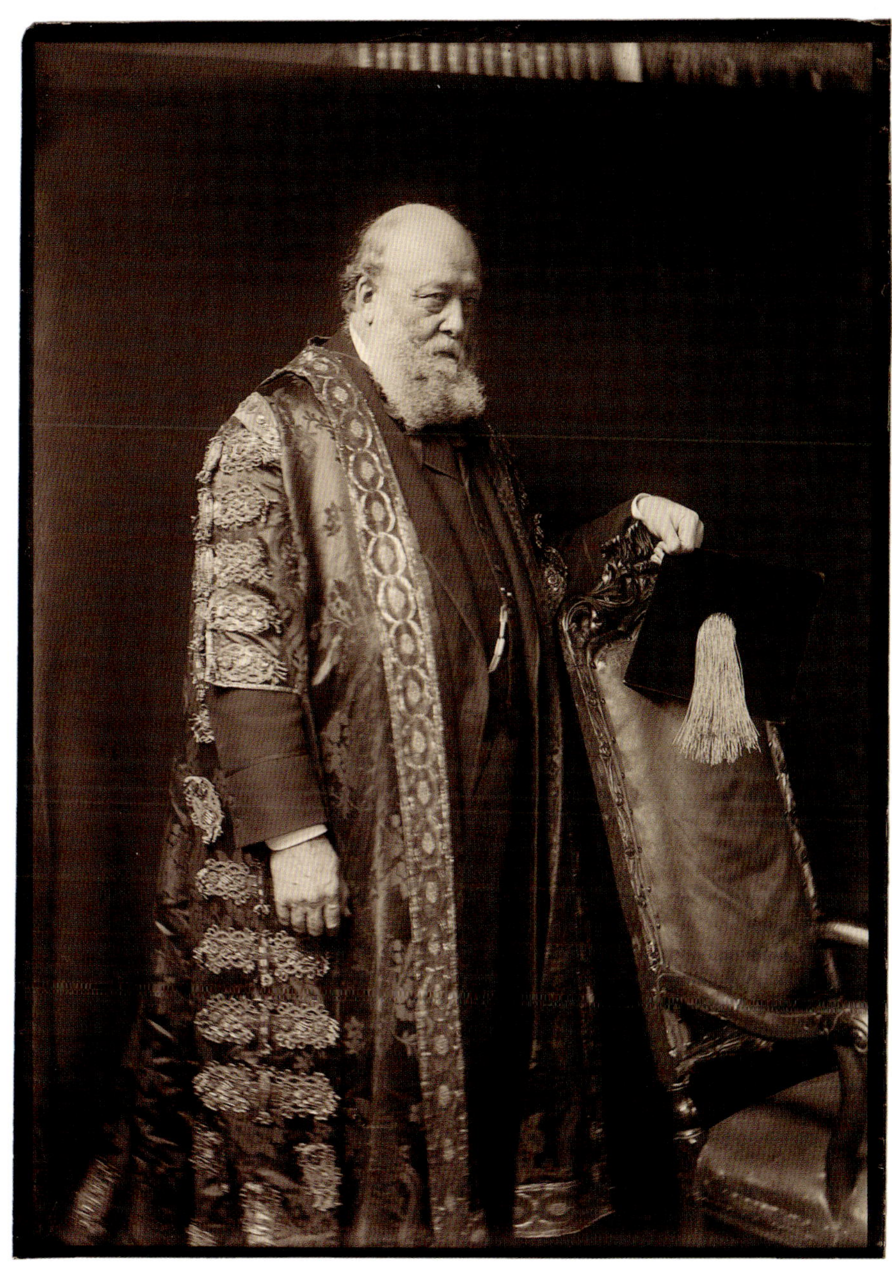

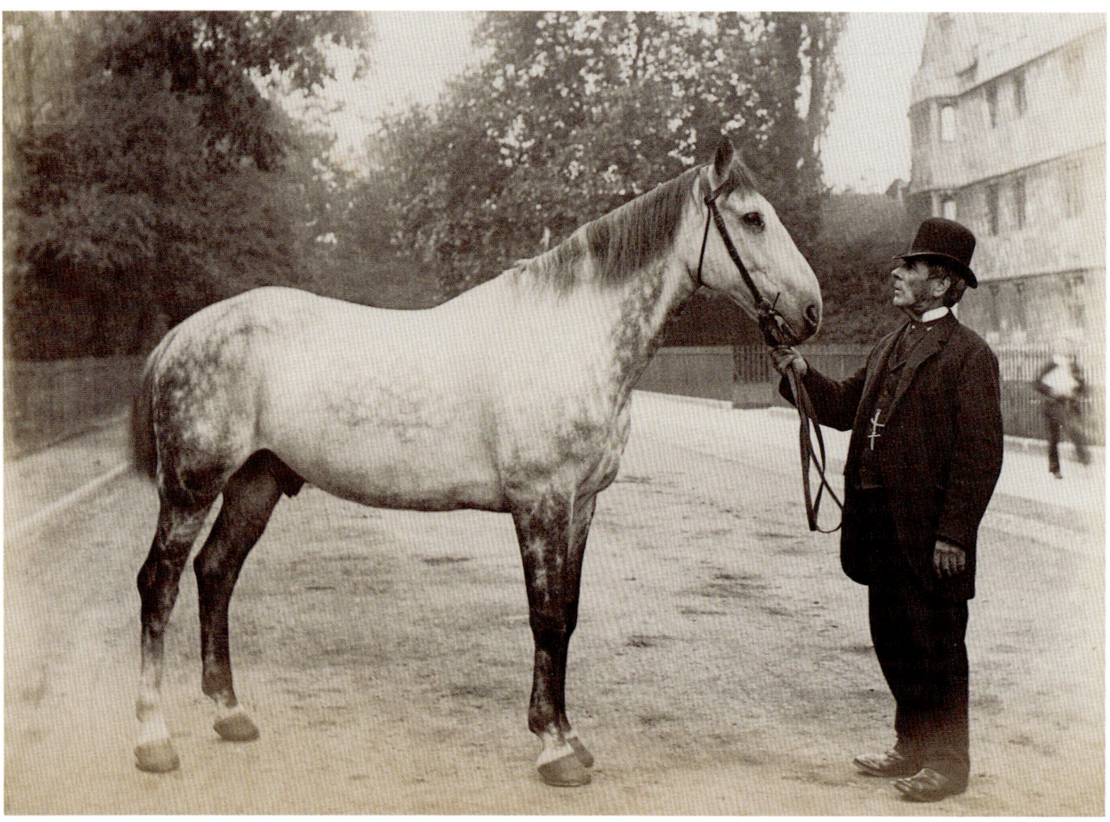

37. *Greening and One of the Greys*

George Greening (1839–1927) and one of the Aclands' grey horses, standing in Park Street outside Wadham College Oxford, summer 1894?

Albumen print from half-plate negative
Bodleian Library, MS. Photogr. c. 177, fol. 144

Miss Acland's love of horses began when she was given a pony — Woodbine — for her fifth birthday. Ina Liddell became her riding companion, trusted to take Woodbine out when she was away from Oxford. In April 1859 Ina wrote with news of their steed:

> My dear Angie
>
> I am afraid you will think I have quite forgotten you but I have not had time before. How soon will you be home? I have seen Woodbine. I shall be so glad when you come home to have a ride with me. I send you some fethers that I have saved for you that came of Poly. I can not write any more so Good bye dear Angie. With love and kisses to Harry and Theodore and Mary and you yourself. Bleve me yours very truly Lorina Charlotte Liddell

Woodbine was succeeded by 'Gammel', a sage pony given to Miss Acland by the historian Charles Henry Pearson (1830–1894). She drove Gammel in a specially adapted carriage left to her by Prince Leopold, who often visited the Aclands whilst a student. One of her regular passengers was the doyen of High Church Oxford, Henry Parry Liddon (1829–1890), whom she took on outings to Wytham and Bagley Wood. When Gammel got old he was sent to Brantwood for the Severn children, where Ruskin bought him a donkey for companionship.

The Aclands' stables were at the back of the house, linked by a passage to Park Street opposite Wadham College. Acland would sometimes travel 70 miles a day visiting patients, his coachman George Greening driving him in a barouche with a pair of greys (jobbed from London) or post horses from local inns.

MS. Acland d. 173, fols. 185–6.

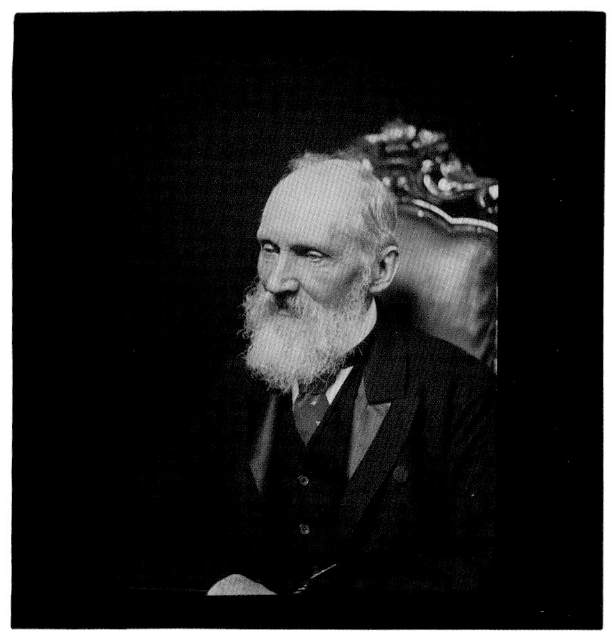

38. *"Lord Kelvin, President of the Royal Society"*

William Thomson, Baron Kelvin (1824–1907)
Oxford, 10 August 1894

Lantern slide
Museum of the History of Science, Inventory no. 85681

Thomson ranks as the third most eminent personage to sit for Miss Acland, after Gladstone and Salisbury. As she remarked when describing this portrait, "Lord Kelvin is so well known for his very distinguished and varied work that there is no need to give details of it here." The circumstances in which he appeared for his portrait were less than ideal, although they did provide her with a useful anecdote of his character:

> He came late in the afternoon to be photographed and as I had no studio only an ordinary room, though it had a skylight, I told him that it might not be a success, to which he replied "Is not the light of my countenance enough?"

The negative of the portrait is so underexposed that it is almost unprintable today, highlighting Miss Acland's skill as a maker of the lantern slides. The sixty-seven slides she exhibited during her Home Portraiture lecture, of which this is one, were specially prepared for the occasion as a coherent set on warm tone lantern plates. The attention she gave to the task reflected the view of many leading photographers that lantern slide making was an important art in its own right. In 1897, for example, the figurehead of the American pictorial movement Alfred Stieglitz offered prizes to the value of $65 at the Camera Club of New York "as an incentive to lantern slide making", while in 1903 the renowned architectural photographer Frederick Evans, who signed his own slides, promoted the practice in an article on "Artistic Photography in Lantern Slides" in the journal *Amateur Photographer*.

Miss Acland shared her birthday with Lord Kelvin: he was exactly twenty-five years her senior.

MS. Don. d. 14, fol. 31v; Ibid.; *Photographic Life*, vol. 1, no. 8 (24 March 1897), p. 173; *Amateur Photographer*, vol. 37, no. 959 (19 February 1903).

39. *"Lord Selborne"*

Roundell Palmer, Earl of Selborne (1812–1895)
Oxford, 13 August 1894

Half-plate negative
Bodleian Library, Minn negative 191/12

In describing this portrait, Miss Acland explained that Lord Selborne

> was a great friend of my Uncle, Sir Henry Cotton, one of the Lord Chief Justices of Appeal. Lord Selborne was educated at Rugby, Winchester and Christ Church. He was Lord Chancellor from 1868–1874 and again 1880–1885. He refrained from entering Mr. Gladstone's third government as he was against Home Rule in Ireland. He was a good Churchman writing often on Ecclesiastical subjects and also composed some hymns.

Selborne was a Tractarian, known for his piety, which no doubt made him especially welcome in the Acland house.

The uncle mentioned by Miss Acland, Henry Cotton (1821–1892), was one of four on her mother's side (her father had six brothers). The others were William Charles Cotton (1813–1879), Joseph Edward Cotton (1823–1842), and Arthur Benjamin Cotton (1832–1918). William was chaplain to Bishop Selwyn in New Zealand and a writer on bees; 'Teddie' died at 19; Arthur became the first vicar of St Paul's, Bow Common (a church in the East End of London endowed by his father), but according to his sister preferred photography to preaching.

Selborne's portrait is typical of Miss Acland's mature work. She adopts essentially the same approach as used from the outset of her photography, lighting the face more from one side than the other, but the range of contrast is much less severe than in her early portraiture. The effect was achieved by a setup very different from that found in the commercial studios of previous decades, and one that instead became characteristic of 'home portraiture' in the 1890s, codified in recommendations in treatises on the subject, including by Miss Acland in her lecture. Her advice to the would-be home portraitist was to choose a long room with two north-facing windows. The sitter should be placed opposite one window, the camera the other. The first provided the 'key' light (in modern terminology), the second a diffuse 'fill' across the whole subject. From this starting point precise control over the desired effect could be achieved by varying the position of sitter and camera, reducing the size of the windows with blinds or curtains, and arranging reflectors on the shadow side.

As a consequence of his office Selborne regularly sat for his portrait. However, Miss Acland's head study, made only a year before his death, outdoes any other likeness of him by a wide margin and is one of her finest works. The portrait gets behind his public face as one of the Great Officers of State to offer an insight into the inner character of the man: the purpose of pictorial portraiture as conceived by artist-photographers in the late nineteenth century.

MS. Don. d. 14, fol. 33v.

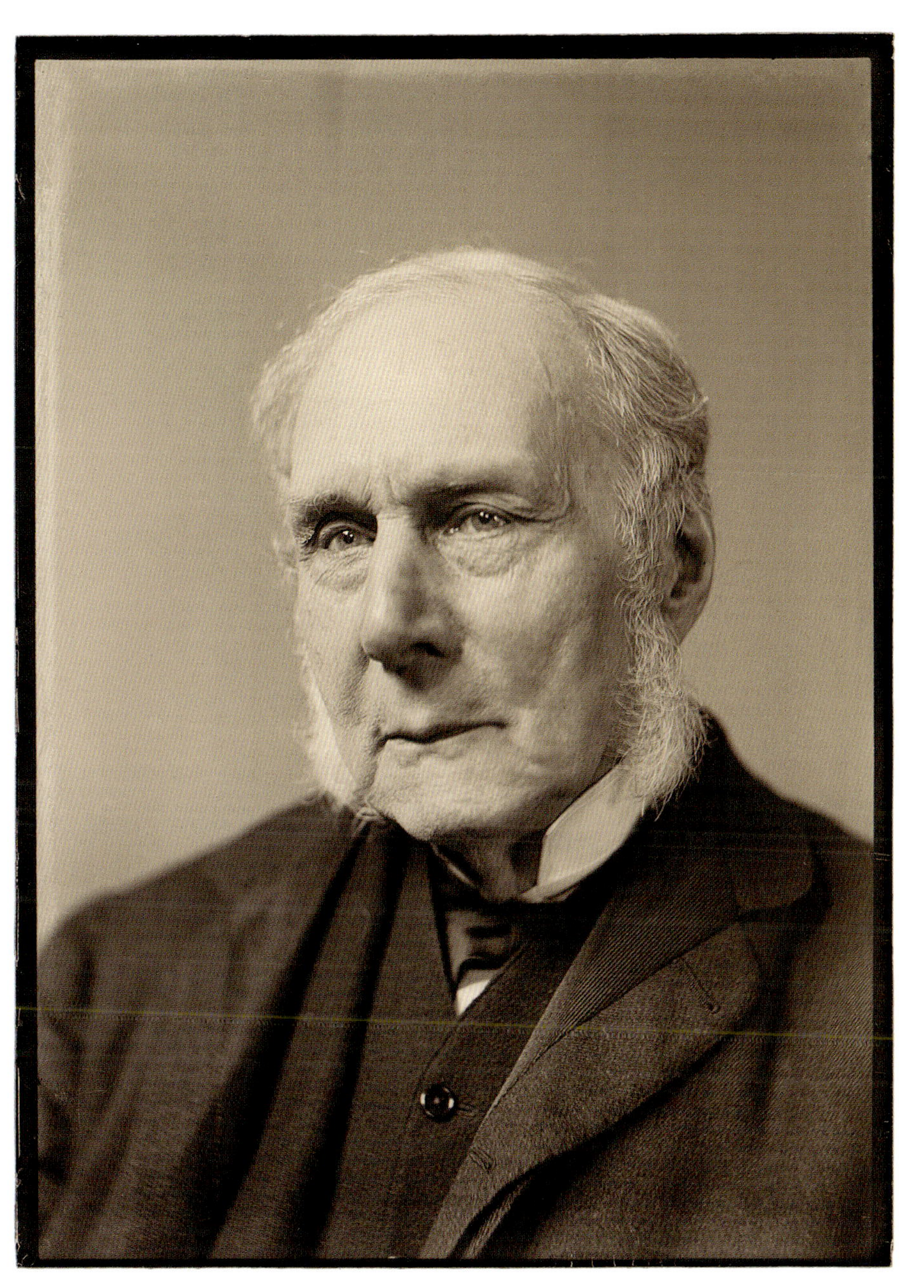

40. *"Mr. Pridgin Teale"*

Thomas Pridgin Teale (1831–1923)
Oxford, 15 August 1894
Half-plate negative
Bodleian Library, Minn negative 169/10

Thomas Pridgin Teale is described in his obituary in *The Times* as "A Great Surgeon and Sanitarian". He was educated at Winchester and Brasenose College, graduating in 1852 with a degree in Mathematics. He then proceeded to King's College, London, to study medicine, where he was later elected a fellow. Most of his professional life was spent as Lecturer in Surgery at the Leeds School of Medicine and as Surgeon to the Leeds General Infirmary, where he specialized in diseases of the eye.

Depicting her sitters with a book, letter or sometimes a photograph, was a tactic Miss Acland used effectively in many of her portraits. As well as giving purpose to the pose, the device helped to distract her subjects from their self-consciousness, as did the home surroundings in which the portraits were taken. According to received opinion, amateurs also had an advantage over professionals in rarely having a sitter they did not know well.

Miss Acland's opportunity to photograph Teale arose as a result of his long-standing professional ties to Oxford as one of the Medical Examiners, who were put up in the Acland house. His status as "an apostle of domestic sanitation at a time when the public gave little thought to drains, ventilation, and fogs" also gave him a passion shared with Acland.

Teale should not to be confused with his father, Thomas Pridgin Teale (1801–1867), also an eminent surgeon.

The Times, no. 43498 (14 November 1923), p. 10f.

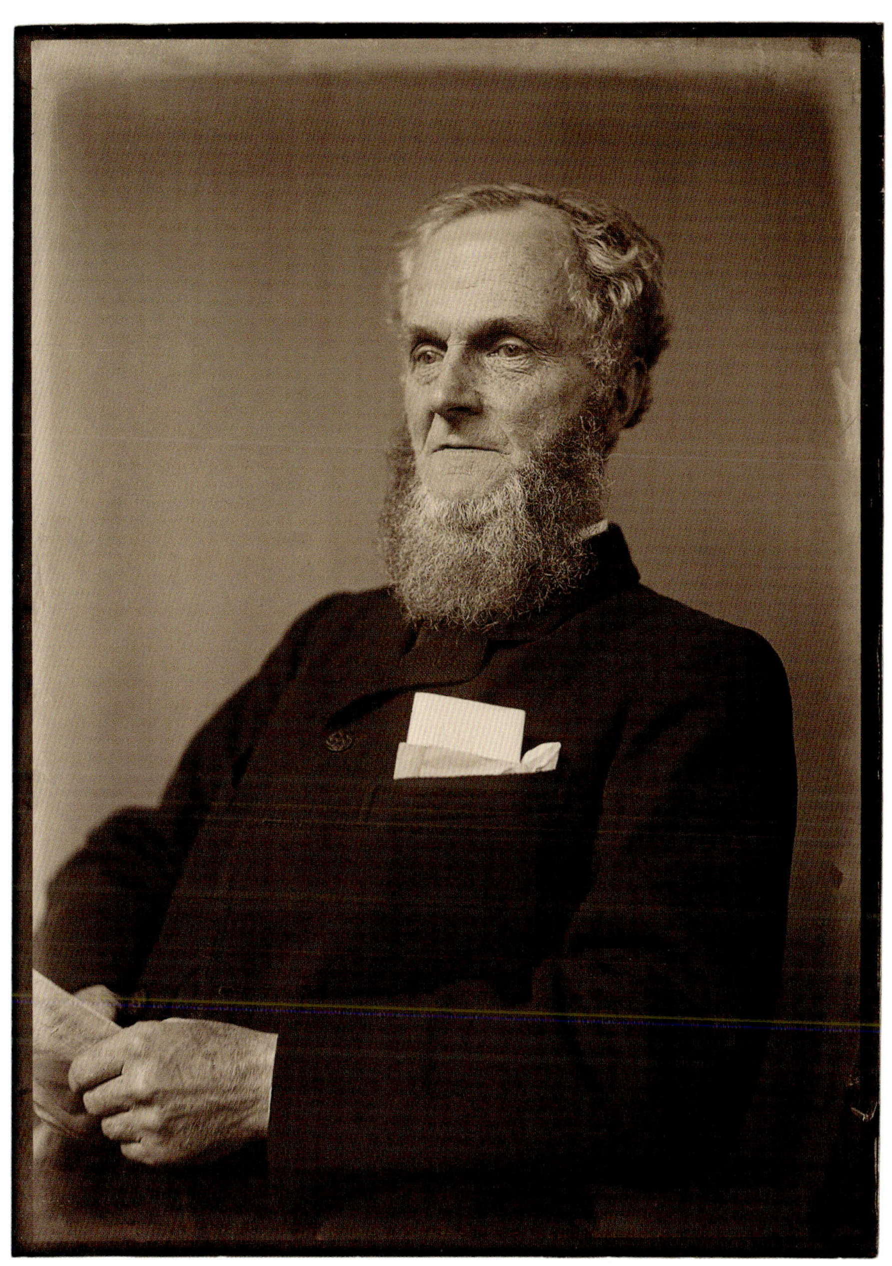

41. *"Miss M.A. Hope"*

Mary Agnes ('Maggie') Hope, afterwards Mrs Wilfred Brinton and Mrs Carl Wolf (b. *c.* 1872, d. after 1923)
Oxford, October 1894

Albumen print from half-plate negative
Bodleian Library, MS. Minn 226, fol. 28r

Maggie Hope was Miss Acland's god-daughter and one of her most frequent sitters, also featuring in a number of early Autochrome and Omnicolore plates. The circumstances of her birth remain a mystery. Miss Acland knew her as the ward of Agnes Cotton (1828–1899), her aunt. In 1865 Cotton founded the 'Home of the Good Shepherd' in Leytonstone, an industrial school for the training of girls (usually under the age of 13) rescued from prostitution and other vice. Maggie, however, lived apart from the others at the school, in Miss Cotton's own home. She appears in the 1891 census as a "musical student", her place of birth stated vaguely as "midland counties", suggesting she may have been an orphan. Her surname was also probably adopted.

On her death Cotton left Maggie the bulk of her personal effects and property. Two years later, on 15 May 1902, Maggie married the Christ Church graduate and barrister Wilfred Brinton (1855–1903). Wilfred was the son of William Brinton (1823–1867), physician and F.R.S., and Mary Brinton, née Danvers (1830–1891), the sister of Willie Acland's mother-in-law, Emily Smith, née Danvers, Viscountess Hambleden (1828–1913). He died on 19 April 1903, less than a year into the marriage, leaving an estate valued at £7,793 (about £650,000 at 2012 values). In 1911 Maggie married Carl Wolf, an Austrian or Swiss, and emigrated with him to Zurich.

Miss Acland's compositional approach in this portrait is unusual among her surviving œuvre — the camera placed behind her sitter — but highly effective in capturing the grace and beauty of Maggie as a young woman, pearls around her neck. Much of the mood of the image is created by the reduced contrast and relatively high tone compared to her other portraits. Maggie has a hint of melancholy in her eyes, perhaps an echo of the tragic circumstances of her childhood.

Census Returns of England and Wales, 1891, RG12/1347, fol. 41, p. 29.

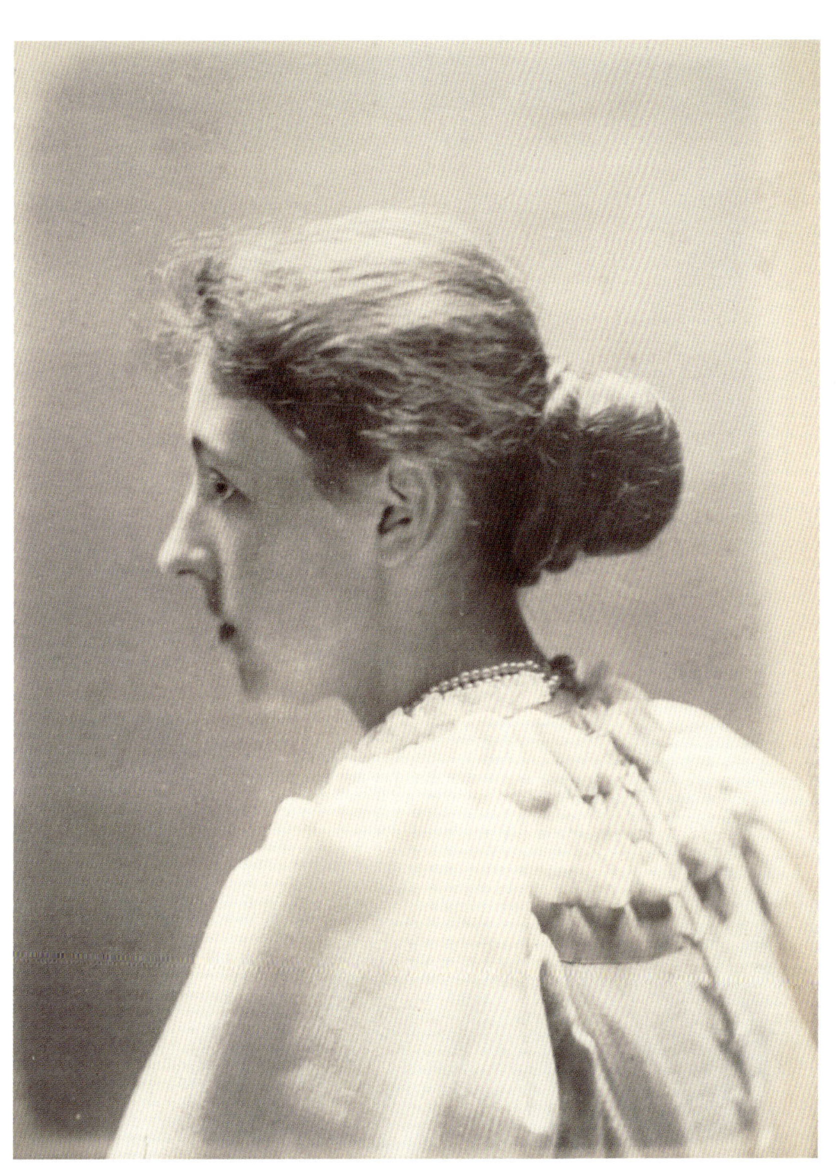

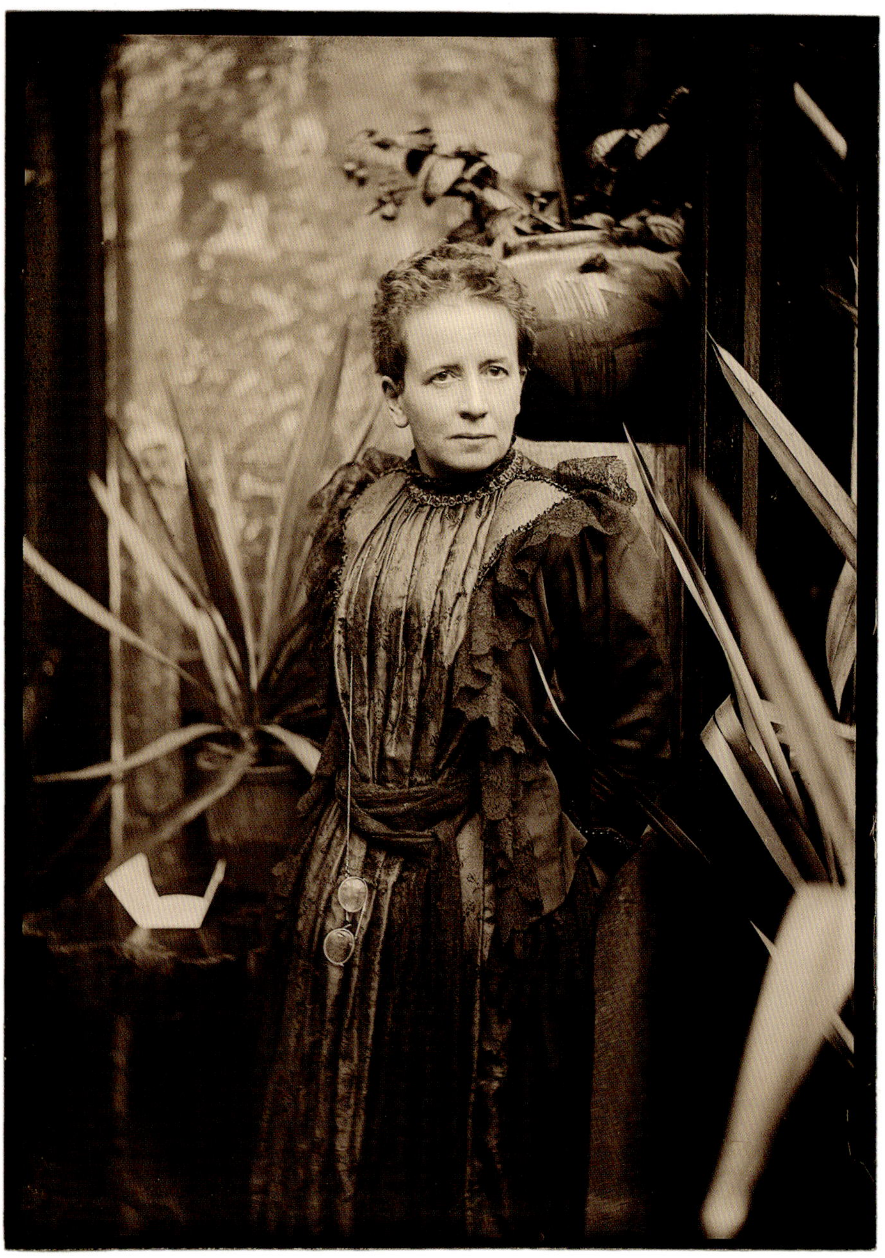

42. *"The Operator"*

Sarah Angelina Acland (1849–1930)
Oxford, October 1894

Half-plate negative
Bodleian Library, Minn negative 201/8

Miss Acland is aged 45 in this self-portrait. She is pictured in a loose-fitting tea-gown: a type of dress worn at home by more artistic women, enhanced here by the sash freely wrapped around her waist. Although invisible in monochrome, the colours of the pleated silk front, which is edged with lace, would have been bright and rich, as would her necklace of green scarab beetles set in gold. She has her hair cut short to show its natural wave and may also have taken the rational decision to dispense with a corset. Her striking appearance, at the height of her success as a portraitist, reflects the creative independence she gained through photography.

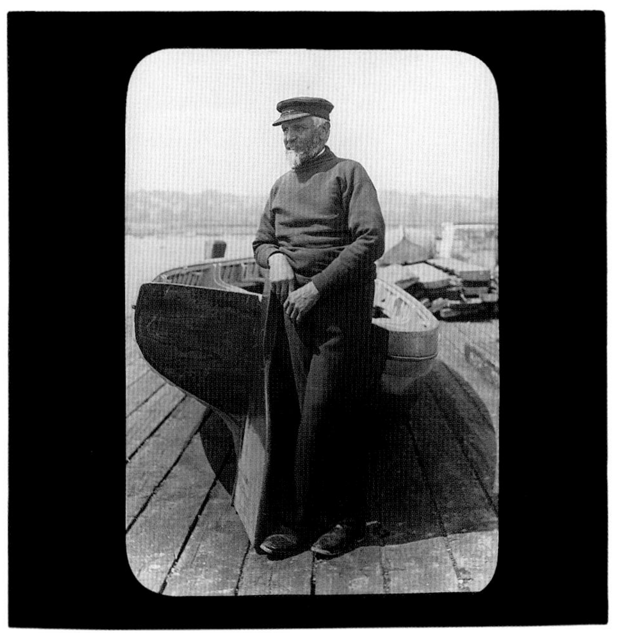

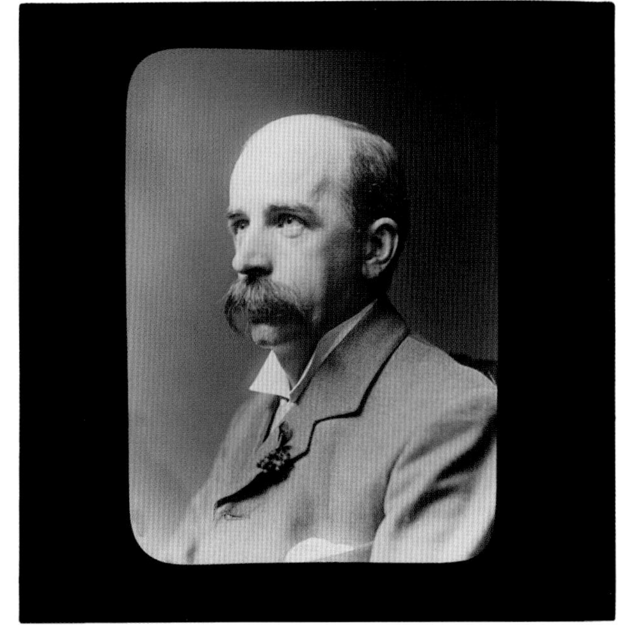

43. *"Theodore Brown"*

Theodore Furneux Brown (1838–1925)
Torquay, 1895?
Lantern slide
Museum of the History of Science, Inventory no. 28222

Theodore Brown was a boatman at Torquay. He lived at 1 Marine Cottages, Rock Walk Steps, just below Florence Villa on Warren Road, where Miss Acland sometimes stayed whilst overwintering in the seaside town for the benefit of her health.

Miss Acland exhibited this slide at her Home Portraiture lecture as evidence that "a better effect could sometimes be obtained by taking the sitter amidst his own surroundings, and at his usual occupation" — a strategy she also used to great effect in a number of other portraits of working men and women. The strong perspective in the boards of the quay and the boat suggest the photograph was taken with a more wide-angle lens than she used for formal portraiture, probably as supplied with one of her Kodak cameras. The result is refreshingly different in style from her studio portraits, having a great sense of place as well as personality, and of a man at one with his vocation.

Proceedings of the Oxford Camera Club, no. 1 (April 1899), p. 5.

44. *"Mr. John Barrow of Backworth"*

John Usher Barrow (1861–1915)
Oxford, August 1895
Lantern slide
Museum of the History of Science, Inventory no. 19698

John Barrow was an engine driver at the Murton Row colliery in Backworth, Northumberland. Backworth was home to a flourishing centre of the University Extension Movement, which aimed to bring higher education to adults of all classes. Lectures were organized in the village, which also had a 'Classical Novel Reading Union' and 'Literary Conversation Class'. Barrow visited Oxford for the Extension Summer School, where Miss Acland got to know and like him.

In 1892 a letter from Barrow describing the effect of the lectures on the men appeared in the *Official Organ of the American Society for the Extension of University Teaching*. "The Northumberland miners as a body are distinctly in advance of those of a similar class in other countries, in point of intelligence," he claimed, "and also, though not to the same extent, in moral character."

Depicting a sitter looking upwards was not something Miss Acland normally recommended. In the case of Barrow, however, it was "typical of the man".

Official Organ of the American Society for the Extension of University Teaching, vol. 1 (1891–92), p. 184; *Proceedings of the Oxford Camera Club*, no. 1 (April 1899), p. 5.

45. *"Dr. Magrath, Provost of Queen's College"*

John Richard Magrath (1839–1930)
Oxford, shortly before 10 September 1895

Half-plate negative
Bodleian Library, Minn negative 144/4

As an undergraduate in the 1850s Magrath had been a friend of Miss Acland's cousin Charles Thomas Dyke Acland (1842–1919) and "in those early days used to be a good deal in Broad St." He later served as Provost of Queen's College for more than half a century and as Vice Chancellor of the University from 1894 to 1898.

Miss Acland's study of Magrath is reminiscent of an iconic portrait of Ruskin by Frederick Hollyer, the "pose arranged by Holman Hunt". Ruskin's portrait was taken at Brantwood in September 1894, a year after Miss Acland visited, and was christened *Datur hora quieti* — "The hour is given for rest" — by his biographers Cook and Wedderburn. Hollyer and Hunt were undoubtedly aware of Miss Acland's work, Hunt being mentioned in *The Oxford Museum* where her portrait of Ruskin and her father was reproduced.

Hollyer and Hunt's portrait of Ruskin was exhibited to great acclaim at the Photographic Salon in October 1895. By this date, however, Miss Acland had probably already seen it. Shortly before 26 June 1895 Hunt and his wife Marion, née Waugh (1846–1931) visited Broad Street for tea, when Miss Acland presented them with a copy of her photogravure. After returning home Hunt dispatched a letter of thanks to Acland:

> Mrs Holman Hunt has not forgotten the light return which she has to make for Miss Acland's esteemed present of her photograph of Professor Ruskin and yourself. The order for the photograph decided upon has been given and I doubt not it will be here to send before many days.

The photograph decided upon was probably Hollyer's portrait of Ruskin. Miss Acland would therefore have seen it not only in advance of the general public, but also two months before her sitting with Magrath.

MS. Don. d. 14, fol. 28v; H.D. Rawnsley, "John Ruskin", *Outlook*, vol. 64, no. 9 (3 March 1900), pp. 511–18, p. 511; E.T. Cook and Alexander Wedderburn (eds.), *The Library Edition of the Works of John Ruskin* (39 vols, London, 1903–12), vol. 35, frontispiece; MS. Acland d. 71, fols. 22–3.

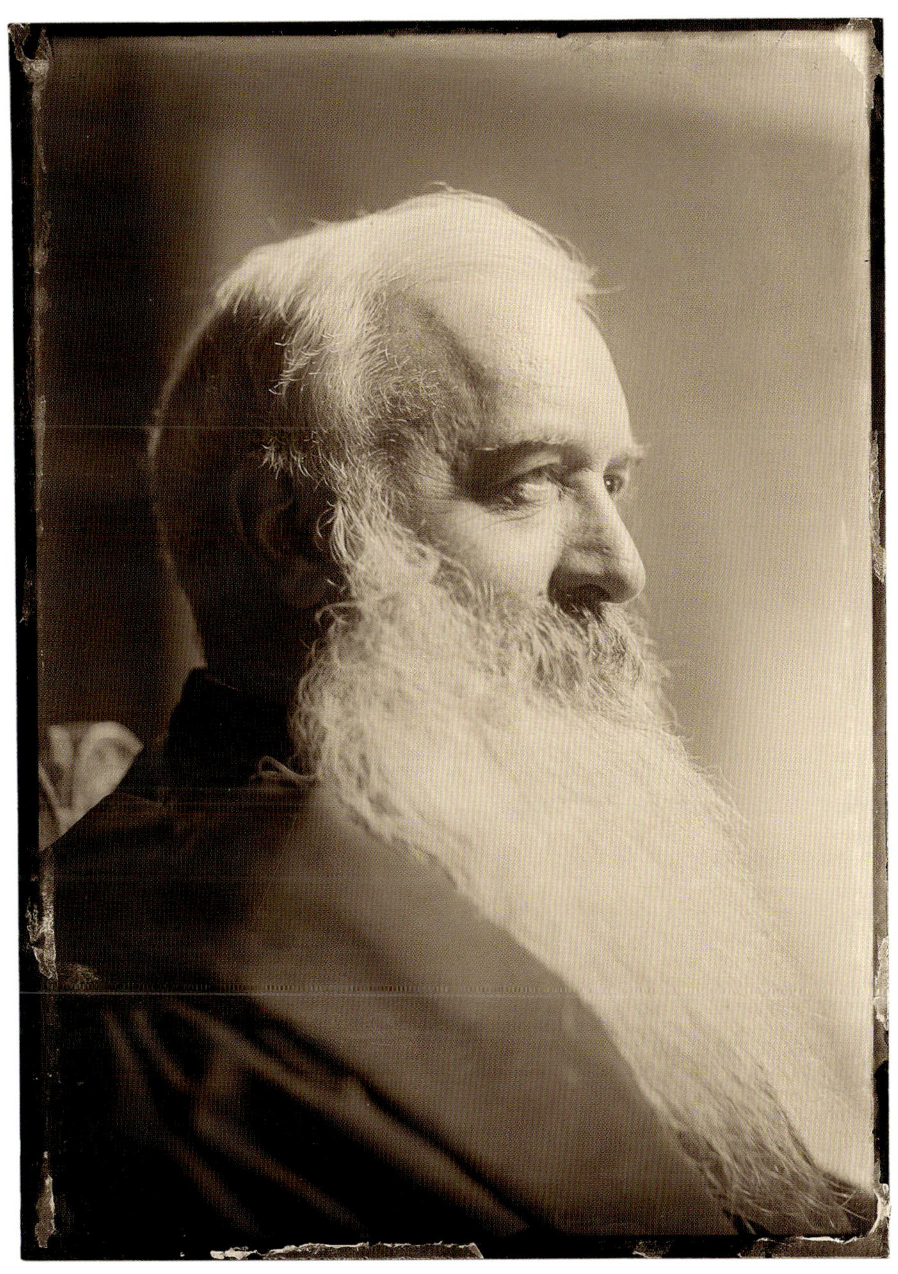

46. *"Superintendent Head"*

Charles Head (1840–1902)
Oxford, 23 September 1895

Albumen print from half-plate negative
Bodleian Library, MS. Minn 226, fol. 29r

Charles Head was the first Superintendent of the unified Oxford police force, created by the *Oxford Police Act, 1868*. Prior to 1869 "the Power of Watch and Ward" had been exercised by two separate forces: during the night as the responsibility of the "Chancellor, Masters and Scholars of the University of Oxford"; at day by the "Mayor, Aldermen and Citizens of the City Oxford" This created difficulties, not least because the University Police went off duty at 4 a.m. but the City Police did not come on until 6 a.m., "so that they did not communicate", as Miss Acland put it. After its creation the combined Constabulary Force of thirty-five men remained under the control of a joint Police Committee, with representatives from both City and University.

Head was described on his appointment as "a comparatively young man", with "every appearance of being 'smart' and 'shrewd'". According to the Constabulary records he had a "fair complexion, hazel eyes, brown hair, [and] proportionate figure". In Miss Acland's photograph he is wearing his police tunic, with its brass buttons and finely embroidered sleeves and collar, the latter partly obscured by his impressive side-whiskers, which extend all the way under his chin.

Miss Acland was a close friend of Head, who carried her in his arms to a waiting ambulance for transfer to London for an operation in 1898. She also kept on good terms with his successors, Chief Inspectors Oswald Cole (1861–1924) and Charles Richard Fox (1891–1972). Head died only a few years after retiring, due to erysipelas, which spread from an infection on his toe.

A surviving print of this portrait in the Oxfordshire History Centre is mounted on a cabinet card of Albert Jenkins (b. 1870) who practised as a photographer in Oxford in the 1890s and in Eynsham from 1900. The pinhole in the bottom right-hand corner reveals the negative was celluloid, the hole used to hang the film to dry. The original has since been destroyed.

31 & 32 Vict., c. lix; Devon Records Office, 1148M/7/1, p. 49; *Jackson's Oxford Journal*, no. 6036 (2 January 1869), p. 5d; Carol Richmond (comp.), *Oxford City Police Register, 1857–1904* (Witney, 2004), p. 19.

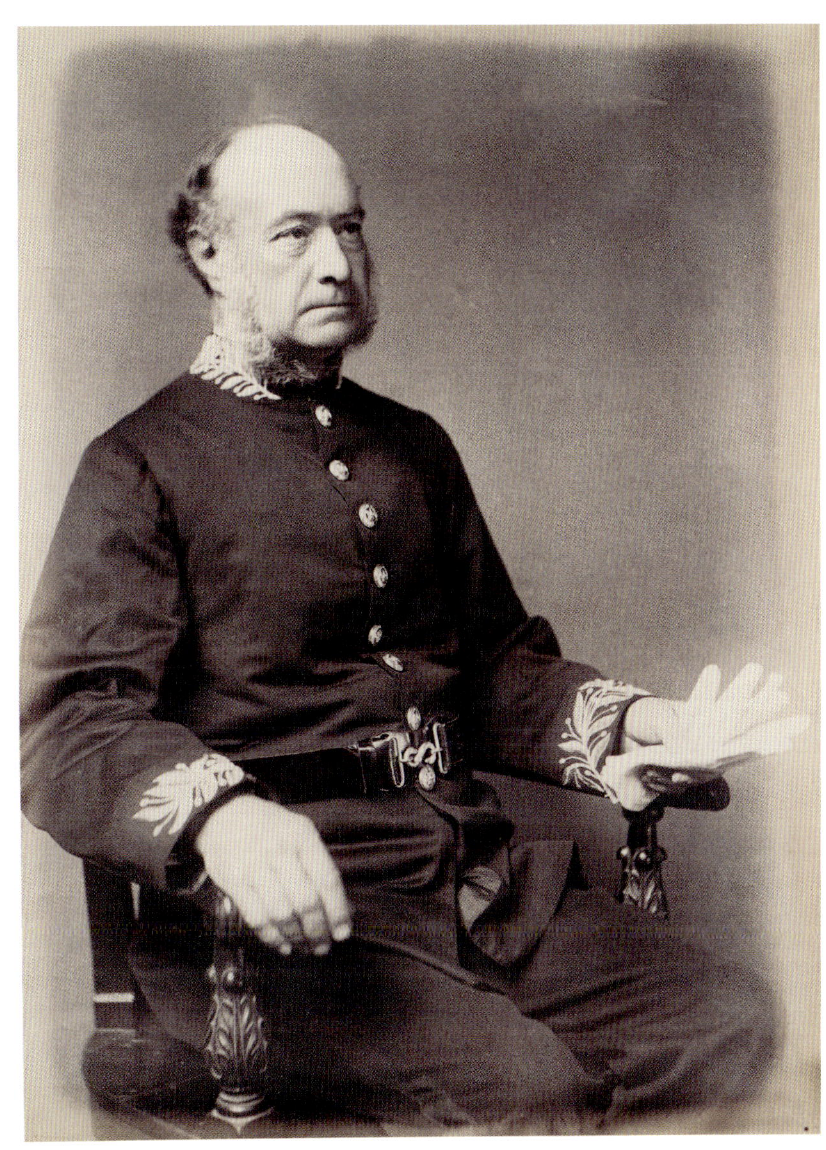

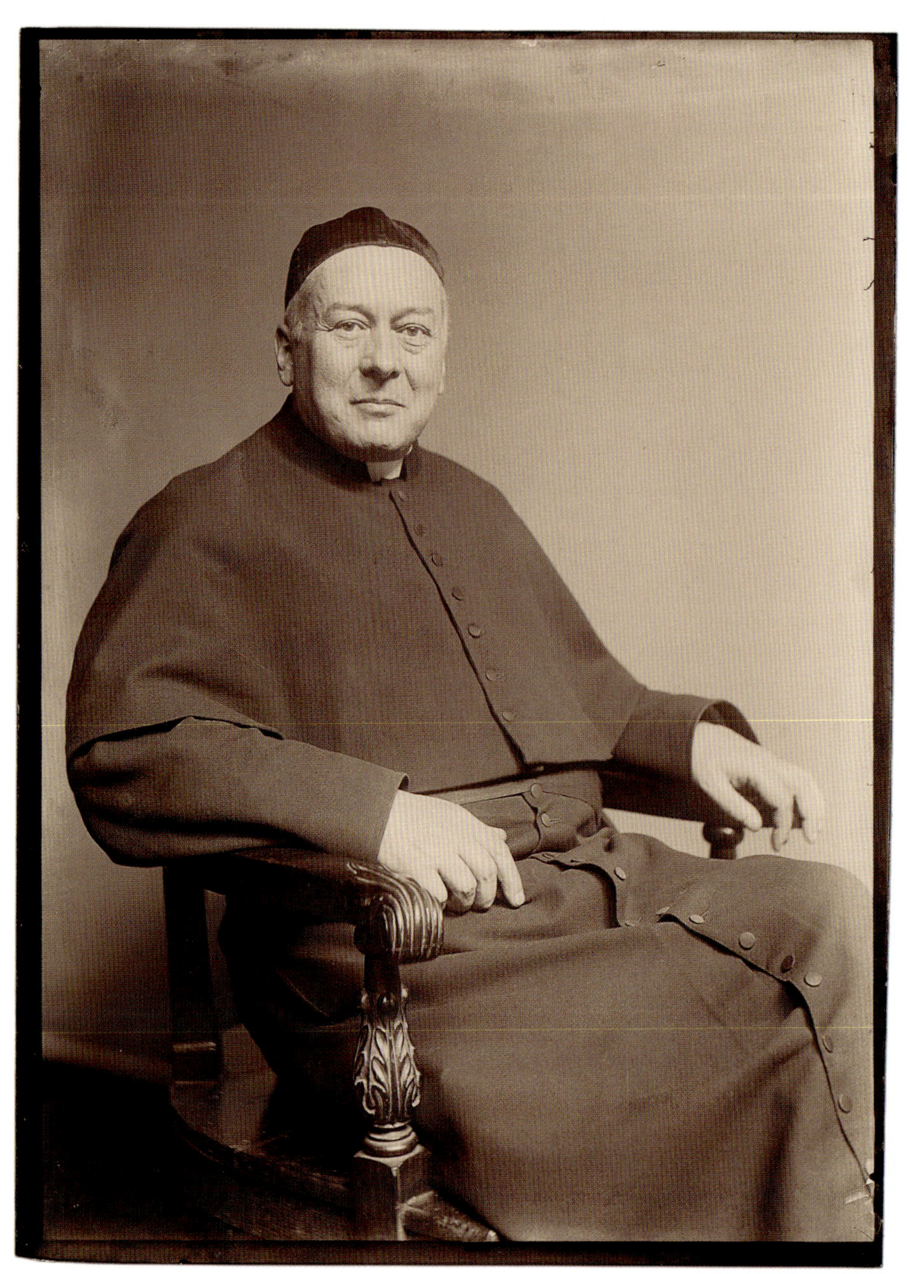

OPPOSITE

47. *"The Rev. Montague Henry Noel"*

Montague Henry Noel (1840–1929)
Oxford, *circa* 23 September 1895

Half-plate negative
Bodleian Library, Minn negative 183/10

'Father Noel' was the first vicar of St Barnabas, the Byzantine-revival church in Jericho, Oxford, endowed by Pre-Raphaelite patron Thomas Combe (1796–1872) and his wife Martha, née Edwards (1806–1893). He served as incumbent for thirty years, "greatly beloved and greatly missed when in 1899 he resigned the living". St Barnabas was the Anglo-Catholic bastion of Oxford, Noel's churchmanship reflected in his choice of cassock, shoulder cape and zucchetto-like cap.

Miss Acland worshipped in St Barnabas when not attending Holywell Church, St Mary Magdalen, or, on special occasions, the chapel at the Radcliffe Infirmary (also endowed by Combe). Her faith was fundamental to her outlook on life. She shared her High Church sympathies not only with her father, but with her extended family and many of her sitters. During her childhood she had been a favourite of Canon Pusey; on his death she was treated almost as a member of the family, attending his funeral with Edward Stuart Talbot (1844–1934), first Warden of Keble College. John Keble (1792–1866) himself held the living of Hursley, Hampshire, under the patronage of William Heathcote (1801–1881), father of Miss Acland's great friends Helena Mary ('Ellie') (1853–1925) and Beatrice Henrietta ('Be') Heathcote (1856–1909) (Ellie was his god-daughter). Miss Acland's most cherished clerical friend was John Henry Newman (1801–1890), whom she entertained to tea in 1880 and sent a birthday card to every year thereafter.

Visible in the left-hand corner of this portrait is the bottom of the "roller back-ground of woollen material and slate colour" Miss Acland used for many of her portraits. This could be made to appear anything from white to black, depending on the lighting. Here she has deliberately placed it at an angle to achieve a graded effect.

Miss Acland was related to Noel through his aunt, Louisa Elizabeth Hoare, née Noel (1786–1816), wife of William Henry Hoare (1776–1819), her grandmother's brother.

MS. Don. d. 14, fol. 45v; *Proceedings of the Oxford Camera Club*, no. 1 (April 1899), p. 4.

OVERLEAF

48 & 49. *"An Old Friend"*

Domenico Guastelli (1815–1902)
Oxford, 1 October 1895

Half-plate negatives
Bodleian Library, Minn negatives 183/8 & 183/9

In April 1878 Mrs Acland wrote to Angie with news of her father's sculptures:

> Rather to Papas horror, I had the very dirty casts taken down out of the dining room and put into the Mess room, in hopes of being allowed to clean them somehow. In order to save them from worse, Papa brought in the Italian, that tall man who sells images in the Streets, and they have come out lovely to behold. It is a relief not having to look upon their smutty noses. I hope that Undine is going to be done also.

Domenico Guastelli is listed in the 1891 census (under the enumerator's Anglicization of his name, "Dominico Whatsley") as a "Maker of plaster statues", aged 75. He was born in Tuscany but had married Eliza, née Sumner (1826–1895) in Bath in 1847, and had a daughter or granddaughter, also Eliza, aged 8. In 1891 the family was living in a house on Marlborough Road in Oxford.

Guastelli's striking physiognomy made him an excellent subject for photography, his head study proving to be one of Miss Acland's most memorable portraits. In the three-quarter length she portrays him with his casts, her œuvre thus spanning the whole breadth of the Victorian art market, from the high society portraiture of Millais to the merchandise of a street hawker.

MS. Acland d. 142, fols 160–2; *Census Returns of England and Wales, 1891*, RG12/1167, fol. 55, p. 18.

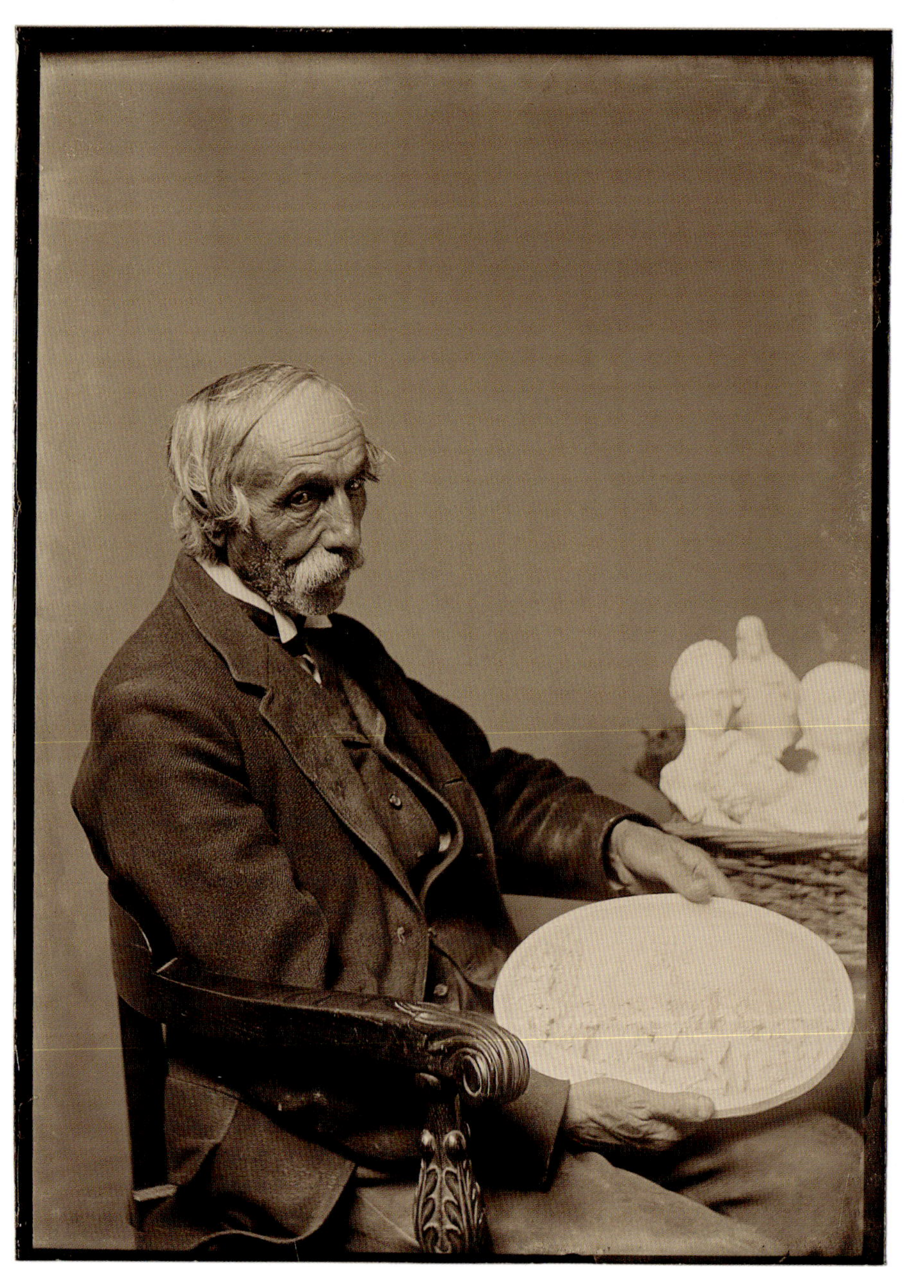

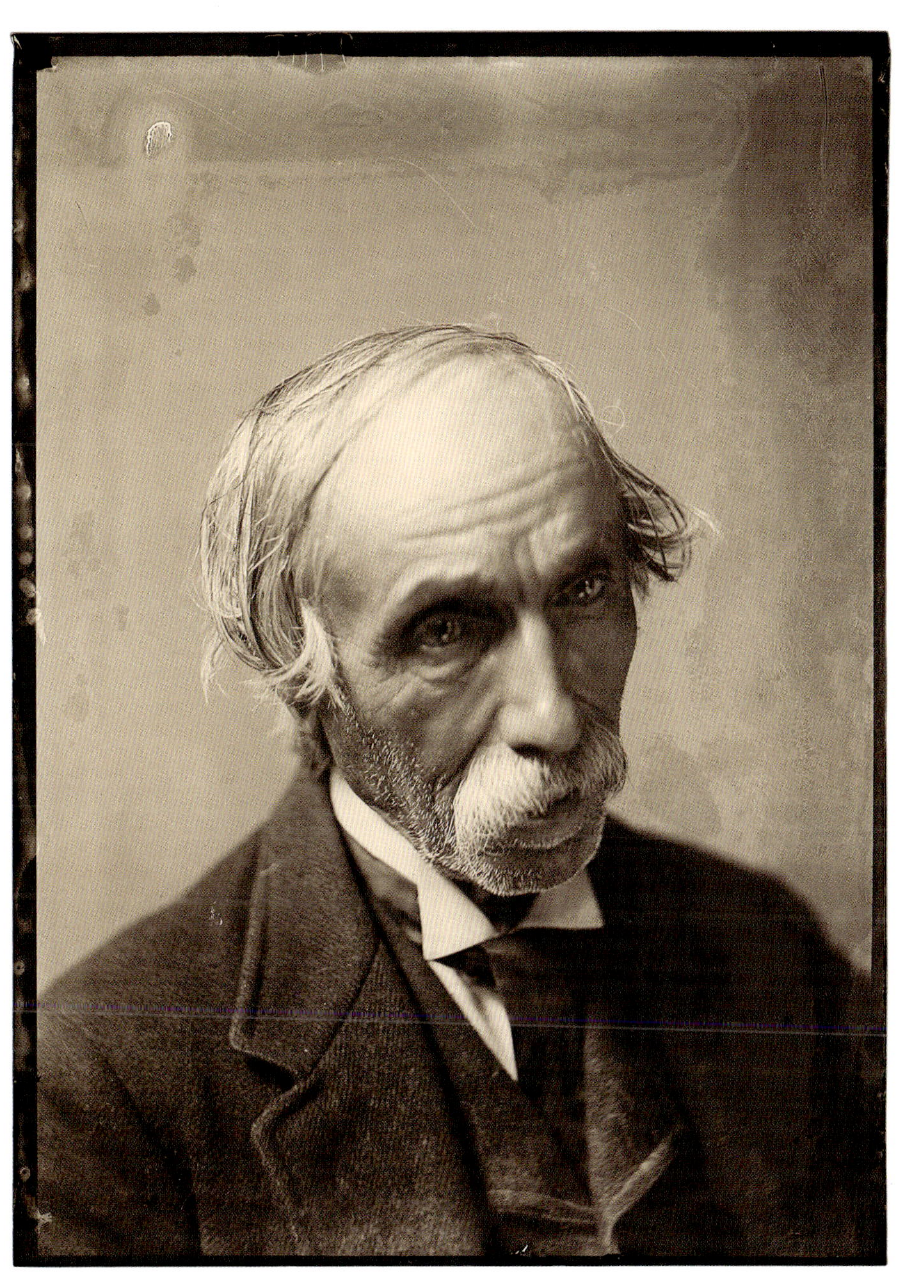

50. *"Miss Denniston"*

Gertrude Jane Denniston (1846–1920), standing by the Mess-room fireplace, 39–41 Broad Street
Oxford, 4 October 1895

Half-plate negative
Bodleian Library, Minn negative 92/7

Gertrude Denniston was the Lady Superintendent of the Sarah Acland District Nurses and the Acland Nursing Home. Born in Durham, the daughter of shipowner John Denniston, she was appointed to the Home in 1883 from the Royal Infirmary, Liverpool. She retired in 1902, but stayed on with the nurses until September 1904.

Miss Denniston was Miss Acland's closest friend in Oxford outside her own household. On her death in July 1920 Miss Acland composed a tribute to her for the *Oxford Times*, writing of how "her gracious presence and charm of manner endeared her to all with whom she came in contact ... including many of the poor who had cause to be grateful to her." These qualities are clearly communicated by the portrait.

The fantastic zoomorphic chimney-piece in the Mess room was carved by James O'Shea, mason on the University Museum. Inscribed on the mantel was a statement of the principle that ruled the lives of the Acland family: 'There is no place like home.'

In one of her albums Miss Acland dates this portrait 4 October 1895. Perplexingly, the calendar on the shelf in the background is set to 20 July, but the ashes in the grate and the hint of a flame point to the autumn date.

Oxford Times, no. 3088 (23 July 1920), p. 6c.

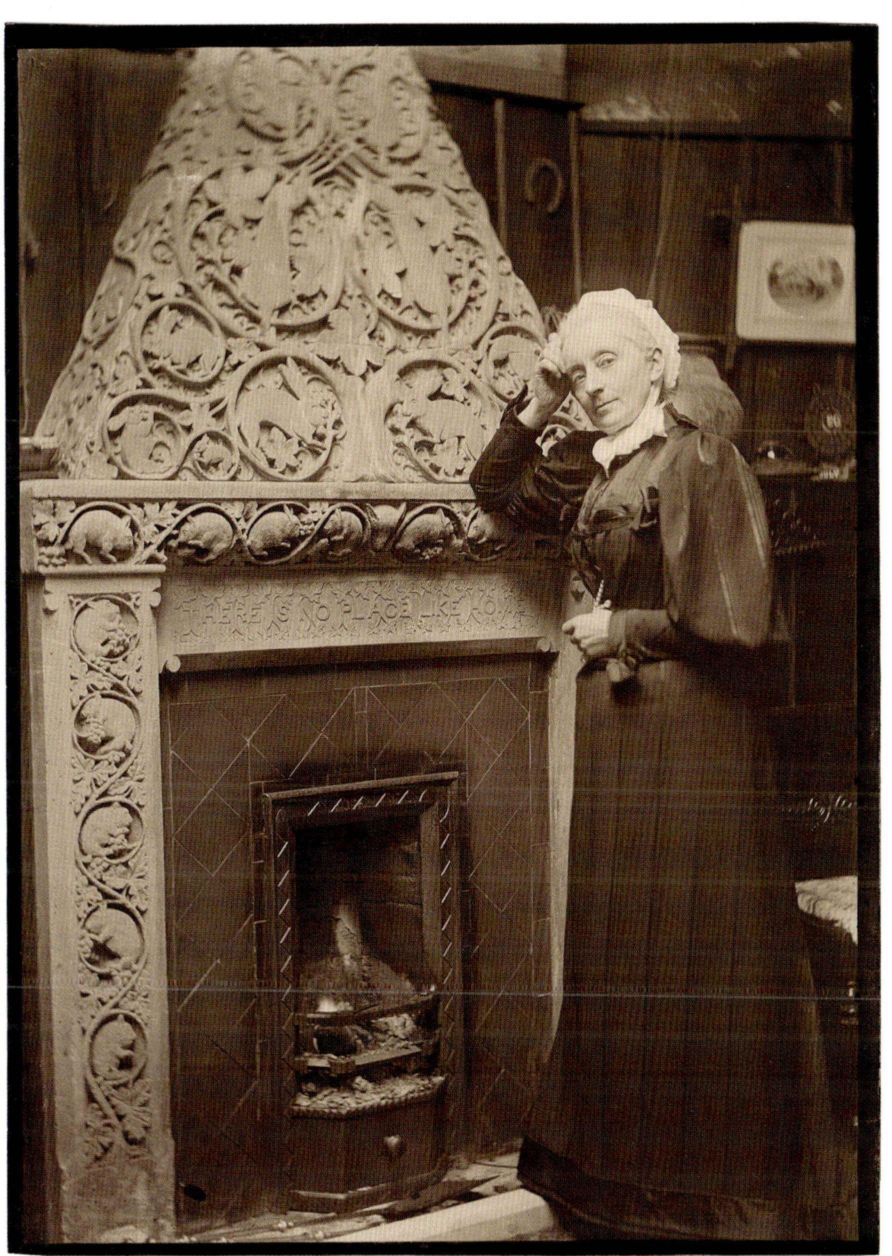
THERE IS NO PLACE LIKE HOME

51. *"Miss Eleanor Smith"*

Eleanor Elizabeth Smith (1822–1896)
Oxford, November 1895 ?

Half-plate negative
Bodleian Library, Minn negative 183/1

Four days after her death on 15 September 1896 a notice, written anonymously by Miss Acland, appeared in the *Oxford Chronicle* celebrating the life of 'Miss Smith of Oxford', or Aunt Ellen, as she was known to the family:

> In Miss Smith's death Oxford has lost a great personality, and her place can never be filled. She was one of Oxford's most splendid and distinguished daughters. … There was probably no one who had a greater number of friends in Oxford, both in the University and the City, and amongst rich and poor alike. Few persons could be less well spared.

Her loss was certainly keenly felt by the early photographer Nevil Story Maskelyne, who wrote to Miss Acland from Basset Down on 16 September to thank her for informing him so promptly

> of the passing away of perhaps the greatest woman I have ever known as well as of a friend so long so dear to me and all my family that I cannot trust myself yet to give my thoughts scope as they arise in me.

Another notable Oxford personality to correspond was Emilia Frances, Lady Dilke (1840–1904), who, unable to attend the funeral, asked Miss Acland to arrange a wreath "as beautiful as it can be made".

Miss Smith was born in Dublin on 30 September 1822. Her father, a barrister, died in 1828, after which she moved to England, settling in Oxford in 1840. On her mother's death she took charge of the house of her brother, Henry John Stephen Smith (1826–1883), Savilian Professor of Geometry after Baden Powell and Keeper of the University Museum in succession to John Phillips (1800–1874) (an appointment he owed to Acland and which sent Miss Smith into "a state of elastic ecstasy", according to Mrs Acland). The two principal causes to which she devoted her life were the education of women and the health of the poor. She was a powerful force on the management committee of Bedford College, London, for example, on which she sat with Maskelyne and Miss Acland's photographer cousin, Arthur Herbert Dyke Acland, Vice-President of the Committee of Council on Education. In Oxford she was the first woman on the School Board and a founder member of the council of Somerville College. For seven years before the Acland Home came into being she funded a district nurse out of her own pocket. This naturally made her an ally of Acland, as did her place on the committee of the Radcliffe Infirmary.

When not looking after the Acland children, Miss Smith could often be found in the company of Mrs Acland, Mrs Liddell, Mrs Combe and Felicia Skene (1821–1899), who together were the moving forces of female philanthropy in Oxford. At Ruskin's inaugural lecture, for example, Mrs Acland, Mrs Liddell and Miss Smith sat together on the steps of a crowded Sheldonian Theatre. After Mrs Acland's death Miss Smith remained a counsellor and confidant to Miss Acland and her father. She was an "adventurous person", according to Acland, often travelling abroad to such exotic places as the "wilds of Brittany". Mrs Acland was also impressed by her daring, in 1877 commenting to Angie that "her intention is to visit all the remarkable places of Spain. Is it not a spirited idea?"

In the nineteenth century older women invariably wore a cap indoors. Miss Smith's has a velvet base and is decorated with 'white work' embroidery flounces and beads.

The quality of this portrait speaks for itself, the only blemish the residue of retouching fluid around Miss Smith's face left by Minn when printing the negative for Miss Acland's presentation albums in 1928. Miss Acland was particularly pleased with the lighting, which was "soft and tender", as befitted a lady. The portrait was reproduced in Miss Smith's obituary in the *Queen*.

Oxford Chronicle, no. 3185 (19 September 1896), p. 8c; MS. Acland d. 167, fols. 48–9; Ibid., fol. 26; MS. Acland d. 19, fol. 19; MS. Acland d. 138, fol. 14; Ibid.; MS. Acland d. 142, fols. 60–62; *Proceedings of the Oxford Camera Club*, no. 1 (April 1899), p. 4.

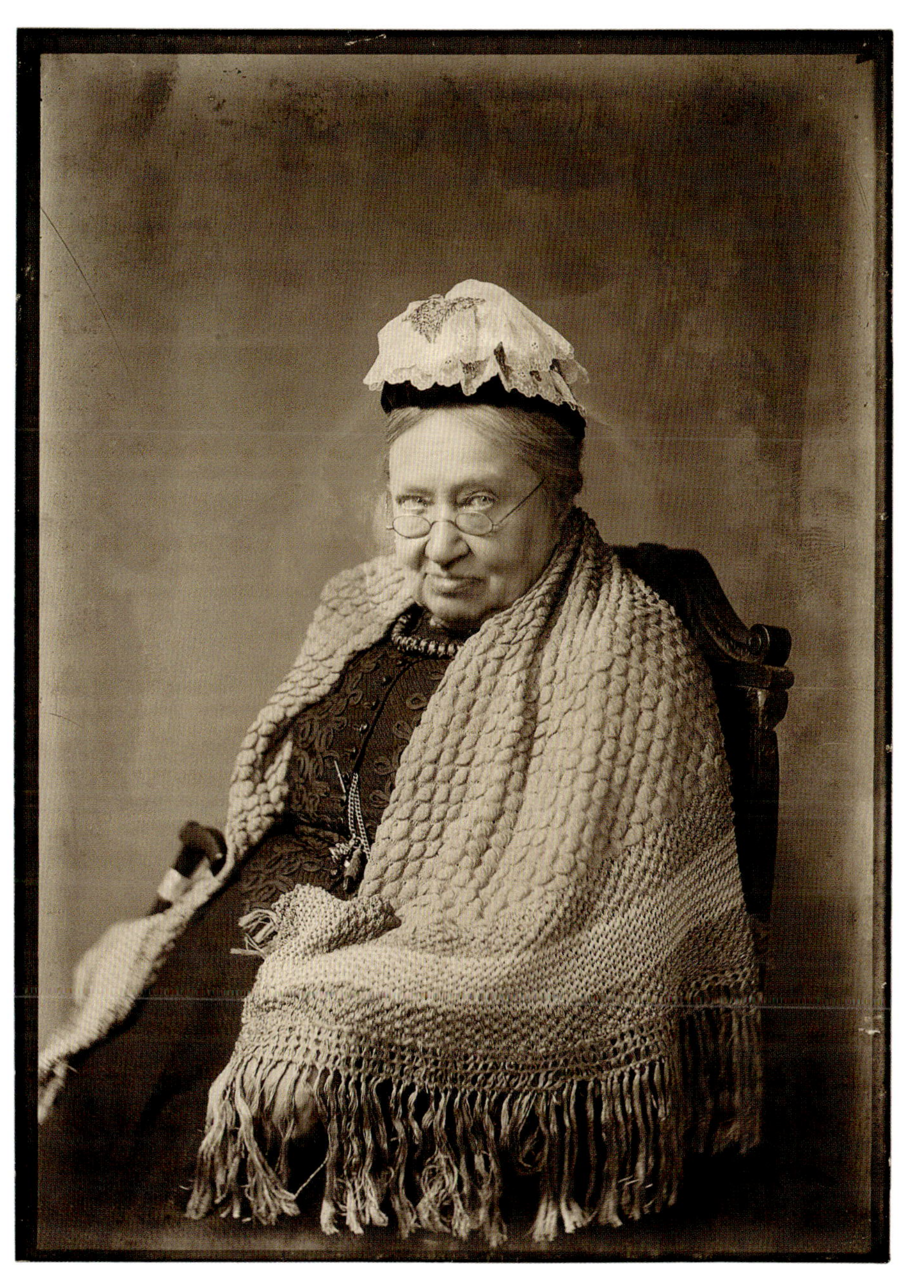

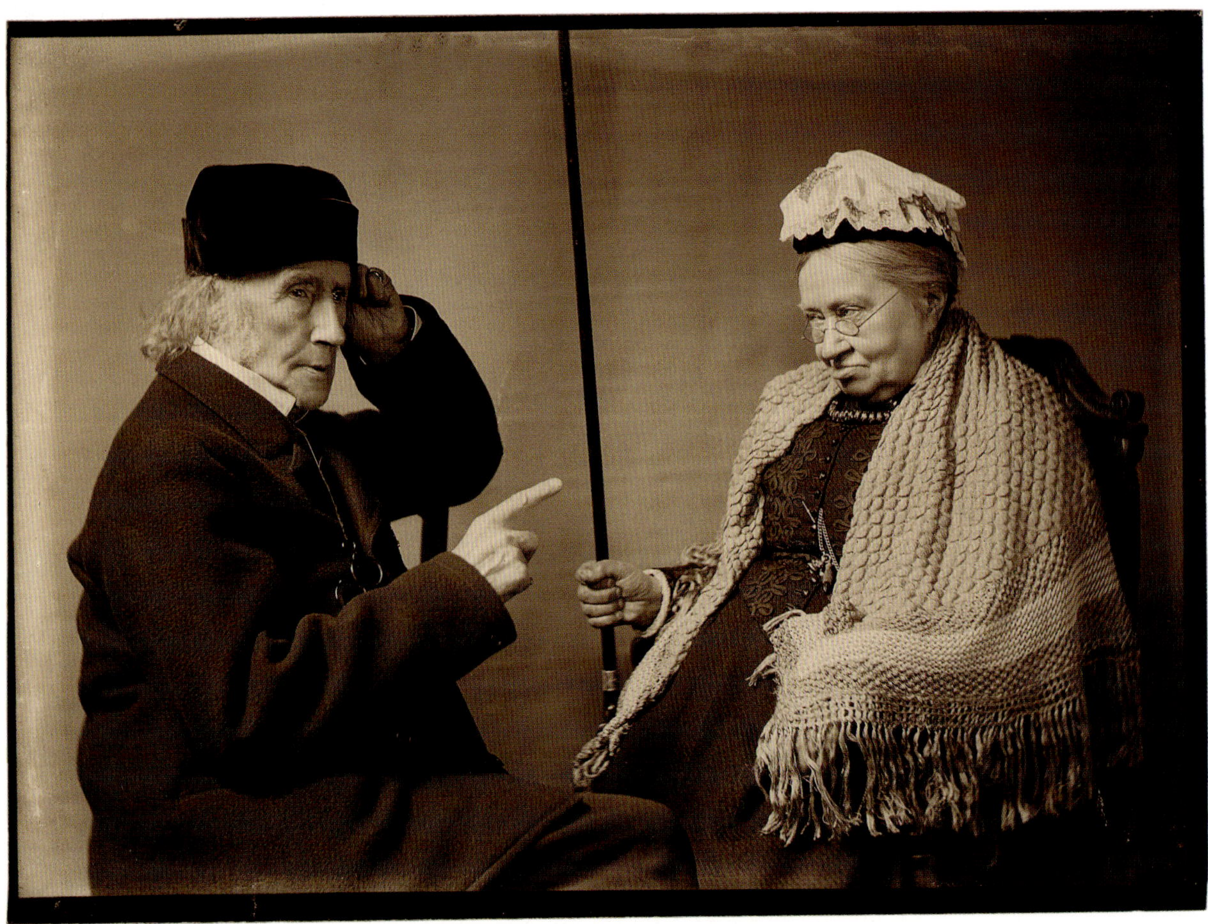

52. *"Sir Henry Acland & Miss Smith"*

Henry Wentworth Acland (1815–1900) and Eleanor Elizabeth Smith (1822–1896)
Oxford, November 1895 ?

Half-plate negative
Bodleian Library, Minn negative 202/6

Miss Acland's surviving photographs include a number of unusual studies of her father "in conversation with various old friends of note". Conversation pieces can be found from the earliest days of photography, but rarely are two sitters depicted with so much character as here. Miss Acland claimed the scene was typical:

> Miss Smith had supper with us on Sunday evenings and she and my Father used to have great discourses. One night my Father asked her whether she read Thomas à Kempis each day. Dr. Liddon's edition had just come out. Yes she answered but I never read it in English but of course in the original Latin. 'Oh I am not up to that' my Father exclaimed, to which Miss Smith said 'And may I ask my dear Sir what is the use of an University Education?' When she died she left him a small legacy and her Latin Thomas à Kempis.

Proceedings of the Oxford Camera Club, no. 1 (April 1899), p. 5a; MS. Don. d. 14, fol. 37v.

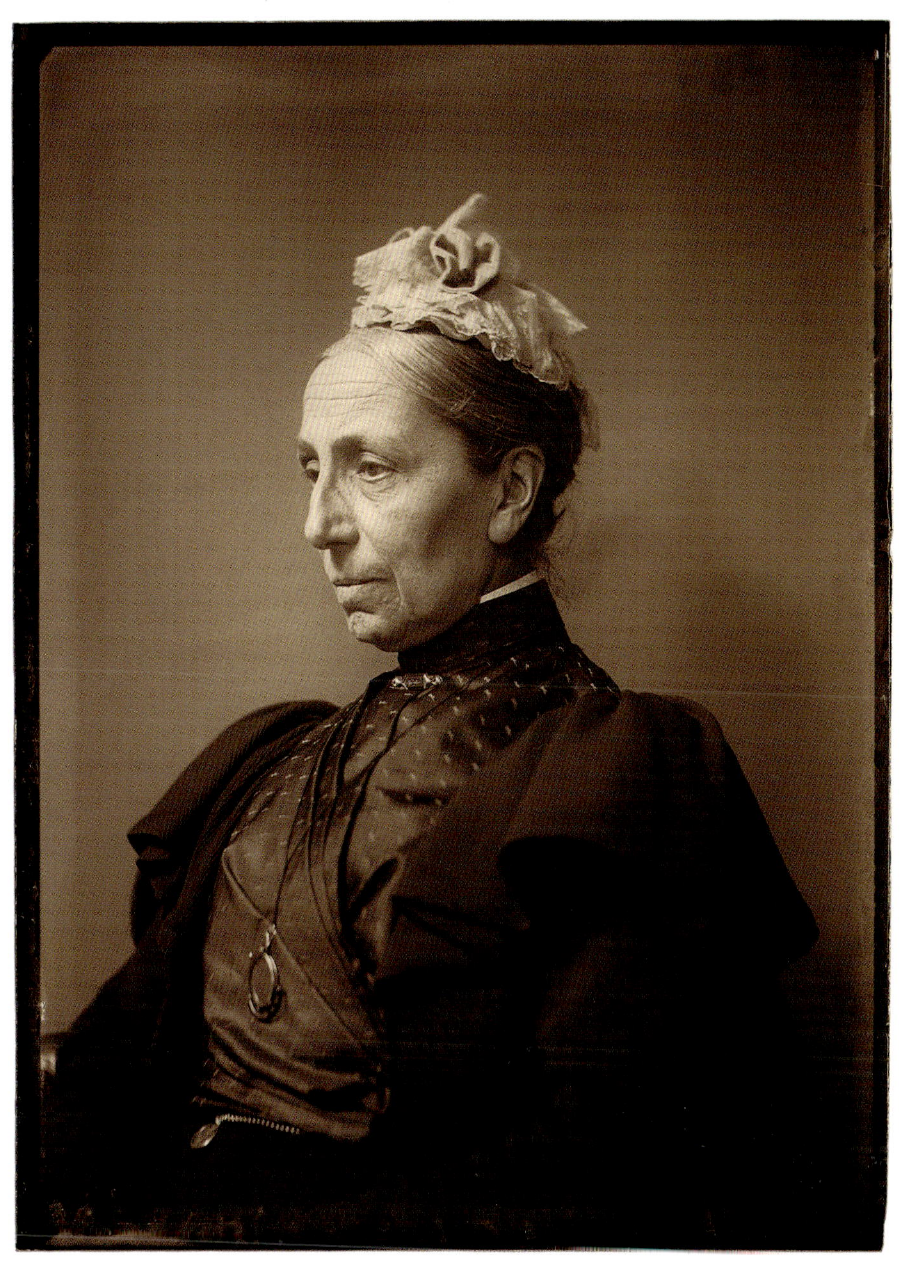

53. *"Miss Harriet Martin"*

Harriet Martin (1830–1899)
Oxford, May 1896 ?

Half-plate negative
Bodleian Library, Minn negative 183/5

'Mi Mar' was the Aclands' third governess, joining the family in February 1859 when Miss Acland was nine. She stayed only until autumn 1862, leaving when Angie went away to school at Killerton, but remained an honorary member of the household for much longer. The daughter of a surgeon, "she had had to go out & earn her living because the gentleman, a clergyman, had died to whom she was engaged to be married". From 1871 to 1893 she was employed as the Lady Resident of Bedford College, a post obtained through Miss Smith.

MS. Acland d. 111, fols. 105–6.

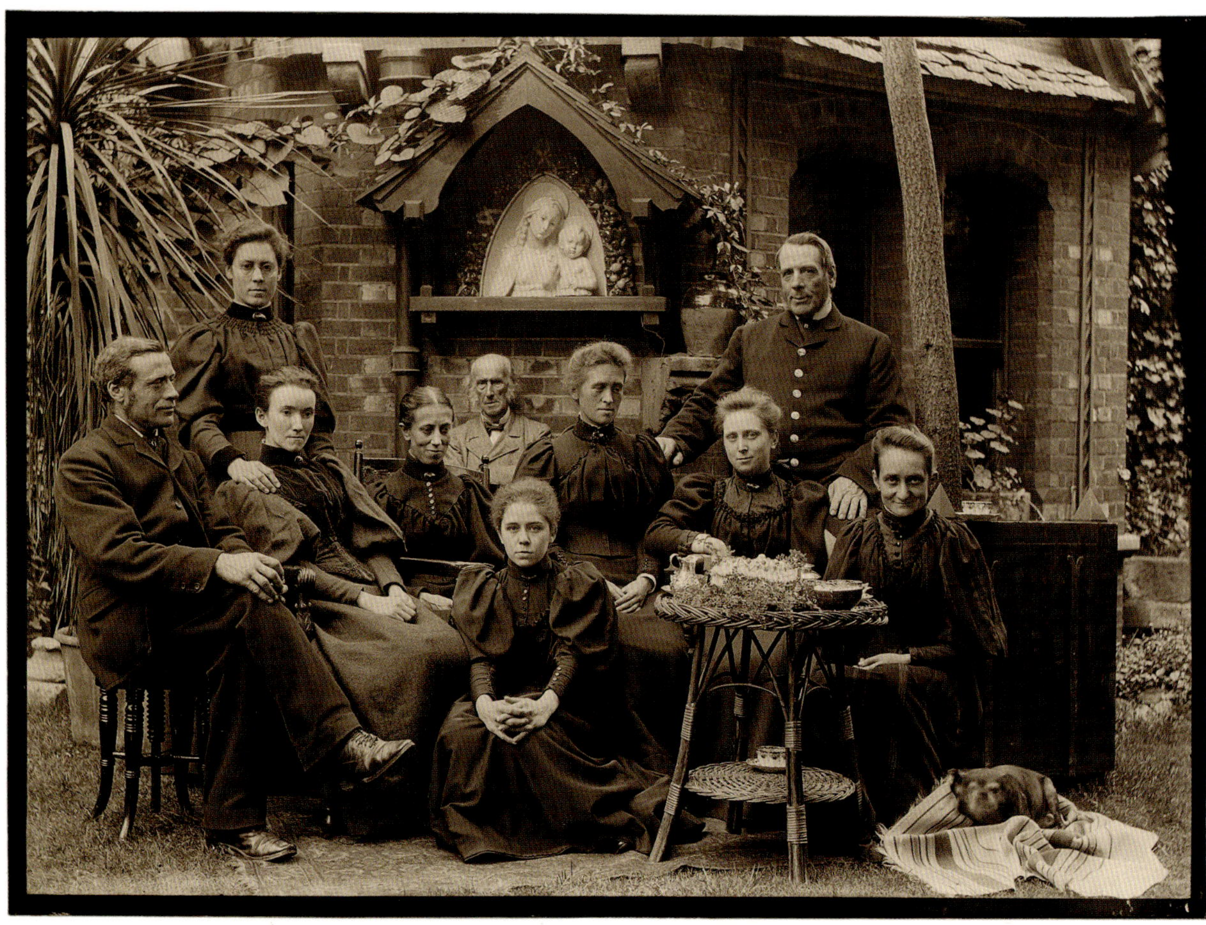

ABOVE & OPPOSITE

54 & 55. *The Acland Household*

Henry Wentworth Acland (1815–1900) and his servants in the garden of 39–41 Broad Street
Oxford, June 1896?

Half-plate negatives
Bodleian Library, Minn negatives 177/1 & 177/2

By the 1890s the Acland household had reduced in size but was still relatively large, especially since Miss Acland and her father were the only members of the family living at home. The servants depicted above are, from left to right: Acland's butler (identity unknown); his nurse Margaret Annie Pappin (1870–1912); an unknown maid; housemaid Fanny Baxter (b. 1852/3); an unknown maid, possibly Alice Cherry; parlourmaids Emma Minall (1863–1940) and Ellen Wicks (b. 1873); the Aclands' coachman George Greening; and Caroline Lawrence (1855–1930), Miss Acland's nurse. The dog is Miss Acland's pug Bogie (d. before 1897). Acland looks gaunt, but has not yet grown the beard seen in later portraits. Although hard to make out in the reproduction, several of the aprons the servants are wearing in the second photograph are exceptionally finely embroidered.

Group portraits are among the most difficult subjects in photography, but in these examples Miss Acland has achieved a harmonious balance of figures, marred only by Bogie's fidgeting. The *Virgin and Child* by Luca della Robbia watching over the household was a gift from Ruskin in 1877 and became the subject of one of Miss Acland's earliest colour photographs (cat. no. 126).

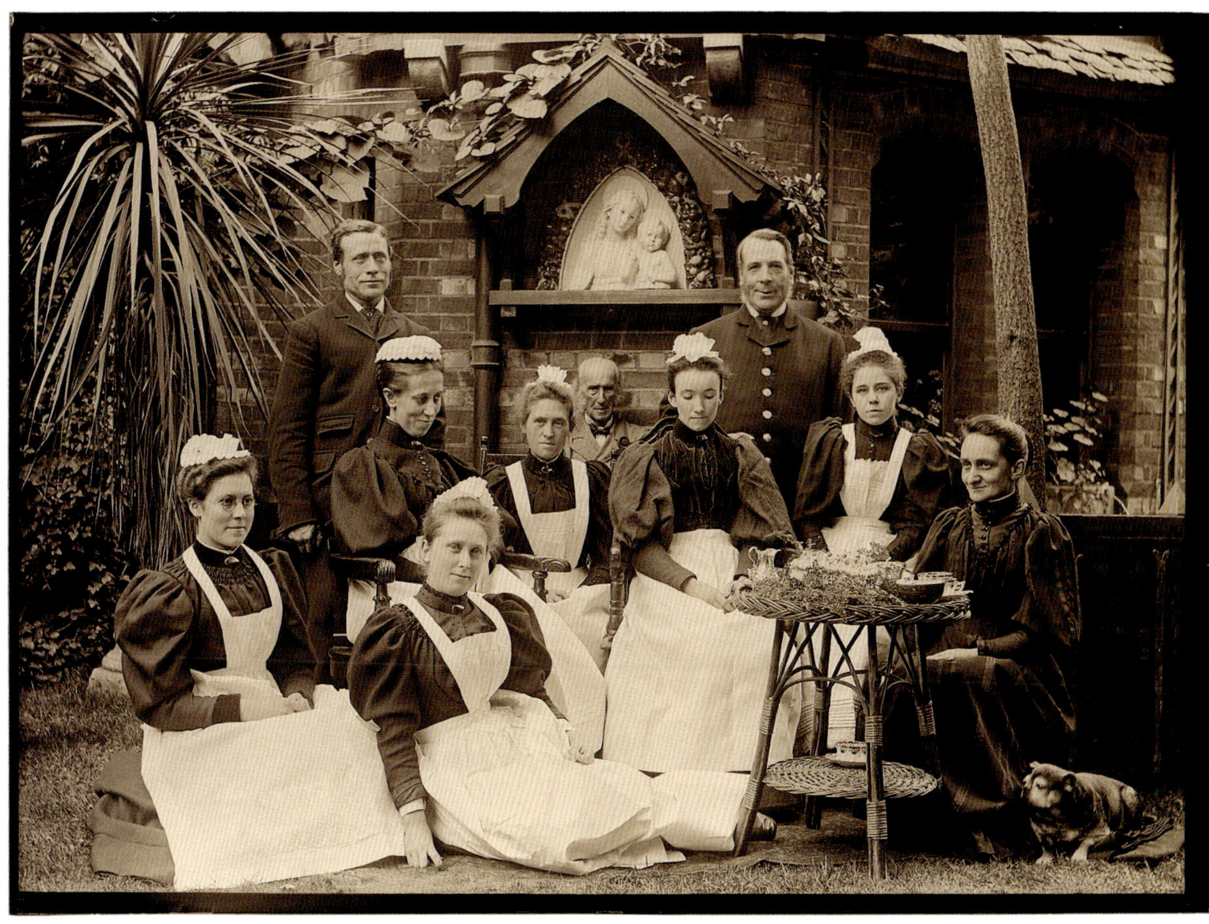

OVERLEAF

56. *"Sir Henry Acland, Bart., M.D., K.C.B."*

Henry Wentworth Acland (1815–1900), in gown and habit
Oxford, June 1896 ?

Half-plate negative
Bodleian Library, Minn negative 176/9

Acland is wearing a laced black doctoral gown, convocation habit, and hood in this portrait. The habit is scarlet, but looks darker than it should due to the insensitivity of the ordinary (non-orthochromatic) plate to red light. In a portrait published in *Black & White* in November 1896 he is seen in the same gown, but without the habit. The author of the accompanying article described him as "a fair-haired, distinguished looking man, with a highly intellectual cast of countenance" and listed his many qualifications: fellow of All Souls, Regius Professor of Medicine, Radcliffe Librarian, Curator of the University Galleries, President of the General Medical Council, etc.

Black & White, vol. 12, no. 302 (14 November 1896), p. 627.

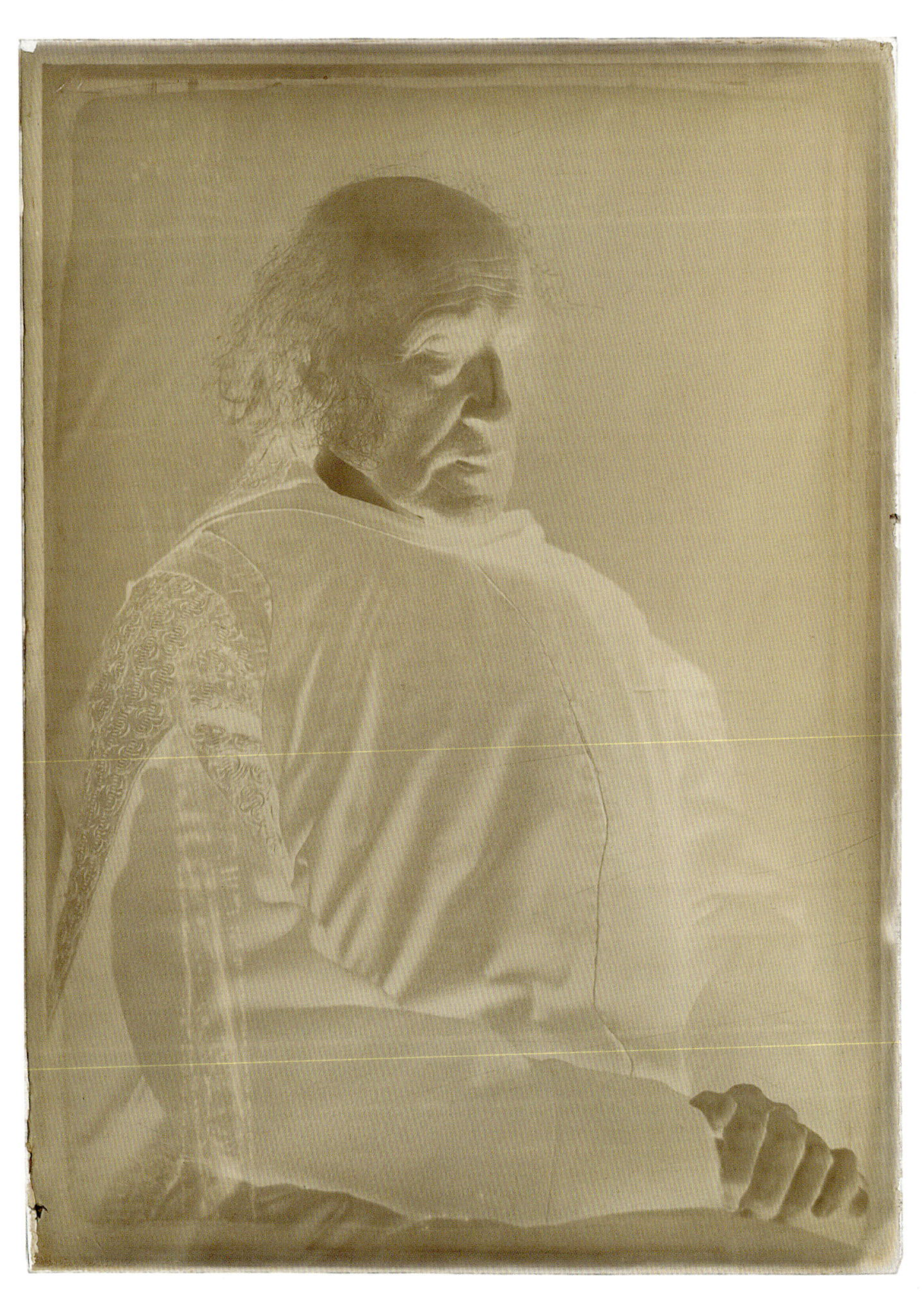

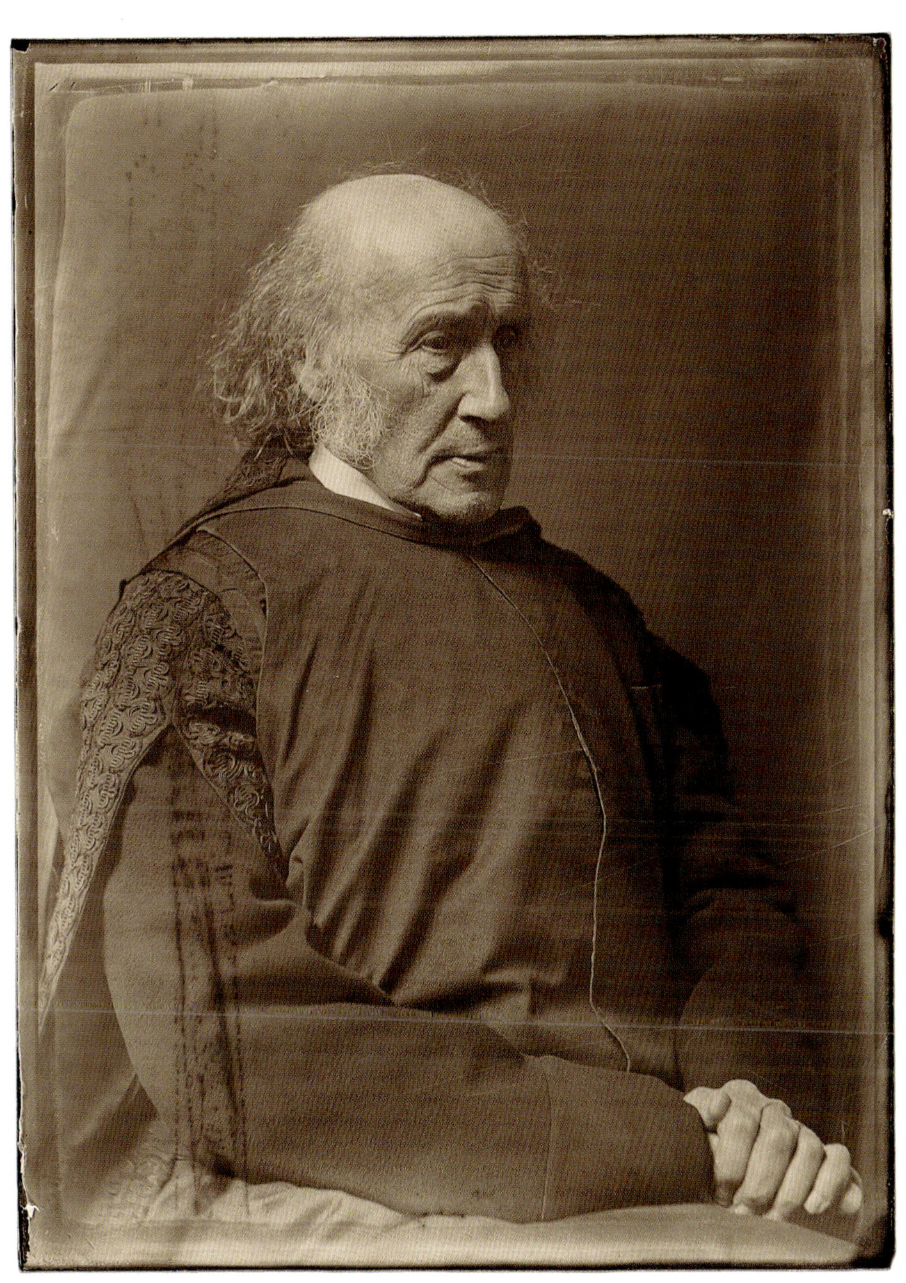

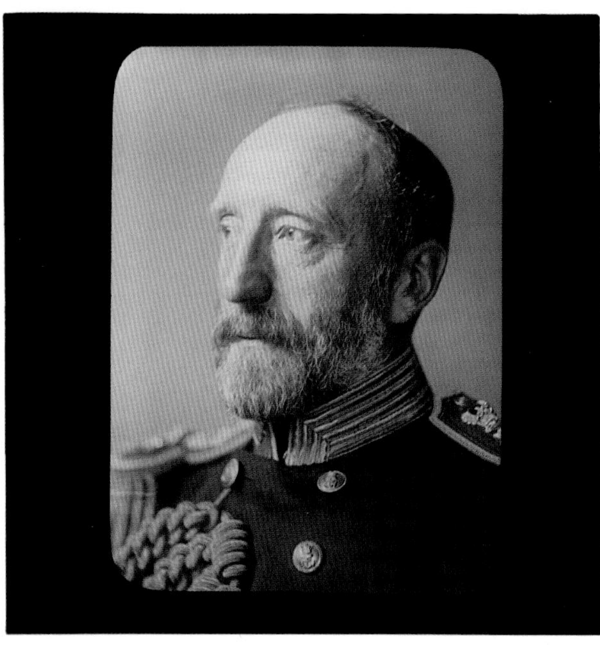

57. *"Captain Acland, R.N., A.D.C."*

William Alison Dyke Acland (1847–1924)
Oxford, 1 June 1896

Lantern slide
Museum of the History of Science, Inventory no. 19896

In her presentation albums Miss Acland described her brother as "the greatly beloved eldest son" and "a distinguished Naval officer". She listed his most important appointments as Naval Attaché to the Chilean Army in 1880, advisor to the Colonial Government of Sydney in 1883, and Naval Aide-de-Camp to Queen Victoria in 1896, the year this portrait was taken.

Willie was eighteen months older than his sister, who saw relatively little of him after he entered the Navy as a cadet in September 1861, aged only 14. In July 1887, aged 38, he married the Honourable Emily Anna ('Emmie') Smith (1859–1942), daughter of newsagent William Henry Smith (1825–1891). Eighteen years earlier his heart had been broken by Ina Liddell, the most desirable of the Liddell sisters (whom Dodgson was also accused of courting). In May 1869 he asked the Dean for Ina's hand in marriage, but it was not to be, as Mrs Acland explained to Angie:

> It was, as we expected, quite out of the question. Of course it is a great trial to dear old Willie, but he is very good. Mrs Liddell says that even if Willie were rich, and living at home, she knows it could not be. So I conclude that Ina's heart is set elsewhere. The Dean has been very kind. Willie spoke to him not Mrs L.

Not to be put off, Willie asked the question again in 1873, receiving the same answer. Soon afterwards a minor rift opened between the families, when Alice informed Angie of Ina's engagement to William Baillie Skene. "I am afraid that I felt quite angry," Mrs Acland told Willie, "for at Commemoration I was told that Mr. Skene wanted to marry Alice." The fallout was enough for the Dean to write to Acland with an explanation. When the wedding took place in February 1874, the Aclands tactfully stayed away, except Angie, who attended in order to prevent "any unfriendly appearance". A week later the Dean visited Broad Street to help heal the wounds, staying until after 10 o'clock, "a wonder for him".

Private collection, n.p.; MS. Acland d. 138, fols. 76–9; MS. Acland d. 42, fols. 393–6; MS. Acland d. 42, fols. 426–8; Ibid.

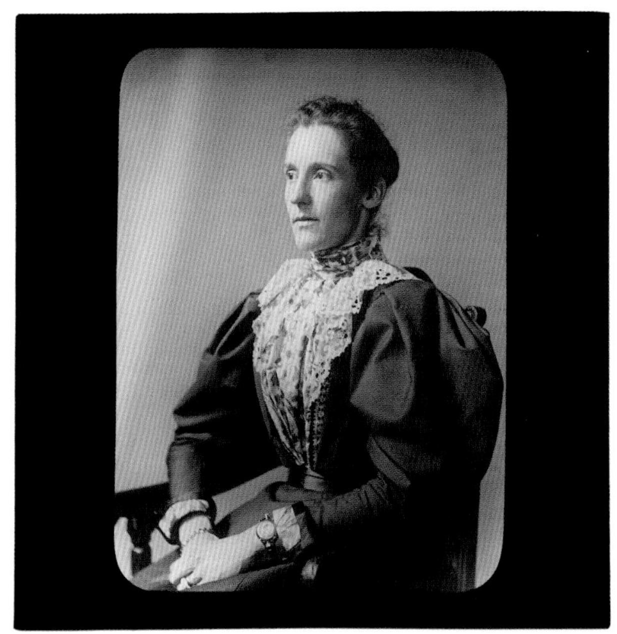

ABOVE

58. *"Mrs Frank Acland"*

Marion Sarah Acland, née Macrorie (1864–1937)
Oxford, *circa* 1 June 1896 ?

Lantern slide
Museum of the History of Science, Inventory no. 45721

Marion Macrorie married Frank Acland on 8 January 1885. She was the daughter of William Kenneth Macrorie (1831–1905), Bishop of Maritzburg, South Africa, and his wife Agnes, née Watson (1836–1917). On first meeting the Macrories in July 1884 Miss Acland was unimpressed (despite the bishop being an uncompromising High-Churchman). "The Macrories visit is over", she wrote to Willie, "I think the result is that I feel rather depressed. I like them all very much personally, but they are rather harum scarum & unpunctual & 'colonial'".

Ironically, given Miss Acland's comments, this photograph is said to be one of the earliest in which anyone is seen wearing a wristwatch. Marion's half-hunter reveals the portrait was taken at 11.45 a.m. Her summer bodice has a front of printed silk finished with machine-made lace. The 'stand' collar is typical of the period.

The Macrories' former home in Pietermaritzburg is now the Macrorie House Museum, a fine example of colonial architecture.

MS. Acland d. 107, fols. 121–2.

OVERLEAF

59. *Francis Acland*

Francis Edward Dyke Acland (1857–1943)
Oxford, *circa* 1 June 1896 ?

Half-plate negative
Bodleian Library, Minn negative 201/14

As an officer in the Royal Artillery Frank served in Natal and Zululand during the Transvaal War, before being appointed Superintendent of Experiments at Shoeburyness. After retiring from the army he became Director of the Maxim-Nordenfelt gun company. In World War I he was involved in a secret Admiralty project to develop the 'Still engine' (a combination of steam and internal combustion engine). He is remembered as a pioneer of modern gunnery and a prominent consulting engineer.

As this example suggests, Miss Acland's negatives are beautiful objects and images in their own right. Her approach was to "expose fully, and use a normal developer, as fairly thin negatives were most satisfactory". The strategy produced soft images without grain in the highlights (by normal developer she presumably meant pyro-soda, as opposed to the newer, rapid solutions such as Metol and Adurol, which increased the effective speed, grain and sharpness of the emulsion). The black borders are the areas masked by the edges of her dark slides and serve as 'fingerprints' for identifying her plates.

Proceedings of the Oxford Camera Club, no. 1 (April 1899), p. 5.

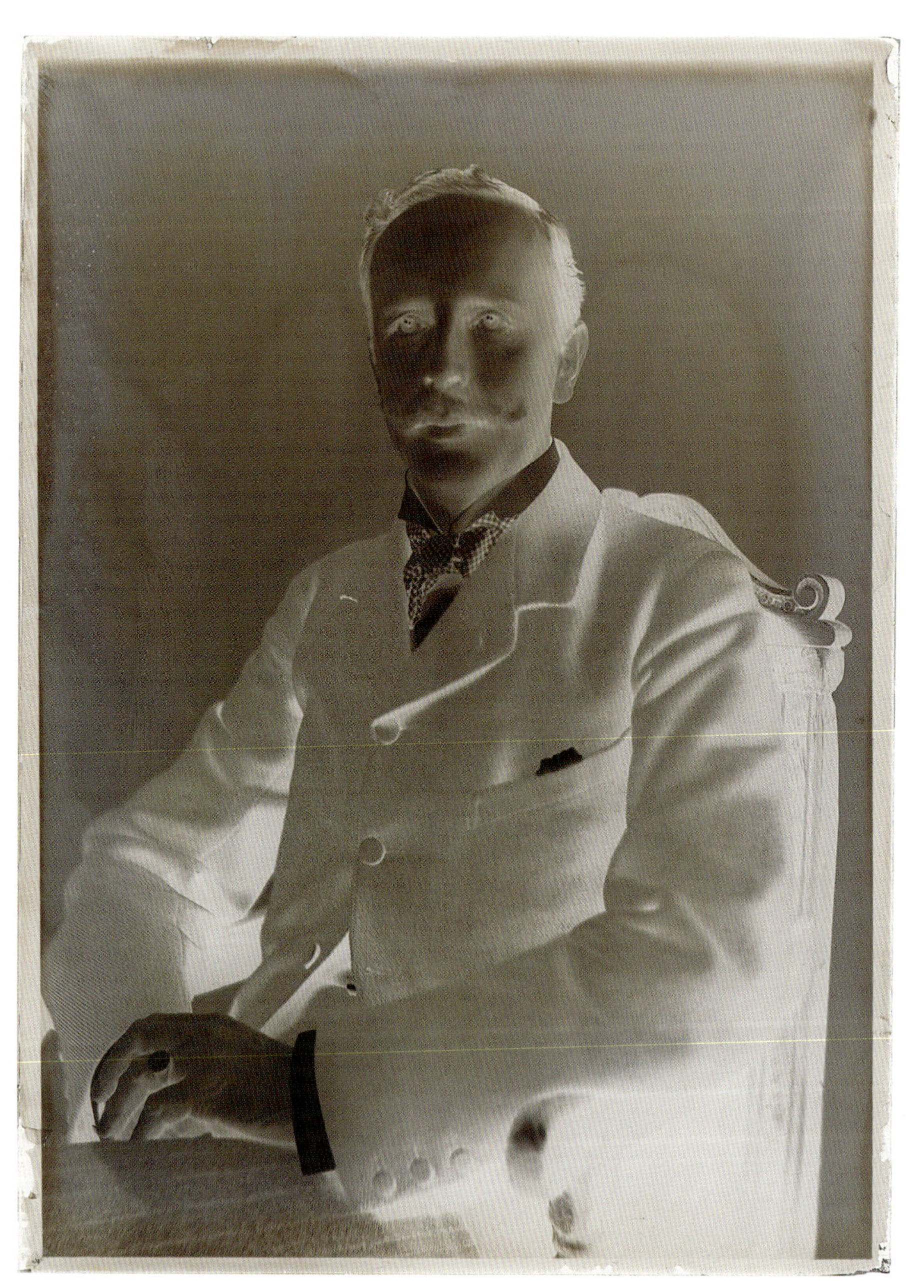

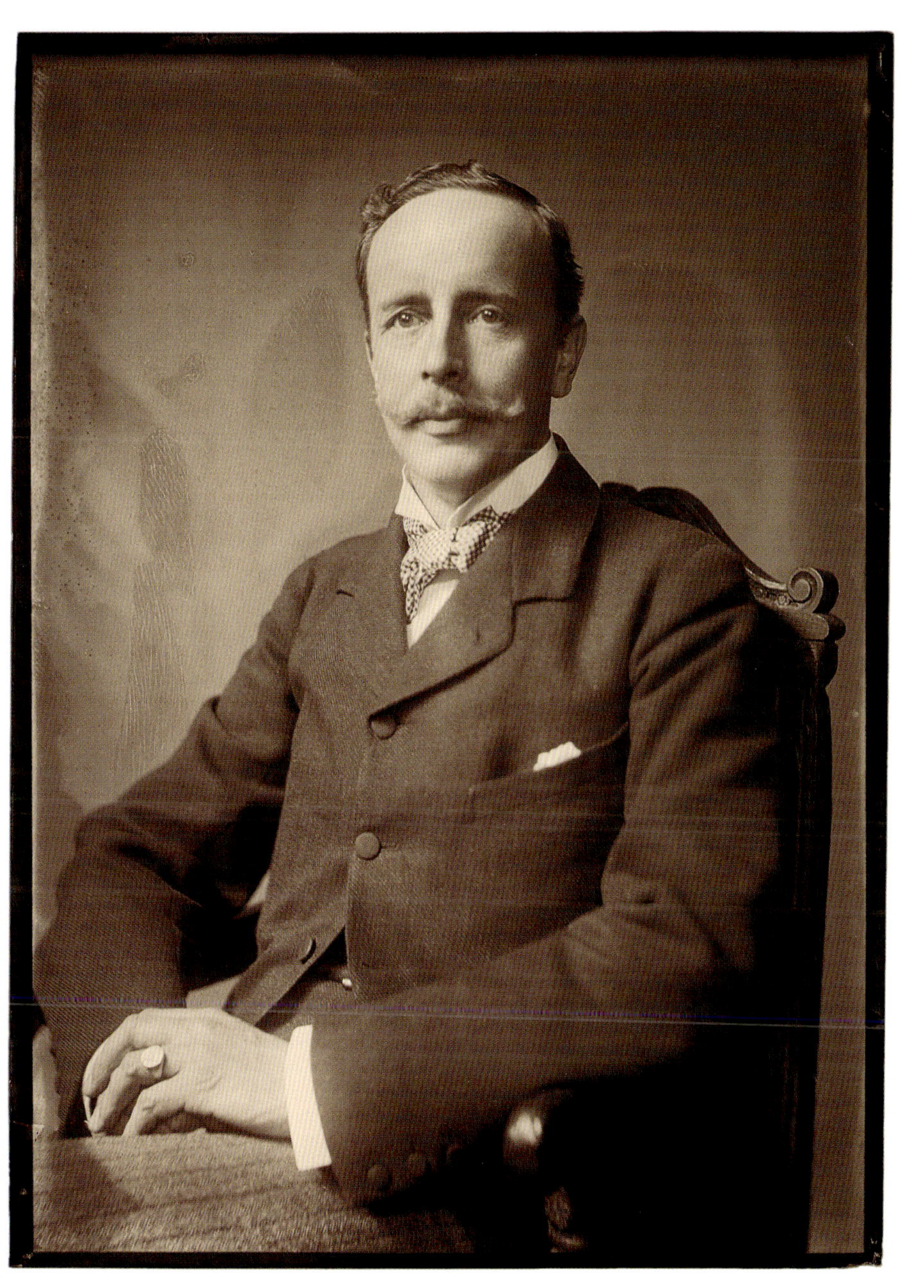

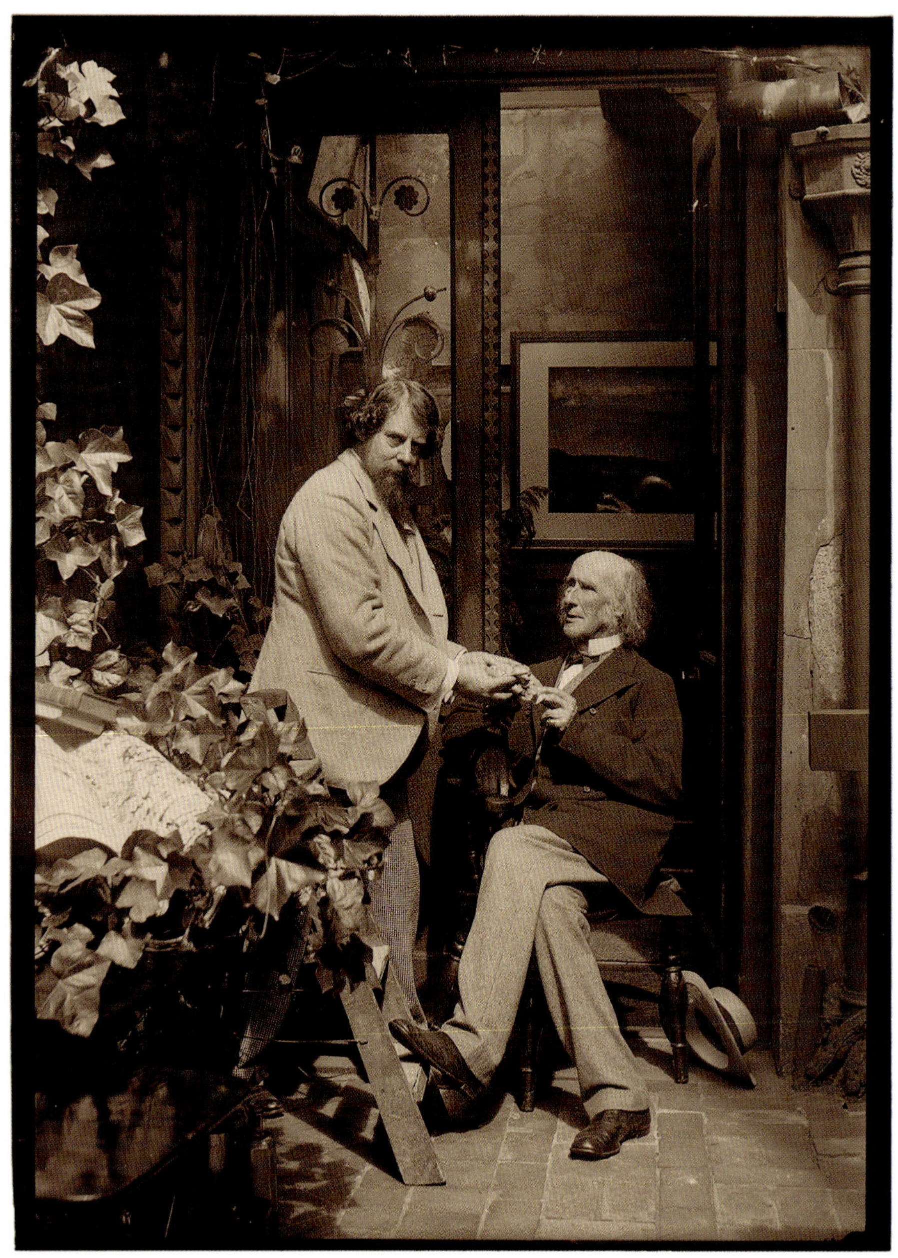

OPPOSITE

60. *"Sir Henry Acland and Mr. Richmond"*

William Blake Richmond (1842–1921) and
Henry Wentworth Acland (1815–1900)
Oxford, June 1896 ?

Half-plate negative
Bodleian Library, Minn negative 202/4

Willie Richmond's friendship with the Acland family originated with his father, George Richmond, whom Acland got to know in Rome in 1838 in the company of Samuel Palmer (1805–1881) and Joseph Severn. In 1840 Miss Acland's uncle Thomas Dyke Acland gave George his most important commission, the first of a series of portraits for the Grillion's Club, which established him as one of the leading portraitists of the Victorian age. In 1879 Acland offered him the chair of Slade Professor of Art in succession to Ruskin, but he declined in favour of his son.

By 1879 Willie Richmond had already benefitted from Acland's patronage, painting a double portrait of Frank and Alfred in April 1864, which was said to be his first commission (cat. nos. 98 & 99). In the same year he portrayed Ina, Alice and Edith Liddell in *The Sisters*, the Dean no doubt engaging him on Acland's recommendation. Portraiture aside, he is remembered chiefly for the mosaics in St Paul's Cathedral, which he undertook, according to Miss Acland, "at a very modest stipend".

Although he surrendered the Slade chair to Ruskin in 1883, during Miss Acland's active period of photography Richmond was often to be found in Broad Street. This, the best of six portraits in which he appears, was taken outside the garden door, looking east, the library out of sight on the left, the dining room on the right. Visible on the edge of the frame is part of a giant clam shell that was a permanent fixture of the courtyard. Behind Richmond is ironwork, probably by Skidmore of Coventry; behind Acland a framed photograph of mountain peaks, likely to be by Miss Acland's uncle Arthur Cotton or her neighbour Willie Donkin.

The pose Miss Acland has chosen for this portrait is unusual: Richmond is giving Acland his glass eye. Whether this is intended to have allegorical meaning, as between artist and patron, is unclear.

Presentation album, private collection, n.p.

OVERLEAF

61. *"Dr. John Shaw Billings, D.C.L."*

John Shaw Billings (1838–1913)
Oxford, between 29 June and 5 July 1896

Half-plate negative
Bodleian Library, Minn negative 182/1

This magnificent head study of Billings, taken soon after his appointment as Superintendent-in-Chief of the New York Public Library, earned Miss Acland first place in the portraits class of the 1896 Oxford Camera Club exhibition. In the opinion of the *Oxford Times* the class was "far and away the best" of the show, largely due to her "grand series of head studies", Billings being "rightly placed first".

Billings's portrait can be dated from his letters. On 3 July 1896 he wrote to his wife from Oxford, commenting that he found Acland well. On 8 July, after leaving, he reported that he had been there three days, adding that "my 'English Cousin' is also in fair condition and took a new photograph of me of which you are to have a copy." The epithet was explained by Miss Acland in her reminiscences for Fielding Garrison's *Memoir* of Billings:

> When I was quite a girl and had a long illness, Dr. Gross of Philadelphia was most kind to me and lodged near me in London, coming daily to see me. He then always called himself my American cousin. One day, I think in 1896, Dr. Billings was staying with us after Dr. Gross had died and we were talking of this. Dr. Billings said, "Is the post of American cousin still vacant?" To which I replied "Yes," rather shyly. He said, "May I apply for it?" "Yes," I replied, "but you must send in a formal application which will be duly considered." The appointment was made and from that date his letters began, "My dear English cousin," and the friendship thus commenced was only ended by his death.

On returning to America in 1896 Billings took a gift from Miss Acland for the Library of "6 books, 62 pamphlets, and one special collection of pamphlets relating to the granting of degrees to women at Oxford".

Billings had expertise of his own in an unusual form of portraiture, having published papers on composite photography as applied to craniology in the 1880s.

Oxford Times (21 November 1896), p. 7e; Billings quoted in Fielding H. Garrison, *John Shaw Billings: A Memoir* (New York & London, 1915), p. 294; Ibid., p. 388; MS. Acland d. 174, fol. 36.

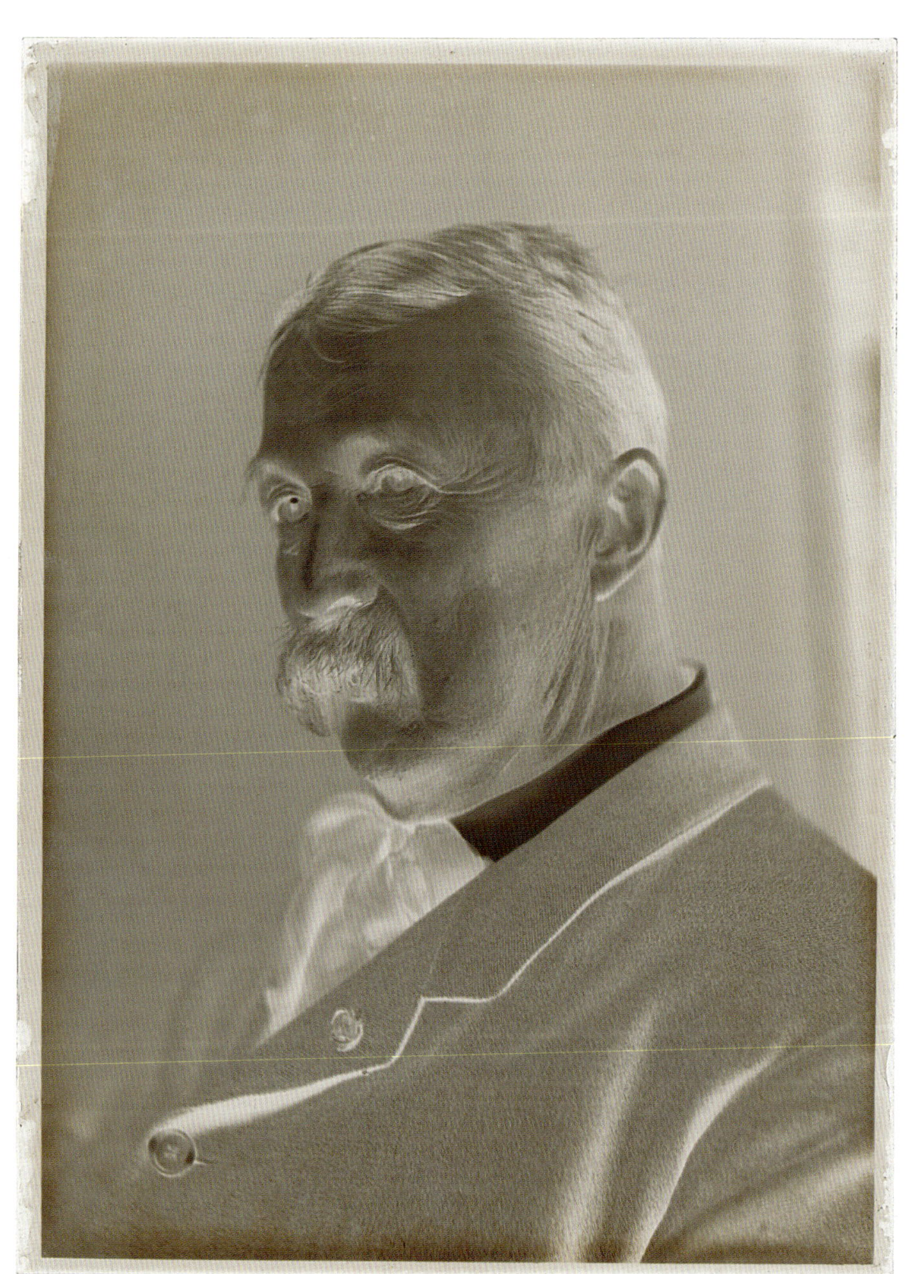

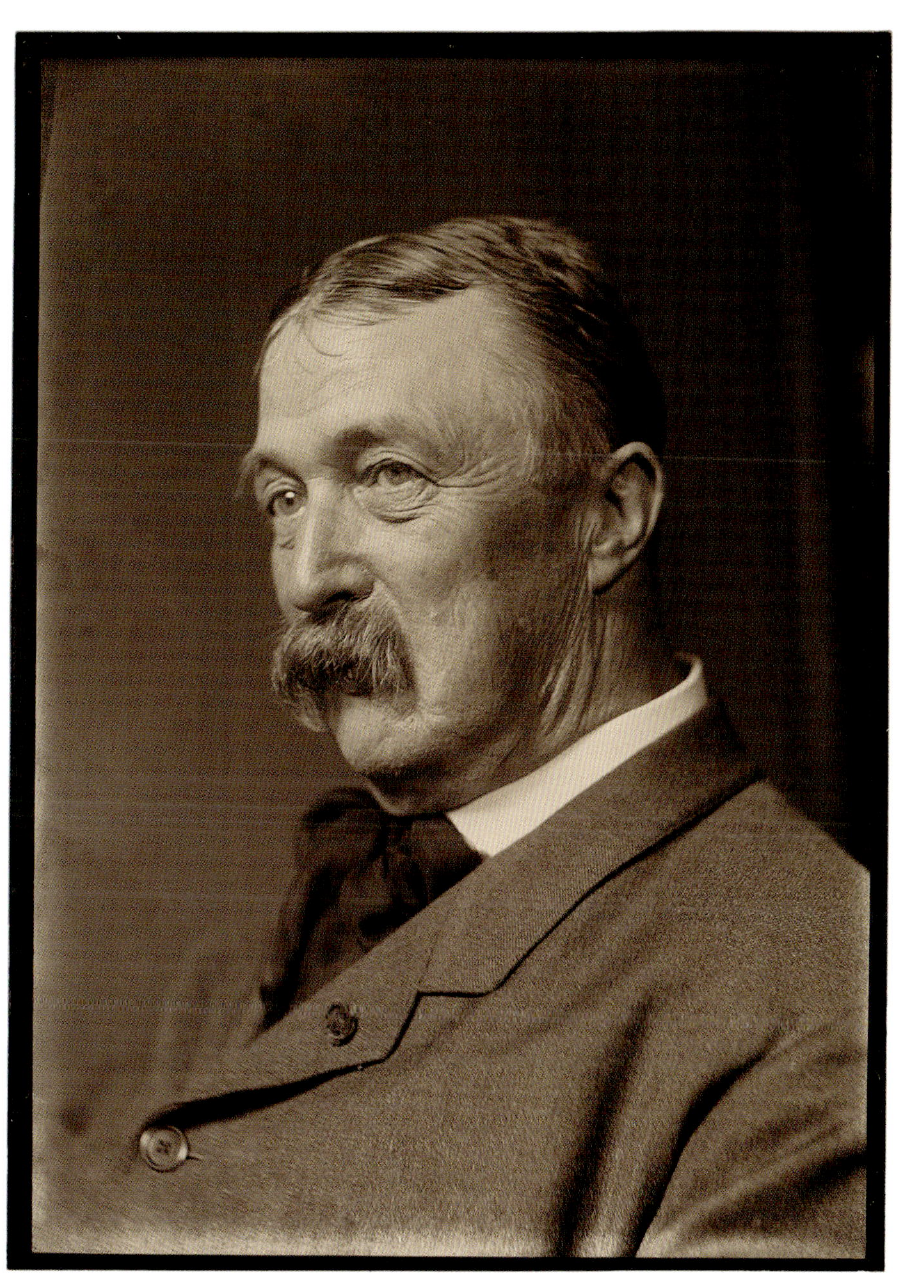

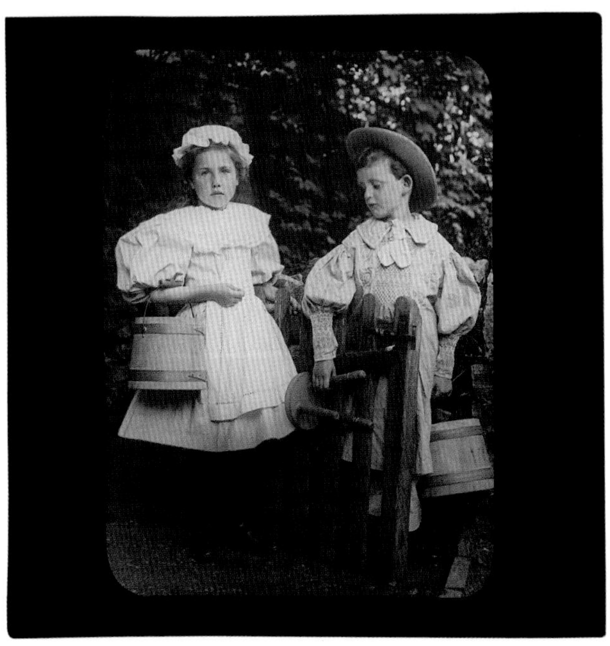

62. *"Little Milkman and Little Milkmaid We"*

A niece and nephew of Sarah Angelina Acland
Oxford ?, shortly before 12 July 1896

Lantern slide
Museum of the History of Science, Inventory no. 26484

This photograph is a rare surviving example by Miss Acland of a 'genre study' — a photograph that 'tells a story or expresses a sentiment' (she took many, but few come down to us). A print from the negative was exhibited in the genre class of the Oxford Camera Club exhibition in November 1896, where it won first prize, Miss Acland exhibiting under the pseudonym 'Acorn'. The study also received a mention in the *Oxford Times*, the paper's correspondent writing that "Miss Acland is to be congratulated on her prize print, 'Little Milkman and Little Milkmaid we'."

The niece and nephew in the slide may be Herbert Arthur Dyke Acland (1886–1968) and his sister Charis Agnes Acland (1888–1968), daughters of Frank and Marion. The children do not look overly enamoured with their roles, a state of affairs confirmed in a letter to Miss Acland from her father, in which he wrote that he was glad "that you have accomplished the milkmaids tho' they were not happy in the process". The main purpose of the gate propped up between the children, Miss Acland revealed, was as an aid in posing.

In 1905 Miss Acland exhibited *Alice in Wonderland* at the Camera Club. Now lost, this too was presumably a genre study, rather than a portrait of Mrs Hargreaves, as Alice became after her marriage. It was also probably a costume study: a style popular with Oxford photographers, whether in portraying adults or children.

Oxford Times, no. 1786 (21 November 1896), p. 7e; MS. Acland d. 134, fols. 146–7.

OVERLEAF

63 & 64. *Sir Henry Acland, Bart.*

Henry Wentworth Acland (1815–1900), wearing a fur-lined coat
Oxford, shortly after 5 September 1896

Half-plate negatives
Bodleian Library, Minn negatives 176/8 & 176/6

On 5 September 1896 Acland wrote to his eldest son that "Angie appeared with the splendid fur which you my dear children have given me to try and keep me going during the time allotted me yet to come." This portrait presumably dates from shortly afterwards.

Miss Acland took more portraits of her father than any other sitter, reflecting the central place he occupied in her life. After the death of her mother in 1878 she dedicated herself to his care, becoming a model example of the 'dutiful daughter'. When he died in October 1900 the loss was traumatic:

> I feel an old woman now that my only object in life is gone. I cannot imagine what I shall do — if I still have to live on — All my interest in life has so entirely gone during the long nursing of Father. My great comfort has been that he clung to me more & more to the end.

Acland was not, contrary to some suggestions, ungrateful or unaware of the sacrifice his daughter was making. In the same letter in which he mentioned the fur, for example, he remarked that he felt she would benefit from "a more lively companion than the octogenarian". In some respects Miss Acland's relationship was more difficult with her mother, who often found her illness, far removed from the "ordinary routine of young Ladyism" enjoyed by the other Oxford girls she chaperoned, a disappointment and a burden.

The left-hand side of the negative of the head study is covered in a thick blue masking compound, in which numerous fingerprints and scratches have been deliberately made. Whether this improves the portrait is questionable. When she compiled her presentation albums Miss Acland claimed proudly that her negatives were all 'untouched' (despite accepting in her portraiture lecture that retouching was occasionally necessary). This suggests the masking compound was added by Harry Minn while the plates were in his possession.

As a photographer, Miss Acland could hardly hope for a more rewarding subject than her father, his distinguished features immediately giving her work the gravitas that was admired in portraiture of men in the late nineteenth century. In most of his portraits Acland is seen from his right-hand side, for the simple reason that his left eye had been removed in 1888.

MS. Acland d. 26, fols. 68–9; MS. Acland d. 108, fols. 64–5; MS. Acland d. 26, fols. 68–9; MS. Acland d. 42, fols. 247–8.

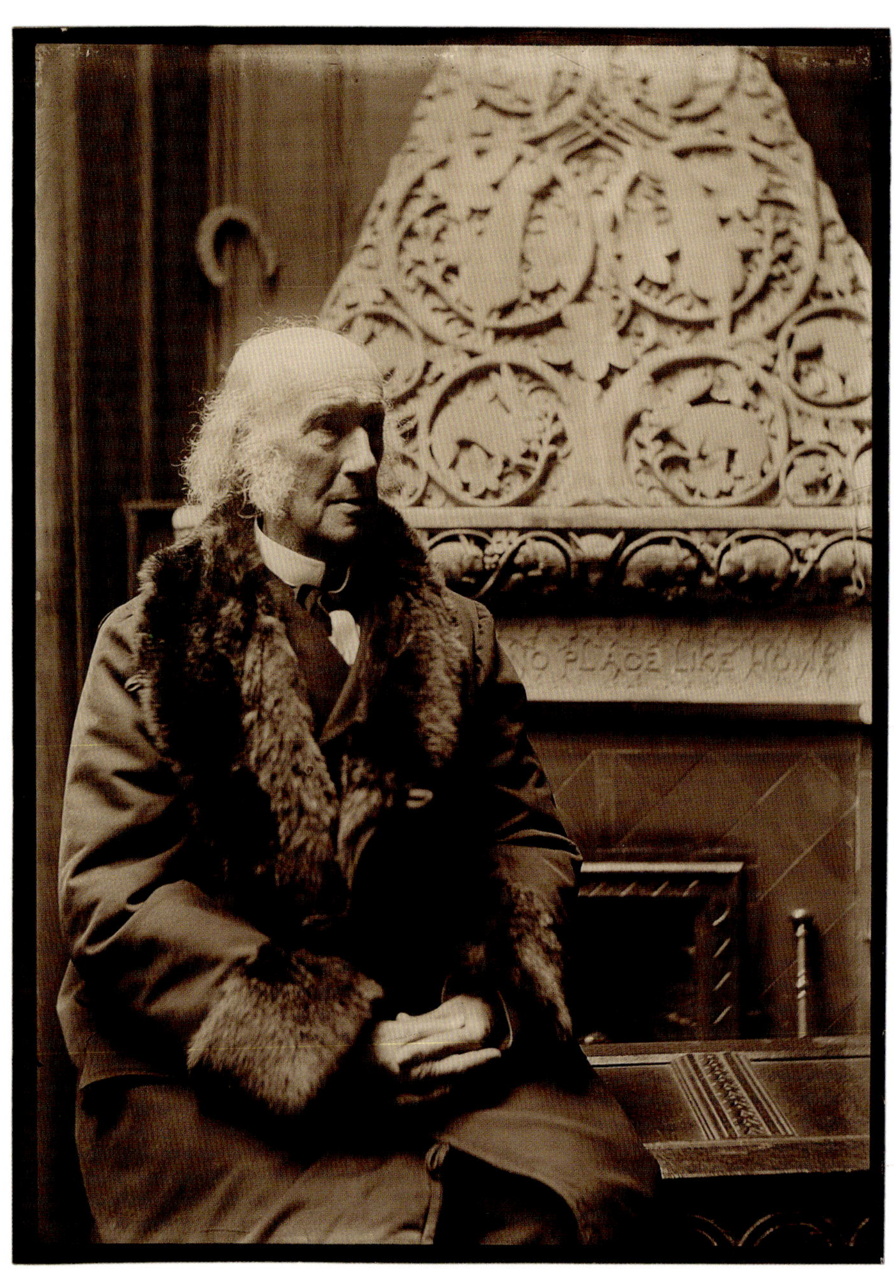
PLACE LIKE

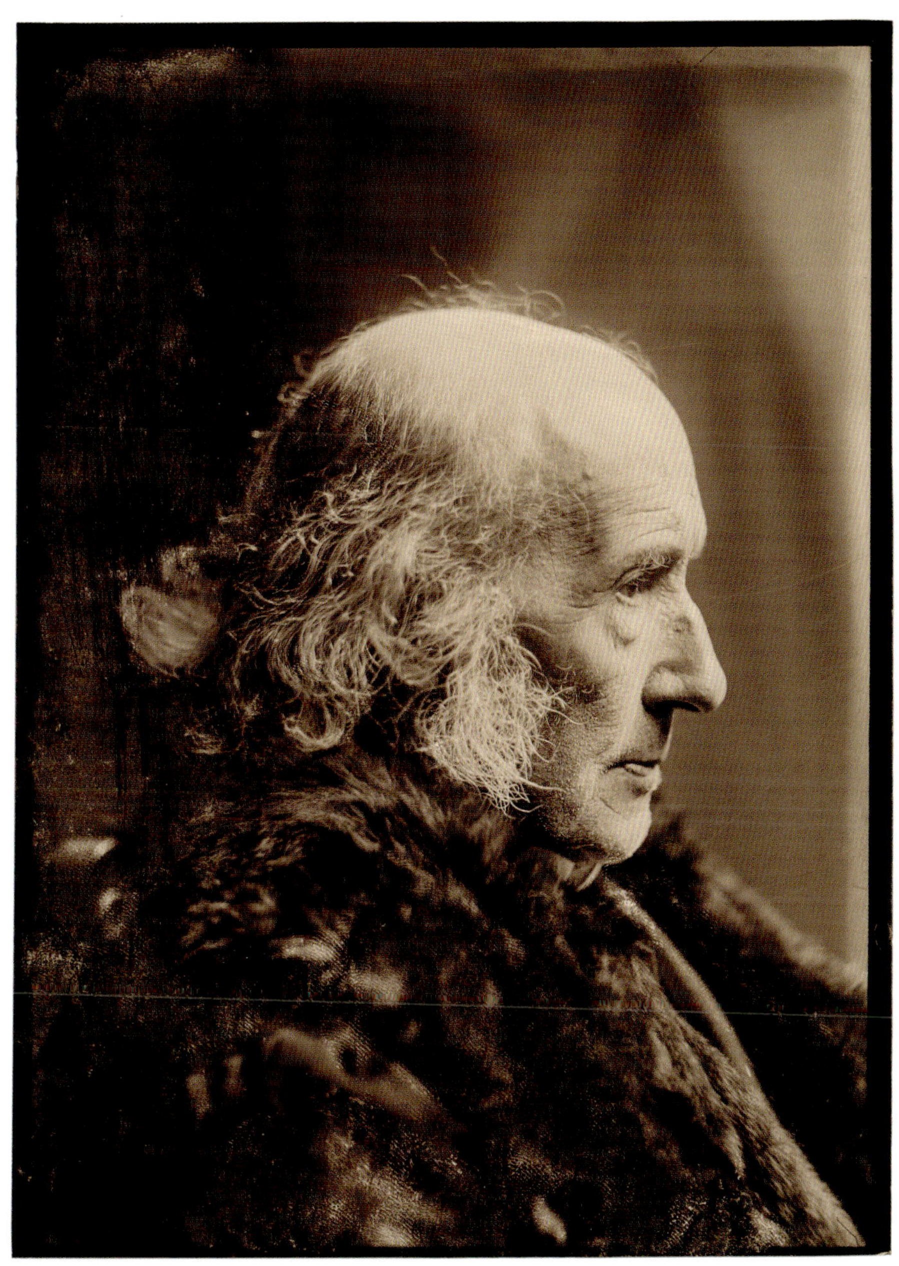

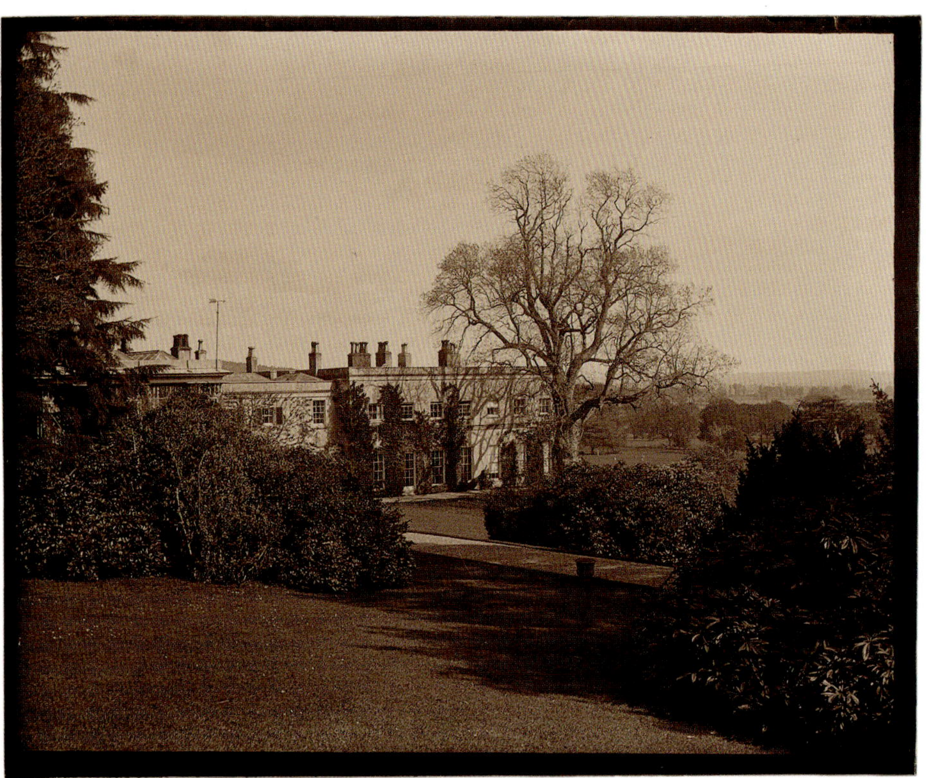

65. *"Killerton"*

Killerton House, from the north-west
Broadclyst, Devon, January 1897 ?
5 × 4 inch negative
Bodleian Library, Minn negative 199/1

Killerton House was the ancestral seat of the Acland family and the birthplace of Miss Acland's father. Built between 1778 and 1779, it was designed by John Johnson (1732–1814), who was also responsible for the Shire Hall and ceiling of St Mary's Church (now Cathedral) in Chelmsford. The 6,000 acre estate of Killerton, which has fine landscape gardens by John Veitch (1752–1839), is located in the countryside north of Exeter.

Killerton was almost a second home to Miss Acland, who spent several years of her childhood in the schoolroom of her uncle's house in neighbouring Sprydoncote. During this time she saw much of her grandfather, Thomas Dyke Acland, 10th baronet. "Grandpapa was a real old Norman & quick tempered", she claimed in her memoirs, but she was "never a scrap afraid of him". Being in his atmosphere was the greatest possible boon, her mother felt, notwithstanding his reputation as the most unpunctual of men.

When Killerton was given to the National Trust in 1944 by Richard Thomas Dyke Acland, 15th baronet (1906–1990), prior to his joining the Labour Party, it was the largest single acquisition in the Trust's history.

Devon Records Office, 1148M/7/1, p. 133.

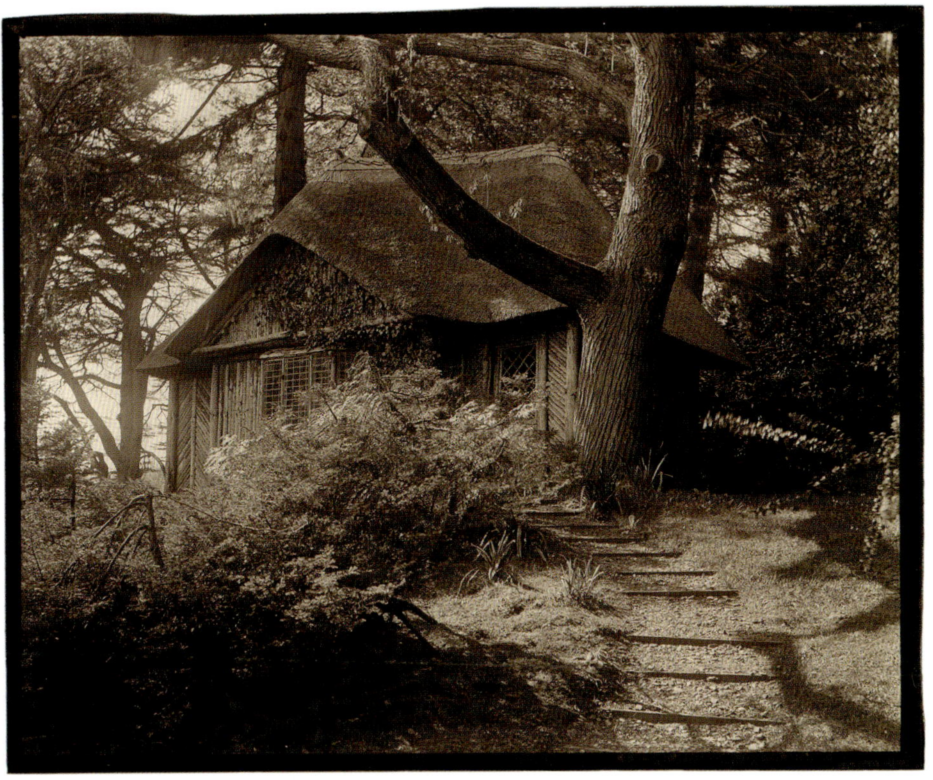

66. *The Bear's Hut*

The Bear's Hut, Killerton
Broadclyst, Devon, January 1897 ?
5 × 4 inch negative
Bodleian Library, Minn negative 199/3

The Bear's Hut, a summer house, was only ever occupied by humans. However, Miss Acland's cousin Francis Gilbert Dyke ('Gibby') Acland (1843–1874) did keep a bear at Killerton, of whom she had fond memories:

> What very happy days we had, with ponies, Tommy the bear, our gardens & so many interests. Tommy had been brought home as a cub by Gibby who was in the Rifle Brigade, from Canada. He had a long chain of about 18 feet which was fastened to an elm tree near the front door at Sprydon & he used to climb up & sit on the branches. His fur was so very thick that one could not part it so as to see the skin. He would sit in the middle of his back holding his hind paws with his front ones & sway himself backwards & forwards. He used to come out with us for walks & if he disapproved of where we were going he would sit down in this way & refuse to move. One day I remember when Grandpapa wanted some friends at Killerton to see him Tommy did this & Pussy & I pulled him all the way there. Oh! how tired & hot we were! We used to take sugar in our pockets to tempt him to do what we wanted. He was very fond of Spanish chestnuts also. One day I had a number I had picked up in a basket & I wanted to give them to him one by one but he wanted the whole basket so we had a disagreement & he pulled me over down the slope in front of the drawing room windows. Soon after this he was sent to the Zoo. I went to see him there where they called him Sir Thomas. He was most delighted to see me & the keeper let me take him out of his cage in his chain for a little walk. I do not suppose it would be allowed now.

Devon Records Office, 1148M/7/1, pp. 128–9.

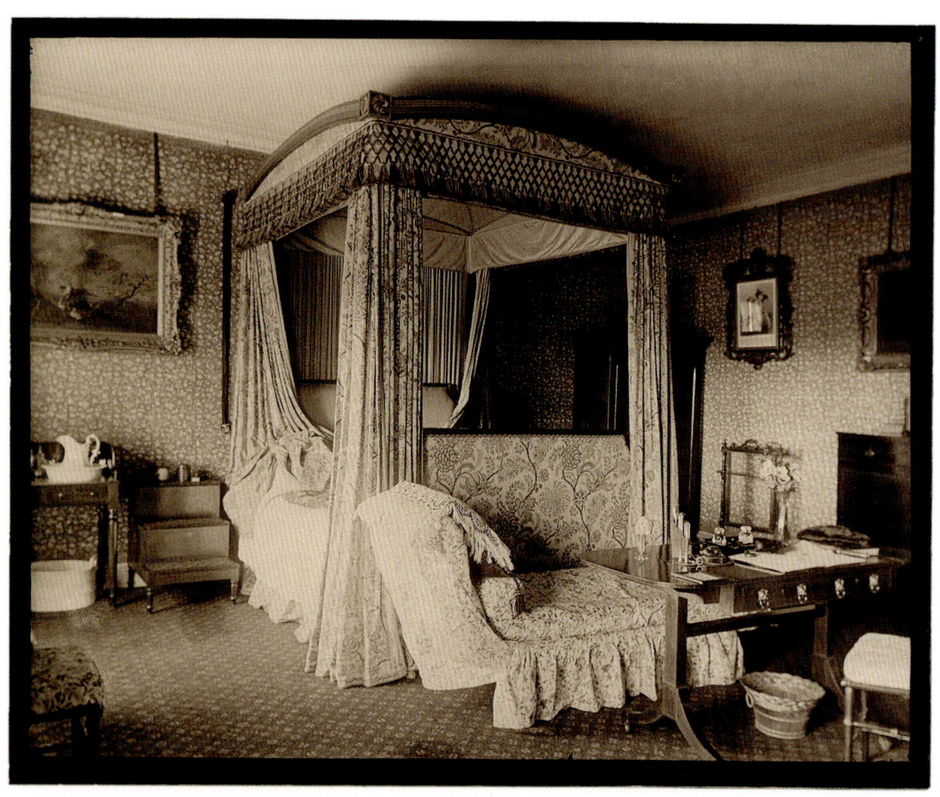

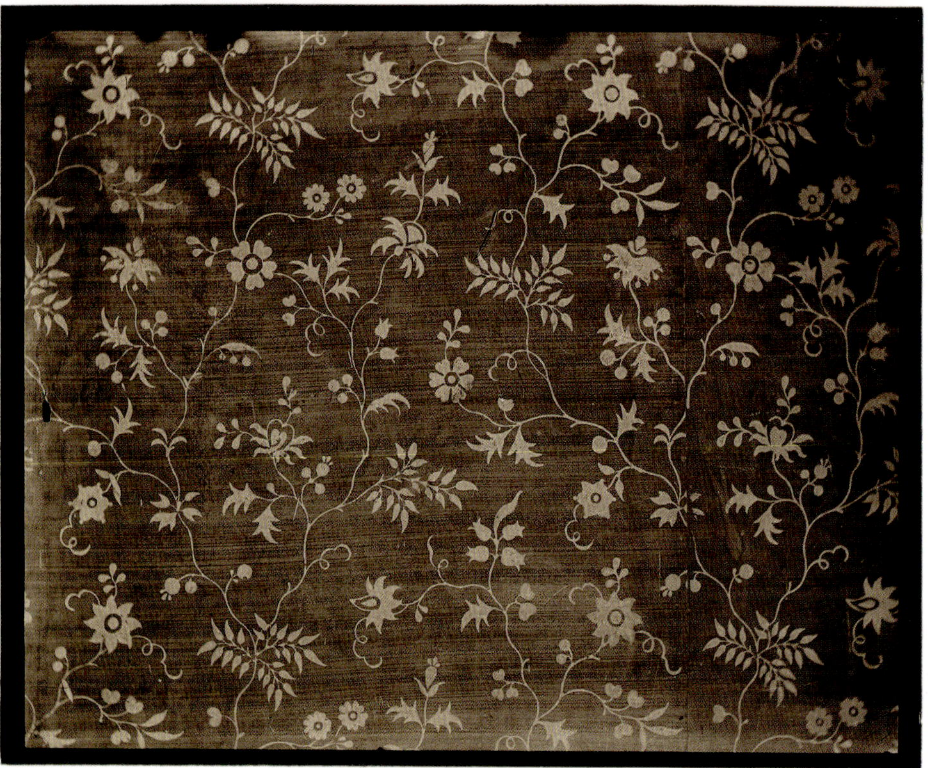

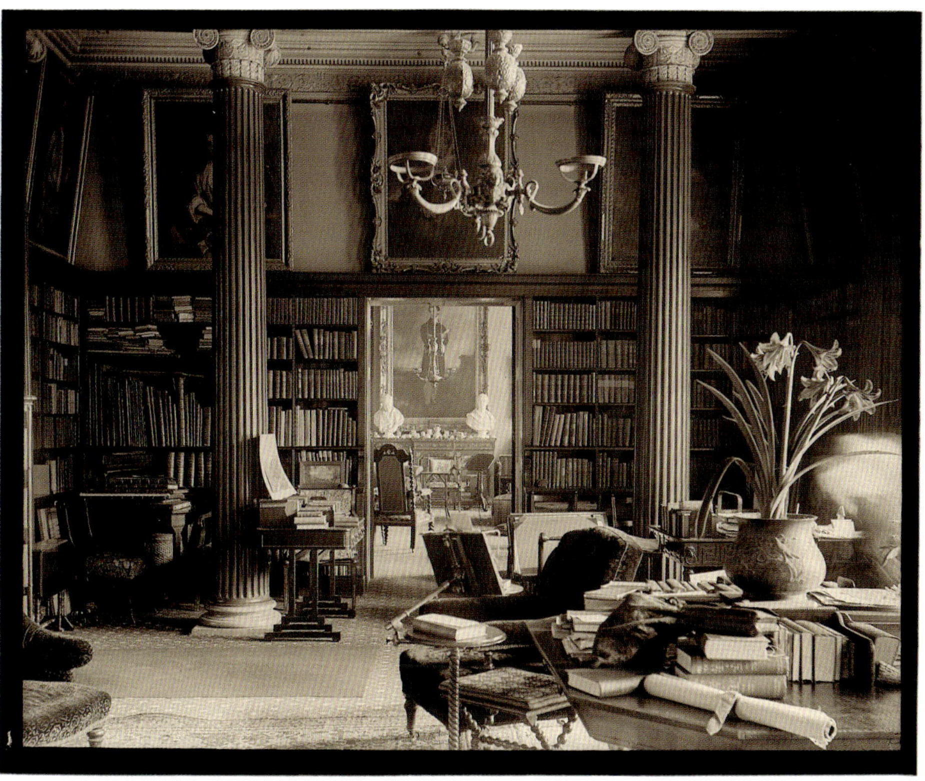

OPPOSITE

67 & 68. *"Bedroom at Killerton"*

Archduke John's bedroom; Wallpaper in the room
Killerton House, Broadclyst, Devon, January 1897 ?

5 × 4 inch negatives
Bodleian Library, Minn negatives 199/9 & 199/6

In her memoirs, which were illustrated by beautiful hand-made prints from these negatives, Miss Acland explained the significance of the subjects depicted:

> In the front bedroom opposite to Aunt Agnes' or Aunt Mary's was a room which had been prepared for the Archduke John when he was to stay at Killerton, but I do not feel clear whether he even did so. There was a four poster bed with carved posts & the paper was interesting fairly dark green with a white pattern on it printed from old square blocks. I took a photograph of it.

Miss Acland's grandfather met Johann von Österreich (1782–1859), Archduke of Austria, at the Congress of Vienna in 1814.

Devon Records Office, 1148M/7/1, p. 135.

ABOVE

69. *"Library at Killerton"*

The old library, Killerton House, looking south
Broadclyst, Devon, January 1897 ?

5 × 4 inch negative
Bodleian Library, Minn negative 199/9

The interiors of middle-class houses only became popular subjects for photography in the 1880s. The stately homes of England, in contrast, had long been sought out by photographers for their pictorial qualities.

The library at Killerton, now the dining room, and the drawing room beyond, are both dominated by portraits. Above the doorway, mostly obscured by the chandelier in this photograph, is a portrait by Henry William Pickersgill (1782–1875) of the social reformer Hannah More (1745–1833), commissioned in 1821 by her friend Thomas Acland, 10th baronet. Through the doorway is a portrait of Thomas himself, by William Owen (1769–1825), known to the children as 'grandpa in a thunderstorm'. The January date for the photograph is suggested by the flowering amaryllis on the table.

OPPOSITE & OVERLEAF

70 & 71. *"Colonel E. C. Impey, C.I.E., Hon. M.A."*

Eugene Clutterbuck Impey (1830–1904)
Oxford, summer ?, 1897

Half-plate negatives
Bodleian Library, Minn negatives 183/12 & 183/11

Impey, the elder statesman of the Oxford Camera Club, was born in Paris, the grandson of Pierre Antoine, Chevalier de l'Étang (1757–1840), and of Elijah Impey (1732–1809), Chief Justice of the Supreme Court of Bengal. After studying at Wadham College he received a commission in the 5th Regiment of the Bengal Native Infantry, going out to India in 1851. He later became military secretary to the Viceroy, John Lawrence (1811–1879), before retiring to England in 1879 and moving to Oxford in 1884.

By 1863, the year in which his cousin Julia Margaret Cameron acquired her first camera (their mothers were sisters), Impey was already an accomplished photographer. During the 1860s he captured every aspect of India on collodion plates: temples, tombs and palaces; the flora, fauna and geology; landscapes and townscapes; military installations; and the indigenous people and their colonial administrators. In 1863 he submitted at least thirty-nine photographs to the Amateur Photographic Association, his *Hill and Tank*, taken at Ulwar, Hindostan, earning him fourth prize in the annual awards. Two years later eighty examples of his architectural photography were published as a portfolio by Cundall & Downes, *Delhi, Agra, and Rajpootana*. In 1871, as 'Major Impey', he exhibited numerous "Views in India" at the Photographic Society.

Miss Acland's head study of Impey (overleaf), which is reminiscent of Cameron's portrait of Henry Taylor given to the University Galleries through her father, is among her finest works. In 1898 it was one of twelve slides, along with Impey's *Window in Haddon Hall*, selected by popular vote as the Oxford Camera Club's contribution to the Royal Photographic Society's International Photographic Exhibition at Crystal Palace — the blockbuster photographic exhibition of its day.

Impey served on the City Council from 1889 to 1893 and from 1895 until his death in 1904. During the first period his fellow Conservative in the North Ward was Charles Miskin Laing, husband of the autochromist Etheldreda Janet Laing. In 1890 Impey and Laing were joined on the Council by Camera Club members Edmund Augustine Bevers (1849–1921) and Hugh Hall (1848–1940); in 1892 by Edmund John Brooks (1860–1937). The Club counted at least ten councillors in its ranks before 1909, no fewer than seven of whom went on to serve as Mayor: Bevers, Brooks, Clement James Victor Bellamy (1880–1946), George Claridge Druce (1850–1932), James Hastings (1857–1928), Samuel Hutchins (b. 1849), and John Henry Salter (1853–1930). The high number reflects the Club's prominent position in the civic landscape and the importance of photographic societies as a microcosm of wider Victorian society.

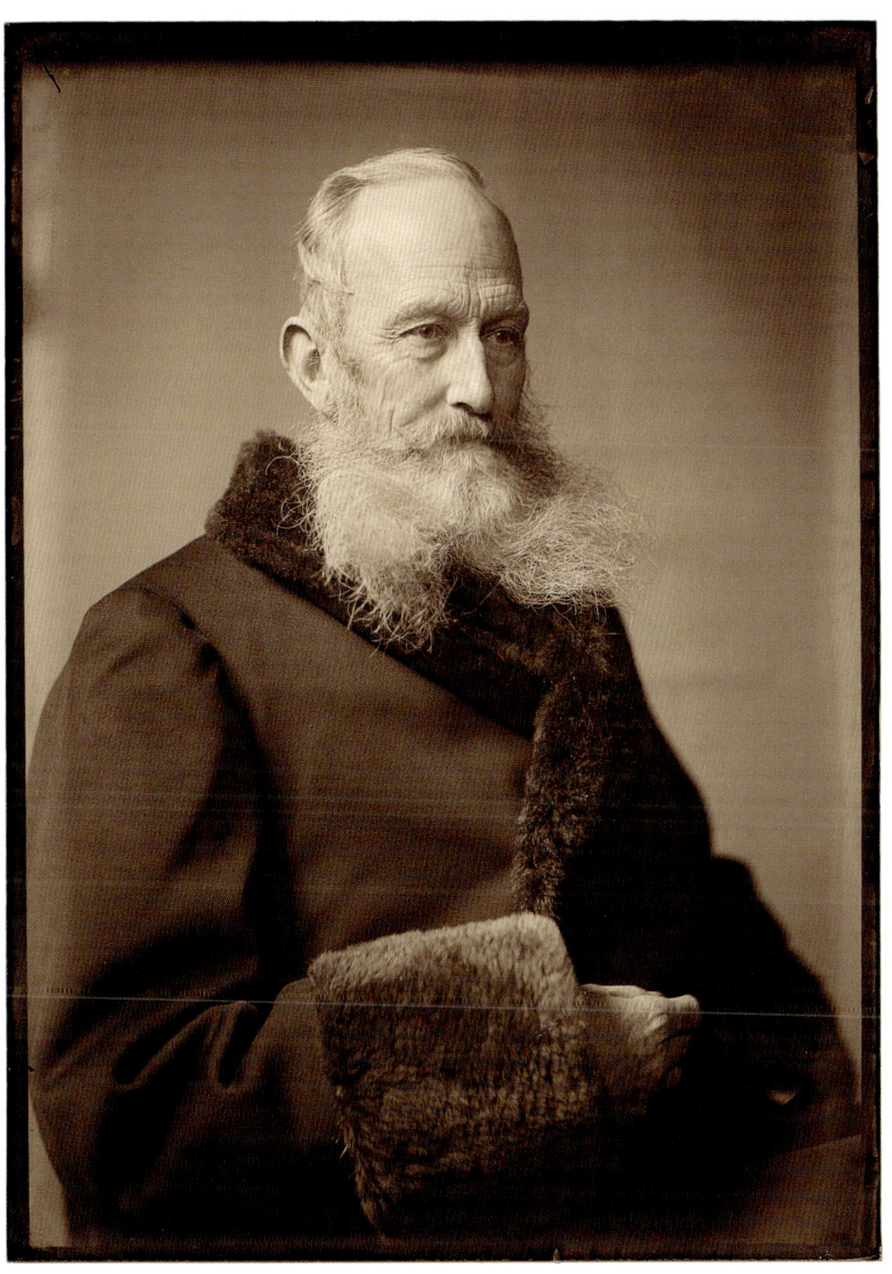

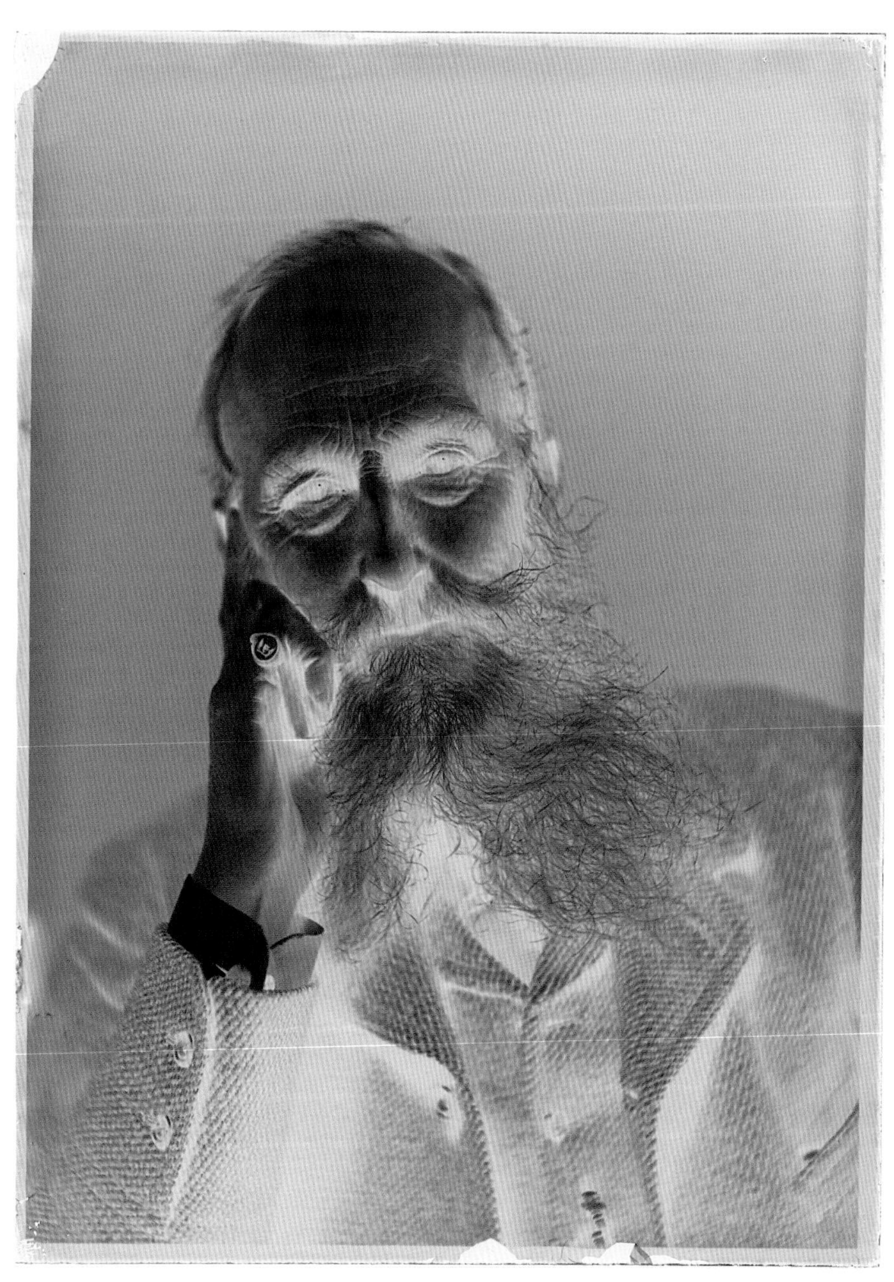

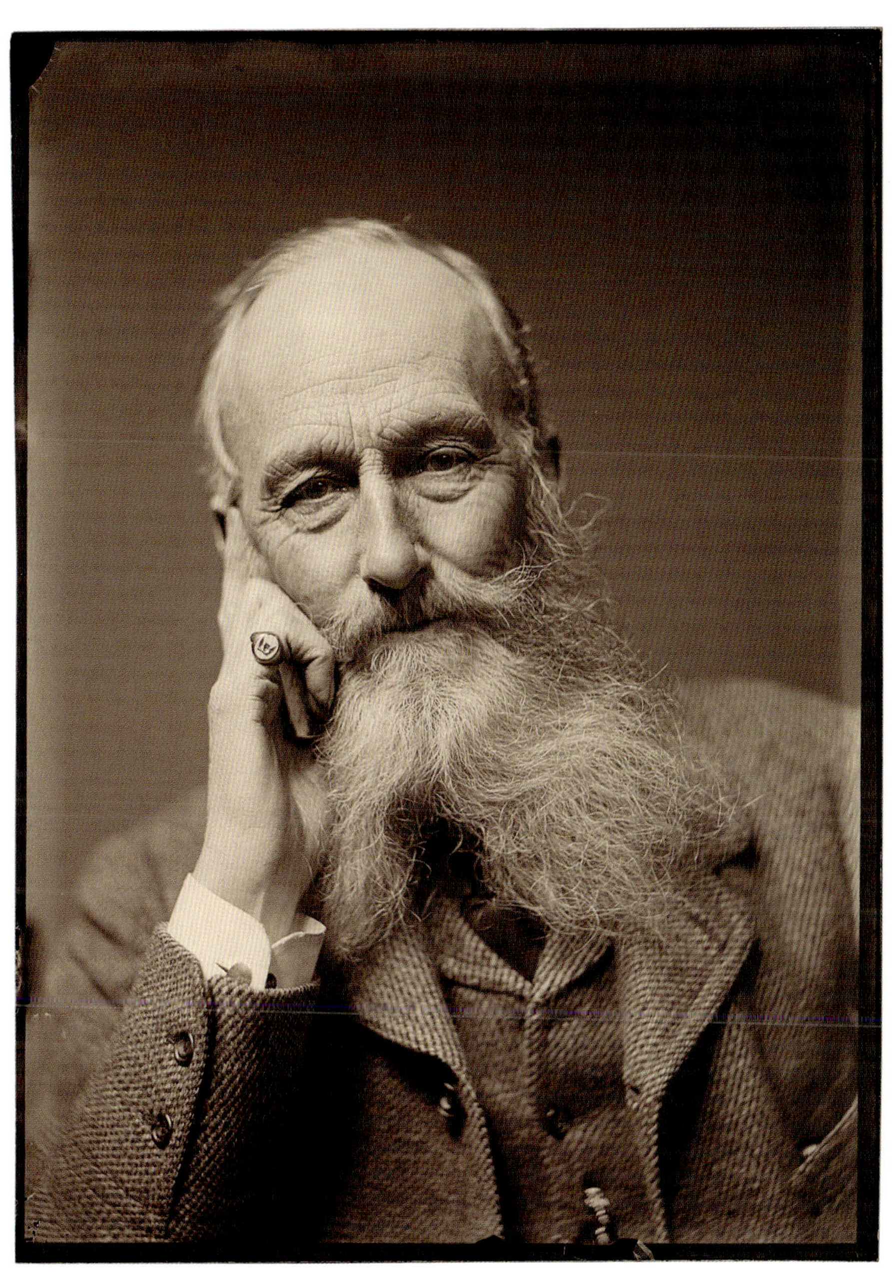

72. *"Mrs Barney"*

Mary Trinder Barney, née Allen (1825/6–1903)
Oxford, summer 1897?

Half-plate negative
Bodleian Library, Minn negative 183/14

Mary Barney was the widow of Robert George Barney (1823–1888), a master chimney sweep. She was born in Oxford and met her husband whilst a servant in the house of Thomas Buckland (d. 1877), to whom Robert was apprenticed. They married in 1845.

Mrs Barney lived her whole life in Castle Street, in the parish of St Peter-le-Bailey, where she was a churchwarden. She suffered deep poverty and was a long-standing recipient of Miss Acland's charity.

With Mrs Barney's portrait Miss Acland is at the height of her artistic skill as a photographer, making use of diffusion of focus, a narrow depth of field, and mastery of the manipulation of light to achieve an image of great tenderness. As well as a work of art, the portrait is a social and moral statement, embodying Miss Acland's powers of sympathy for those less well-off than herself and her willingness to embrace as friends members of the lowest class in society. The dignity with which Mrs Barney is portrayed also speaks to Miss Acland's belief in the power of faith and nobility of spirit in conquering the struggles of daily existence.

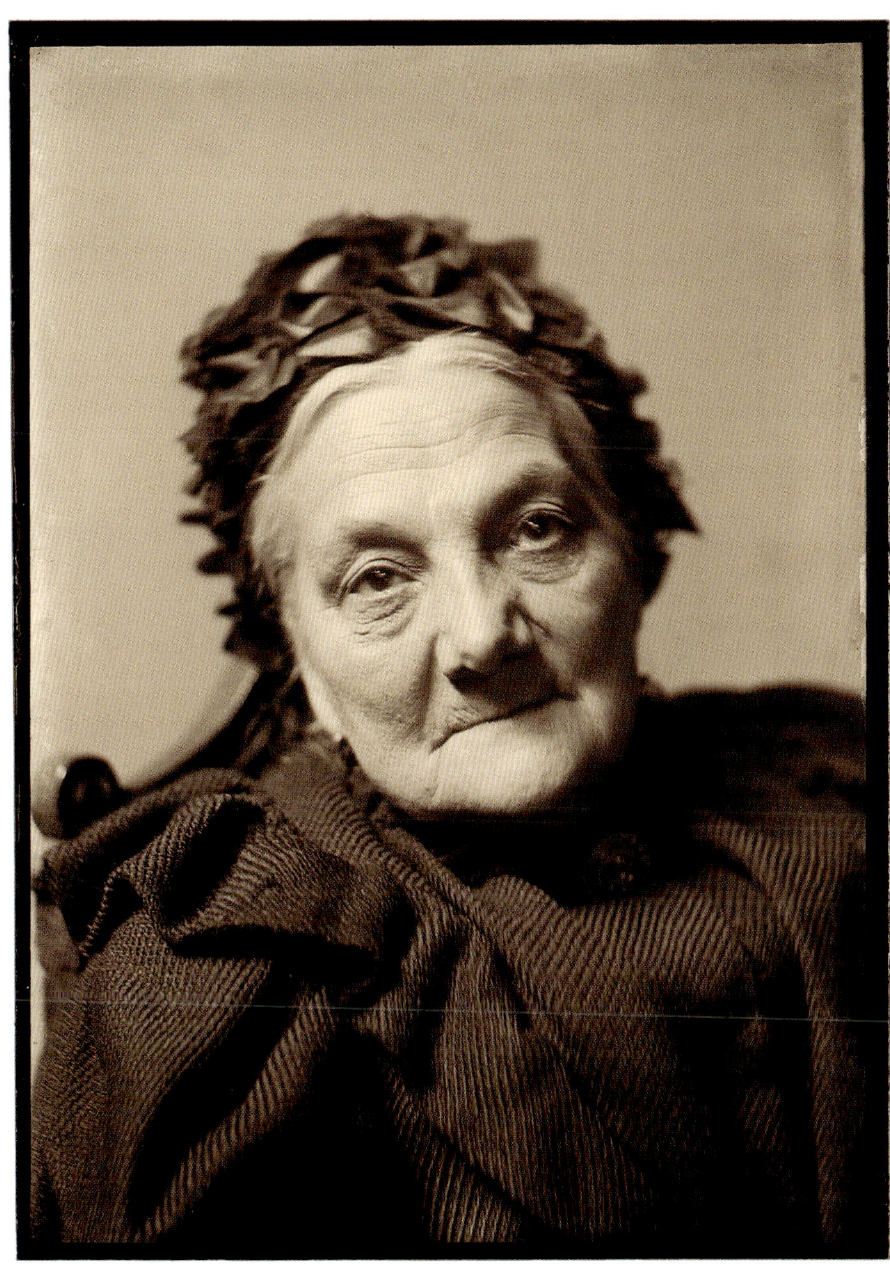

73. *Nurses of the Sarah Acland Memorial Home*

Gertrude Jane Denniston (1846–1920) and seven nurses, outside 37 Wellington Square
Oxford, September or October 1897 ?

Half-plate negative
Bodleian Library, Minn negative 92/1+

The Sarah Acland Memorial Home for Nurses was founded in memory of Miss Acland's mother, Sarah Acland, née Cotton (1815–1878). Mrs Acland was highly esteemed in Oxford among all classes for her charitable work. After her death her friends set about "to raise some lasting memorial of her worth, as an expression of the affection and reverence with which her life and character are regarded". This memorial, it was felt, should be "of practical usefulness, so as to promote some good work of the kind which Mrs Acland cherished, rather than be one of a purely personal character, which she would have deprecated". It was therefore decided to establish an 'Institution for Nurses' in her memory, the principal object of which would be to provide free nursing for the poor in their own homes, at a time when little other provision of the kind existed.

On 1 January 1879, by which time funds of £3,889 had been raised by public subscription under the patronage of Prince Leopold, an Acland district nurse and assistant started work out of Broad Street. In May, after the advice of Florence Nightingale (1820–1910) and Florence Sarah Lees (1840–1922) had been taken, 37 Wellington Square was opened, where an additional staff of five 'trained nurses' were given rooms. In 1882 the neighbouring house at 38 Wellington Square became a 'Medical and Surgical Home' for paying in-patients (principally undergraduates). Five years later a 'Middle Class Home' was added at No. 36, for patients unable to pay the fees of the Surgical Home, and a 'Maternity Branch' established, in the form of a midwifery nurse. By its 25th anniversary in 1904, the Home had five district nurses and three midwives, who were conducting 25,000 visits a year. A further twenty nurses were employed directly by patients. The private practice had become so large that it was decided to split the institution (a move that proved divisive), the two sides of which became known as the 'Sarah Acland Memorial District Nurses' and the 'Acland Medical and Surgical Home', although the distinction was still somewhat blurred.

Miss Acland, naturally, was closely involved in the Acland Home, stepping down from the committee in March 1907 after twenty-seven years' service. She knew the nurses personally, as reflected in the relaxed manner with which they posed for her in this group portrait on the steps of 37 Wellington Square.

This negative is one of the few among Miss Acland's plates to show any sign of deterioration: the emulsion is flaking away at the top in a manner more reminiscent of wet collodion. The gelatine dry plates she used were considerably easier to handle and more reliable than the earlier process, but still had to be varnished after development to protect the surface. Varnishes were usually shellac-based, requiring the plate to be warmed both before and after application. Flaking would result if the gelatine was not completely dry before coating.

Jackson's Oxford Journal, no. 6556 (9 November 1878), p. 5f.

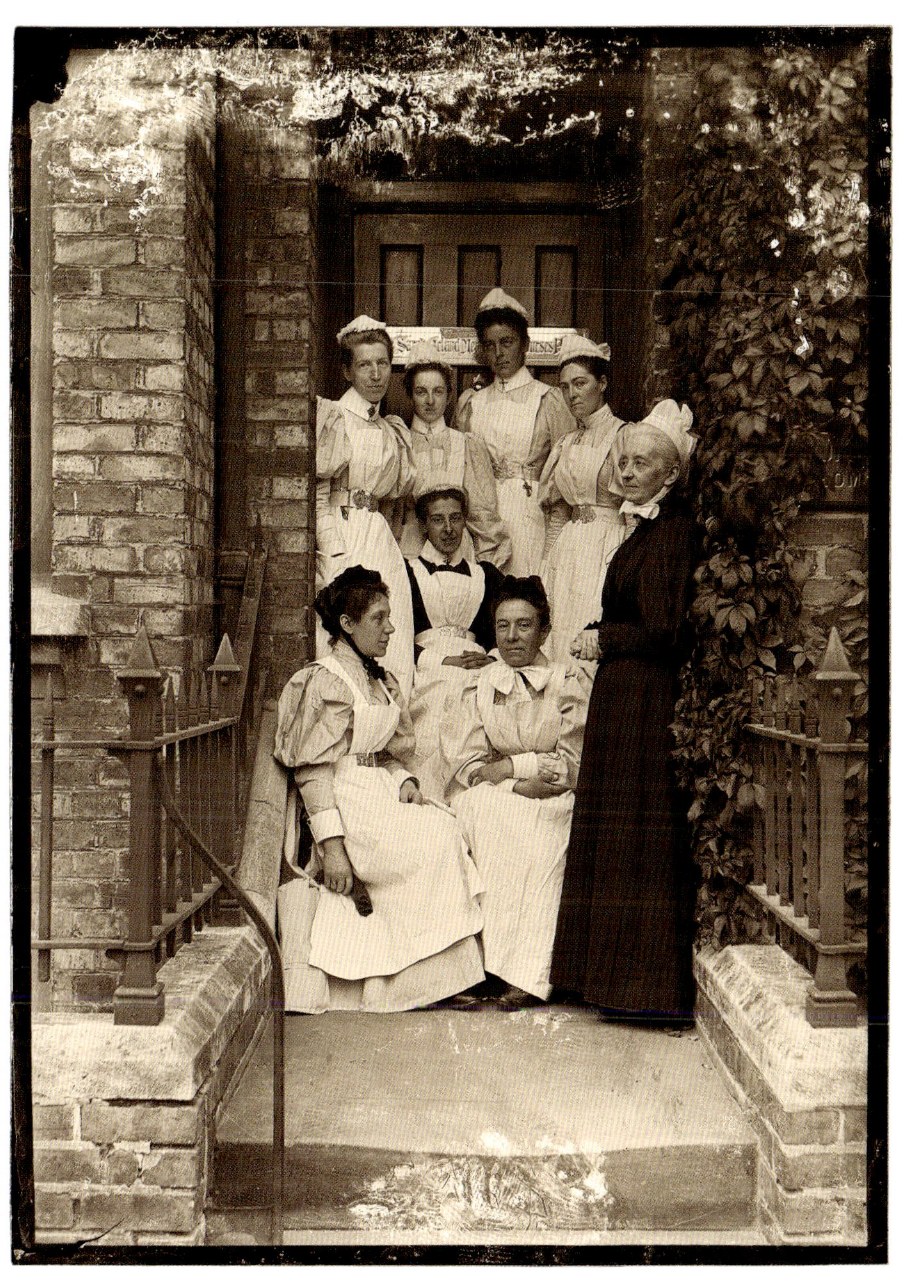

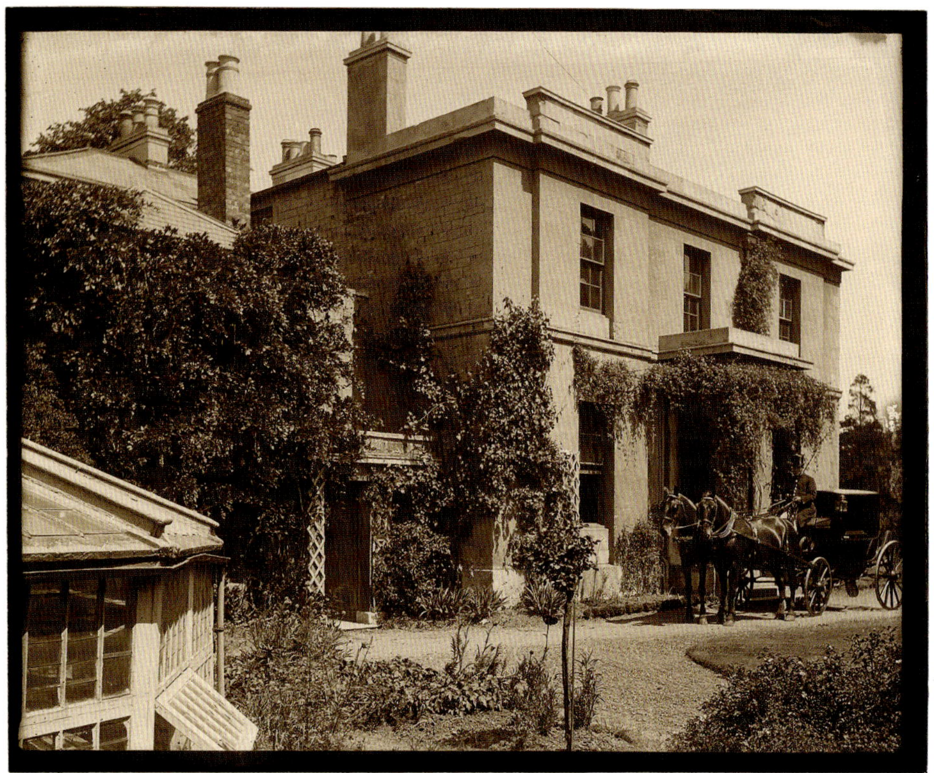

74–76. *The Sarah Acland Home for Nurses*

Northgate House; 25 Banbury Rd.; 36–38 Wellington Sq.
Oxford, 1895 or 1896; 1897 ?; 1897 or 1898

5 × 4 inch negatives
Bodleian Library, Minn negatives 25/2 & 25/1

Half-plate negative
Bodleian Library, Minn negative 184/11

By 1895 the Acland Home was outgrowing its premises in Wellington Square. The committee therefore took a lease from Lincoln College for 25 Banbury Road, the former residence of Bodley's Librarian, Henry Octavius Coxe (1811–1881). Thomas Graham Jackson (1835–1924) was then asked to draw up plans for an extension to Northgate House, as it was known, while funds were raised through a testimonial to Acland on his retirement as Regius Professor of Medicine. The new buildings were opened by the Prince of Wales in May 1897 but only became ready for occupation in October.

Catalogue no. 74 (above) shows Northgate House before the extension was added, with George Greening waiting by the door with the Aclands' brougham. In catalogue no. 75 (opposite top) the extension, which consisted of a three-storey administrative block and two-storey wing with patients' rooms, has recently been completed (the roof is pristine). Catalogue no. 76 (opposite bottom) shows Miss Denniston standing by the steps of 37 Wellington Square. Three doors down a large black dog lies on the pavement. The same nurse and pony cart are seen outside both properties.

A further extension to the Home, built with funds raised by Miss Acland and designed by Robert Langton Cole (1858–1928), opened in October 1906. In 2004 the Acland Hospital, as it had become, moved to Headington and was renamed the Manor Hospital, the district nurses having already been absorbed by the NHS. The Banbury Road site now belongs to Keble College, which would no doubt have met with Miss Acland and her parents' approval, given their close association with the college's founders.

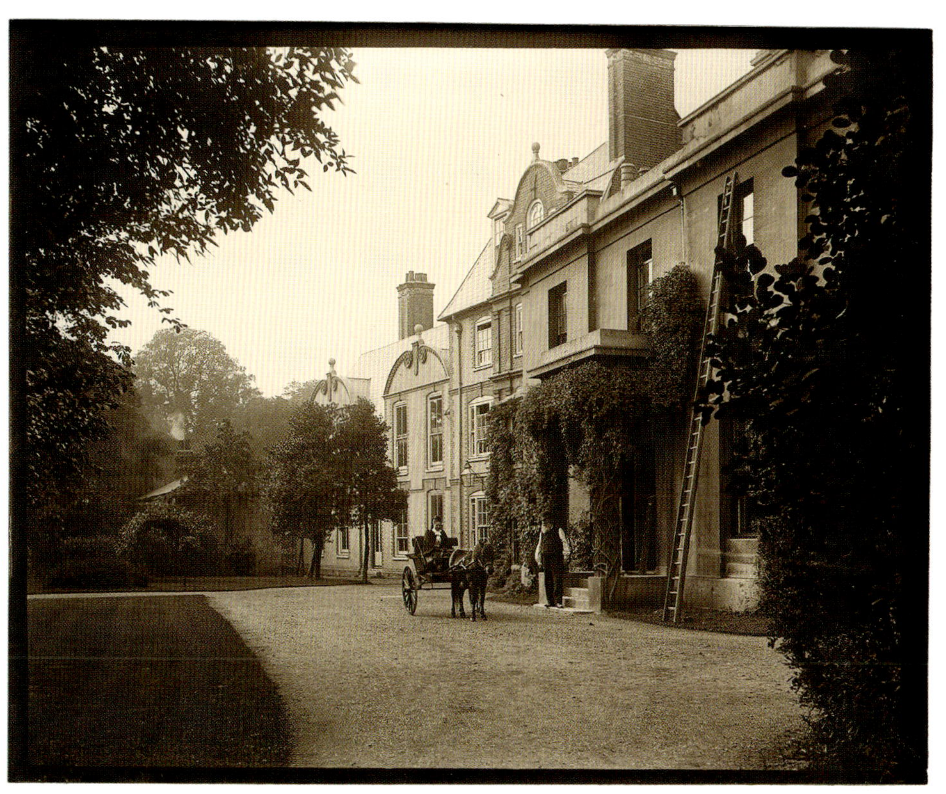

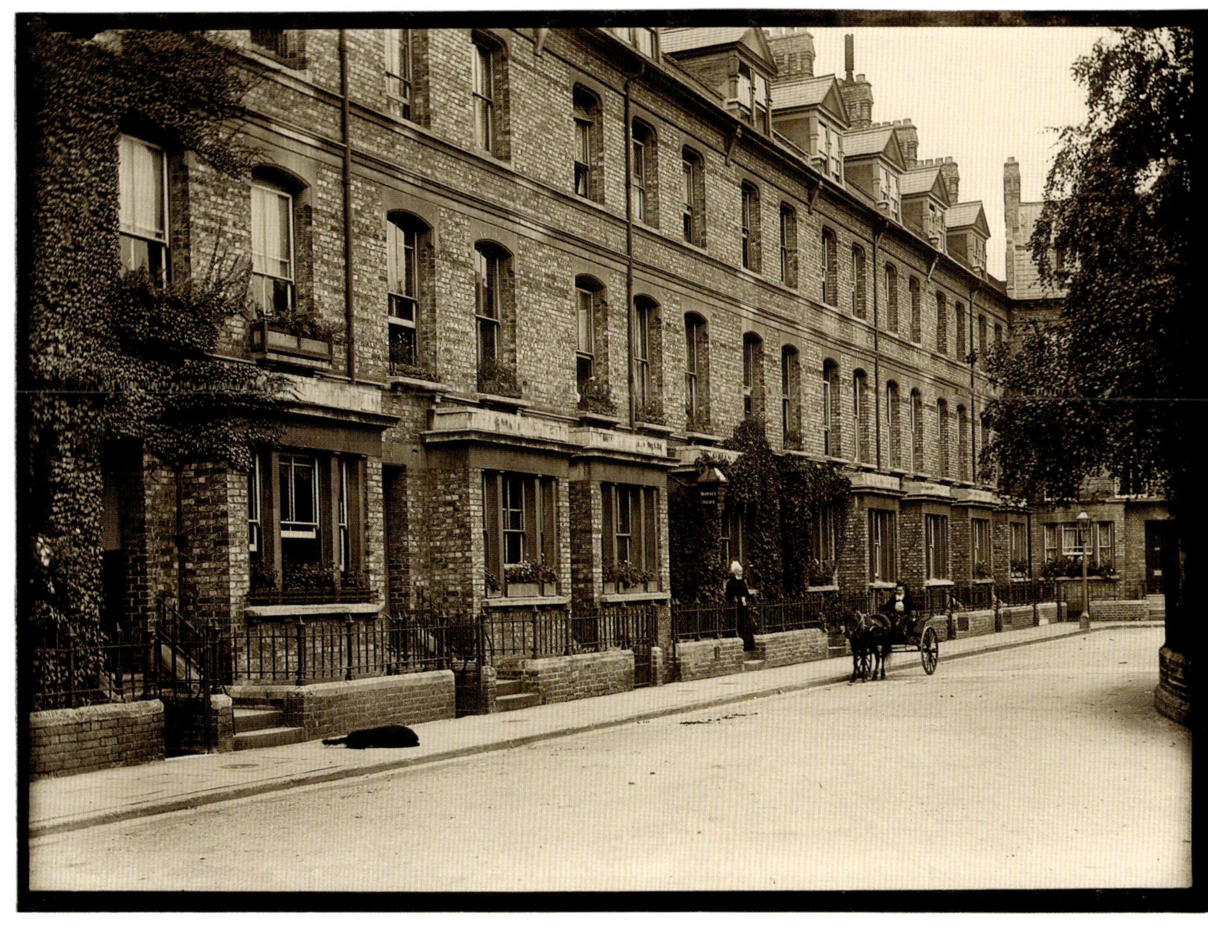

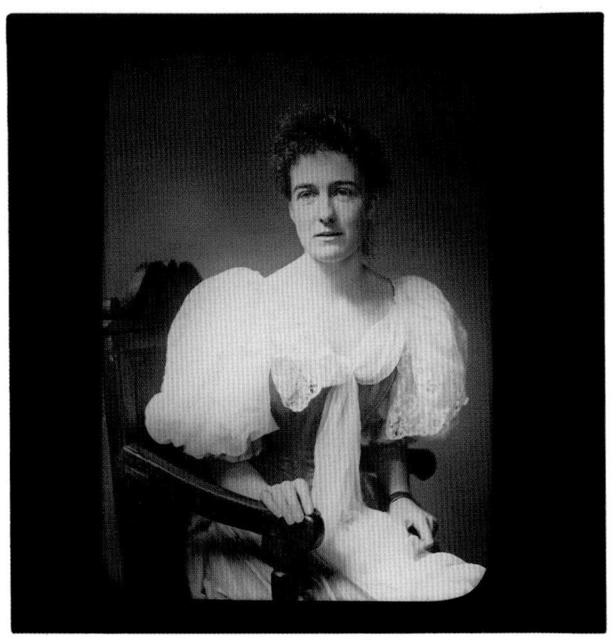

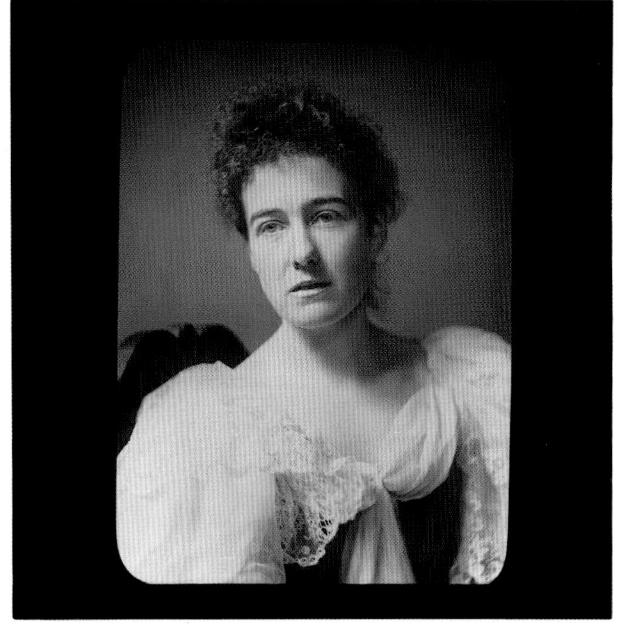

77 & 78. *"Miss de Lacy"*

Helen de Lacy (1864/5–?1949)
Oxford, *circa* 14 to 20 September 1897 ?
Lantern slides
Museum of the History of Science, Inventory nos. 76630 & 30830

Part of Miss Acland's advice to the Camera Club during her portraiture lecture concerned the different approach required for men and women, the latter being far more difficult, she argued, as "everything depended on pose and lighting". These portraits of Helen de Lacy are examples of her practice of treating young female subjects with the lips apart, a strategy also recommended by the leading society portraitist William Crooke.

Helen stayed with the Aclands on several occasions during the 1890s, including in Torquay and Boars Hill, either as a companion for Miss Acland or to help with the nursing of her father. Although she was absent for the lecture, Miss Acland sent her the proceedings of the Camera Club for February 1899, for which she returned thanks, expressing the "surprise and honour I felt yesterday to see my name amidst such distinguished company and in a lecture given by yourself!"

Helen's identity is problematic. Her address on writing in 1899 was Kenilworth House, Ealing, the home of Clare Mary Goslett, née Toomer (1857–1943), a prolific author and lecturer on hygiene and health. She was there to nurse Clare's daughter, Mildred Beatrice Goslett (b. 1876), but in what capacity is unclear. In the 1891 census she was listed as a "friend" of the Gosletts, when they were living in Babbacombe, Torquay, but her profession, if she had one, goes unrecorded.

Helen's 'reception dress' is fashionably artistic and consists of a form-fitting bodice of striped satin, the neckline and puffed sleeves decorated with Limerick lace, the tulle collar extending in a scarf down the front.

Proceedings of the Oxford Camera Club, no. 1 (April 1899), p. 4; MS. Acland d. 166, fols. 22–3; *Census of England and Wales, 1891*, RG12/1705, fol. 90, p. 20.

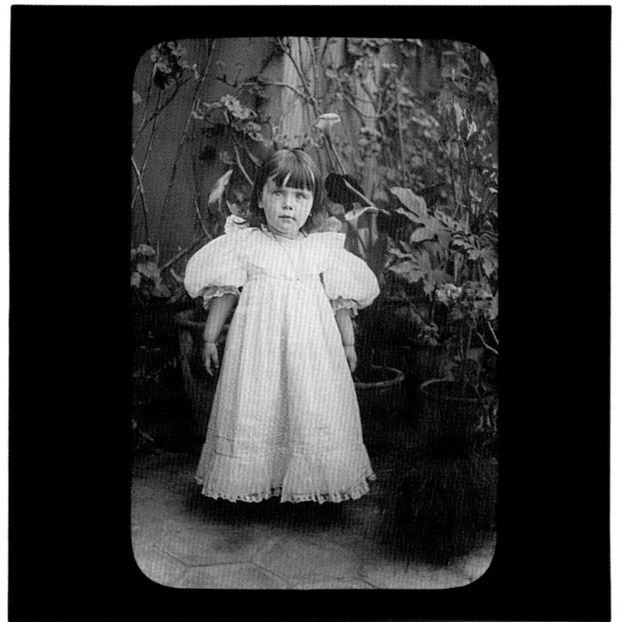

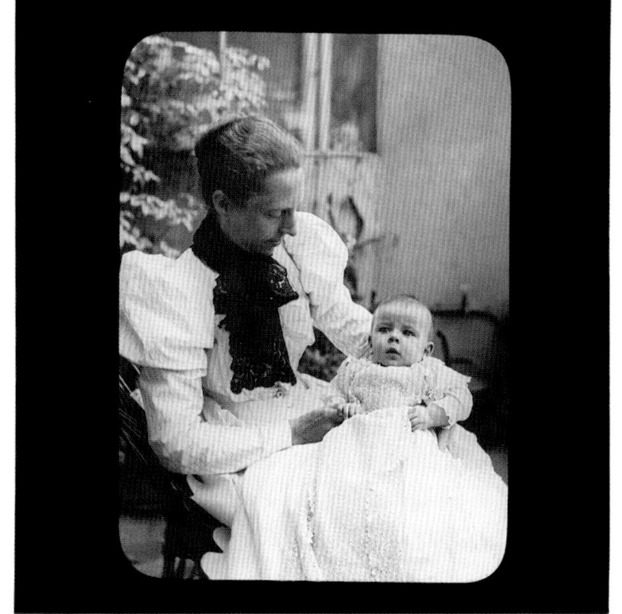

79. *"Sally"*

Sarah Beatrice ('Sally') Acland (1896–1979)
London, March 1898?

Lantern slide
Museum of the History of Science, Inventory no. 24062

Like Dodgson, who exhibited *Group of Children from Life* and *Portrait of a Child* at the Photographic Society in 1858, Miss Acland delighted in child portraiture. Her picture of Sally at 18 months was achieved "by getting everything ready, then as the child passed the spot marked, she was spoken to and the shutter snapped".

Sarah Beatrice Acland was Alfred's second child. Born on 11 September 1896, she married Cecil William Francis Stafford-King-Harman (1895–1987), a breeder of horses with a large estate at Rockingham Castle, County Roscommon. Her dress is sheer cotton woven with a spot and she is wearing a cross.

Proceedings of the Oxford Camera Club, no. 1 (April 1899), p. 5.

80. *"Harvey and the Boy"*

Margaret Mary Harvey (1855–1940) and Arthur William Acland (1897–1992)
London, March 1898?

Lantern slide
Museum of the History of Science, Inventory no. 27371

Arthur was the eldest son of Miss Acland's youngest brother, Alfred. He served in the Grenadier Guards in both World Wars, receiving the Military Cross in 1917 and the OBE in 1945. Harvey was described in her death notice in *The Times* as "for 52 years nurse and friend in the family of the late Colonel A. D. Acland and the Honourable Mrs. Acland".

Miss Acland photographed Harvey and Arthur using an exposure of 1⅖ seconds. Harvey's blouse has the 'gigot' (leg of mutton) sleeves that were a hallmark of the 1890s. Arthur, who was born on 20 November 1897, is wearing an unusually fine gown, decorated with Irish crochet lace, suggesting the portrait may have been taken on the occasion of his christening.

The Times, no. 48692 (12 August 1940), p. 1a.

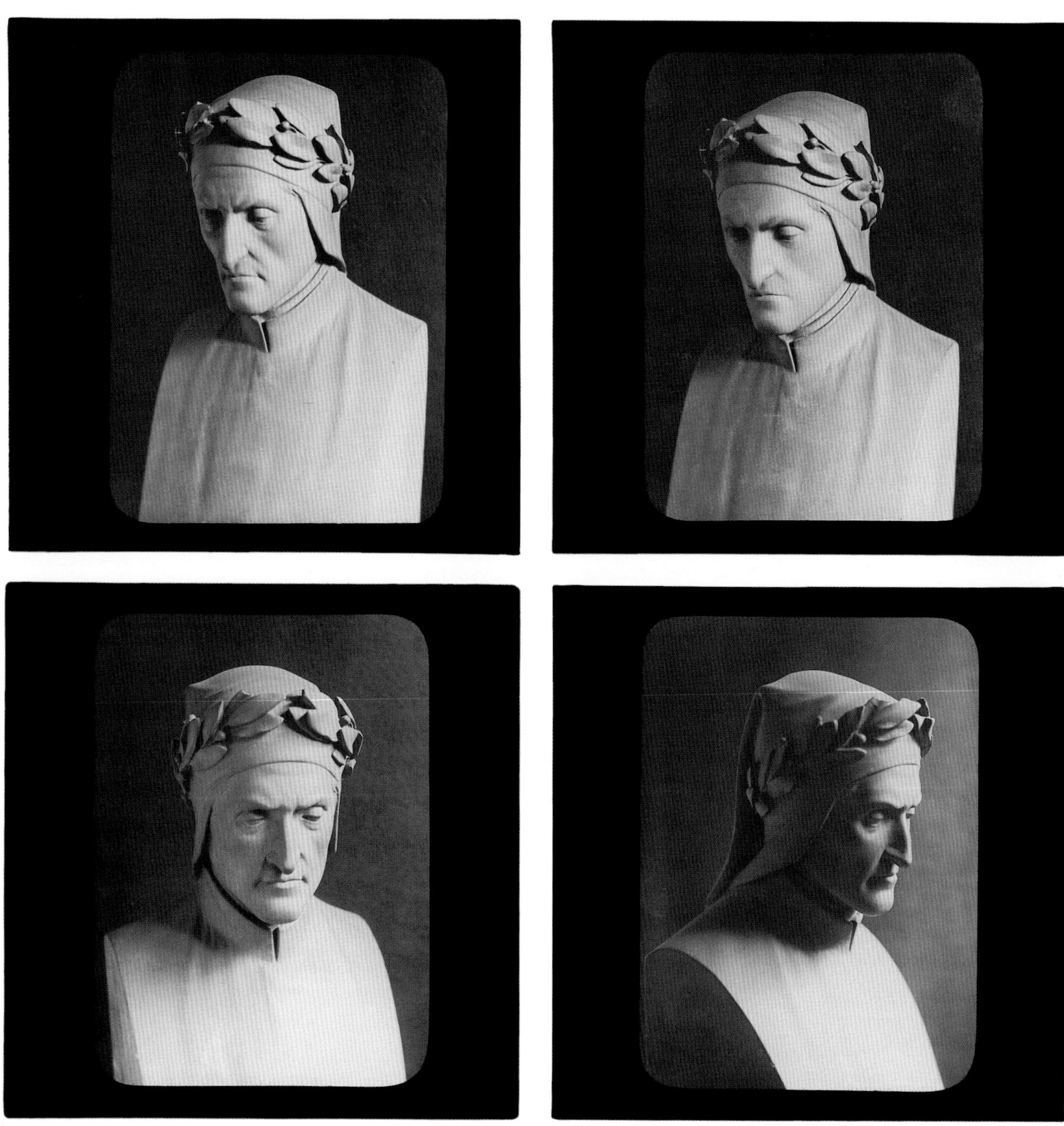

OPPOSITE

81–84. *"Dante"*

Four studies of a bust of Dante by Alexander Munro
Oxford, 1898 or 1899 (before 27 February 1899)

Lantern slides
Museum of the History of Science, Inventory nos. 85313, 81267, 27439 & 85966

These four studies of Alexander Munro's bust of Dante were used by Miss Acland in her Home Portraiture lecture to teach the principles of lighting. Mastery of chiaroscuro was an essential skill for the photographic portraitist, the successful portrayal of character depending on the precise manipulation of light and shade delineating the sitter's features. In her studies of Dante, Miss Acland argued, the difference in the lighting had "so changed the expression of the face" that had they been photographs of a living person "everyone would have said that the expression of the face had in truth changed".

In reporting Miss Acland's lecture the *British Journal of Photography* described the studies as "remarkable". "In one," the reviewer enthused, "Dante appeared with his usual lugubrious expression, while in another he appeared to be smiling". For John Andrews (1837–1906), Camera Club member, Estates Bursar of Wadham College, and the author of *Studies in Photography* (London, [1892]), they offered "an object lesson to all".

On 22 February 1858, a little over forty years before Miss Acland took these photographs, Dodgson called at the Acland house, at Mrs Acland's request, to show Munro his portraits. "He suggests that I should photograph his bust of Dante, which Dr. Acland has", Dodgson wrote in his diary after returning to his rooms. Later in the summer he acted on the suggestion, albeit preferring, it seems, the sculptor's own cast of the bust, photographed during a visit to his studio in Pimlico, to the copy in Oxford Miss Acland would later put to such good use.

Proceedings of the Oxford Camera Club, no. 1 (April 1899), p. 4; *British Journal of Photography*, vol. 46, no. 2027 (10 March 1899), p. 151b; MS. Acland d. 166, fols. 14–15; Edward Wakeling (ed.), *Lewis Carroll's Diaries*, vol. 3 (1995), p. 157.

OVERLEAF

85. *"Sir Henry Acland"*

Henry Wentworth Acland (1815–1900), in a smoking cap, writing at a table
Oxford, July 1898 ?

Whole-plate negative
Bodleian Library, Minn negative 138/1

"With all his work & manifold interests my Father was often greatly overworked & the strain was a very severe one", Miss Acland wrote in the second sentence of her memoirs. Acland's medical practice encompassed much of Oxfordshire. His first consultation outside the City had been to Samuel Wilberforce, at the Bishop of Oxford's Palace in Cuddesdon. Here he is wearing a smoking cap and looking frail: the portrait is the last in which he appears by himself.

Acland has been identified by some commentators as the inspiration for the White Rabbit in *Alice's Adventures in Wonderland* (London, 1865) — an idea suggested by the Rabbit's habit of dispensing potions and the brass nameplate at his door. The identification has much to recommend it. The Rabbit's anxious, busy, absent-minded manner is certainly reminiscent of Acland, as is his relationship with the King and Queen of Hearts, who are surely thinly veiled caricatures of the Dean and Mrs Liddell. One of Acland's nameplates, removed from Broad Street in February 1901 by Miss Acland's builder, Thomas Axtell (1926–1901), is now in the Museum of the History of Science, as is his medicine chest.

According to Miss Acland this undated portrait was her first whole-plate negative. The camera she used belonged to her brother Willie. When she finally gave it back in January 1919 she referred to it as being on "about a 20 year loan". The brown colour of the plate is either due to ageing of the varnish used to protect the emulsion or the effect of the developer. 'Pyro-soda' (a mixture of pyrogallic acid, sodium sulphite and sodium carbonate) was said to stain the highlights of negatives yellow, while 'pyro-ammonia' left blue tones. Miss Acland's negatives display a range of hues, from warm to cold.

Devon Records Office, 1148M/7/1, p. 4; MS. Acland d. 113, fols. 148–51.

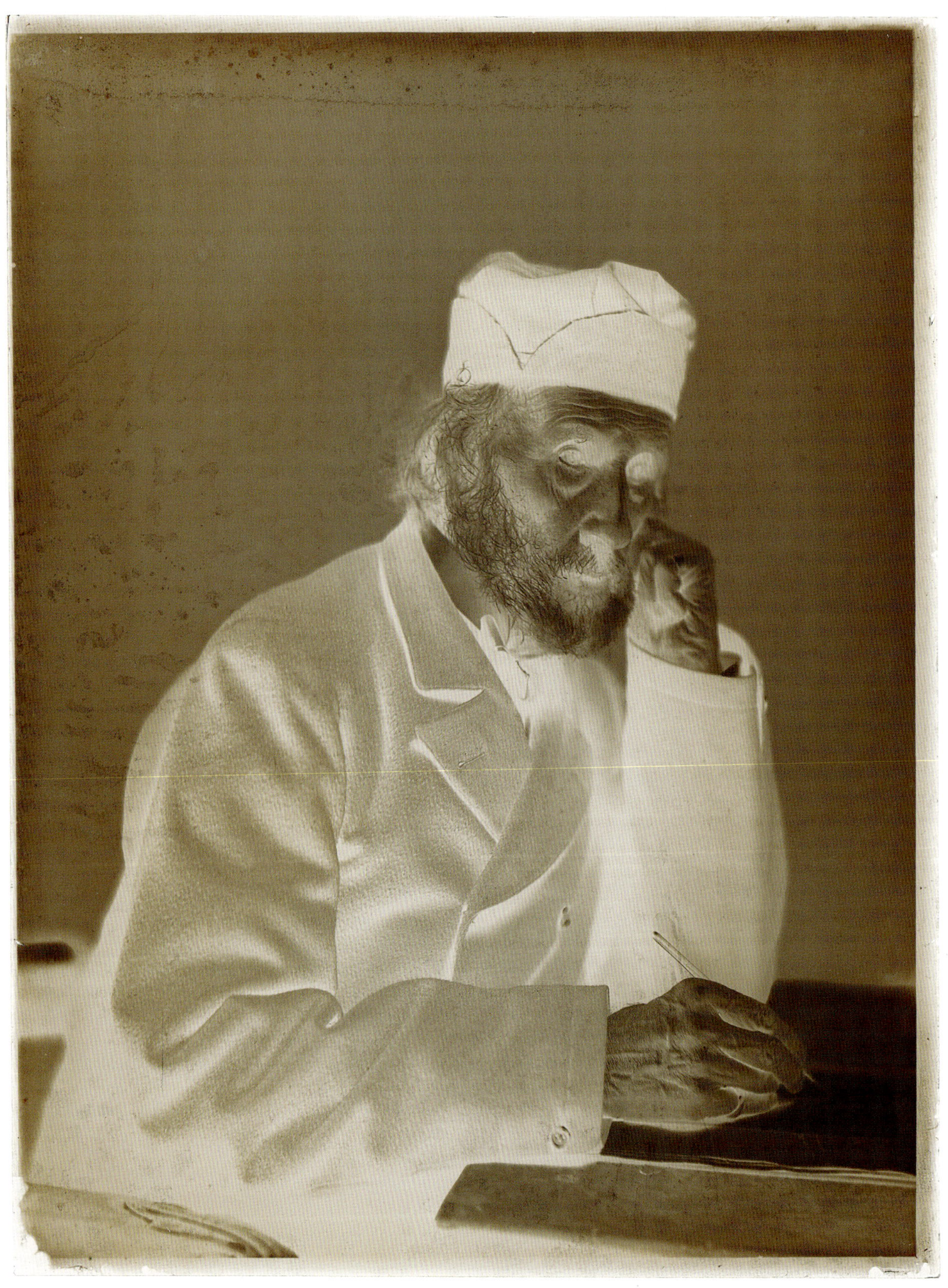

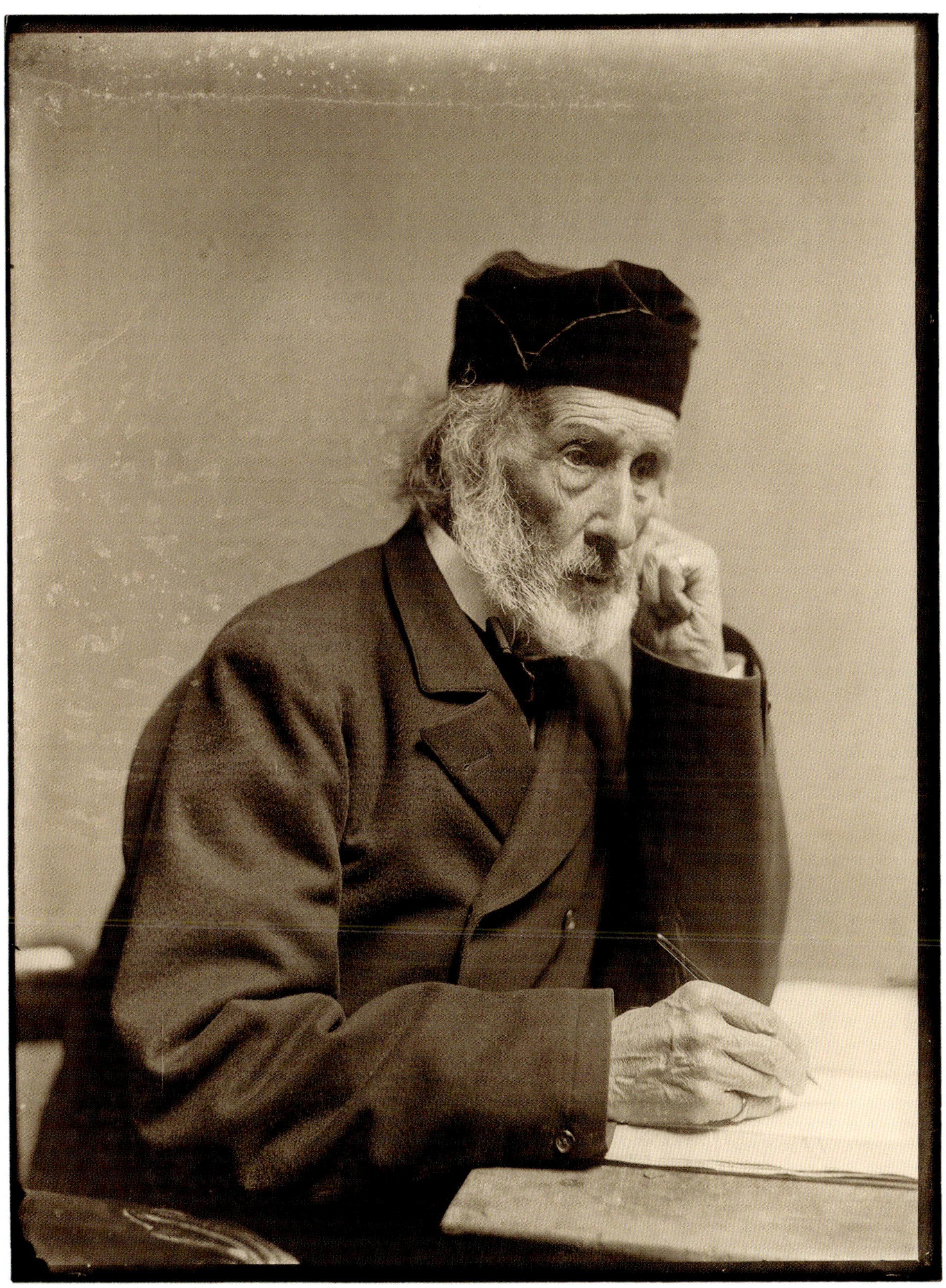

86. *"Sir William James Herschel, Bart."*

William James Herschel (1833–1917)
Oxford, between 16 and 19 February 1899

Whole-plate negative
Bodleian Library, Minn negative 196/6

William James Herschel was the son of John Frederick William Herschel, inventor of photographic fixer and the cyanotype. His grandfather, William Herschel (1738–1822), discovered Uranus (which was first referred to as the 'Herschel planet'). He therefore belonged to one of the most illustrious scientific families of the age. During his twenty-two years as President of the Oxford Camera Club he became a close friend of Miss Acland.

Herschel had a special interest in colour photography, no doubt inherited from his father, who in the early 1840s conducted experiments on the effect of different coloured light on a wide range of compounds, including tinctures extracted from flower petals. Although he lectured on colour photography on several occasions before 1900, W. J. Herschel took few colour photographs himself until some years after the release of the Autochrome. When he did do so much of his work was carried out in collaboration with his niece, Marjory Theodora Hardcastle, who lived with him at Lawn Upton in Littlemore, near Oxford. Marjory exhibited nine Autochromes at the R.P.S. between 1910 and 1915, several of which were taken in Switzerland and Egypt.

Miss Acland arranged this sitting in order to be able to show Herschel's portrait at the end of her Home Portraiture lecture. An earlier attempt, on 15 or 16 February, had been unsuccessful, apparently due to "the fault of the lens". In the lecture she claimed her first portraits had been taken with "an old-fashioned Wray lens", while noting that a "good portrait lens" was the best of all. Whether by 'old-fashioned' she meant a singlet, single combination ('landscape') lens, or symmetrical doublet is unclear. In the 1890s single lenses were recommended for artistic portraiture precisely because of their failings (chromatic aberration and poor definition). Her comments may therefore have been an attempt to reinforce the artistic credentials of her work, rather than entirely dispassionate advice.

In Miss Acland's albums the earliest portraits for which exposure details are recorded tend to be half and three-quarter length studies taken with a Rapid Rectilinear lens — a symmetrical doublet design by Dallmeyer of 1866 that was still very popular in the 1890s. Miss Acland's had a maximum aperture of f/8 and focal length of 8 inches (43 mm at 35 mm equivalent). In 1893, before going on holiday to the Lakes, she invested in a Ross 'Extra Rapid Universal Symmetrical' lens of 9 inches focus (48 mm equivalent) and f/5·6 aperture. After its introduction in late 1897 or early 1898 she then procured a 'No. 4 Dallmeyer Stigmatic Series II' lens, 7·6 inches in focus (41 mm equivalent) and f/6 aperture (a triplet and doublet pair). However, by 1899 she was back to taking large head studies with the "common lens supplied with her enlarging lantern": a Petzval-type portrait objective. For interiors and architecture she also owned a 4 inch (23 mm equivalent), f/16 'wide angle landscape lens'.

One of the issues Miss Acland addressed in her lecture was the best side of the sitter's face to photograph. She recommended the side with the greatest distance between the eye and corner of the mouth, or the side away from which the bridge of the nose inclined. "Few faces were sufficiently symmetrical to look best from the front", she argued. Herschel's was an exception: this is the most satisfactory of eight plates, six of which show him in profile or three-quarter face (cf. fig. 40).

MS. Acland d. 137, fols. 43–4; *Proceedings of the Oxford Camera Club*, no. 1 (April 1899), p. 5; *British Journal of Photography*, vol. 46, no. 2027 (10 March 1899), p. 152a; *Proceedings of the Oxford Camera Club*, p. 4.

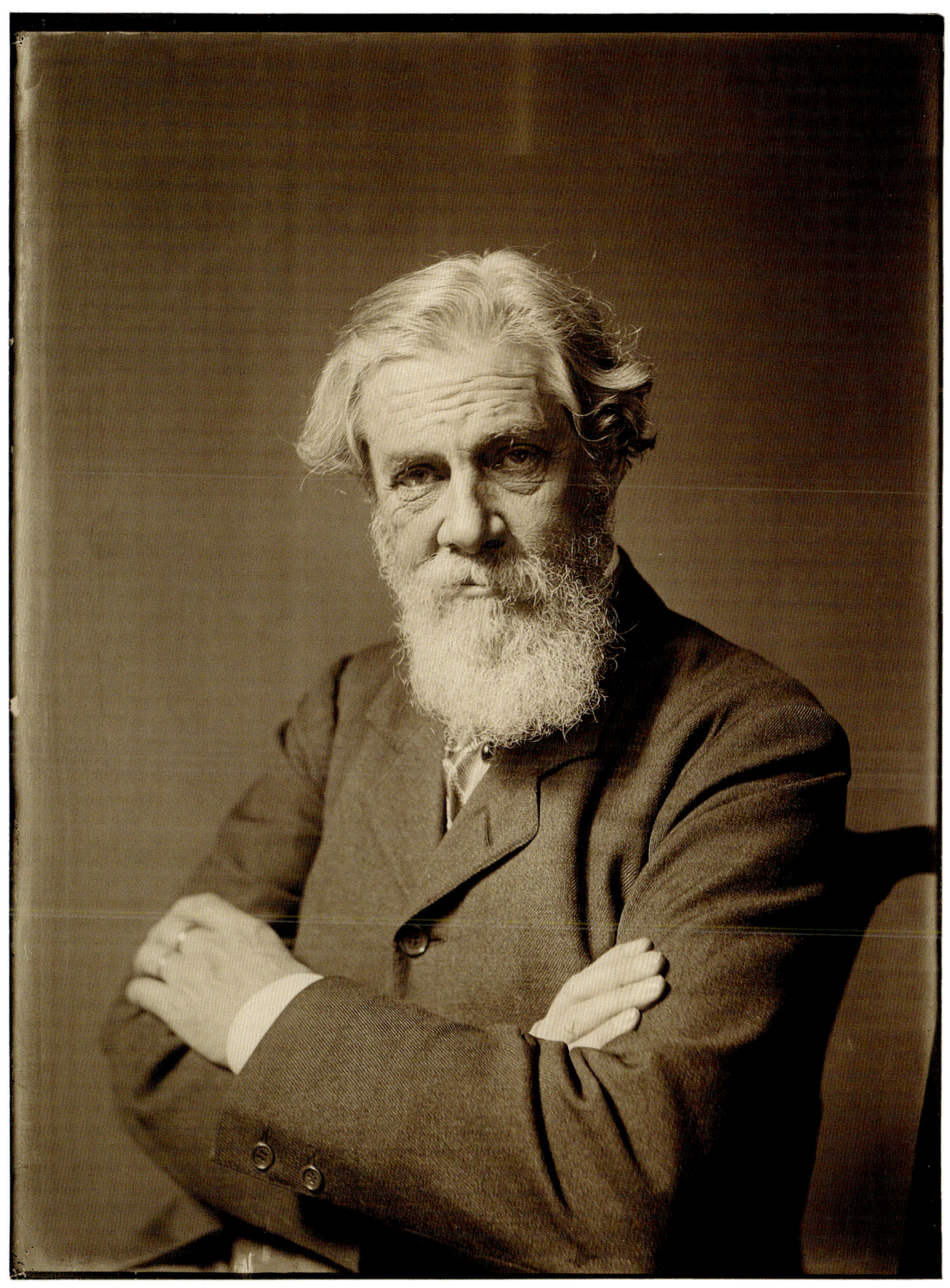

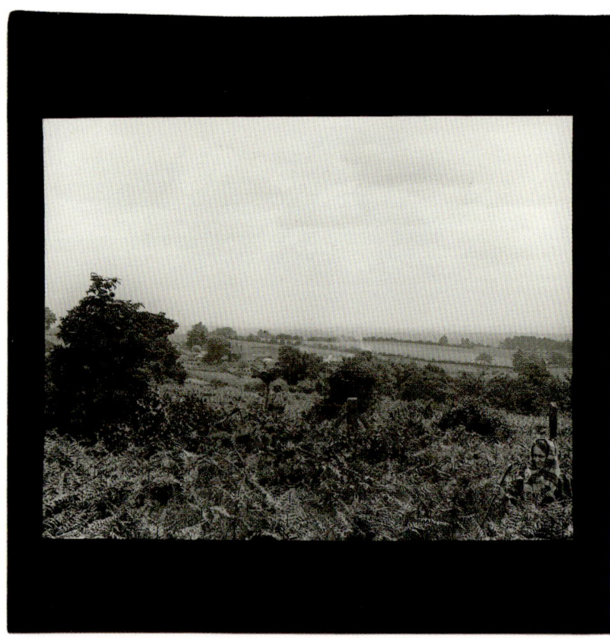
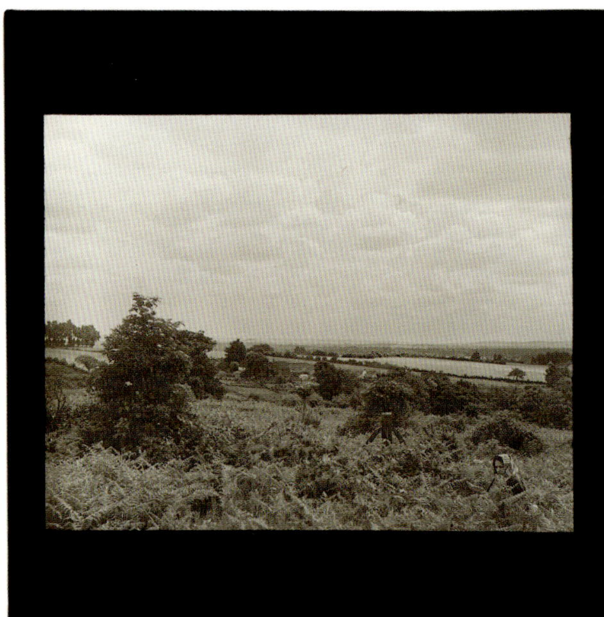
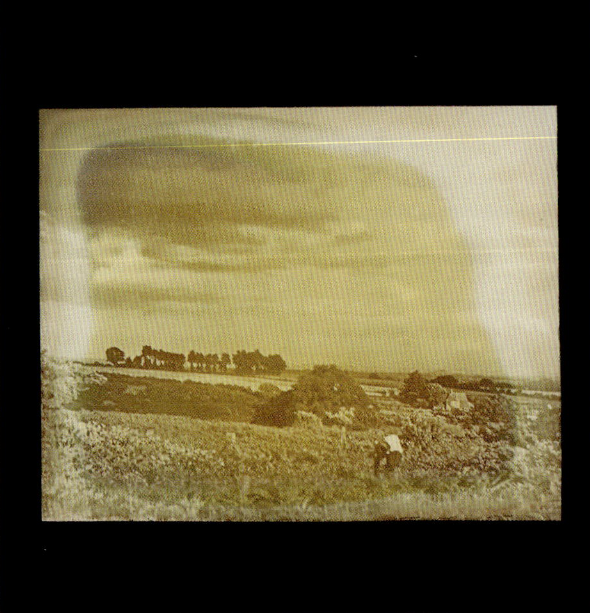
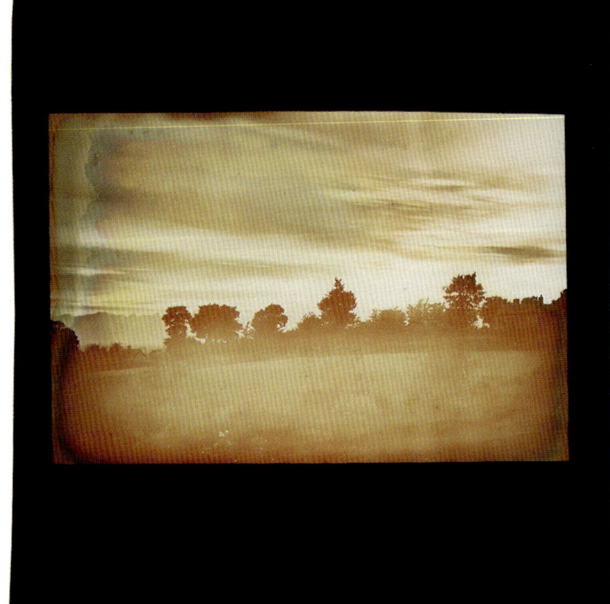

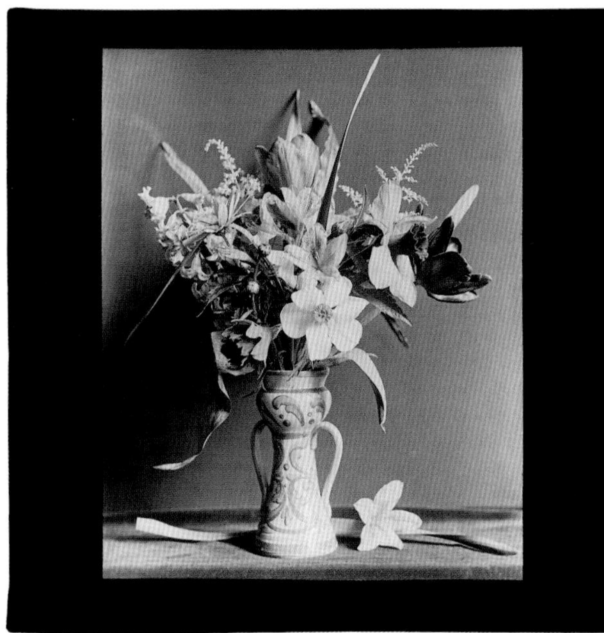

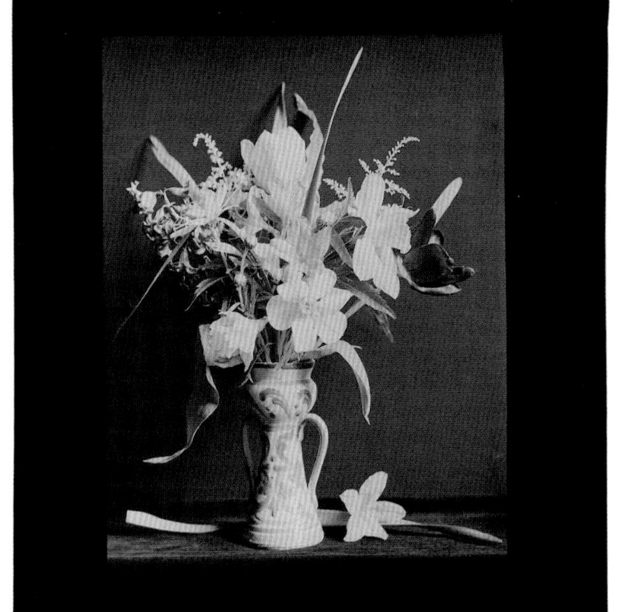

OPPOSITE TOP

87 & 88. *"From Boars Hill"*

View south-west from Boars Hill over the Fox Public House, with Wittenham Clumps in the far distance
Oxford, between 5 June and 9 August 1899
Lantern slides
Museum of the History of Science, Inv. nos. 27189 & 31221

OPPOSITE, BOTTOM LEFT

89. *"Clouds"*

View east by south-east from Boars Hill
Oxford, between 5 June and 9 August 1899
Lantern slide
Museum of the History of Science, Inventory no. 17761

OPPOSITE, BOTTOM RIGHT

90. *"Afterglow"*

View west by north-west from the Heath, Boars Hill
Oxford, between 5 June and 9 August 1899
Lantern slide
Museum of the History of Science, Inventory no. 53405

ABOVE

91 & 92. *"Posy"*

A posy of tulips, daffodils, bluebells and lilies in a vase before 23 April 1900
Lantern slide
Museum of the History of Science, Inv. nos. 44310 & 85102

After the success of her Home Portraiture lecture Miss Acland began a series of experiments in orthochromatic photography with James Cadett's Spectrum plate. These lantern slides were made for her second lecture at the Oxford Camera Club, on 23 April 1900, when she presented her results. The effect of the Spectrum plate, with its increased sensitivity to orange and red light compared to ordinary plates, is immediately apparent in *Posy*. In the ordinary plate, on the left, the orange and yellow of the daffodils and tulip are rendered as muddy greys; with the Spectrum plate they are almost white. *From Boars Hill* shows the benefit of orthochromatic plates for landscape work, especially in translating the golden sward of the cornfield in the distance and the clouds against the sky.

The orange tone of *Clouds* and *Afterglow* is evidence of Miss Acland's interest in another innovation of colour chemistry: copper toning by the 'Ferguson process'. William Bates Ferguson (1853–1937) was a former natural science student of her father and graduate of Merton College. His process, using solutions of copper sulphate, potassium ferricyanide and potassium citrate, was announced in 1900 and championed by *Photography*, which in September noted that Miss Acland was sending a print toned by the method to the R.P.S. exhibition. Miss Acland's enthusiasm for the technicalities of photographic chemistry belies the stereotype of her sex.

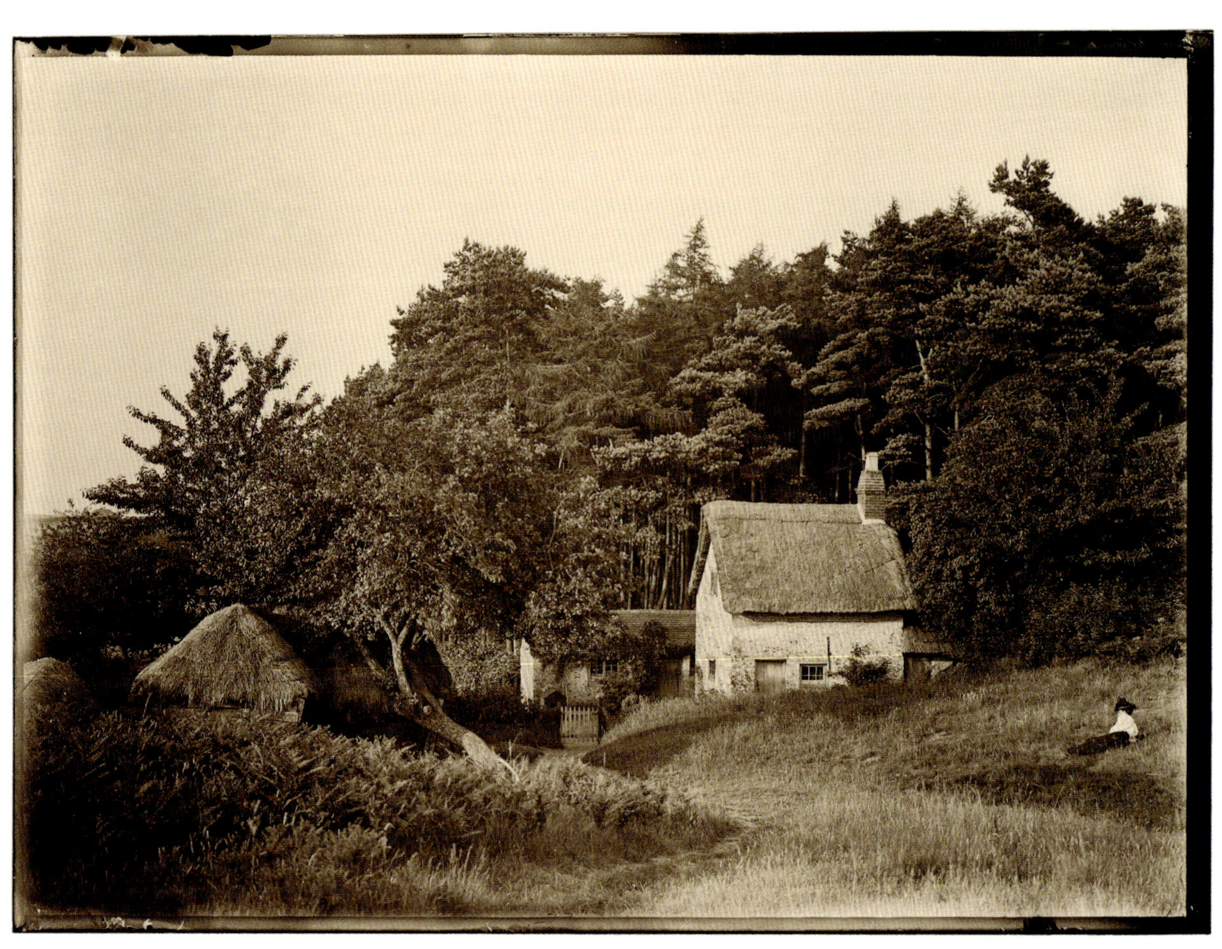

OPPOSITE

93. *Muckle's Hut, Boars Hill*

Muckle's Hut, Bedwells Heath, Boars Hill
Oxford, between 5 June and 9 August 1899

Half-plate negative
Bodleian Library, Minn negative 154/5

Muckle's Hut is the oldest building in Boars Hill, a prosperous hamlet south-west of Oxford. Miss Acland decamped to Boars Hill with her father and the whole household in June and July 1899 in order to escape the unremitting social demands placed on them in Oxford. "The view here is most beautiful & it is a most complete change from Oxford life", she told Willie. The vacation was a great success, especially for her trials in orthochromatic photography with the Spectrum plate. It would be the last time her father left the 'Old Home' in Broad Street.

In Boars Hill the Aclands rented 'The Heath', a large house owned by Randal Thomas Mowbray Rawdon Berkeley, 8th Earl of Berkeley (1865–1942). Berkeley was a chemist and had a laboratory at neighbouring Foxcombe Hall (now part of the Open University). He was also a photographer, and was interested to see Miss Acland's results: "All seem to be very successful any how to my untutored eye & what a difference the screen filter makes! I certainly shall go in for the Cadet spectrum plate when we come home again & will gladly avail myself of your kind permission to ask you for help."

MS. Acland d. 108, fols. 33–4; MS. Acland d. 171, fol. 89.

OVERLEAF

94. *"Broad Street at Night"*

The Clarendon Building and No. 30 Broad Street
Oxford, *circa* July or August 1899

Half-plate negative
Bodleian Library, Minn negative 148/4

Although at first sight mundane, this view of the east end of Broad Street is one of the most remarkable of Miss Acland's photographs. That something is unusual about the image is betrayed by the tone of the sky, the glow of the lamps hanging on the roadworks, the light from the stove where an invisible man sits at a makeshift shelter brewing his tea, and the bright windows of Mrs Williams's 'New & Secondhand Clothing Stores'.

The key to the unusual qualities of the photograph lies in the fact that it was taken during twilight and darkness, in an exposure of four hours from 8 p.m. to midnight (one hour at f/11, the remainder at f/5). Miss Acland used a Spectrum plate for the task, her intention being to assess the (disputed) capabilities of orthochromatic emulsions for recording the orange light of the evening. She exhibited the image as a lantern slide in her Spectrum Plates lecture and as an enlargement at the Camera Club in 1900, when it was described as "quite one of the curiosities of the exhibition".

Broad Street at Night is related to a genre of 'night photography' that became popular in Britain in the 1890s. In 1893, when she attended the R.P.S. exhibition for the first time, Miss Acland particularly admired a series of photographs taken in a mine. Three years later she could enjoy medal-winning views of *London by Gas Light* by Paul Martin (1864–1944). At a time when amateurs were vying with each other "like the Athenians of old" for new forms of artistic expression, photography in low light was a field ripe for exploitation. The use of orthochromatic plates was more faithful to the photographic medium than some of the new processes favoured by photographers on the extreme wing of the 'Pictorial Movement' in photography, who preferred to imitate the graphic arts with bichromated gums and other materials capable of direct manual manipulation.

Jackson's Oxford Journal, no. 7669 (10 March 1900), p. 4c; *Amateur Photographer*, vol. 27, no. 692 (7 January 1898), pp. 9–10.

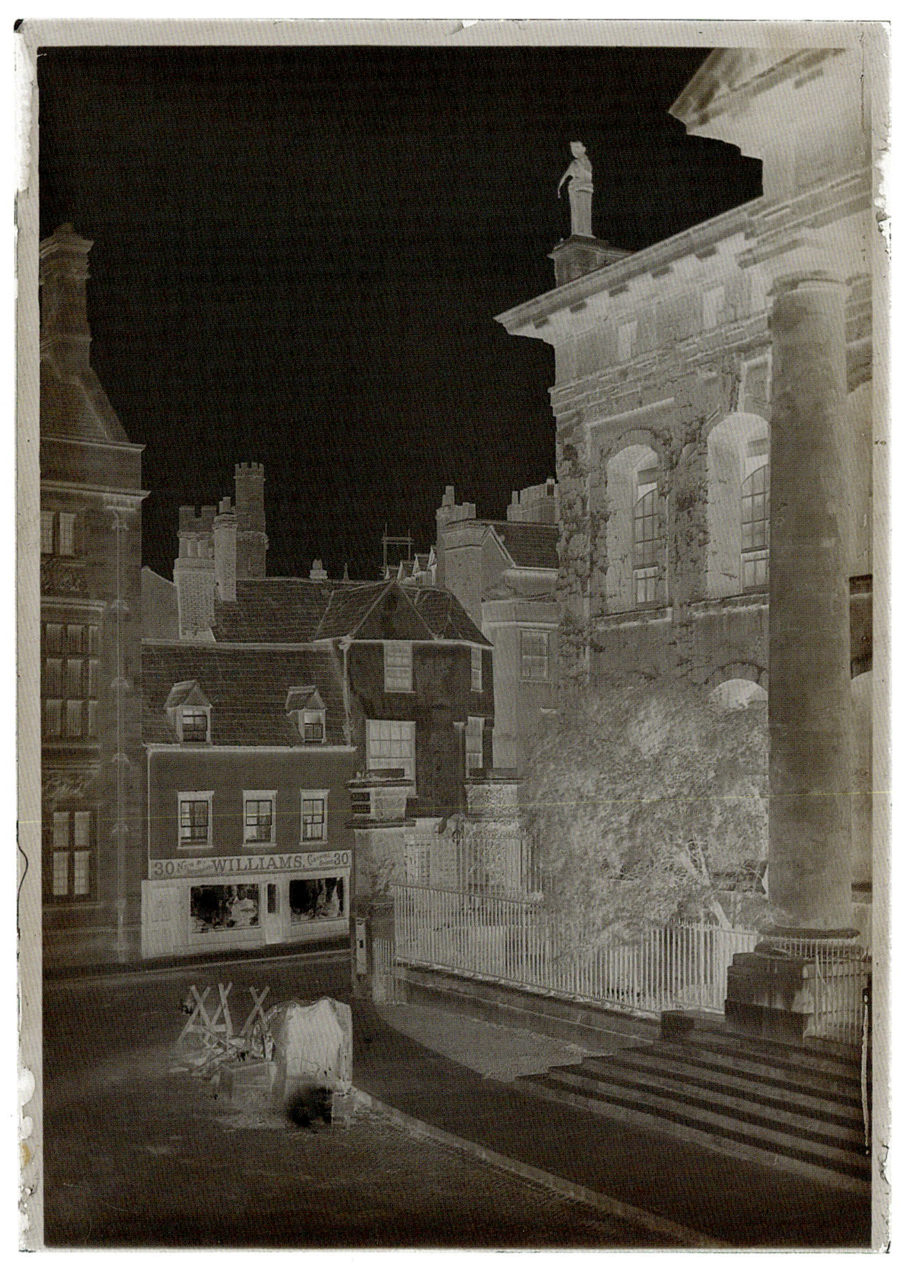
30 WILLIAMS, 30

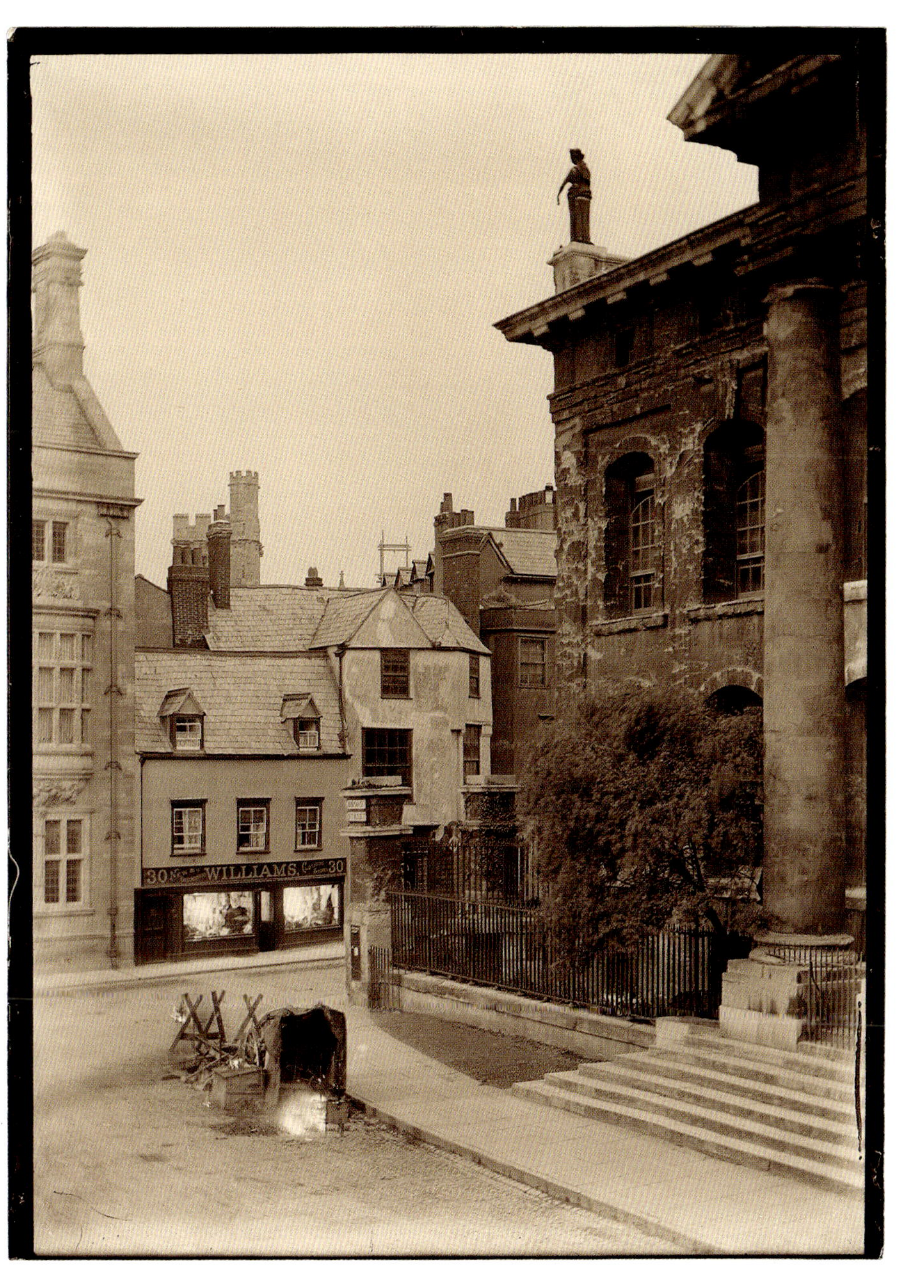
30 WILLIAMS. 30

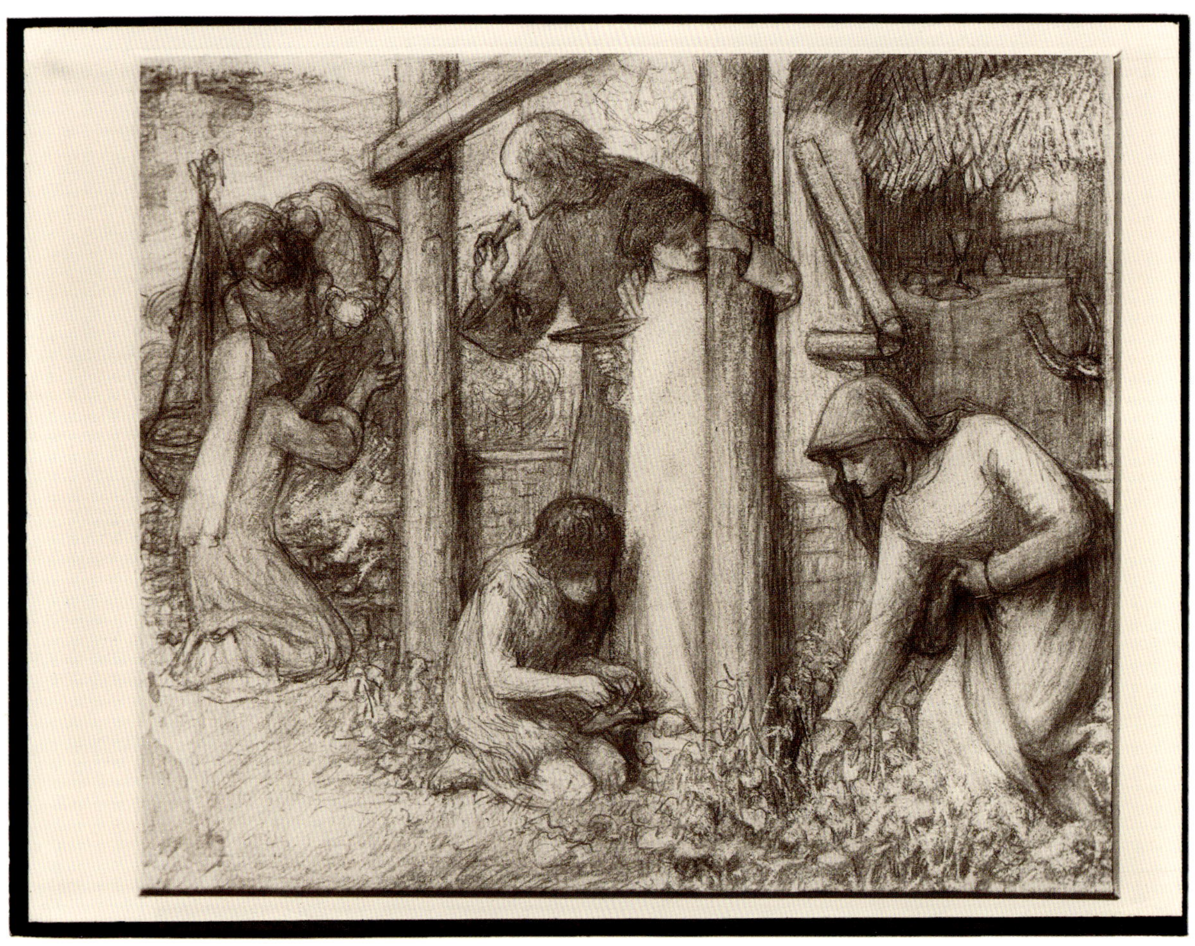

95. *"Gathering the Bitter Herbs"*

Pencil drawing by Dante Gabriel Rossetti (1828–1882)
Oxford, between 5 and 23 August 1899
Whole-plate negative (reduced ×0·75)
Bodleian Library, Minn negative 138/10

In 1855 Ruskin persuaded Acland to take Elizabeth Siddal, Rossetti's model and future wife, under his care. Siddal's stay in Broad Street was not without its problems, Ruskin finding the need to write to Mrs Acland with an apology for Siddal's ungratefulness and failure to keep her room in order. To thank Acland on Rossetti's behalf Ruskin gave him this drawing and a companion piece, *The Holy Family Eating the Passover*. A watercolour from the Passover design is now in Tate Britain.

Miss Acland made this copy of *Gathering the Bitter Herbs* at the request of art historian Henry Currie Marillier (1865–1951), for his *Dante Gabriel Rossetti: An Illustrated Memorial of his Life and Work* (London, 1899). She also photographed Rossetti's *La Belle Dame Sans Merci* and *Michael Scott's Wooing*, drawings that belonged to her friend John Arthur Ruskin Munro, fellow of Lincoln College, who inherited them from his father, sculptor Alexander Munro. J.A.R. Munro was also a photographer, with a talent for landscape work.

Miss Acland photographed Rossetti's drawing upside down, as revealed by the shadow of the mount, which is at the bottom rather than the top of the picture. The trick meant the image appeared the right way up on the ground glass of her camera as she aligned the frame.

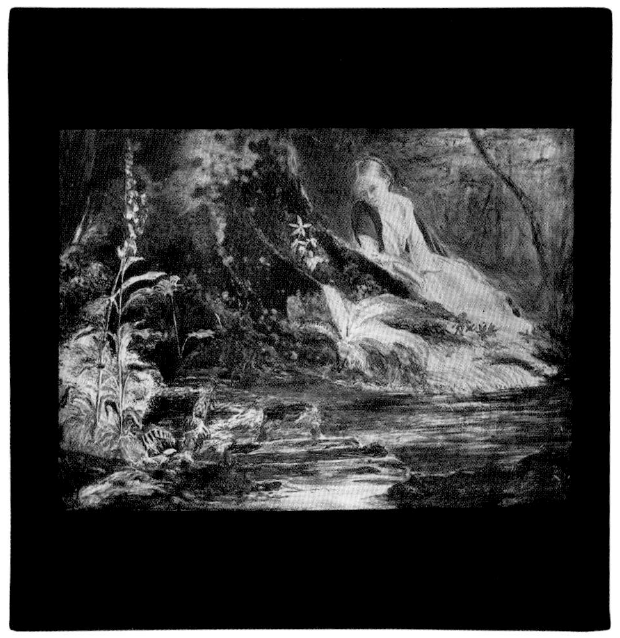

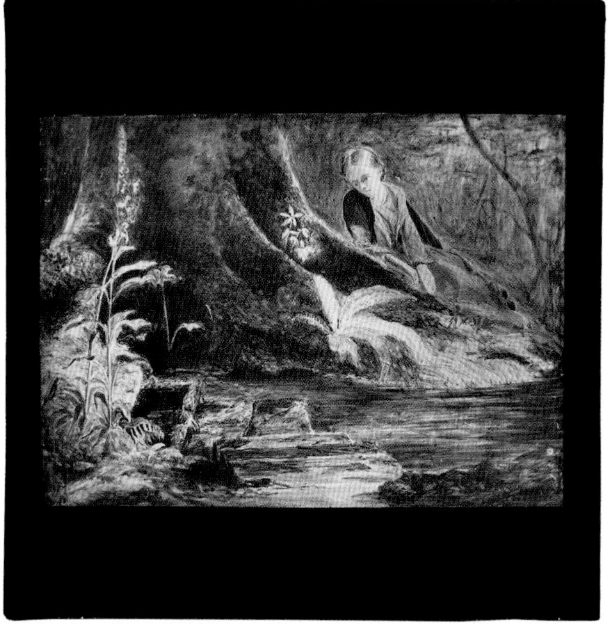

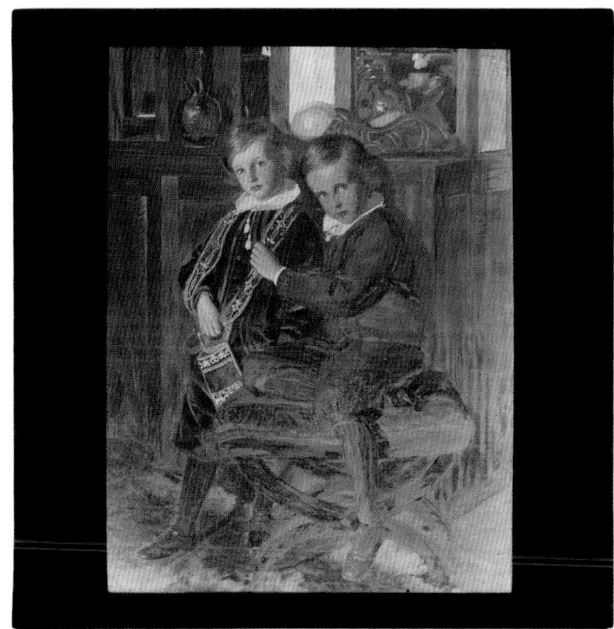

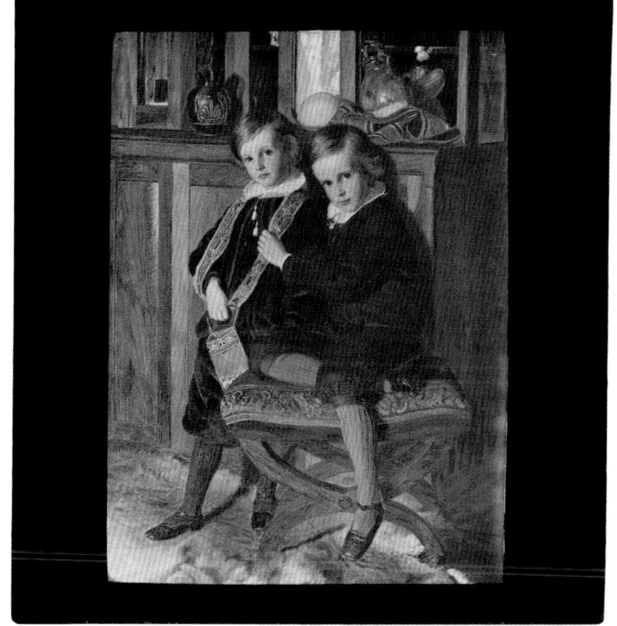

96–99. *The Spectrum Plate as Copyist*

Paintings by Henry Wentworth Acland and William Blake Richmond, on ordinary and Spectrum plates
September or October 1899 ? (before 23 April 1900)
Lantern slides
Museum of the History of Science, Inventory nos. 17431, 99516, 77488 & 60560

Copying artworks was a challenge that fascinated Miss Acland and one she examined at length in her Spectrum Plate lecture. Richmond's portrait of Frank and Alfred can be seen in the drawing room in catalogue no. 5 and was said to be his first commission. In her paper Miss Acland explained that the boys' coats were dark blue, their stockings and the pouch (embroidered with beads and porcupine quills) bright red, the shadows brown.

Acland's *The Maid of Wallington Wells* was painted in August 1855 at Wallington Hall, Northumberland, the home of his friends the Pre-Raphaelite patrons Sir Walter (1797–1879) and Pauline Trevelyan (1816–1866). Lady Trevelyan was a keen amateur photographer.

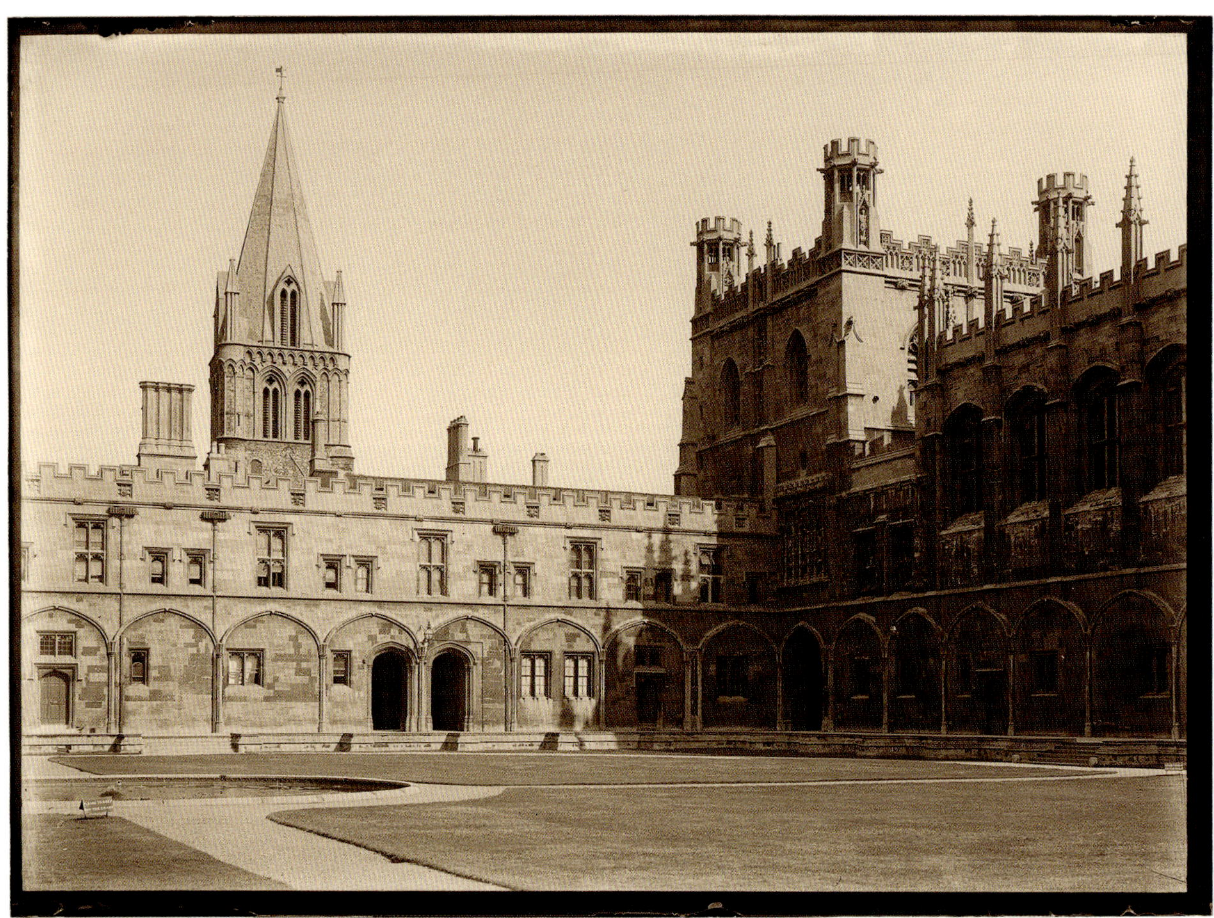

ABOVE *&* OPPOSITE

100. *Tom Quad*

South-east corner of the Great Quadrangle, Christ Church Oxford, August or September 1899 ?

Half-plate negative
Bodleian Library, Minn negative 187/5

In 1897 the Oxford Camera Club entered into an agreement with the London publisher F. E. Robinson to provide photographs for a series of histories of the Oxford colleges. On dividing up the work Miss Acland was allocated Christ Church, for which she made this and the following plates. When the Christ Church history was published in August 1900 the photographs were credited to the Camera Club rather than to her as an individual, reflecting its members' strong collaborative ethos. Nevertheless, she was thanked by the author, Henry Lewis Thompson (1840–1905), husband of her great friend Katie Paget.

Surprisingly, the majority of the stonework visible was still new when the photograph was taken. Liddell had undertaken an extensive programme of restoration during his time as Dean which saw the complete remodelling of Tom Quad: the terrace lowered, pinnacles added to the Hall, battlements substituted for a balustrade, and a new entrance made to the Cathedral. The curtain wall of the bell tower, with its faux louvres, hides the 'meat safe' that still contains the bells, as parodied by Lewis Carroll in *The New Belfry of Christ Church* (Oxford, 1872).

The open windows suggest the photograph was taken in the summer months. Shadows visible in a view of the interior of the Cathedral probably taken on the same occasion give the sun's elevation as 41° at noon and therefore point to a date around 15 September.

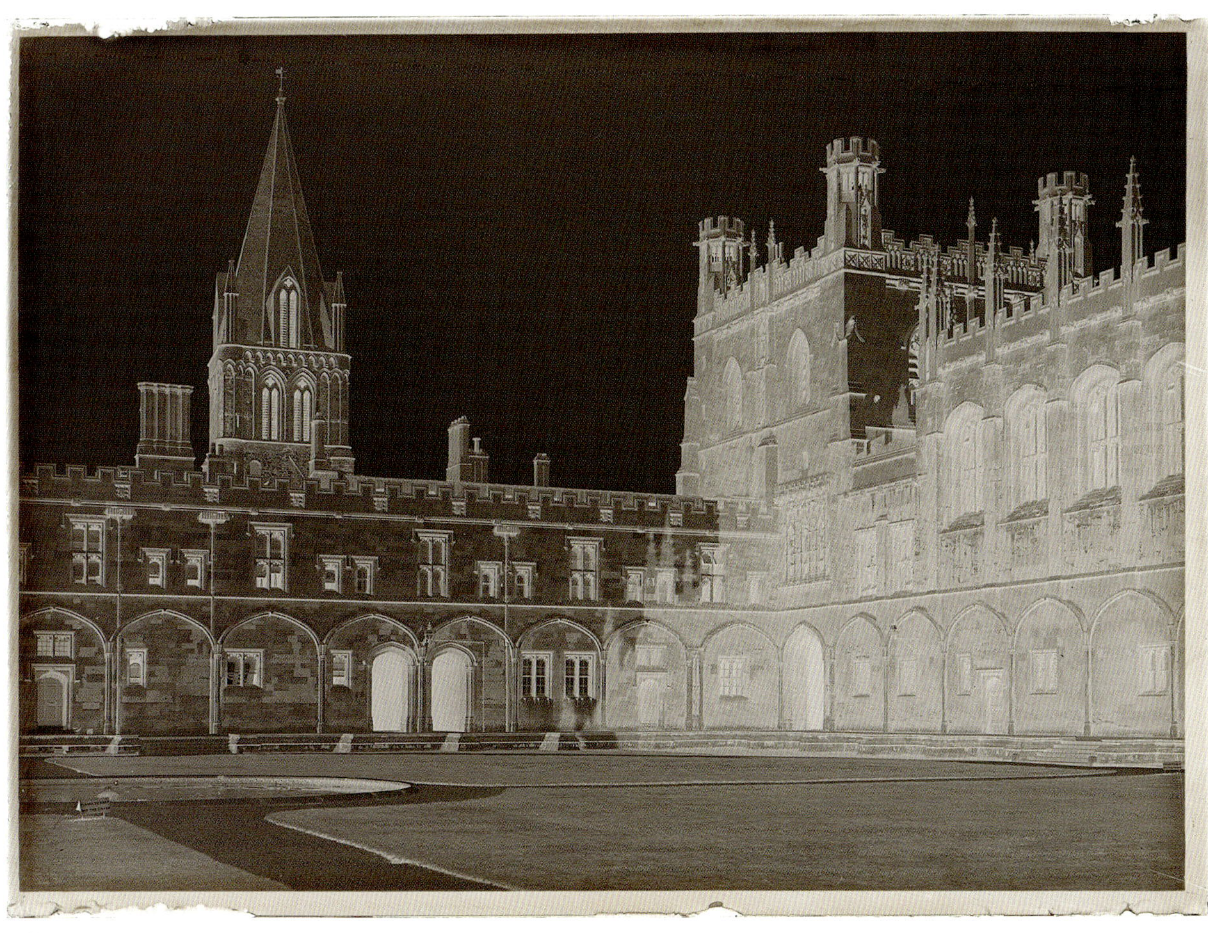

OVERLEAF

101. *Interior of Christ Church Cathedral*

North transept, Christ Church Cathedral
Oxford, August or September 1899 ?
Half-plate negative
Bodleian Library, Minn negative 171/8

This is not, as appears at first sight, the nave of Christ Church, but a more visually interesting view across the north transept. In Miss Acland's hands the scene has become an essay in mass and tone, and light and shade, extending across the full range of gradation. In the architecture class of the 1900 Camera Club exhibition she won first prize with *Christ Church Kitchen*, but most thought her photograph of the Cathedral "far better, both in technique and composition".

Ecclesiastical interiors was a genre in which Oxford Camera Club members could claim a certain distinction. When Caleb Court Cole (1847–1905) showed views of Christ Church at the Philadelphia Exhibition in 1893, for example, Alfred Stieglitz called them "absolutely above criticism" and "the most marvelous bit of technical work in the whole exhibition". Cole was succeeded by J.R.H. Weaver, a close friend of Frederick Evans, who made a speciality of Spanish ecclesiastical architecture.

A beautiful platinum print by Miss Acland of this exquisite photograph survives, but the image was not one chosen for publication in the college history.

Oxford Times, no. 2044 (10 March 1900), p. 11f; "The Joint Exhibition at Philadelphia", *American Amateur Photographer*, vol. 5 (1893), p. 250.

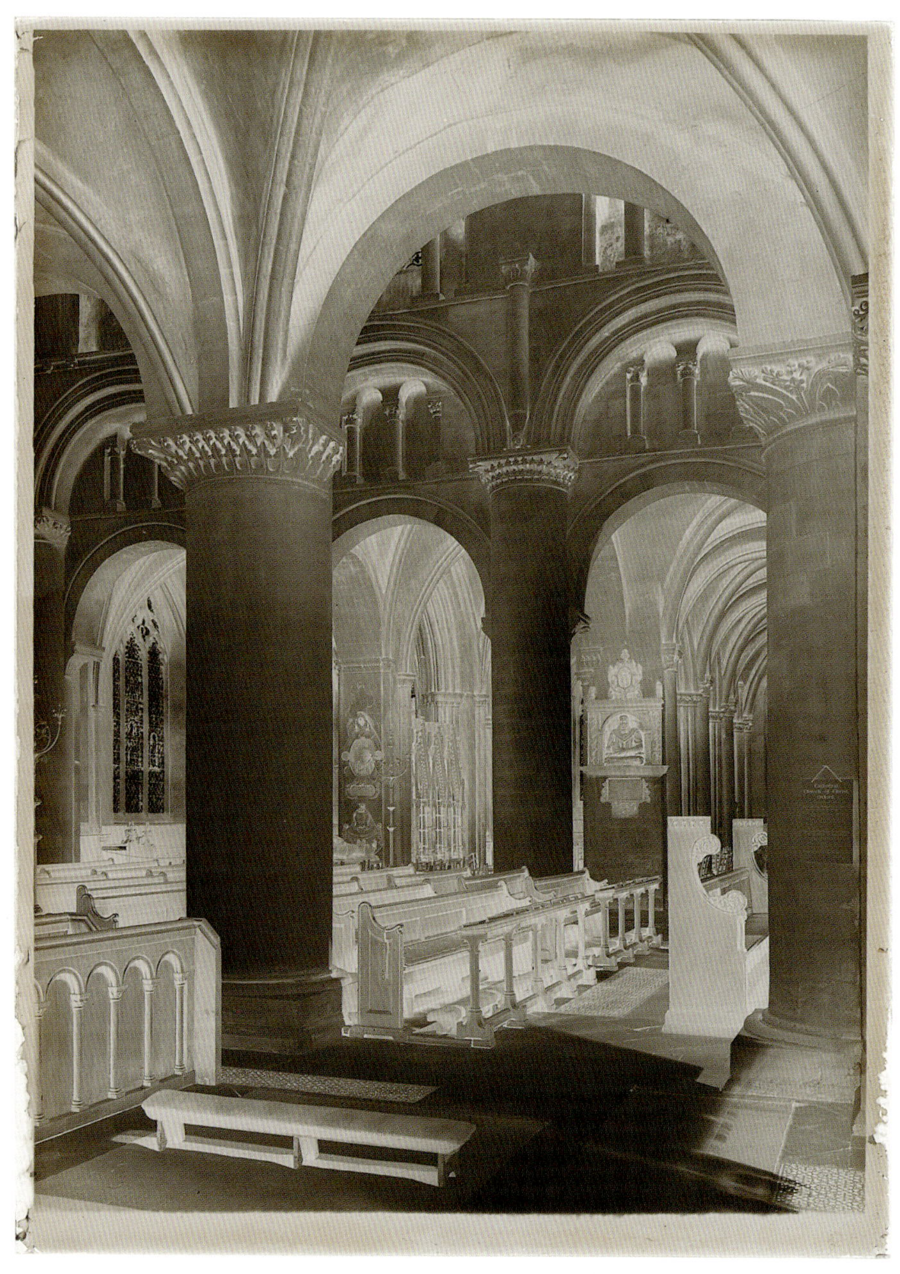

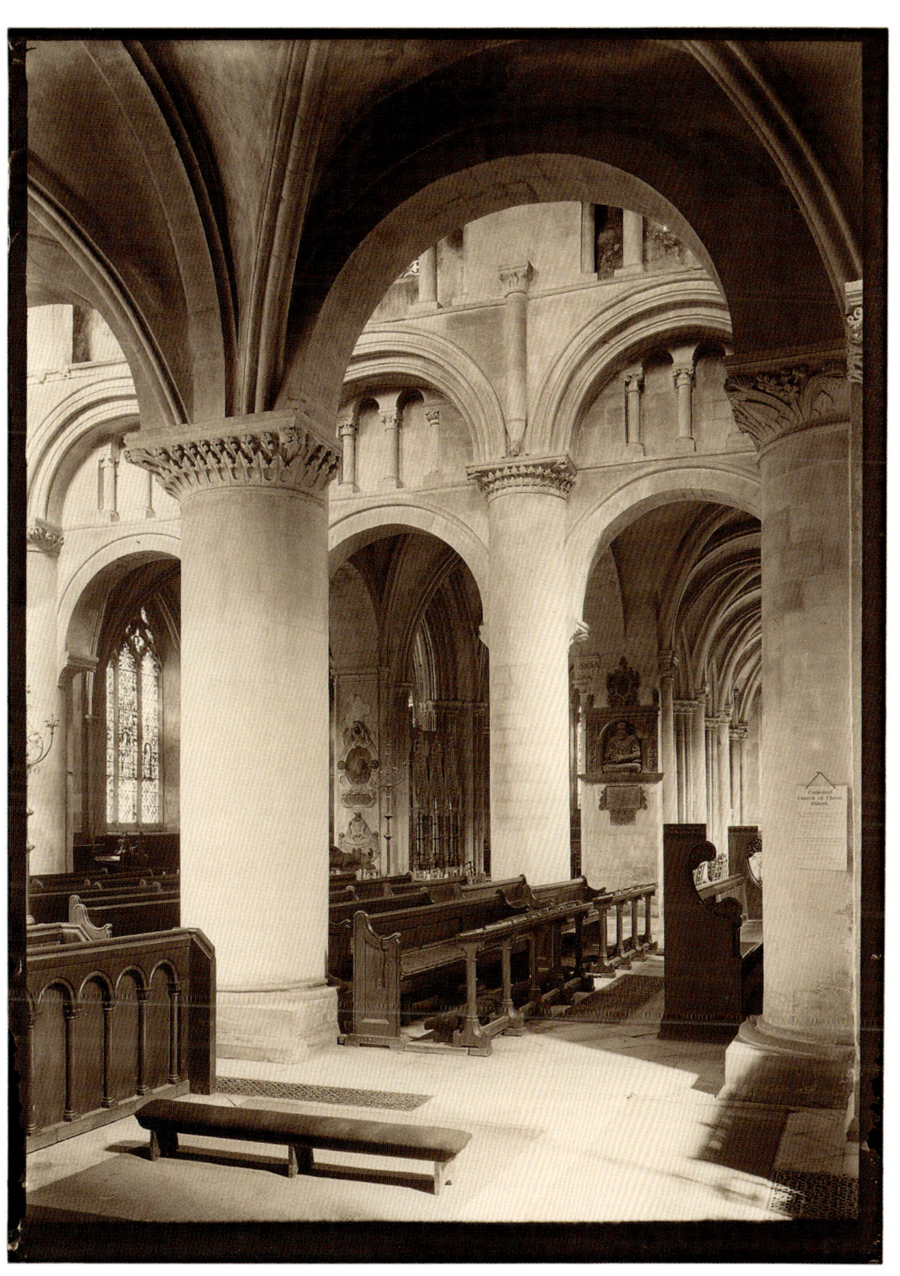

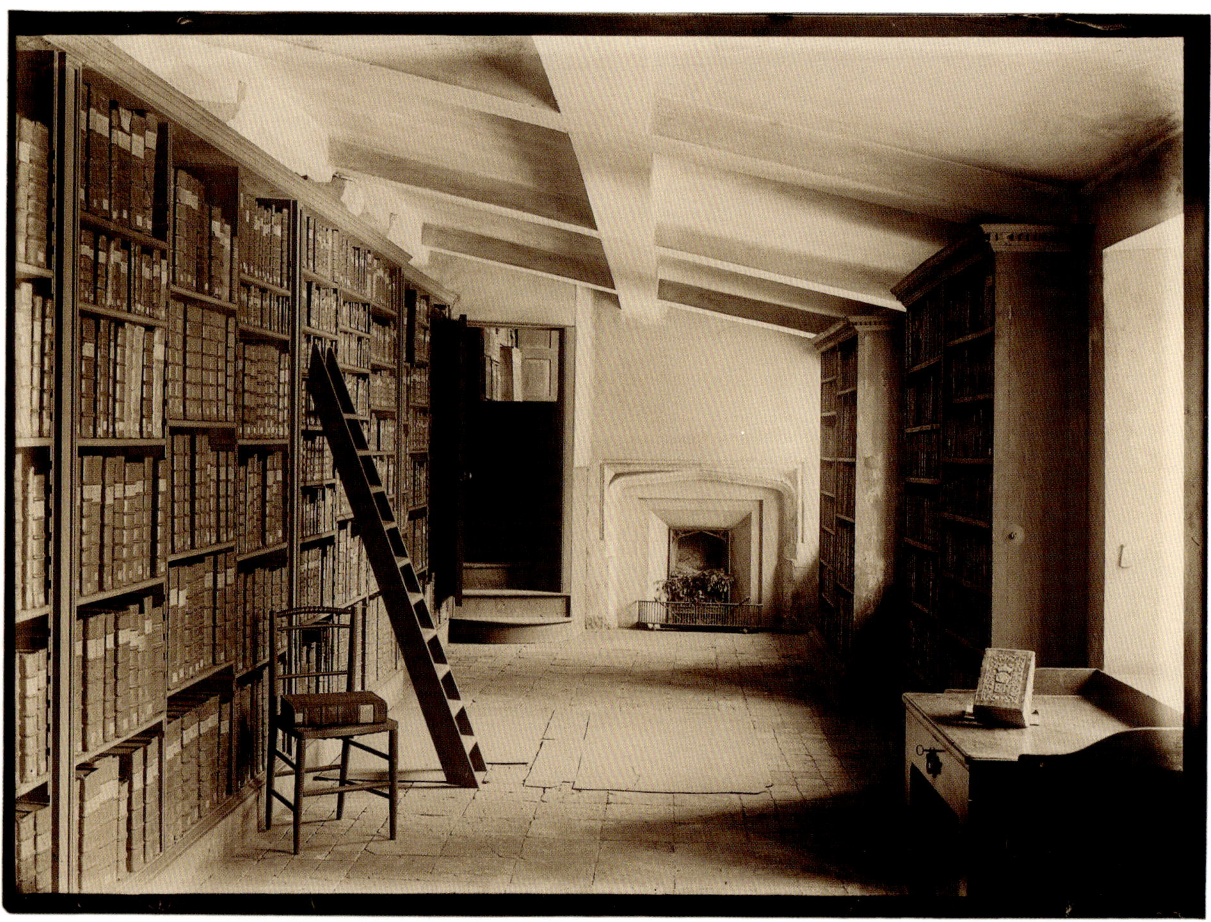

ABOVE & OPPOSITE

102 & 103. *"The Allestree Library"*

The Allestree library and antechamber, Christ Church Oxford, August or September 1899?

Half-plate negatives
Bodleian Library, Minn negatives 171/2 & 171/9

Thompson gave an account of these rooms in his Christ Church history, where the photographs were reproduced:

> Over the south cloister is a row of windows belonging to an apartment which has probably been entered by very few Christ Church men. It is the Allestree library, and the only person who has access to it is the Regius professor of divinity. It contains the library of Dr. Richard Allestree, the loyal churchman and close friend of John Fell and Dolben, who with them maintained the services of the Church of England at Beam Hall during the days of the Commonwealth ... It was probably soon after Allestree's death that the present chamber, or rather two chambers, were fitted up in close proximity to the college library as it then existed in the old refectory; and there the books have remained ever since that time for the private use of the Regius professor of divinity.

Referring directly to the illustrations, he went on to explain that the book on the table is a bible of 1547, decorated with the Tudor rose and crown and the letters 'E.R.', the title-page illuminated with Elizabeth I's arms.

The antechamber (opposite) is the room glimpsed up the stairs in the view of the main chamber. The well-trodden spiral staircase leads to the ringing room and belfry.

Henry L. Thompson, *Christ Church* (London, 1900), p. 241.

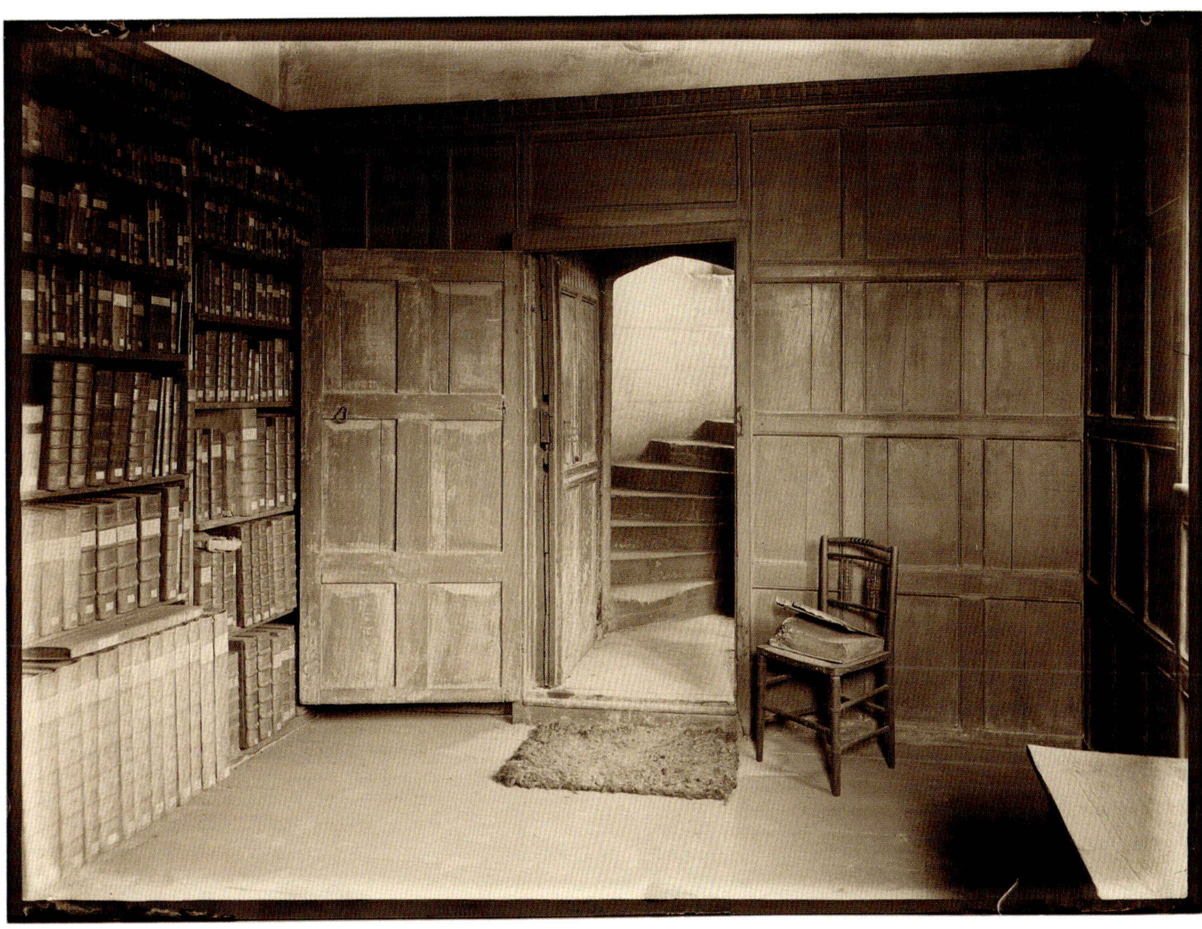

OVERLEAF

104. *Part of Queen's College, Oxford*

Queen's Lane, looking north
Oxford, August 1899 or later?

Half-plate negative
Bodleian Library, Minn negative 172/7

By the time Miss Acland photographed this view, Queen's Lane had already secured a place in the history of photography as Fox Talbot's choice for the first plate of *The Pencil of Nature* (6 parts, London, 1844–46). Talbot's vantage point was the upper storey of the Angel Inn on High Street. Miss Acland positioned herself at street level, half way up the lane, outside the gates to St Peter-in-the-East, thereby achieving a more harmonious composition than the inventor of her art. In the half-century between the two photographs the scene had changed little.

The incumbent of St Peter's from 1843 to 1858 was Edmund Hobhouse (1817–1904), later Bishop of Nelson, New Zealand. The Hobhouse family were old friends of the Aclands. Hobhouse's wife, Anna Maria, née Williams (1824–1925), was the daughter of the Warden of New College. In 1865 Anna presented Angie with a portrait of her husband for her photograph album, he matching it with one of her. Anna lived to the age of 101. Her son Edmund Hobhouse (1860–1933), one of Acland's medical students, sat to Miss Acland in 1893.

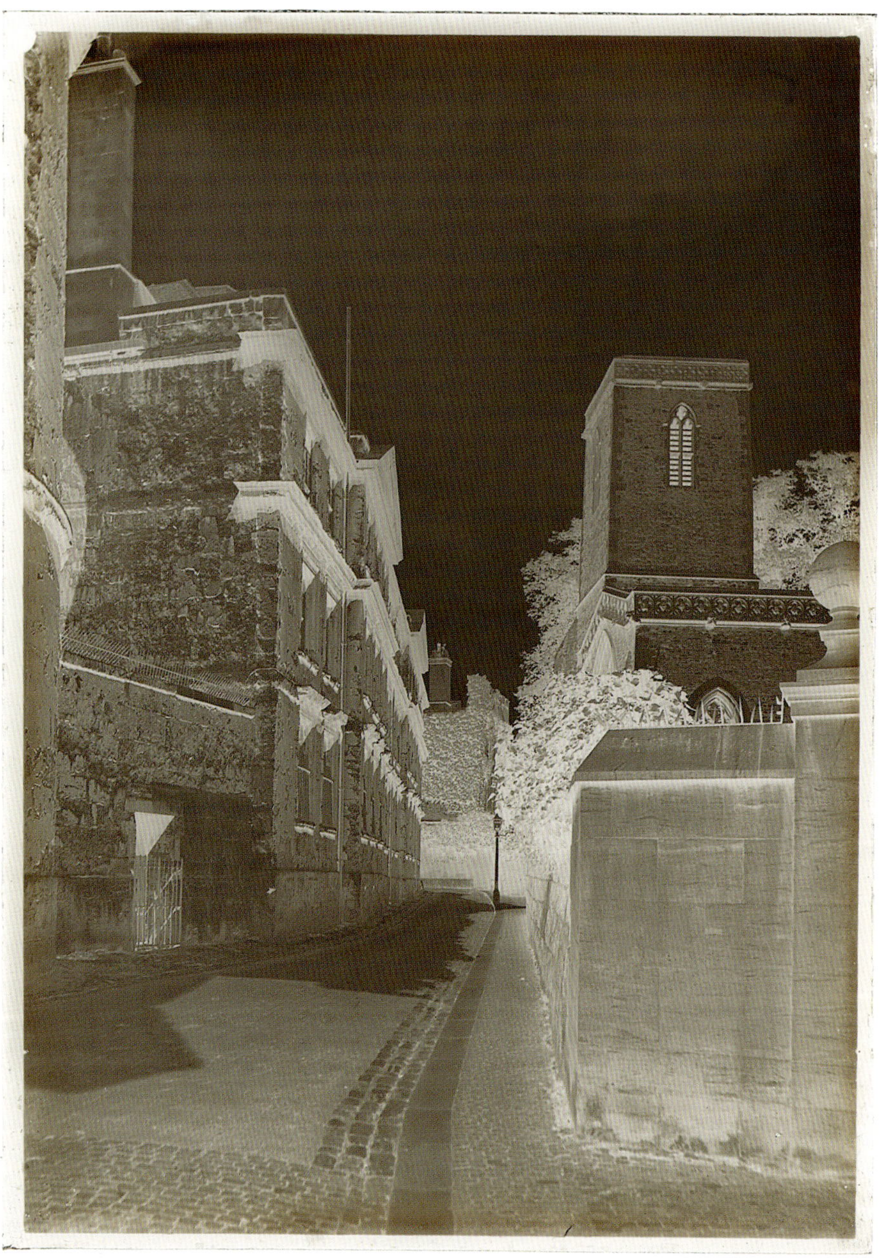

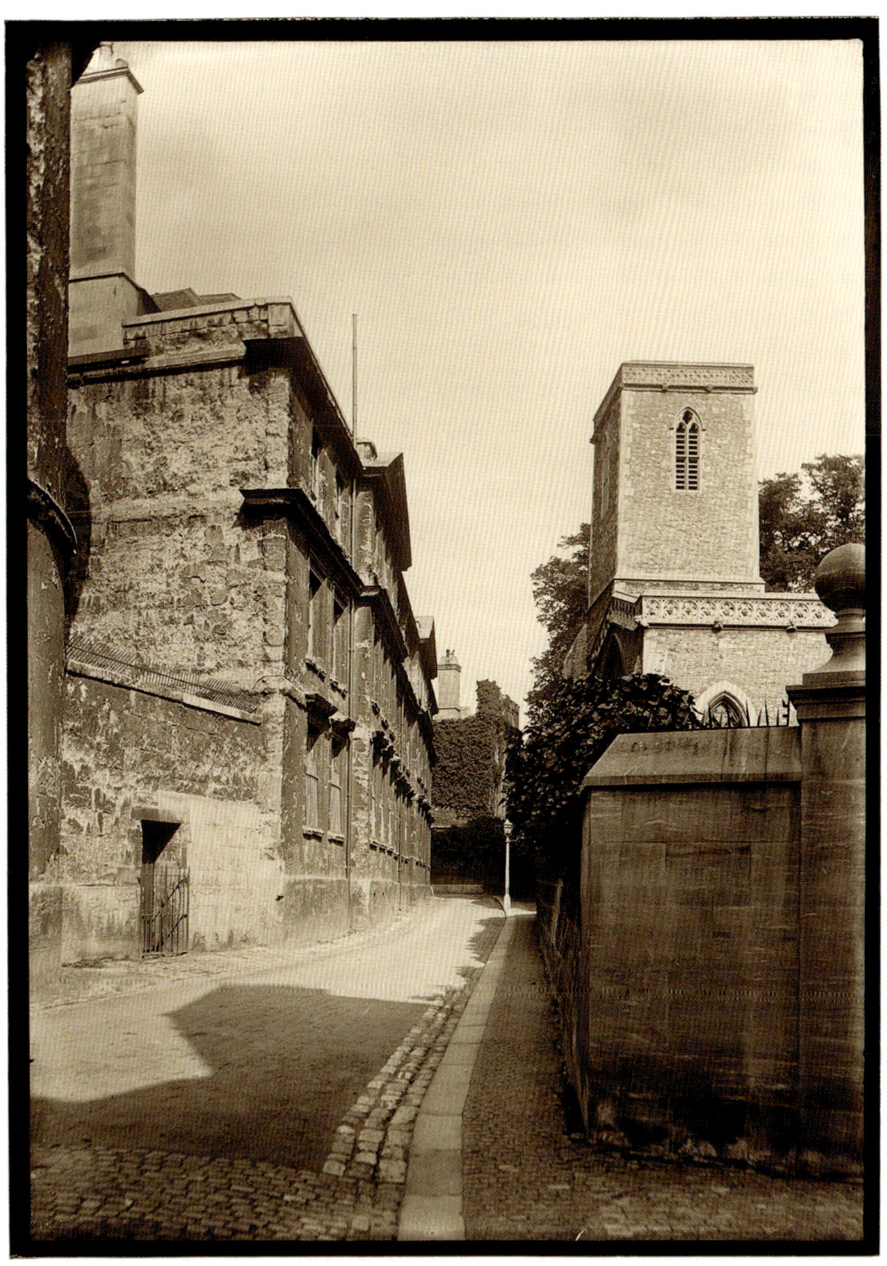

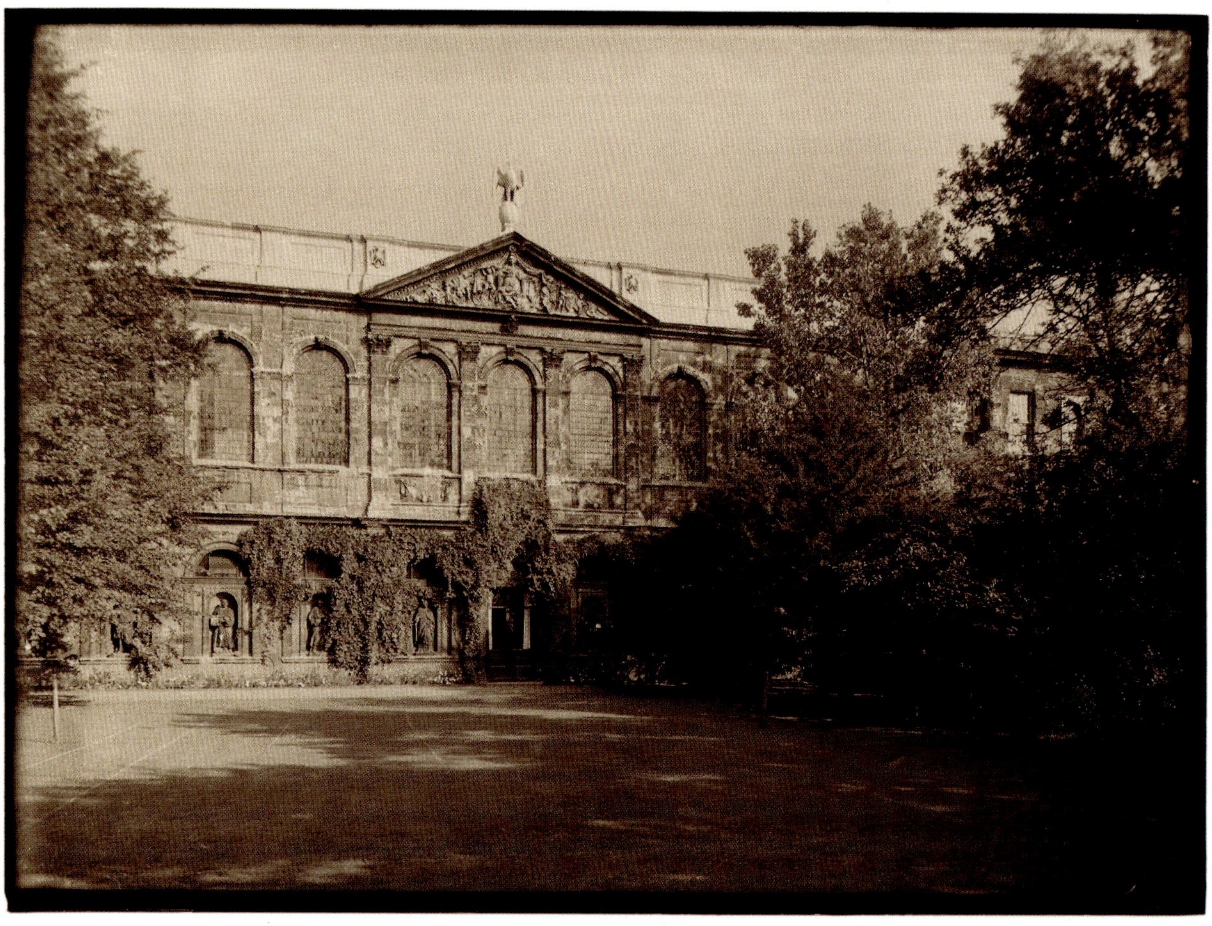

105 & 106. *The Library, Queen's College*

Exterior of Queen's College library, from the west;
Interior, looking south
Oxford, August 1899 or later

Half-plate negatives

Bodleian Library, Minn negatives 17/48 & 172/5

In the original division of work for the college histories Miss Acland was allocated Queen's College as well as Christ Church. Robinson commissioned the text for the history from the Provost, John Richard Magrath (cat. no. 45). Unfortunately, Magrath failed to produce a manuscript, so neither the volume, nor Miss Acland's photographs, were ever published.

The library of Queen's College was built between 1692 and 1695 and was once attributed to Christopher Wren. Seen in the interior are a monitor lizard (significance unknown), large celestial and terrestrial globes by John Senex (1678–1740), a telescope by Dollond, and a leopard skin. In the external view the ground to the west of the building is marked out as a tennis court.

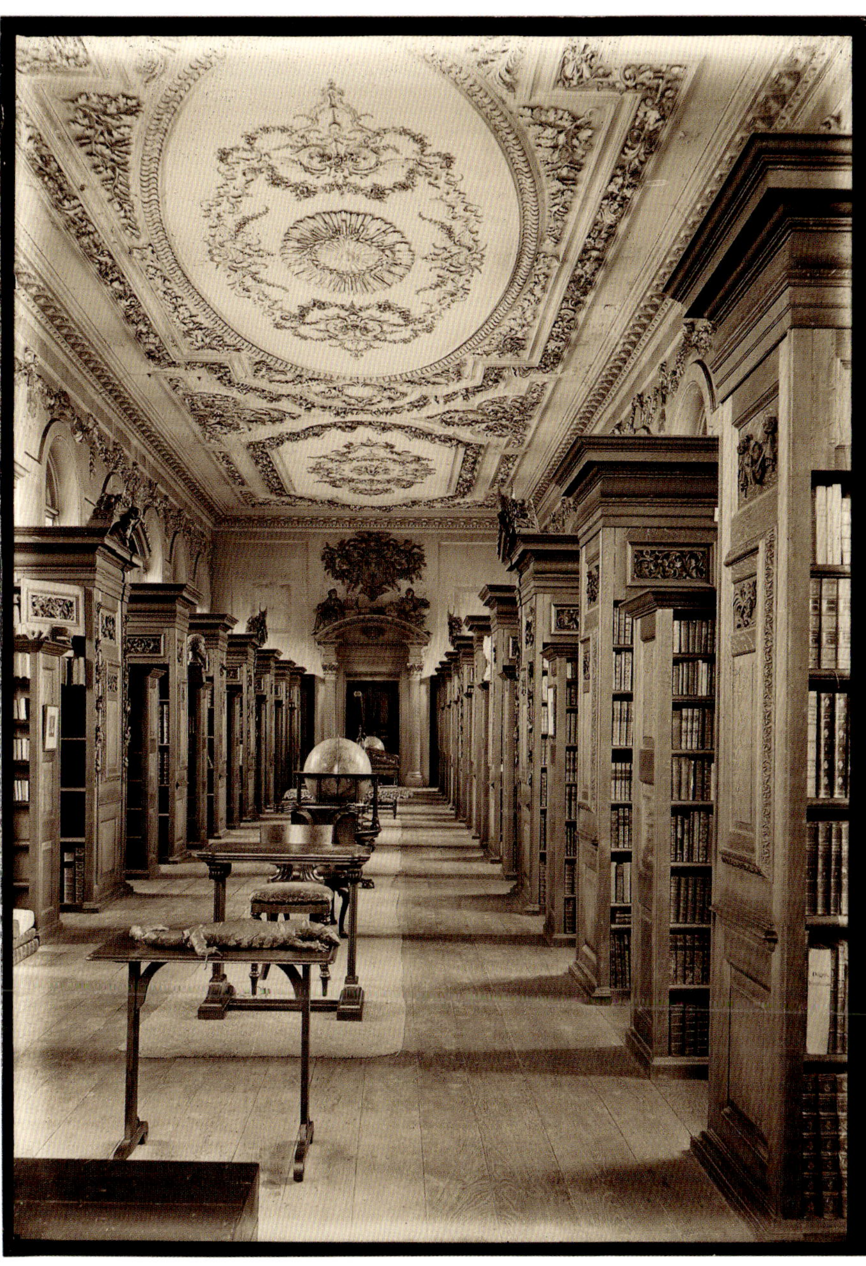

107. *Trooper Sidney Peel*

Sidney Cornwallis Peel (1870–1938), wearing an army jacket and slouch hat, and holding a rifle
Oxford, between 22 and 27 January 1900

Whole-plate negative
Bodleian Library, Minn negative 196/8

Sidney Peel was the third son of Arthur Wellesley Peel, Viscount Peel (1829–1912), speaker of the House of Commons. His grandfather was the former Prime Minister Robert Peel (1788–1850). He was a graduate of New College and later became a fellow of Trinity.

On the outbreak of the Second Anglo-Boer War in 1899 Peel joined the 40th (Oxfordshire) Company of the 10th Battalion of the Imperial Yeomanry, the designations for which — 'XIY' and '40' — can be seen on his collar and shoulder. On his return from South Africa he recounted his experiences in a popular memoir, *Trooper 8008, I. Y.* (London, 1901). In the memoir he described his fellow yeomanry as a "miscellaneous multitude of all ages from twenty to forty, with coats of every degree of newness and shabbiness". They ranged from barristers to butchers: "men of all classes, professions, and trades, and men of none", levelled by the uniform of khaki serge and Bedford cords. Peel began and ended his time as "nothing more than an ordinary trooper". "To have been able to go at all", he wrote, "was the most extraordinary piece of good luck that ever was. I would not have missed the months during which I wore her Majesty's uniform for anything in the world."

Miss Acland and her father took a close interest in any Oxford men going out to South Africa. When the first contingent left in December 1899 Miss Acland presented them with a Christmas card containing good wishes and a view of Oxford, presumably from one of her photographs. After they had gone she coordinated the collection of 'comforts' and clothing to send out, occasionally receiving gifts in return, such as the *Queen's Chocolate Box* that featured as one of her first colour lantern slides at the Royal Photographic Society in 1901.

Miss Acland had to wait until good weather in February 1900 before making prints from this negative, which she did by contact printing under the light of the sun. Most of her prints were produced by one of the silver chloride based 'printing-out' processes, in which the image appears directly during exposure without the need for development, although they still needed to be fixed in 'hypo'. After fixing they also benefitted from toning in a gold solution, which shifted the colour from an unpleasant red towards brown and purple-black. For day-to-day work she favoured albumen papers (including high-gloss 'double albumenized paper'), but she also experimented with the newer matt, gelatino-chloride media, as well as with bromide printing: a 'developing out' process that enabled enlargements to be made by artificial light with an enlarging lantern. For her finest work she chose platinotype and carbon printing, the latter forming the basis of her early colour photography.

As was her habit, Miss Acland sent copies of this portrait to her sitter's family and friends. "The face photographed of the Khaki man gave great satisfaction this morning", Viscount Peel wrote on receiving examples. "It brings him vividly before me and when I think of him I recall the many acts of friendship which he received from you & from your Father." The portrait certainly finds Miss Acland in full mastery of the photographic medium, shortly before she turned away from portraiture to concentrate on colour. Peel's facial features and the fabric of his uniform are modelled in soft, sympathetic shadows, the narrow plane of focus positioned on his left eye.

Peel is another of Miss Acland's sitters seen wearing a wristwatch, or rather a pocket-watch strapped to his arm. This is a Goldsmiths' Company 'Service' watch. Such timepieces proved invaluable for coordinating military manoeuvres and their use in the Boer War made the wristwatch an acceptable accessory for men.

Sidney Peel, *Trooper 8008, I. Y.* (London, 1907), p. 3; Ibid.; p. vi; p. vii; MS. Acland d. 148, fol. 141; Ibid.

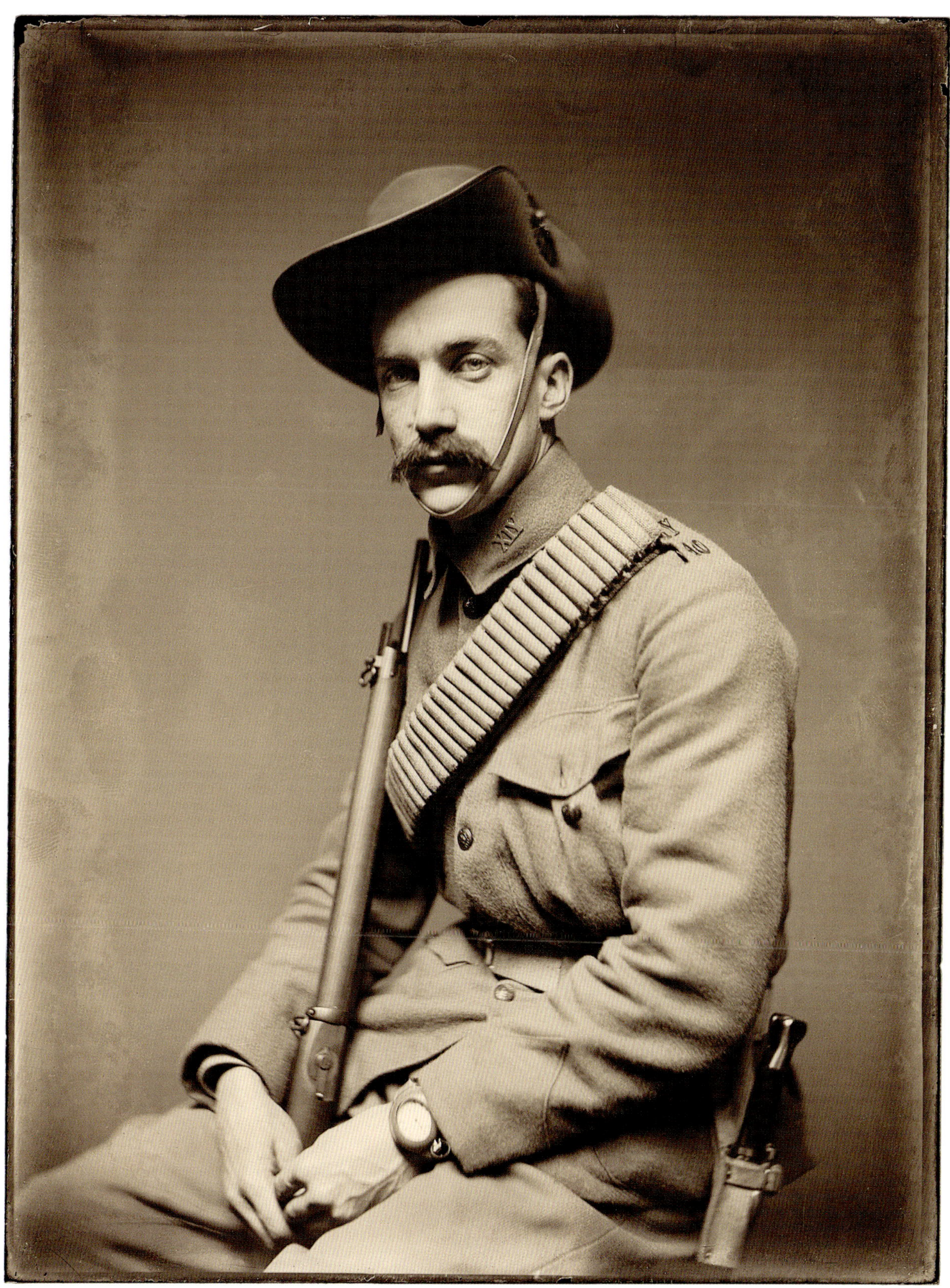

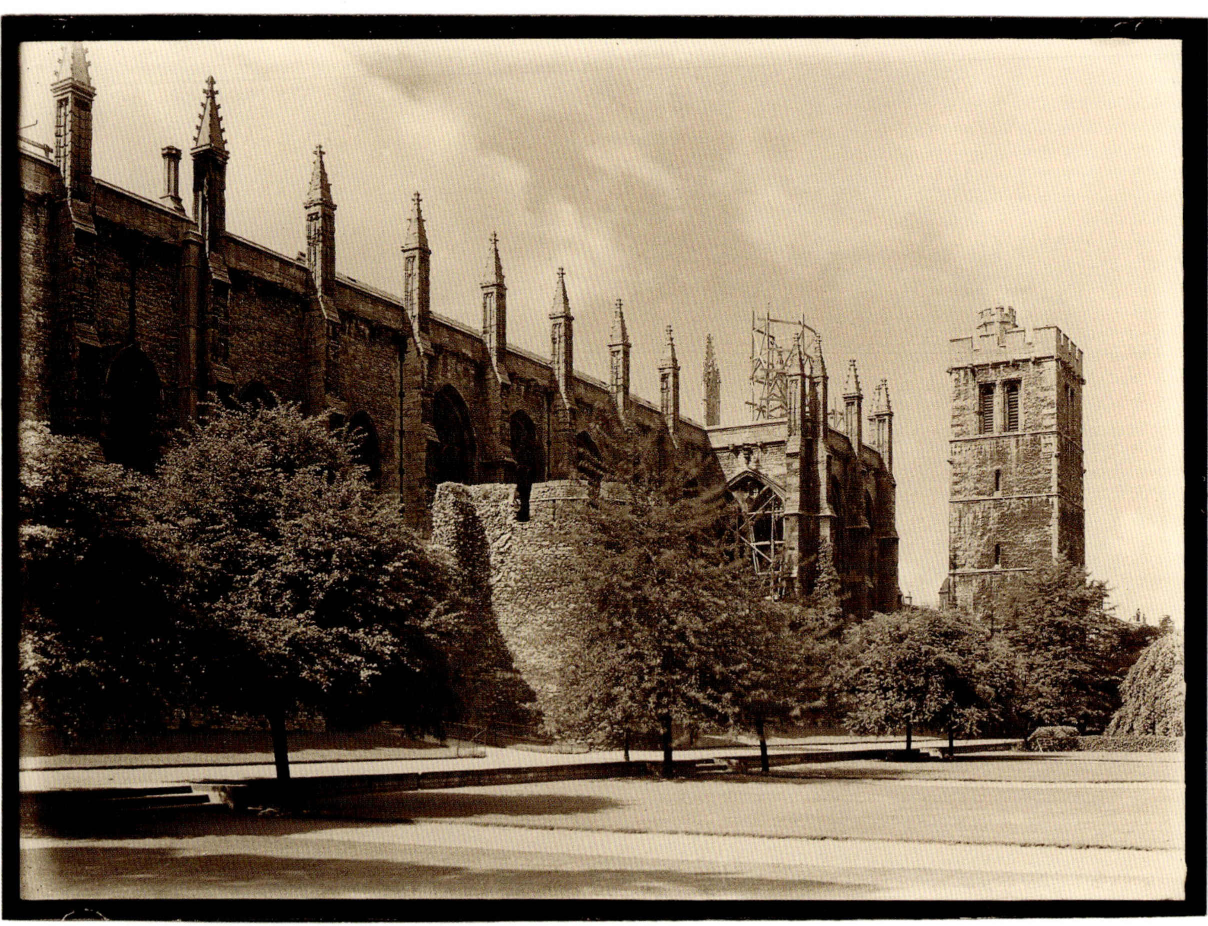

108. *"The Hall and Chapel, from the New Buildings"*

New College hall, chapel and bell tower, looking south-west
Oxford, *circa* July 1900

Half-plate negative
Bodleian Library, Minn negative 189/5

When work for the college histories was first allocated Vincent Perronet Sells (1858–1907), a University Extension lecturer, was given New College, where he had been an undergraduate. Later the commission was transferred to Miss Acland, probably due to Sells's declining health.

This is a view from inside the Holywell Street entrance to New College. The large range of 'New Buildings' by Basil Champneys (1842–1935) and George Gilbert Scott (1811–1878) is out of sight behind the camera. The hall and chapel, divided where the windows change height, were part of the original quadrangle, completed in 1386, a mere 514 years before Miss Acland took the photograph. The bell tower is from the same date and is now detached, except to the thirteenth-century city wall, which can be seen in the centre of the plate. The scaffolding on the roof was for the restoration of the pinnacles, which was still ongoing when Miss Acland took her first colour photographs (cat. nos. 127, 155 & 156).

Miss Acland knew the Dean of New College, William Archibald Spooner (1844–1930), of Spoonerism fame, having been at school at Mayfield with his sister, Janet Sarah Spooner (1849–1922).

OVERLEAF LEFT

109. *"The Chapel, East End"*

Chancel and reredos of New College chapel
Oxford, *circa* July 1900

Half-plate negative
Bodleian Library, Minn negative 189/9

Like Miss Acland's view of Tom Quad, almost everything in this photograph, including the hammer-beam roof, is a Victorian restoration. The original reredos escaped the first ravages of the Reformation but was condemned by Elizabeth I, who regarded New College as a hotbed of popery.

George Gilbert Scott, who breakfasted with the Aclands in April 1870, began the restoration of the reredos in 1879, but it was only completed in 1892 with the addition of the statues. These are arranged according to the following scheme:

> Under a representation of the Lord in Glory is the top tier of niches, containing a representation of the Agnus Dei, with angels on each side. The centrepiece of the second tier is the Crucifixion, and to the right and left are Apostles and Saints. In the third row is a figure of the Virgin and Child, with, on the one side, King Richard II., a benefactor of the founder, and the following martyrs: St. John, St. Jude, St. Simon, St. James the Greater, St. Thomas, and St. Philip. On the other side are leading representatives of the Church in England: William of Wykeham, St. Augustine, the Venerable Bede, St. Anselm, the Wykehamist Archbishop Warham, and the Wykehamist Bishop Ken. The lowermost tier represents Prophets and Christian Teachers.

Miss Acland entered a print of the reredos in the architecture class of the 1902 Camera Club exhibition.

Hastings Rashdall & Robert S. Rait, *New College* (London, 1901), p. 76.

OVERLEAF RIGHT

110. *Muniment Room, New College*

Upper room of the Muniment Tower, New College
Oxford, *circa* July 1900

Half-plate negative
Bodleian Library, Minn negative 188/12

New College had four muniment rooms (medieval strongrooms), arranged above each other in the Muniment Tower in the north-east corner of the main quadrangle. The lower room was originally used to store vessels of brass, the first floor charters and documents, the upper two rooms college plate and jewels. By the time Miss Acland took this photograph the documents had been moved to the upper rooms. The various packages on the floor and the volumes on the table still contained the college deeds and Papal bulls of privilege, all apparently in "perfect preservation". The room itself has a simple stone vault and encaustic tiles.

Interiors such as this make challenging subjects for photography, the darkness of the room and bright window giving the subject a huge contrast range. To deal with the problem Miss Acland probably used a 'Sandell plate' Patented in 1891 by John Tyack Sandell (1853–1906), Sandell plates were coated with three emulsions, the uppermost rapid, the lowest extremely slow. The layers extended the contrast range of the negative and reduced 'halation' — the scattering of light in the glass of the plate exhibited as flare around the brightest parts of the image. The same fault could also be minimized by 'backing' the plate with black card or a sticky dark-brown masking compound sold as 'Caramel'.

Hastings Rashdall & Robert S. Rait, *New College* (London, 1901), p. 32.

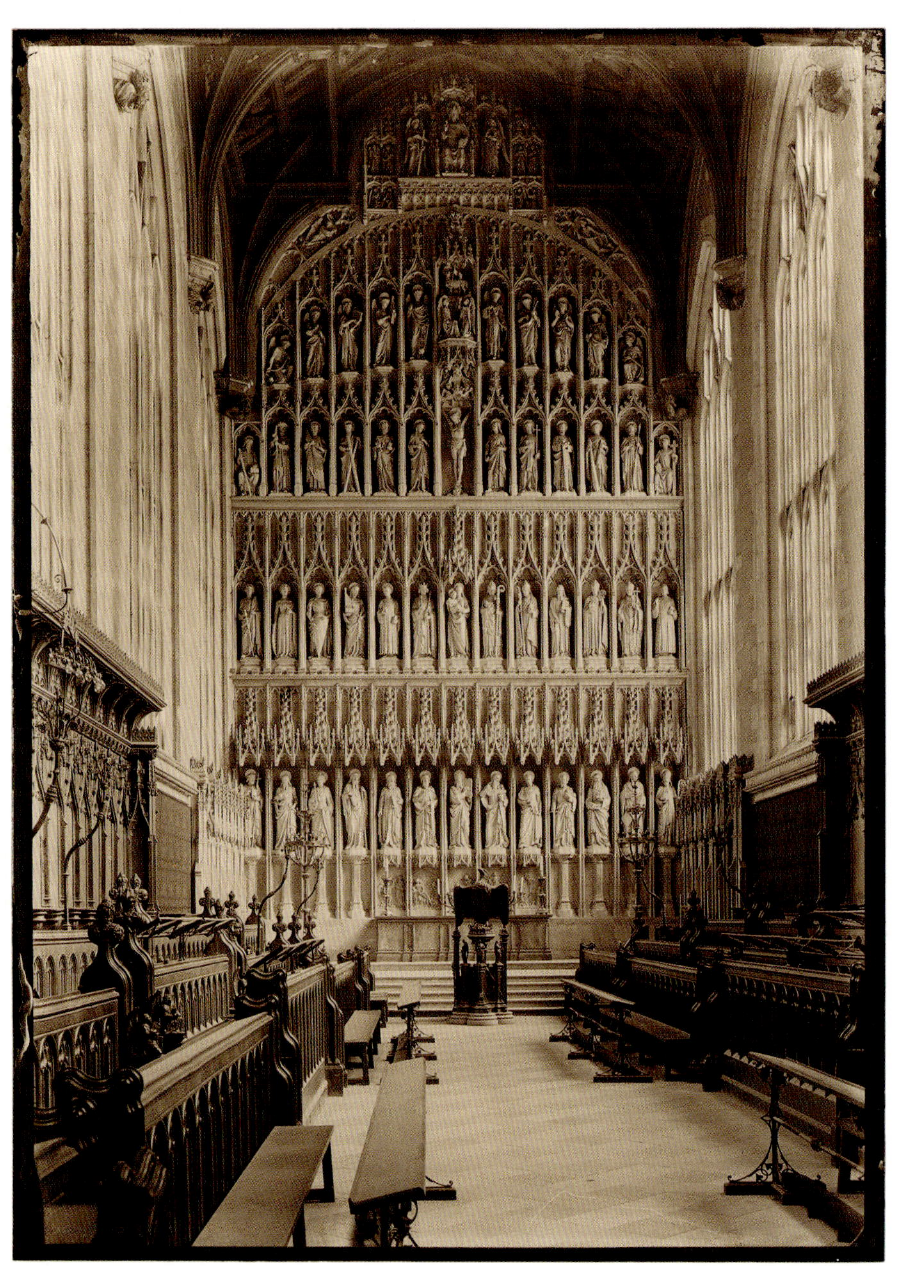

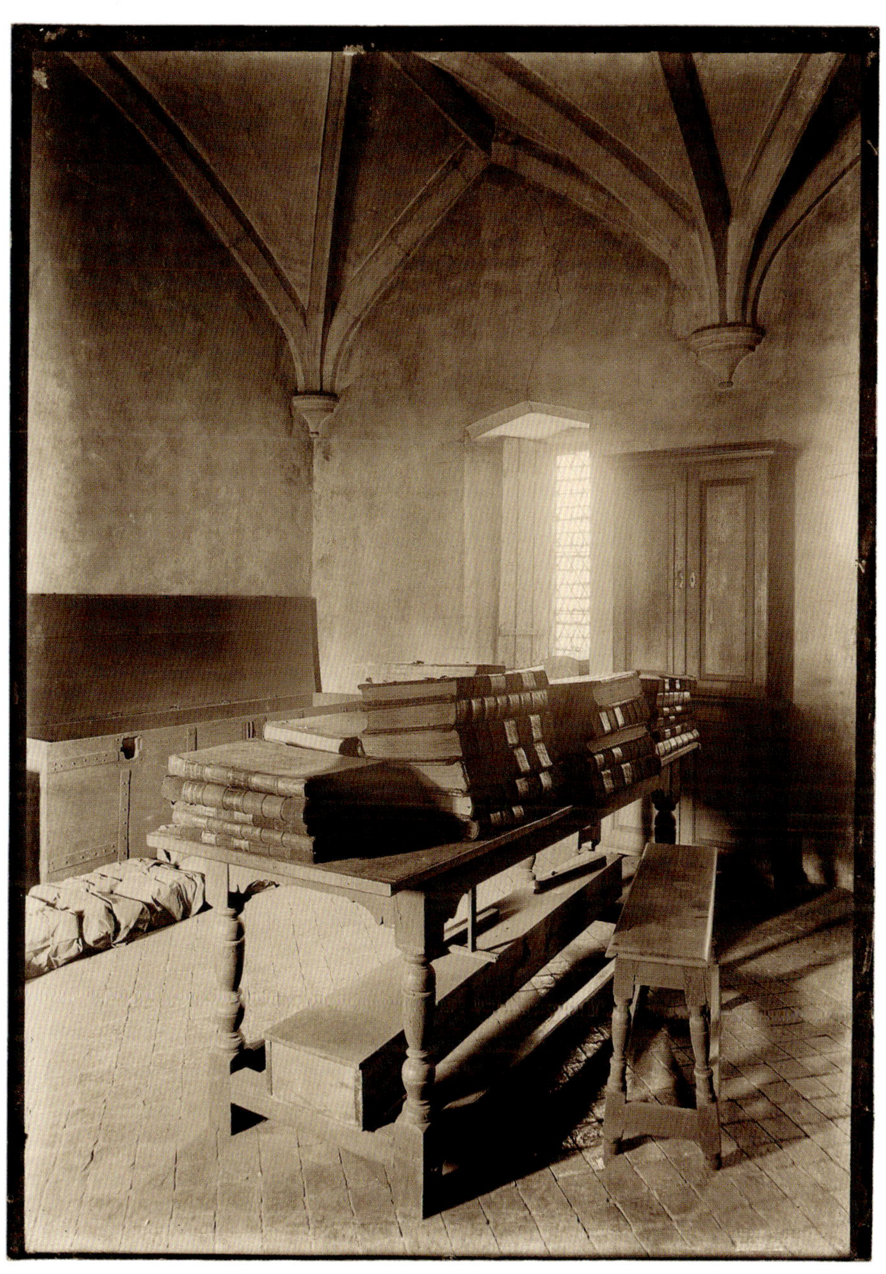

111. *A Corner of the Drawing Room*

Miss Acland's desk in the little drawing room
Oxford, March 1901

Half-plate negative
Bodleian Library, Minn negative 191/2

The desk in this photograph has sometimes been identified as Acland's, but was actually his daughter's (his was in the Maalstofa). This corner of the house, at the west end of the drawing room, had long been Miss Acland's domain. "We are going to make a nest for you in your Pussy Corner where you may have company or not as you like", her mother wrote in December 1868 during the worst of the problems with her foot.

The most extraordinary feature of the room is the picture above the desk: John Everett Millais's portrait of Ruskin at Glenfinlas. The painting is one of the most celebrated in the history of British art. Its importance was recognized by Acland, who wrote that "for many reasons it is a unique national picture of the Century." Acland had held the canvass when the portrait was begun at Brig o'Turk in 1853, where he also witnessed Millais' "wondrous free" manner with Ruskin's wife Effie. Effie would later petition for the annulment of her marriage (on the grounds of Ruskin's 'incurable impotency') in order to be with the artist.

Ruskin left his portrait to Acland in a will made out during his mother's lifetime, transferring it to Oxford on her death in 1871. The picture owed its place above Miss Acland's desk to the closeness of her friendship with her 'Cricket'. "The fact is your relations to Ruskin are very special", her father commented when discussing what should happen to the portrait, "with all its touching associations", on his own death. Although he left it to Willie as an heirloom, Acland wished to see the picture remain in Oxford in the Ruskin School in the University Galleries (rather than go to the National Gallery, as some had proposed). In the event, it went with Miss Acland to Park Town, where she hung it above her writing table in the drawing room: "a very good dry place on an inner wall" (cat. no. 198). There it proved something of a magnet for visitors, when not on loan to exhibitions (before she went to Madeira in 1911 she lent it to the Ashmolean; in 1919 Thomas Herbert Warren (1853–1930), President of Magdalen, persuaded her to allow the Royal Academy to borrow it for the Ruskin Centenary). Whenever the question of its return was raised with her brothers she was unambiguous about wanting to keep it, even if her custodial responsibilities were sometimes a worry. In 1921, for example, a year after she had it re-varnished by Alec Macdonald (1862–1930), Alexander's son, the plate-glass front fell out. "No one could blame you if it was burgled", Harry later reassured her, "nor if it was burnt as that would be by accident. In any case it is insured" (for £5,000 in 1897, but only £2,000 in 1919). At some point between Willie's death in 1924 and her own it was reclaimed by Robin Acland, Willie's heir. In 1965 it was sold at auction for 24,000 guineas (about £350,000 at 2012 values).

Other works of art seen in the photograph include a medallion by Alexander Munro of Harry Acland shown at the Royal Academy in 1855; watercolours by George Richmond of Miss Acland's grandparents, William and Sarah Cotton; and her own 1878 portrait of Acland Sahera of Zanzibar, a liberated slave who was the god-child of her parents. On the desk is a reproduction of *The Light of the World* and photographs of Canon Pusey, Acland in yachting oilskins, and the grave of Mrs Acland shortly after her interment in Holywell Cemetery.

Miss Acland took a number of photographs of the interior of her old home shortly before moving to Clevedon House in Park Town. Four negatives of the little drawing room survive, this being the example she chose to illustrate her memoirs. In one of the variants a birdcage rather than a plant is positioned on the bookcase by the window, its door left open, as if to suggest the bird had finally flown the nest.

MS. Acland d. 139, fols. 85–8; MS. Acland d. 137, fols. 31–2; MS. Acland d. 9, fol. 130; MS. Acland d. 137, fols. 29–30; MS. Acland d. 137, fols. 27–8; MS. Acland d. 108, fols. 115–18; MS. Acland d. 144, fols. 115–16; Ibid.

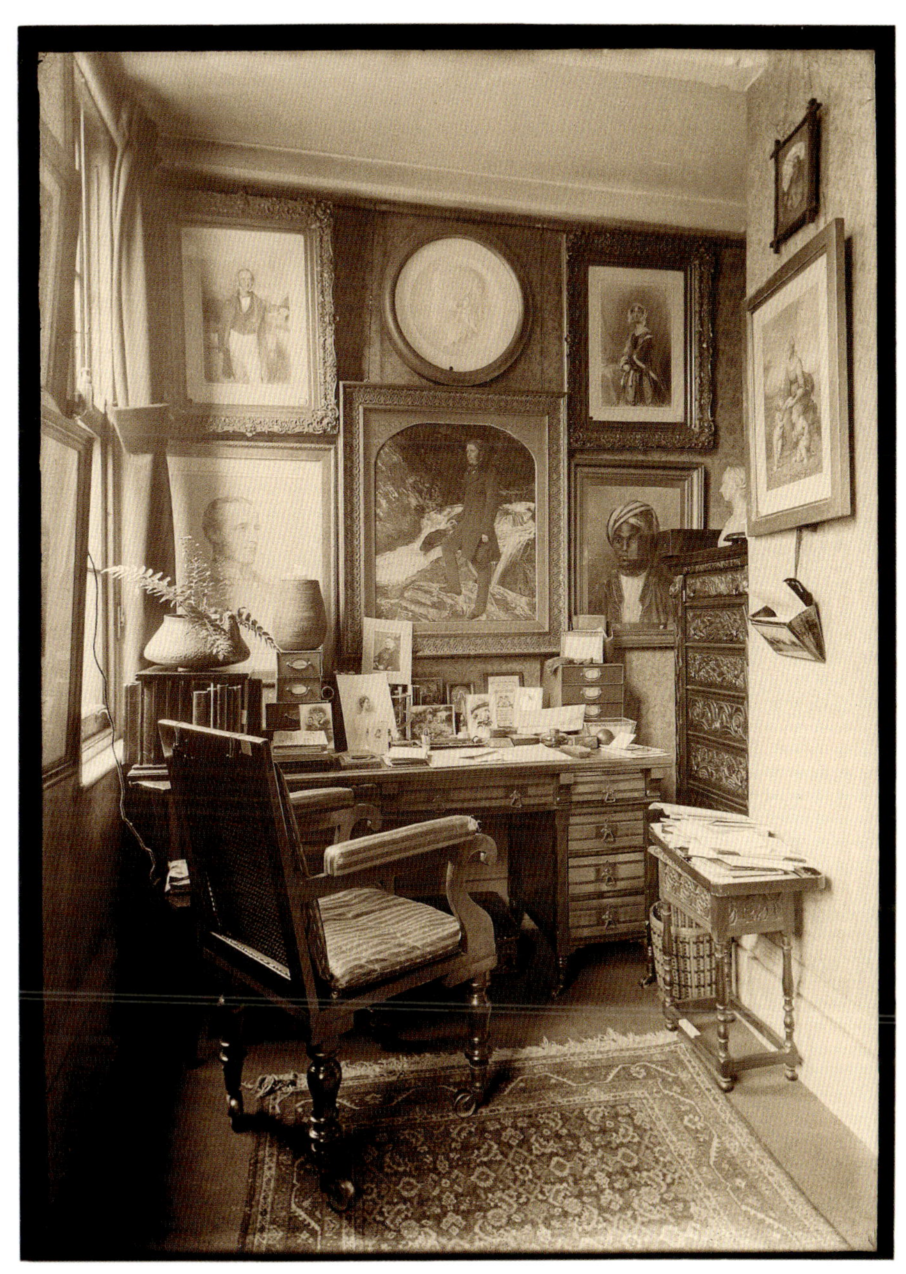

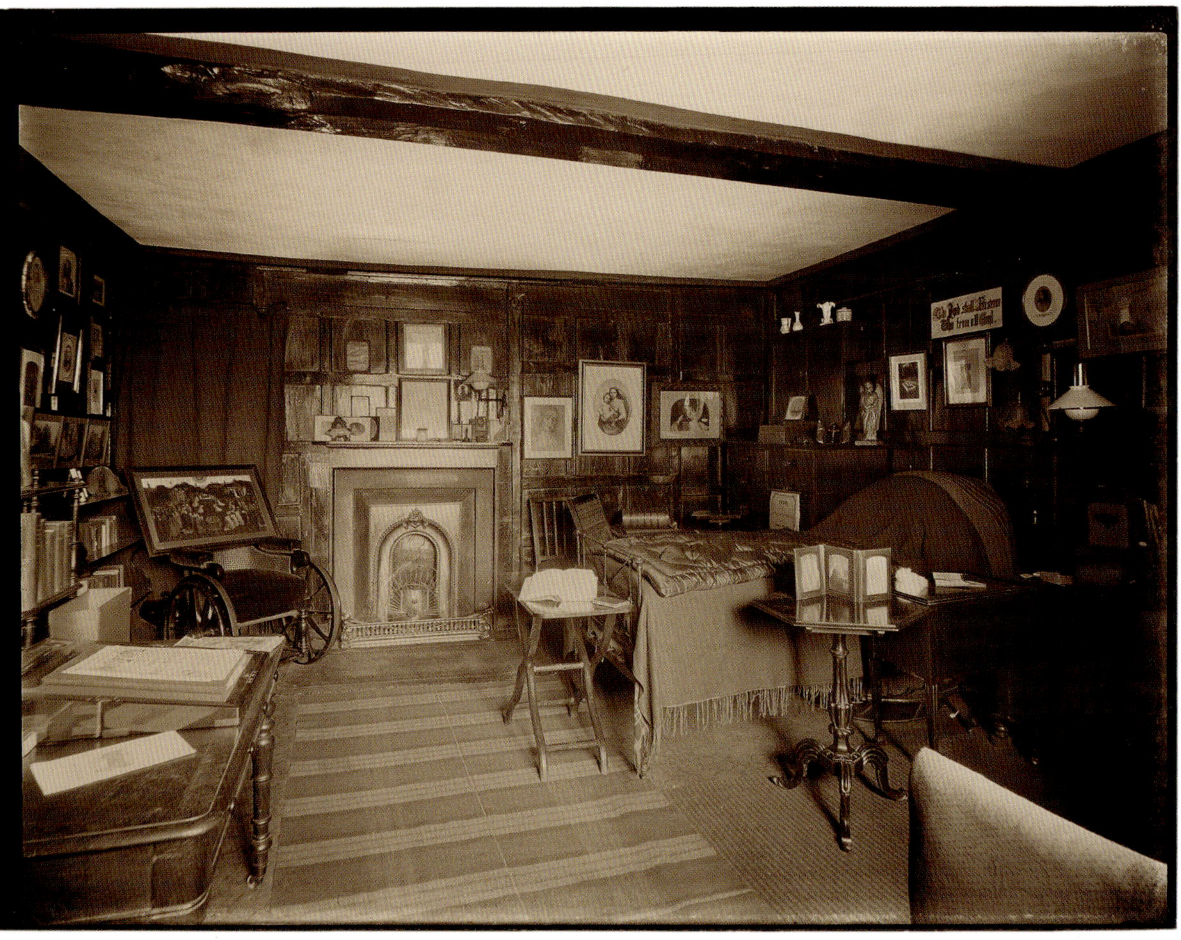

112. *"Bedroom in Broad St., Oxford"*

Acland's bedroom, 39–41 Broad Street, looking south-west
Oxford, between September 1900 and 23 May 1901

Whole-plate negative (reduced ×0·75)
Bodleian Library, Minn negative 195/4

The "old panelled room", as Miss Acland referred to it in her memoirs, was her parents' bedroom and also the place of her birth. The panelling dated from the seventeenth century. On the Davenport on the table on the left is the August 1900 issue of *Photography* in which her Spectrum Plate paper appeared. The photograph must therefore have been taken shortly before her father's death on 16 October 1900, or perhaps as he left the room.

In the corner of the room is Miss Acland's rollstuhl, purchased in Wildbad in 1869 and lent to Prince Leopold during his time in Oxford. Propped on the chair is a print from Jan van Eyck's *Adoration of the Mystic Lamb* in St Bavo's Cathedral, Ghent. Acland had visited Ghent in 1876 with Frank, Theodore and the artist Lionel Boulton Campbell Lockhart Muirhead (1844–1925). Lionel was the great-grandson of Matthew Boulton, James Watt's partner; his sisters Beatrix Marion (1849–1944) and Eleanor Anne Muirhead (1855–1916) were friends of Miss Acland. Their aunt, botanist Mary Anne Robb, née Boulton (1829–1912), who lived at Tew Park, Great Tew, was one of the four women to exhibit at the first exhibition of the Photographic Society in 1854, showing *A Country House, Oxon*.

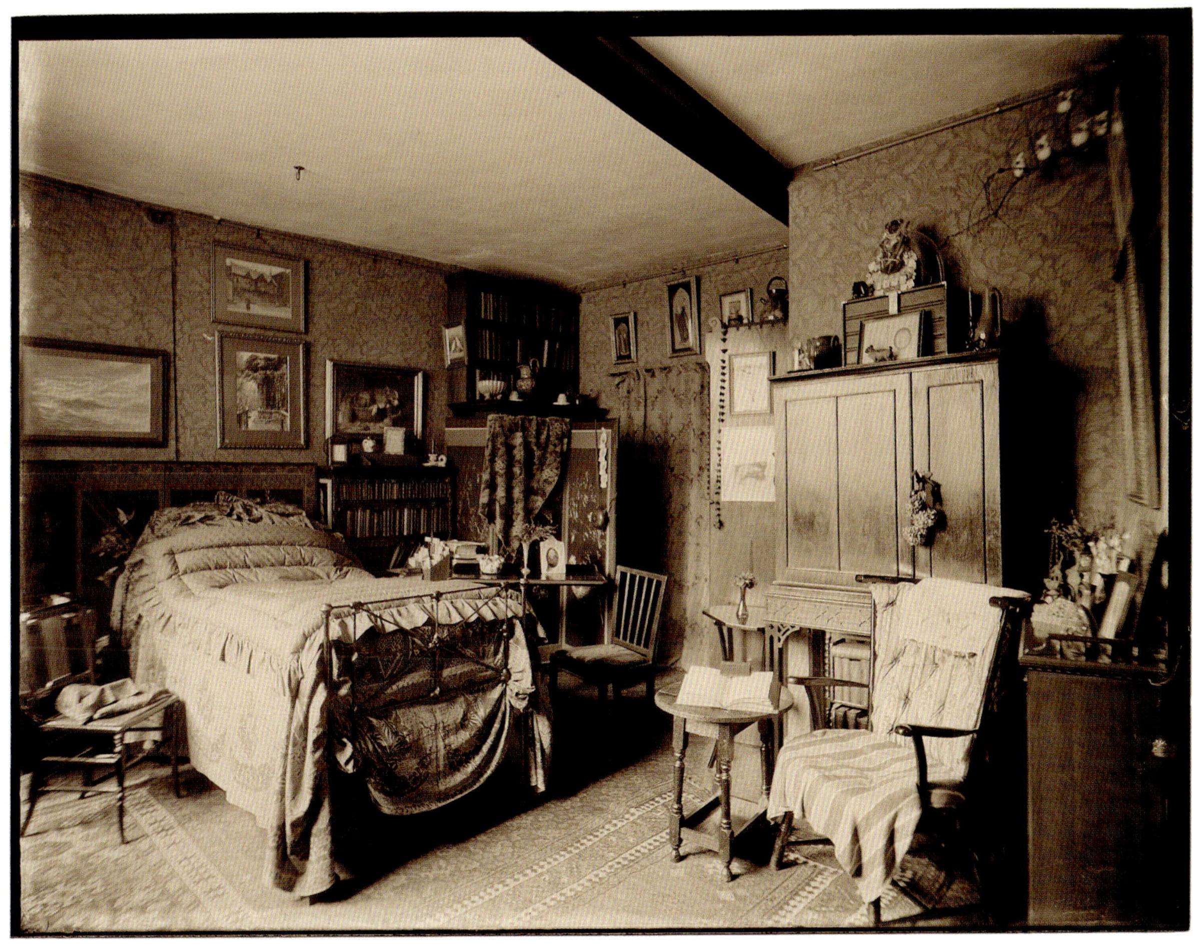

113. *The Best Room*

Miss Acland's bedroom, looking south-west
Oxford, between September 1900 and 23 May 1901
Whole-plate negative (reduced ×0·75)
Bodleian Library, Minn negative 195/7

Miss Acland's bedroom was an exercise in womanly good taste, decorated with a large-pattern arts and crafts wallpaper, simple furniture, and Japanese screens. Formerly the 'best room', it had been Ruskin's during his first term as Slade Professor. "Mr. Ruskin used to say that he liked this room as it had the ugliest outlook he ever knew & he was not tempted to look out of the window when he ought to be at work!", she wrote in her memoirs.

On the wall above Miss Acland's bed is a watercolour by her father, *A Coming Squall in the Bay of Biscay*, painted in 1889 and exhibited at the Oxford Art Society in 1892. To the right is a study by Alexander Macdonald of a fresco on the south (external) wall of the library at Broad Street. The original depicted Angie and Willie watching a sunset and was painted by their father. When Macdonald's watercolour was reproduced by Miss Acland in collotype for her 1923 Christmas card she gave it the title *"It will rise again!"* The phrase derived from her conversation with her brother: "I said 'Tiney we shall die some day.' Tiney replied 'We shall rise again Angie, like the Sun' and I answered 'And go to Heaven.'" Also on the wall is her own painting of the family dog Bustle, a Pomeranian who leapt to fame in March 1872 when he was mentioned by Ruskin in his lecture on "The Relation to Art of the Sciences of Organic Form", having broken his leg jumping out of a window.

Devon Records Office, 1148M/7/1, p. 51; Presentation album, private collection, n.p.

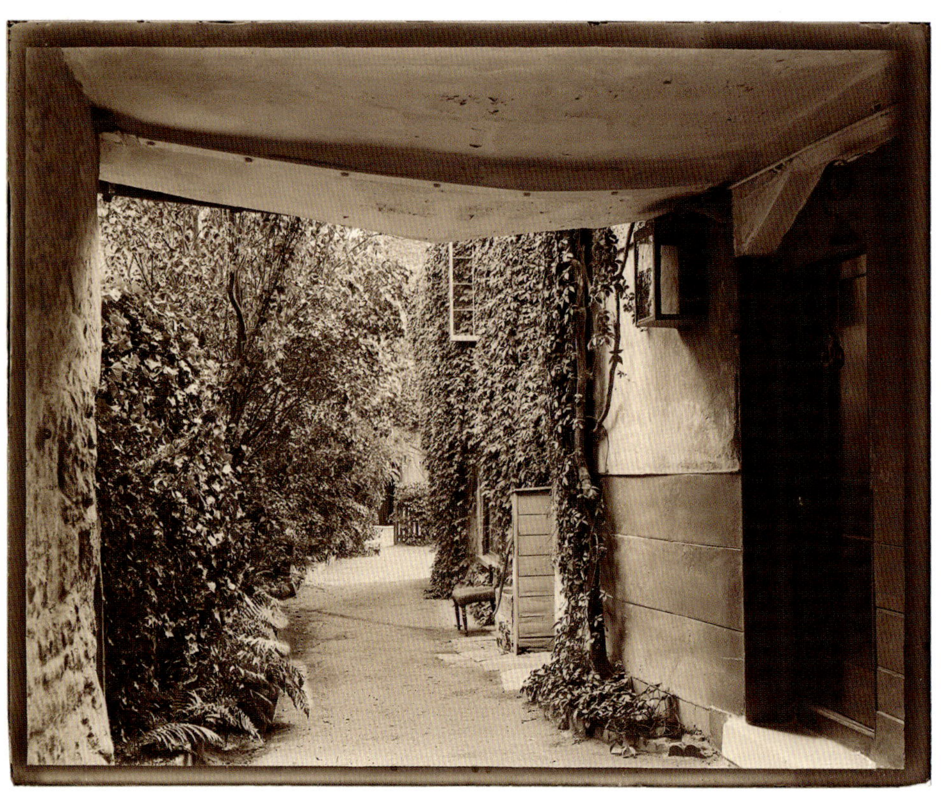

114 & 115. *Old Houses in Oxford*

Coachway of No. 65, Holywell Street; Bath Place
Oxford, shortly before 14 July 1902
5 × 4 inch negatives (×1; enlarged ×1·3)
Bodleian Library, Minn negatives 25/6 & 25/5

These are two of only twelve 5 × 4 inch negatives by Miss Acland known to survive. They depict buildings on the south side of Holywell Street that back on to, and are now incorporated within, New College. Both were probably part of her contribution to the Photographic Survey of Oxfordshire. Conceived in June 1897, the Survey took its inspiration from a successful project in Warwickshire and a proposal at the 1894 Congress of Archæological Societies to obtain "a permanent pictorial record of all objects of general or of local interest". It predated (by a month) and remained independent from Benjamin Stone's National Photographic Record Association, Oxford's photographers preferring to organize themselves on a local basis. An ambitious scheme, by 1901 it was already faltering. In April 1902 Miss Acland was appointed to a sub-committee tasked with restarting work, but by 1906 the Survey had died a death, only to be replaced by a similar project organized under the auspices of a campaign for the 'Preservation of Old Houses in Oxford'.

The cottage beyond the gate in the distance of catalogue no. 114 (above) was the family home of Jane Burden (1839–1914) on her marriage to William Morris in 1859. Morris, who co-founded the Society for the Protection of Ancient Buildings, had known Mrs Acland from Leytonstone before going up to Oxford in 1853. "Mrs Morris", Miss Acland recalled, "used to be a matter of great surprise to my young mind as she would wear a bonnet with apple green strings next to her brilliant pink cheeks and a purple shawl."

In Miss Acland's hands simple topographical views were capable of becoming beautiful pictorial photographs. The compositional strategy she adopts for Bath Place is essentially the same as catalogue nos. 94 and 104. The camera is slightly off centre, looking at an angle to the main perspective, the image divided, both horizontally and vertically, into three zones along the lines of thirds.

Dep. d. 524, fol. 76; Devon Records Office, 1148M/7/1, p. 23.

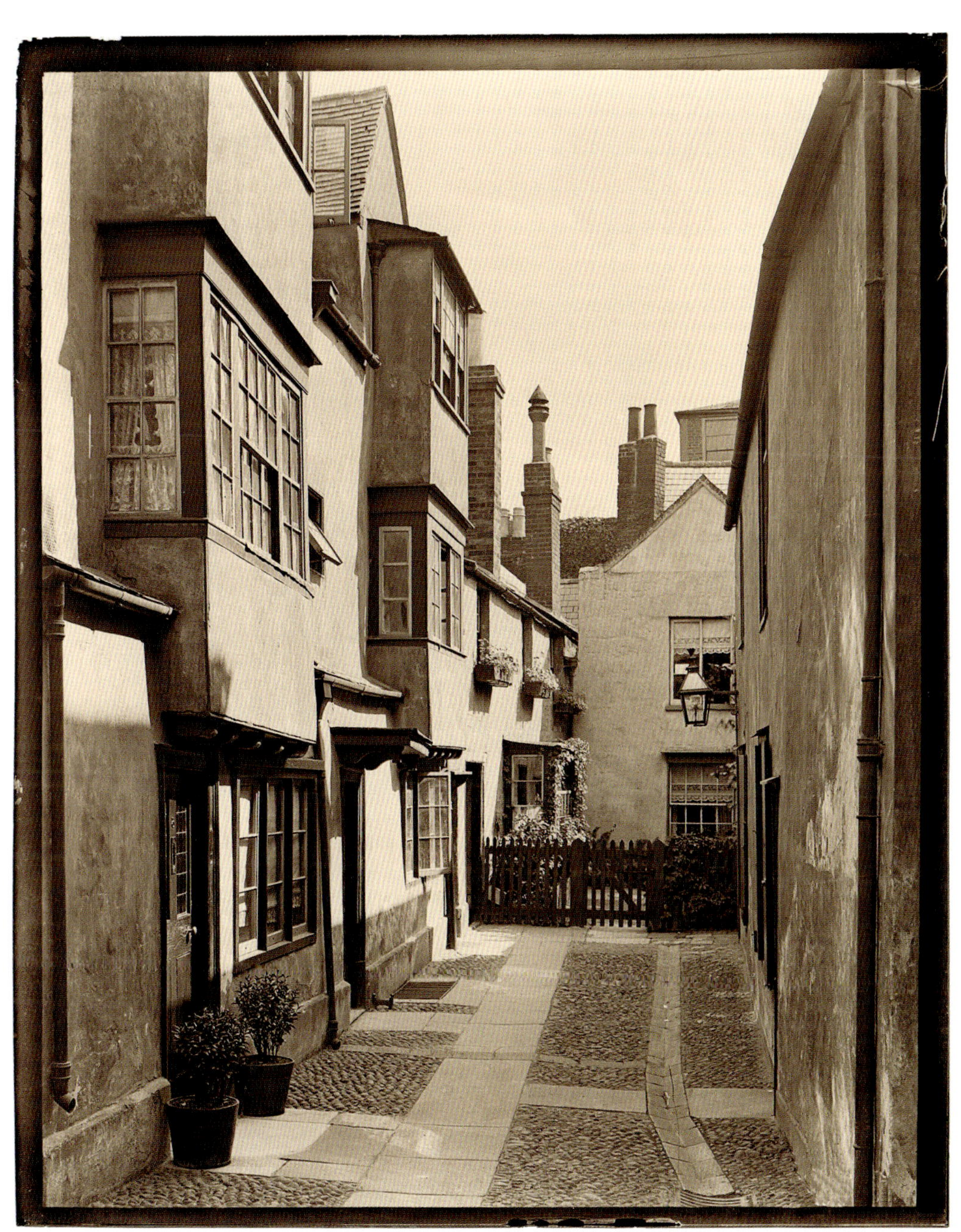

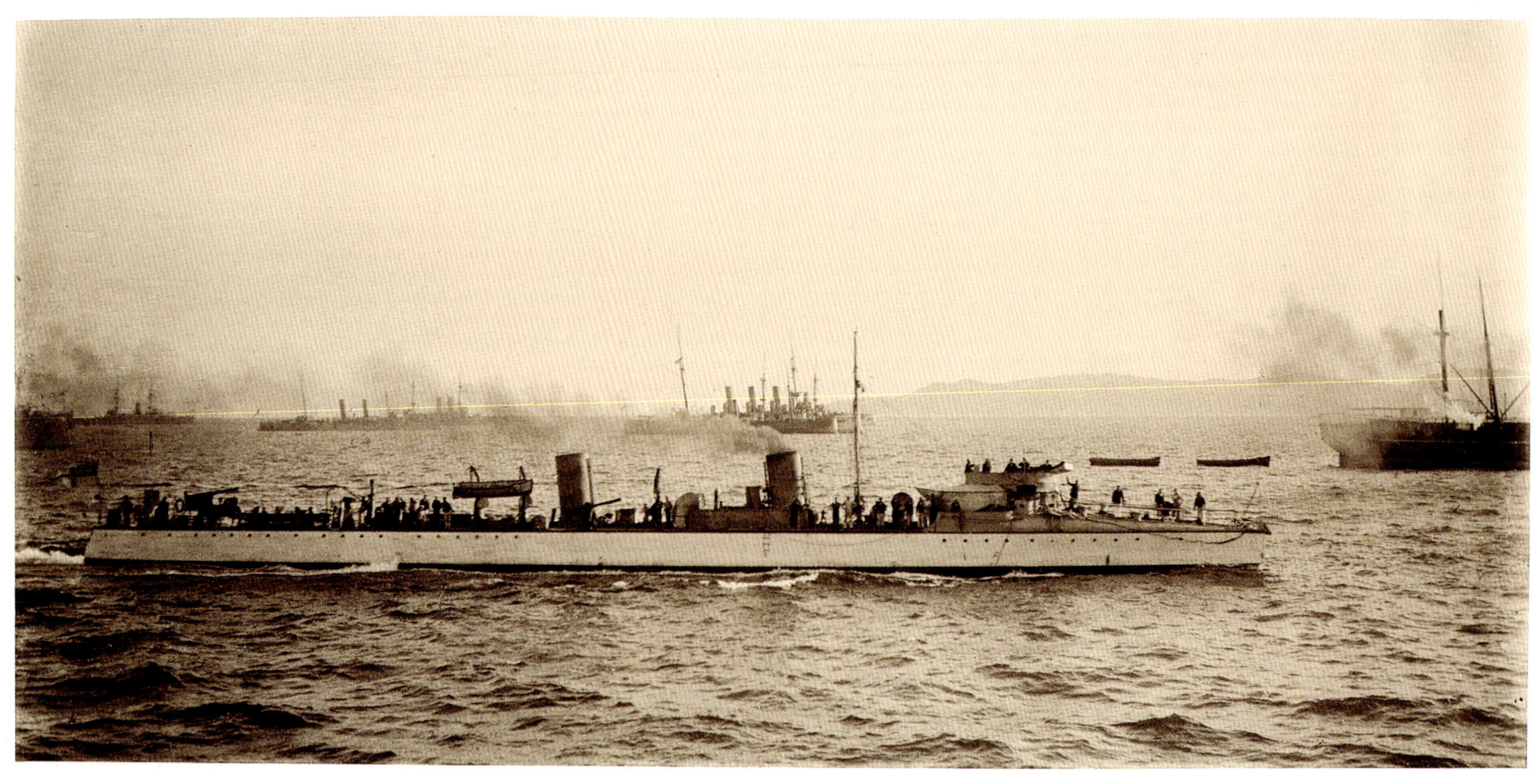

116. *The X Fleet in Torbay*

Ships of the Royal Navy on exercise, Berry Head beyond Torbay, Devon, August 1901

Whole-plate negative
Bodleian Library, Minn negative 110/7

The ship in the foreground of this seascape is a Thornycroft 30 knotter, a *Desperate* class torpedo boat destroyer. The photograph was taken from the gallery of H.M.S. *Magnificent*, Willie's flagship, during the 1901 naval manoeuvres. The manoeuvres pitted the 'X Fleet' against the 'B Fleet', which were both tasked with obtaining the command of the English Channel.

Miss Acland exhibited several slides of war vessels at the Camera Club in November 1901. A colour slide of the whole fleet was also shown and was presumably the same as the colour print she sent to the R.P.S. in 1902, when it became the first colour photograph to be seen in the Pictorial rather than the Scientific section of the exhibition. Naval matters interested Miss Acland greatly. One of the slides in her Gibraltar lecture was a panorama of three negatives showing the combined Mediterranean Fleet, Channel and Cruiser Squadrons, taken from the signal station at the top of the Rock.

117. *The Kasbah Mosque, Tangier*

Entrance to the Kasbah Mosque, Tangier
Morocco, May 1903

Whole-plate negative
Bodleian Library, Minn negative 110/1

During her stay in Gibraltar Miss Acland went on several excursions, including to Algeciras and Tarifa in Andalusia, and across the Strait to Morocco, carrying a camera with her. This photograph was taken outside the seventeenth-century Kasbah Mosque in Tangier, its elaborate doorway with horseshoe arch visible on the left. Out of sight above is a beautiful brick minaret.

Miss Acland achieved the narrow aspect of this and the previous image by masking the whole-plate negatives with several strips of binding tape. The originals were probably taken on film stock with a hand camera light enough to be carried on expeditions (the images display noticeable grain and larger than expected dust marks). She would then have copied the small-format negatives onto glass in order to be able to make enlargements by contact printing.

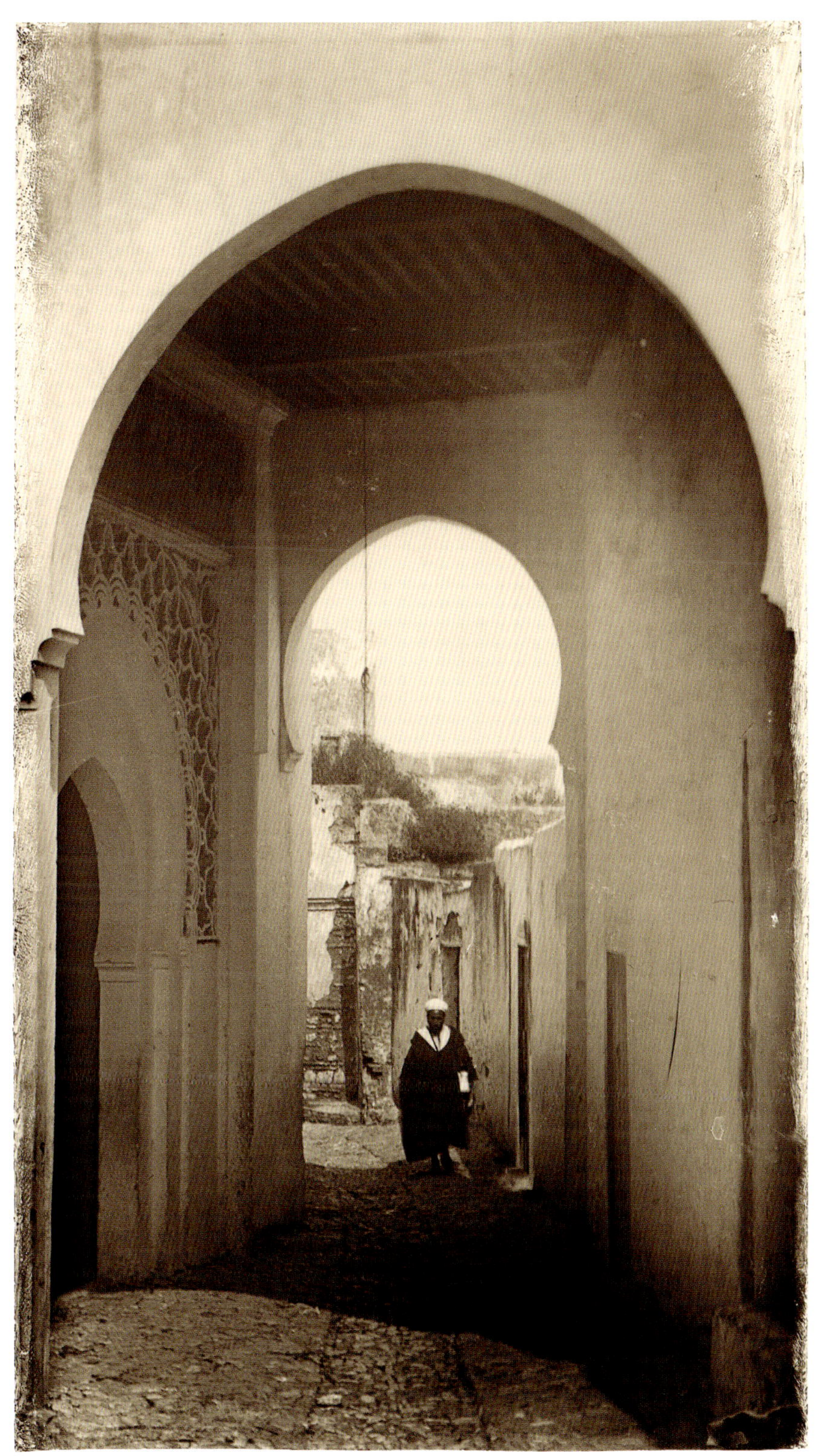

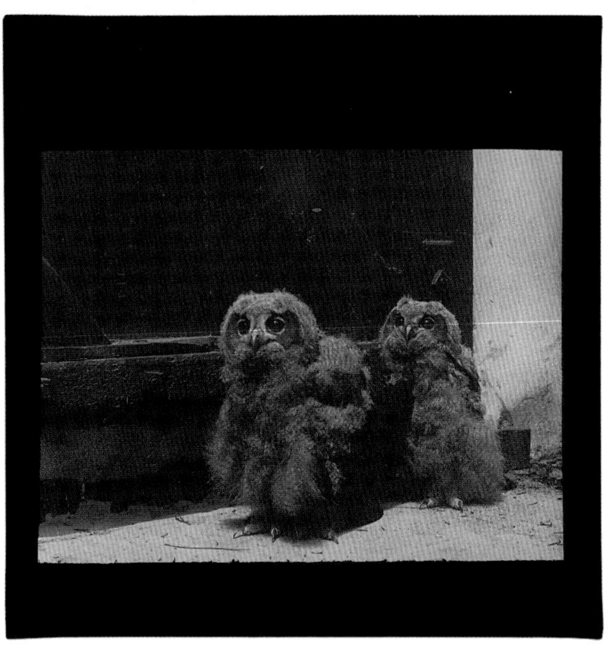

118. *"Eagle Owls Aged Six Weeks"*
Two Eagle-owl chicks
Winchfield, Hampshire, June 1903
Lantern slide
Museum of the History of Science, Inventory no. 76438

Miss Acland photographed these eagle-owl chicks after her return from Gibraltar in 1903 at the home of William Willoughby Cole Verner (1852–1922) (cat. no. 141). Verner discovered the chicks in their nest high on the east side of the Rock. Fearing for their survival he removed them to The Mount, Willie Acland's official residence, where, according to Emmie Acland, they "greatly interested Angie". The slide was shown after a lecture by Verner on "Bird-life in Spain", given to the combined forces of the Oxford Camera Club and Ashmolean Natural History Society in October 1903, at Miss Acland's invitation. Another photograph of the chicks, presumably also by her, was included in Verner's *My Life Among the Wild Birds in Spain* (London, 1909).

The Aclands were a family of animal-lovers. Miss Acland's pets ranged from dormice to dogs, but birds were favourites. Her greenfinch was killed in the schoolroom by the cat in 1858 but received a royal burial under a stone from the Museum on which its 'history' had been written in red letters. Her first dog, a Pomeranian named Jess, was a gift from Thomas Combe. One of Jess's puppies went back to the Combes and was painted by Holman Hunt with his son Cyril Benoni Holman Hunt (1866–1934) in a portrait of 1874. Later Miss Acland acquired fawn and black pugs named Toby and Bogie, who appear in her early Kodak snapshots.

In 1896 Miss Acland took several photographs of her father with a rhesus monkey, labelling one "A Philosopher and one of his Friends". The monkey was not, as sometimes claimed, Acland's pet, but had been brought to Broad Street by a boy attending St Giles's Fair. She later sent prints of the monkey to the *British Journal of Photography* as a contribution to a discussion about the effects of printing negatives under green glass.

'Hon Lady Acland', *Mi Ricordo* (London, 1932), p. 226; *Proceedings of the Oxford Camera Club*, no. 10 (January, 1904), pp. 85–6; MS. Minn 226, fol. 33v.

119. *"Annula Eclipse of the Sun"*

The sun and moon during annular eclipse
Oxford, 8 April 1921

Quarter-plate negative
Museum of the History of Science, Inventory no. 92809

Miss Acland had already developed an interest in astronomical photography by the partial eclipse of the sun on 28 May 1900, six lantern slides of which she sent to the Royal Photographic Society later in the year. She also tried to photograph the total eclipse of 21 August 1914.

Several factors no doubt motivated Miss Acland to turn her camera to the heavens. Oxford had a tradition of astronomical photography, established with the De La Rue reflector at the University Observatory. A second instrument by Grubb was used for the University's contribution to the Carte du Ciel and *Astrographic Catalogue*, much of the work for which was carried out by Frank Arthur Bellamy (1863–1936), a founder member of the Oxford Photographic Society. This local expertise aside, astronomical photography attracted a wide following among amateur photographers. Articles about how to photograph eclipses appeared in all the photographic journals, as well as the regular "Camera Notes" column in the *Oxford Times*.

Miss Acland's curiosity in astronomy was one of several scientific interests absorbed from her father. Acland had an impressive observatory at Broad Street, where he entertained guests. In June 1869, for example, he showed Saturn after an evening party; in February 1877 the eclipse of the moon to Alexander Macdonald and his daughters. After her father's death Miss Acland developed a passion for comet spotting, observing Halley's comet over Funchal in 1910 and the arrival of Brooks', Quenisset's, and Beljawsky's comets in Oxford in 1911.

The 1921 eclipse was visible at its peak magnitude of 0·975 only from northern Scotland. Miss Acland made six negatives from Oxford, tracking its progress until just after the maximum at about 8.46 a.m.

120. *Sarah Angelina Acland*

Sarah Angelina Acland (1849–1930), in the drawing room of Clevedon House, Park Town
Oxford, 1928

Half-plate negative
Bodleian Library, Minn negative 206/5

Whoever released the shutter to take this photograph, whether Miss Acland's collaborator Harry Minn, a niece or nephew, or one of her maids, it has the character of a self-portrait. Miss Acland is lying on her couch in the east side of the drawing room at Clevedon House. The plate was one of six taken for her 1928 Christmas card.

Many of the objects surrounding Miss Acland are familiar from her photographs of Broad Street. Of other items of interest, a copy of *The Richmond Papers*, published in 1926, can be seen on the table: Miss Acland often read the memoirs of old friends and would have found several references to her father in Richmond's biography. Titles visible on her bookshelves include Kipling's *Just So Stories*, Laurence Housman's *The Death of Socrates*, and *My Life Among the Bluejackets* by Agnes Weston (1840–1918), with whom she corresponded. Over the mantel is the inscription 'Rest and Be Thankful', borrowed from above the Maalstofa fireplace.

By 1928 Miss Acland had long since given up active photography. She made the decision to dispose of her equipment in early 1919, giving most of it away to Minn and her nephew Robin, who even took her "beloved little Sibyl with its splendid lens". The Sibyl was a quarter-plate camera, released in 1908 by Newman & Guardia and fitted with a Zeiss 'Tessar' lens. No photographs by Miss Acland taken with it are known. Robin declined his aunt's enlarging lantern, which was sold instead to a Mr A. Podmore of Amicable Street, Burslem, for the princely sum of £20 (having cost only £10 twenty-five years earlier). Podmore wrote afterwards to ask Miss Acland's profession and the price she charged for 'finishing' photographs, much to her amusement.

This is the last-known portrait of Miss Acland, taken two years before her death on 2 December 1930. Notices of her passing appeared in, amongst other places, the *British Journal of Photography* and *The Times*, the latter writing that she "gained distinction in photography, especially in portraiture" and was "one of the, if not the first, to take a portrait in colour photography". Her funeral was held on 5 December in Christ Church Cathedral and she was buried in Holywell Cemetery with her mother, father and eldest brother.

Miss Acland bequeathed her "Negatives, Colour Prints and Transparencies" to Minn, who left them in turn to the Bodleian Library in 1961. In 1988 the colour screen-plates were transferred to the Museum of the History of Science, where they were reunited with her camera equipment, Gibraltar separation negatives, and the medals she won for photography.

MS. Acland d. 113, fols. 226–8; *The Times*, no. 45687 (4 December 1930), p. 18e; Sarah Angelina Acland, "Last will and Testament", 26 March 1928.

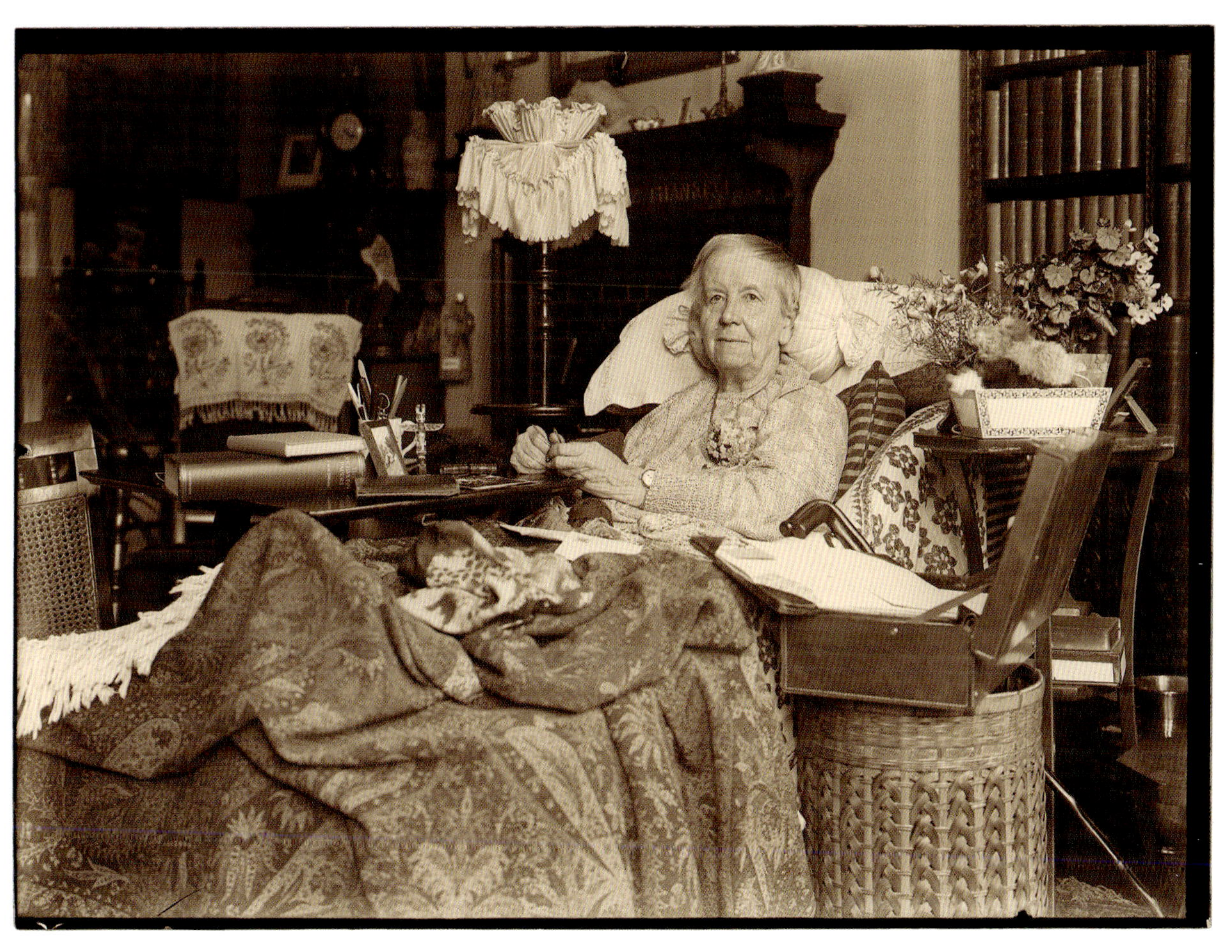

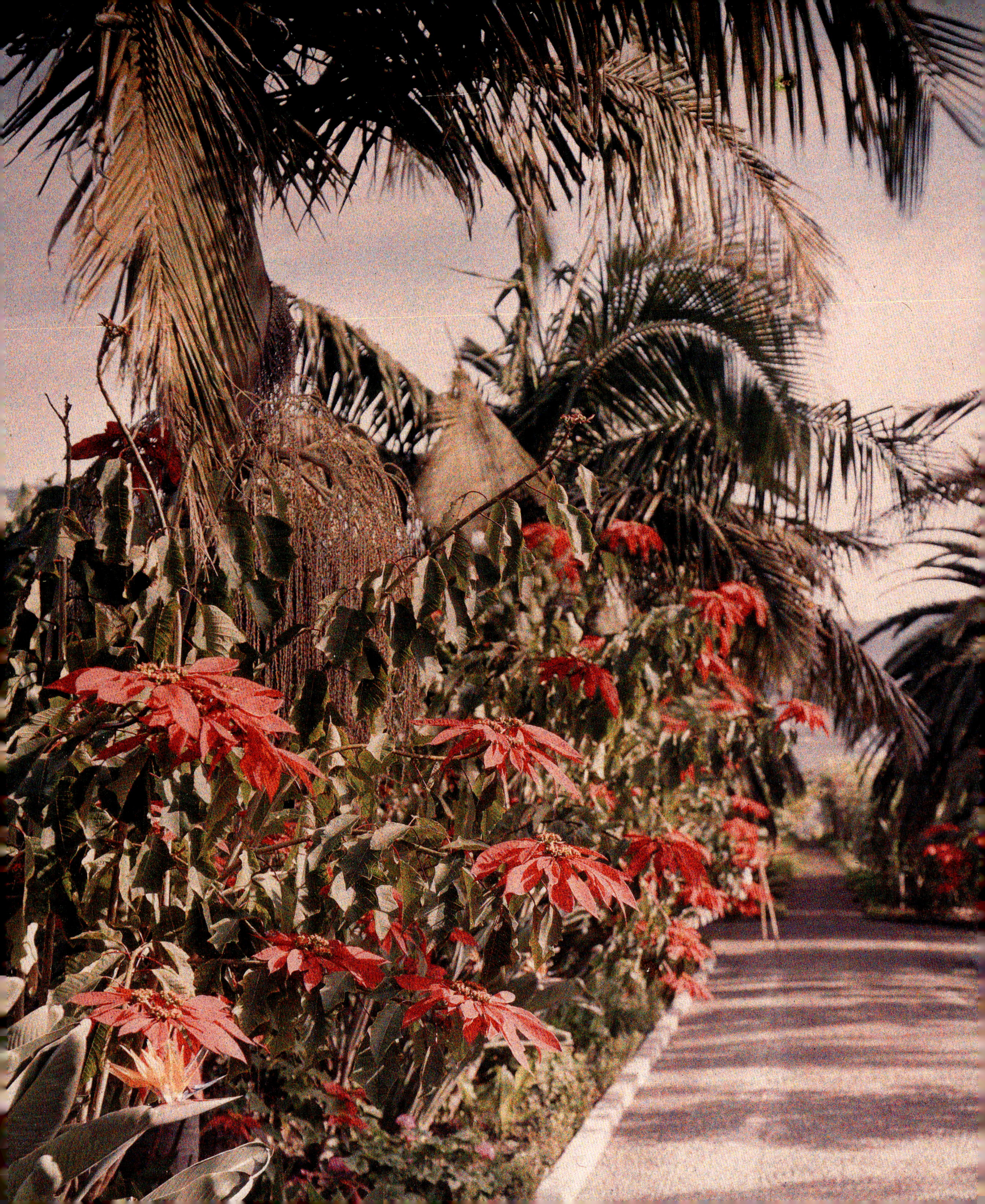

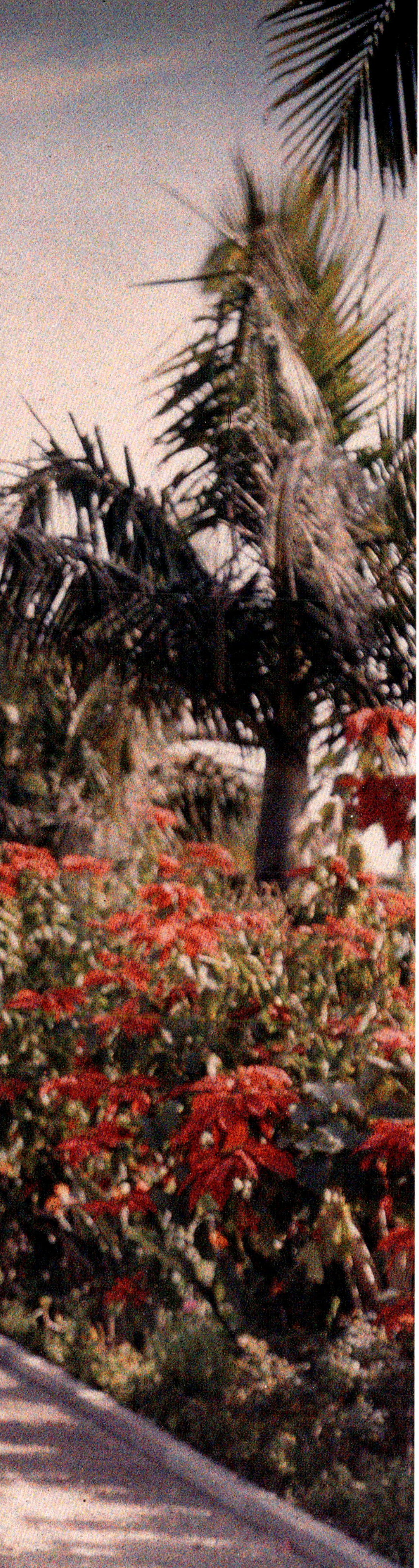

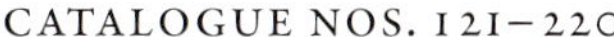

CATALOGUE NOS. 121–220

COLOUR PHOTOGRAPHS

Except where stated, the Kromaz, Krōmskōp and Sanger Shepherd photographs that follow are digitally recomposed from Miss Acland's original three-colour separation negatives, as discussed in cat. no. 163. Inventory numbers are those of the negatives; magnification factors are given where applicable.

Autochrome, Omnicolore, Dufay Dioptichrome and Paget Colour plates are designed to be viewed by transmitted light. Their reproduction in ink on paper therefore presents a challenge, the saturated luminosity of the originals being difficult to convey and many of the colours lying beyond the range of the primaries used in commercial printing (especially the blues that give the Omnicolore process much of its character). The illustrations here aim to capture the impression the originals make on the eye and mind in the flesh, conceding that a precise match is impossible. The plates are reproduced as composites of two scans: a scan of the mount by reflected light and a scan of the picture as a transparency, in an attempt to communicate a sense of the photographs as objects as well as merely images, the weight of which can be felt in the hand.

KROMAZ & KRŌMSKŌP PLATES

Miss Acland gave the first hint of her interest in colour photography after her Home Portraiture lecture in February 1899, when the Camera Club's Krōmskōp was on display. A year later, in April 1900, she spoke at some length on the principles of the Sanger Shepherd process during her Spectrum Plates lecture, exhibiting colour slides lent to her for the event. Prior to exhibiting Sanger Shepherd slides from her own hand in public she experimented not only with the Krōmskōp but with the Kromaz system. Both were 'indirect' methods of colour photography, requiring separate exposures through red, green and blue filters. Positives from the negatives were then combined optically (rather than physically as slides or prints), using a bespoke viewing instrument.

The Kromaz system was patented by the Englishmen Thomas Knight Barnard (1869–1956) and Frederick Gowenlock (1876–1952). It sold from July 1899 through Watson & Sons, manufacturers of Miss Acland's half-plate camera. In the system a full-colour stereoscopic photograph was created from only two pairs of images: a stereo pair taken through red and blue filters; and a stereo pair taken through green filters. The red and green left eye images, and the blue and green right eye images, were then combined optically in a viewer, leaving the illusion of full colour to be formed in the mind of the observer. Apparatus consisted of the colour filters, mirrors to place inside the camera, an attachment for the back, and the 'chromo stereoscope' viewer. Examples of each survive with Miss Acland's equipment, as do four pairs of Kromaz slides.

Ives's Krōmskōp system was released in autumn 1897, although a camera for taking the negatives did not become available for at least another year. In use, a ribbon of three stereograms from separation negatives was placed on the Krōmskōp instrument and the images optically superimposed by means of mirrors. The Oxford Camera Club acquired a viewer from the 'Photochromoscope Syndicate' shortly after its release, together with a box of sample Kromograms.

OPPOSITE

121. *"Frogbowl, Ribbon and Fruit"*

Still life of fruit and a ribbon, arranged in a bowl
Oxford, between July 1899 and August 1900
Blue-red Kromaz slide; green slide; digital composite
Museum of the History of Science, Inv. nos. 22608 & 96219

Three black and white illustrations of this still life were reproduced as half-tones in Miss Acland's Spectrum Plate paper in *Photography*. If treated as red, green and blue plates, these can be combined to create a colour image. Perplexingly, however, in the journal they are described not as colour separation negatives, but as images taken on an ordinary plate, a Spectrum plate with Gilvus (yellow) filter, and a Spectrum plate with Absolutus (orange) filter. Exposures made in this way would approximate to separation negatives — the ordinary plate being sensitive mainly to blue and the Spectrum plate more to red — but not as perfectly as seen in the figures, so they must have been mixed up somewhere along the line.

It is possible these slides were created from Miss Acland's early separation negatives at a later date, as a historical demonstration of the Kromaz system. Nevertheless, the publication of the original negatives dates the exposures to August 1900 at the latest and indicates how early Miss Acland was experimenting in colour. She exhibited the same still life as a Sanger Shepherd lantern slide at the Royal Photographic Society exhibition in 1901.

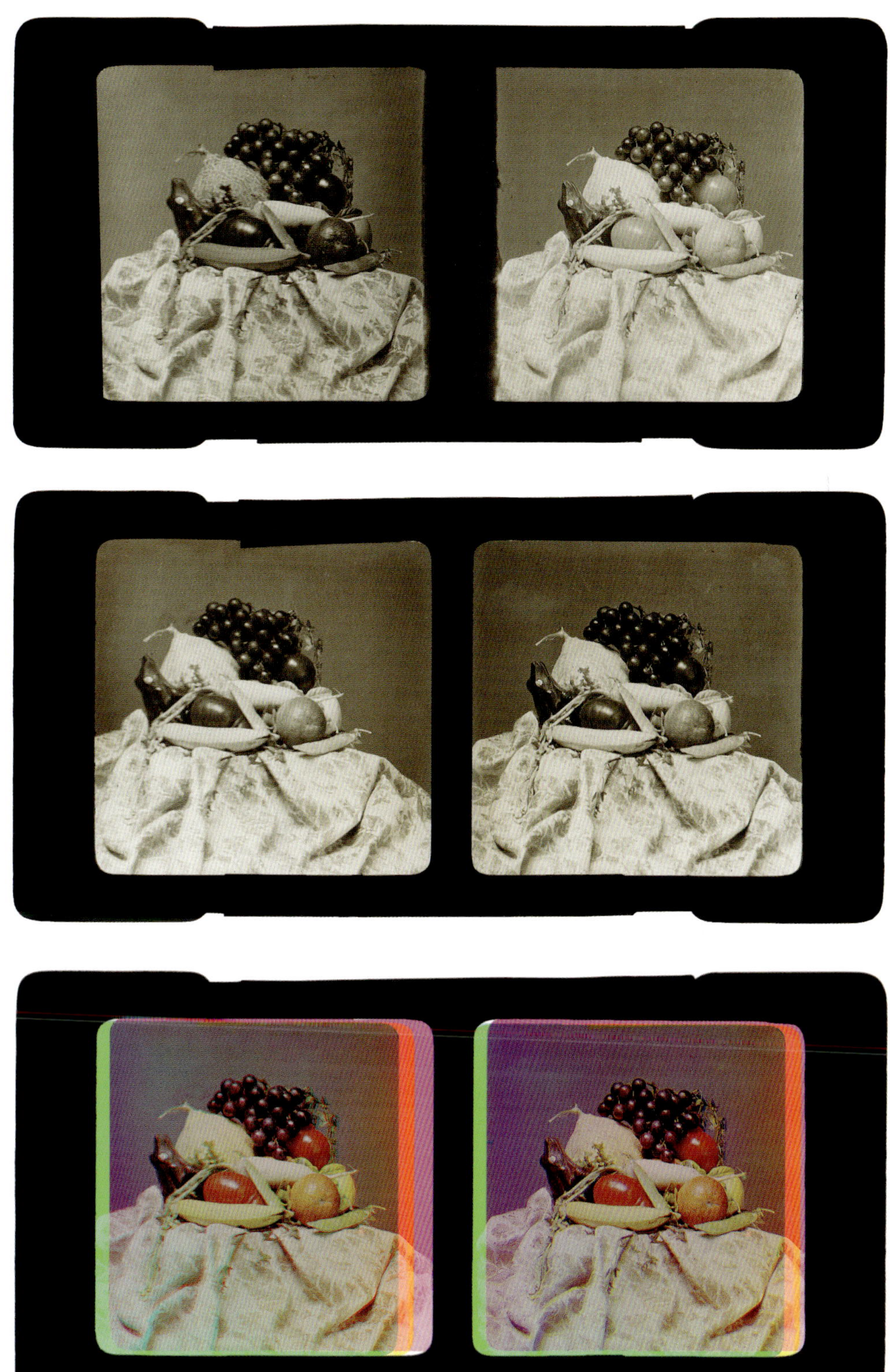

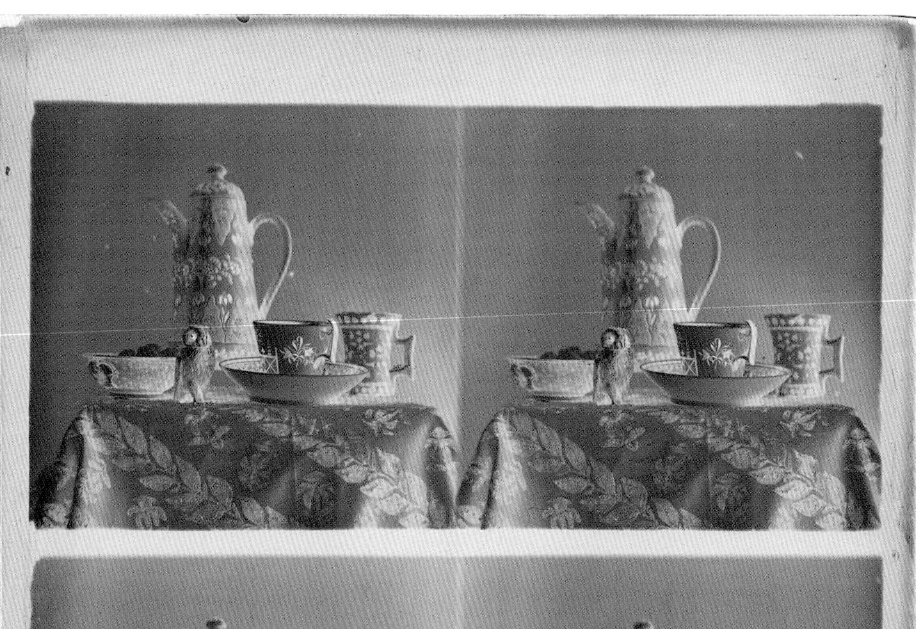

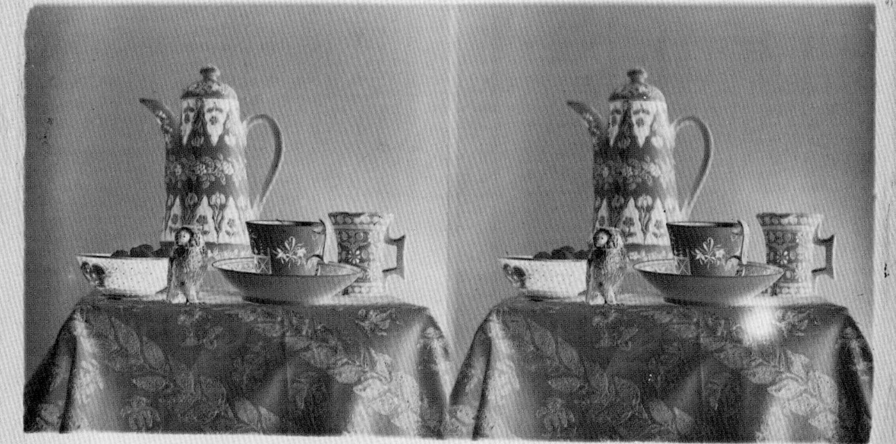

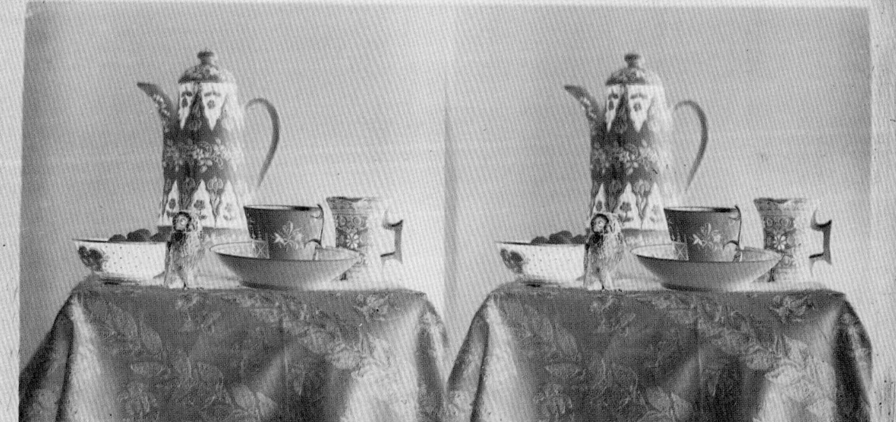

Print Blue
Print Blue

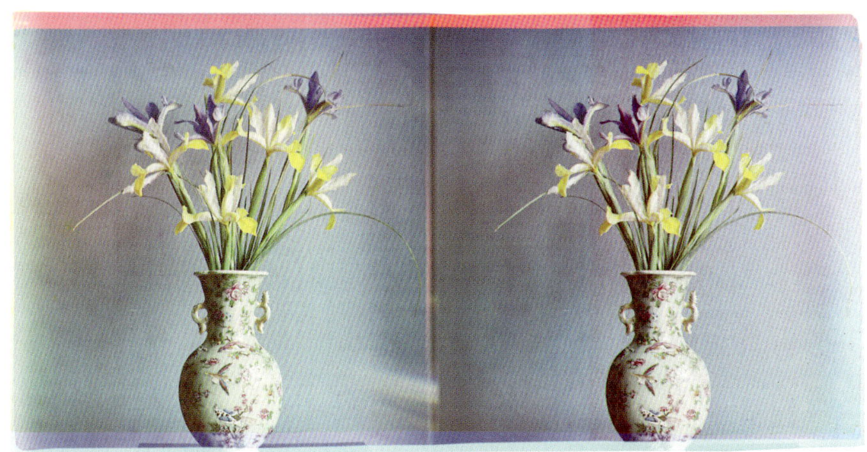

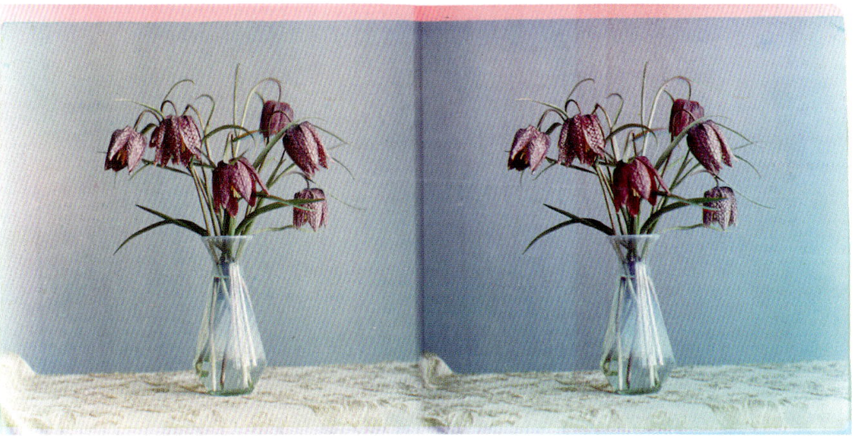

122–124. *Kromograms*

Breakfast service; Irises; Fritillaries
Oxford, between July 1899 and August 1900?

8 × 5 inch 3-colour stereo separation negative & composites
Museum of the History of Science, Inventory nos. 46431, 59089 & 68187

Among Miss Acland's plates are twelve 8 × 5 inch stereo separation negatives for making Kromograms. With the negatives is the camera in which they were taken: a simple, wooden, box-form device, with two lenses, flap shutter, and sliding back. The camera has no maker's label, but the design and workmanship is similar to Sanger Shepherd's, suggesting it dates from before he founded his company in September 1899, possibly while he was working as an assistant to Ives.

Miss Acland's Kromogram negatives appear to have been taken before she left Broad Street on 23 May 1901. The breakfast service and fritillaries are arranged on the same gold-embroidered cloth as her frogbowl still life and therefore probably date from before August 1900. Fritillaries flower in the second half of April in Oxford, irises slightly later, which points to a spring date. In March 1899 she enquired of Harry "where the breakfast service is made", which could be a reference to the crockery. That she chose such mundane subjects, and paid little attention to the composition, is indicative of the experimental nature of colour photography at the time.

MS. Acland d. 144, fols. 42–3.

SANGER SHEPHERD PROCESS

The original Sanger Shepherd process was a 'simplified' method of making colour lantern slides for viewing in the hand or with an ordinary lantern projector. The process was announced by its inventor at the London Camera Club on 5 October 1899, shortly after a company had been formed for its commercial exploitation, Sanger Shepherd & Co., of 5, 6 & 7, Gray's Inn Passage, Red Lion Street, Holborn.

As worked by Miss Acland, the three negatives from which Sanger Shepherd lantern slides were made were arranged side by side on a "one-plate triple negative", 8 × 3⅓ inches in size. The plate was exposed three times, through red, green and blue filters, using a 'repeating back'. This could be attached to a normal field or studio camera and consisted of a dark slide and filter assembly that moved in a wooden trough. Between exposures each successive filter and the unexposed portion of the plate below was moved to align with the image in the camera. Exposure times were long, typically lasting 2 minutes in bright light outdoors, including the time to move the plate: the red exposure might take 60 seconds, the green 10, and blue 2 seconds, but the exact ratio varied with each batch of plates. Any movement of camera or subject during the exposures would result in colour fringes in the final image.

Assuming successful negatives had been obtained, Sanger Shepherd slides were assembled by printing the negative from the red exposure on glass by a variant of the cyanotype process, and those from the green and blue exposures as unpigmented carbon prints on pieces of transparent celluloid, which were then stained magenta and yellow respectively. All three positives were varnished, cemented together in 'optical contact' using Canada balsam (a resin from the balsam fir, *Abies balsamea*), a cover glass added, and the slide bound up with paper tape. The process was fraught with difficulty at every stage. The celluloid had to be sensitized in a special solution before being dried overnight in a warm darkroom, for example, while the carbon prints required development in water at exactly 100°F, pinned downwards to a piece of cork for a length of time recognizable only by experience.

In 1899 the idea of producing colour photographs by superimposing coloured carbon prints was nothing new. During the 1890s several experimenters had attempted to convert the concept into a workable process, including Gustav Adolph Selle (1854–1902) in Brandenburg, the Lumière brothers in France, and the Austrian chemist Arthur Freiherr von Hübl (1853–1932). In Britain in 1897 John Wallace Bennetto (1857–1931), a Newquay professional, attracted praise and ridicule in equal measure for his claim to have solved the whole problem of colour photography by the technique. However, it was not until Sanger Shepherd that the process was transformed into a fully practicable, commercial proposition. Sanger Shepherd's success was partly due to his use of a transparent celluloid that had only just become available, and partly to his application of scientific principles of accuracy and measurement to the design, manufacture and testing of the component parts of his system — a strategy he took pains to stress in the rhetoric that accompanied his advertisements.

Materials and apparatus for the Sanger Shepherd process were placed on the market in July 1900. Miss Acland's first negatives date from soon after, or possibly shortly before this date, but it was not until 25 March 1901 that she exhibited completed colour slides at the Oxford Camera Club, the delay being due to the death of her father on 16 October 1900.

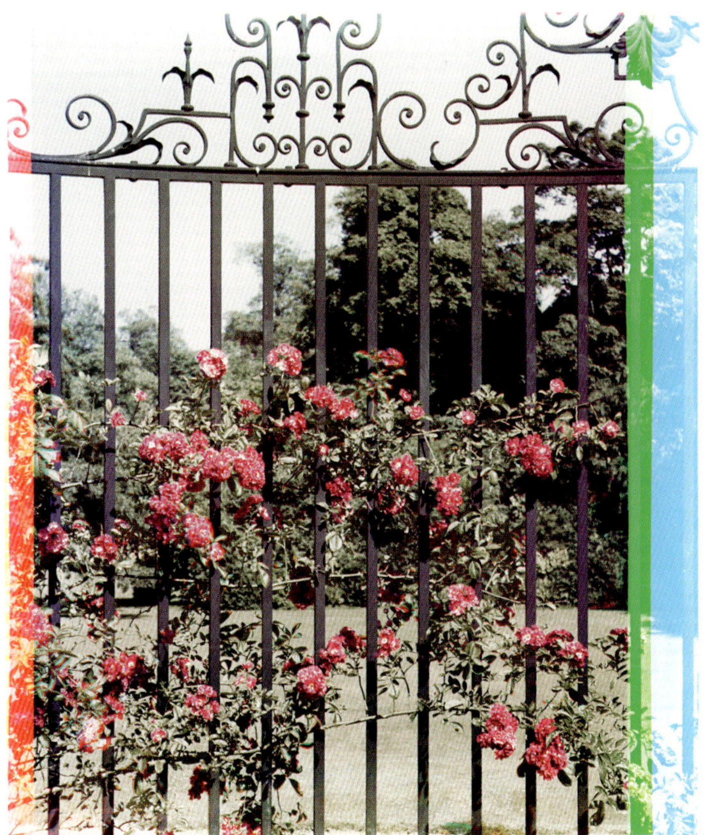

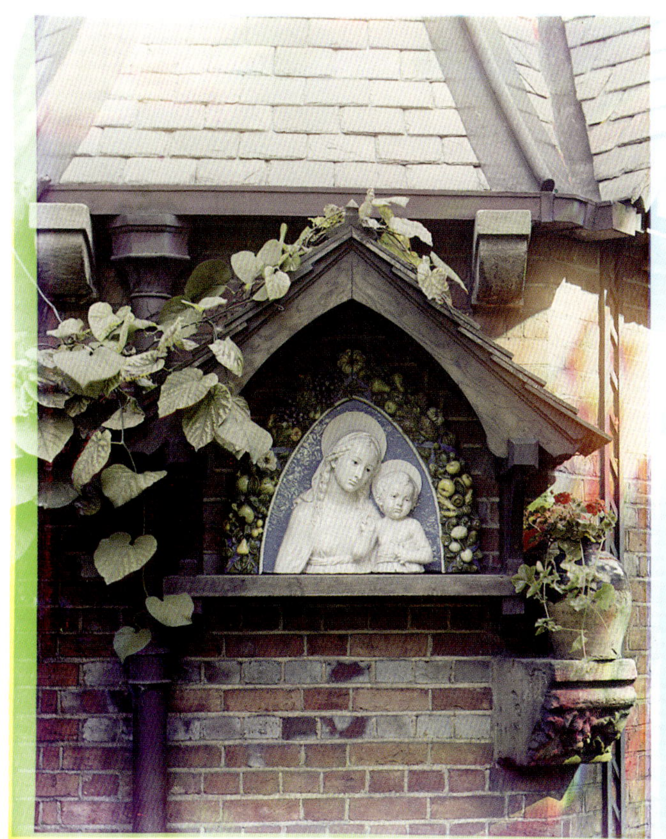

125. *"Crimson Rambler in New College Gardens"*

Turner's Crimson Rambler rose
Oxford, June or July 1900

Composite from 8 × 3⅓ inch 3-colour separation negative (×1·4)
Museum of the History of Science, Inventory no. 15114

This was one of six slides Miss Acland sent to the Oxford Camera Club on 25 March 1901, marking her public debut as a colour photographer. Crimson Rambler flowers in June in Oxford, so the negatives must have been taken nine months earlier, in 1900. The slides were "much admired, especially the very fine one of the roses trailing over the entrance to the Gardens".

Turner's Crimson Rambler was the superstar rose of its day. Introduced to Europe from China in 1878, it became popular after being placed into commercial cultivation by Arthur Turner (1849–1930), of the Royal Nurseries, Slough. Miss Acland knew Turner, having been introduced to him by William George Baker (1861–1945), Curator of the Oxford Botanic Garden.

Proceedings of the Oxford Camera Club, no. 7 (May 1901), p. 58.

126. *Virgin and Child*

Virgin and Child, by or after Luca della Robbia
Oxford, June or July 1900 ?

Composite from 8 × 3⅓ inch 3-colour separation negative (×1·4)
Museum of the History of Science, Inventory no. 16886

The bold, polychrome glaze of Miss Acland's Della Robbia provided a suitable subject for her early experiments with the Sanger Shepherd process. When she came to demonstrate the process at the Camera Club in 1903 (see p. 34) she claimed that Ruskin, who gave her the sculpture, had once attempted colour photography himself, in collaboration with Alexander Macdonald, but had failed due to the insensitivity of ordinary plates to red light. For Christmas 1905 she gave Macdonald one of her own colour prints. "I am very much interested to see what advance has been made towards reproducing the colours of nature, and it is most interesting to find that these are so much like what painters produce, for effect, as is generally supposed, but really as being what they see", he wrote in his letter of thanks.

MS. Acland d. 174, fols. 13–14.

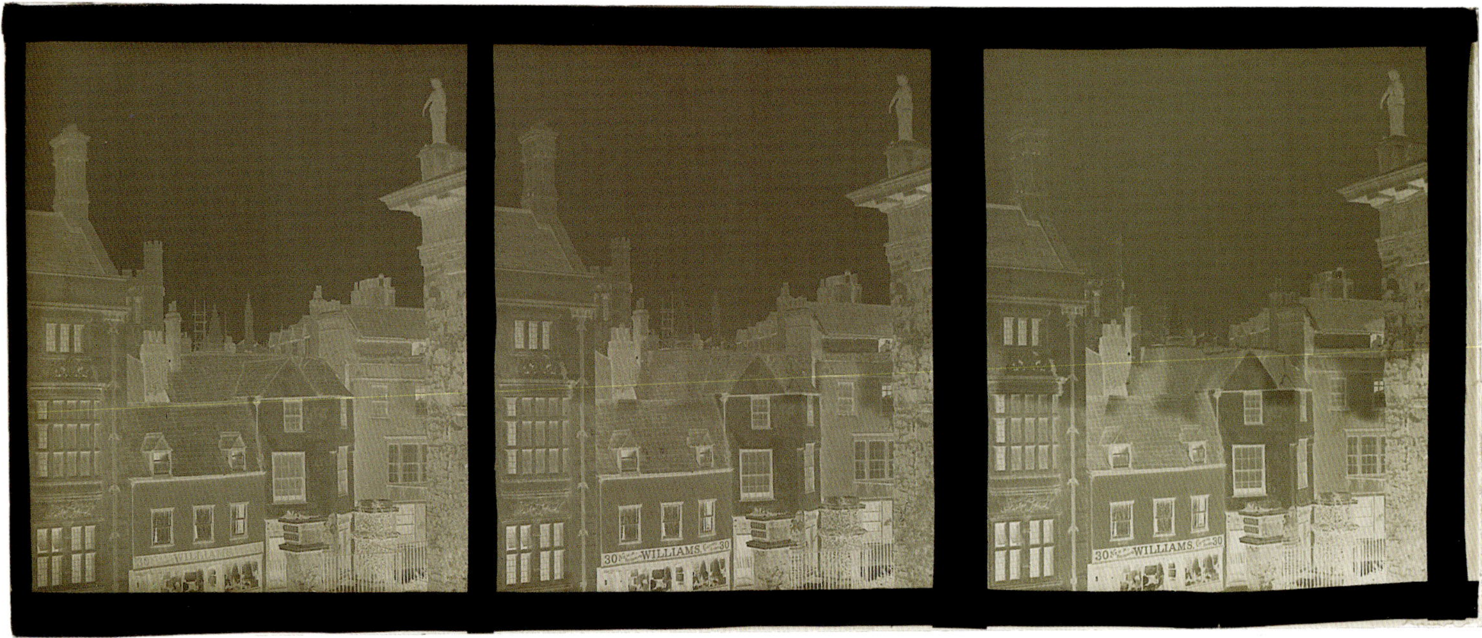

127. *Evening Light in Broad Street*

Rooftops in Broad Street and the tower of New College
Oxford, July or August 1900?

8 × 3⅓ inch 3-colour separation negative and composite (×2)
Museum of the History of Science, Inventory no. 51603

The sun is setting in the north-west in this photograph of the east end of Broad Street from the first floor of the Acland house, and the windows in the attic of Mrs Williams's 'Fancy Repository' are open, suggesting it was taken on a warm summer's evening. As a much-loved view, seen almost daily for the first fifty-two years of her life, it was probably one of the first Miss Acland attempted in colour. Little more than a year's growth is seen in the ivy on the pillars by comparison with *Broad Street at Night* (cat. no. 96). Beside the pillar on the left in both photographs, lined up in the window of the 'Athletic Outfitters' at No. 29 Broad Street, is a row of cricket bats.

In common with most of the illustrations in this section, the image opposite has been digitally recomposed from Miss Acland's original three-colour separation negative (reproduced above, showing, from left to right, the blue, green and red exposures). That the colours are imperfect is due to a combination of factors, including the imprecision of Sanger Shepherd's trichromatic filters and the inadequate isochromatic response of the Cadett Spectrum plate. The colour fringes are caused by the movement of the sun and shadows during the three exposures. The red fringes are the widest because the red plate required the longest exposure.

This is undoubtedly the first colour photograph ever taken of Oxford. The sun was setting for Miss Acland on Broad Street in more ways than one: she would leave her beloved home for the last time on 23 May 1901, moving a mile north to Clevedon House in Park Town.

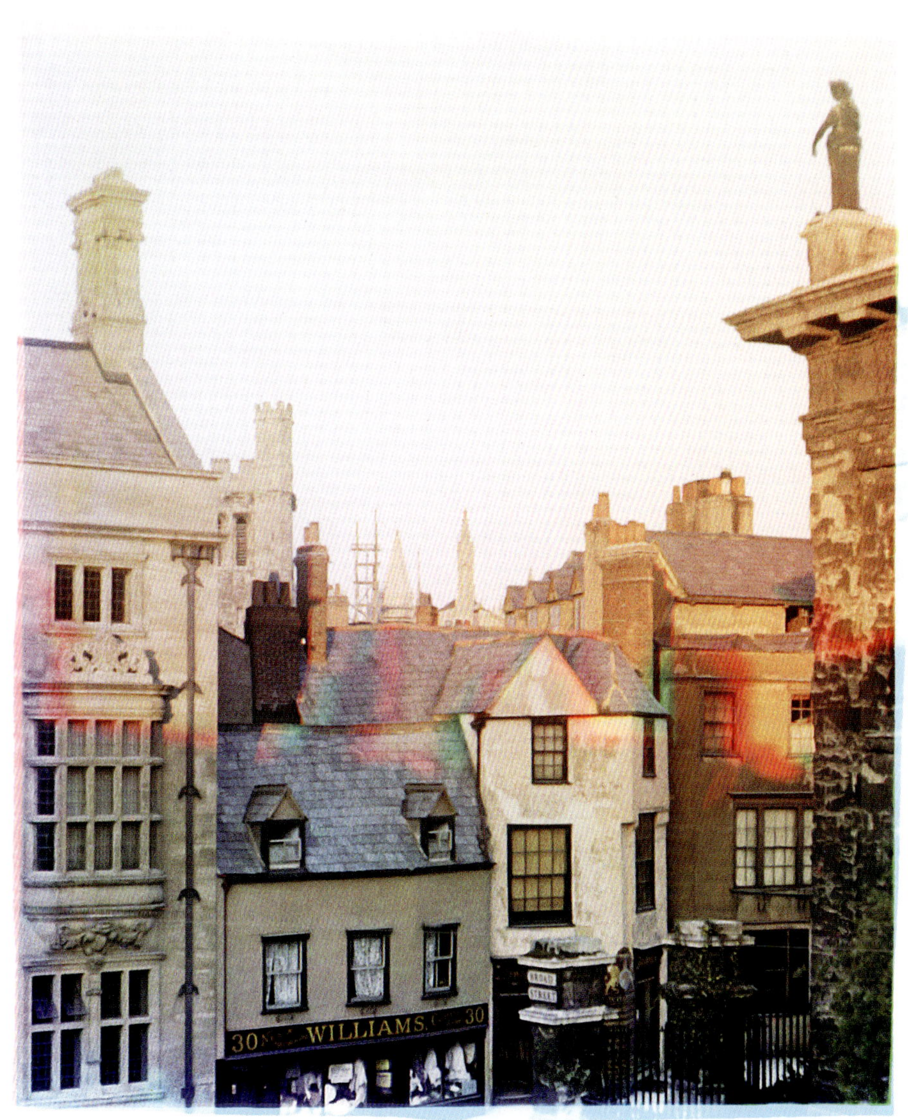
30 WILLIAMS 30
BROAD
STREET

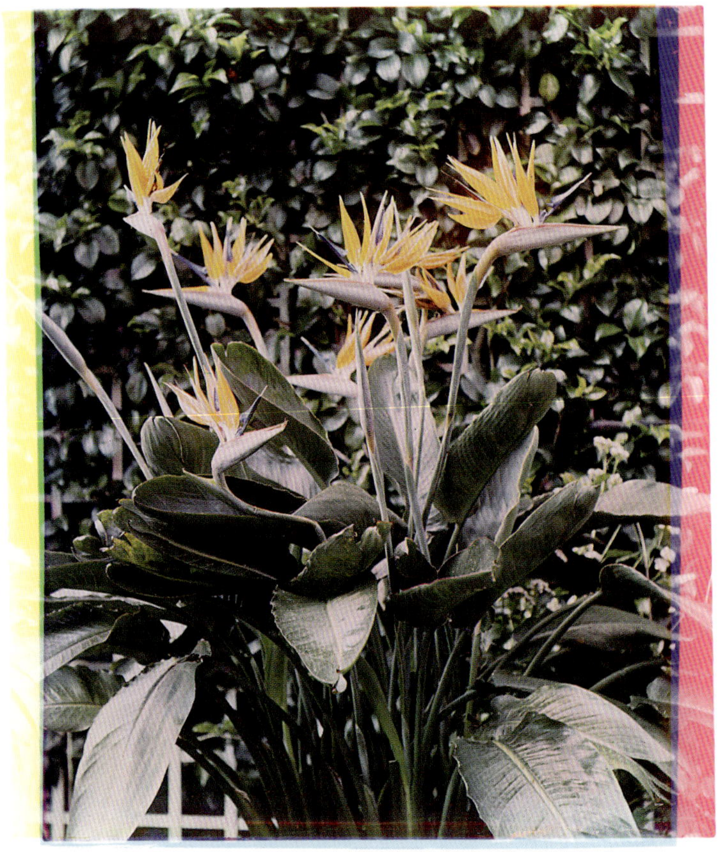

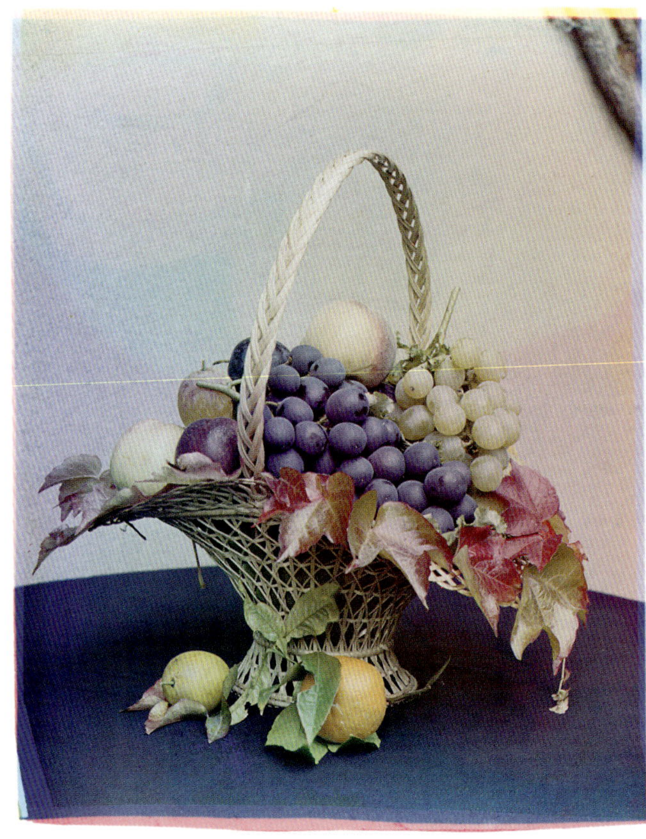

128. *"Strelitzia Reginae"*

Bird of Paradise flower (Crane Lily)
Oxford, between March and May 1901 ?

Composite from 8 × 3⅓ inch 3-colour separation negative (×1·4)
Museum of the History of Science, Inventory no. 68337

In March 1888 the *Journal of Horticulture* reported that *Strelitzia juncea* had recently been in bloom on the front stage of the Palm house at the Botanic Garden in Oxford. This specimen of its close relative was probably located in the same place, if not in New College or Miss Acland's own garden. A photograph of *Strelitzia reginae* was one of the six colour slides Miss Acland submitted to the R.P.S. exhibition in September 1901. Six years later, in October 1907, she sent a colour slide of the same subject to the first exhibition of the Society of Colour Photographers.

Colour photographs of botanical specimens, aside from being of special interest to Miss Acland as a woman, were of commercial value: one of the earliest applications of colour photography was the illustration of seedsmen's catalogues.

129. *"Basket of Fruit"*

Still life of grapes and other fruit, in a wicker basket
Oxford, between March and May 1901 ?

Composite from 8 × 3⅓ inch 3-colour separation negative (×1·4)
Museum of the History of Science, Inventory no. 65438

When Miss Acland showed this still life in Oxford the editor of the Camera Club's *Proceedings* commented that "the bloom on the grapes was beautifully brought out". Other critics were less convinced by early versions of the three-colour process. Commentating on the 1901 R.P.S. exhibition one reviewer wrote that "the colouring of many of the colour slides is, to our thinking, far too vivid." The criticism can perhaps justly be levied against this example: the lighting is indirect (the shadow below the basket diffuse) and therefore likely to have been less saturated than it appears. Improvements in filters for three-colour work would later address this problem, as testified to by the praise Miss Acland received for the neutral tones of her Gibraltar slides (see cat. no. 135).

Proceedings of the Oxford Camera Club, no. 9 (October 1903), p. 81; *Photography*, vol. 13, no. 674 (10 October 1901), p. 690.

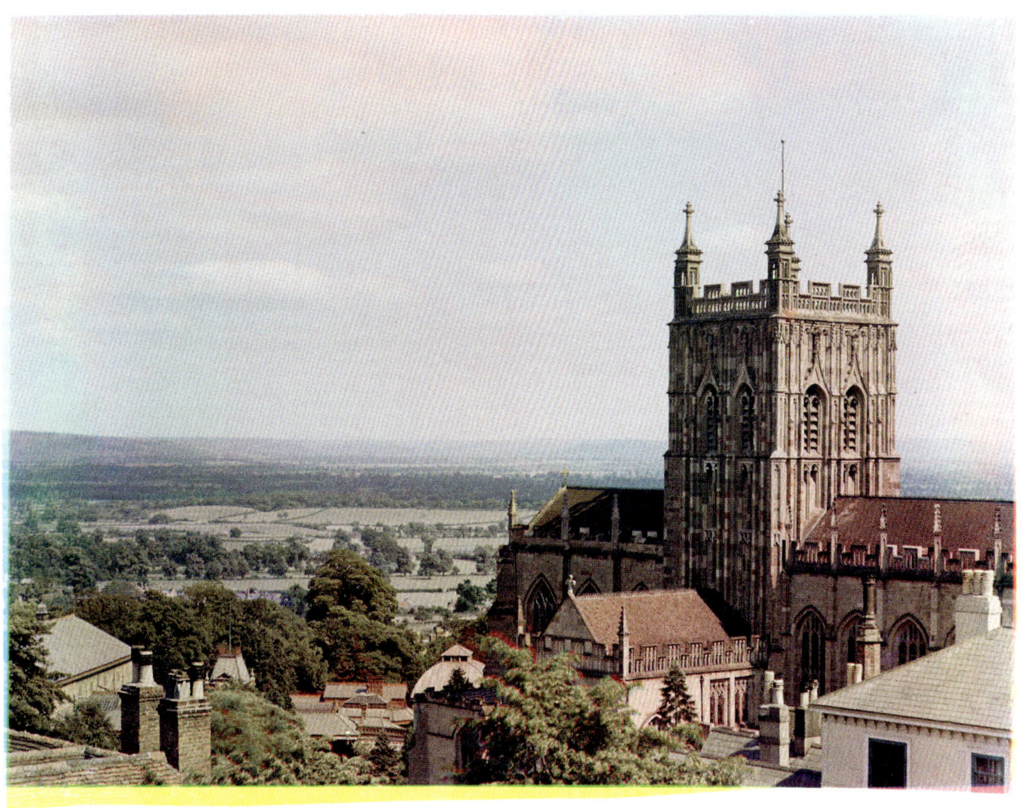

130. *"View from Great Malvern"*

Malvern Priory from the Old Bank, looking south-east
Malvern, *circa* 6 June 1901 or earlier

Composite from 8 × 3⅓ inch 3-colour separation negative (× 1·8)
Museum of the History of Science, Inventory no. 22160

This panorama was taken from an upper window of the Worcester Old Bank in Malvern, where Harry Acland was manager. The view was a favourite with Harry's father, who wrote that it had "never been surpassed in beauty in any part of the world I have ever seen".

Harry was Edward Elgar's bank manager, golfing partner and the dedicatee of *Sursum Corda*, Op. 11. Another link between Elgar and the Acland family operated through Miss Acland's first cousin once removed: Arthur Troyte ('Artie') Griffith (1864–1942), son of George and Ettie Griffith. Artie is the subject of the seventh movement of the *Enigma Variations*. By coincidence Miss Acland also knew the subject of the third variation, Richard Baxter Townshend (1846–1923), who was a member of the Oxford Camera Club. Richard's sister was the noted amateur portrait photographer Susan Hodgson.

When taking colour photographs Miss Acland had to judge the correct time for three exposures, through three different filters. As a guide she used an 'actinometer' (probably 'Wynne's 'Infallible' exposure meter'), timing how long a piece of printing-out paper took to darken to a particular tint. To determine the exact ratio for each colour she first exposed a test plate on a black focussing cloth, coloured ribbon, and white origami frog.

On 8 July 1901 Herschel exhibited a lantern slide from this photograph during his Presidential lecture on colour photography at the Oxford meeting of the Photographic Convention of the United Kingdom. An "exceedingly beautiful" result, it "opened up a most hopeful field for work", he told the delegates.

MS. Acland d. 136, fol. 182; *Oxford Times*, no. 2117 (13 July 1901), p. 8.

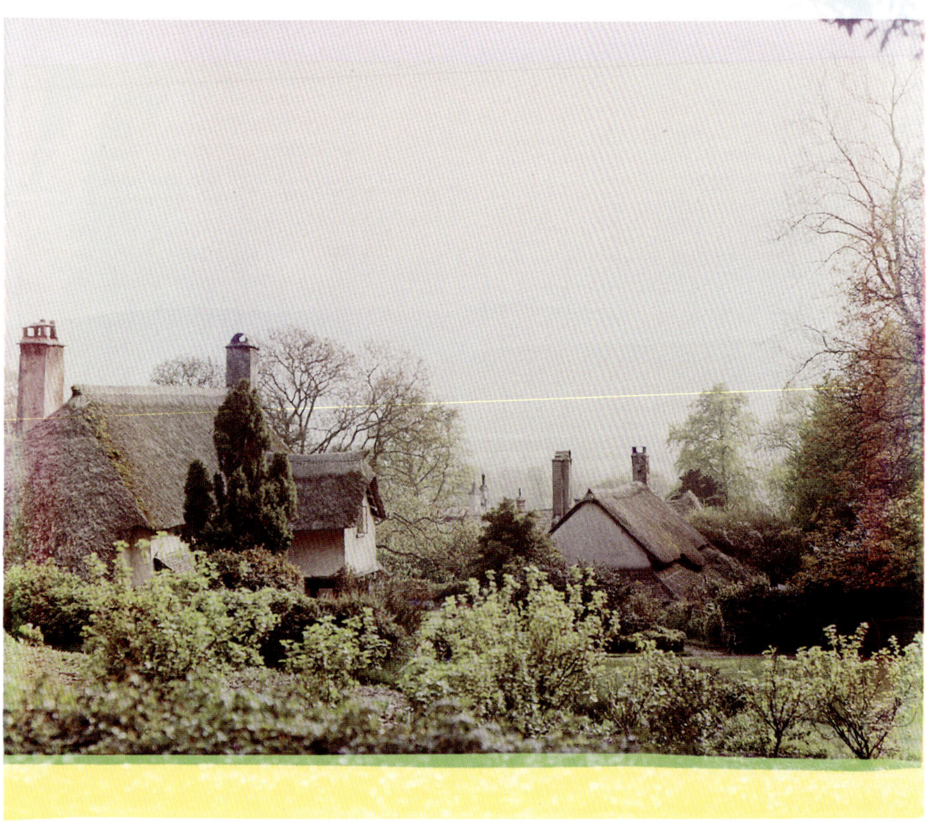

ABOVE

131. *Selworthy Green*

Workers cottages, Selworthy, from the north
Somerset, spring 1902 ?

Composite from 8 × 3⅓ inch 3-colour separation negative (× 1·6)
Museum of the History of Science, Inventory no. 38861

Holnicote House, in Selworthy, Somerset, had been the second home of Miss Acland's grandfather. By the time she took this photograph it was occupied by her cousin, Charles Thomas Dyke Acland, 12th baronet. Selworthy is situated in an idyllic spot, known to the family as the 'Happy Valley'. The cottages on the Green were built in 1828 for pensioners of the estate.

In 1876 it was to Holnicote that Miss Acland accompanied the Liddell family after the tragic death of Edith. "Give my love to Mrs. Liddell and Alice and indeed to all, and tell them how much we think of them and hope that they may be comforted, and that their stay at Holnicote may be a time of soothing & rest", Mrs Acland wrote to her on 6 July.

MS. Acland d. 139, fols. 191–2.

OPPOSITE

132. *Walled Garden*

An unidentified walled garden
England, *circa* 1902

Composite from 8 × 3⅓ inch 3-colour separation negative (× 2)
Museum of the History of Science, Inventory no. 68878

The location of this garden is a mystery. From other photographs we learn that the gate leads to a large lawn planted with bedding in an armorial design. The lawn slopes down to water, where a small boat with a funnel is moored, suggesting it borders a canal, river or estuary.

Miss Acland's Sanger Shepherd photographs are reproduced here uncropped, showing the full extent of each colour plate. The plates are different sizes and overlap different parts of the image due to the way the filters were mounted in her repeating back, the bottom of the blue being stuck to the top of the green and the bottom of the green to the top of the red with tape, which obscured different parts of the image. Some of the composites have narrower coloured borders because she masked the negatives in certain cases and remounted the filters with thinner tape before taking others.

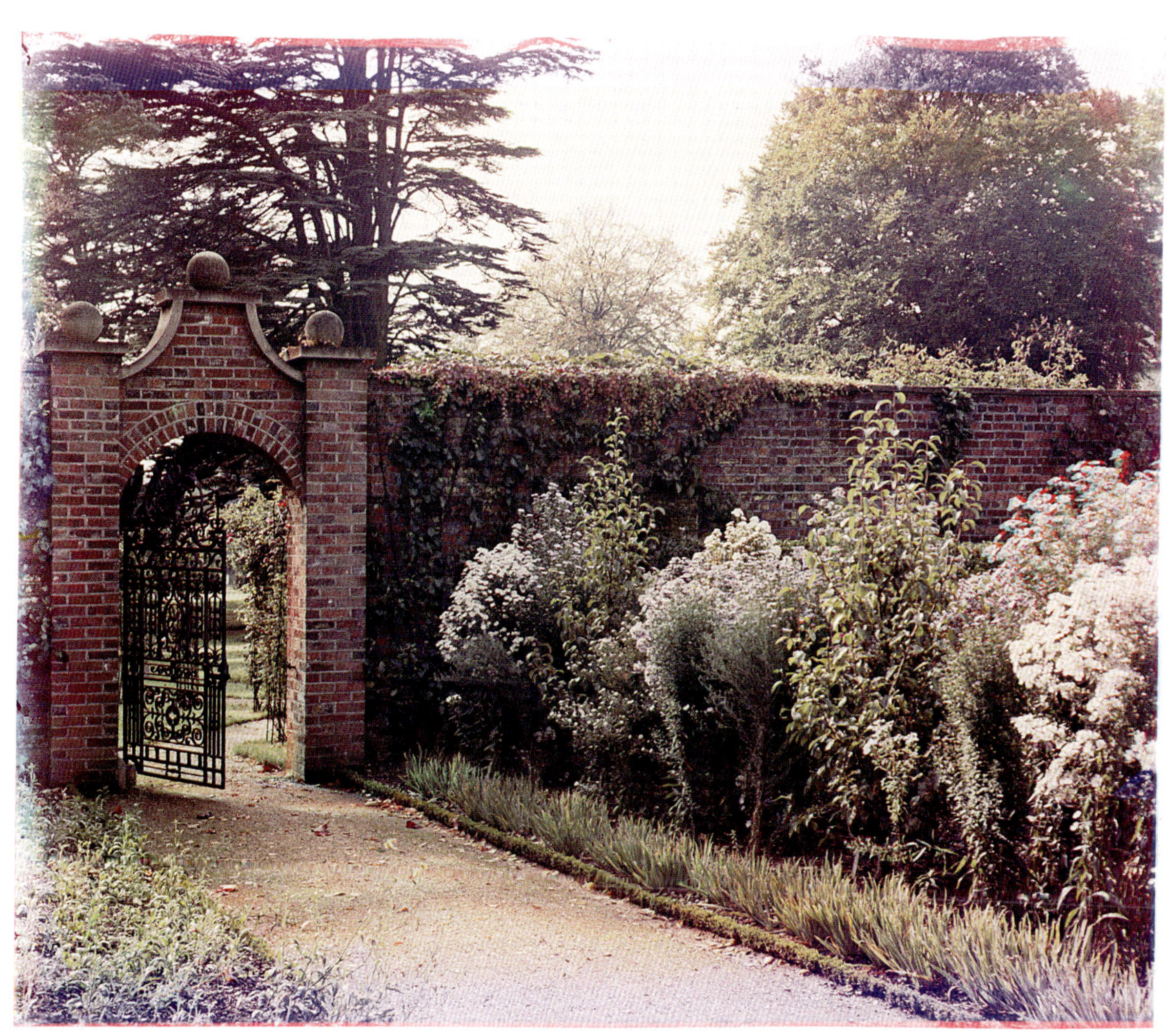

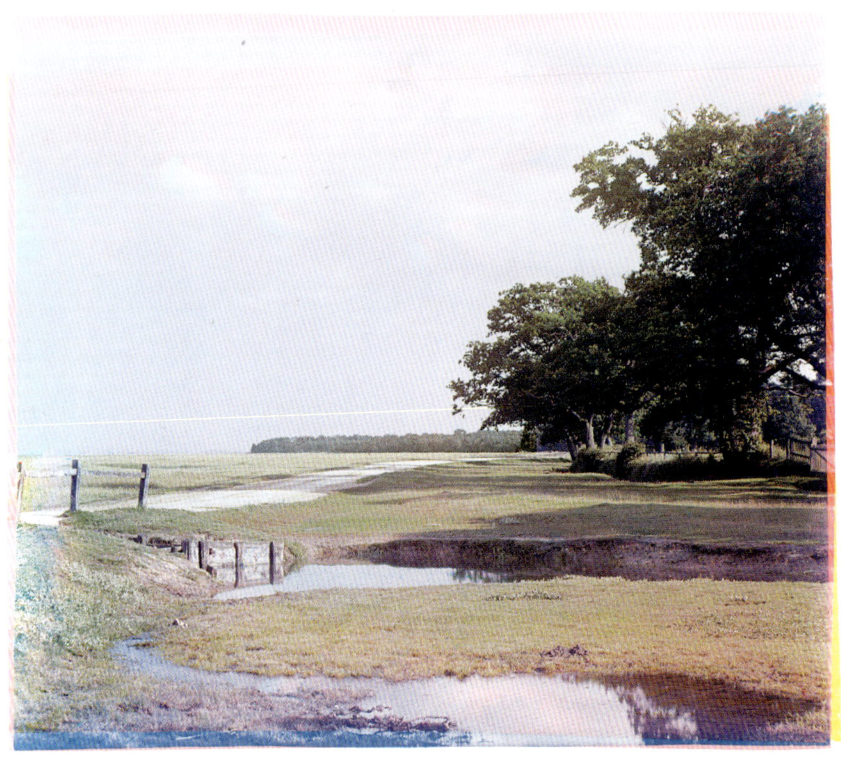

133 & 134. *"Foreshore, Southampton Water"*

Foreshore, Hythe, looking south-east towards Tate's Copse; Looking north towards Southampton and the docks Hampshire, between 9 and 20 August 1902

Composites from 8 × 3⅓ inch separation negatives (×1·5, ×2) Museum of the History of Science, Inv. nos. 89997 & 22613

These two photographs were taken from the same point, just south of Hythe in Hampshire, but looking in opposite directions. The view south-east (above) is practically unchanged today, the individual trees even identifiable, albeit the road tarmacked and the culvert reinforced with concrete. The view north (opposite) is now almost unrecognizable. During World War I the area in the foreground became the location of the Admiralty shed for the construction of flying boats; later it was occupied by Vickers Supermarine and R.A.F. Hythe. The flag visible by the hut is a blue ensign, suggesting the jetty was being used as a Navy sailing club in 1902.

Miss Acland rarely photographed urban scenes in colour, preferring more conventionally picturesque subjects. However, in the distance of catalogue no. 134 the Port of Southampton is visible, with its cranes and chimneys, and the masts and funnels of ships at berth on the quays. The docks are unusually busy with transports and troopships involved in the Boer War supply; the presence of the *Kildonan Castle* and *La Plata* allows the photograph to be dated to between 9 and 20 August 1902.

In 1903 Miss Acland entered *Foreshore, Southampton Water* in the R.P.S. 'Affiliation Societies' lantern slide competition, winning a certificate. The Society kept the winning slides for its permanent collections, giving competitors a small fee in return. However, at a meeting of the Affiliation Committee on 12 February a letter from Miss Acland was read "in which exception was taken to the purchase of colour slides at 2/6 each when the market price was so much higher". Unfortunately, her plea for an increased fee fell on deaf ears.

National Media Museum, R.P.S. Archives (Affiliation of Photographic Societies, Committee minutes, 29 November 1898 to 21 June 1907), n.p.

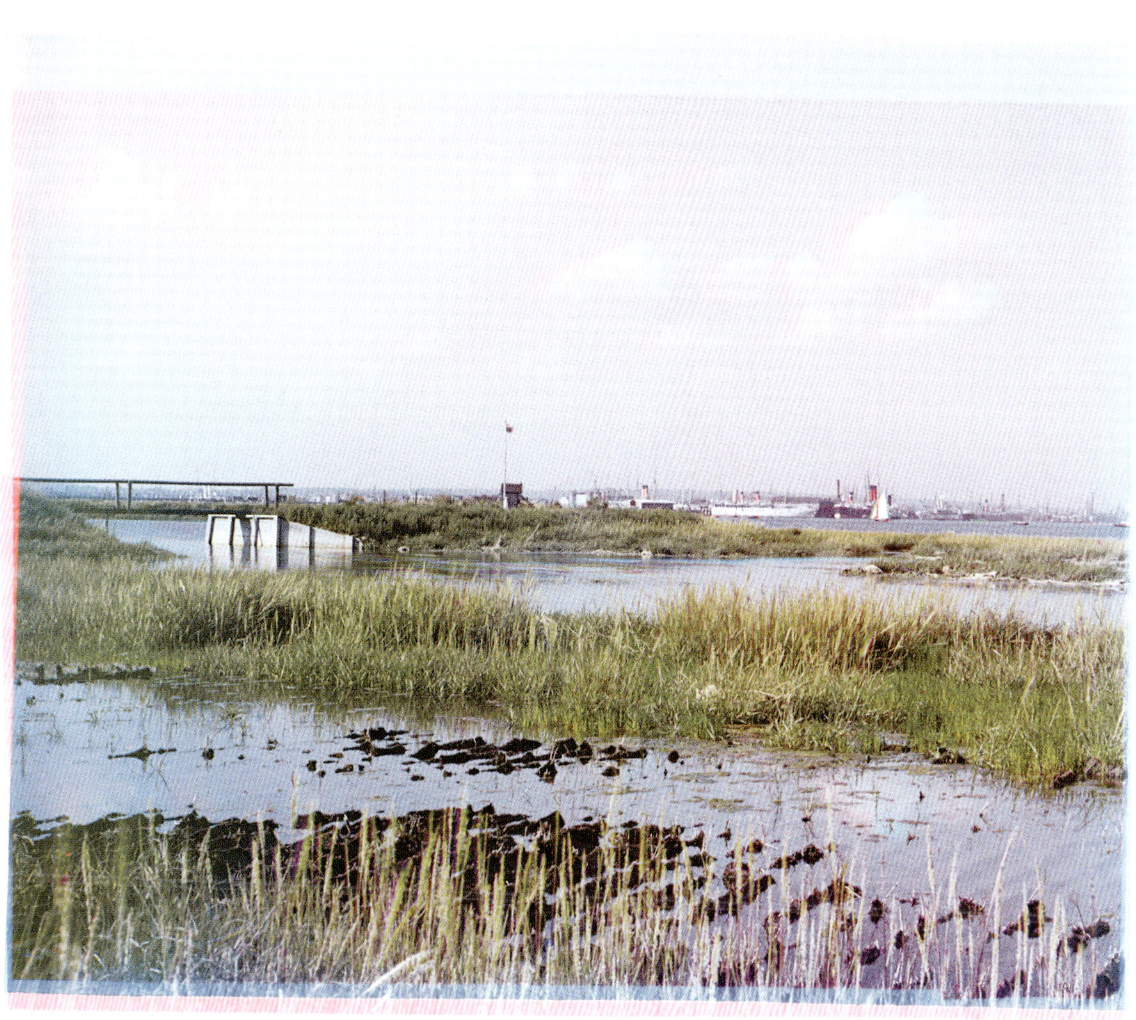

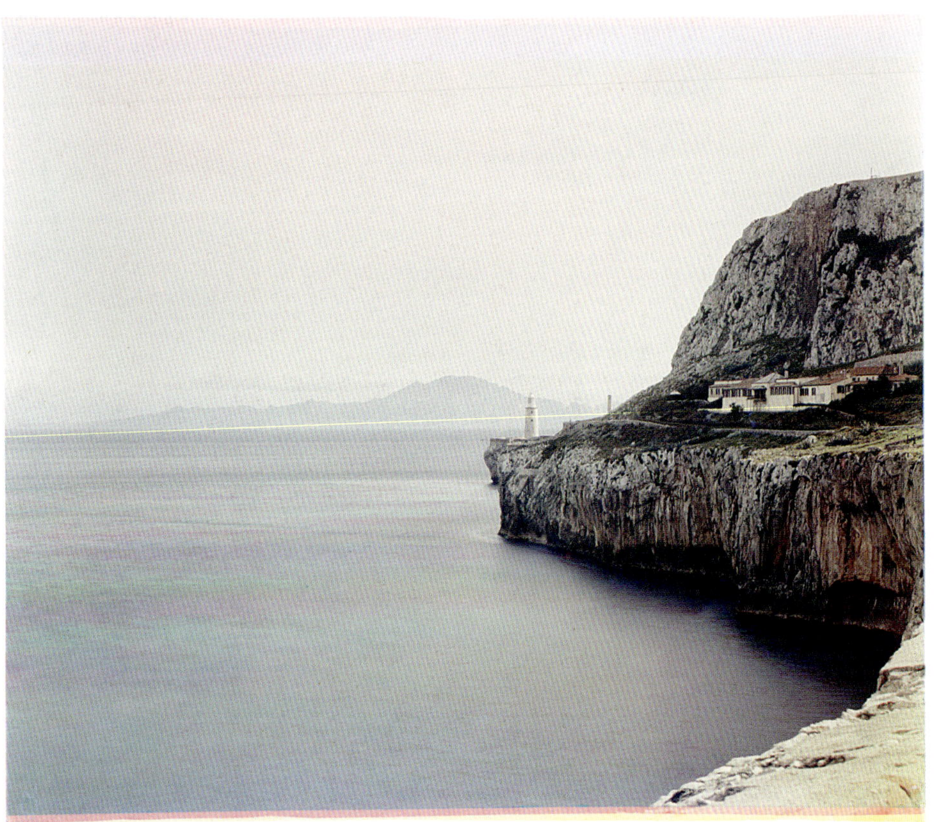

135. *"Europa Point, Gibraltar"*

Europa Point, the coast of Morocco in the distance
Gibraltar, May 1903 or May 1904

Composite from 8×3⅓ inch 3-colour separation negative (×1·6)
Museum of the History of Science, Inventory no. 14858

The colour photographs that brought Miss Acland to notice were taken during two visits to Gibraltar in May 1903 and 1904. In autumn 1903 she showed the results from her first visit at the R.P.S. exhibition as colour prints, in 1904 results from both as prints and lantern slides. This view was shown as one of the lantern slides.

The slides that most impressed the colour aficionados in Miss Acland's audiences were those in which neutral tones predominated. The editor of *Photography*, for example, spoke of the

> acclamation for the subtler effects, in which Miss Acland seemed supreme. Portraits with the most faithful renderings of flesh colour, distances grey or blue, as the case might require, and hardest of all whites and blacks that were white and black, testified to the skill and knowledge brought to bear upon the most difficult process photography has to offer the enthusiast.

The *British Journal of Photography* also offered a "special word of praise" for the scenes with neutral tones, noting that certain slides of the sea in grey weather were excellent and a "severe test" of her mastery of the process.

Miss Acland's vantage point is the Europa Advance Battery, a gun emplacement on the eastern side of the Rock. The building in the middle distance is Governor's Cottage, a summer retreat sheltered from the sun by the cliffs. The faint colouration in the sea is due to the movement of the waves during the exposures.

Photography, vol. 19, no. 866 (13 July 1905), p. 548; *British Journal of Photography*, vol. 52, no. 2353 (9 June 1905), p. 456.

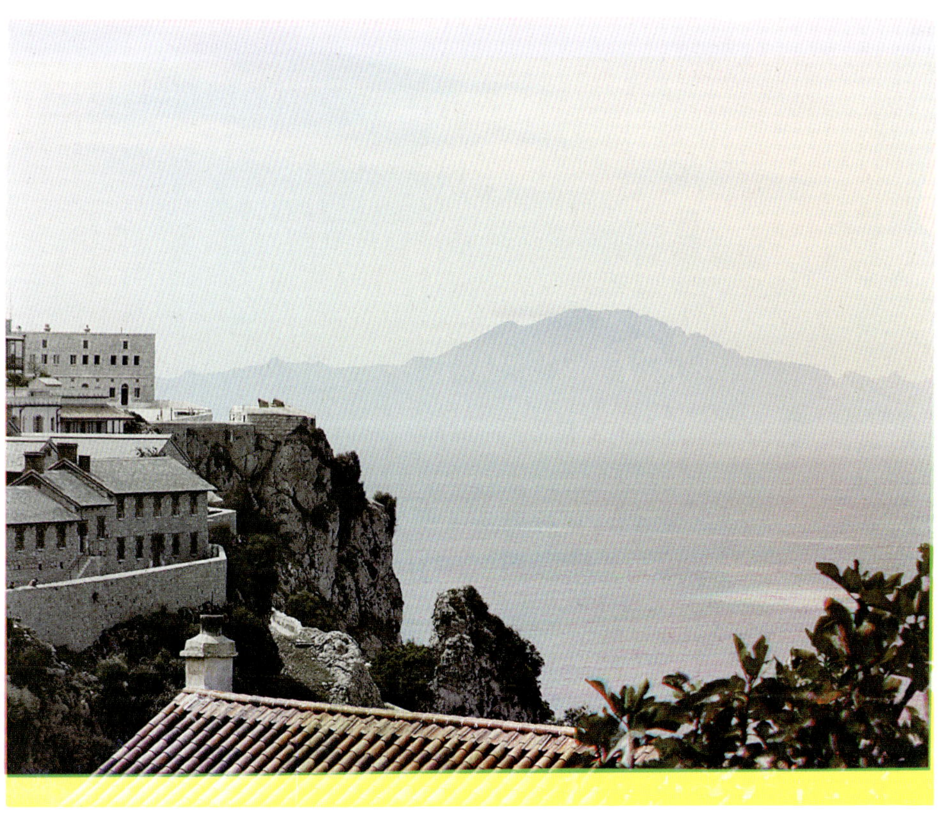

136. *Across the Strait*

Jebel Musa and the coast of Africa from The Mount Gibraltar, May 1903 or May 1904

Composite from 8×3⅓ inch 3-colour separation negative (×1·6)
Museum of the History of Science, Inventory no. 72649

Miss Acland took this photograph of the coast of North Africa, ten miles from Gibraltar, using a Dallmeyer 'Adon' telephoto lens, which has foreshortened the perspective significantly. The Adon was a popular telephoto attachment, first released in 1902, effectively inaugurating the field of amateur telephotography.

The rectangular building top left is the Buena Vista Barracks. Several tiny figures are seen walking in the forecourt (literally, as they move during the exposures). On the edge of the cliff are two guns. Below the barracks are buildings of the Buena Vista hutment, where a man leans over the parapet of the retaining wall.

Miss Acland missed out on being the first person to photograph Africa in colour to Campbell Hausburg (1873–1931), who in 1899 accompanied Halford John Mackinder (1861–1947), Reader in Geography at Oxford, on the first ascent of Mount Kenya, taking an Ives colour camera with him. His photographs were later reproduced in the *Geographical Journal*. The School of Geography moved into the Acland house in 1910.

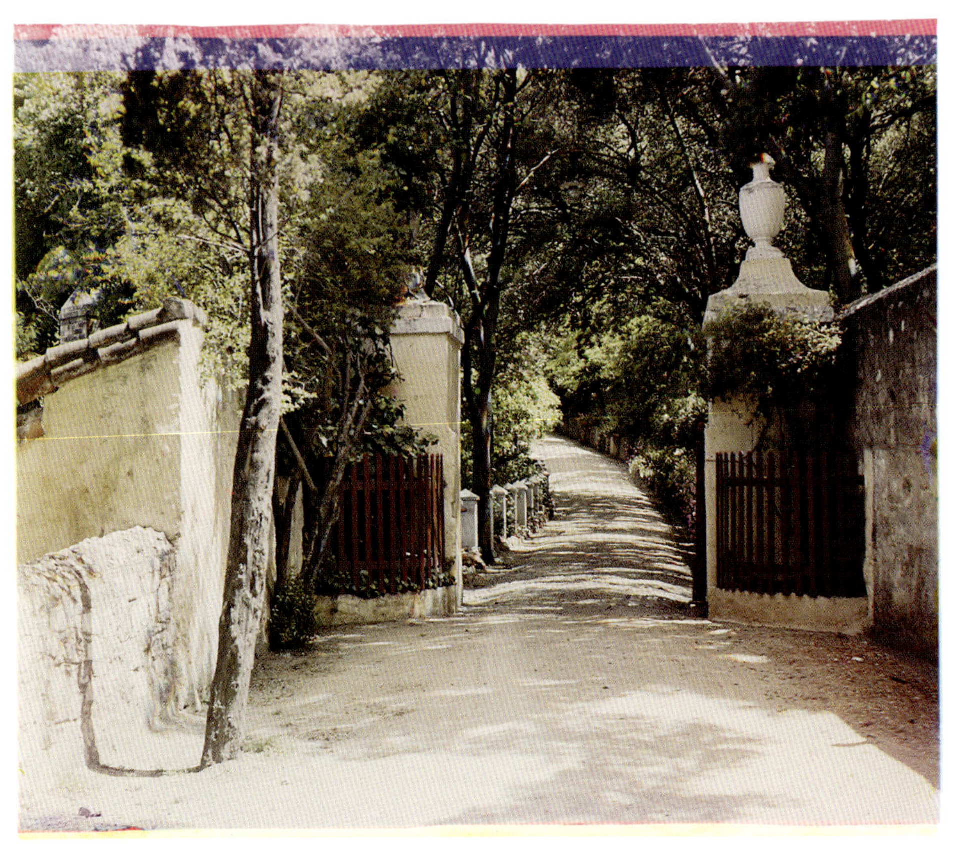

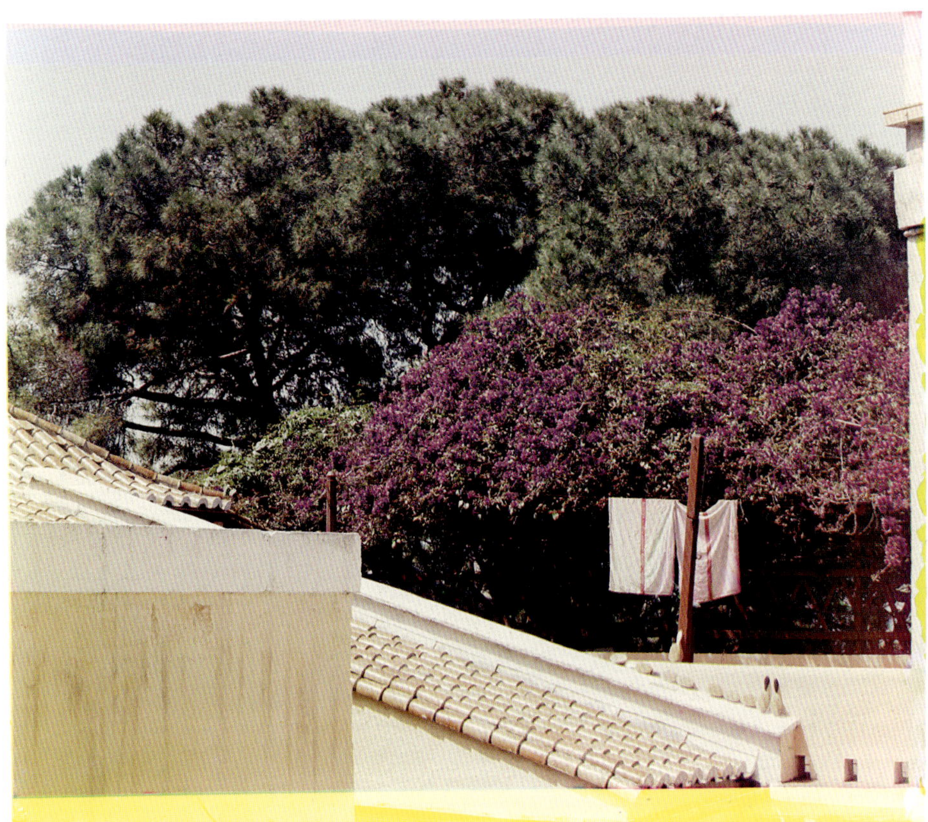

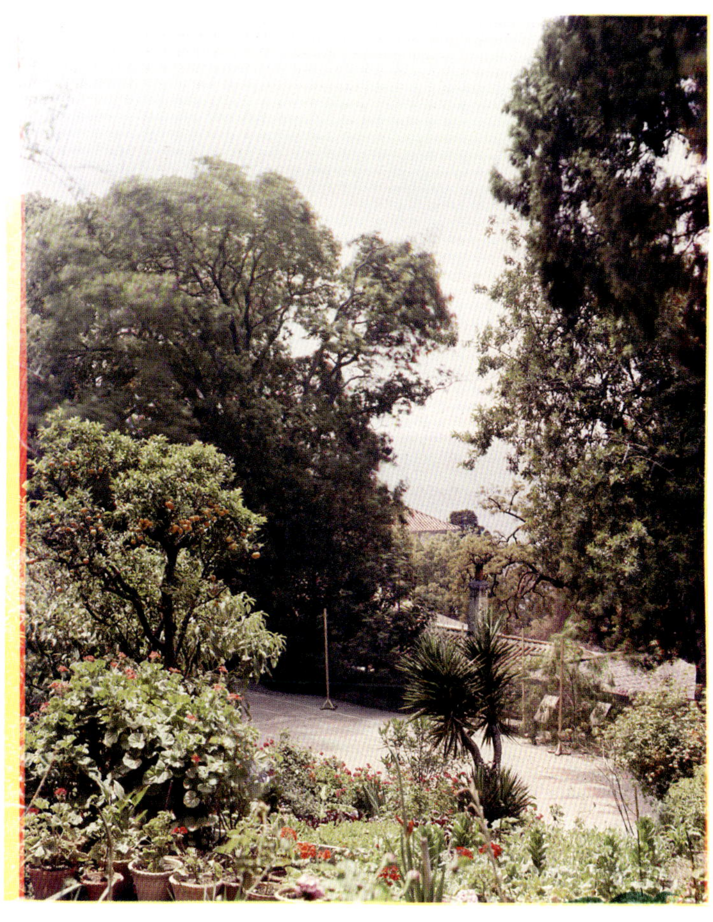

137–139. *The Mount*

South lodge gates, The Mount; View from the guest bedroom; View from the dining room
Gibraltar, May 1903 or May 1904

Composites from 8 × 3⅓ inch negatives (×1·6, ×1·6, ×1·5)
Museum of the History of Science, Inventory nos. 74610, 45128 & 59467

In Gibraltar Miss Acland stayed with her brother in The Mount, the Admiral's residence nestled high on the west side of the Rock. The house was approached by a drive to the south, which she described thus:

> It is quite a relief to get inside the lodge gates into the cool shade of the trees with their undergrowth of brilliant flowers. ... Proceeding up the drive towards the house you pass masses of geraniums, monthly roses, and yellow-eyed daisies. ... The shade deepens as we go further up the drive and get under the heavy pines. The Pinus maritima I believe they are. The road is laid with a small greyish pebble, not yellow gravel as with us.

In her lecture to the Camera Club one of the first colour slides Miss Acland exhibited was "the flora as seen from the windows of the dining-room", which was probably the view above. A slide with a similar title, *From My Window, Gibraltar* which she exhibited at the R.P.S. in 1904, may be the scene looking over the roofs towards the purple bougainvillea and pines (opposite bottom). The photograph repays close inspection: under the two tea towels, lined up on the stub wall, are ten sponges (three with handles), put out to dry in the baking sun.

Photographic Journal, vol. 45, no. 7 (July 1905), p. 234; *Proceedings of the Oxford Camera Club*, no. 12 (April 1906), p. 104.

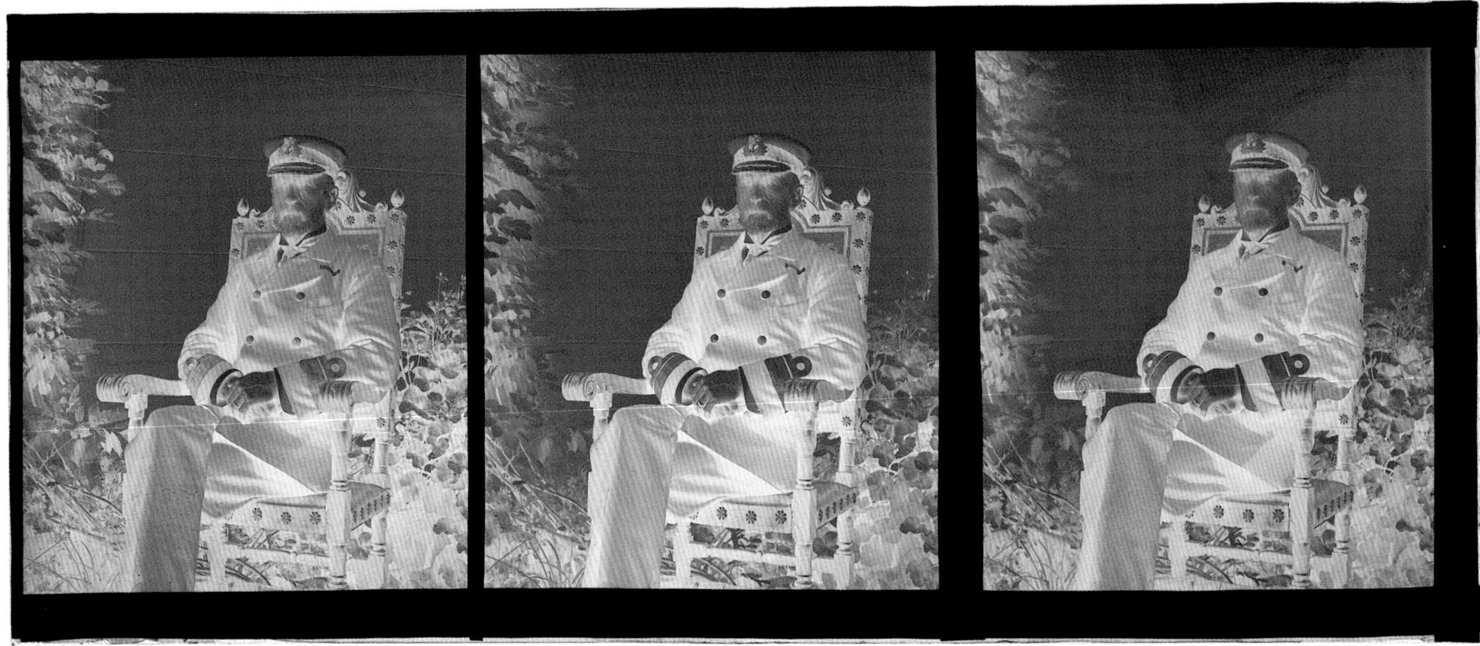

140. *"The Admiral"*

William Alison Dyke Acland (1847–1924)
Gibraltar, May 1903
8 × 3⅓ inch 3-colour separation negative and composite (×2)
Museum of the History of Science, Inventory no. 62989

Willie Acland was appointed Admiral Superintendent of the Gibraltar Dockyard on 8 August 1902. Once established he extended an invitation to his sister to visit. "I am greatly looking forward to coming out to you", she wrote in January 1903, "would about the middle of April suit you?" April did not in fact suit, as Willie had a more important guest to entertain: Edward VII, the first British monarch to visit the colony. However, on 24 April, after the King's departure, Miss Acland sailed for the Rock, arriving five days later and staying for a month. She returned for a second visit on 22 April 1904, arriving back on 2 June.

Miss Acland has masked each exposure on this 'triple negative' with black binding tape, presumably to provide the 'safe edge' necessary for carbon printing. She exhibited a print from the negative at the Royal Photographic Society in 1903, when it was described as "enlarged three diameters" (almost as large as this page). Creating an enlarged colour print from separation negatives added to the difficulty of an already challenging process. Although Miss Acland owned a Watson 'Acme' enlarging lantern, with a hefty 10⅝-inch condenser and incandescent lamp fittings, as a printing-out process colour carbon prints could only be made by contact printing from an enlarged copy negative under daylight.

At the R.P.S. in 1904 Miss Acland exhibited Willie's portrait again, but as a transparency. It was also seen from 19 January to 17 March 1906 as part of her contribution to the first exhibition of colour ever held in Britain, at the *British Journal of Photography*. Reviewing the exhibition the *Morning Advertiser* wrote that "Miss S. A. Acland, F.R.P.S., working with the Sanger-Shepherd process, has produced (as a transparency) a notable portrait of her brother, Admiral Acland, and her scenes of Gibraltar also deserve attention."

Willie remained admirably still during the two-minute exposure, helped by the back of his chair. The slide was the last Miss Acland showed in her lecture at the Camera Club, when she described Willie as "a fine officer, a true friend, and the best of brothers—my Admiral!"

MS. Acland d. 108, fols. 124–6; *British Journal of Photography*, vol. 50, no. 2266 (9 October 1903), p. 814; *British Journal of Photography*, vol. 53, no. 2386 (26 January 1906), p. 64; *Proceedings of the Oxford Camera Club*, no. 12 (April 1906), p. 105.

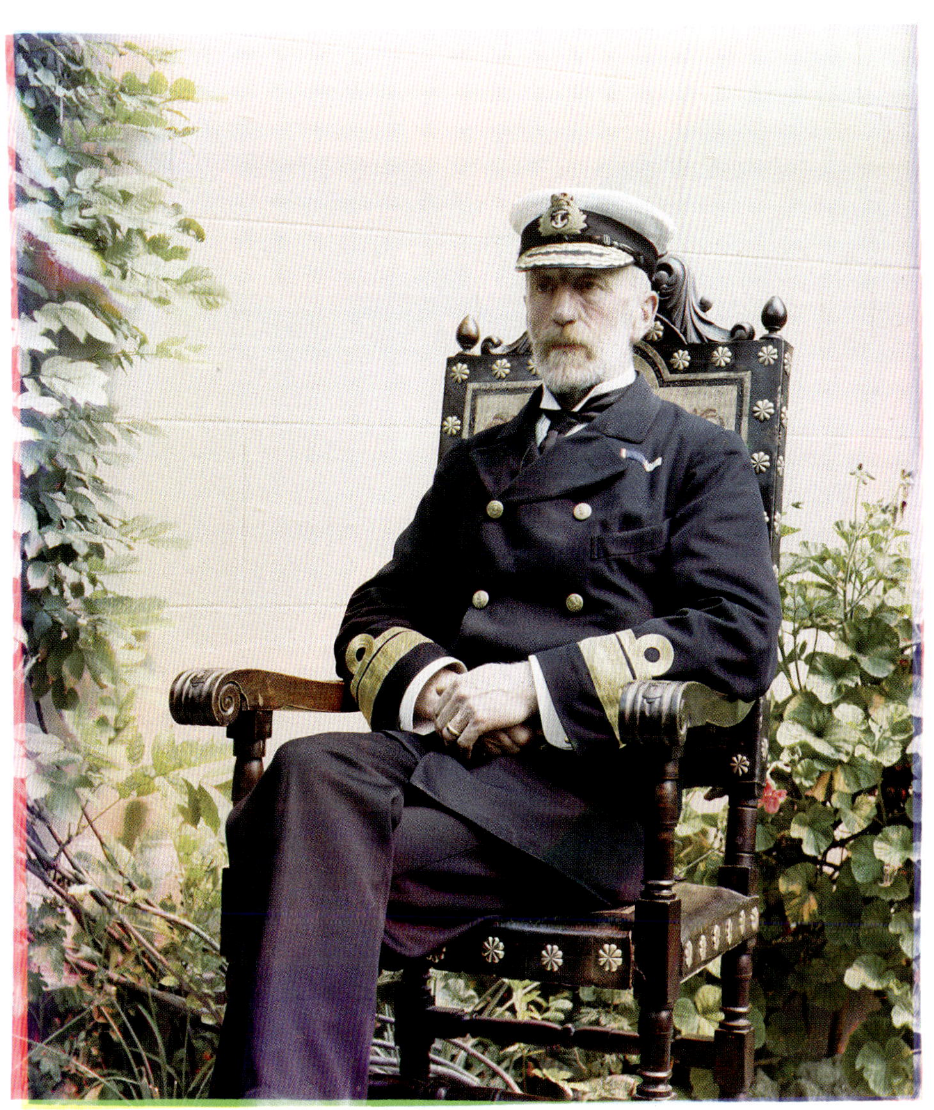

141. *"Sir Willoughby Verner"*

William Willoughby Cole Verner (1852–1922), seated in the garden of The Mount, holding a butterfly net
Gibraltar, May 1903

Composite from 8×3⅓ inch 3-colour separation negative (×2)
Museum of the History of Science, Inventory no. 75687

With pinstriped suit and Homburg hat, red lily for button-hole and butterfly net in hand, Colonel Verner's choice of dress for Gibraltar was as remarkable as his life. As an officer in the Rifle Brigade he served on the Nile Expedition in 1884 and in South Africa during the Second Boer War; as Professor of Military Topography at Sandhurst he invented a balloon for aerial photography and the ubiquitous Verner-pattern prismatic compass. After his retirement he built a house in Algeciras, across the bay from Gibraltar, from where he pursued his great passion: ornithological photography. This led him to many daring exploits, related in two lectures to the Camera Club in 1903 and 1905. After the first, Herschel spoke of how the members had been "virtual participators in the explorations in Spain that evening, and if they had not actually encountered the dangers and taken part in the adventures, they had been thrilled by the experiences given".

When Miss Acland exhibited this and several other Gibraltar portraits as prints at the R.P.S. exhibition they were listed as being "by the three-colour process with her own modifications". In its review of the 1902 exhibition the *British Journal of Photography* described her modified process in detail:

> The foundation blue print consists of an ordinary bromide print, bleached in ferricyanide of potassium, washed, treated with perchloride of iron, rinsed, followed by a hyposulphite of soda bath, again washed, cleared in a dilute sulphuric acid bath, and finally washed. The pink and yellow prints are made upon bichromated gelatine tissue, containing a small quantity of silver bromide for the purpose of assisting the dissolution of the gelatine in the subsequent operations. These bichromated gelatine prints are squeegeed to pieces of glass, edged with rubber solution, in order to keep the gelatine films firmly on the glass supports. The prints so mounted are soaked in cold water, developed with warm water, fixed, and washed. When dry, the prints are faintly stained pink and yellow respectively, coated with rubber solution, to hinder the dye from running, and finally covered with collodion. The blue bromide print is then mounted on card and coated with thin varnish. A particular gelatine solution is then flowed over the print, and the pink print placed in register above it. When dry, the two prints are stripped away from the glass and made ready for the yellow print as before.

Some felt that women were peculiarly fitted for work of this complexity. Cadett, for example, argued that "the many details to be carried out in three-colour photography were best done by ladies; men were too impatient to study them as they required to be studied."

In 1890, thirteen years before Verner sat for Miss Acland, his sister, the artist Constance Ida Verner (1851–1937), had been one of the three women judges of the first *Amateur Photographer* Ladies' Photographic Competition, sitting on the panel with Eveleen Myers and the illustrator Edith Maud Susanna Scannell (1852–1940).

Miss Acland's portrait of Verner is a magnificent achievement, accomplished at a date before the received history of photography acknowledges the existence of a practicable colour process. As such it underlines why conventional assumptions about colour photography need to be reassessed in light of her results prior to 1907.

Proceedings of the Oxford Camera Club, no. 10 (January 1904), p. 86; *British Journal of Photography*, vol. 50, no. 2266 (9 October 1903), p. 814; Ibid., vol. 49, no. 2214 (10 October 1902), pp. 812–13; *Photographic Journal*, vol. 45, no. 7 (July 1905), p. 238.

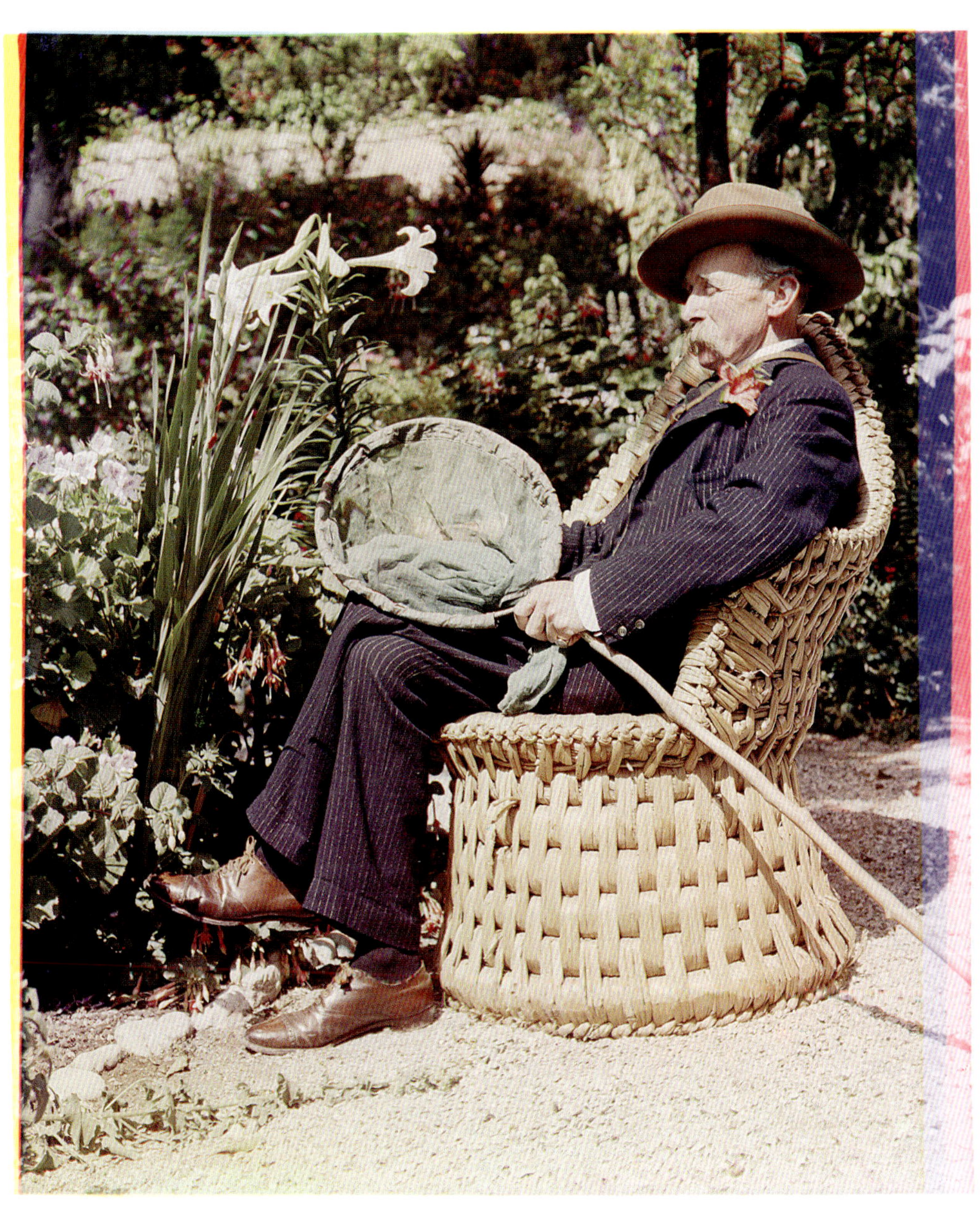

142 & 143. *"Conda the Moor"*

A man named Conda, sitting in The Mount gardens Gibraltar, May 1903

Composites from 8×3⅓ inch separation negatives (×1·5, ×2)
Museum of the History of Science, Inv. nos. 95405 & 74058

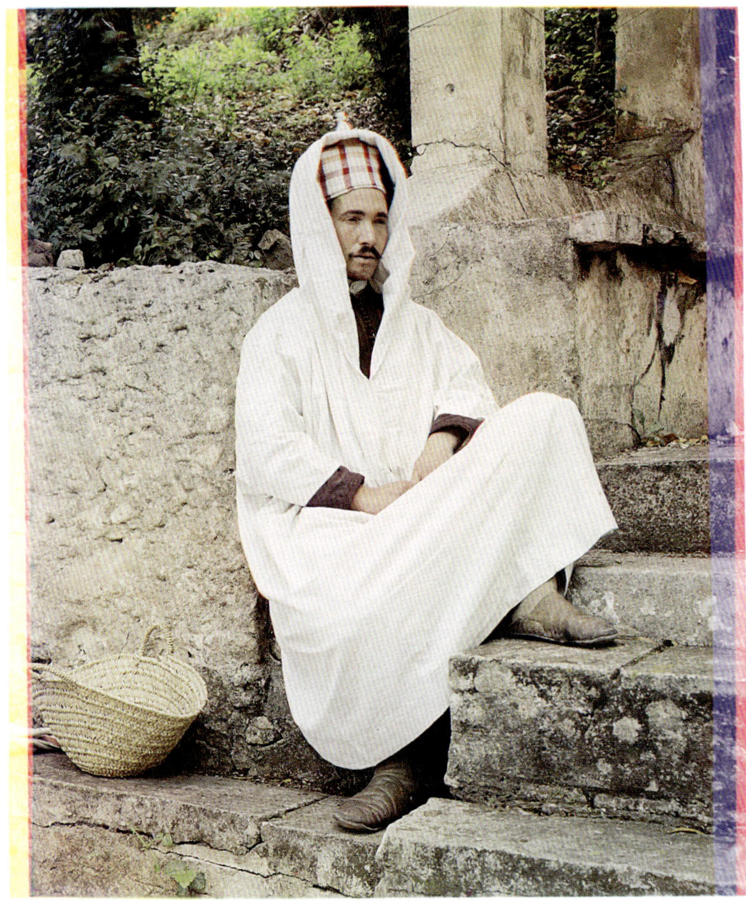

Conda was employed as a gardener at The Mount. Miss Acland described him as wearing the "ordinary dress of his country" in catalogue no. 143 (far right). This was supplemented in winter by a long thick brown burnous with hood, and in summer by a long white burnous, which he pulled over his head "the instant that the sun shines" (catalogue no. 142, near right). The turban around his fez was the sign of a married man, he assured her. However, on exhibiting the slides she was careful to warn her audience that what they saw was partly an illusion: "Conda had been for many years in Gibraltar and loved to dress himself up in any old clothes that he could pick up so that he was not always so tidy as the picture represents him to be."

In October 1903 Miss Acland wrote to Willie that a 'Mr. Bewicke' had visited her in Oxford, to whom she had promised "photographs in colour of the Moors for Kait MacLean to take out to the Sultan of Morocco". William Standert Bewicke (1851–1912) was British Vice-Consul in Tétouan; Harry Aubrey de Vere Maclean (1848–1920) colonel of the Sultan of Morocco's bodyguard. The photographic enthusiasms of the Sultan, the young Mulai Abd al-Aziz (1878–1943), were already well known in England. In 1901 an article had appeared in the *British Journal of Photography* detailing his "expensive tastes in the matter of cameras" and his propensity to confiscate property "whereby his expensive tastes may be gratified". According to Bewicke, these tastes extended to colour photography. "H.S.M. knows the process", he reported, "& has taken & developed colored photographs." Miss Acland attempted to establish which colour process, but without success: "I have forgotten to say that kind Sir Harry Maclean tried to find out what system of coloured photography the Sultan had followed but failed", Bewicke told her.

Conda's photograph walks the thin line between a portrait of an individual and an ethnographic study of a racial type. Ethnographical portraiture was an important genre of photography in the nineteenth and early twentieth centuries. Miss Acland had learnt its value from her father, who visited Gibraltar and North Africa thirteen years before her. Writing from Algiers in October 1890, Acland enthused about prints he had seen in the local studios:

> I studied at a first rate Photographers the Photographs of Races — children of the Desert — Kabyles of the Atlas, Arabs of the Plains. Negroes — half caste Berber. The people are to me more interesting than all else ... I was long looking them over & bought a very few & thought what shall we do with them! Yet I liked to bring some home to talk over.

Acland's fascination with ethnographical portraits had also been in evidence in 1860, when he returned from Canada with the daguerreotype and two ambrotypes of Ojibwe which Miss Acland exhibited after her Home Portraiture lecture.

Photographic Journal, vol. 45, no. 7 (July 1905), pp. 235–6; Ibid.; Ibid.; MS. Acland d. 108, fols. 158–161 *British Journal of Photography*, vol. 48, no. 2149 (12 July 1901), p. 447; MS. Acland d. 171, fols. 94–7; MS. Acland d. 171, fols. 99–104; MS. Acland d. 127, fols. 96–101.

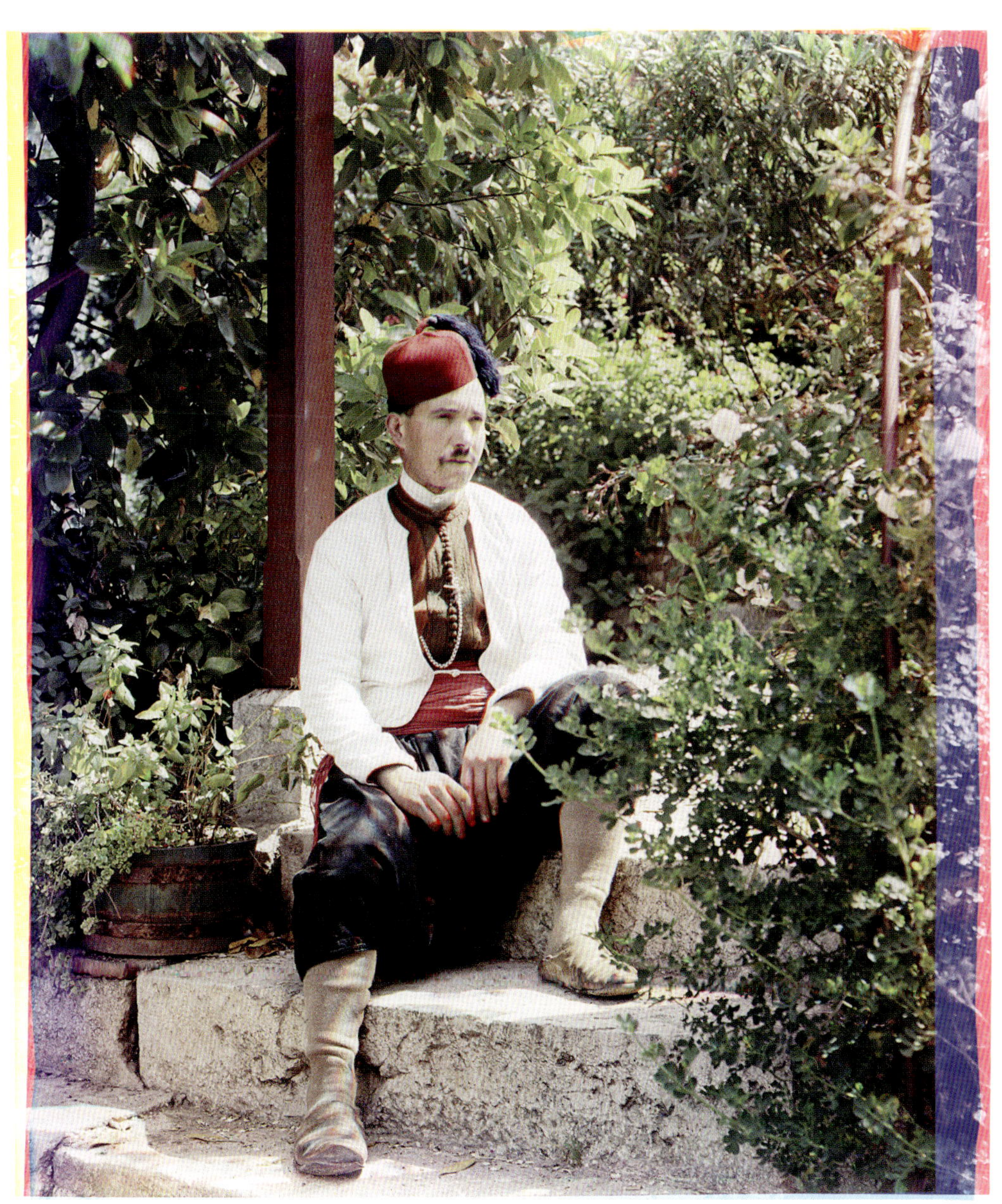

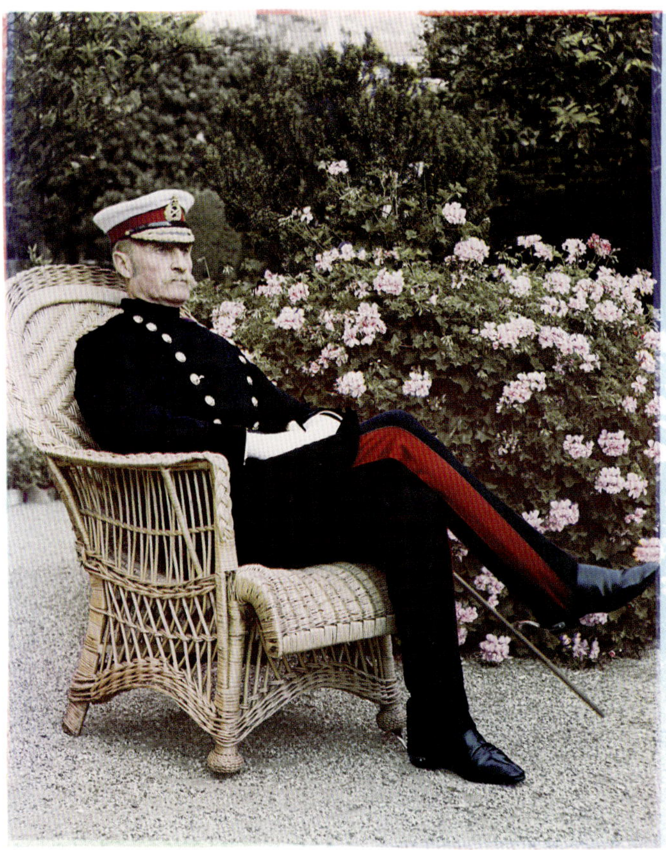

ABOVE

144. *"Sir George White"*

George Stuart White (1835–1912), in The Convent garden
Gibraltar, between 29 April and 15 May 1903

Composite from 8×3⅓ inch 3-colour separation negative (×1·5)
Museum of the History of Science, Inventory no. 75111

Sir George White was Commander-in-Chief and Governor of Gibraltar, the only officer to outrank Willie. Miss Acland took his portrait in less than ideal conditions:

> The day on which this portrait was taken was a very unfortunate one, as it had just drenched with rain and a heavy cloud hung over the Rock, so that the exposures were long and might with advantage have been longer. But it was my only chance of photographing Sir George White as he was shortly leaving for England.

On the same occasion she also photographed White's youngest daughter, Georgina Mary White (1897–1985), but Georgie moved during the exposure. The Whites hailed from Broughshane, near Ballymena, Co. Antrim.

Photographic Journal, vol. 45, no. 7 (July 1905), p. 234.

OPPOSITE

145. *"Spanish Gypsies"*

An unidentified man and woman, with baskets
Gibraltar, May 1903

Composite from 8×3⅓ inch 3-colour separation negative (×2)
Museum of the History of Science, Inventory no. 98762

Miss Acland photographed these 'Spanish gypsies' sitting on horse mounting blocks close to the front door of The Mount. They proved excellent sitters:

> The time occupied in taking the negatives of the gipsies including the changing was nearly 1½ minutes, and it was wonderful therefore that my patients, as in this case I think they may be truly called, managed both to sit still at once. Twice one in such a case is, I think, much more than two.

Although pleased with how still her sitters had kept, she was unhappy with the composition: "As it was necessary to use an interpreter, it was difficult to pose them so as to obtain an artistic photograph."

Photographic Journal, vol. 45, no. 7 (July 1905), p. 235; Ibid.

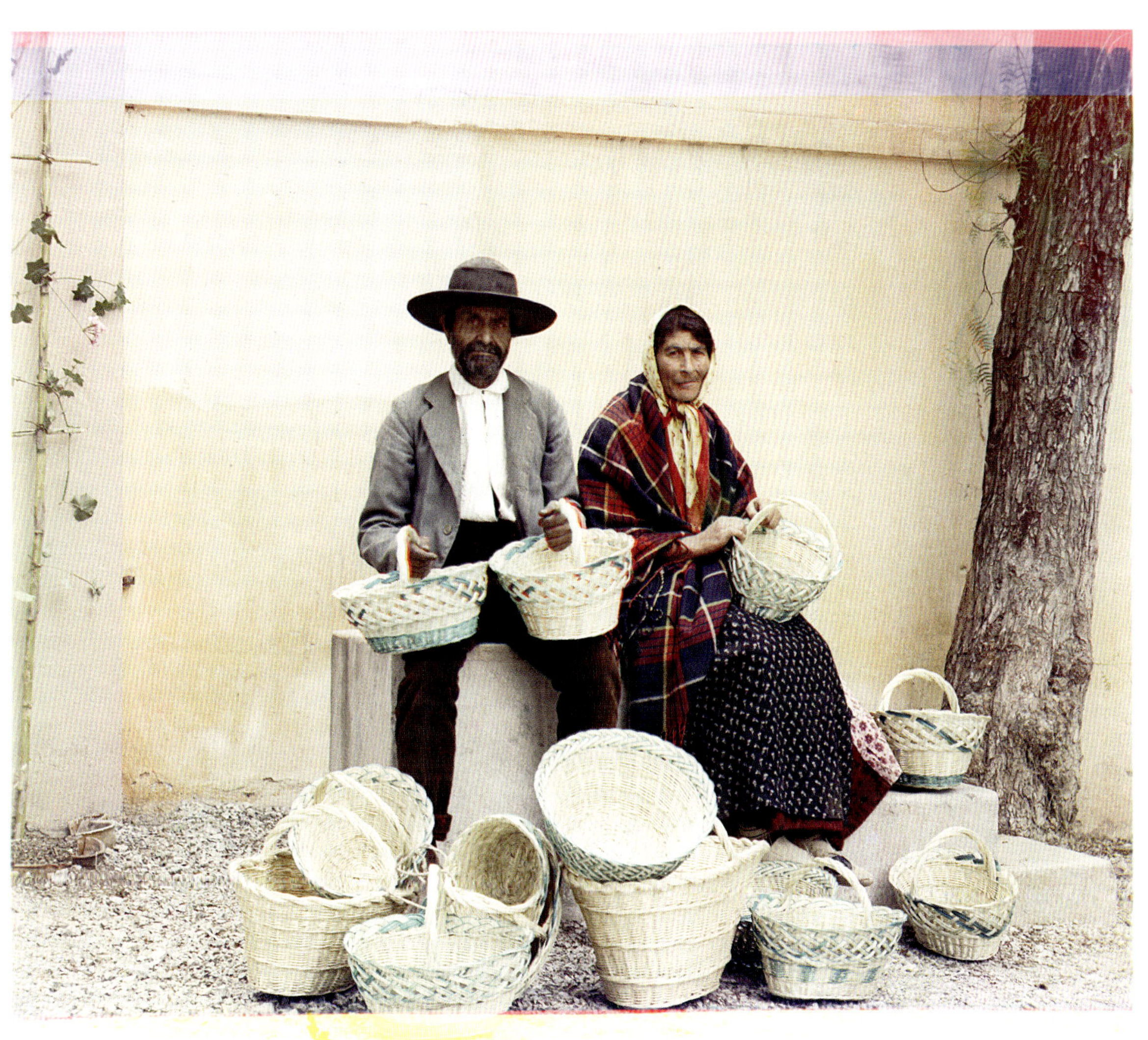

OPPOSITE & OVERLEAF

146–148. "*Solomon's Gardens of Old*"

The Mount gardens
Gibraltar, May 1903 or May 1904

Composites from 8 × 3⅓ inch 3-colour separation negatives (×2)
Museum of the History of Science, Inventory nos. 62044, 64406 & 88508

The majority of Miss Acland's colour photographs of Gibraltar were taken in the grounds of The Mount, which she described as "a carefully tended wilderness ... arranged liked Solomon's hanging gardens of old". A floral paradise, crammed to overflowing with beautiful plants, the gardens were arranged in a series of terraces clinging to the west side of the Rock.

Although it was primarily due to her brother that Miss Acland found herself in Gibraltar, according to *Photography* "she might have gone much farther and fared much worse in selecting a spot to portray thoroughly in colour. For Gibraltar in May is a mass of colour". Her "foreground studies" of the luxurious flora were her most popular slides, the *British Journal of Photography* describing them as "magnificently reproduced".

Catalogue no. 146 is taken close to the house, looking south. Purple verbena and pelargoniums in various shades of pink can be seen on the bank, in front of bright red gladioluses. Overhanging the path is an orange tree and by the steps a datura, with its delicate yellow trumpet-shaped flowers. Catalogue no. 147 is also looking south, but from above the house. The orange flowers on long stalks are inflorescences of *Aloe saponaria*. Catalogue no. 148 is higher up in the garden, looking north. The steps by the large aloe led to the 'upper walk', above which a wire fence marked the boundary of the garden. The beauty of this photograph is enhanced by the dappled patches of light on the path, with their strong colour fringes caused by the movement of the sun and the leaves in the trees during the exposure. Gibraltar was "a veritable temple of winds", Miss Acland lamented, making three-colour work all the more challenging.

Miss Acland's photographs of The Mount were taken in the afternoon, when the sun had come round to the west of the Rock, the indirect morning light being insufficient for colour work even at such southern latitudes.

Photographic Journal, vol. 45, no. 7 (July 1905), p. 234; *Photography*, vol. 19, no. 846 (24 January 1905), p. 154; *British Journal of Photography*, vol. 52, no. 2353 (9 June 1905), p. 456; *Proceedings of the Oxford Camera Club*, no. 12 (April 1906), p. 104.

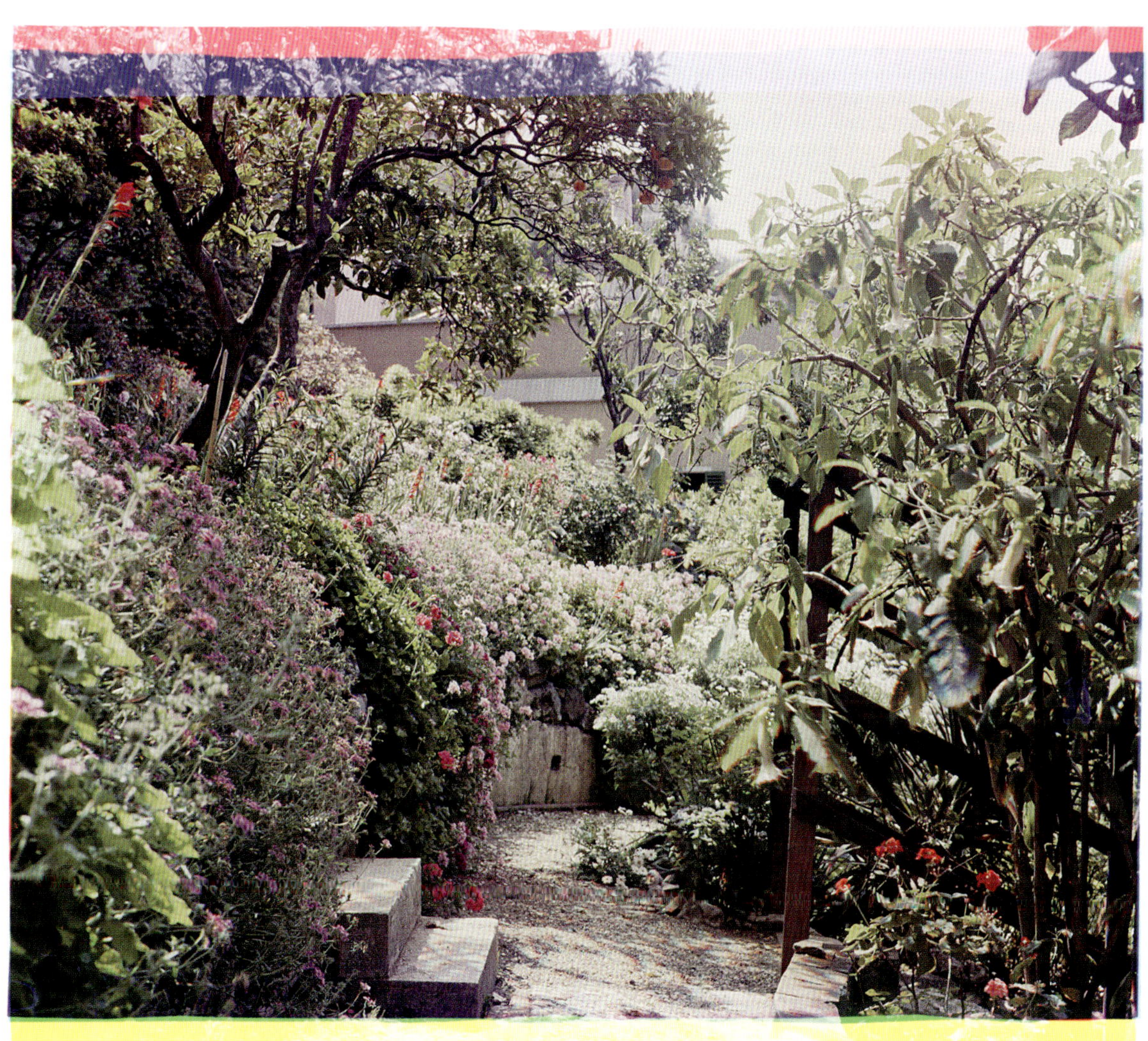

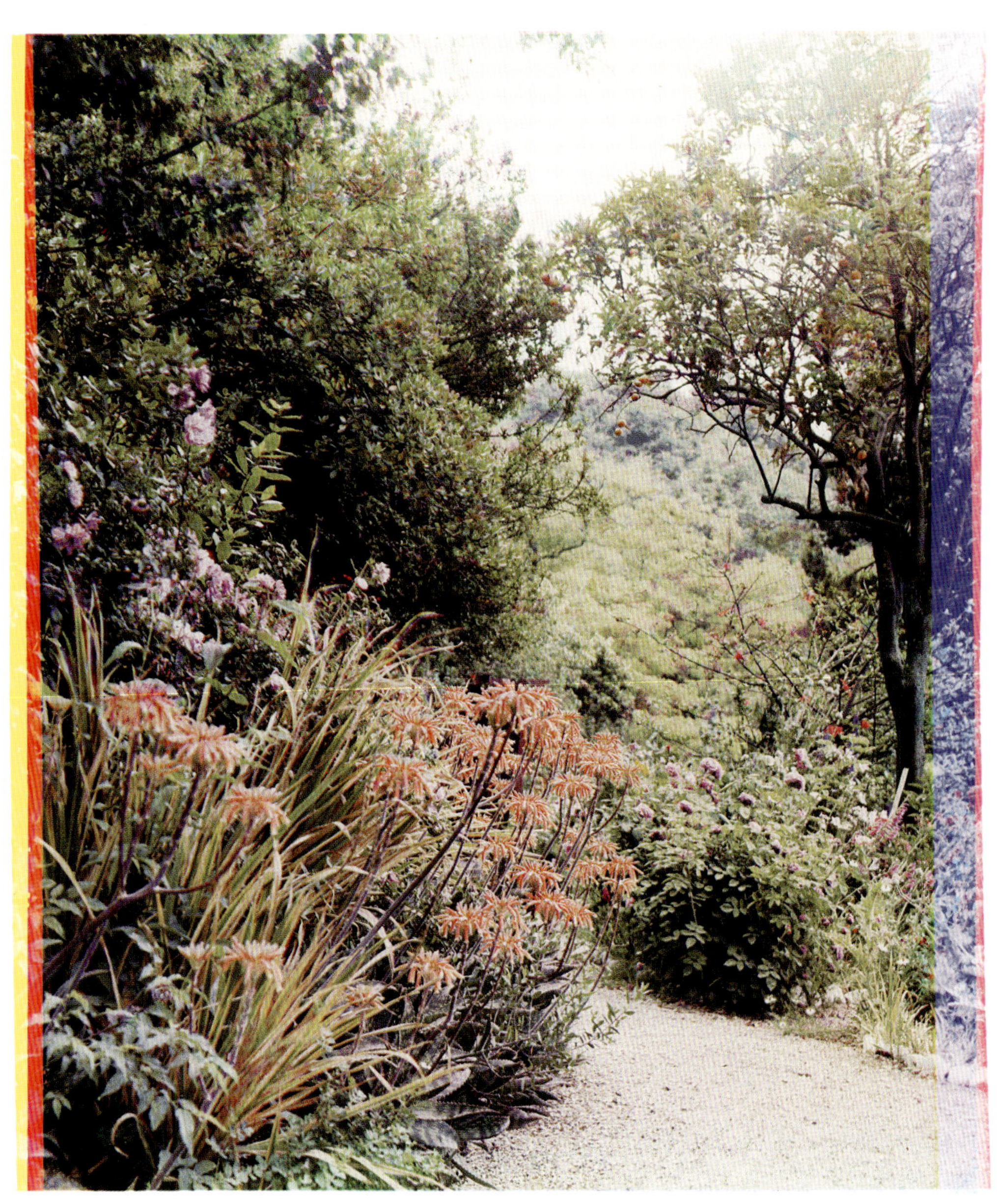

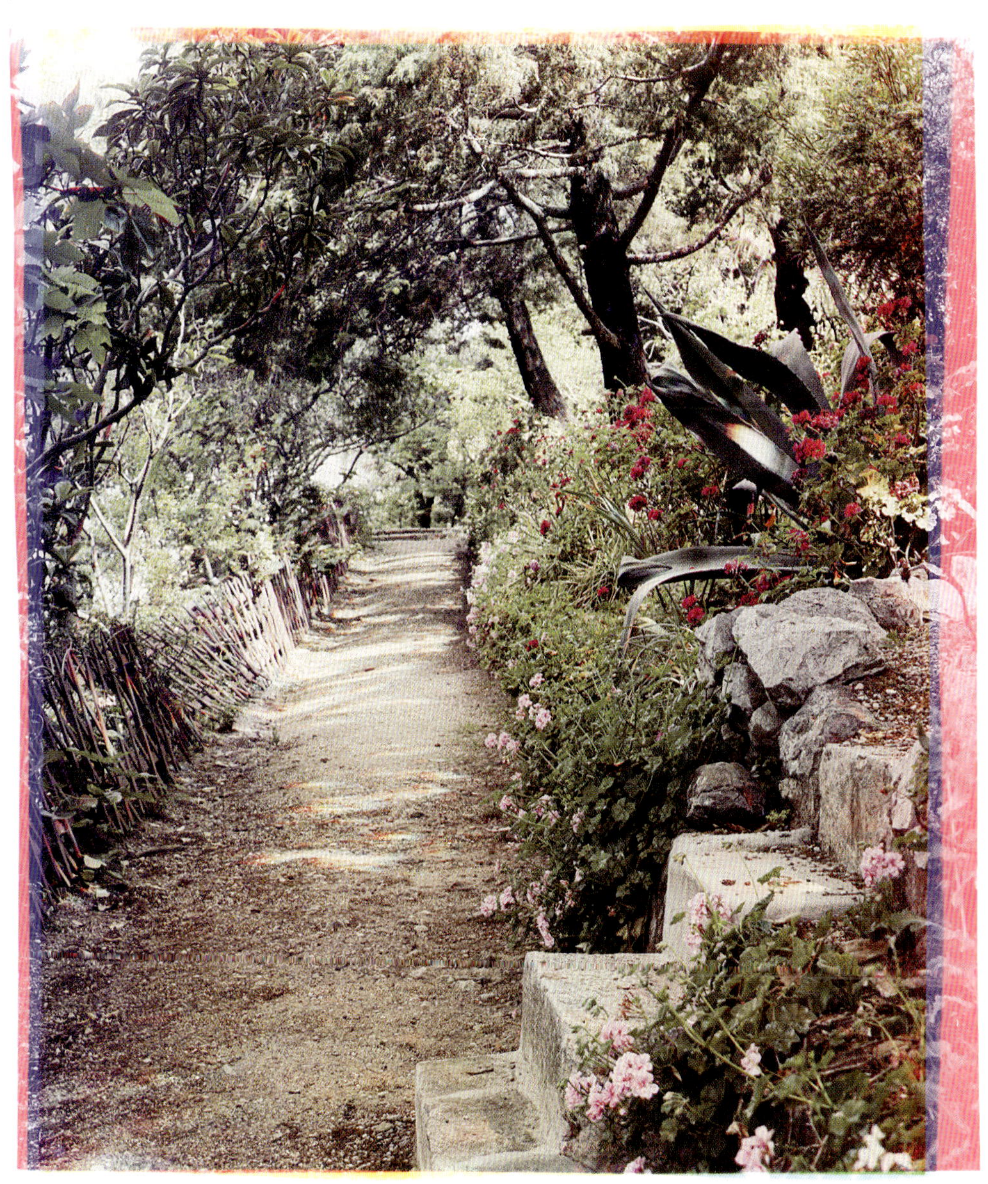

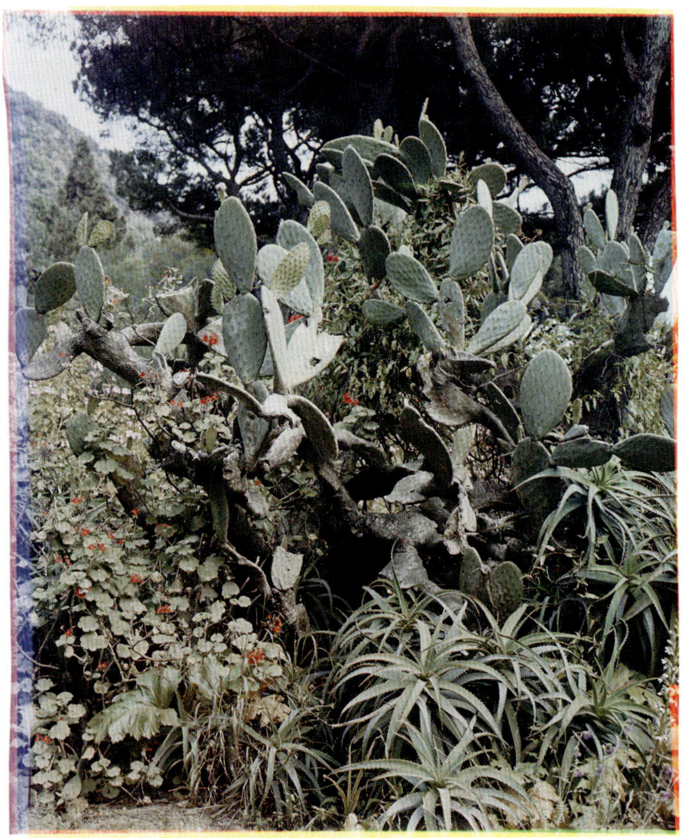

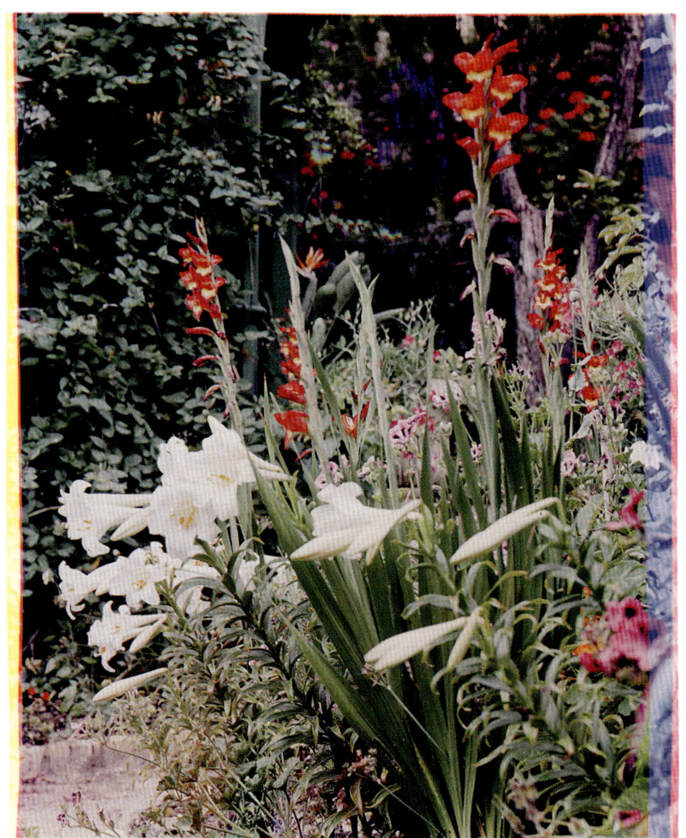

149–152. *Plant Portraits*

Opuntia; *Lilium* and *Gladiolus*; *Pelargonium*; *Begonia*
Gibraltar, May 1903 and May 1904

Composites from 8× 3⅓ inch separation negatives (×1·4, ×1·4, ×1·5 & ×1·5)
Museum of the History of Science, Inventory nos. 35044, 27317, 99818 & 42428

Miss Acland photographed numerous individual plant specimens in Gibraltar, not only at The Mount, but in the Alameda Gardens, now the Botanic Gardens. She had been fascinated by botanical illustration even before turning to photography. Whilst overwintering on the French Riviera from 1875 to 1877, for example, she compiled a book of watercolours of Mentone flowers, which was much admired back home in Oxford, including by Ruskin.

"Before we came away the white Bermuda lilies which grew up everywhere in the garden were in full beauty", Miss Acland recalled of The Mount. Prickly pears and agaves were common throughout southern Spain, she also pointed out, especially in hedges.

One of the difficulties of gardening on the Rock was the rapidity with which plants reverted to their original type, ivy-leafed geraniums, for example, quickly defaulting to lilac from their cultivated pink. Gibraltar's colonial administrators no doubt faced analogous problems to her gardeners. An imperialist subtext ran throughout Miss Acland's lectures, Gibraltar's status as an outpost of Empire being one of the factors that made them so interesting to her public back at home. Her photographs functioned as a visual metaphor of the advantages of British civilization, interpreted from a woman's point of view: the transformation of a barren wilderness into a cultivated flower garden.

Photographic Journal, vol. 45, no. 7 (July 1905), p. 237.

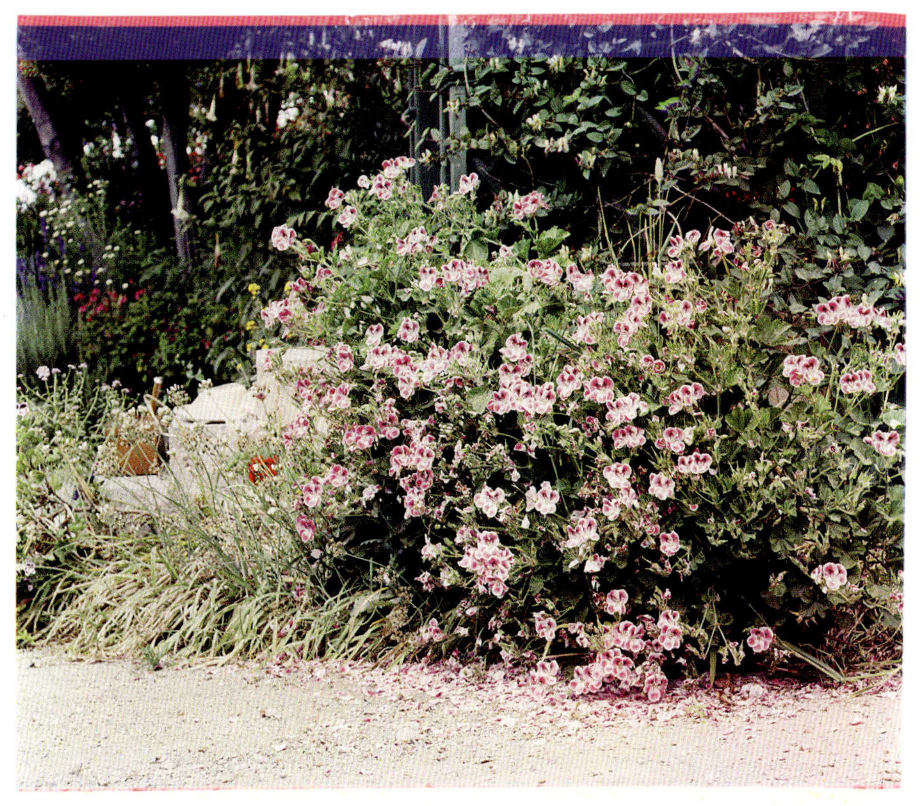

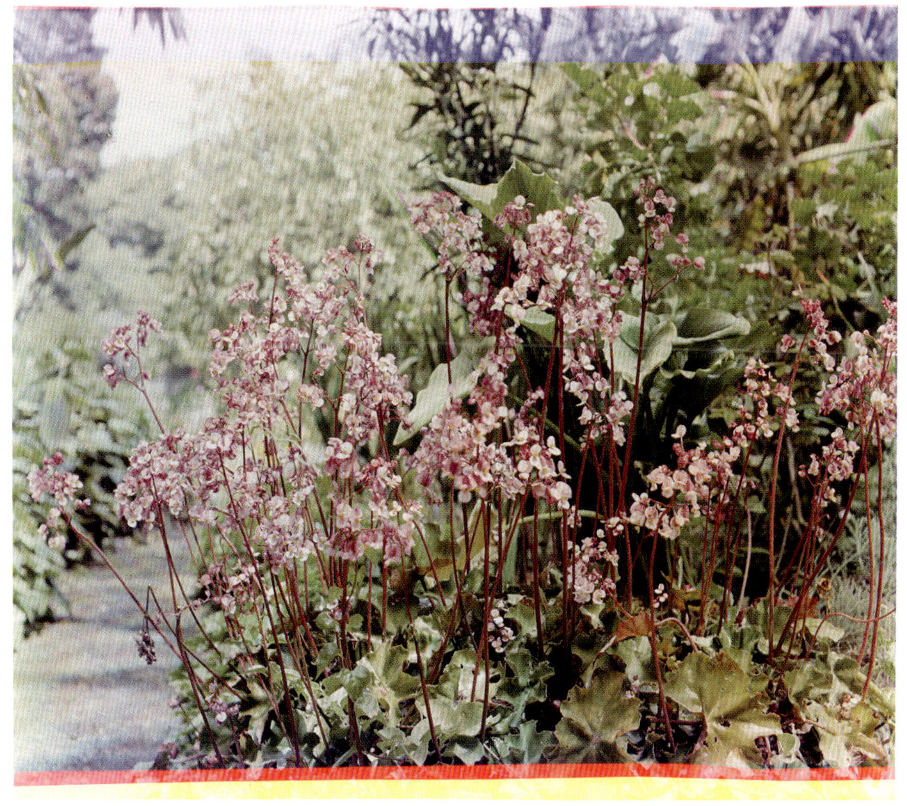

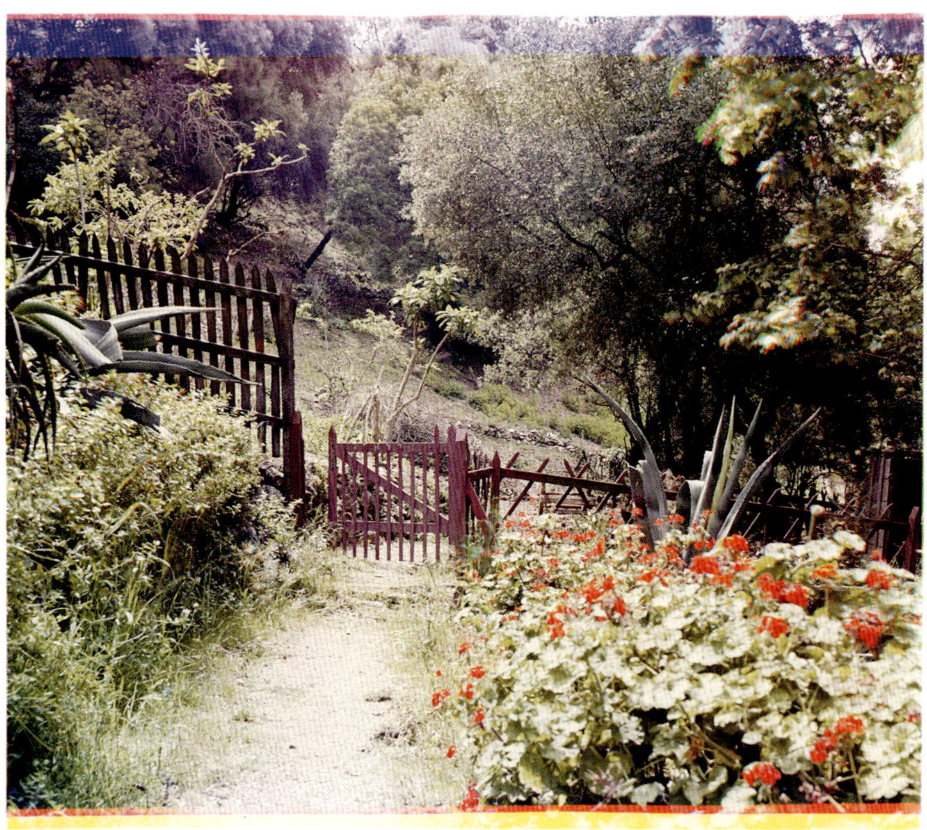

ABOVE

153. *The Wilderness*

A gate in The Mount gardens
Gibraltar, May 1903 or May 1904

Composite from 8 × 3⅓ inch 3-colour separation negative (× 1·6)
Museum of the History of Science, Inventory no. 47495

Situated on the steep west-facing slopes of the Rock of Gibraltar overlooking water, the terrain of The Mount was similar that at Ruskin's home on Coniston Water. This photograph echoes one Miss Acland took ten years earlier, in black and white, of *The Professor's Garden Gate* at Brantwood. A watercolour of the same subject by Arthur Severn now hangs in the house.

A colour lantern slide by Miss Acland with the title *The Wilderness, The Mount, Gibraltar* appeared as catalogue number 694 in the 1904 Royal Photographic Society exhibition.

OPPOSITE

154. *Flora Calpensis*

Flowers in The Mount gardens
Gibraltar, May 1903 or May 1904

Composite from 8 × 3⅓ inch 3-colour separation negative (× 2)
Museum of the History of Science, Inventory no. 98071

The emulsion of the three-colour negative from which this composite is assembled has completely detached from the glass in places, resulting in several indistinct areas in the recombined image. Happily, the effect is in keeping with the subject matter, lending the photograph a beautiful impressionistic quality.

The photograph brings to mind paintings of Giverny by Claude Monet (1840–1926). Monet's studies were contemporaneous with Miss Acland's colour photography and share her preoccupation with light and colour over composition and form.

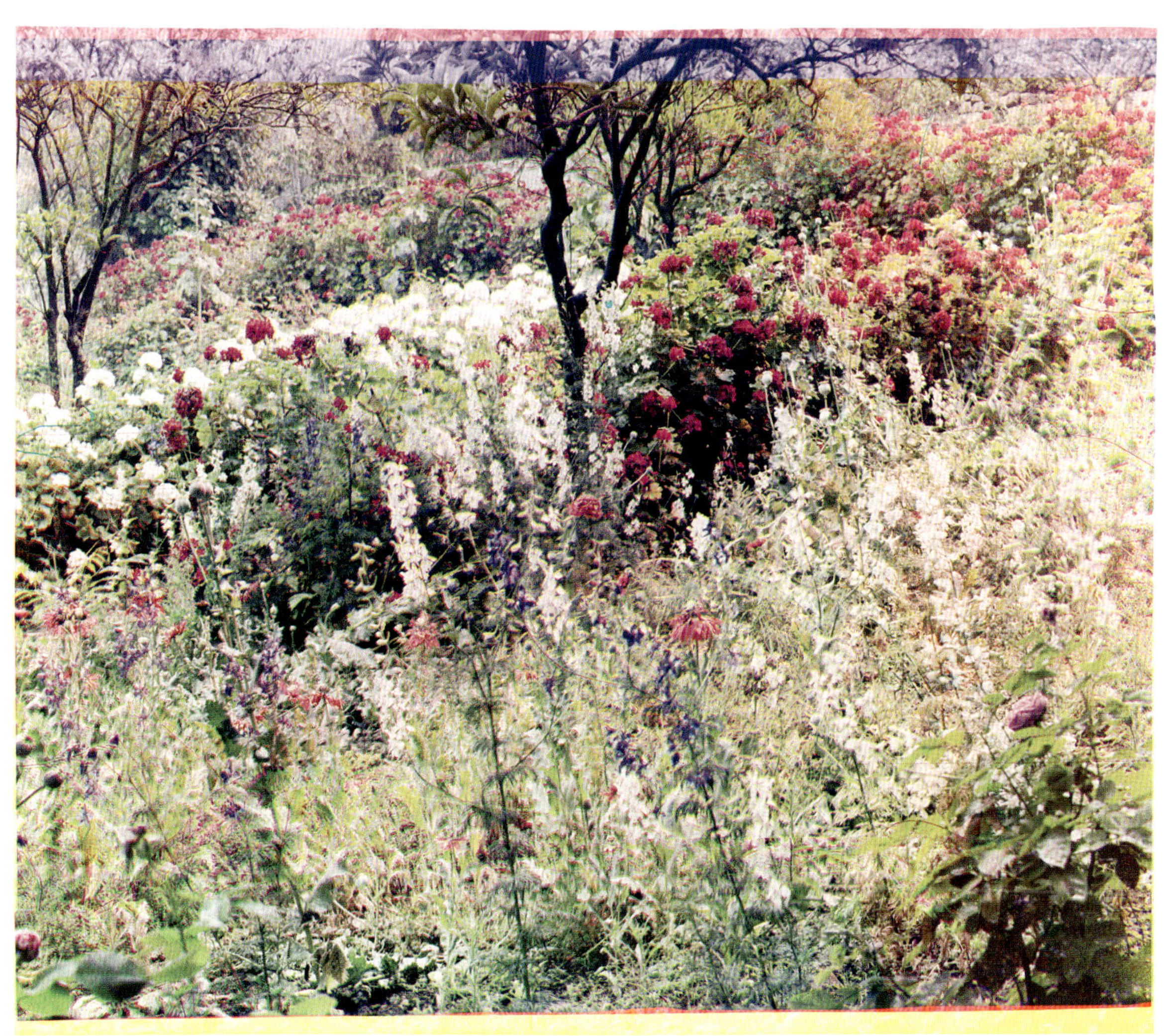

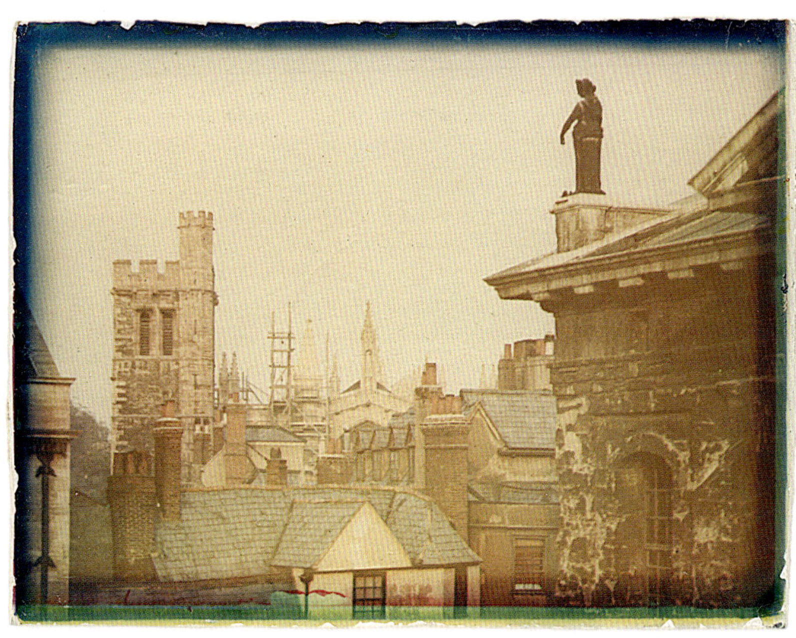

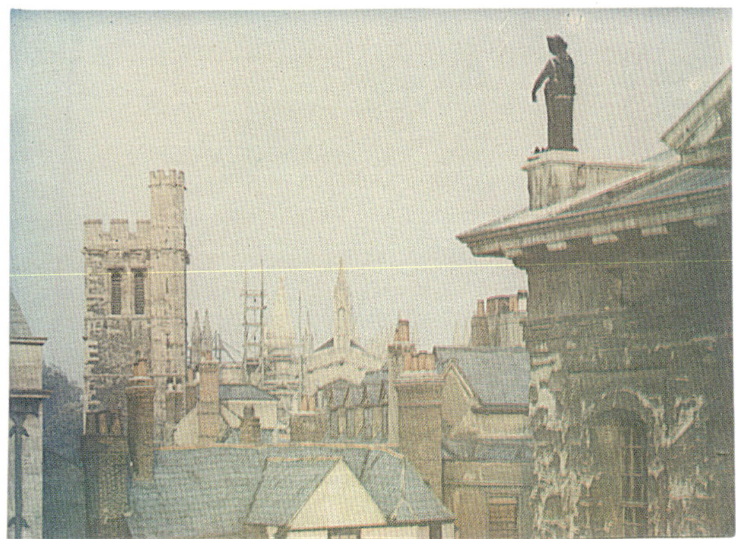

155 & 156. *Dreaming Spires*

Rooftops and New College tower from the Acland house
Oxford, *circa* 1900 or 1901, printed *circa* 1903 or 1904

Three-colour carbon print; imbibition print
Museum of the History of Science, Inv. nos. 25293 & 52537

This photograph was taken from one floor higher than catalogue no. 127, but around the same date. The prints must have been made several years later, as one is a three-colour carbon print, the other an imbibition print. The imbibition process was patented by Sanger Shepherd in December 1902 and relied on the transfer of dye from hard to soft gelatine — a phenomenon noticed by his employee, Owen Mortimer Bartlett (1879–1955). Imbibition prints were highly admired, one critic describing them as having "a softness of colouring and texture which is really very remarkable, partaking rather of the character of an oil painting than a colour photograph".

British Journal of Photography, vol. 53, no. 2386 (26 January 1906), p. 65.

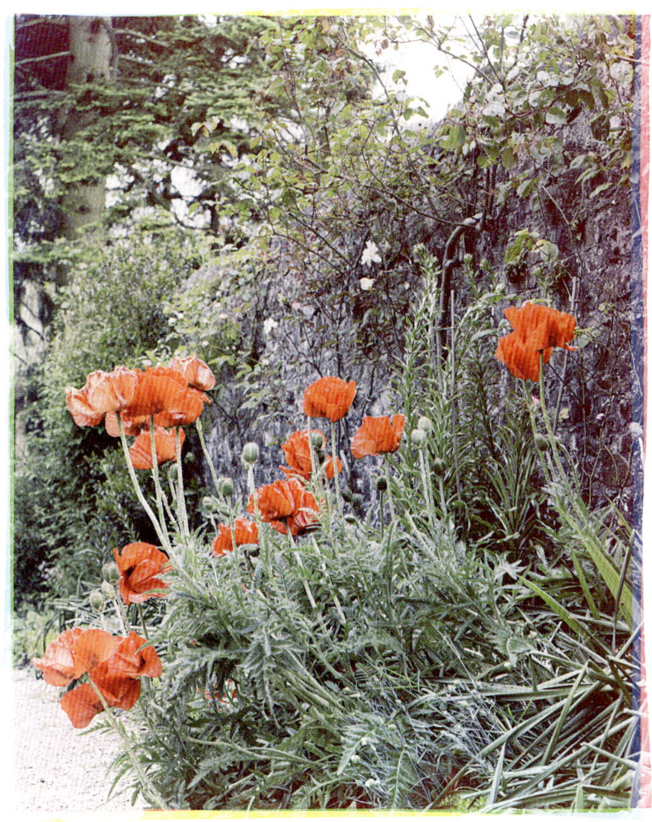

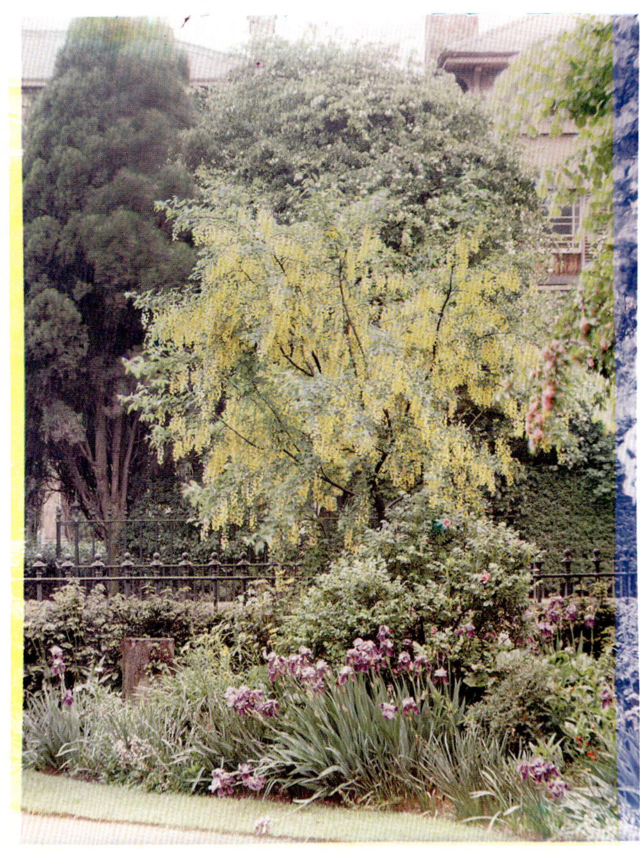

157 & 158. *Oxford Gardens*

Papaver orientale, in the Botanic Garden ?; *Iris* and *Laburnum*, in the communal gardens, Park Town Oxford, *circa* 1905

Composites from 8× 3⅓ inch separation negatives (×1·4)
Museum of the History of Science, Inv. nos. 54707 & 55491

Photographs of poppies were popular with early colour photographers, for obvious reasons. At least ten were submitted to the R.P.S. exhibition before 1915, including by Alice Worsley (1870–1940), an early experimenter with the Joly process from Bristol who would go on to write "Colour Photography: A Visit to the Home of the Autochrome" for *Amateur Photographer* in 1912. The Joly process, in which the colour was created by a screen of parallel red, green and blue lines, was a potential rival to Sanger Shepherd's system. However, although widely tested by photographers, including in Oxford by Herschel and Alfred Robinson (1862–1938), assistant at the University Museum, it was never a success, commercially or practically. Robinson, for example, in showing a slide of poppies at the Camera Club in December 1898, complained that "very small differences in working caused the resulting colours to vary greatly from those of nature", while Sanger Shepherd, perhaps a little biased, pointed out that "the results look as if they had been photographed on a sheet of corrugated paper."

Miss Acland had a front and back garden at Clevedon House, but could also enjoy the communal gardens in the centre of Park Town, which had been laid out by William Baxter (1787–1871), Curator of the Botanic Garden. The Park Town Estate, which was begun in 1853, is a notable example of the Victorian garden suburb. One of the first developments in north Oxford, it was also among the few to be built on land not owned by St John's College.

Amateur Photographer, vol. 55, no. 1422 (1 January 1912), p. 10; *Proceedings of the Oxford Camera Club*, no. 3 (January 1900), p. 22; *Journal of the Camera Club*, vol. 15, no. 176 (January 1901), p. 5.

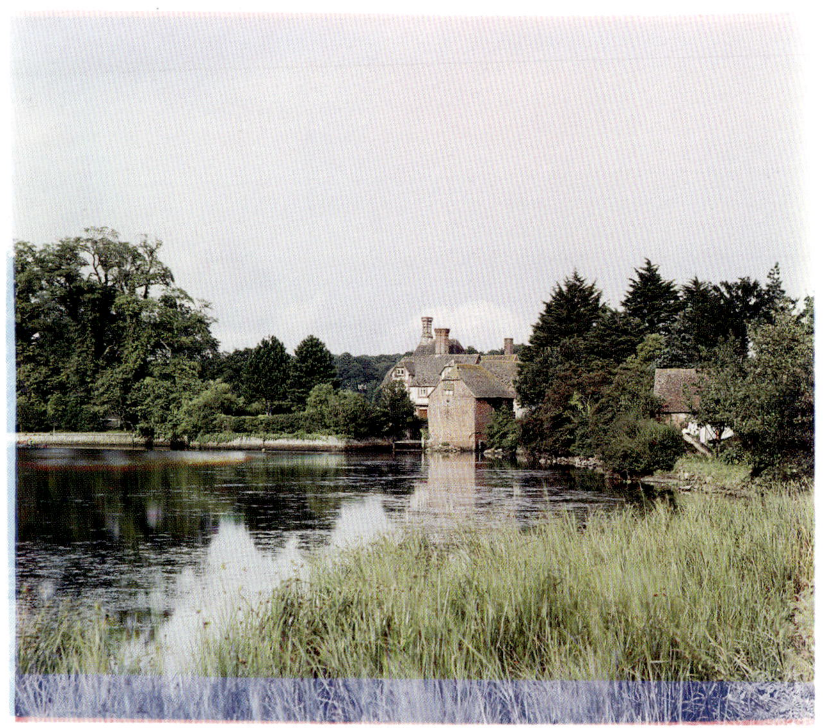

159 & 160. *Time & Tide*

Tide Mill, Beaulieu; Peaked Tor, Torquay
Hampshire and Devon, 1906?

Composites from 8 × 3⅓ inch separation negatives (×1·5)
Museum of the History of Science, Inv. nos. 50734 & 35600

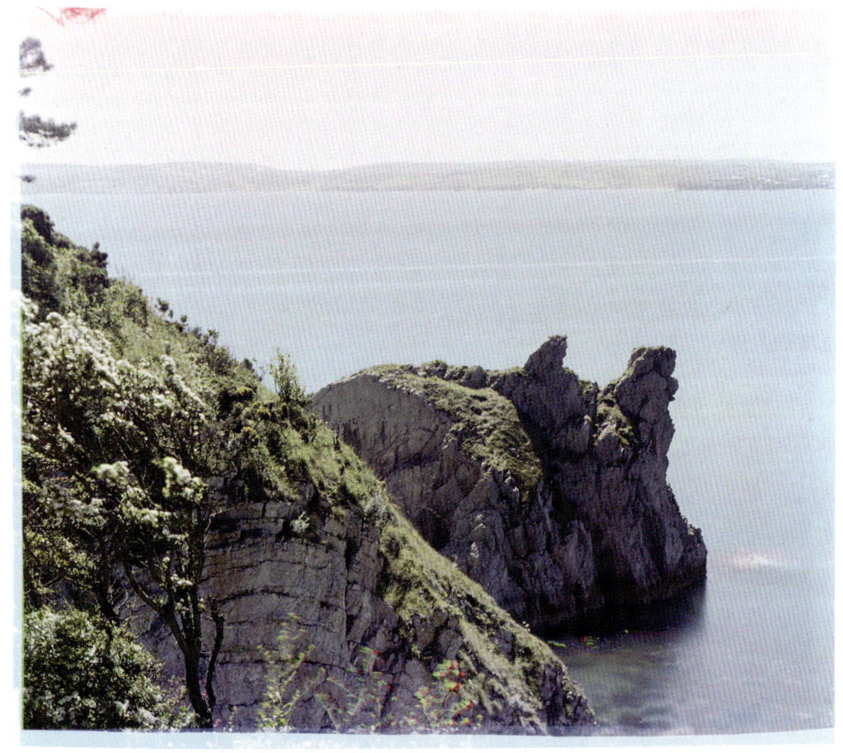

These negatives are undated but were taken in Beaulieu, Hampshire, near Lyndhurst, where Miss Acland's friends the Heathcotes lived (as did Alice Liddell after her marriage) and at Torquay, Devon, where she often overwintered. Colour fringes are visible in both due to the movement of the water during the exposures.

The weakness of the Sanger Shepherd process was in the greens, a fault shared with other early three-colour processes. In commenting on W. E. Brewerton's *Poppy Field* in the 1902 Royal Photographic Society exhibition, for example, *Amateur Photographer* complained that "the red of the poppies is fairly rendered, but the greens are very far from true". "To succeed in an effort like this", the reviewer went on, "would be to redeem three-colour work from the reproach that it cannot at the same time reproduce vivid red and true green, together with a range of other tints."

Amateur Photographer, vol. 39, no. 939 (2 October 1902), p. 263.

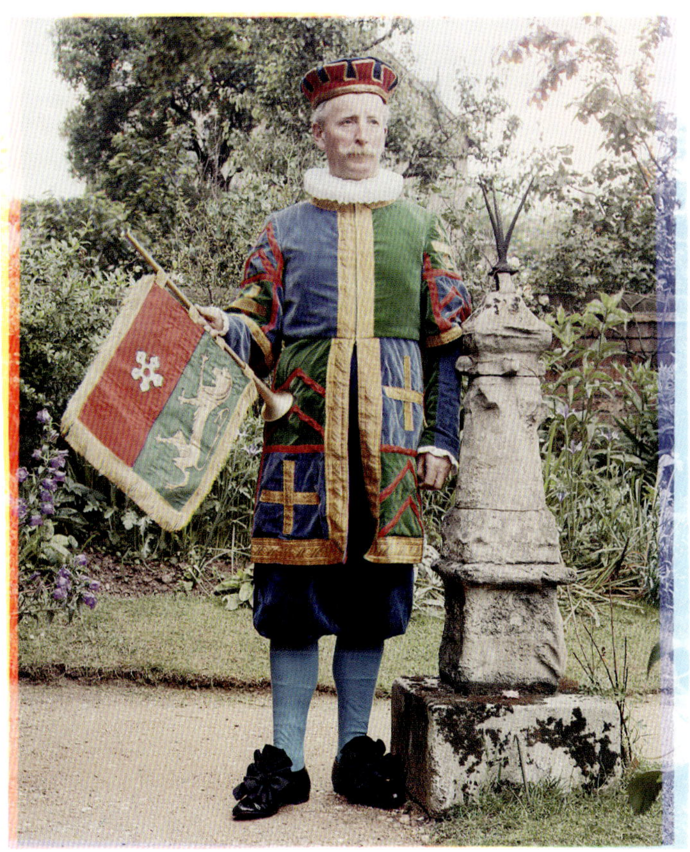

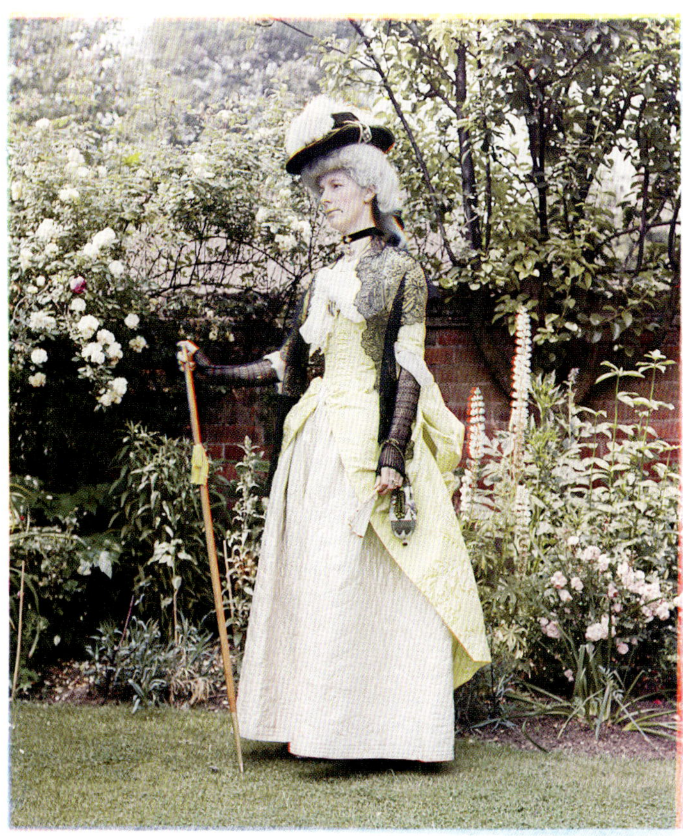

161 & 162. *Pageant Portraits*

Henry Dyke Acland (1850–1936) as the Lancaster Herald; Mary Agnes Brinton, née Hope (b. *c.* 1872, d. after 1923), as a Lady in Powder

Clevedon House, Oxford, *circa* 27 June to 3 July 1907

Composites from 8 × 3⅓ inch separation negatives (×1·6)
Museum of the History of Science, Inv. nos. 55989 & 84973

The Oxford Historical Pageant took place from 27 June to 3 July 1907. A large undertaking, in which several hundred local people re-enacted episodes from the City's history, it was part of a craze that began with the Sherborne Pageant in 1905. Maggie Hope played a 'Lady in Powder' in a dramatization of the visit of George III to Oxford in 1785. Her staff helped her stand still for the portrait. Harry, who is leaning against an old pinnacle from the Bodleian Library, featured in the Funeral Procession of Amy Robsart (wife of Robert Dudley, Elizabeth I's favourite), who had been found dead at Cumnor Place, near Oxford, in suspicious circumstances in 1560. Miss Acland served on the Ladies' General Committee of the Pageant, but did not perform.

By the time these photographs were taken the Autochrome had been released in France (although not in England), and would soon become the medium of choice for Miss Acland and a new generation of colour photographers. The Sanger Shepherd process, meanwhile, had reached a high degree of perfection since its release seven years earlier, as these portraits prove.

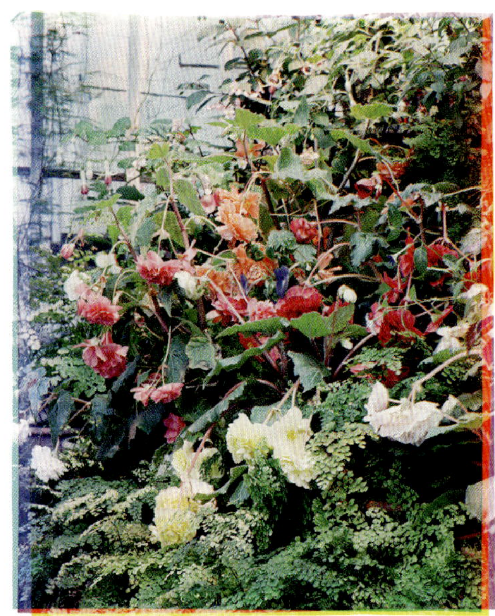
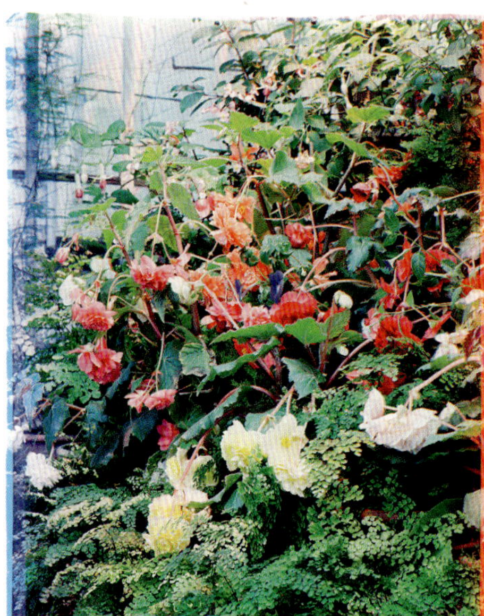
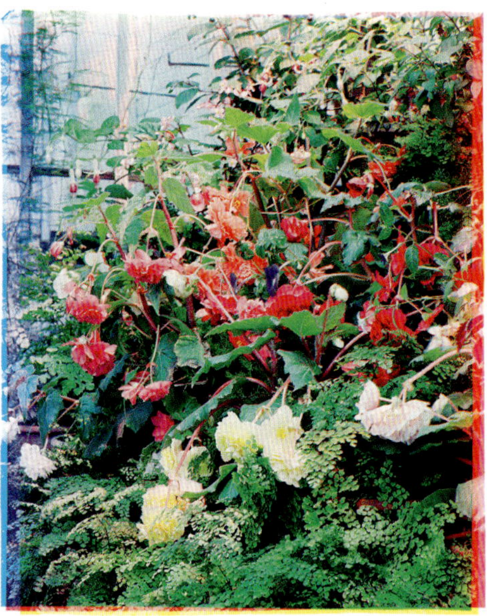

163. *Primary Colours*

Begonia, *Fuchsia* and *Adiantum capillus-veneris*
Oxford, 1907 ?

Composites from 8 × 3⅓ inch separation negative
Museum of the History of Science, Inventory no. 38530

With the advent of modern digital imaging technologies the re-creation of colour images from Miss Acland's three-colour separation negatives is relatively straightforward: positives from a scan of each monochrome negative are simply pasted into the corresponding red, green or blue channel of an RGB digital image. Registration can then be fine-tuned by nudging and warping areas of each colour plate, with contrast and exposure also adjusted individually. The techniques are analogous to those available to Miss Acland, albeit workable with a greater degree of control and precision.

Despite (and because of) its ease, the digital reproduction of separation negatives raises a number of historical issues. Inaccuracies of registration between the separations, for example, are due to such factors as the aberration of the lens with which they were taken, the imperfect optical qualities of the filters, camera and subject movement, and shrinkage of the emulsion. Some, but not necessarily all of these faults are integral to the historical character of the image and arguably should be preserved. A more fundamental problem arises due to the different primaries used in the modern and historic processes. The appearance of the recomposed image will therefore differ depending on the colour space used for the digital surrogate, particularly in its level of saturation. The effect is illustrated above, where all three images are reassembled from the same negative (shown at the size of the original), but assigned (from left to right) the sRGB, Adobe RGB and Wide Gamut RGB colour spaces.

In theory it ought to be possible to reproduce three-colour negatives more accurately by measuring the spectral absorption of the filters through which they were taken or by creating a colour profile for the set. Unfortunately, Miss Acland's filters do not survive with her negatives. The original colours as 'analysed' by the filters will, in any case, be obscured by the printing process by which they are reproduced. In this catalogue, for example, any attempt at objectivity is subverted by the transformation in colour gamut that occurs when printing by offset lithography, using the subtractive primaries, cyan, magenta and yellow. Here, therefore, the aim has been to bring out the best of the negatives, rather than imitate how they might have appeared if printed by the carbon or imbibition processes. The sRGB colour space has been chosen for this task, with the balance of each colour adjusted as necessary to obtain a convincing translation of the subject.

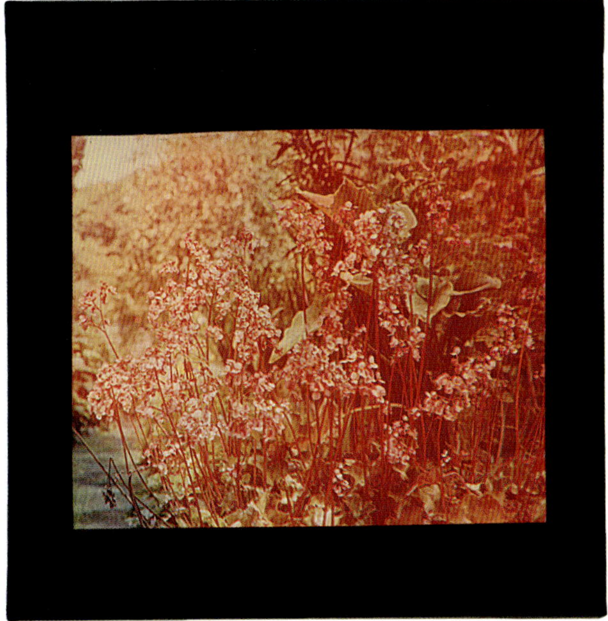

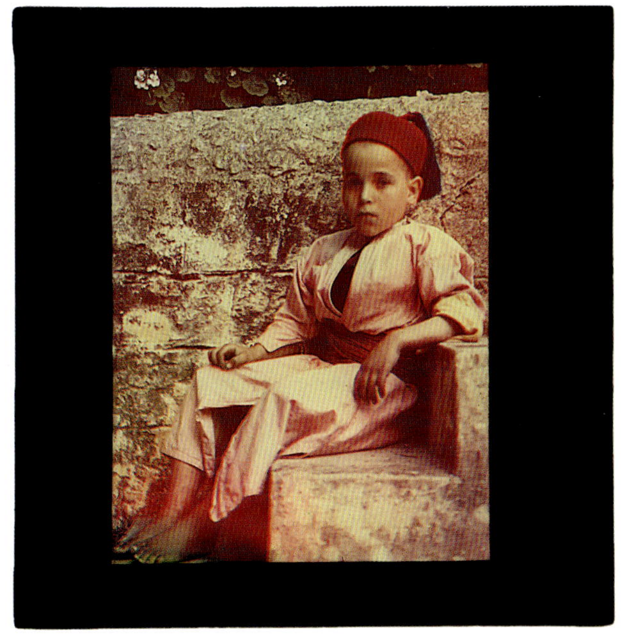

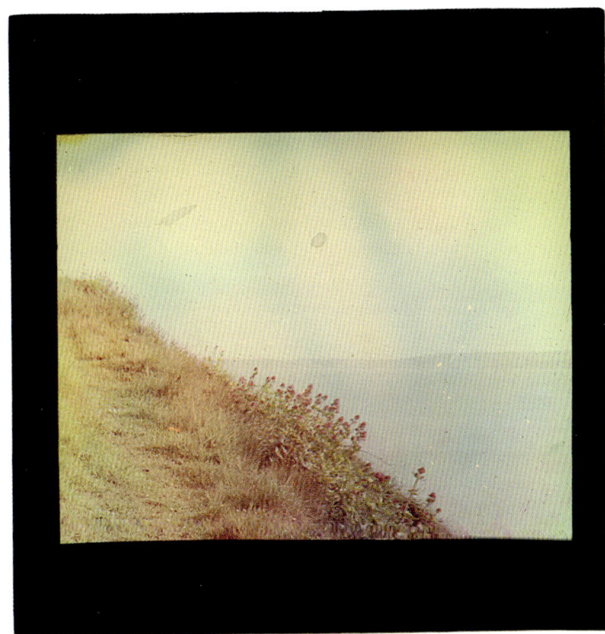

164–166. *Decayed Sanger Shepherd Lantern Slides*

Miniature begonia; *"Mustapha"*; Cliff path, Babbacombe ?
Gibraltar, 1903 or 1904; Gibraltar, 1903; Torquay, *circa* 1903

Original Sanger Shepherd lantern slides
Museum of the History of Science, Inventory nos. 63098, 33100 & 38613

Few of Miss Acland's original, assembled Sanger Shepherd lantern slides survive. One of the reasons why was revealed by the *Oxford Times* in January 1908: "We regret to hear that Miss Acland's magnificent set of Gibraltar slides, made under the Sanger Shepherd process, and which represented nearly two years' work, have been ruined during an exhibition in London". Miss Acland named the guilty party in a letter to Willie thirteen years later: "It is such a pity that the Royal Photographic Society burnt out my lecture in their powerful lantern."

Any blame for this unfortunate accident is mitigated today by the poor state of the slides that do come down to us, as these illustrations show. Sanger Shepherd slides by other workers invariably display similar faults. Their poor condition is due to the yellow carbon print turning liquid over time, perhaps due to a reaction between the yellow dye and the celluloid or Canada balsam. All detail is lost in the yellow as a result and the image takes on an orange cast, although this can often be removed digitally.

Oxford Times, no. 2463 (11 January 1908), p. 10f; MS. Acland d. 114, fols. 138–9.

AUTOCHROME PLATES

On 10 June 1907, nine months after Miss Acland had given her fourth lecture on colour photography at the Royal Photographic Society, the Autochrome process of Auguste and Louis Lumière was launched in Paris. The Autochrome caused a sensation and made 1907 the *annus mirabilis* of colour photography. Although not, as often erroneously stated, the first commercially successful colour process, nor the first capable of being worked by amateurs (these honours belonging to Sanger Shepherd), the Autochrome opened the field of colour to many more photographers than anything that had gone before.

The Autochrome had long been expected. "That it is a revolution is unquestioned, yet, paradoxically enough, it is not novel", Roger Child Bayley commented in July 1907. The *Oxford Times* had given a detailed account of the technical basis of the system as early as January 1905:

> In this process potato starch granules having a diameter of 1–15,000th to 1–20,000th of a millimetre are stained in three colours, red-orange, green, and violet. The coloured powders thus obtained are mixed together and spread upon glass. After isolating the colours with a varnish, the plate is coated with a panchromatic emulsion. Exposure is carried out in the ordinary manner, but with the glass side of the plate facing the lens, so that the light has to pass through innumerable microscopic colour screens, formed by the potato grains, before reaching the sensitive film.

The surprising result of this organic process, as it were, is invariably images of great beauty, in which the starch grains act as luminous pinpricks of intensely coloured light, giving Autochromes pointillistic qualities.

Photography, vol. 24, no. 975 (16 July 1907), p. 44; *Oxford Times*, no. 2307 (7 January 1905), p. 10d–e.

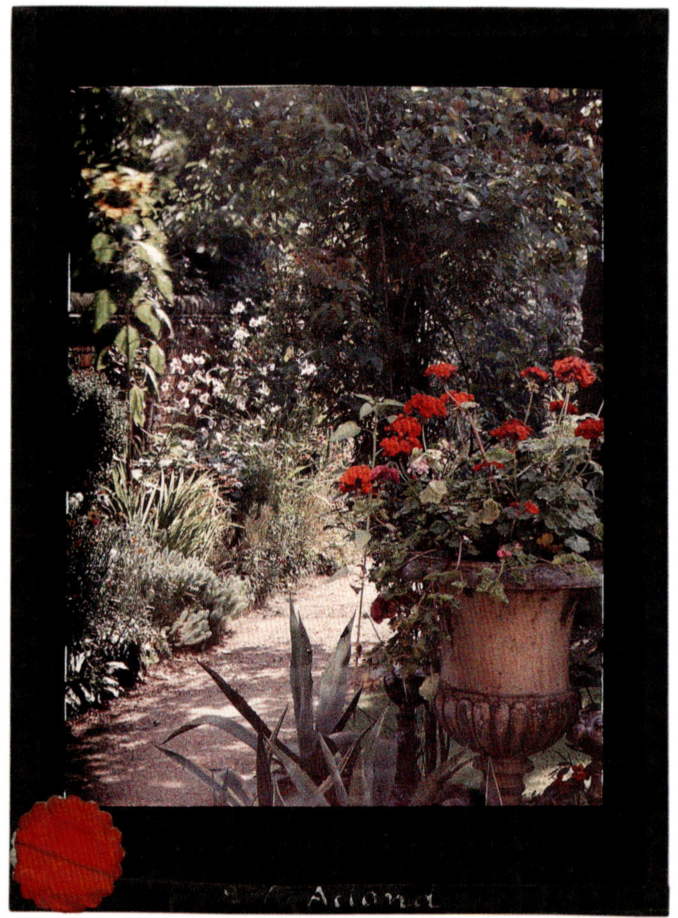

167. *"A Garden Study"*

The garden of Clevedon House, Park Town
Oxford, September 1907

9 × 12 cm Autochrome plate
Museum of the History of Science, Inventory no. 29565

Miss Acland began with the Autochrome where she left off with the Sanger Shepherd process: photographing flowers. The colourful flora in her garden at Park Town provided a convenient test of the capabilities of the new plate. With its rich, dense colours, this example is typical of the Autochrome and its strengths.

The red rosette visible in the bottom left-hand corner was awarded to the photograph when it was shown at the Oxford Camera Club exhibition in March 1908.

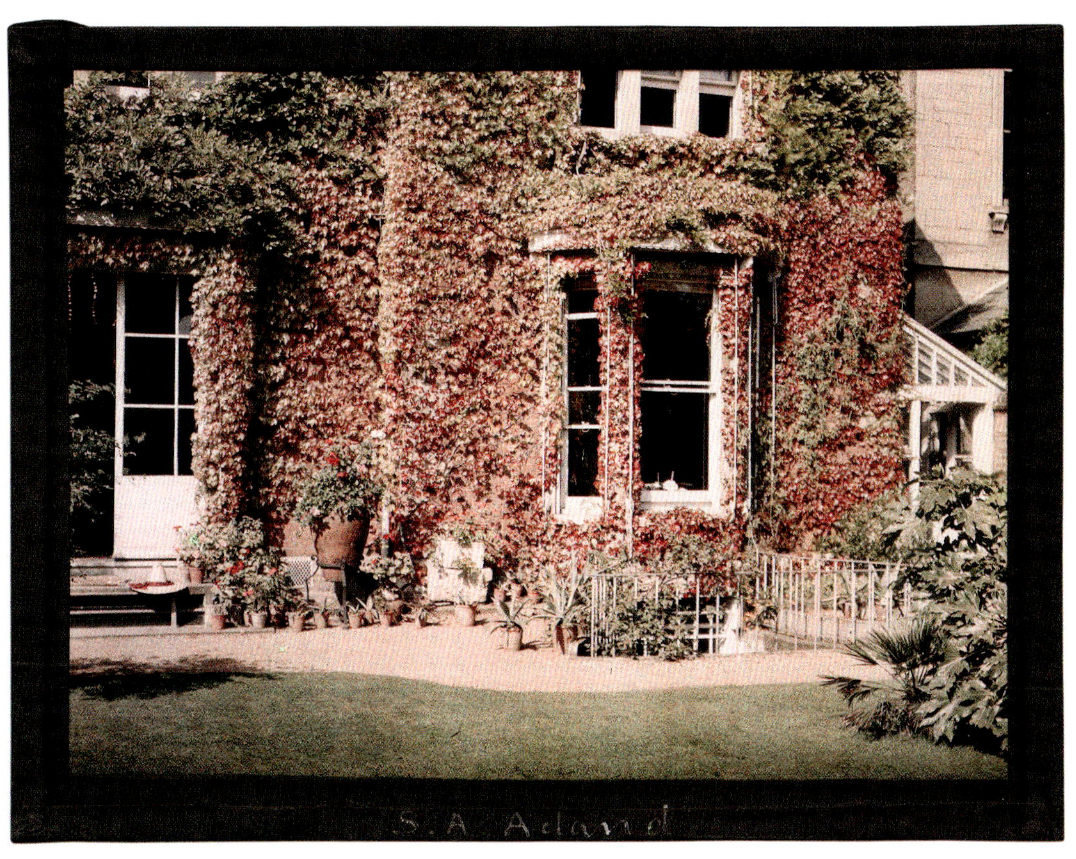

168. *"First of House"*

Clevedon House, Park Town, from the back garden
Oxford, week of 8 September 1907

9 × 12 cm Autochrome plate (×1·2)
Museum of the History of Science, Inventory no. 32614

One of the earliest subjects to which Miss Acland turned with the Autochrome was her own home, just as she had with her monochrome photography. Clevedon House, or 7 Park Villas as it was numbered in her day, had been built in 1855. Various University dignitaries lived there before Miss Acland including Montagu Burrows (1819–1905), Chichele Professor of Modern History, and Edwin Hatch (1835–1889), Vice-Principal of St Mary Hall. During Hatch's time the house was the venue for amateur theatricals penned by Lewis Carroll. Hatch's daughters sat to Dodgson for their photographs, Evelyn Maud Hatch (1871–1951) having been photographed by him 'undraped'.

Immediately prior to Miss Acland, Clevedon House was occupied by the Liddon Memorial Orphanage for 'upper class' boys, conducted by the Sisters of the Church. Miss Acland made several alterations after taking possession, installing electric lights and building an extension by Langton Cole (see cat. no. 75). In 1907 she acquired a telephone ("234 Oxford"), in 1924 a wireless set.

This plate was exposed in the afternoon, around 3 or 4 o'clock. The Boston Creeper has already begun to turn, signalling the imminent arrival of autumn.

MS. Acland d. 177, fol. 156.

169. *"A Portrait Outdoors"*

Mary Agnes Brinton, née Hope (b. *c.* 1872, d. after 1923), on the garden steps of Clevedon House
Oxford, week of 8 September 1907

9 × 12 cm Autochrome (×1·3)
Museum of the History of Science, Inventory no. 29152

On the announcement of the Autochrome Miss Acland could justifiably claim to be the leading colour photographer in Britain. She maintained this status for a brief period after its release, this portrait of her god-daughter Maggie Brinton (see cat. no. 41) being, as far as is known, the earliest Autochrome by a woman ever exhibited in public. Entitled simply *Portrait*, it was shown at the Society of Colour Photographers First Annual Exhibition, which took place at the 'Little Galleries' of the *British Journal of Photography* from 30 September to 26 October 1907. In reviewing the exhibition the annalist of colour photography, Edward John Wall (1860–1928), referred to the plate as "a model of what should be attempted in a portrait of a lady by the process", adding that "Miss Acland's long practice in colour photography by the Sanger-Shepherd process has kept her from the common mistake of indulging the appetite for colour to excess."

Miss Acland's first experiments with the Autochrome were conducted soon after plates became available in England in early September 1907. The weather was poor throughout the first week of the month, but improved on Sunday 8th, when Oxford enjoyed 6·45 hours of bright sunshine. Monday was also "very fine". The deadline for entry forms for the Society of Colour Photographers exhibition fell on 10 September, exhibits being required to reach the offices of the *British Journal* by the 13th. The portrait therefore almost certainly dates from between 8 and 12 September 1907.

Maggie is sitting on the garden steps of Clevedon House. The plate is labelled on the back "By Miss Acland. F.R.P.S.", as required for submission to the Society of Colour Photographers exhibition, and in the same form as given in the catalogue. The inscription "S. A. Acland" on the front was added when Miss Acland entered the portrait in the Oxford Camera Club exhibition in March 1908, where it was referred to as *A Portrait Outdoors* and awarded the red rosette visible in the top left-hand corner.

British Journal of Photography Monthly Supplement on Colour Photography, vol. 1, no. 10 (4 October 1907), p. 73; *Results of Meteorological Observations made at the Radcliffe Observatory, 1906–1910* (Radcliffe Observations, vol. 50, 1912).

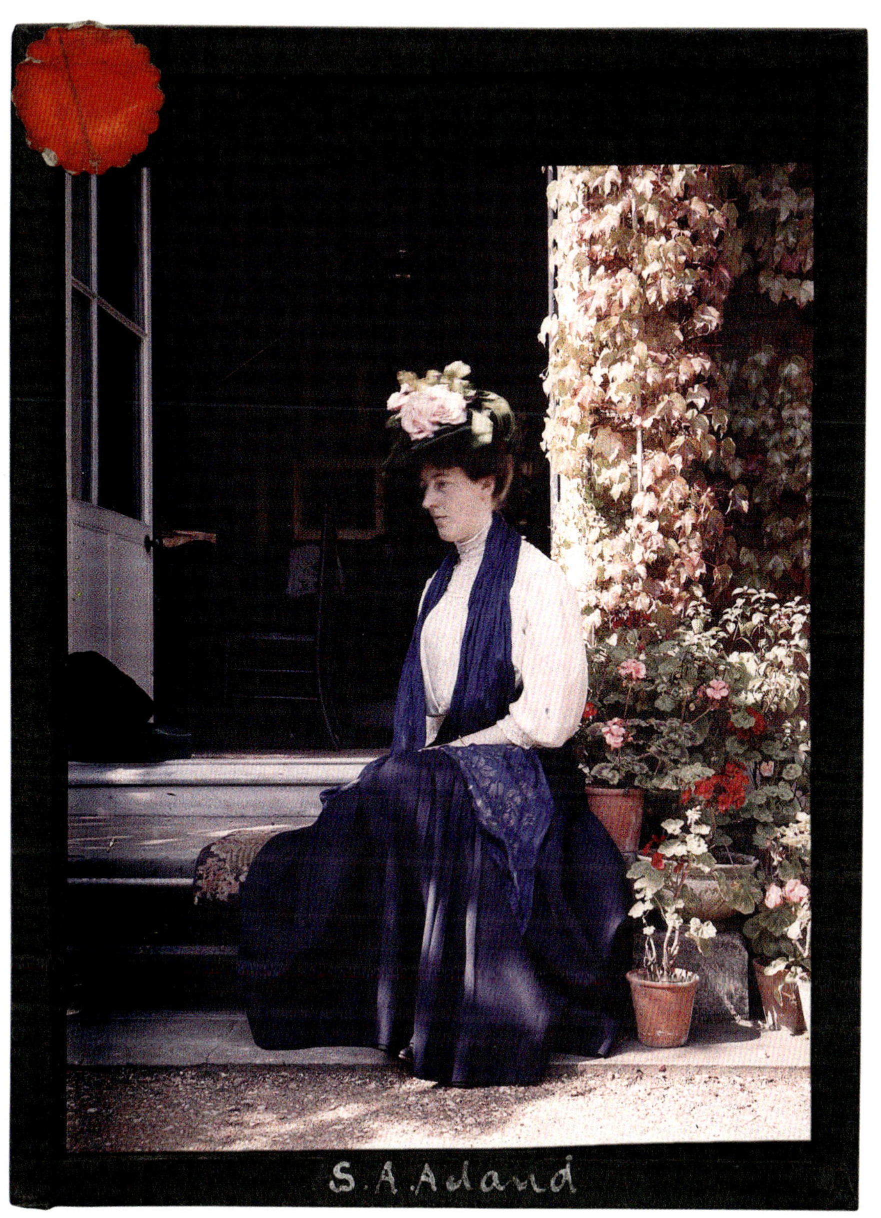
S. A. Acland

170. *"Worcester Old Building"*

The Old Buildings, Worcester College
Oxford, *circa* 10 September 1907

9 × 12 cm Autochrome plate (×1·3)
Museum of the History of Science, Inventory no. 24890

The Old Buildings in Worcester College, which are part of the original Gloucester Hall, a Benedictine foundation of 1283, face almost due south. The chimneys serve as perfect gnomons, making it straightforward to determine the time and date this photograph was taken: between noon and ten minutes past, four or five days either side of 10 September (1907).

The vast majority of Miss Acland's Autochromes were taken on 9 × 12 cm, continental-sized plates. The camera she used was an 'Una', introduced in 1905 by James A. Sinclair & Co., London, purveyors of "high-class apparatus and materials". Sinclair advertised the Una heavily, often side by side with Autochrome plates, which he was among the first to supply. Constructed of "selected Spanish Mahogany", the Una was designed as a compromise between a 'hand' and 'stand' camera, being light and portable, but sporting bellows, rising front, and an interchangeable lens board. Complete with three dark slides it sold for £7-10-0. A Goerz sector shutter added £3-10-0, a 5¾-inch Aldis 'Anastigmat' lens £3-5-0, a Zeiss Protar lens of 6½ and 11½ inch focus £11-10-0, and a leather case £1-7-6 (a grand total of £27-2-6, or £2,000 at 2012 values). The Aldis lens was moderate wide angle, 42 mm in focal length at 35 mm equivalent; the Protar normal angle and moderate telephoto, 45 mm and 84 mm equivalent.

The writer of the "Matters Photographical" column in the *Oxford Times* had seen this plate by 28 September 1907, writing that "the grey buildings and tiled roofs are reproduced with accuracy of shade and colouring." The beauty and subtlety of the colours must have pleased Miss Acland and it is easy to see why the Autochrome process created such excitement on its release. The banding in the sky is a manufacturing fault seen in early Autochromes (left by the rollers that flattened the starch grains). The vignetting in the top corners is due to Miss Acland's use of a lens with inadequate covering power.

British Journal Photographic Almanac, 1905, p. 1543; Ibid.; *Oxford Times*, no. 2449 (28 September 1907), p. 10e.

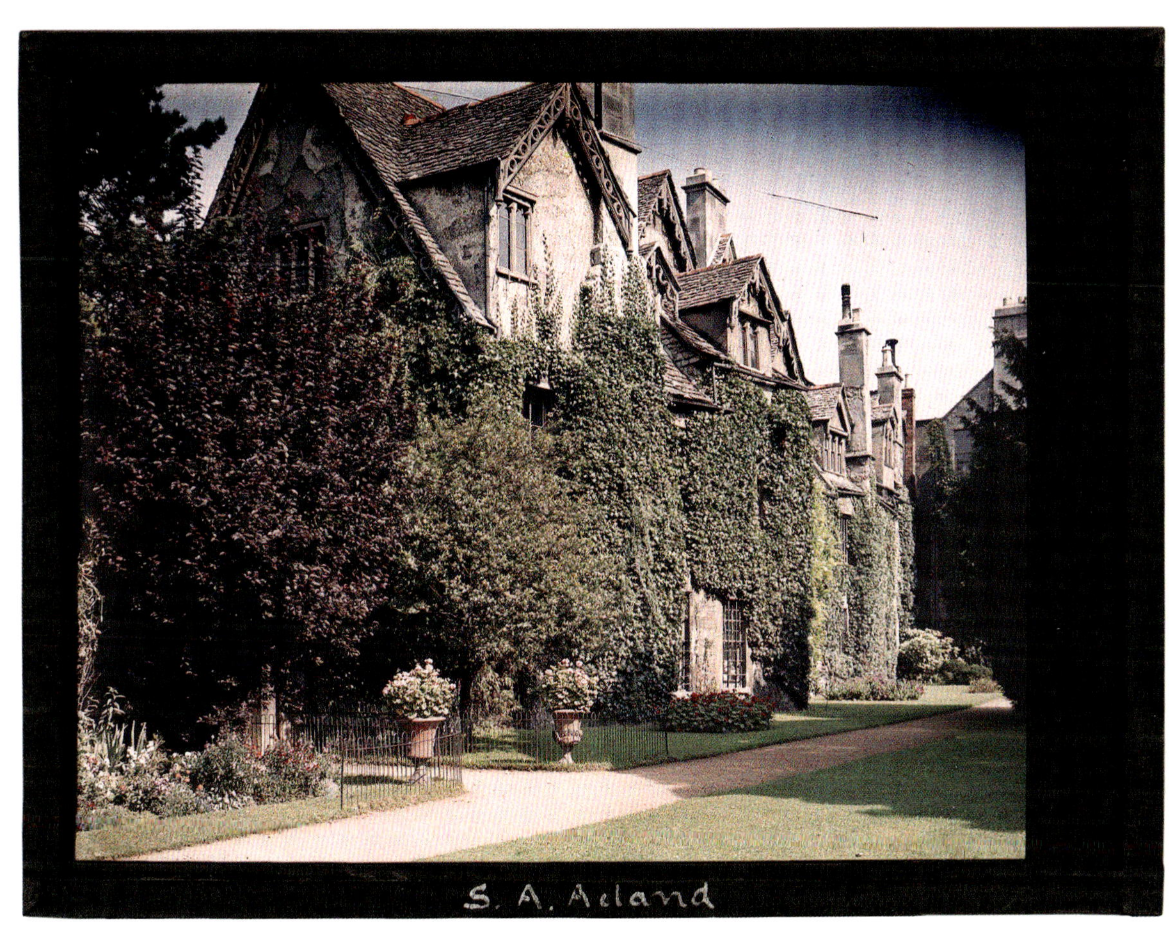
S. A. Acland

171. *"Botanic Garden"*

Buildings of the Botanic Garden, looking west
Oxford, week of 8 September 1907

9 × 12 cm Autochrome plate (×1·3)
Museum of the History of Science, Inventory no. 14780

The Botanic Garden in Oxford had been a favourite with photographers since it was photographed by Fox Talbot in the early 1840s. The two storey building in the foreground of Miss Acland's Autochrome post-dates Talbot's calotypes, having been constructed in 1848 by the Professor of Chemistry, Charles Giles Bridle Daubeny. Daubeny incorporated the principles of photographic chemistry in his introductory lectures on 'Heat and Light', delivered in these buildings to several notable Oxford photographers, including William Thomson, Arthur Cotton, and Reginald Southey. Photography also interested him as Professor of Botany, the action of light on silver salts, mediated by the so-called 'actinic rays', appearing to operate by a similar mechanism to the light of the sun on the green parts of plants, and therefore to offer support for his belief in "the analogy which runs throughout the whole of creation".

The original box in which this plate is stored is labelled "Botanic Garden not intensified" in Miss Acland's hand. Intensification was a stage in the development of Autochromes that increased the contrast and richness of the colours. In August and September 1907 considerable confusion surrounded the technique, due to an error in the instructions issued by the Lumière company (whereby 3 rather than 30 grammes of citric acid were stipulated for 'Solution F' in the ninth stage of development). *Amateur Photographer* published a correction on 27 August, but this was not reported in *Photography*, the journal Miss Acland took, until 17 September. That she labelled the plate retrospectively as developed with the incorrect formula is suggested by the fact that "not intensified" is written in pencil. Nevertheless, the reduced contrast adds greatly to the beauty of the image.

Historians have often claimed that the Autochrome was of the utmost simplicity, that it worked automatically if the instructions were followed to the letter, and that it could be carried out successfully by all but the most incompetent of photographers. The reality was rather different. Development was a fourteen-stage process, using ten separate solutions. Early workers encountered numerous problems, from the image disappearing completely, to staining, blistering and 'frilling' (the emulsion detaching from the glass). The unreliability of the system challenged even the most experienced colour photographers: on 14 October 1907 Harry told Willie that he had watched their sister develop a plate but it was "not a success unfortunately as some water got inside the film".

Miss Acland has captured an idyllic scene in this photograph, the brightness and warmth of the Indian summer enjoyed by England in 1907, so beneficial to colour work and so crucial to the early success of the Autochrome in the country, being almost palpable.

Charles Daubeny, *An Introduction to the Atomic Theory* (Oxford, 1850), p. 421; MHS Inventory no. 89211 [box]; MS. Acland d. 48, fol. 30.

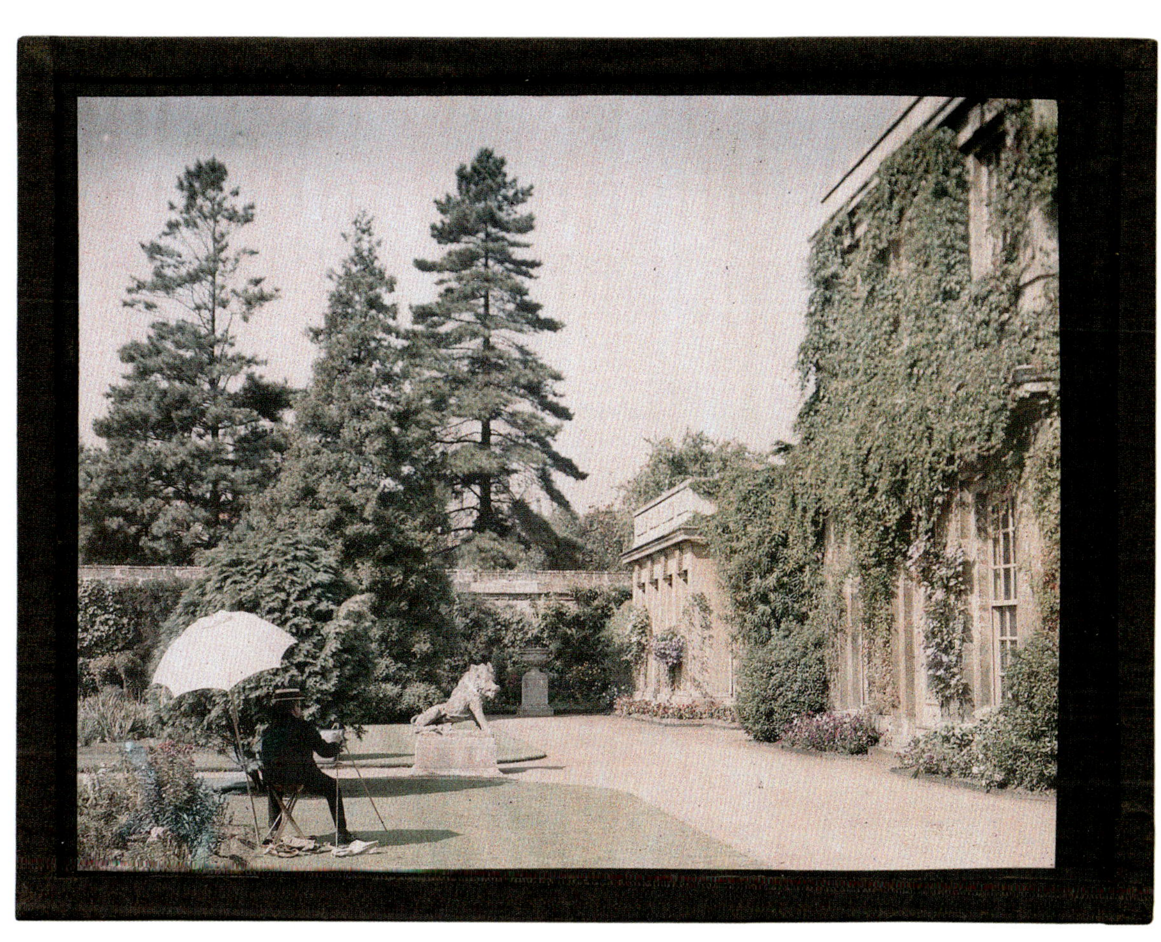

172. *"Autumn Colours in New College Gardens"*

New College bell tower, gardens, and the old city wall
Oxford, between 8 and 28 September 1907

9 × 12 cm Autochrome plate (×1·3)
Museum of the History of Science, Inventory no. 27301

When the photographic correspondent of the *Oxford Times* first saw specimens of the Autochrome process he was unimpressed. "The pictures were interesting as examples," he wrote, "but could not be considered in any way perfect. The colouring appeared to lack tone and gave a wash effect". This plate, taken in New College gardens by Miss Acland, forced him to change his view:

> On writing a week or two ago on the capabilities of the new Autochrome plate, as demonstrated by two examples in a shop window in Glasgow, we did this, the last word but one in colour photography, considerable injustice. ... This week we have seen the results of local experiments with the Autochrome plate and the majority were really splendid. One, in particular, reproduced without exaggeration and yet in all its beauty, the autumn richness of the college gardens.

However, no doubt having Miss Acland's difficulties in mind, he added a caveat: "Early workers in any process expect to find difficulties, but there is a limit to patience when plates about quarter-plate size and costing 5s. for four develop freaks without warning that entirely spoil the picture." "As a novelty", he concluded, "the Lumiere process will certainly receive attention from the opulent."

Miss Acland took considerable pride in this beautiful plate, choosing to take it to the Camera Club on 7 January 1908, when Thomas Knight Grant (1870–1940), the Lumières' London representative, visited to demonstrate the 'Autochrome System'. His demonstration was the first "outside the metropolis", as befitted Oxford's status as the provincial capital of colour photography.

Visible on the right in the photograph is part of the old city wall. In the middle distance a lady is enjoying the shade on a strategically placed bench. Light can be seen through the louvres of the bell tower, which Miss Acland photographed from the opposite side with the Sanger Shepherd process. Just to the left of the tower smoke is visible rising from a chimney, highlighted by the sun against the shadowed wall of New College hall. The scene remains almost unchanged today.

Oxford Times, no. 2446 (7 September 1907), p. 10h; Ibid., no. 2449 (28 September 1907), p. 10e; Ibid., no. 2463 (11 January 1908), p. 10f.

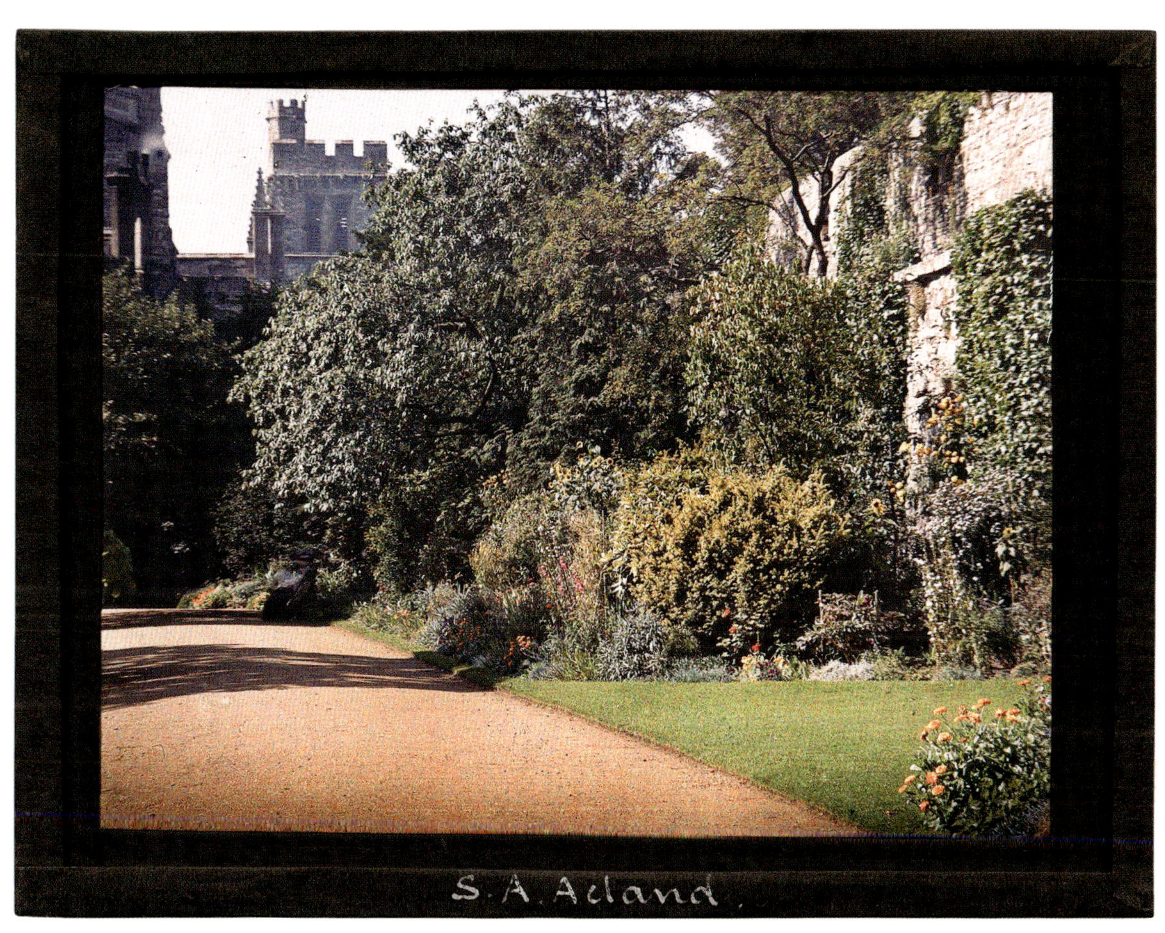
S. A. Acland.

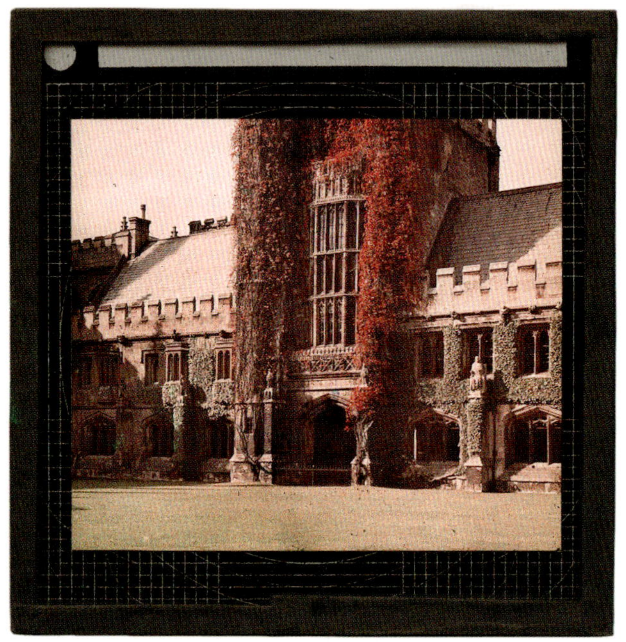

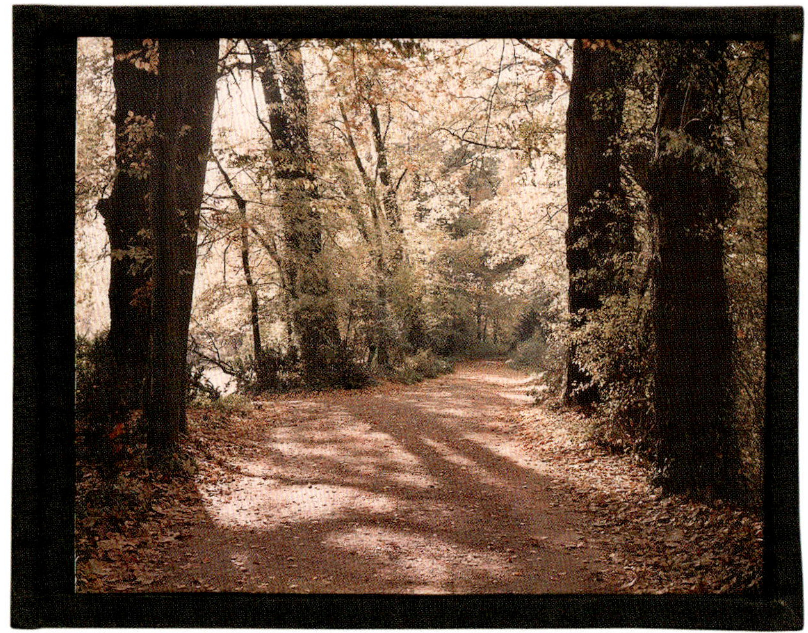

173. *"Magdalen — Founders Tower"*

Founder's Tower, Magdalen College, from the cloister
Oxford, 8 October 1907 or shortly after

3¼ × 3¼ inch Autochrome plate
Museum of the History of Science, Inventory no. 17479

On 8 October 1907, shortly after visiting Willie, Miss Acland wrote to her brother anxiously:

> I am in great trouble because I have not got the Vice Chancellors permission to Photograph in Magdalen. I have not as far as I remember seen it since I left Bolham. I have written to Isabel as I knew you were going to Hayne yesterday to ask her to look in the blotting book & the drawers in my room. There was a very nice note from him & the permission to photograph on a card. Did I show it to you or Robin? If so I may have left it downstairs. I shall be very thankful if it is found as it seems very careless after his kindness to have lost it.

On 11 October she wrote again with the news that Herbert Warren, who was also President of Magdalen and a personal friend, had kindly provided a replacement card, "so the first is not of so much value but I should like to have it & the letter back if it is found".

MS. Acland d. 109, fols. 33–4; Ibid., fols. 35–6.

174. *Autumn Leaves*

Mesopotamia Walk, looking south ?
Oxford ?, autumn 1907

4¼ × 3¼ inch Autochrome plate
Museum of the History of Science, Inventory no. 23317

Miss Acland succeeded in obtaining several magnificent photographs during her early trials with the Autochrome, of which this is one. The russet tones of the leaves, the fall of light through the branches, and the atmosphere of approaching autumn are perfectly captured by the process.

Only eight quarter-plate Autochromes by Miss Acland are known. Autochromes did not become available in English, imperial sizes until the end of September 1907, lantern-plates two weeks later. At 4¼ × 3¼ inches (8·3 × 10·8 cm), quarter-plates are slightly smaller than the equivalent French, metric plates (9 × 12 cm). However, Autochromes in both sizes were eventually sold at the same price, which may explain why Miss Acland persevered with the format for the majority of her photography with the process.

The path depicted is probably Mesopotamia Walk, just south of the University Parks, between the upper and lower Cherwell. A glint of the sun reflected off the river can just be glimpsed through the trees.

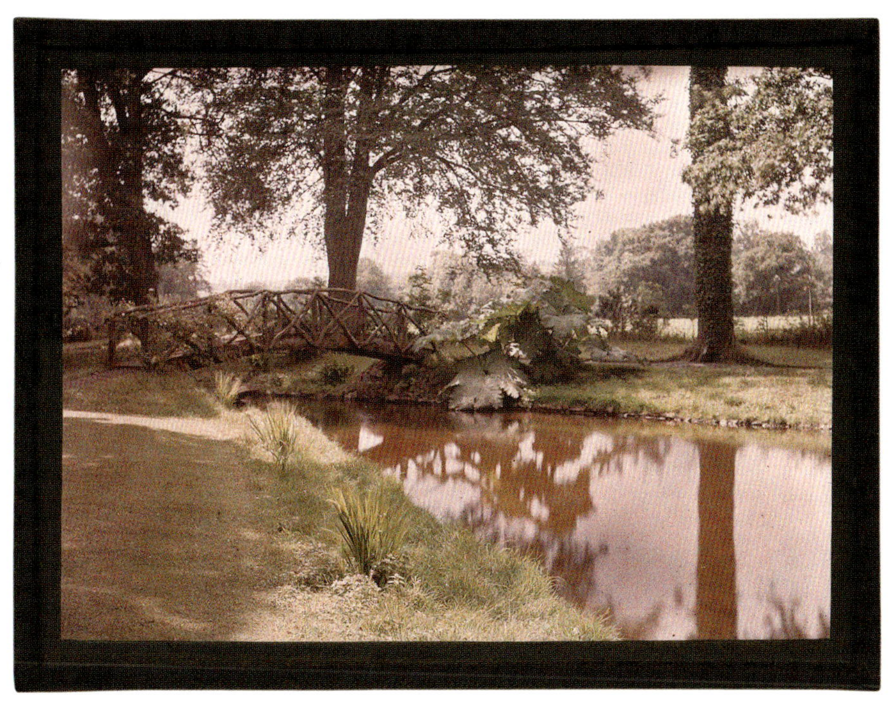

175. *On the Exe at Bolham*

A bridge in the garden of Bolham House
Tiverton, Devon, 1907 or later

9 × 12 cm Autochrome plate
Museum of the History of Science, Inventory no. 30502

In late September 1907 Miss Acland visited Willie at his new home in Bolham, near Tiverton, Devon. Whilst there she was given "the freedom of the darkroom", an opportunity she used to develop Autochromes of the nearby River Exe. This view of one of the river's feeders in Willie's garden may have been taken on the occasion or during a later visit.

After returning to Oxford Miss Acland reported to the Camera Club that Autochromes required a 16-second exposure at f/12 under white cloud (guidelines suggested 1 second at f/8 in bright sun and 6 seconds under cloud). The slowness of the plates was only part of the problem: many photographers had trouble determining the correct exposure in the first place and controversy raged for some time over the Autochrome's true speed. To complicate matters slight variation from the optimum led to significant colour casts in the final image.

MS. Acland d. 109, fols. 31–2.

176. *Councillor Merivale*

Mary Sophia Merivale (1853–1928), in the garden of Clevedon House, Park Town
Oxford, 1908 or later

9 × 12 cm Autochrome plate (×1·3)
Museum of the History of Science, Inventory no. 31931

Sophia Merivale was Oxford's first woman councillor, elected at the head of the poll for the North Ward on 1 November 1907. She stood as an independent, displacing the sitting Conservative. Her election followed the passing of the *Qualification of Women (County and Borough Councils) Act*, which saw seven other women elected, notably Elizabeth Garrett Anderson (a decade would pass before they could stand for parliament).

Miss Acland was one of Miss Merivale's nominators: a fact she was quick to point out in a letter to *The Times* in 1909 in response to a column on "Women at the Municipal Elections". She was also her neighbour, Sophia living with her sister Judith Ann (1860–1945) at 4 Park Town. Daughters of Charles Merivale (1808–1893), Dean of Ely, Sophia and Judith were brought up in the Ely Cathedral Close but moved to Oxford in 1894 with their mother, Judith Mary Sophia Merivale, née Frere (1817–1906). One of their neighbours in Ely had been the autochromist-to-be, Etheldreda Janet Laing, whose father Richard Winkfield (1836–1929) was headmaster of the Cathedral School.

Miss Merivale was also a photographer, joining the Oxford Camera Club on 8 October 1900. A little over a year later, on 2 December 1901, she seconded Laing's nomination for membership. As a member of the Club Laing would certainly have seen and been influenced by Miss Acland's Autochromes; as a friend of Sophia she may well have been shown this portrait.

That Miss Acland, Miss Merivale and Mrs Laing prospered in the Camera Club was testimony to the efforts made from its foundation to develop an ethos attractive to women. The Club was a place where women were able to partake on more equal terms with men than in other areas of Victorian life, including by seeking election as officers, as Miss Acland had done in 1896, eleven years before her friend's electoral success in the wider public sphere.

On Miss Merivale's left in the photograph is a terracotta oil jar, planted with a geranium, which Miss Acland took to Park Town from Broad Street. An identical jar is visible in a number of Dodgson's photographs of the Acland and Liddell children (see, for example, p. 287).

Miss Merivale is portrayed in her councillor's robes.

The Times, no. 39107 (3 November 1909), p. 10c.

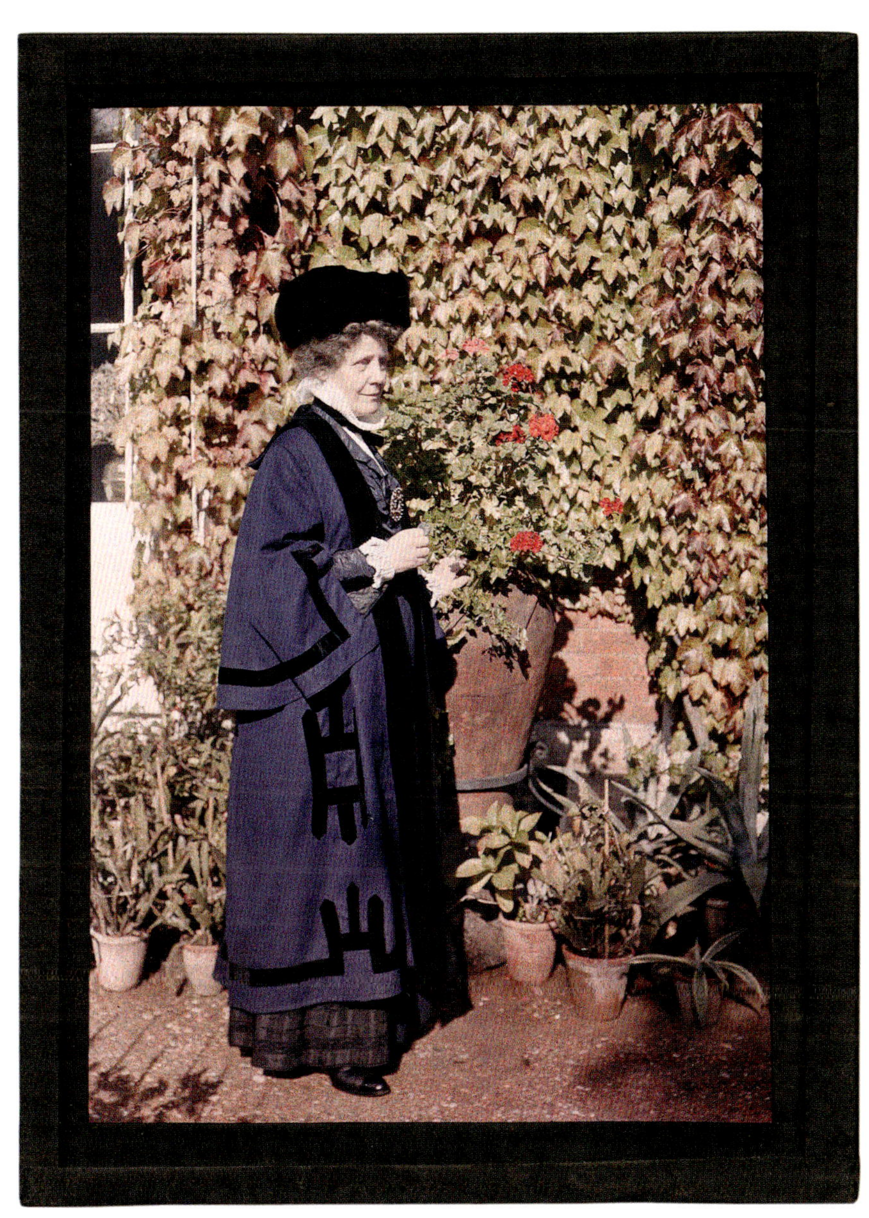

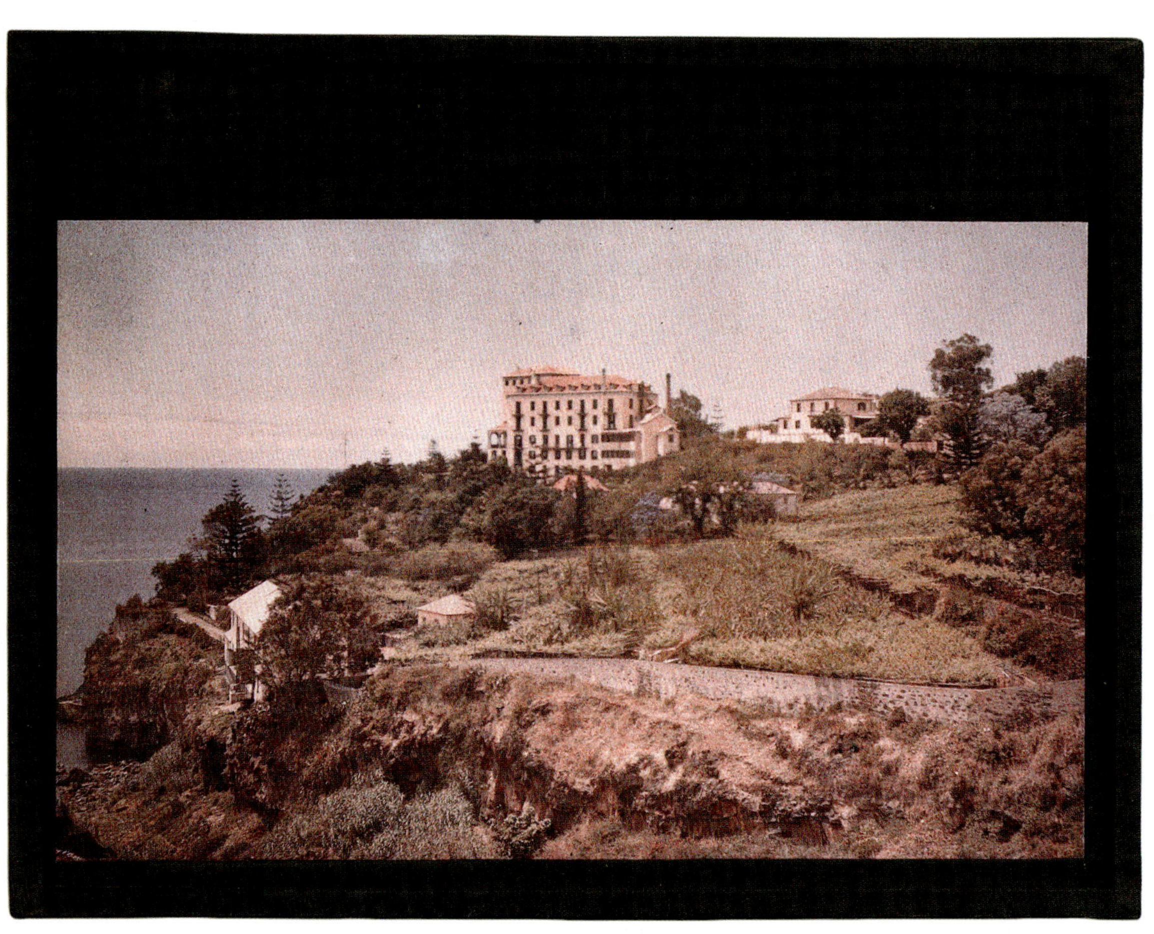

OPPOSITE

177. *Reid's Palace Hotel*

Reid's Hotel, from the New Road
Funchal, between March and May 1908 ?

9 × 12 cm Autochrome plate (×1·3)
Museum of the History of Science, Inv. nos. 19122 & 18035

Reid's Hotel would be Miss Acland's surrogate home for a combined total of three and a half years between 1908 and 1915. Opened in November 1891 as the New Hotel ('and annexes'), by the time Miss Acland took up residence it was known as the New Palace Hotel, Reid's Palace Hotel or simply 'Reid's'. The building was "perched up on a cliff above the sea" a mile to the west of the centre of Funchal, in what was then open country-side. A British establishment, the largest in Madeira, it was said to have done much to increase the popularity of the island as a destination. Miss Acland regarded the hotel as almost empty when sixty or seventy guests were staying, but the influx of 125 day-trippers for lunch, from passing liners, made the place unbearably crowded.

Miss Acland's first impressions of Reid's were bad. "A great disappointment awaited us when we reached the Hotel, as instead of our promised rooms Miss Grimston and I have one between us", she wrote. A "barrack" with two beds, the room had no view and was in the basement where everyone could see in. "It was quite a shock on the top of our tiredness." Nevertheless, when they had "shaken down" it proved quite comfortable.

The sloping ground in front of Reid's, covered in vegetation, was part of the hotel's impressive terraced gardens, which were a great delight to Miss Acland. The blue bloom of the *Jacaranda mimosifolia* helps to date the photograph to the spring months.

Like other hotels on the island, Reid's was equipped with a darkroom for the use of guests.

Museum of the History of Science, MS. Gunther 30, fol. 1r; Ibid., fol. 5r; MS. Acland d. 109, fols. 54–6; Ibid.; MS. Gunther 30, fol. 5r.

OVERLEAF

178 & 179. *"Green Ixias"*

Ixia viridiflora, Quinta do Bom Sucesso
Funchal, between 11 and 23 March 1908

9 × 12 cm Autochrome plates (×1·3)
Museum of the History of Science, Inv. nos. 28536 & 17731

These inflorescences of *Ixia viridiflora* were chosen by Miss Acland as early Autochrome subjects on account of their spectacular turquoise colour. In her diary on 24 March 1908 she described how she came across them:

> Twice we have been up to Mr. Reid's Quinta to try to get a photograph of his great green Ixias. They are I believe Cape flowers. This also is a wonderful garden and Mrs. Reid has quite a large menagerie of Parrots, Monkeys, Chameleons etc. Some very rare parrots. Lady Maude Wilbraham is staying with them and took care of us.

The Reids' quinta, known as the Quinta do Bom Sucesso, is now the Botanical Gardens, situated in a dramatic position in the hills above Funchal. The Mr Reid mentioned was either Alfred Edward Reid (1865–1946) or William James George Reid (1851–1928), who together ran the hotels established by their father William Reid (1822–1888). Both took good care of Miss Acland in Madeira, but she was fondest of William, describing him as "such a very nice man, very superior to his brother".

Museum of the History of Science, MS. Gunther 30, fol. 10r; MS. Acland d. 111, fol. 122.

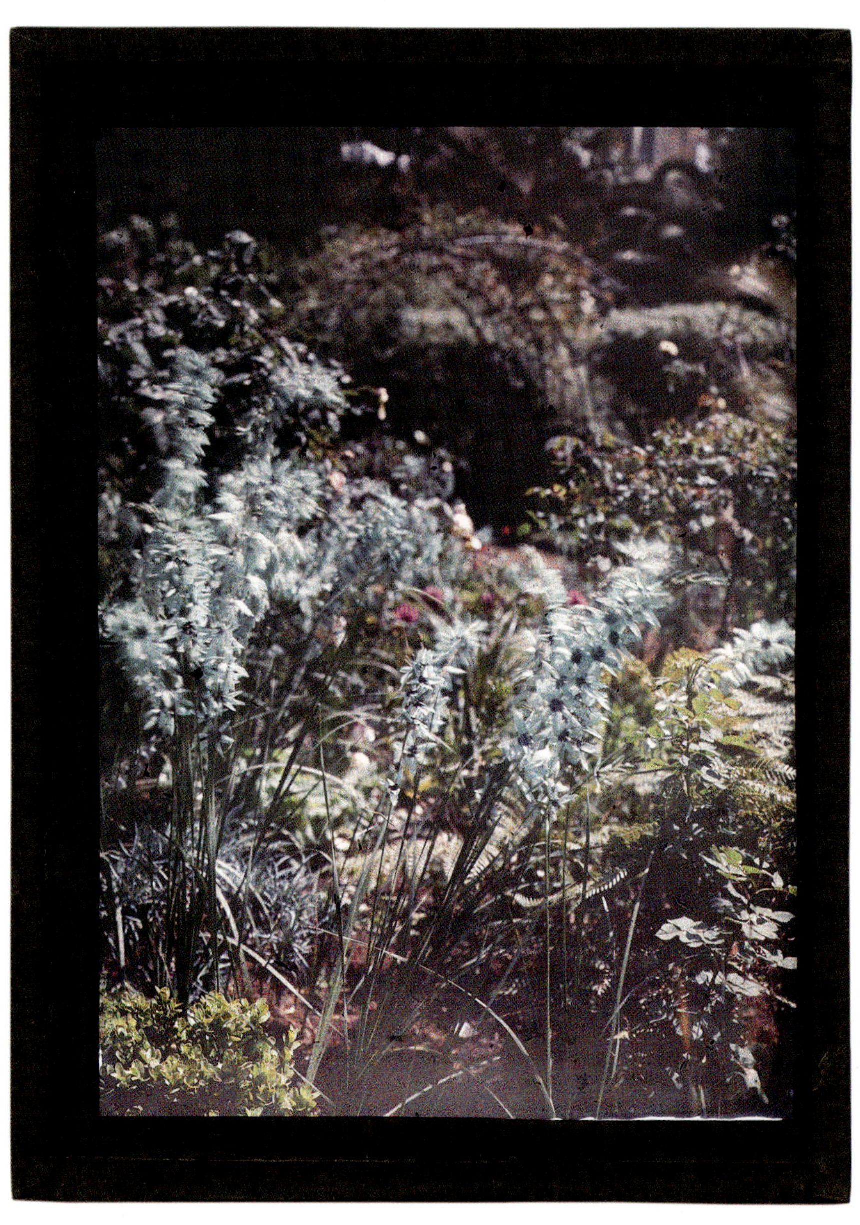

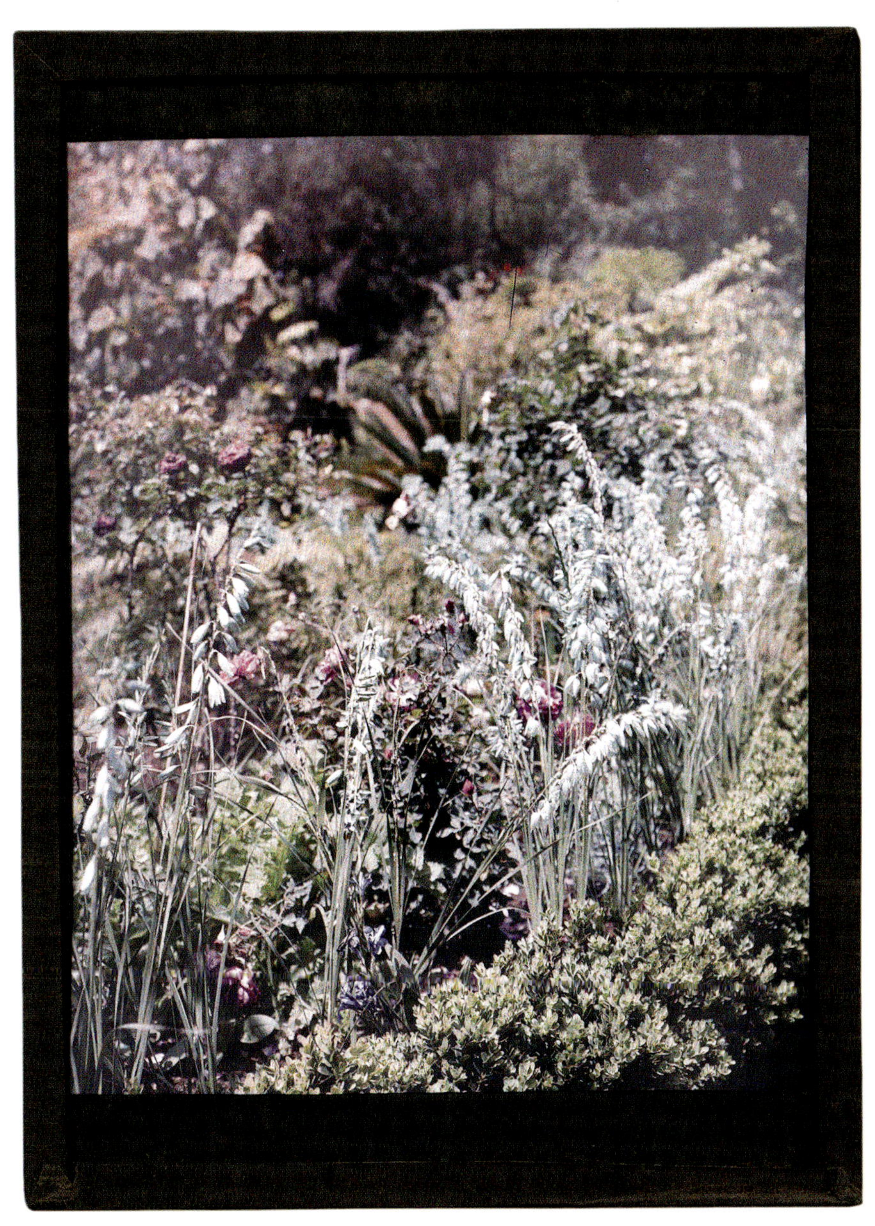

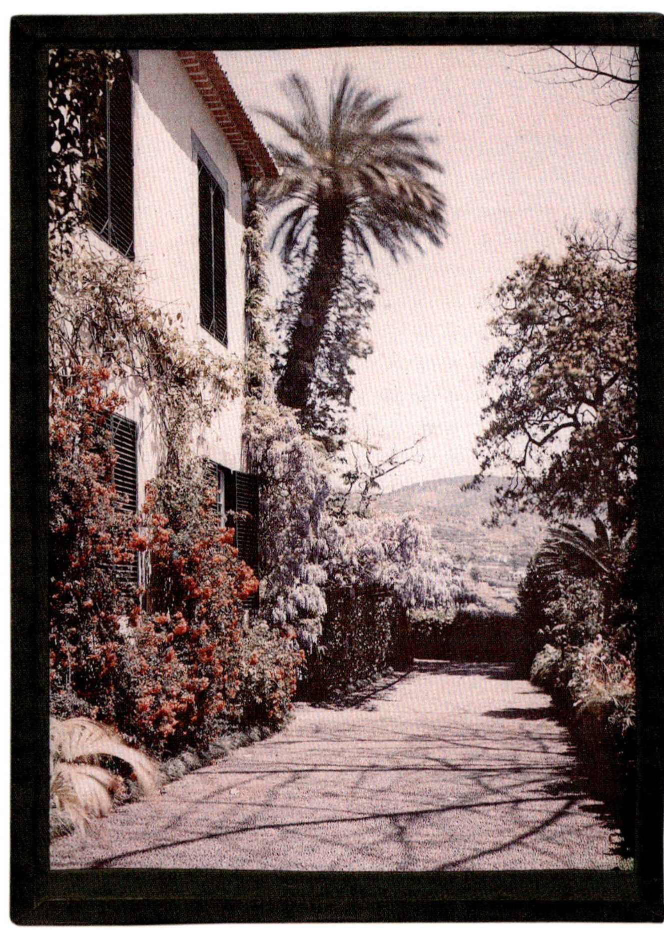

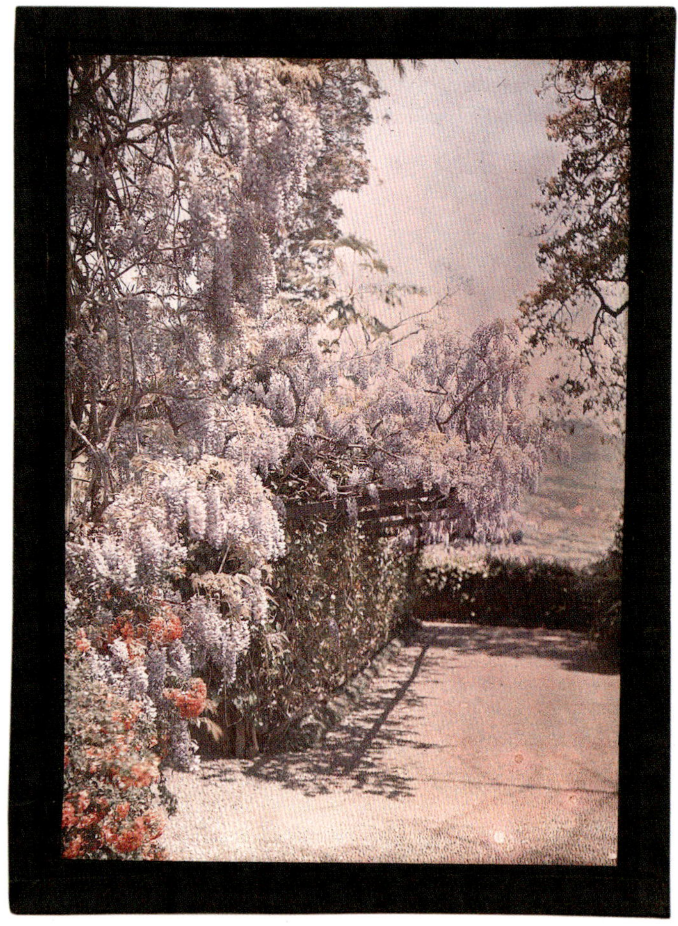

ABOVE

180 & 181. *The Quinta da Levada*

Bougainvillea and *Wisteria sinensis,* Quinta da Levada
Funchal, April 1908 ?

9 × 12 cm Autochrome plates
Museum of the History of Science, Inv. nos. 15253 & 24661

During her first visit to Madeira Miss Acland was given an introduction to Anna Mary Furber Cossart, née Blandy (1849/50–1939). "Mrs. Cossart is a great gardener and their garden contains the best Wistaria I have seen climbing right up an immense palm tree", she wrote in her diary. Later she got to know the Blandys' daughter, Mildred Blandy Cossart (1879–1966), "a very nice girl but alas very deaf which is most sad for her". Mildred shared Miss Acland's passion for photography and practised it with some success, 100 of her photographs being reproduced in W. H. Koebel's *Madeira: Old and New* (London, 1909).

Museum of the History of Science, MS. Gunther 30, fol. 11r; fol. 24r.

OPPOSITE

182 & 183. *Aloe arborescens*

Aloe arborescens, on the cliff outside Reid's Hotel
Funchal, 1909 or 1910 ?

9 × 12 cm Autochrome plates
Museum of the History of Science, Inv. nos. 17538 & 17057

"Sometimes outlined against the blue azure main might be seen the orange-red spikes of *Tritoma*, of which my friend Miss Acland had produced the most beautifully effective colour-photograph I have yet seen, but which, alas, was accidentally broken", the Oxford pharmacist and camera retailer George Claridge Druce wrote in an article on Madeira after holidaying on the island in 1909. These plates remain intact, but Druce's accolade is equally appropriate. They depict not Red Hot Pokers, but the scarlet spikes of *Aloe arborescens*, with which *Tritoma* is often confused.

"A Pharmacist's Holiday", *Chemist and Druggist*, vol. 78, no. 1631 (29 April 1911), pp. 149–50, p. 149.

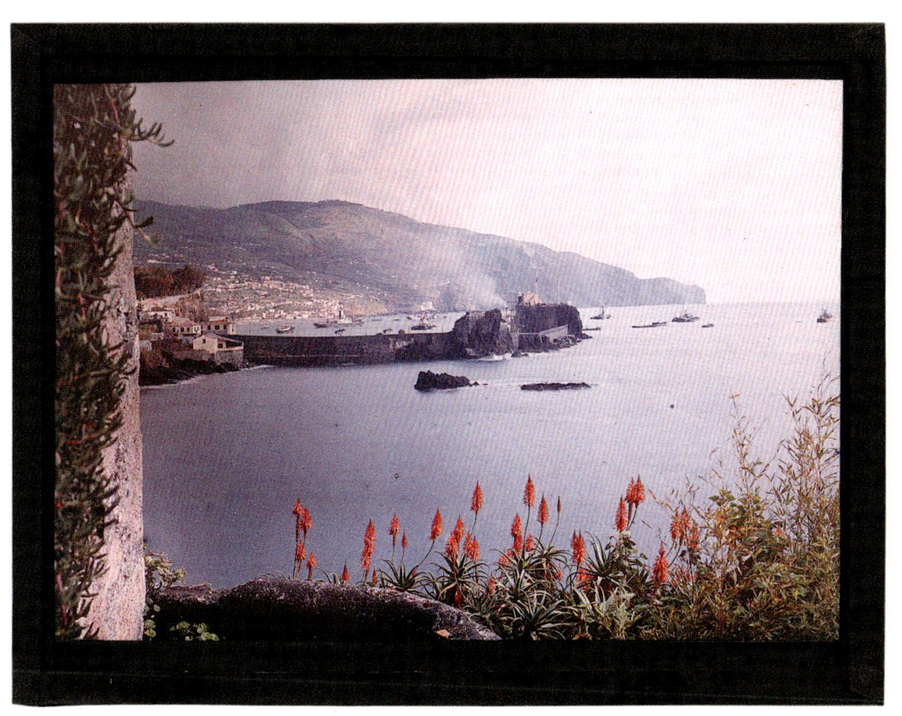

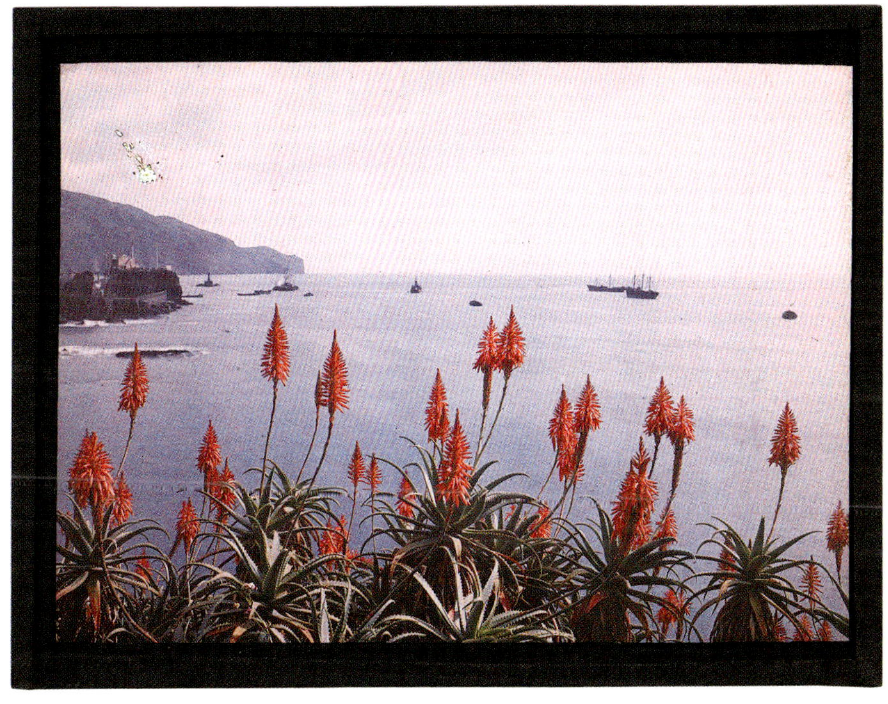

184. *The British Cemetery, Funchal*

British Cemetery, looking towards the Rua da Carreira
Funchal, April 1909 ?

9 × 12 cm Autochrome plate (×1·3)
Museum of the History of Science, Inventory no. 21429

This picturesque view is taken, rather incongruously, in the grounds of the British cemetery in Funchal. Ferns in pots line the drive, fully bearing out the statement in *Brown's Madeira* that the cemetery was "prettily laid out and carefully tended by the Foreign Residents".

Unfortunately, the spectre of death hung over Madeira all too frequently during Miss Acland's time there. In February 1910 an epidemic of typhoid broke out at Reid's, claiming the lives of several foreign residents, including Emeline Crocker (1858–1910), a lady gardener out collecting for Kew whom Miss Acland had befriended. Alice, the maid of a Mrs Cleveland Thomas, also succumbed to the bacillus. Miss Acland nursed her during her last days, after she was left to die by her mistress, who was reported to have said that "she brought her out to work & not to be ill". Miss Acland's own maid Mabel was also laid up with the infection, but survived.

The typhoid epidemic prompted Miss Acland to take advice before deciding whether to return to Madeira the following season. One of those she consulted was her friend, the bacteriologist and former assistant to Pasteur, Wolfgang Aaronoich Mordecai Wolff Haffkine (1860–1930). Haffkine advised that an outbreak of sixty typhoid cases in a hotel of 200 residents was a "frightful incident, & should put the whole island on the black list." Nevertheless, return Miss Acland did. The decision was a bad one. No sooner had she arrived back, in November 1910, than an epidemic of Asiatic cholera broke out, closing the port and seeing troops deployed to quell the rioting against the sanitary measures. Within two weeks 600 cases had been reported, a third of which proved fatal. However, the cholera affected tourists less than the Madeirenses, with no cases arising in the hotel.

In many respects Miss Acland was in her element during both crises. Not only was she able to pass on advice from Haffkine, who sent his *Notes on the Methods of Mitigating the Death-rate from Cholera,* compiled a few months earlier in Simla, but she could also seek guidance from Theodore, who served in Egypt during the cholera epidemic of 1883. Theodore in turn could draw on knowledge passed down from his father, whose medical reputation was established by the experiences he described in his *Memoir on the Cholera at Oxford, in the Year 1854* (London & Oxford, 1856).

Samler Brown, *Brown's Madeira* (9th ed., London, 1908), p. 135; MS. Acland d. 110, fols. 30–3; MS. Acland d. 161, fols. 117–18.

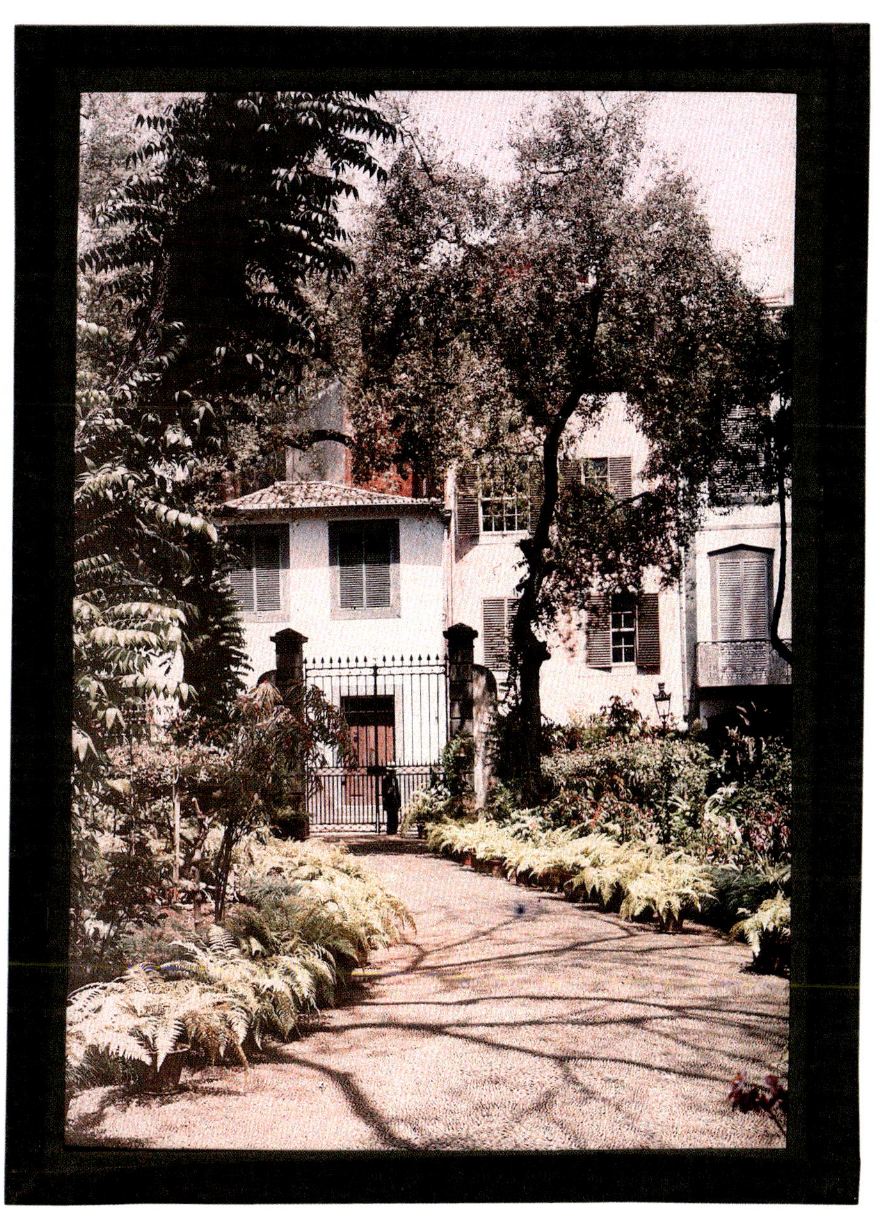

185. *"Avenue of Poinsettias"*

The Avenue of Poinsettias, Casa Branca
Funchal, December 1909 ?
9 × 12 cm Autochrome plate (reverse, ×1·3)
Museum of the History of Science, Inventory no. 89628

The Casa Branca, which is located about 250 metres north of Reid's Hotel, was the home of the merchant John Milberne Leacock (d. 1915) and his wife Mary Silence Leacock, née Erskine (1860–1945). In November 1913 Miss Acland travelled out to Madeira with the Leacocks on board the R.M.S. *Balmoral Castle*.

Florence Du Cane (1869–1955), in *The Flowers and Gardens of Madeira* (London, 1909), described in words the scene photographed by Miss Acland:

> almost opposite to the hotel in the grounds of Casa Branca for a few short weeks in the year the avenue of *Poinsettia pulcherrima* interspersed with date palms and clumps of strelitzias is worth seeing. The poinsettia blooms are almost the largest I have ever seen, measuring quite eighteen inches in diameter from point to point of the scarlet leaves. ... Poinsettias seem to rejoice in rich soil, and they appear to revel in the liberal feeding of the adjoining banana plantations, which, no doubt, they deprive of a good deal of nourishment; but they well repay their owner, as in the glow of the western sun they provide a veritable feast of colour all through December.

Miss Acland's hammock is hidden halfway down the avenue: one end can just seen sticking out, standing on its forks. In the far distance is the blue smudge of the sea.

This plate is numbered as the third in a group of six, the other members of which also survive. The labelling is on the reverse, as required for submission to the Society of Colour Photographers exhibition. As well as in October 1907, the Society held exhibitions in summer 1908, 1910 and 1912. Unfortunately, the only recorded catalogue is for the inaugural exhibition, making it difficult to confirm Miss Acland's contributions in subsequent years.

Florence and Ella Du Cane, *The Flowers and Gardens of Madeira* (London, 1909), p. 38.

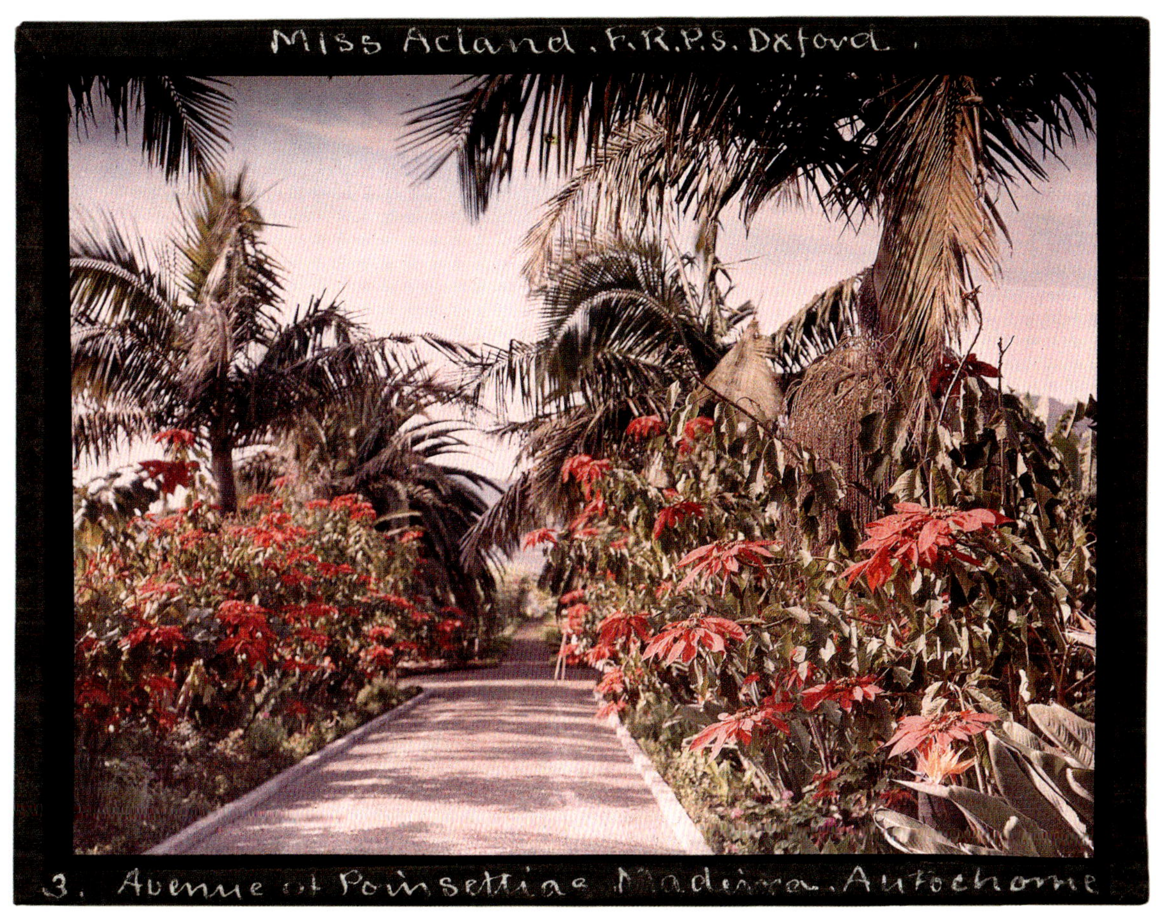
Miss Acland. F.R.P.S. Oxford.
3. Avenue of Poinsettias Madeira. Autochome

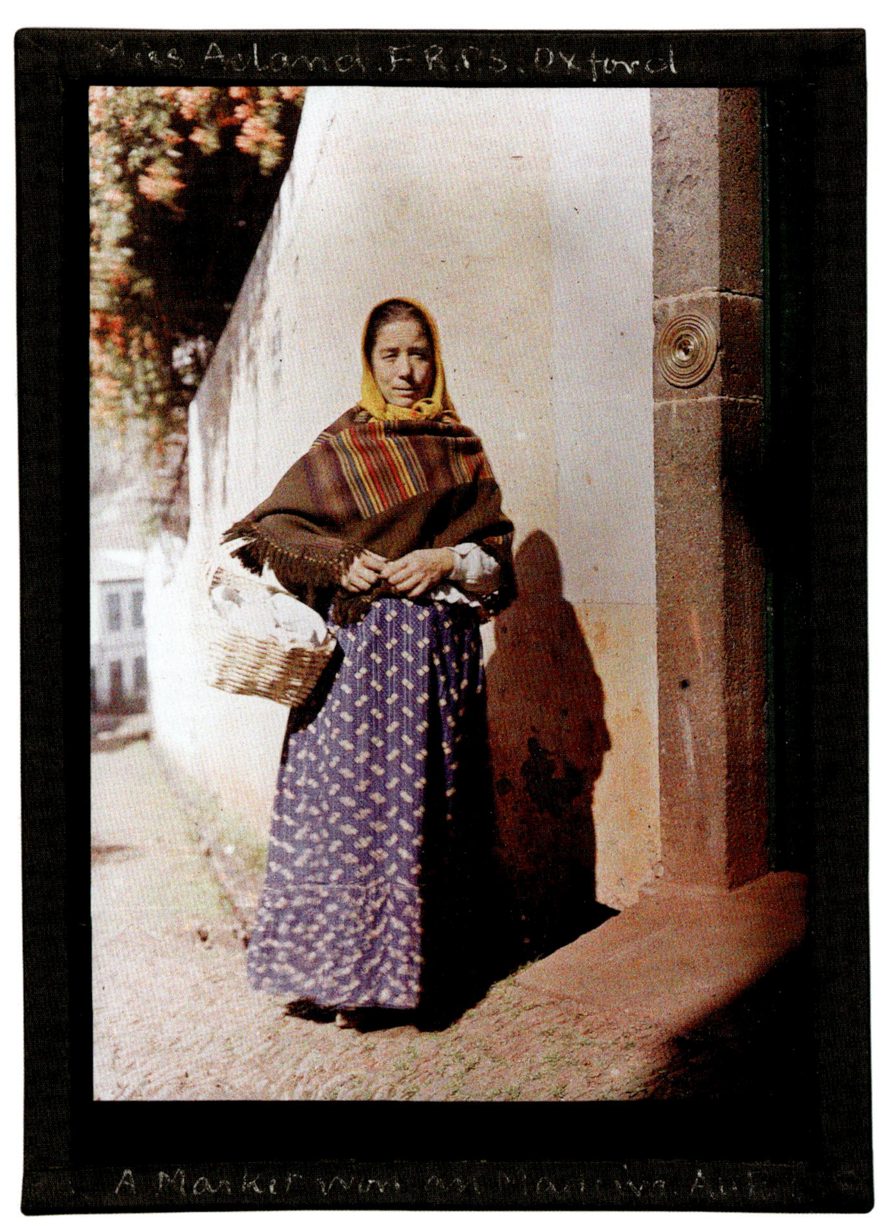
Miss Acland. F.R.P.S. Oxford

OPPOSITE

186. *"A Market Woman"*

A woman by a doorway on the Calçada da Cabouqueira
Funchal, January 1910 ?

9 × 12 cm Autochrome plate (reverse, ×1·3)
Museum of the History of Science, Inventory no. 20827

According to Ellen M. Taylor, in *Madeira: Its Scenery and How to See It* (1882), the dress of the women of the island was "picturesque, but expensive, as the striped petticoats of many bright colours are finely spun and closely woven". This woman appears to be wearing everyday clothes, but the colours of the fabric are bold and beautiful all the same. She is standing by a doorway of a quinta on the Calçada da Cabouqueira, the street disappearing out of sight to the north-east. The contents of her basket are difficult to make out, but are probably loaves of bread or other baked goods.

Like Miss Acland's other screen plates, the labelling on this Autochrome is on the reverse (the side of the plate away from the emulsion, which is protected with a cover glass). The image as reproduced is therefore laterally reversed: to be seen in the correct orientation Autochrome plates must be viewed from the emulsion side, which is the opposite to a normal negative. Autochromes were exposed back-to-front in the camera, which is to say through the glass, rather than directly onto the sensitive surface — a consequence of the fact that the light had to pass through the filter screen before reaching the emulsion, the screen having been applied to the glass first during manufacture (and rolled under enormous pressure to squash the starch grains). The thickness of the glass required a tell-tale correction to be made to the focussing scales of cameras used for Autochrome work and the ground glass focussing screen to be mounted in reverse, matt surface towards the photographer.

Ellen M. Taylor, *Madeira: Its Scenery and How to See It* (London, 1882), p. 62.

OVERLEAF LEFT

187. *The Guitar Player*

Grace Helen Douglas (1885–1984) ?, playing a guitarra
Funchal, between November 1911 and May 1912 ?

9 × 12 cm Autochrome plate (×1·3)
Museum of the History of Science, Inventory no. 19113

The beautiful twelve-stringed instrument this woman is holding is a Portuguese guitar (guitarra de Lisboa). Miss Acland acquired a guitarra in January 1910, by which time she was already taking lessons on the Machete de Braga (a ukulele with four strings) and the Rajão (a small six-stringed guitar). The guitarra was "a lovely instrument", but finding music for it was difficult.

This portrait is an excellent example of the Autochrome's ability to render neutral tones faithfully.

OVERLEAF RIGHT

188. *A Young Girl in Traditional Costume*

An unidentified child in traditional costume
Funchal, Christmas 1911 ?

9 × 12 cm Autochrome plate (×1·3)
Museum of the History of Science, Inventory no. 29246

The dress of this girl is typical of the elaborate costumes worn by the Madeirenses on festival days. Her distinctive conical hat is known as a *carapuça*. The location of the portrait is recognizable as Reid's Hotel from the steps. The reason the girl visited the hotel is suggested by a letter from Miss Acland in which she mentions the Christmas celebrations in 1911. "There was some good music", she wrote, "& children from a school did Madeira dances & songs in costume which was very pretty & then they did some tableaux — Scenes of Life in Madeira".

MS. Acland d. 110, fol. 221.

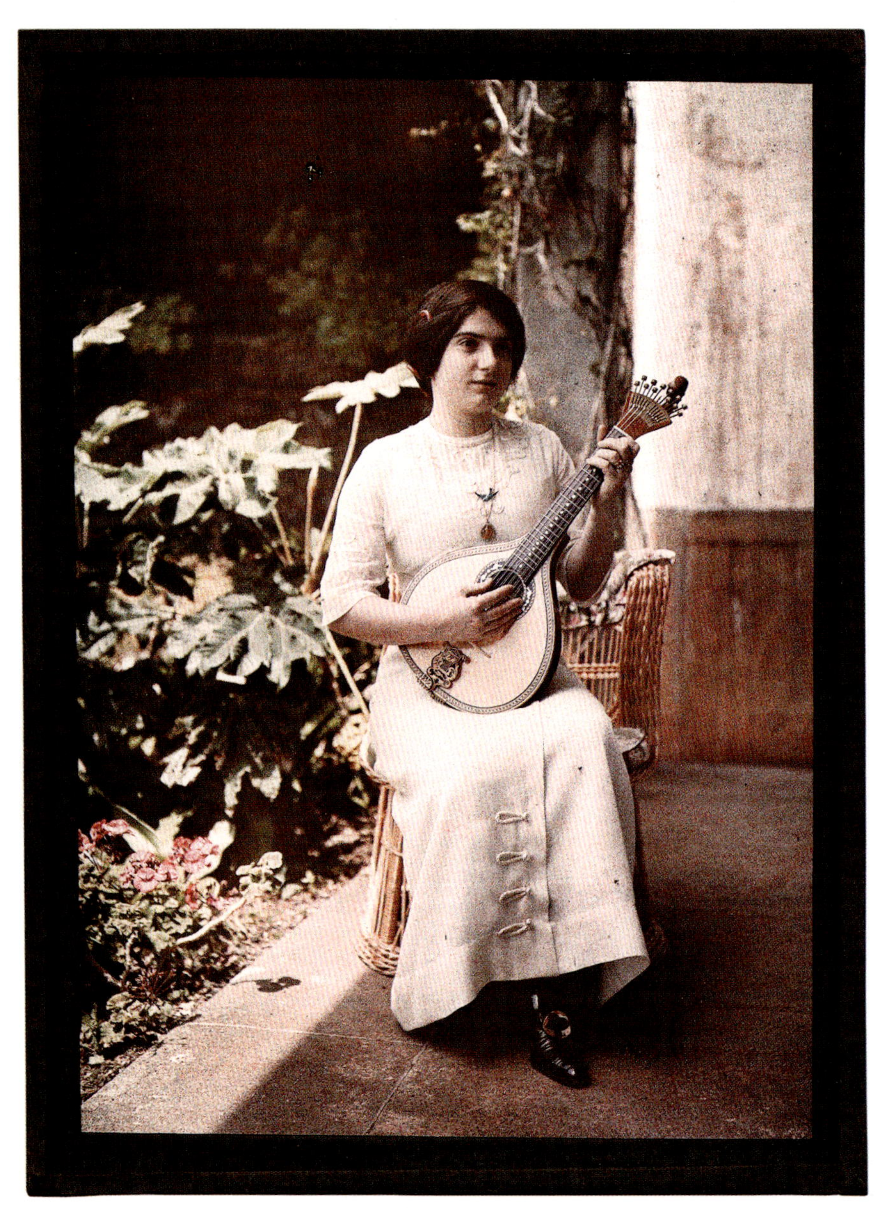

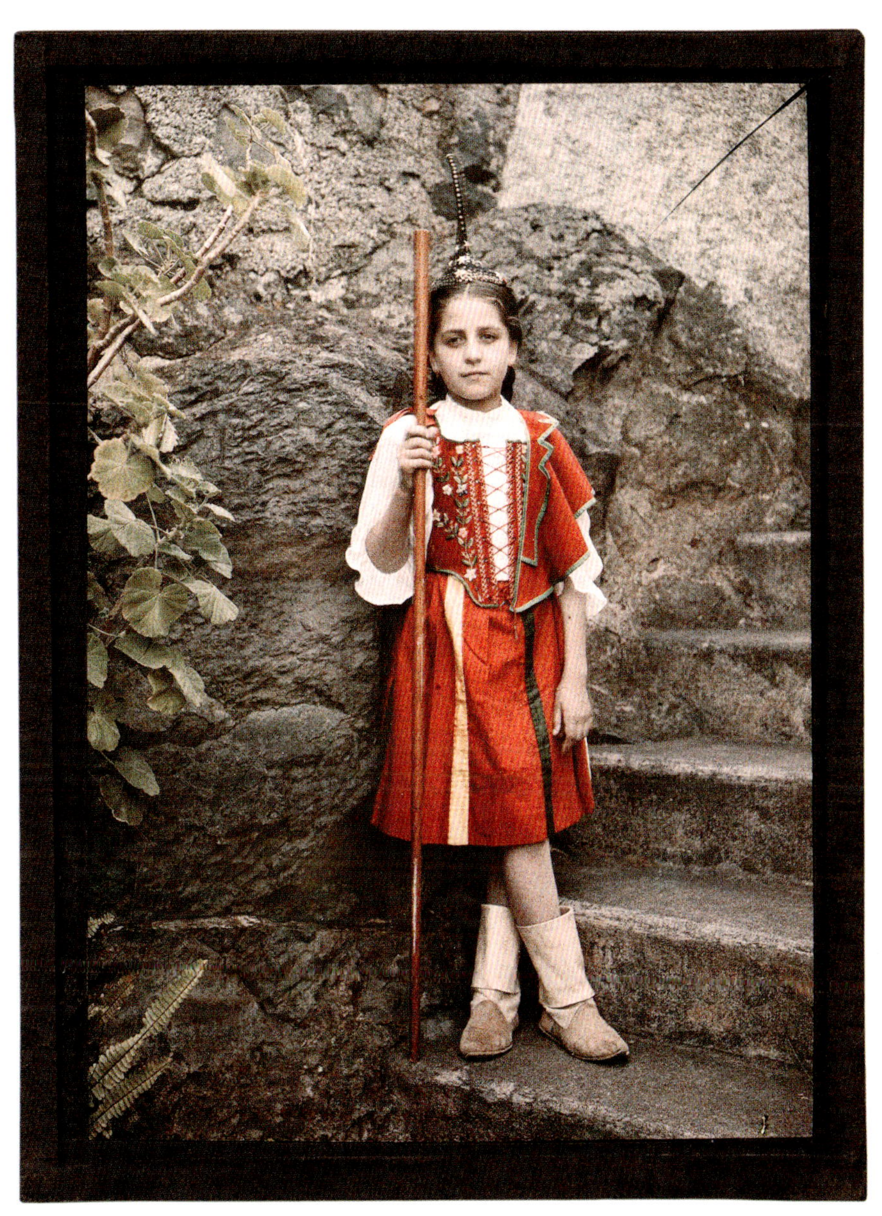

189. *Among the Flowers*

A view in the garden of the Quinta Stanford ?
Funchal, between December 1909 and May 1910 ?

9 × 12 cm Autochrome plate (×1·3)
Museum of the History of Science, Inventory no. 25604

This artfully framed view was probably taken in the Quinta Stanford, which has a fountain matching the one just visible at 9 o'clock in the image. There is no record of Miss Acland visiting the Quinta, but it was barely a quarter of a mile from Reid's and belonged to Charles Thomas-Stanford (1858–1932), a graduate of Oriel College. In 1909 Stanford published *Leaves from a Madeira Garden*, in which he described his home's advantageous position, to the west of Funchal:

> This may now be described as the Strangers' quarter, for here, as elsewhere, those who are free to select their own place of residence seem to be drawn by some mysterious law to move westwards. ... In this direction are the hotels frequented by visitors, and here, on a slope above the Dry River, is the Quinta in which we live among our flowers. It faces south-east, and looks across the bay ... and across such portions of the city as are not hidden by the intervening ridges to the great hills beyond. ... It would be difficult to find a fairer setting for a garden, a nobler combination of sea and mountain, with just the sufficient evidence of man's neighbourhood and handiwork to emphasize the natural grandeur of the scene.

When Stanford took over the house from a Portuguese man "more concerned with farming than with flowers" it was known as the Quinta Pitta. It is now the Quinta da Vista Alegre.

Many of Miss Acland's photographs adopt a compositional language foreign to the modern eye, but one of great subtlety nevertheless. The care she has taken in positioning the component parts of this picture, in multiple layers, is easily overlooked, as is the ease with which the eye is led through the garden to the distant mountains, the view framed both by the trellis-work in the centre and the trees on the edges of the plate.

Charles Thomas-Stanford, *Leaves from a Madeira Garden* (London, 1909), pp. 33–5; Ibid., p. 35.

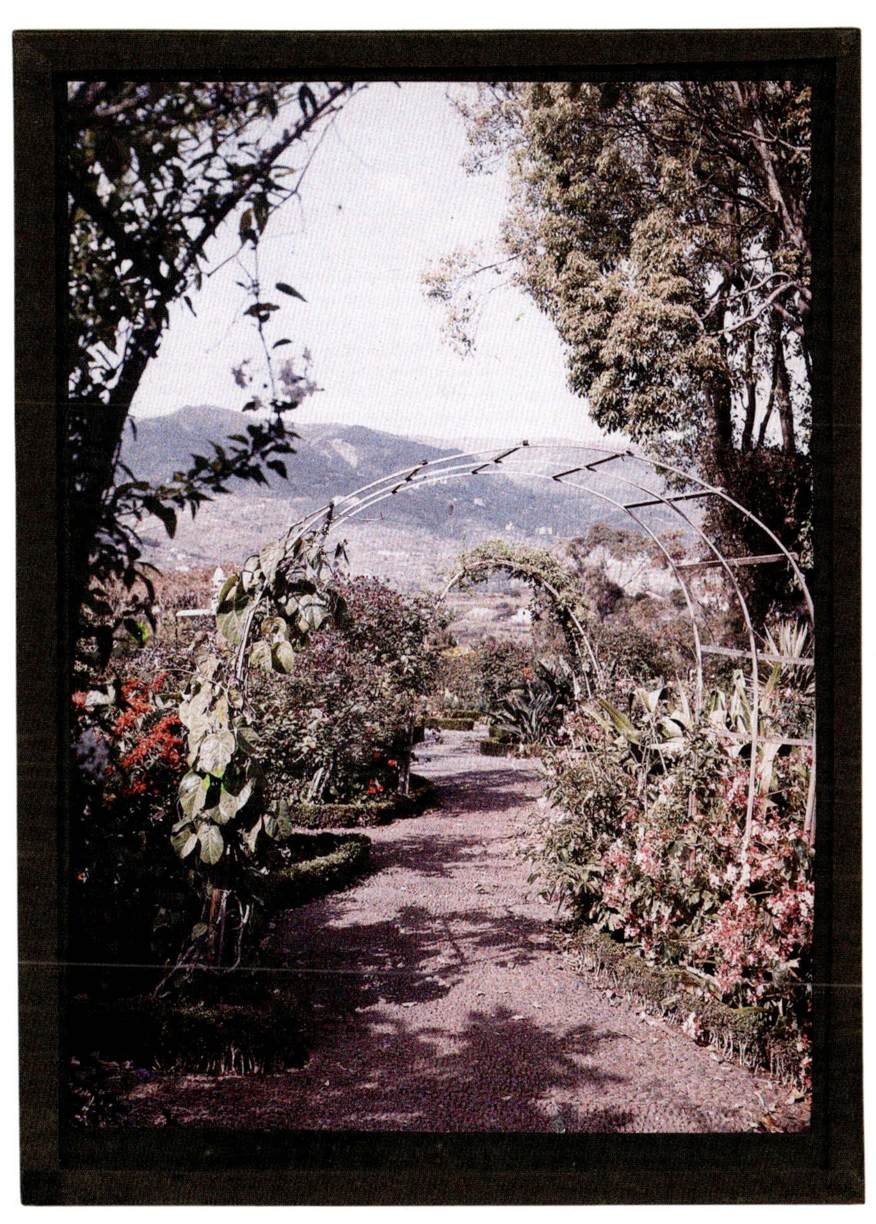

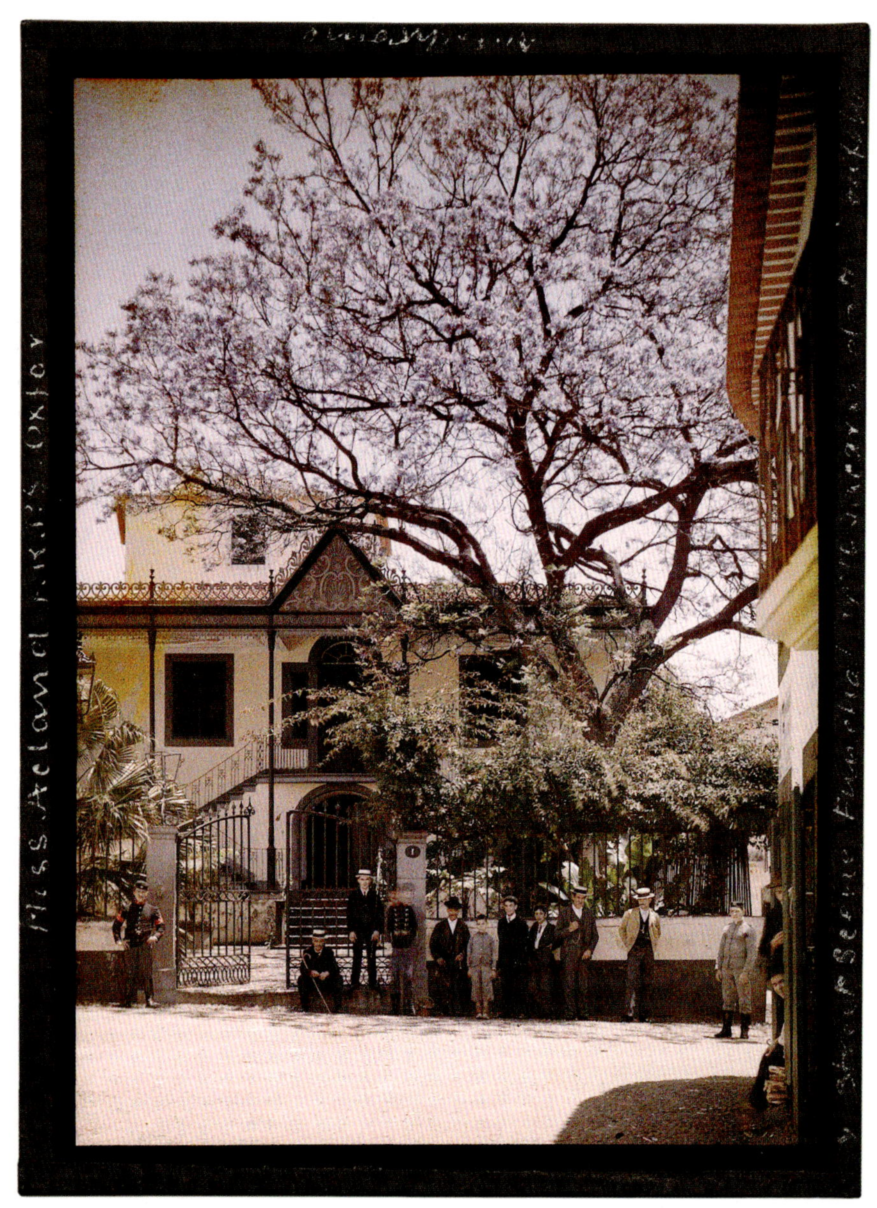

OPPOSITE

190. *"Street Scene Funchal with Jacaranda mimosafolia"*

Rua das Mercès 1, from the Rua dos Netos
Funchal, April 1910 or later ?

9 × 12 cm Autochrome plate (reverse, ×1·3)
Museum of the History of Science, Inventory no. 19451

Street scenes are as rare among Miss Acland's photographs of Madeira as they are of England, but equally fascinating. In this example thirteen men can be seen watching her make the exposure. Three are soldiers from a nearby barracks, the man on the far left identifiable as a sergeant from his red armbands and gold buttons. Another, on the right, is wearing a plain grey uniform, with black cap and leather boots. The third soldier, in front of the pillar, failed to stand to attention long enough to be recorded on the plate other than as a ghostly blur. Of the other men, several are dressed in three-piece suits and straw boaters. The man standing in the gateway is holding a mace with an ornate silver top, the significance of which is unknown.

None of Miss Acland's Autochromes is labelled with a date, although some can be dated from her correspondence or annotations on the boxes in which they are stored. The order in which the rest are presented here is tentative and based partly on an estimate of the number of plates she used each year, as deduced from the batch numbers (*No. de Fabrication*) and expiry dates (*à employer avant*) stamped on the boxes. In the future it may be possible to derive a more definitive chronology from a forensic examination of the similarities and differences that exist between groups of plates in such characteristics as the size of the starch grains, the spectra of the dyes used, and the amount of carbon black present as filler.

The building in the background in the photograph is the Clube Funchalense, a Portuguese social institution where afternoon receptions and balls were held. Miss Acland's principal interest in the scene was the jacaranda tree, which remains one of the largest in Funchal.

OVERLEAF LEFT

191. *The Serras in Shadow*

The Villa Victoria and the Serras, from Reid's garden
Funchal, between December 1909 and May 1910 ?

9 × 12 cm Autochrome plate (×1·3)
Museum of the History of Science, Inventory no. 14234

This photograph was taken from below the garden gate of Reid's. The view is looking north towards the Serras (the mountains surrounding Funchal) enshrouded in violet shadows typical of early Autochromes. The building in the foreground is the Villa Victoria, where the exiled Charles I, Emperor of Austria, would later take up residence. Lining the path are vibrant red and purple varieties of bougainvillea. Miss Acland returned to this spot regularly, also photographing the mountains under snow with the Paget Colour process.

OVERLEAF RIGHT

192. *"Barberton Daisies"*

Still life with *Gerbera Jamesonii* and avocados
Funchal ?, between December 1909 and May 1910 ?

9 × 12 cm Autochrome plate (reverse, ×1·3)
Museum of the History of Science, Inventory no. 25315

Barberton daisies are native to South Africa and the hills surrounding the town of the name in what is now Mpumalanga, formerly Eastern Transvaal. Their botanical name honours Robert Jameson (1832–1908), who collected the first specimens sent to Kew in 1884. The plant only came into common cultivation after 1900, making the blooms still something of a novelty, and a colourful one, when photographed by Miss Acland.

Avocados were also rare in England, except at Christmas, suggesting the photograph was taken in Madeira. The jug is the same as other pottery only seen in Miss Acland's rooms in Reid's — in Oxford she collected Aller Vale ware from Torquay.

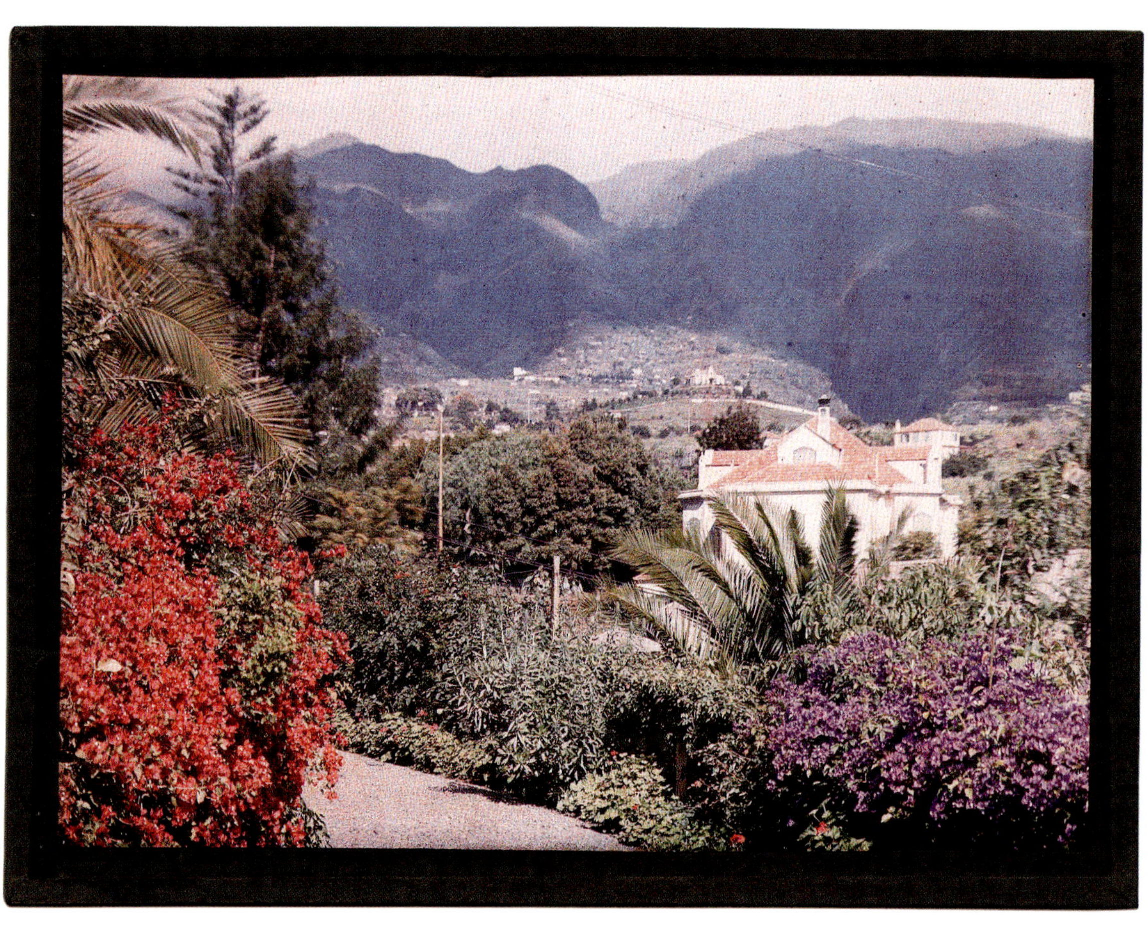

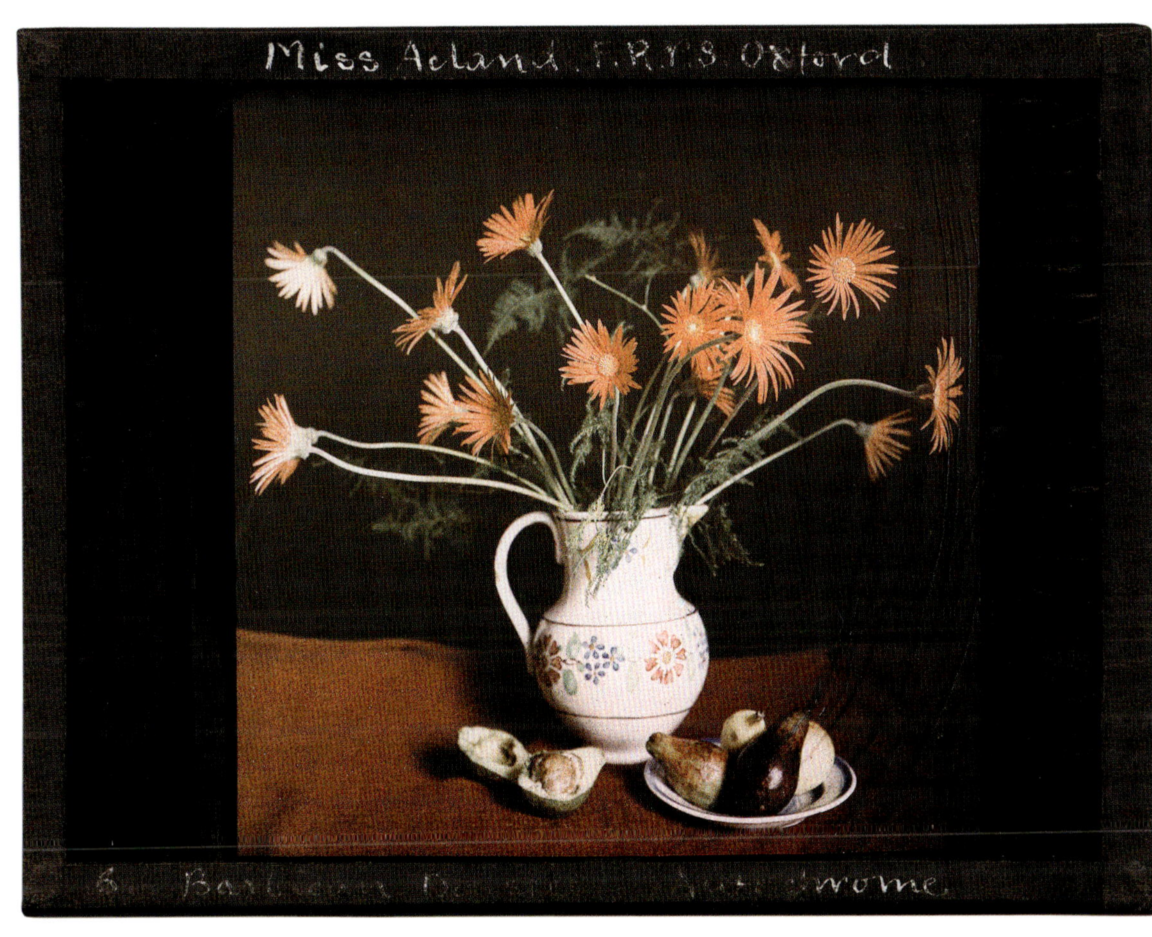
Miss Acland. F.R.P.S Oxford

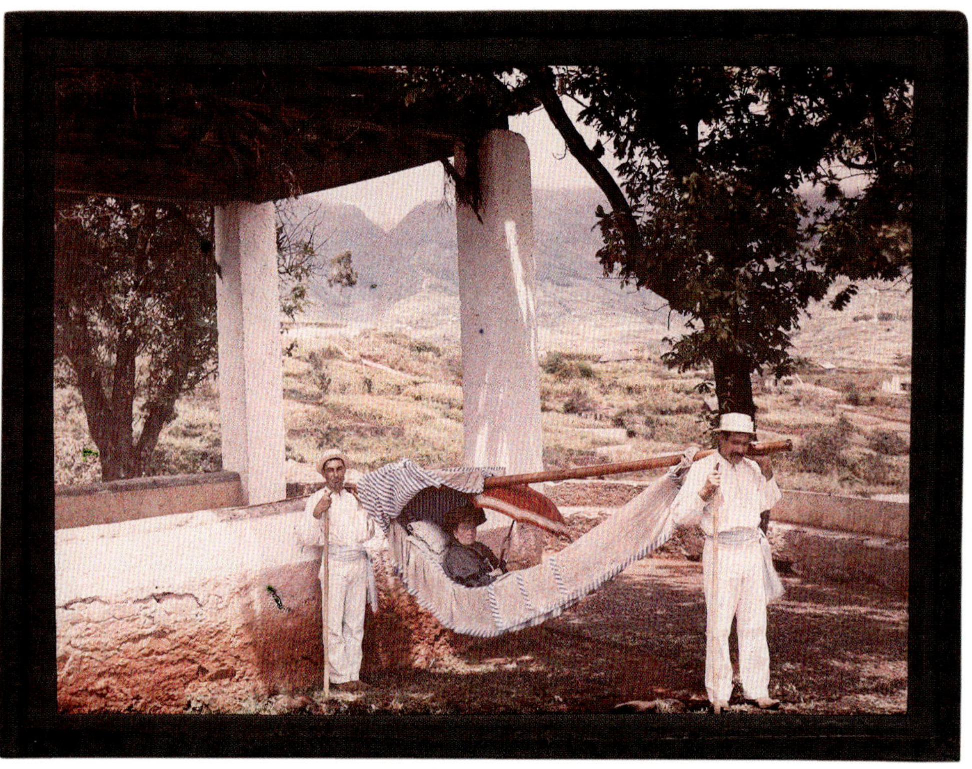

ABOVE

193. *Hammock Party*

Sarah Angelina Acland, carried by Jacintho Fernandes and Sousa Calceteira, at the Capela da Nazaré
Funchal, 1910 or 1911 ?

9 × 12 cm Autochrome plate (×1·1)
Museum of the History of Science, Inventory no. 17810

The *rêde*, a traditional form of transport on Madeira, was one of the island's great attractions for Miss Acland. "It is such a gain to me having it as I can do what I have never done in my life before", she wrote. Her bearers, Jacintho and Sousa, were delightful men, "most faithful & devoted", fast walkers and punctual.

From 1900 Miss Acland employed a 'lady's companion' in addition to her nurse (Caroline Lawrence). Jenny Grimston, her first, was a useful photographer but left in 1911, taking up with another lady in Madeira, much to Miss Acland's distress and embarrassment. Helen Douglas, her replacement, was "a remarkably nice girl", but with her "striking appearance" Miss Acland doubted whether she ought to be about so much in a hotel.

MS. Acland d. 110, fols. 11–13; MS. Acland d. 111, fol. 23; MS. Acland d. 110, fols. 269–70; MS. Acland d. 111, fols. 34–5.

OPPOSITE

194 & 195. *Telephoto Views*

A Union Castle ship, from the Avista Navios; The Forte da Penha de França, from Reid's gardens
Funchal, between December 1913 and May 1914 ?

9 × 12 cm Autochrome plates (×1·1)
Museum of the History of Science, Inv. nos. 15225 & 18222

These views were taken with Miss Acland's Dallmeyer Adon lens. Autochrome telephotography was far from trivial due to the slow speed of the plates and the need to use a correcting filter over the lens to compensate for the imperfect panchromatic response of the emulsion. The photograph of one of the Union Castle steamers on which Miss Acland travelled to Madeira suffers from the long exposure. In her view of the Forte da Penha de França (the barracks at the end of the breakwater), on the other hand, the movement of the sea and the surf adds to the charm of the picture.

Visible on the far left edge of the second plate is the tower of the Capela da Penha de França. In the middle, on the cliff top, the gardens of the Quinta Vigia glow in the golden light of the evening.

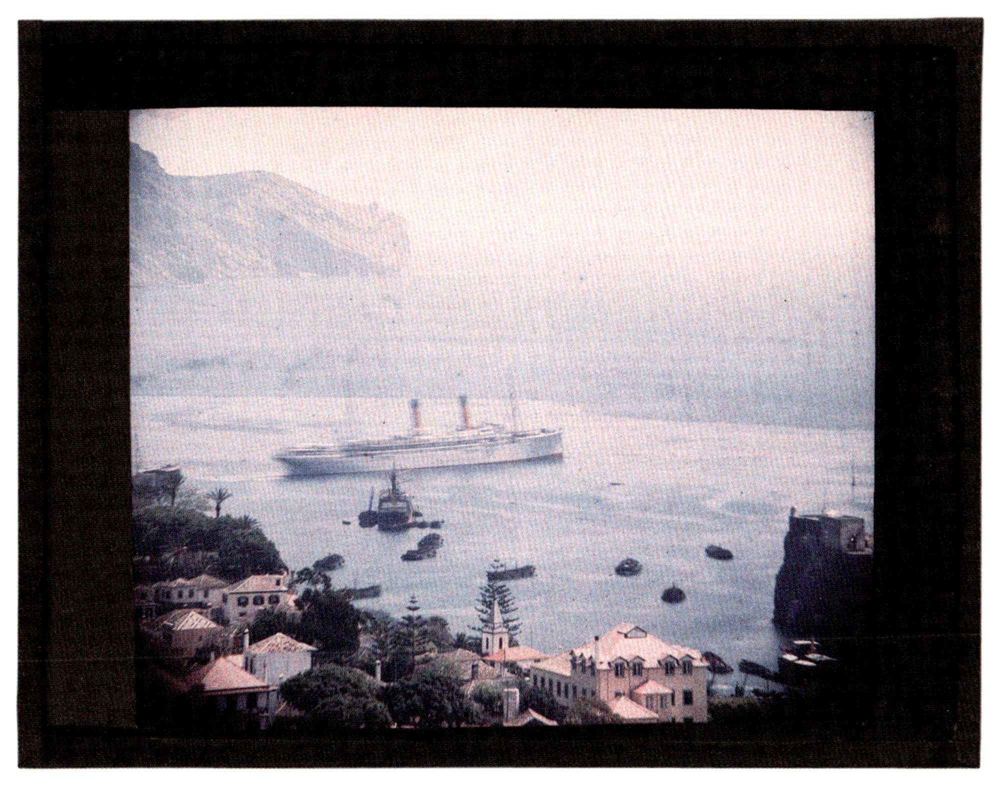

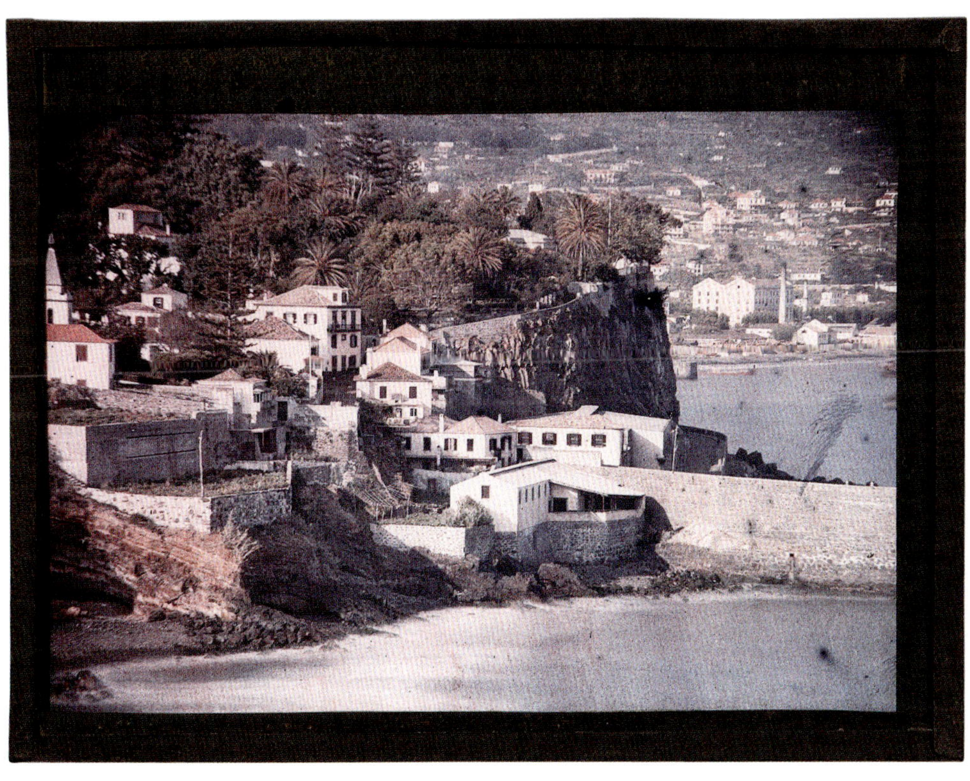

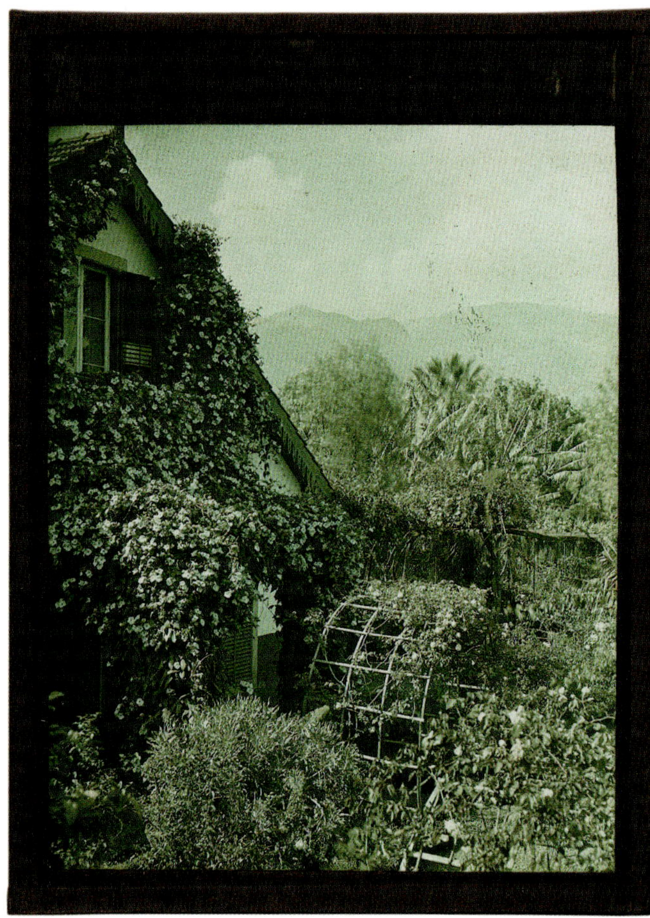

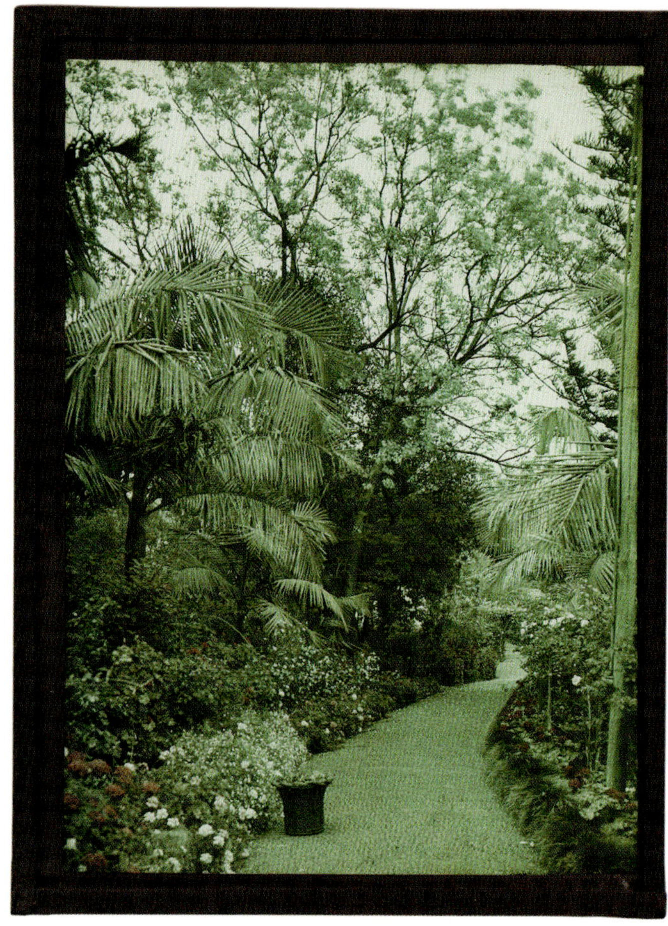

ABOVE & OPPOSITE TOP

196–198. *Spoiled Autochrome Plates*

Unknown quinta; Reid's garden; Ruskin at Glenfinlas
Madeira, 1908 to 1915; Oxford, June 1913 to May 1917

9 × 12 cm Autochrome plates, one shown digitally restored
Museum of History of Science, Inv. nos. 27826, 18689 & 29265

Most Autochromes contain a range of minor flaws, some present at manufacture, others arising during exposure and development. These examples are more unusual in having turned completely green, although a hint of colour still remains in places. The transformation has probably occurred over several decades due to the green dye spreading. This is unfortunate, as the landscapes were once fine pictures and the interior is the earliest colour photograph of Millais's famous portrait of Ruskin. Digital restoration is partly successful in reviving the Ruskin plate (opposite, top right). The portrait is hanging over Miss Acland's writing table in Clevedon House. The frame above is Elizabeth Siddal's *We Are Seven*, a drawing based on Wordsworth's poem of the same title.

OPPOSITE BOTTOM

199. *Rainbow over Park Town*

A rainbow from Clevedon House, Park Town
Oxford, autumn 1907?

9 × 12 cm Autochrome plate (×1·15)
Museum of the History of Science, Inventory no. 16181

The colours have survived well in this Autochrome but the extensive tape masking the image is showing signs of deterioration. Rainbows were considered a tour de force of early colour photography. In 1901, when Herschel was given a MacDonough (Joly) process plate of a *Rainbow in the Bois de Boulogne* by Charles N. Crewdson (b. 1870), he labelled it "very precious", adding that "to the best of my belief this is the only photograph of a rainbow hitherto obtained". Miss Acland also photographed the weather over Funchal. Her interest in the subject was due to the artistic influence of Ruskin, who recommended studying clouds, and the scientific legacy of her father.

Private collection.

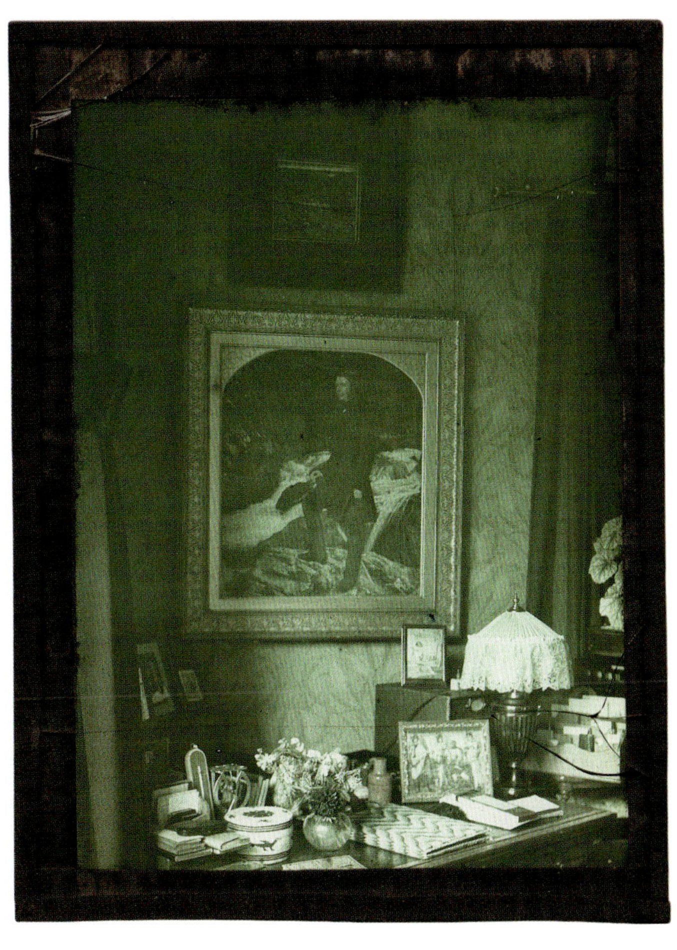

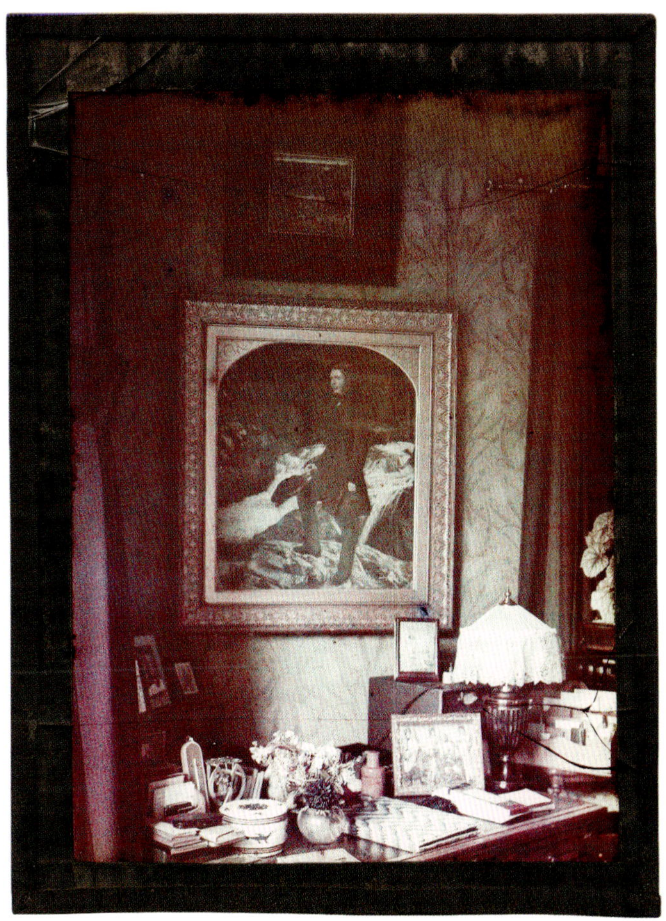

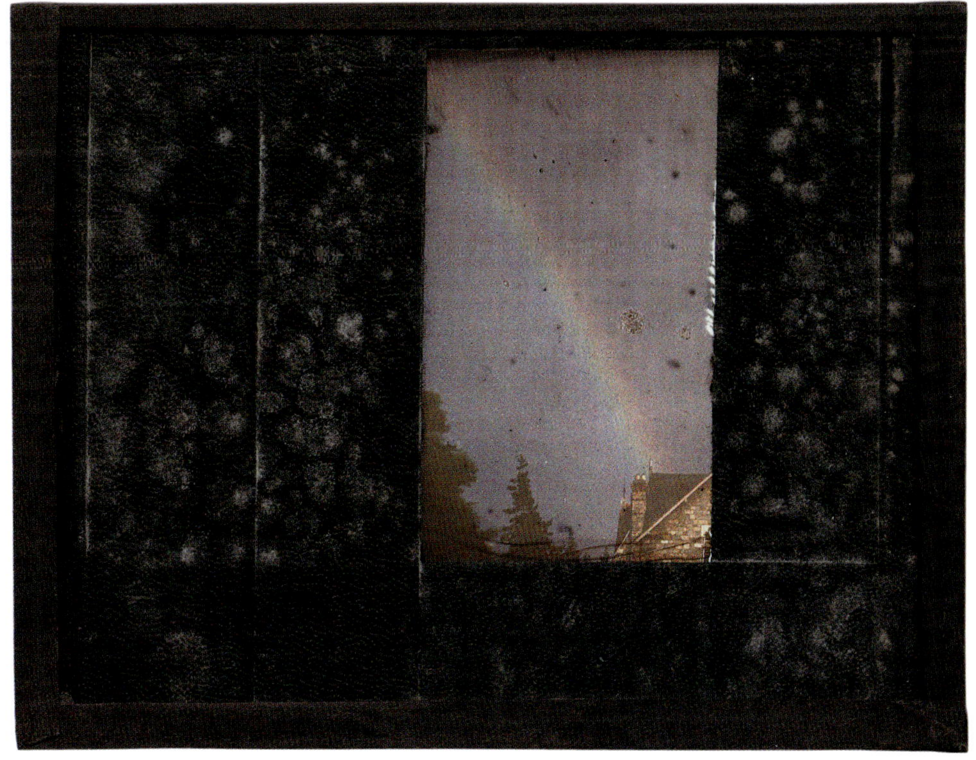

OMNICOLORE PLATES

The sensational success of the Autochrome prompted the release of numerous rival screen-plate processes by the Lumières' competitors. The first alternative Miss Acland tried was the Omnicolore process, a patent of Ducos du Hauron and his nephew Raymond de Bercegol. The Omnicolore plate had threatened to pre-empt the Autochrome: examples were shown in Paris on 19 April 1907 and an advertisement — the first to be seen for a screen-plate process — appeared in the *British Journal of Photography* in May, announcing their sale from 1 June. In the event it was not until January 1909 in France, and May in England, that the plates actually reached the market. Nevertheless, they were well received, in stark contrast to earlier pretenders to the Autochrome's throne. Had the Omnicolore been fortunate enough to appear first, it was claimed, it might have created just as much of a stir.

Omnicolore plates are similar to Autochromes in consisting of a monochrome panchromatic emulsion coated over a screen of microscopic coloured filters. However, rather than randomly distributed potato starch grains, the screen is arranged as a geometric mosaic of coloured gelatine squares. This was created by printing a gelatine plate with two perpendicular series of parallel lines in mutually repellent coloured inks, then staining the interstices a third colour. The main benefit of this method was the increased transparency of the plates, which allowed shorter exposure times and dispensed with the need for an extra-bright lamp when exhibiting them by projection.

Although the Omnicolore generated a good deal of excitement when released, in Britain practitioners of the process were few and far between, making Miss Acland's specimens all the more noteworthy.

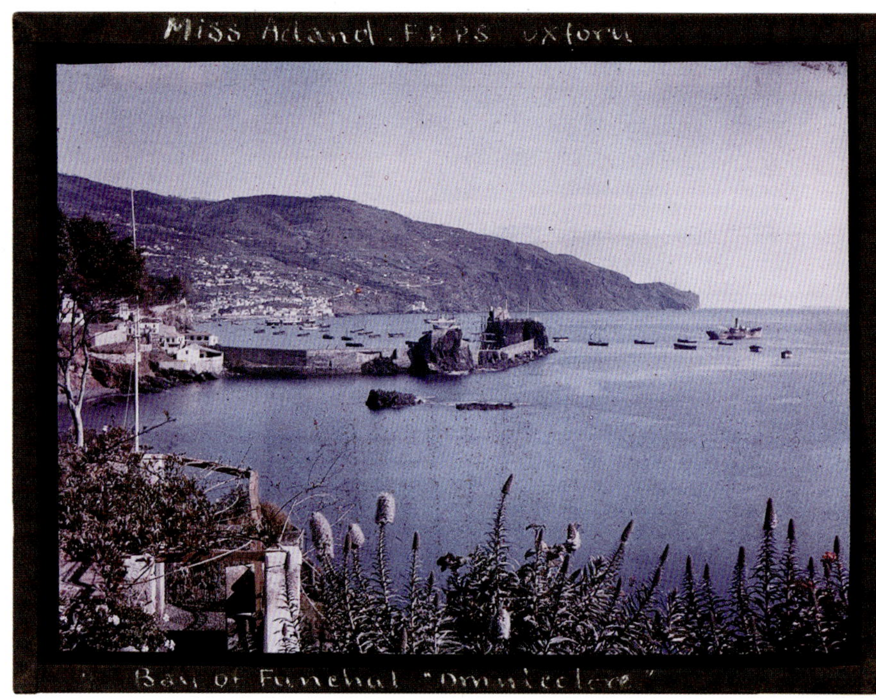

200. *"Bay of Funchal"*

The Bay of Funchal, from Reid's gardens
Madeira, between December 1909 and May 1910 ?
9 × 12 cm Omnicolore plate (reverse, image reversed)
Museum of the History of Science, Inventory no. 27772

The grounds of Reid's Hotel command an impressive view over the Bay of Funchal. The existence of an almost identical exposure to this on an Autochrome suggests the scene was one of the first Miss Acland turned to when assessing the capabilities of the new Omnicolore plates. The predominance of blue is typical of the process and in this case eminently fitted to the subject.

The breakwater visible in the scene is the Pontinha, where visitors landed on arriving at Madeira. At the sea end is the Loo Rock, surmounted by the seventeenth-century Fortaleza de Nossa Senhora da Conceição do Ilhéu; halfway along is the smaller, eighteenth-century Forte de São José. The headland in the distance, about four miles off, is the Ponta do Garajau (Tern Point). In the foreground are seed-heads of Pride of Madeira, *Echium fastuosum*.

In the reproduction above the image has been digitally reversed in the mount to allow the inscription to be visible while preserving the correct orientation of the scene.

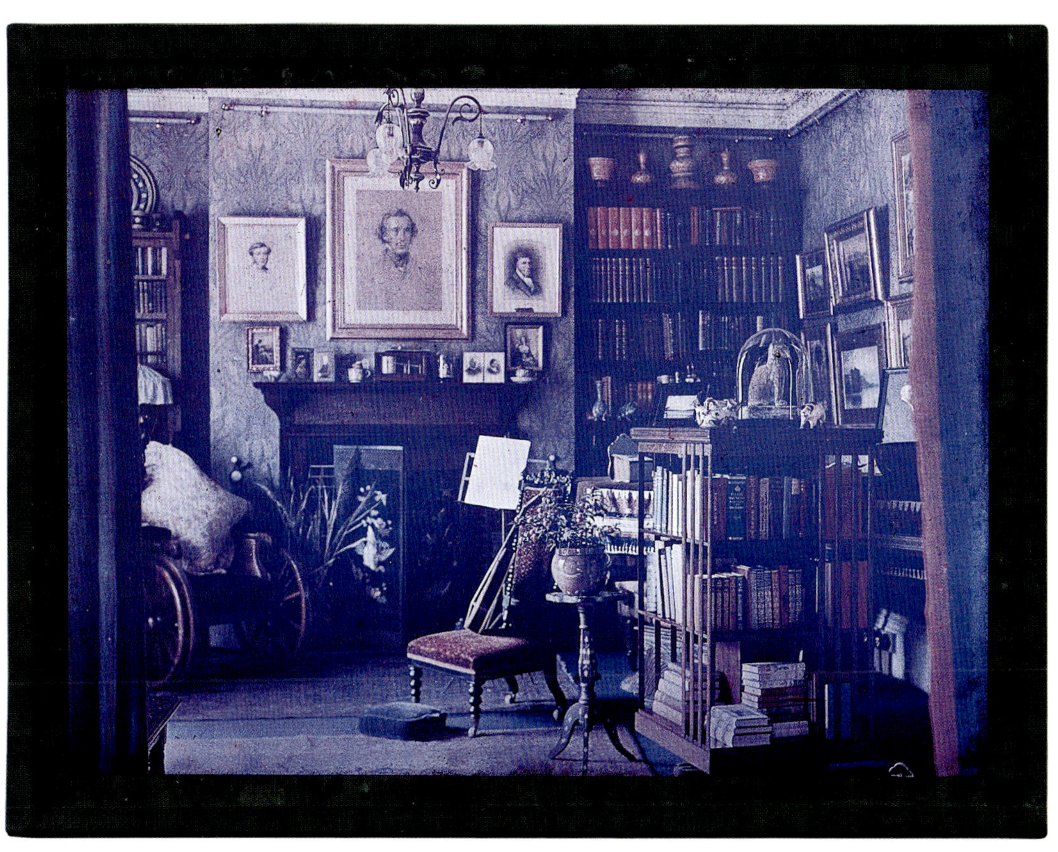

201. *An Elegant Interior*

Drawing room, Clevedon House, looking west
Oxford, August 1910?

9 × 12 cm Omnicolore plate (× 1·2)
Museum of the History of Science, Inventory no. 21644

The interior of Miss Acland's house in Park Town was as tastefully arranged as her Broad Street home had been. This is a view of the drawing room, looking west. Although the resolution of Omnicolore plates is relatively poor, some of the titles on the revolving bookcase can be made out: the large blue volume is Whitaker's *Peerage, Baronetage, Knightage and Companionage* for 1910; to the left is *Who's Who*; to the right Whitaker's *Almanac*. On top of the bookcase sits a wooden effigy of a cat from Sakkara, Egypt, said to date from 2000 B.C. In the middle of the mantel is Miss Acland's barograph, under a crayon drawing of Acland by George Richmond. The inscription below is from Wordsworth's poem "To A Skylark", the same as in the library at Broad Street: "Type of the wise, who soar, but never roam, True to the kindred points of heaven and home".

For women, the cultural functions of interior photography were reciprocal, allowing them to exercise artistic skill and taste in both the arrangement of the room and the taking of the photograph. In Clevedon House Miss Acland had sole responsibility for the furniture and fittings of her drawing room; in Broad Street she had inherited the legacy of her mother, whose own ideas were tempered by those of her husband (even if his primary domain was the library). Acland promoted the domestic ideal as much as the women in his household did: indeed, when Ruskin first read Coventry Patmore's *The Angel in the House* to Mrs Acland in 1854, she disliked it, much to his "annoyment", so he persuaded Acland to buy a copy instead.

MS. Acland d. 72, fol. 67.

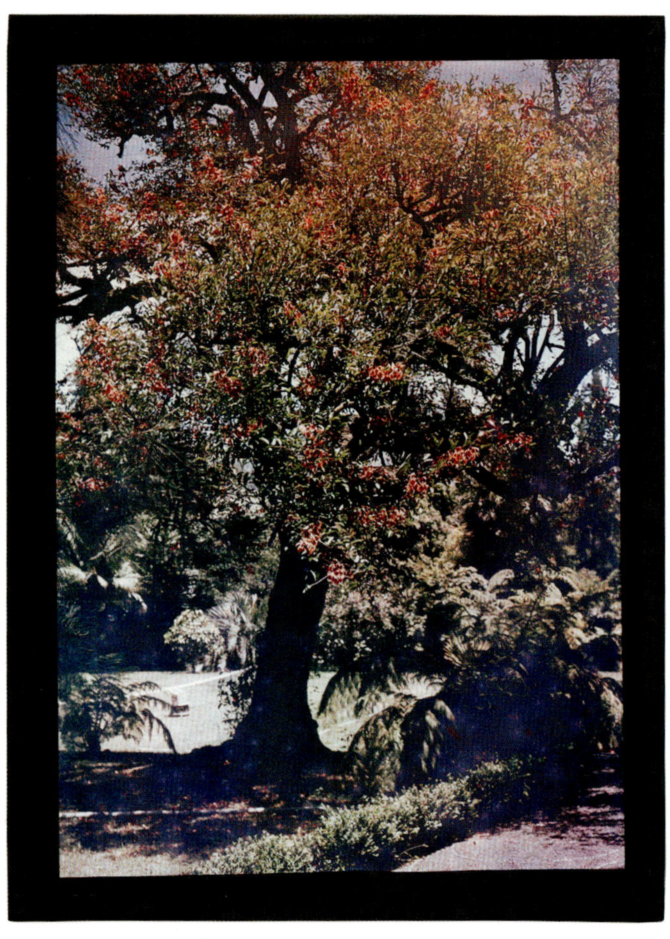

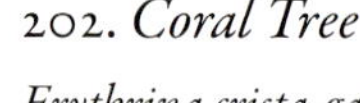

202. *Coral Tree*

Erythrina crista-galli, in the Quinta Vigia gardens ?
Funchal, May 1910 ?

9 × 12 cm Omnicolore plate
Museum of the History of Science, Inventory no. 22154

Although typified by its blues, the Omnicolore process could also capture vivid reds, such as displayed by the flowers of this Coral Tree. A Sanger Shepherd separation negative of the blooms of *Erythrina crista-galli* also survives amongst Miss Acland's photographs, but must have been taken in Gibraltar since she submitted it to the Society of Colour Photographers exhibition in 1907.

Omnicolore plates were manufactured by the 'Société anonyme des Plaques, Pellicules & Papiers Photographiques J. Jougla', of Joinville-le-Pont, in the Paris suburbs. In 1911 the Jougla company was taken over by Lumière & Cie, whereupon both types of plate were marketed by the 'Union Photographique Industrielle, établissements Lumière et Jougla réunis'.

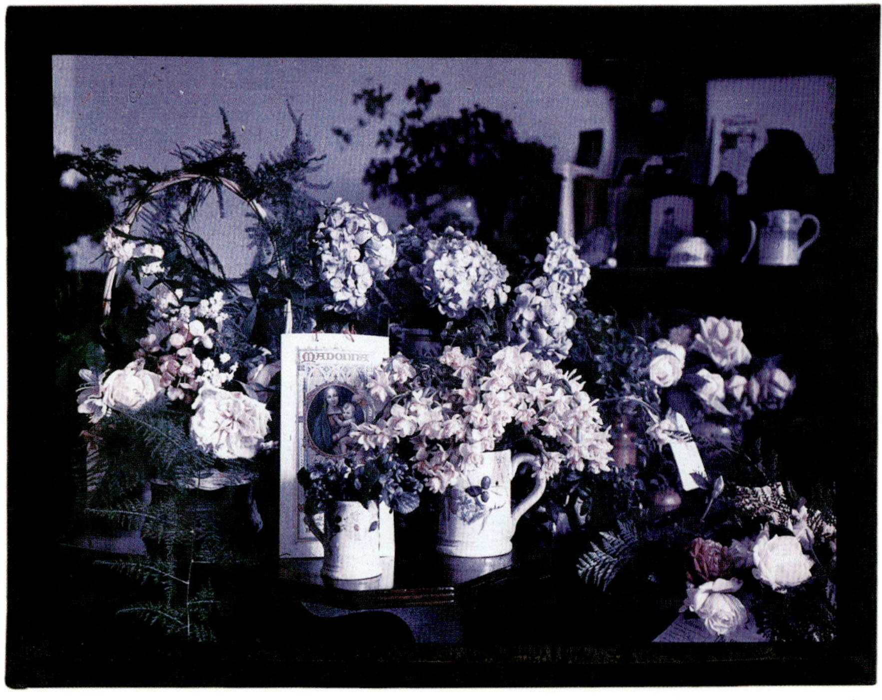

203. *Christmas Flowers*

Still life with *Viola*, *Narcissus* and *Hydrangea*
Funchal, Christmas 1910

9 × 12 cm Omnicolore plate
Museum of the History of Science, Inventory no. 16781

Miss Acland was obliged to lead a quiet life on Madeira in the winter of 1910 to 1911, due to the cholera. She took only two colour photographs, one of which was this still life, the other an Autochrome of the same subject. The photograph was taken at Christmas — several of the baskets of flowers are gifts, labelled with tags. In the bottom right-hand corner is the edge of a Western Telegraph Company telegram, presumably conveying Christmas greetings from one of her brothers back in England. On the mantel are various photographic prints, including a copy of one of Miss Acland's own portraits of her father.

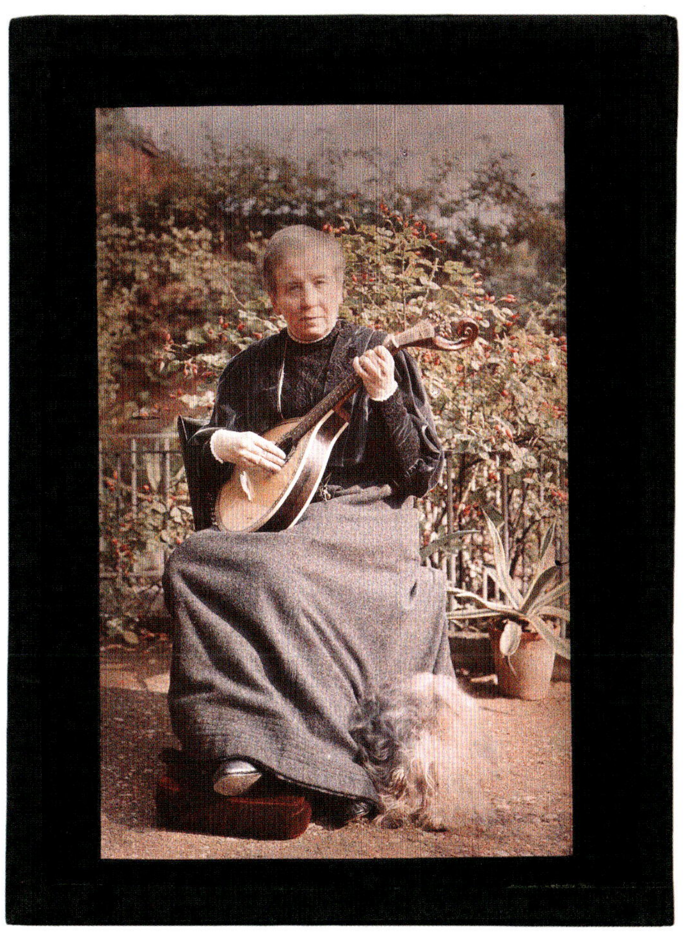

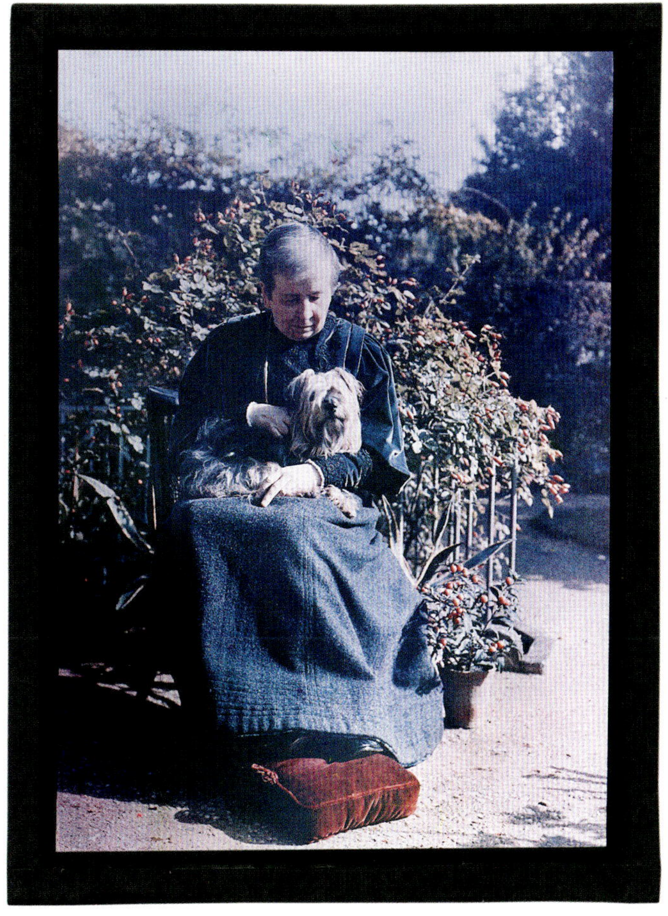

ABOVE

204 & 205. *Companions*

Sarah Angelina Acland (1849–1930) and her dog Chum
Oxford, August 1910 ?

9 × 12 cm Autochrome and Omnicolore plates
Museum of the History of Science, Inv. nos. 17853 & 25554

These self-portraits were taken by Miss Acland on the same day, on Autochrome and Omnicolore plates. The Omnicolore allowed a shorter exposure: Chummy appears as a blur in the Autochrome and even Miss Acland's face is smudged. The colour characteristics of the two processes are very different.

Chummy was Miss Acland's last dog. A tablet in his memory in the wall at the end of the garden at Clevedon House reads "My Devoted Chum / August 1909 / Laid to Rest March 30 1920".

OVERLEAF

206 & 207. *Flora*

Mary Agnes Brinton, née Hope (b. *c.* 1872, d. after 1923)
Oxford, August 1910 ?

9 × 12 cm Autochrome and Omnicolore plates (×1·3)
Museum of the History of Science, Inventory nos. 23051 & 19252

Miss Acland's inspiration for these portraits, whether Roman mythology or medieval legend, can only be guessed, but the result is beautiful examples of the use of the Autochrome and Omnicolore in portraiture, and an instructive comparison of the two processes. The Autochrome displays its typical warm pink tone and granular filter structure, the Omnicolore cooler tints, but cleaner highlights and shadows. The portraits are among Miss Acland's most memorable colour photographs, especially in light of her family's long association with the Pre-Raphaelites and their patrons.

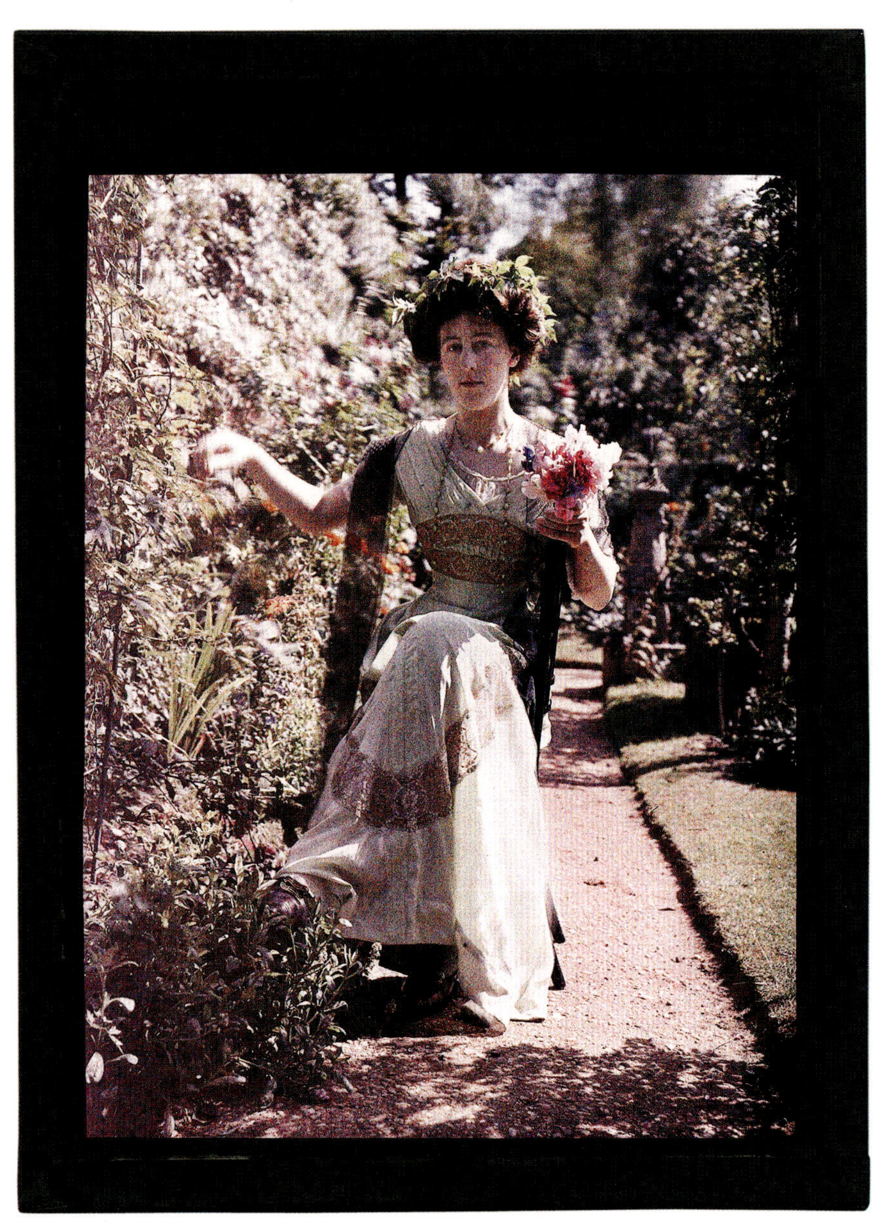

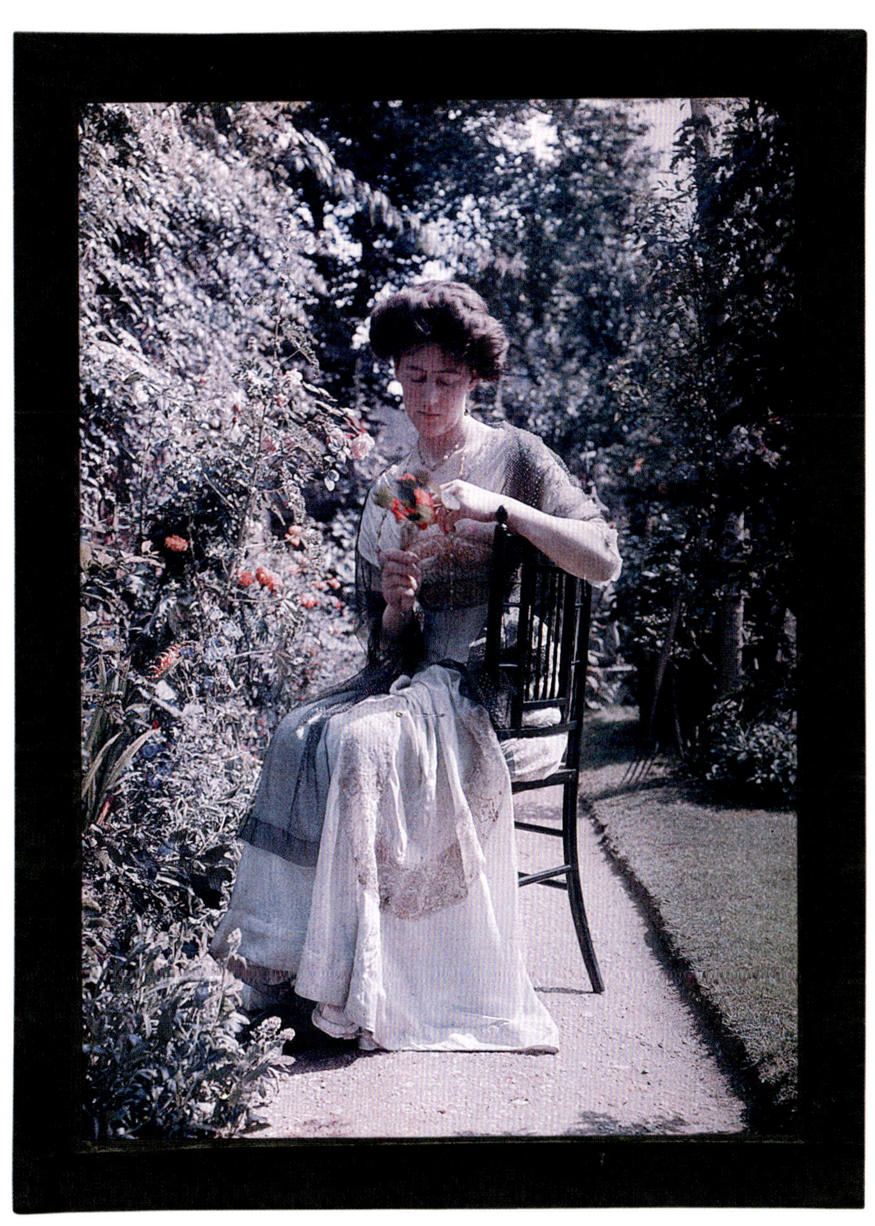

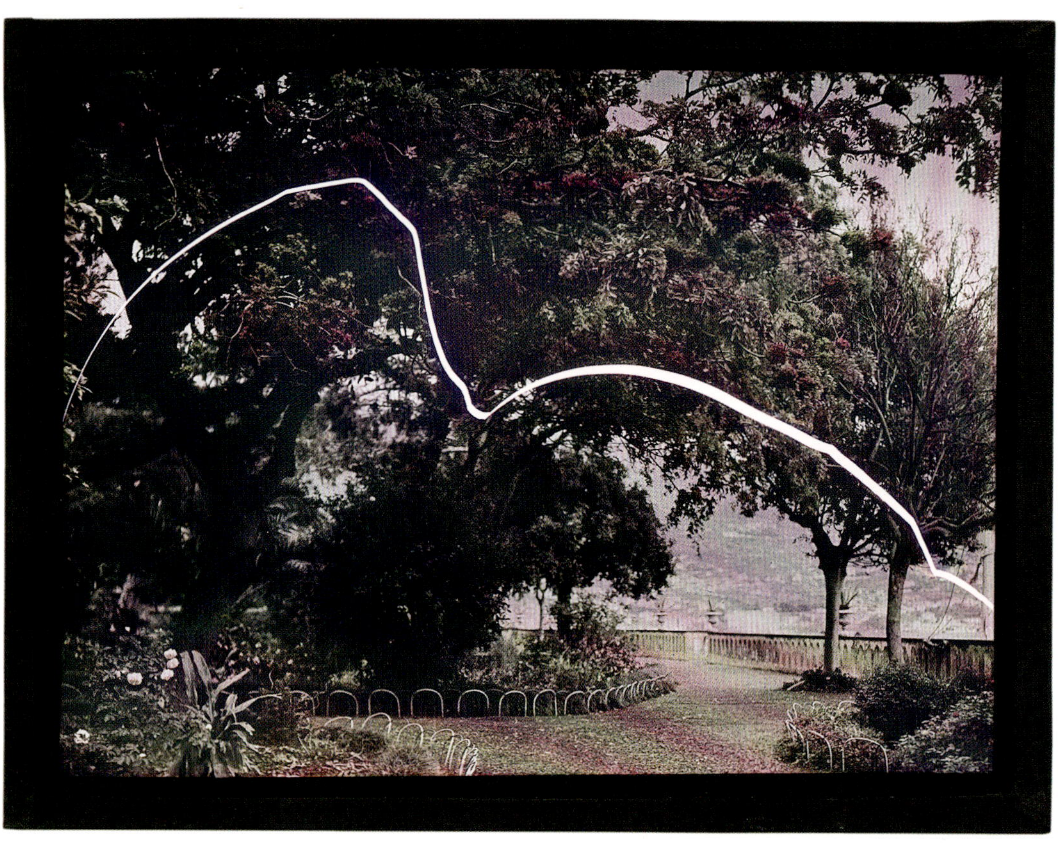

DUFAY DIOPTICHROME PLATES

The Dioptichrome plates of Louis Dufay (1874–1936), which were manufactured in Chantilly, France, first became available in Britain between May and July 1910, through the Autotype Company. Like Omnicolore plates, they were based on a geometric filter screen. The method of creating the screen was complex, involving staining a bichromated colloid, over-printing parallel lines in a greasy resist, bleaching, over-printing with a varnish, removing the greasy resist, and staining in the next colour. The result was a highly transparent filter in a single layer, which was finer and more 'mechanically perfect' than anything else on the market, according to its inventor.

"The most perfect solution of the difficult problem of Colour Photography yet attained", according to its makers, the Dioptichrome process attracted a stronger following in Britain than Omnicolore plates, being seen at the Royal Photographic Society every year from 1910 to 1915, as well as at exhibitions of the Society of Colour Photographers. From 1912 they were seen by large audiences after the natural history photographer Henry Essenhigh Corke (1883–1919) included examples in his popular lectures on 'Garden Flowers and their Wild Relatives'. Unfortunately, the process had limited commercial success, at least until after the First World War, when it was revived on a film base as 'Dufacolor'. This was widely used in colour cinematography and manufactured in England by Ilford.

British Journal of Photography Monthly Supplement on Colour Photography, vol. 4, no. 43 (1 July 1910), supplement p. C.

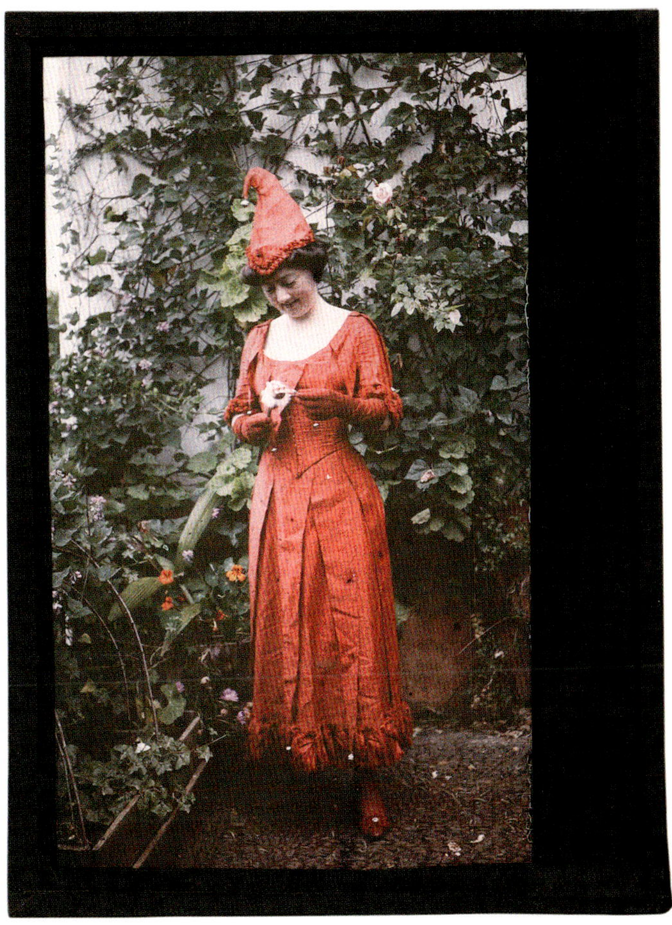

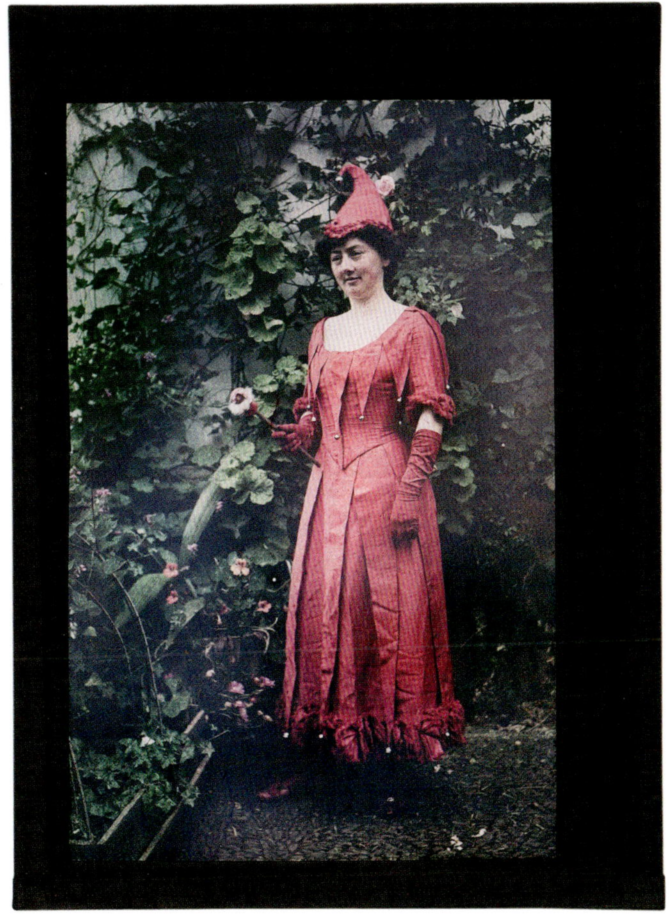

OPPOSITE

208. *A Terrace in the Quinta Vigia*

The garden of the Quinta Vigia
Funchal, between November 1911 and May 1912 ?

9 × 12 cm Dufay Dioptichrome B plate (×1·2)
Museum of the History of Science, Inventory no. 17828

The Quinta Vigia ('House of the Watch-tower') was situated on the cliff directly overlooking Funchal harbour. A former residence of Elizabeth of Bavaria, Empress of Austria, in the 1910s the house was owned by the Portuguese government. It has since been flattened to make way for the Funchal Casino and should not be confused with the current Quinta Vigia, formerly the Quinta Lambert or Quinta das Angústias.

The emulsion of this Dufay plate has shrunken badly, causing a split across the middle, which has left the filter elements exposed in places and produced an interference pattern between the screen and emulsion in others. Such faults are common with examples of the Dioptichrome.

ABOVE

209 & 210. *"The Poor Thing"*

A woman dressed as a jester, holding a bauble
Funchal, Christmas 1911 ?

9 × 12 cm Autochrome and Dufay Dioptichrome B plates
Museum of the History of Science, Inv. nos. 29878 & 29935

The woman depicted here may have been one of the maids Miss Acland brought to Madeira from England. She is photographed on an Autochrome on the left, a Dufay plate on the right. The portraits were taken at Reid's, presumably on the day of a fancy-dress ball.

Dufay released at least two variants of the Dioptichrome process, in addition to a version in which the filter screen was separate from the sensitive plate. The variants are inadequately differentiated in the secondary literature. Miss Acland used both. The example here is a 'Dioptichrome B' plate, released in April or May 1911. The B plate had a finer screen than its predecessor and was said to show less predominant green.

PAGET COLOUR PLATES

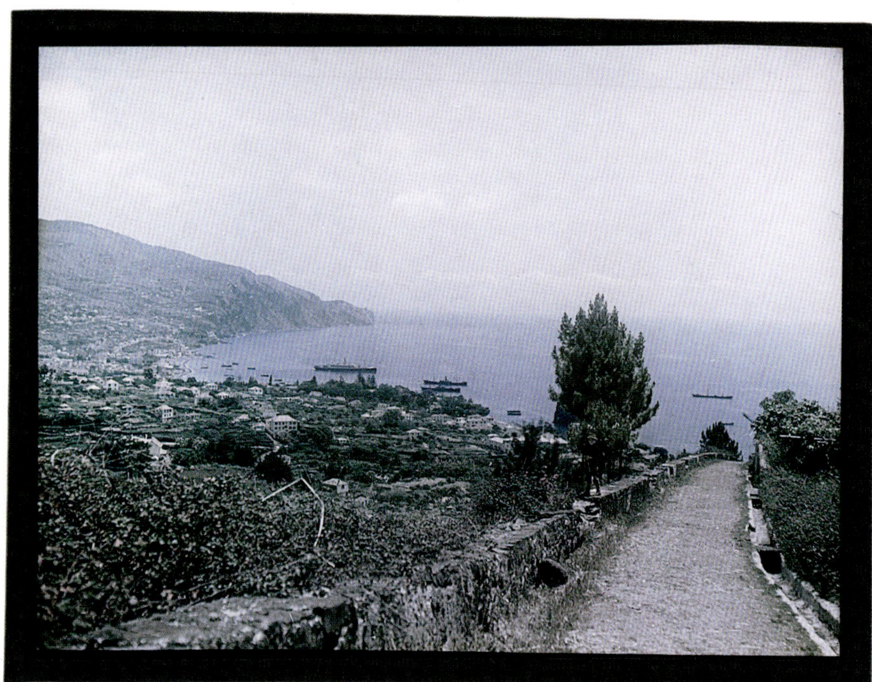

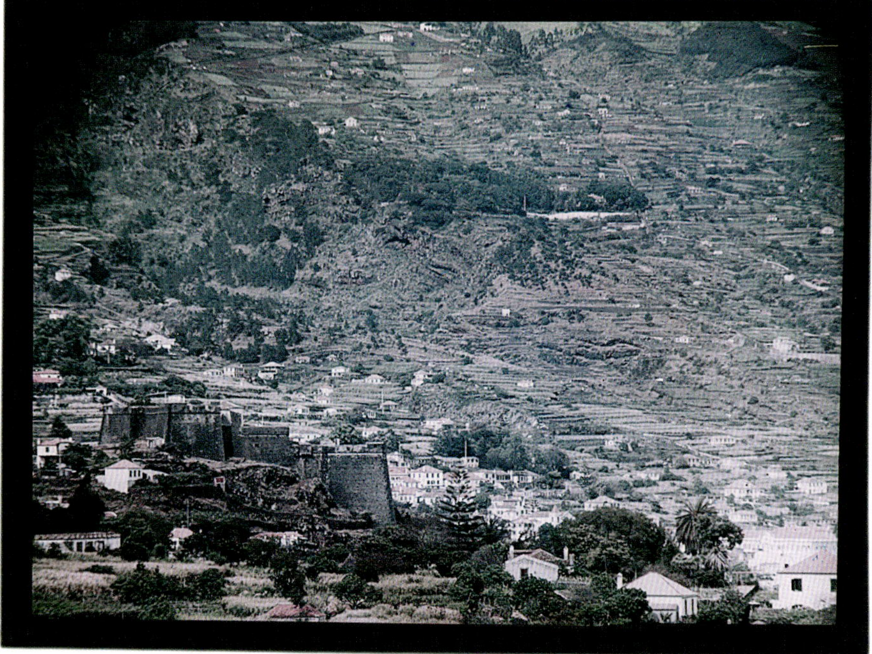

The 'Paget Colour' process was the first screen-plate of English manufacture to achieve commercial success. It was devised by George Sydney Whitfield (1860–1937), son of George Corpe Whitfield (1831–1917), co-founder of the Paget Prize Plate Company. The process was promoted by Whitfield's nephew, Geoffrey Ernest Whitfield (1888–1960), a graduate in chemistry from New College and one of many photographers to attend lectures in the Daubeny Laboratory. Geoffrey was assisted in the task by Clare Livingstone Finlay (1877–1936), the man behind the earlier, unsuccessful, Thames Colour plate.

The Paget process differed from other screen-plate processes in being available as a 'duplicating' method, in which the colour 'taking screen' and 'viewing screen' were separate from the black-and-white negative on which the image was recorded. A single master negative, exposed in the camera through the taking screen, could therefore be used to print off any number of monochrome positives, which were then bound up with viewing screens to create colour slides. This made the process cheaper than its rivals. Quarter-plate taking screens were priced at 8d, but could be reused, viewing screens at 8d a pair, and negatives 8d for six, making a total of less than 6d per plate, which compared with 9d a plate for Autochromes (about £2.75 at 2012 values).

By 8 May 1913 Miss Acland had already exposed her first Paget plates in Madeira, even though the process had only been released on 4 April. However, she waited until her return to Oxford before developing them.

Despite being largely passed over by historians, in Britain Paget plates were a popular alternative to the Autochrome. At the Royal Photographic Society exhibition in 1913 at least eighteen were shown by nine different workers, including Oxford Camera Club member Albert Hamm, who exhibited *Orange-tipped Butterfly* and other entomological subjects.

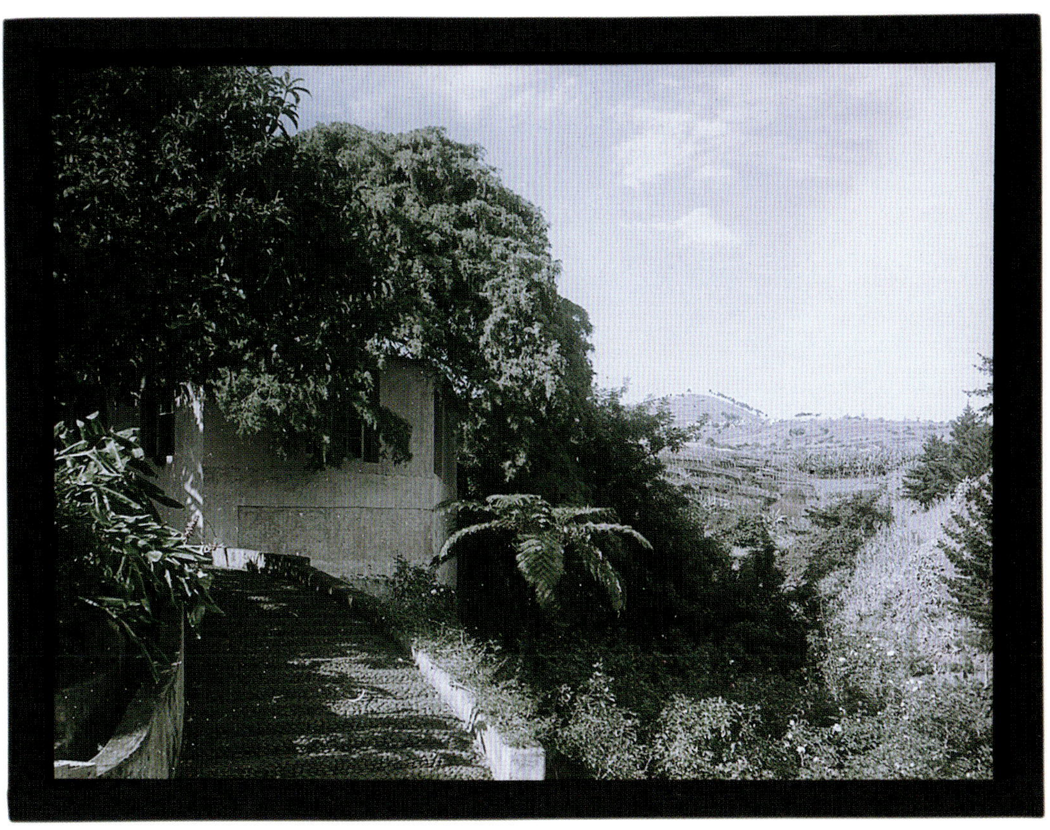

OPPOSITE

211 & 212. *Avista Navios*

Funchal and the bay; Fortaleza de São João Baptista do Pico, from the Avista Navios
Funchal, May 1913 ?

9 × 12 cm Paget Colour plates
Museum of the History of Science, Inv. nos. 15505 & 20472

Both of these views were taken from a point close to the Avista Navios (View of the Ships) on the Caminho da Nazaré, a path leading from behind Reid's Hotel to the Capela da Nazaré (Chapel of the Nativity), one of Miss Acland's favourite destinations for excursions. In the first practically the whole of Funchal east of the Ribeiro Seco (Dry River) is visible. The area immediately below the path became a football pitch in 1927 and is now the Estádio dos Barrieros. The second view, which Miss Acland took with her Adon lens, shows the characteristic terraces of the volcanic slopes above Funchal, looking north-east towards the Fortaleza de São João Baptista do Pico (Fort of St John the Baptist on the Hill).

ABOVE

213. *In the Foothills*

An unidentified quinta above Funchal
Madeira, May 1913 ?

9 × 12 cm Paget Colour plate (×1·2)
Museum of the History of Science, Inventory no. 21182

The unmistakable green bias and blue cast of the Paget process is plain to see in this and many of Miss Acland's other plates. The popularity of the process is surprising given the fault, but its ease of working seems to have outweighed its imperfections in contemporary eyes.

The identity of the quinta depicted is unknown, if indeed the octagonal building is a quinta. The location is a picturesque spot above Funchal, with the Pico dos Barcelos in the background. The cobbles are typical of Madeira. Miss Acland's choice of camera subject was rarely arbitrary but in some cases the stories behind the images have yet to be discovered.

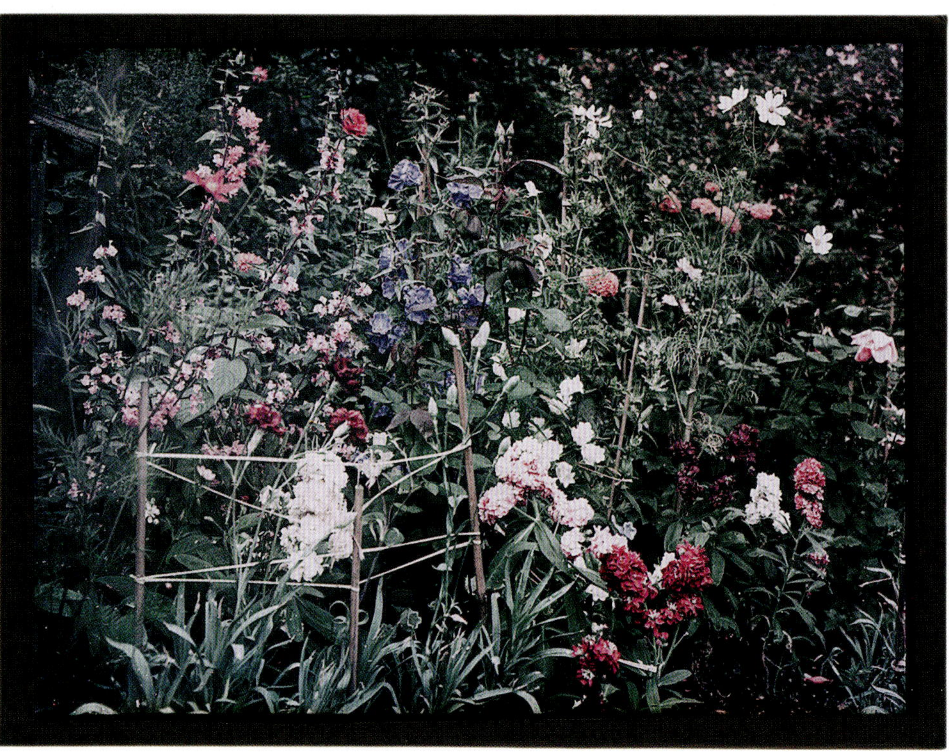

ABOVE

214. *"Hedge in Garden"*

Campanula and *Cosmos* in Clevedon House garden
Oxford, 4 July 1913

9 × 12 cm Paget Colour plate (×1·1)
Museum of the History of Science, Inventory no. 18849

The summer of 1913 was as good for Miss Acland's garden as it was for her colour photography. Her Canterbury Bells had never been so large, she claimed, one measuring nearly 4½ feet in height. The Paget process made it easier to capture such beauties in colour: "With the new Paget plates colour photographs can be taken at 1/30 of a second under certain conditions with an aperture of 4.5", she enthused to Willie.

The proliferation of screen-plate patents of the 1900s and 1910s has many parallels with the digital revolution of recent years. The similarities are particularly striking because the principle behind the historic processes and modern digital cameras is the same: a mosaic filter over a black-and-white sensor. Then, as now, the success of competing systems depended not only on technological advances, but also on more complex and impalpable factors, social, economic, and even meteorological.

MS. Acland d. 111, fols. 38–9.

OPPOSITE

215. *Rose Arbour*

The garden of Clevedon House, Park Town
Oxford, 4 July 1913

9 × 12 cm Paget Colour plate (×1·3)
Museum of the History of Science, Inventory no. 22417

Miss Acland was assisted in her horticultural endeavours by her gardener, Albert Victor Tuffrey (1866–1922), and by William Baker, who gave her surplus stock from the Botanic Garden. She also exchanged plants further afield: the eminent Japanologist Ernest Mason Satow (1843–1929) presented her with a Japanese maple on one occasion, for example, she having sent him an *Eccremocarpus*. "My garden is quite a Museum of curiosities", she remarked in 1922.

A little over a year after this photograph was taken the tranquillity of Oxford life was broken by the outbreak of the First World War. Several years passed before the hardships began to bite, but in 1917 Miss Acland took the decision to erect a henhouse in the garden and turn the lawn over to potatoes. The change in her priorities presaged her retirement from active photography in 1919.

MS. Acland d. 115, fols. 102–3.

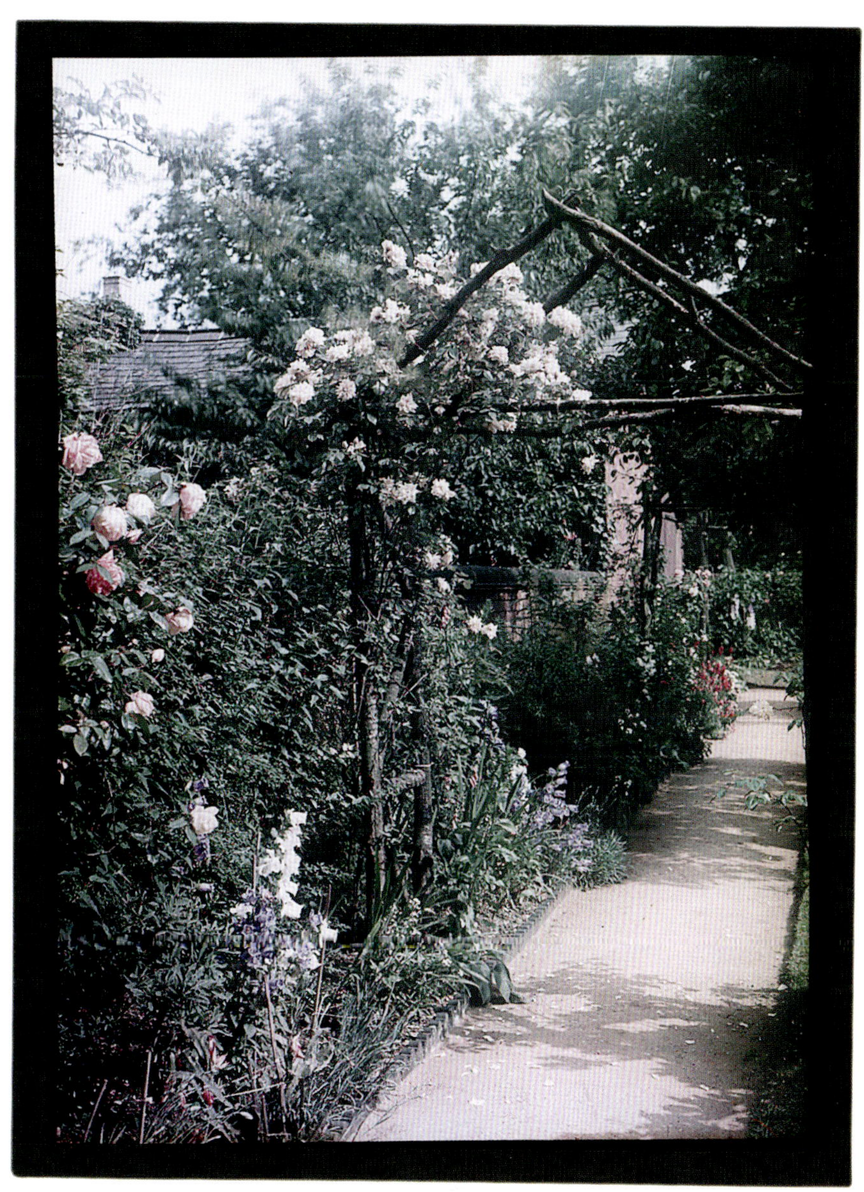

216. *A Child Friend*

An unidentified boy in a Madeira garden
Funchal, between December 1913 and May 1914?

9 × 12 cm Paget Colour plate
Museum of the History of Science, Inventory no. 25698

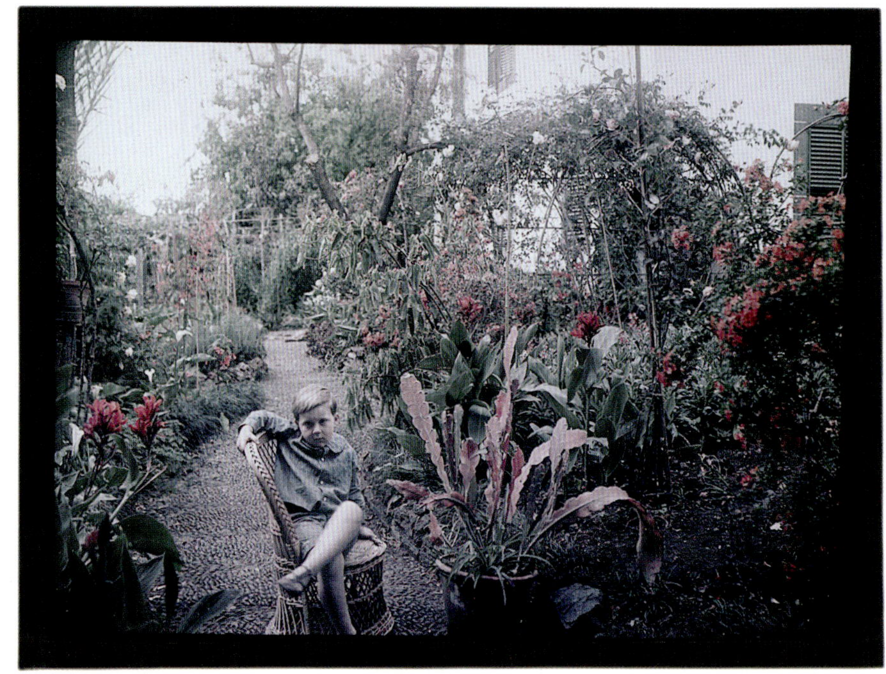

The young boy in this photograph is sitting in the same garden as Miss Acland in catalogue no. 219. It is possible he is William Alfred Reid (1904–1950), son of Alfred Edward Reid, in which case the location is probably a corner of the extensive grounds of his father's hotel. The exotic plants surrounding him include, on the right, the red, leaf-like stems of a species of *Epiphyllum* (orchid cactus), and on the left, the large red blooms of the Canna lily or Indian shot, *Canna indica*.

217. *Madeira Interior*

Miss Acland's sitting room, Reid's Hotel
Funchal, between December 1913 and May 1914?

9 × 12 cm Paget Colour plate
Museum of the History of Science, Inventory no. 29886

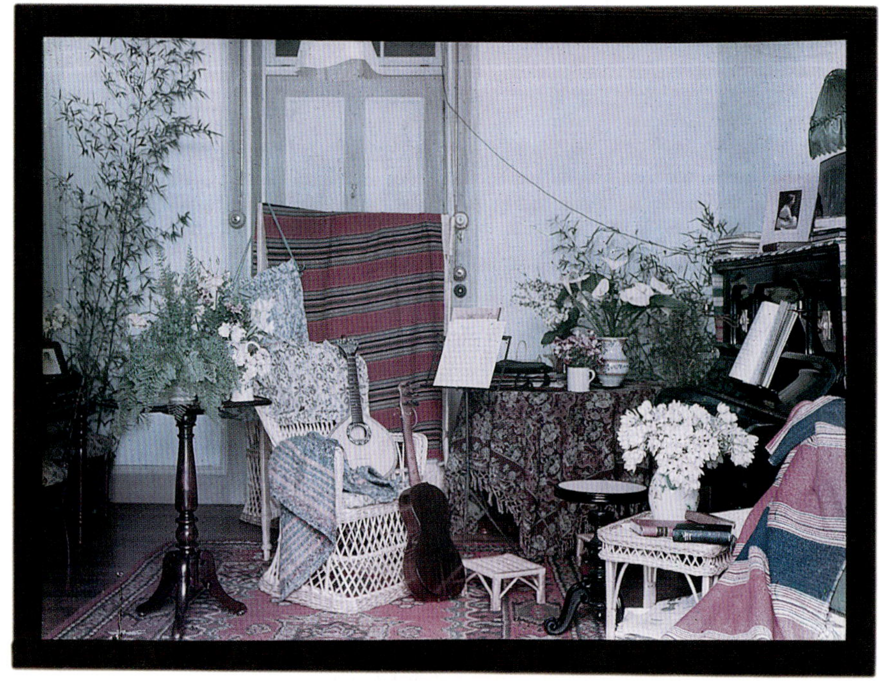

"I wish you could see my little sitting room, now that it is all arranged it looks so very cosy & homelike", Miss Acland wrote to Willie from Madeira on Advent Sunday 1913. One of her home comforts was a piano: she was an accomplished pianist and often invited guests for music. One of her regulars, a Czech baritone of some repute called Bogea Oumiroff (1864–1929), was also a good photographer of stereoscopic views, she claimed.

The volume in the black binding on the wicker table is the *Commemoration Prayer Book*, published to mark the death in 1910 of Edward VII, the highest in rank of Miss Acland's royal acquaintances.

MS. Acland d. 111, fols. 87–8.

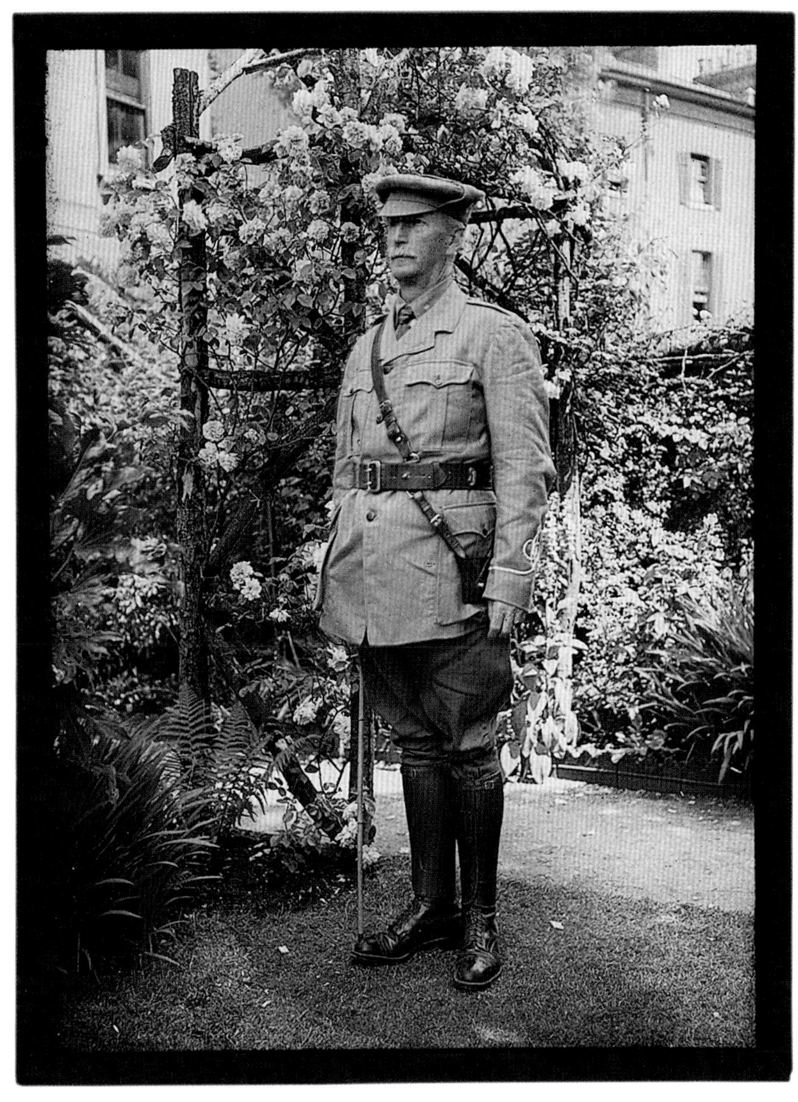

218. *Lieutenant H. D. Acland*

Henry Dyke Acland (1850–1936), in service dress
Oxford, summer 1917 ?

9 × 12 cm Paget Colour plate (×1·2)
Museum of the History of Science, Inventory no. 20325

Unlike his brothers, Harry had no service record before the First World War, the doctors having refused to pass him fit for Sandhurst as a young man. However, in 1917, at the age of 66, he joined the 1st Volunteer Regiment of the Duke of Cornwall's Light Infantry, qualifying as a musketry instructor in pursuit of an enthusiasm for shooting acquired at Rugby School fifty years earlier.

After the War Harry kept up his shooting. In its coverage of the Ashburton Shield in July 1924 *The Times* reported that "Mr. H. D. Acland, who, as a cadet of the Rugby team, opposed Lord Cheylesmore in '66 and still shoots to-day, saw his school compile 226 at 200 yards ... and because of that score Mr. Acland, like Lord Cheylesmore last year, had the pleasure of congratulating his old school upon their victory". Herbert Francis Eaton, Baron Cheylesmore (1848–1925) was the Commandant of the Army Musketry School and an Old Etonian.

The Times, no. 43701 (11 July 1924), p. 16a.

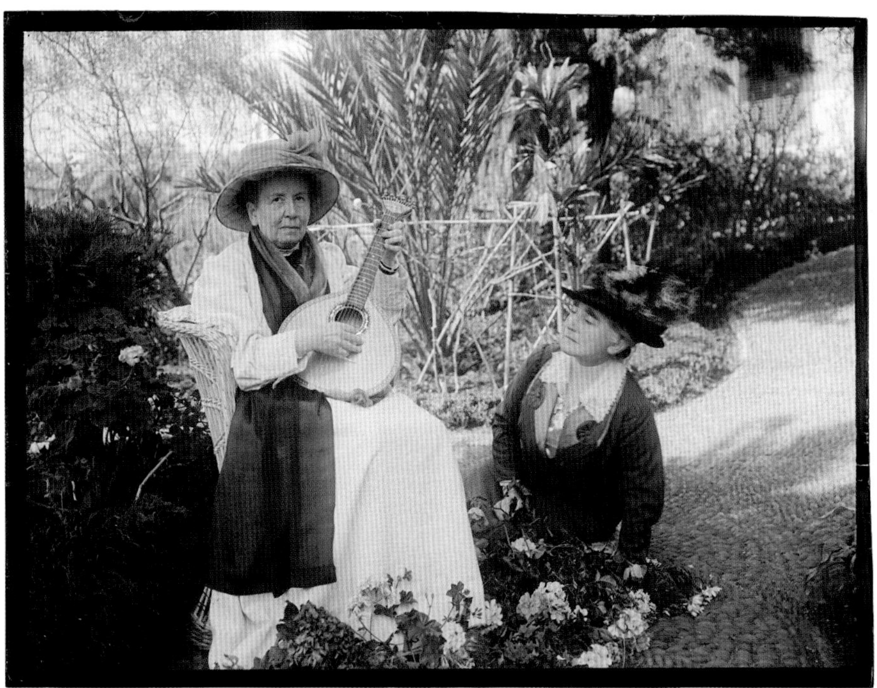

219. *In a Madeira Garden*

Sarah Angelina Acland (1849–1930) and Clara Anne Reid (1867–1924)?
Funchal, between December 1913 and May 1914?
9 × 12 cm Paget screened negative (without viewing screen)
Museum of the History of Science, Inventory no. 86039

The woman depicted with Miss Acland in this photograph is present in a Reid family group portrait taken before 1888. She is therefore presumably a daughter or daughter-in-law of William Reid, founder of Reid's Hotel, possibly the wife of Alfred Reid, Clara Anne (1867–1924), whom Miss Acland knew well. Whoever the woman is, the intimacy of the portrait reflects the strength of the friendships Miss Acland formed in Madeira.

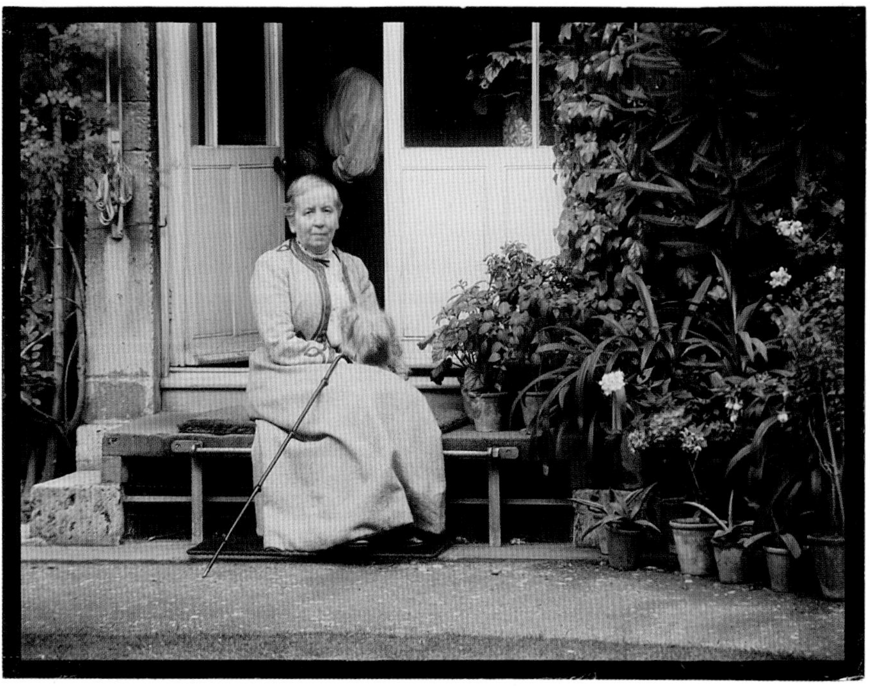

220. *First Lady of Colour Photography*

Sarah Angelina Acland (1849–1930), her dog Chummy, and an unidentified maid
Oxford, July or August 1913 or 1914?
9 × 12 cm Paget screened negative (without viewing screen)
Museum of the History of Science, Inventory no. 62641

Forty-six of Miss Acland's surviving Paget Colour plates were taken in Madeira, twelve in Oxford (fourteen are duplicates). Twenty-six exist as completed transparencies, bound up with a 'viewing screen'. The rest are left bare, as 'screened' black and white negatives, recognizable in the originals by the minute diamond pattern left by the filter elements of the Paget 'taking screen'. The digital re-creation of colour images from these negatives remains a task for the future.

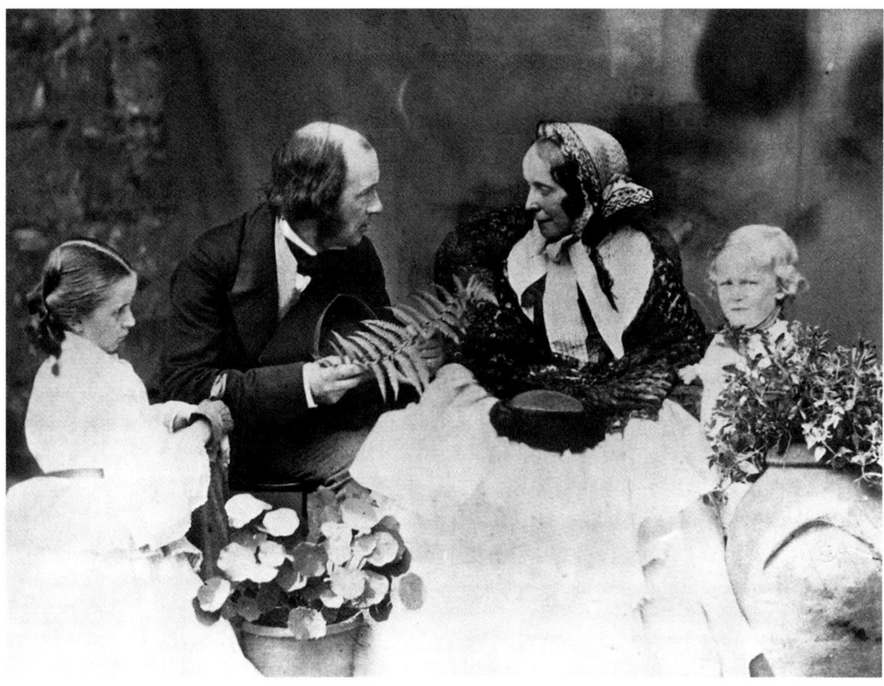

Sarah Angelina, Henry Wentworth, Sarah & Herbert Dyke Acland
Charles Lutwidge Dodgson, albumen print, *c.* 1860

NOTES

1. The Acland children are known to have sat to Dodgson in November or December 1856 from his diary: on 5 November he recorded that Acland had agreed to send them; on 5 March 1857 he promised Mrs Acland "the photographs I did for them last year". It is assumed that fig. 1, which was taken on the same occasion as the portraits of Angie and Harry on page 289, is from this sitting, although none is dated. However, the setting and lighting appear to match portraits of the Liddell sisters dated to summer 1858 in Wakeling's chronological register of Dodgson's photographs (Roger Taylor and Edward Wakeling, *Lewis Carroll Photographer: The Princeton University Library Albums,* Princeton & Oxford, 2002). It is possible, therefore, that the figures are unrecorded portraits from the later date, when Dodgson's diaries are missing. Alternatively, the Liddell portraits may be earlier (in their lighting and setting they closely match a self-portrait of Dodgson usually attributed to June 1857). The fact that the Aclands are dressed in mourning is of little help, as it might be for their grandmother Lydia Elizabeth Acland, née Hoare (1786–23/6/1856), their uncle Arthur Henry Dyke Troyte, né Acland (1811–19/6/1857) or their aunt Lydia Dorothea Acland (1814–14/3/1858).
2. Devon Records Office, 1148M/7/1 (Sarah Angelina Acland, "Memories in my 81st Year" [1930]), p. 21.
3. Ibid.
4. Ibid., pp. 51–2. On Cameron see Julian Cox and Colin Ford, *Julia Margaret Cameron: The Complete Photographs* (London, 2003).
5. Catherine Weed Ward, "Woman in Photography", *Photogram*, vol. 12, no. 144 (December 1905), pp. 373–4, p. 373; "Royal Photographic Society", *British Journal of Photography*, vol. 52, no. 2353 (9 June 1905), pp. 456–7, p. 456.
6. H. O. Klein, "Colour Photography of To-day", *British Journal Photographic Almanac*, 1936, pp. 172–85, p. 173.
7. Devon Records Office, 1148M/7/1, p. 11.
8. Isambard Brunel (ed.), *A Sketch of the Life and Character of Sarah Acland* (London, 1894), p. 14.
9. Devon Records Office, 1148M/7/1, p. 23.
10. "Obituaries / Miss Sarah Acland", *The Times*, no. 45687 (4 December 1930), p. 18e.
11. See MS. Acland d. 170 *passim.*
12. *Alpine Journal*, vol. 12, no. 91 (February 1886), p. 464.
13. *Jackson's Oxford Journal*, no. 4484 (6 April 1839), p. 3f.
14. Thomson, who dropped the 'p' in his name, is probably the William Thompson who corresponded and sent photographs to Fox Talbot in 1841, 1844 and 1845 (cf. Larry Schaaf with Roger Taylor, "Biographical Dictionary of British Calotypists", in Roger Taylor, *Impressed by Light* (New York, 2007), p. 382).
15. Edward Wakeling (ed.), *Lewis Carroll's Diaries* (6 vols, Luton, 1993–2001), vol. 3 (1995), p. 67. Dodgson's diary entry mentioning the tour is confused, suggesting incorrectly that Arthur's brother William was the photographer.
16. MS. Acland d. 142, fols. 115–16.
17. MS. Acland d. 107, fols. 28–31.
18. Acland 1.

19. See Vickie Hearnshaw, "A New Zealand Collection with English Connections: The Photographs of the Misses Acland", *New Zealand Journal of Photography*, no. 46 (Autumn 2002), pp. 4–6.
20. MS. Acland d. 138, fols. 226–7.
21. See Elizabeth Edwards, *Raw Histories: Photographs, Anthropology and Museums* (Oxford & New York, 2001), ch. 5.
22. "Photographic Novelties at the London Stereoscopic Company", *Queen*, vol. 92, no. 2396 (26 November 1892), p. 875.
23. Cuthbert Bede [Edward Bradley], *Photographic Pleasures Popularly Portrayed with Pen and Pencil* (London, 1855), p. 54.
24. "Amateurs at the Photographic Exhibition", *Amateur Photographer*, vol. 1, no. 1 (10 October 1884), pp. 8–19, p. 9.
25. MS. Acland d. 128, fols. 129–32.
26. "Second February Meeting / Miss Acland on Home Portraiture", *Proceedings of the Oxford Camera Club*, no. 1 (April 1899), pp. 3–5, p. 4a.
27. "City Camera Club Exhibition", *Oxford Times*, no. 2473 (14 March 1908), p. 12d.
28. Catherine Weed Barnes, "Photography from a Woman's Standpoint", *American Amateur Photographer*, vol. 2, no. 1 (January 1890), pp. 10–13, p. 11 .
29. 'Lux', "Personal Paragraphs", *Amateur Photographer*, vol. 29, no. 753 (10 March 1899), p. 182.
30. MS. Acland d. 172, fols. 88–9.
31. "New Art Publications", *The Times*, no. 32923 (31 January 1890), p. 14b.
32. Andrew Pringle, "The Naissance of Art in Photography", *Studio*, vol. 1, no. 3 (June 1893), pp. 87–95, p. 92.
33. Charles W. Hastings (ed.), *The 'Amateur Photographer' Home Portraiture Number, 1890* (London, 1890), p. 4.
34. MS. Acland d. 42, fols. 355–7.
35. MS. Acland d. 108, fols. 1–4.
36. "'The Standard' Special Columns for New Books, Recent Editions, &c.", *Standard*, no. 22045 (27 February 1895), p. 4a.
37. Devon Records Office, 1148M/7/1, p. 116.
38. P. B-S., "Miss E. L. Turner" [Obituary], *Nature*, vol. 146, no. 3700 (28 September 1940), p. 424.
39. [Hills & Saunders], *The Oxford Photographic Gallery* (Flysheet, [Oxford, 1860]) [John Johnson Collection, 89/90–103].
40. MS. Don. d. 14, fol. iv.
41. *Proceedings of the Oxford Camera Club*, no. 1 (April 1899), pp. 3–5, p. 5a.
42. "Photographing Children", *Photo-Miniature*, vol. 2, no. 19 (October 1900), pp. 281–304, p. 284.
43. *Proceedings of the Oxford Camera Club*, no. 1 (April 1899), pp. 3–5, p. 4a.
44. "Home Portraiture" [Report of Miss Acland's lecture], *British Journal of Photography*, vol. 46, no. 2027 (10 March 1899), pp. 151b–152a, p. 151a.
45. Harold Baker, "Notes on Portrait work in the Studio", *Photography,* vol. 9, no. 444 (13 May 1897), pp. 295–6, p. 295; H. S. W. [Henry Snowden Ward], "Camera Craft", *Art Journal*, New series, vol. 19, no. 738 (December 1899), p. 381.
46. A. M. [Alfred Maskell], "On Some Methods of Suppression and Modification in Pictorial Photography", *Studio*, vol. 3, no. 13 (16 April 1894), pp. 13–16, p. 14.
47. "Oxford Camera Club / Presentation to Mr. Norton", *Oxford Times,* no. 2487 (20 June 1908), p. 9a–b.
48. MS. Top. Oxon. e. 625, fol. 2v.
49. "Obituaries / Mr. A. H. Hamm", *Nature*, vol. 167, no. 4241 (10 February 1951), p. 220.
50. "Lady Members", *Photographic Review of Reviews*, vol. 2, no. 24 (15 December 1893), p. 390, quoting the *Manchester Courier*.
51. "The Biennial Exhibition", *Proceedings of the Oxford Camera Club*, no. 11 (October 1904), pp. 95–6, p. 96a.
52. [Elizabeth Eastlake], "Photography", *London Quarterly Review*, no. 202 (April 1857), pp. 241–55, p. 249.
53. Advertisement, *British Journal of Photography*, no. 1659, vol. 39 (19 February 1892), p. xii.
54. Advertisement, *British Journal of Photography*, no. 1860, vol. 42 (27 December 1895), p. x.
55. See "George Bernard Shaw on the Use of Orthochromatic Films and Screens", *Amateur Photographer* (14 August 1902), pp. 123–4, p. 123.
56. "Our Table / The Spectrum Plate", *American Amateur Photographer*, vol. 12 (January to December 1900), pp. 526–7.
57. 'A Graduate of Oxford' [John Ruskin], *Modern Painters* (5 vols, London, 1843–60), vol. 1, pt. 2, ch. 2, §1.
58. "Second April Meeting", *Proceedings of the Oxford Camera Club*, no. 5 (October 1900), pp. 38–40, p. 39b.
59. Thomas Bedding, "Colour Au Naturel", *British Journal of Photography*, vol. 37, no. 1548 (3 January 1890), p. 4.
60. H. Snowden Ward, "The McDonough–Joly Process of Colour Photography", *Photographic Journal*, vol. 25, no. 4 (31 December 1900), pp. 141–8, p. 141; William H. Half, "Natural Colour Photography: The Sanger Shepherd Process", *Photographic Times*, vol. 33, no. 3 (March 1901), pp. 104–7, p. 104.
61. MS. Acland d. 108, fols. 45–6.
62. "Photographic Convention of the United Kingdom. Oxford Meeting", *Oxford Times*, no. 2117 (13 July 1901), p. 8, p. 8c.
63. Ibid.
64. "Matters Photographical", *Oxford Times*, no. 2299 (24 December 1904), p. 10c.
65. MS. Acland d. 108, fols. 119–21.
66. "More Color Photography", *Wilson's Photographic Magazine*, vol. 39, no. 545 (May 1902), p. 182.
67. *Proceedings of the Oxford Camera Club*, no. 12 (April 1906), pp. 104–105.
68. "Matters Photographical", *Oxford Times*, no. 2330 (17 June 1905), p. 10c.
69. *Photographic Journal*, vol. 46 (Supplement) (20 September 1906), p. 4.
70. *Oxford Times*, no. 2299 (24 December 1904), p. 10c.
71. R. Child Bayley, *The Complete Photographer* (London, 1906), p. 290.
72. *British Journal of Photography Monthly Supplement on Colour Photography*, vol. 1, no. 1 (January 1906), p. 8.
73. MS. Acland d. 110, fol. 233.
74. Ibid.
75. MS. Acland d. 110, fol. 230.
76. "The War and Colour Photography", *British Journal of Photography Monthly Supplement on Colour Photography*, vol. 8, no. 93 (4 September 1914), p. 35.
77. MS. Acland d. 113, fols. 44–9.
78. MS. Acland d. 113, fols. 226–8.
79. MS. Don. d. 14, fol. 48v; ibid., letter inside cover.
80. "Spirit of the Times", *Photography*, vol. 19, no. 866 (13 July 1905), pp. 548–9, p. 548.

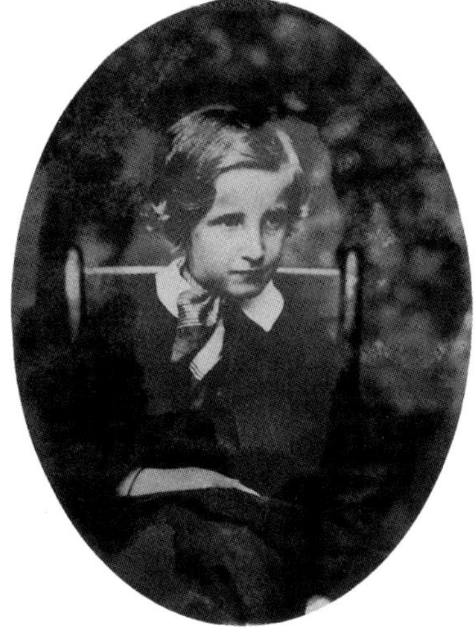
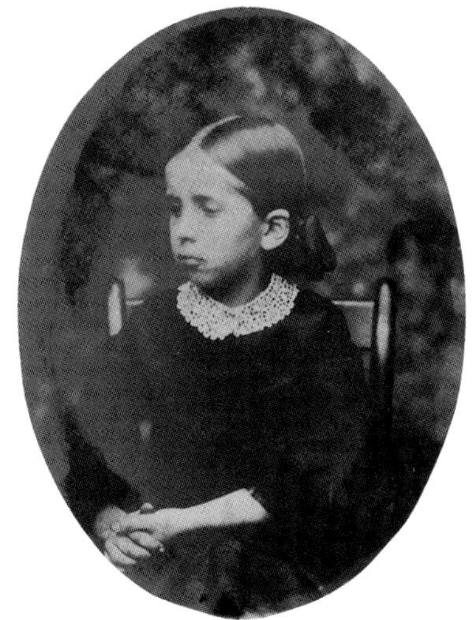

Henry Dyke Acland; Sarah Angelina Acland
Charles Lutwidge Dodgson, albumen prints, 1856

SELECT BIBLIOGRAPHY

Manuscripts, Photographs and Artworks

Bodleian Library, MS. Acland (Acland Papers) [includes 84 volumes of correspondence and approximately 6,175 items to or from Miss Acland].

Ashmolean Museum, WA.RS.UF.44a to c (Watercolours by Sarah Angelina Acland, Mentone, 1877).

Bodleian Library, MS. Minn 226 (Sarah Angelina Acland, Display album of portraits, 1892–96) [albumen prints].

Bodleian Library, MS. Photogr. c. 176 & 177 (Sarah Angelina Acland, Photograph albums, 1891 to *c.* 1895) [mostly albumen prints].

Museum of the History of Science, MS. Gunther 30 (["Holiday Diary of Sarah Angelina Acland, 5 March to 10 April, 1908"]).

Bodleian Library, MS. Eng. misc. d. 214 (Sarah Angelina Acland, "Memories in my 81st Year", [1929–30]) [draft autobiography].

Devon Records Office, Exeter, 1148M/7/1 (Sarah Angelina Acland, "Memories in my 81st Year" [1930]) [presentation copy of the above, illustrated with platino-matt bromide prints].

Bodleian Library, MS. Don. d. 14 (Sarah Angelina Acland, "Photographs taken in my old Home in Broad Street, Oxford between the years 1891 & 1900, with annotations made in 1930") [presentation album of portraits with carbon prints made by Harry Minn].

Private Collection, Presentation Album (Sarah Angelina Acland, "Photographs taken in my old Home in Broad Street Oxford, between the years 1891–1900, with annotations made in 1930 in my 81st year") [near duplicate of the previous item].

Bodleian Library, MS. Photogr. b. 34 (Photographic album of Henry Wentworth Acland, *c.* 1850–1863).

Bodleian Library, MS. Photogr. c. 175 (Photographic album of Sarah Acland, *c.* 1860–78).

Bodleian Library, MS. Photogr. b. 35–37 (Photographs by W. A. D. Acland, *c.* 1883–93).

Bodleian Library, MS. Top. Oxon. e. 624 (Minutes of the Oxford Camera Club, 16 April 1894 to 24 January 1898).

Bodleian Library, MS. Top. Oxon. c. 764 (Minutes of the Oxford Camera Club, 7 February 1898 to 5 April 1909).

Works by or about Miss Acland

'A.' [Sarah Angelina Acland], "Letters from Wildbad", *Churchman's Companion*, New series, vol. 6, no. 32 (August 1869), pp. 137–42; no. 33 (September 1869), pp. 260–5; and no. 34 (October 1869), pp. 363–9.

[Sarah Angelina Acland], ed. Isambard Brunel, *A Sketch of the Life and Character of Sarah Acland* (London, 1894).

"A Correspondent" [Sarah Angelina Acland], "Death of Miss Eleanor E. Smith", *Oxford Chronicle*, no. 3185 (19 September 1896), p. 8c.

'S.A.A.' [Sarah Angelina Acland], "Correspondence / Printing under Green Glass", *British Journal of Photography*, vol. 43, no. 1903 (23 October 1896), p. 687.

"Home Portraiture" [Report of Miss Acland's lecture], *British Journal of Photography*, vol. 46, no. 2027 (10 March 1899), pp. 151b–152a.
'Miss Acland' [Sarah Angelina Acland], "Home Portraiture", *Photography*, vol. 11, no. 540 (16 March 1899), p. 169.
"Second February Meeting / Miss Acland on Home Portraiture", *Proceedings of the Oxford Camera Club*, no. 1 (April 1899), pp. 3–5.
'Miss Acland' [Sarah Angelina Acland], "The Spectrum Plate. Theory: Practice: Result", *Photography*, vol. 12, no. 615 (23 August 1900), pp. 553–60.
"Second April Meeting" [Report of Miss Acland's lecture on the Spectrum plate], *Proceedings of the Oxford Camera Club*, no. 5 (October 1900), pp. 38–40.
"Second November Meeting" [Report of Miss Acland & Minn's "Demonstration of the Sanger-Shepherd Method of Indirect Colour Photography"], *Proceedings of the Oxford Camera Club*, no. 8 (February 1902), pp. 64–5.
"Three-colour Work from Nature / Notes on a Lecture by Miss Acland on Gibraltar, Delivered to the Oxford Camera Club / Illustrated by Lantern Slides by the Sanger Shepherd Process", *Photography*, vol. 19, no. 846 (24 January 1905), pp. 154–5.
"Royal Photographic Society" [Report of Miss Acland's lecture on Gibraltar], *British Journal of Photography*, vol. 52, no. 2353 (9 June 1905), pp. 456–7.
'Miss Acland' [Sarah Angelina Acland], "A Visit to Gibraltar / Demonstrating the Use of Three-Colour Photography in Giving a more Faithful Impression of a Place than could Otherwise be Obtained", *Photographic Journal*, vol. 45, no. 7 (July 1905), pp. 232–8.
[Roger Child Bayley], "Spirit of the Times" [Comments on Miss Acland's Gibraltar lecture], *Photography*, vol. 19, no. 866 (13 July 1905), pp. 548–9.
"Congratulatory" [Letter from Miss Acland], *British Journal of Photography Monthly Supplement on Colour Photography*, vol. 1, no. 1 (4 January 1906), p. 8.
"Second December Meeting" [Report of Miss Acland's lecture on Gibraltar], *Proceedings of the Oxford Camera Club*, no. 12 (April 1906), pp. 104–5.
[Sarah Angelina Acland], "Country Boroughs" [Letter on Miss Merivale's nomination], *The Times*, no. 39107 (3 November 1909), p. 10c.
[Sarah Angelina Acland], "Death of Miss Denniston / Miss Acland's Tribute", *Oxford Times*, no. 3088 (23 July 1920), p. 6c.
"News and Notes of the Week / Death of Miss S. A. Acland", *British Journal of Photography*, vol. 77, no. 3683 (5 December 1930), p. 739.
"Miss Sarah Acland" [Obituary], *The Times*, no. 45687 (4 December 1930), p. 18e.

Works by Other Authors

Robert H. Allshouse (ed.), *Photographs for the Tsar: The Pioneering Colour Photography of Sergei Mikhailovich Prokudin-Gorskii* (London, 1980).
[Amateur Photographer], "George Bernard Shaw on the Use of Orthochromatic Films and Screens", *Amateur Photographer*, vol. 36, no. 932 (14 August 1902), pp. 123–4.
J. B. Atlay, *Sir Henry Wentworth Acland, Bart.: A Memoir* (London, 1903).
Catherine Weed Barnes, "Photography from a Woman's Standpoint", *American Amateur Photographer*, vol. 2, no. 1 (January 1890), pp. 10–13.
R. Child Bayley, *The Complete Photographer* (2nd edn, London, 1906).
R. Child Bayley, "My Own Experiences with the Autochrome Plates", *Photography*, no. 975, vol. 24 (16 July 1907), pp. 41–4.
J. S. Billings & W. Matthews, "On Composite Photography as Applied to Craniology", *Bulletin of the Philosophical Society of Washington*, vol. 7 (1884), pp. 25–6.
[*Black & White*], "Of a Great Physician: Sir Henry Acland, Bart., K.C.B.", *Black & White*, vol. 12, no. 302 (14 November 1896), p. 627.
Evelyn Boden, "Portraiture with Single Lenses", *Photogram*, vol. 6, no. 64 (April 1899), pp. 109–10.
[W. Arthur Boord (ed.)], *Sun Artists* [Mrs. F. W. H. Myers], no. 7 (April 1891).
Stephen Bottomore, "The Sultan and the Cinematograph", *Early Popular Visual Culture*, vol. 6, no. 2 (July 2008), pp. 121–44.
David J. Boullin, "The Earliest Photograph of a Wristwatch?", *Antiquarian Horology*, vol. 18, no. 6 (Summer 1990), pp. 653–6.
[British Journal of Photography], "The War and Colour Photography", *British Journal of Photography Monthly Supplement on Colour Photography*, vol. 8, no. 93 (4 September 1914), p. 35.
[British Medical Journal], "Obituary / Sir Henry Acland", *British Medical Journal*, no. 1281 (27 October 1900), pp. 1281–2.
P. B-S., "Miss E. L. Turner", *Nature*, vol. 146, no. 3700 (28 September 1940), p. 424.
M. C. Burkitt, "Col. Willoughby Verner", *Nature*, vol. 109, no. 2729 (16 February 1922), pp. 213–14.
James Cadett, "Colour Correct Photography and a New Plate", *Photographic Journal*, New series, vol. 20, no. 6 (29 February 1896), pp. 161–70.
James Cadett & Sanger Shepherd, *Orthochromatic and Three-Colour Photography (Simplified)* (6th edn, Cadett & Neall, Ashtead, Surrey, 1901).
[Chuo University, Tokyo], "Founding Principal: Rokuichiro Masujima", *Chuo Online* (www.yomiuri.co.jp/adv/chuo/dy/movie/movie04.htm, [2010]).
A. H. Church, *Colour* (Cassell's Technical Manuals, London etc., [1872]).
Brian Coe, *Colour Photography: The First Hundred Years, 1840–1940* (London, 1978).
E. T. Cook & Alexander Wedderburn (eds.), *The Library Edition of the Works of John Ruskin* (39 vols, London, 1903–1912).
Jack H. Coote, *The Illustrated History of Colour Photography* (Surbiton, 1993).
V. Cremier, "Experiments with the Dioptichrome Colour Screen-Plate", *British Journal of Photography Monthly Supplement on Colour Photography*, vol. 5, no. 53 (5 May 1911), pp. 37–8.
James S. Dearden, *John Ruskin: A Life in Pictures* (Sheffield, 1999).
[De Montfort University], *Exhibitions of the Royal Photographic Society 1870–1915* (http://erps.dmu.ac.uk/, 2008).
C. T. Dent, "In Memoriam / William Frederick Donkin", *Alpine Journal*, vol. 14, no. 102 (November 1888), pp. 128–31.
Frances Dimond, *Developing the Picture: Queen Alexandra and the Art of Photography* (London, 2004).
Florence & Ella Du Cane, *The Flowers and Gardens of Madeira* (London, 1909).
[Elizabeth Eastlake], "Photography", *London Quarterly Review*, no. 202 (April 1857), pp. 241–55.
Elizabeth Edwards, "Time and Space on the Quarter Deck: Two Samoan Photographs by Captain W. Acland", in Elizabeth Edwards, *Raw Histories: Photographs, Anthropology and Museums* (Oxford & New York, 2001), ch. 5, pp. 107–9.
D. W. F. [Douglas William Freshfield], *In Memoriam* [W. F. Donkin] (Exhibition catalogue, Gainsborough Gallery, London, [1889]).
Helmut Gernsheim, *Lewis Carroll: Photographer* (London, 1949).
Malcolm Graham, *Henry Taunt of Oxford: A Victorian Photographer* (Oxford, 1973).
Peter Hamilton & Roger Hargreaves, *The Beautiful and the Damned: The Creation of Identity in Nineteenth Century Photography* (Aldershot, 2001).
Anne Hammond (ed.), *Frederick H. Evans: Selected Text and Bibliography* (World Photographers Reference Series, vol. 1, Oxford, 1992).
John Hannavy (ed.), *Encyclopedia of Nineteenth-century Photography* (2 vols, London, [2007]).
Margaret Harker, *The Linked Ring: The Secession Movement in Photography in Britain, 1892–1910* (London, 1979).
Charles W. Hastings (ed.), *The "Amateur Photographer" Home Portraiture Number, 1890* (Hazel, Watson, & Viney, Ltd., London, 1890).
Vickie Hearnshaw, "A New Zealand Collection with English Connections: The Photographs of the Misses Acland", *New Zealand Journal of Photography*, no. 46 (Autumn 2002), pp. 4–6.
Bernard V. & Pauline F. Heathcote, "The Feminine Influence: Aspects of the Role of Women in the

Evolution of Photography in the British Isles", *History of Photography*, vol. 12, no. 3 (July – September 1988), pp. 259–73.

Liz Heron & Val Williams (eds.), *Illuminations: Women Writing on Photography* (London, 1996).

Robert Hewison, *Ruskin and Oxford: The Art of Education* (Oxford, 1996).

Robert Hewison, Ian Warrell & Stephen Wildman, *Ruskin, Turner and the Pre-Raphaelites* (Tate Gallery, London, 2000).

Tim Hilton, *John Ruskin: The Later Years* (New Haven & London, 2000).

Marjorie Hoare, *The Quintas of Madeira: Windows into the Past* (Funchal, 2004).

Roger Hutchins, *British University Observatories 1772–1939* (Aldershot, 2008).

[Lawrence Impey], *Col. E. C. Impey: The Photography of Col. Eugene C. Impey* (http://ecimpey.info/wordpress, [2010?]).

Frederic Ives, *Krömsköp Color Photography* (London, 1898).

[Jackson's Oxford Journal], "The Sarah Acland Memorial", *Jackson's Oxford Journal*, no. 6608 (8 November 1879), pp. 6a–b.

Patricia Jalland, *Women, Marriage, and Politics, 1860-1914* (Oxford, 1986).

Patricia Jalland, *Death in the Victorian Family* (Oxford, 1999).

Peter James, Tessa Sidey & John Taylor (eds.), *Sunlight and Shadow: The Photographs of Emma Barton, 1872–1938* (Birmingham Museums & Libraries, 1995).

Stephanie Jenkins, *Oxford History* (www.headington.org.uk/oxon, 2000–2011).

Jo Elwyn Jones & J. Francis Gladstone, *The Red King's Dream or Lewis Carroll in Wonderland* (London, 1995).

Judith Keller & Kenneth A. Breisch, *A Victorian View of Rome: The Parker Collection of Historical Photographs in the Kelsey Museum of Archaeology* (Ann Arbor, 1980).

John Know, "Sir George White: Local Hero", in Eull Dunlop (comp.), *Mid-Antrim, Part 2: Further Articles on Ballymena and District* (Mid-Antrim Historical Group, Ballymena, 1991), pp. 113–16.

[Hans P. Kraus & Larry J. Schaaf], *Llewelyn, Maskelyne, Talbot: A Family Circle* (Sun Pictures, catalogue 2, New York, n. d.).

Bertrand Lavédrine & Jean-Paul Gandolfo, *L'autochrome Lumière: Secrets d'atelier et défis industriels* (Comité des travaux historiques et scientifiques, [Paris?], 2009).

Karoline Leach, *In the Shadow of the Dreamchild : A New Understanding of Lewis Carroll* (London, 1999).

Raymond Lister, *George Richmond: A Critical Biography* (London, 1981).

Katherine Macdonald, "Alexander Munro: Pre-Raphaelite Associate", in Benedict Read & Joanna Barnes (eds.), *Pre-Raphaelite Sculpture: Nature and Imagination in British Sculpture 1848–1914* (London, 1991), pp. 46–65.

H. J. Mackinder, "A Journey to the Summit of Mount Kenya, British East Africa", *Geographical Journal*, vol. 15, no. 5 (May 1900), pp. 453–86.

[Ministère de la Culture, France], *La photographie des couleurs: Autochromes Lumière, 1907–1935* (www.autochromes.culture.fr, 2008).

Vanda Morton, *Oxford Rebels: The Life and Friends of Nevil Story Maskelyne* (Gloucester, 1987).

Frederick O'Dwyer, *The Architecture of Deane and Woodward* (Cork, 1997).

Lawrence H. Officer, *MeasuringWorth.com* (www.measuringworth.com, 2008).

David Okuefuna, *The Wonderful World of Albert Kahn: Colour Photographs from a Lost Age* (London, 2008).

[Oxford, Bodleian Library] "Notes and News: The Late Henry Minn", *Bodleian Library Record*, vol. 7 no. 2 (July 1963), pp. 65–6.

[Oxford Magazine], "Oxford University Photographic Club", *Oxford Magazine*, vol. 2, no. 15 (4 June 1884), pp. 285–6.

[Oxford Pageant Committee], *The Oxford Historical Pageant / Book of Words* (Oxford, 1907).

[Oxford School of Art], *School of Art, Randolph Galleries, Beaumont Street, Oxford, 1868: List of Prizes ... and Catalogue of Drawings ... Exhibited in the Town Hall* ([Oxford, 1868]).

[Oxford Times], "Photographic Convention of the United Kingdom, Oxford Meeting", *Oxford Times*, no. 2117 (13 July 1901), p. 8.

[Oxford Times], "Oxford Camera Club Meeting: Autochrome System of Colour Photography", *Oxford Times*, no. 2463 (11 January 1908), p. 9h.

W. A. Pantin, "The Recently Demolished Houses in Broad Street, Oxford", *Oxoniensia*, vol. 2 (1937), pp. 171–200.

[Coventry Patmore], "Walls and Wall Painting at Oxford", *Saturday Review*, vol. 4, no. 113 (26 December 1857), pp. 583–4.

Andrew Pringle, "The Naissance of Art in Photography", *Studio*, vol. 1, no. 3 (15 June 1893), pp. 87–95.

Michael Pritchard, "Cadett and Neall Dry Plate Ltd.", in John Hannavy (ed.), *Encyclopedia of Nineteenth-century Photography* (2 vols, London, [2007]), vol. 1, pp. 234–5.

John A. Randall, "Portraiture in Rooms", *Year Book of Photography and Amateur's Guide*, 1898, pp. 200–226.

Pamela Roberts, *A Century of Colour Photography* (London, 2007).

Everett Roseborough, "Story of a Forgotten Pioneer: E. Sanger-Shepherd", *Photographic Canadiana*, vol. 19, no. 5 (March/April 1994), pp. 10–11.

Naomi Rosenblum, *A World History of Photography* (3rd ed. rev., New York, London & Paris, 1997).

Naomi Rosenblum, *A History of Women Photographers* (3rd ed., New York, London & Paris, 2010).

H. E. Salter & Mary D. Lobel, *The University of Oxford* (Victoria History of the County of Oxford, vol. 3, London, 1954).

E. Sanger Shepherd, "Natural Colour Photography", *Journal of the Camera Club*, vol. 13, no. 163 (December 1899), pp. 195–8.

Larry J. Schaaf, *The Photographic Art of William Henry Fox Talbot* (Princeton & Oxford, 2000).

Larry J. Schaaf and Roger Taylor, "Biographical Dictionary of British Calotypists", in Roger Taylor, *Impressed by Light: British Photographs from Paper Negatives, 1840–1860* (New York, 2007), pp. 283–92.

Simon Schaffer, "Accurate Measurement is an English Science", in M. Norton Wise (ed.), *The Values of Precision* (Princeton, 1995), pp. 135–72.

Grace Seiberling with Carolyn Bloore, *Amateurs, Photography, and the Mid-Victorian Imagination* (Chicago & London, 1986).

A. V. Simcock, *Photography 150: Images from the First Generation* (Oxford, 1989).

The Society of Colour Photographers: First Annual Exhibition (Exhibition catalogue, London, 1907).

Allen Stanley & Christopher Newall, *Pre-Raphaelite Vision: Truth to Nature* (Tate Britain, London, 2004).

Alfred Stieglitz, "The Joint Exhibition at Philadelphia / II", *American Amateur Photographer*, vol. 5, no. 6 (June 1893), pp. 249–54.

[Henry Sturmey (ed.)], "The 'Acme': W. Watson & Sons", *Photography Annual*, 1891, pp. 280–81.

Roger Taylor, *Photographs Exhibited in Britain, 1839–1865* (http://peib.dmu.ac.uk 2004).

Roger Taylor & Edward Wakeling, *Lewis Carroll Photographer: The Princeton University Library Albums* (Princeton & Oxford, 2002).

Wilma Rugh Taylor and Norman Thomas Taylor, *This Train Is Bound For Glory: The Story of America's Chapel Cars* (Valley Forge, Pennsylvania, 1999).

Andrew Topsfield, "Eugene Impey at Mount Abu and Jodhpur", *History of Photography*, vol. 14, no. 3 (July to September 1990), pp. 251–74.

Andrew Topsfield, "Eugene Impey in Rajastan", *History of Photography*, vol. 20, no. 1 (Spring 1996), pp. 94–7

Diane Waggoner, *The Pre-Raphaelite Lens: British Photography and Painting, 1848–1875* (National Gallery of Art, Washington, 2010).

Edward Wakeling (ed.), *Lewis Carroll's Diaries* (6 vols, Luton, 1993–2001).

E. J. Wall, "An Exhibition of Colour Photography" [Review of 1906 British Journal of Photography exhibition of examples of colour photography], *British Journal of Photography*, vol. 53, no. 2386 (26 January 1906), pp. 64–7.

E. J. Wall, "The Exhibition of the Society of Colour Photographers", *British Journal of Photography Monthly Supplement on Colour Photography*, vol. 1, no. 10 (4 October 1907), pp. 73–5.

H. J. Weaver, *Reid's Hotel: Jewel of the Atlantic, 1891–1991* (London, 1991).

Liz Wells (ed.), *Photography: A Critical Introduction* (3rd ed., London, 2004).

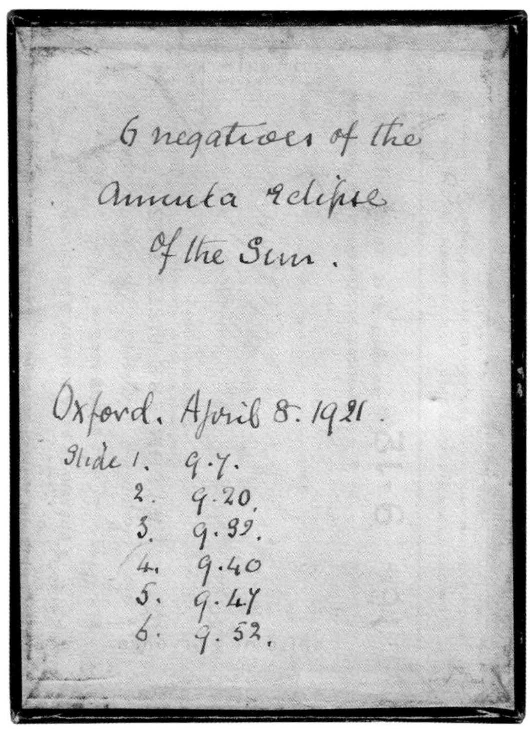

Box of Negatives Labelled by Miss Acland
Miss Acland's label is stuck over the lid of an Autochrome box

INDEX

ACKNOWLEDGEMENTS

I would like to thank the following for the valuable assistance and information they have provided during the preparation of this work: the Acland family; Tony Simcock, Colin Harris and Stephen Rench; Alan and Vanda Morton, Alastair Arnott, Alena Ptak-Danchak, Amanda Saville, Ann Lund, Anne Hammond, Antony Acland, António Abreu, Arthur Jackson, Avner Offer, Beryl Hartley, Bob Pullen, Bob Wyatt, Brian Gasser, Brian Liddy, Bruce Barker-Benfield, Carolinne White, Charles Greene, Chris Morton, Colin Harrison, Constantia Nicolaides, Caroline and John Hodkinson, David Acland, David Thompson, Doris Kloster, Edward Wakeling, Edwina Ehrman, Elizabeth Edwards, Eric J. Johnson, Evelyne Glyne, Gemma Wright, Graham Thompson, Guy Acland, Hannah Thomas, Helen Drury, Helen Trompeteler, Helena Araújo, Hugo Reis, Ian Howdill, Ian West, Jamie Tabor, Jane Cooke, Janet Howarth, Janet McMullin, Janine Freeston, Jeremy and Simon Zino, John Cortes, John Herschel-Shorland, Jon Whiteley, Judith Curthoys, Katherine Macdonald, Kathy Connor, Kelley Wilder, Ken Jacobson, Larry Schaaf, Laurence Mazaud, Linda Briscoe Myers, Lucy Blaxland, Malcolm Walker, Marcos Pinto, Margaret Croft, Margaret Pinsent, Marigold Rei, Mark Jacobs, Mary Burt, Mary Clapinson, Michael Pritchard, Mike Weaver, Nuala LaVertue, Pam Arnold-Foster, Pamela Hunter, Pamela Roberts, Paul Evans, Peter Warren, Rachel Lassam, Robin Darwall-Smith, Roger Mills, Rui Carita, Rupert Shepherd, Seiko Kashiwagi, Simon Bailey, Stella Brecknell, Stephanie Jenkins, Stephen Wildman, Terence Pepper, Victoria Perry, Walter Sawyer; the staff of the Bodleian Library, Radcliffe Science Library, Museum of the History of Science, Ashmolean Museum, Lincoln College, Oxfordshire History Centre, Oxford Brookes University, National Portrait Gallery, St Bride Library, Devon Records Office, National Media Museum, and Alpine Club; many friends who have given advice; those I have neglected to mention; and most importantly of all, my father, wife and daughter, Andrew, Julia and Alexandrina.

FIGURE SOURCES

The source of figures is Bodleian Library, University of Oxford, except where noted below as: Museum of the History of Science, Oxford (MHS); Oxford University Museum of Natural History (OUM); Ashmolean Museum, University of Oxford (ASM); Oxfordshire History Centre, Oxfordshire County Council (OHC); Institute of Archaeology, University of Oxford (IAO); National Media Museum, Bradford (NMEM); or Private collection.

Frontispiece, detail from cat. no. 172; **page 4**, detail cat. no. 68; **p. 6**, OHC 81/4189; **fig. 1**, MS. Photogr. b. 34, f. 127; **2**. MS. Eng. misc. c. 748, f. 29; **3**. MS. Photogr. b. 34, f. 151; **4**. MS. Photogr. c. 175, f. 37; **5**. Ibid., f. 30; **6**. Ibid., f. 152; **7**. MHS 11668; **8**. *Illustrated London News*, vol. 26, no. 750 (30 June 1855), p. 652; **9**. MS. Eng. misc. c. 748, f. 57; **10–11**. Private collection; **12**. ASM WA.RS. UF.44c; **13**. *Alpine Journal*, vol. 10, no. 74 (November 1881), before p. 331; **14**. 20500 c. 4, no. 87; **15**. MS. Photogr. b. 34, f. 86; **16**. G. A. Oxon. c. 222, f. 1; **17**. MS. Photogr. b. 34, f. 79; **18**. Ibid., f. 19; **19**. MS. Photogr. c. 175, f. 474; **20**. Ibid. f. 497; **21**. Ibid., f. 529; **22**. Ibid., f. 116; **23–24**. MS. Photogr. c. 177, f. 29 & 30; **25**. MS. Photogr. b. 36, f. 125; **26**. D. G. Hogarth, *A Wandering Scholar in the Levant* (London, 1896), frontispiece; **27**. MS. Photogr. c. 176, f. 1; **29**. *Photography Annual*, 1892, p. 294; **29**. *Photography Annual*, 1891, p. 280; **30**. NMEM, 2003-5001/2/24311, RPS collection; **31**. MS. Photogr. c. 175, f. 361; **32**. Arch. K. b. 12, f. 53r; **33**. MS. Photogr. c. 176, f. 159; **34**. MS. Photogr. c. 175, f. 372; **35**. W. W. Hunter, *Life of Brian Houghton Hodgson* (London, 1896), opp. p. 333; **36**. *Sun Artists*, no. 7 (April 1891), opp. p. 52; **37**. MS. Photogr. c. 176, f. 182; **38**. *Young Man*, vol. 9, no. 103 (July 1895), cover; **39**. *Black & White*, vol. 12, no. 302 (14 November 1896), p. 627; **40**. *British Journal of Photography*, vol. 48, no. 2148 (5 July 1901), supplement; **41**. *British Medical Journal*, vol. 2 (7 October 1900), p. 1281; **42**. Dew Family Photographs; **43**. Rogers box 7/15; **44**. MS. Photogr. c. 175, f. 463; **45**. Ibid., f. 183; **46**. MS. Acland d. 158, f. 43; **47**. OHC Album 56, f. 17r; **48**. NMEM; **49**. *British Journal of Photography*, vol. 48, no. 2150 (19 July 1901), supplement; **50**. A. H. Church, *Introduction to the Plant Life of the Oxford* District (3 pts, 1922–25, pt. 1), opp. p. 64; **51**. Impey neg. 4(11) ["No. 32"]; **52**. *Photographic Journal*, vol. 84 (April 1944), p. 104; **53**. Op. cit., ser. 1, frontispiece; **56**. *Photographic Journal*, vol. 45 (supplement) (21 September 1905), n.p.; **54**. Private collection; **55**. *Photographic Journal*, vol. 42 (supplement) (27 September 1902), n.p.; **56**. *Photograms of the Year*, 1908, p. 117; **57**. NMEM 1978-497/1; **58**. MHS 19384; **59**. MHS 39802; **60**. MHS 18981; **61**. *Photography*, vol. 12, no. 615 (23 August 1900) opp. p. 556; **62**. MHS 43029; **63**. MHS 15132; **64**. MHS 69657; **65**. *Photography*, vol. 12, no. 615 (23 August 1900), p. 553; **66**. MHS 16335; **67**. MHS 20283; **68**. Private collection; **69**. *British Journal of Photography Monthly Supplement on Colour Photography*, vol. 1, no. 2 (1 February 1907), p. 12; **70–72**. MHS 27896; **73**. *British Journal Photographic Almanac*, 1908, p. 1100; **74**. MHS 31825; **75**. Minn neg. 170/5; **76**. MHS 41415; **77**. OUM, Hope Department of Entomology; **78**. NMEM 1949-172/part; **79**. NMEM; **80**. Private Collection; **81**. IAO; **82**. *British Journal of Photography*, vol. 53, no. 2385 (19 January 1906), p. xix; **83**. *British Journal of Photography Monthly Supplement on Colour Photography*, vol. 1, no. 9 (6 September 1907), p. 67; **84**. *British Journal Photographic Almanac*, 1908, p. 1057; **87**. W. H. Koebel, *Madeira: Old and New* (London, 1909), opp. p. 135; **88**. Ella and Florence Du Cane, *The Flowers and Gardens of Madeira* (London, 1909), opp. p. 76; **89**. *Quarterly Journal of the Royal Meteorological Society*, vol. 43, no. 181 (January 1917), p. 41; **90**. Private collection; **91**. MS. Acland d. 178, f. 131; **92**. MS. Acland d. 177, f. 82; **93**. MS. Don. d. 14; **94**. MS. Top. Oxon. d. 494, f. 56; **page 42**, detail cat. no. 4; **p. 192**, detail cat. no. 185; **p. 287**, Private collection; **p. 289**, MS. Photogr. b. 34, ff. 100 & 99; **p. 292**, MHS 43356.

In Memoriam
Claire Hudson, née Dillamore (1942–1994)

"We shall rise again Angie, like the Sun"
William Alison Dyke Acland to his sister Sarah Angelina, *c.* 1856

gilesmhudson@hotmail.com

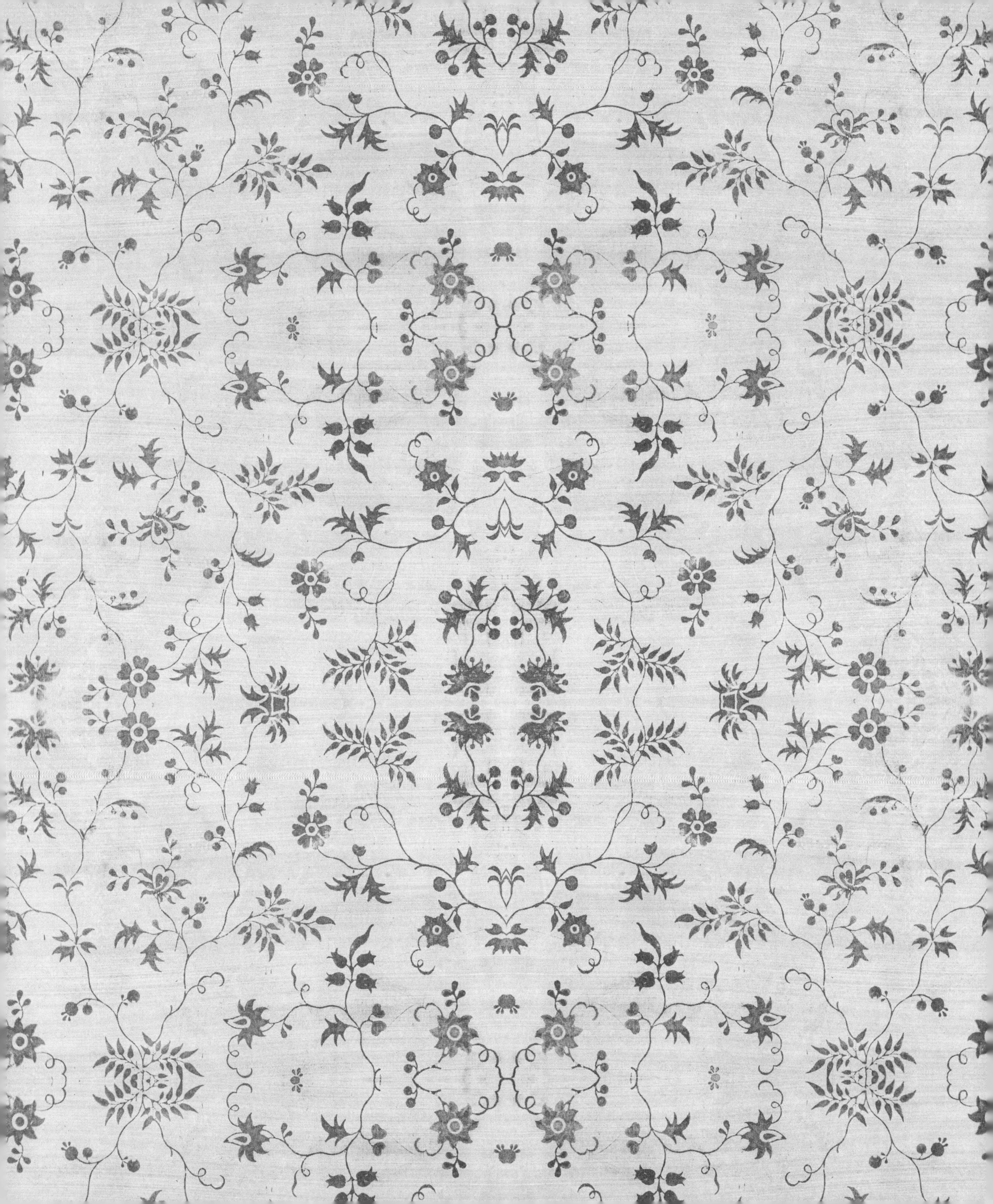

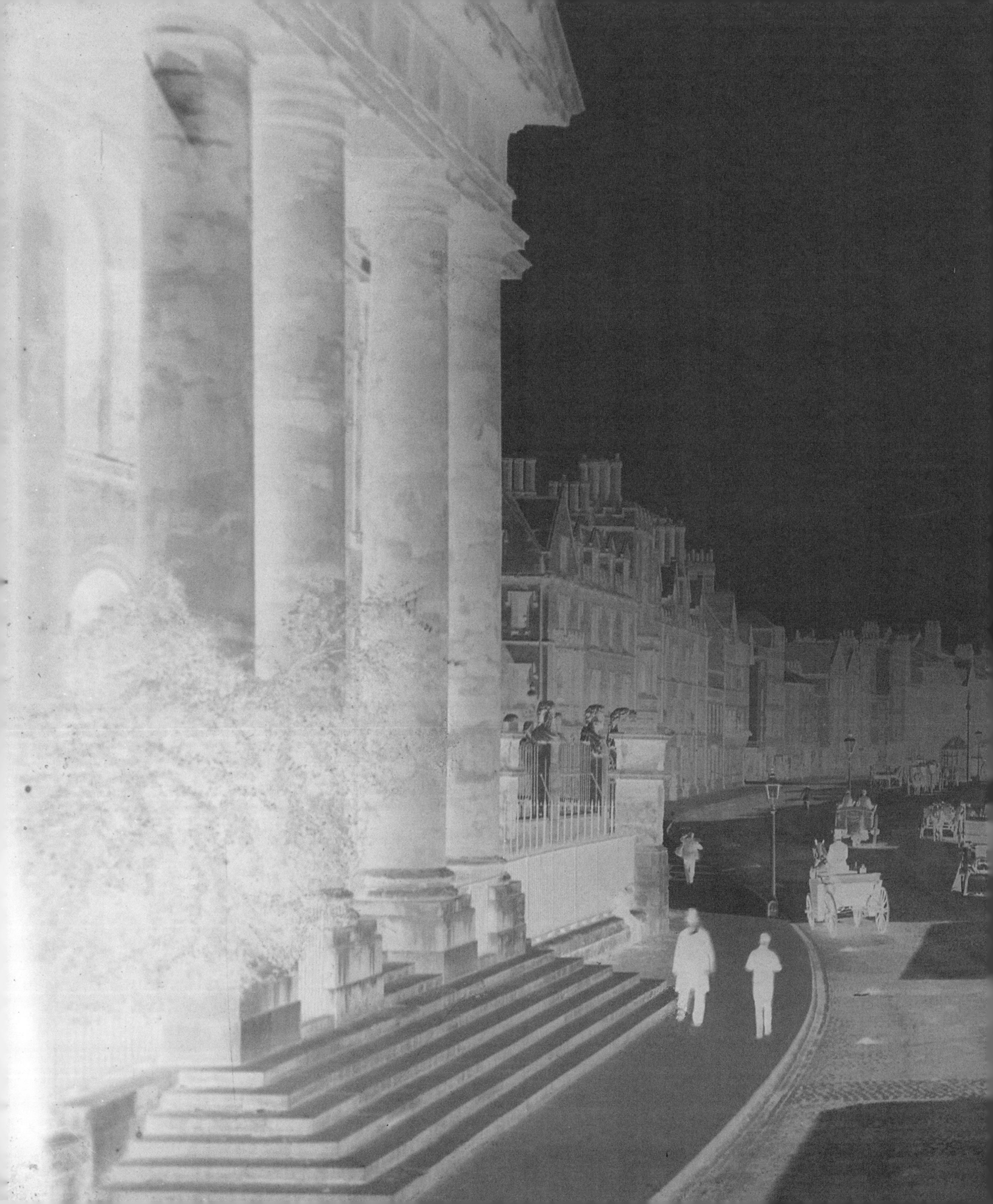